Tort Law in New Zealand

Tort Law in New Zealand

Third Edition

Stephen Todd

This book was originally published as a monograph in the International Encyclopaedia of Laws/Tort Law.

Founding Editor: Roger Blanpain
General Editor: Frank Hendrickx
Volume Editor: Britt Weyts

Wolters Kluwer

Published by:
Kluwer Law International B.V.
PO Box 316
2400 AH Alphen aan den Rijn
The Netherlands
E-mail: international-sales@wolterskluwer.com
Website: lrus.wolterskluwer.com

Sold and distributed by:
Wolters Kluwer Legal & Regulatory U.S.
7201 McKinney Circle
Frederick, MD 21704
United States of America
Email: customer.service@wolterskluwer.com

Printed on acid-free paper

ISBN 978-94-035-2481-8

e-Book: ISBN 978-94-035-2482-5
web-PDF: ISBN 978-94-035-2483-2

This title is available on www.kluwerlawonline.com

Printed in the United Kingdom.

The Author

Stephen Todd LLB, LLM (Sheffield), LLD (Canterbury), Barrister (Inner Temple) is Professor of Law, at the University of Canterbury, New Zealand.

Stephen Todd specializes in the law of torts and has a particular interest in the ambit of the law of negligence. He has an associated interest in New Zealand's accident compensation scheme and its relationship with the common law. He is the general editor and principal author of *Todd on Torts*, published in its eighth edition in 2019. His other main research interest is in the field of contract. He is the joint author with two colleagues of *The Law of Contract in New Zealand*, the sixth edition of which was published in 2018, and of *International Encyclopaedia of Laws: Contracts (New Zealand)* (2003, and revised 2008, 2011, 2013, 2017 and 2019). He also has written *Leading Cases in Song* (2013), a light-hearted rewriting of some leading decisions as songs, with music and illustrations. In 2002 Stephen was awarded an LLD by the University of Canterbury in recognition of his published works in the law of torts. In 2006, he became the fourth recipient of the *John Fleming Memorial Prize for Torts Scholarship*. This international prize is awarded every two years on the recommendation of a Committee whose members are drawn from around the world.

The Author

Table of Contents

Table of Contents

List of Abbreviations

AC	Appeal Cases
Ad & El	Adolphus & Ellis
ALJR	Australian Law Journal Reports
All ER	All England Law Reports
ALR	Australian Law Reports
App Cas	Appeal Cases
Aust Torts Reps	Australian Torts reports
B & C	Barnewall & Cresswell
B & S	Best & Smith
Bing NC	Bingham's new Cases
CB	Common Bench
CBNS	Common Bench New Series
CCLT	Canadian Cases on the Law of Torts
Ch	Chancery
Ch.	Chapter
Ch D	Chancery Division
CJ	Chief Justice
CLR	Commonwealth Law Reports
CP	Common Pleas
CRNZ	Criminal Reports of New Zealand
Cro Jac	Croke
CSIH	Court of Session Inner House
DCR	District Court Reports
DLR	Dominion Law Reports
E & B	Ellis & Blackburn
EG	Estates Gazette
EGLR	Estates Gazette Law Reports
EMLR	Entertainment and Media Law Reports
Eq	Equity
ER	English Reports

List of Abbreviations

ERNZ	Employment Reports of New Zealand
EWCA	England and Wales Court of Appeal
Exch.	Exchequer
Ex D	Exchequer Division
F	Federal Reporter
F & F	Foster & Finlayson
FLR	Federal Law Reports
FRNZ	Family Reports of New Zealand
FMA	Financial Markets Authority
FSR	Fleet Street Reports
GLR	Gazette Law Reports
H & C	Hurlstone & Coltman
HC	High Court
HCR	High Court Rules
HL	House of Lords
HLC	Clark and Finnelly's House of Lords Reports New Series
HL Cas	House of Lords Cases
Hob	Hobart
ICR	Industrial Court Reports
IRD	Inland Revenue Department
ISP	Internet Service Provider
J	Justice
KB	King's Bench
Ld Raym	Lord Raymond Law Reports
LJ Ch	Law Journal Chancery
LJKB	Law Journal King's Bench
Ll Rep	Lloyd's Law Reports
Ll Rep Med	Lloyd's Law Reports Medical
Ll Rep PN	Lloyd's Law Reports Professional Negligence
LQR	Law Quarterly Review
LR	Law Reports First Series
LT	Law Times Reports
LIM	Land Information Memorandum
M & W	Meeson and Welsby
MAF	Ministry of Agriculture and Fisheries
Man & G	Manning & Granger
Marsh	Marshall
MLR	Modern Law Review
Moo & R	Moody & Robinson

MR	Master of the Rolls
NE	North Eastern Reports
NERC	National Environment Research Council
NI	Northern Ireland Law Reports
NICA	Northern Ireland Court of Appeal
NSWLR	New South Wales Law Reports
NSWSC	New South Wales Supreme Court
NZAR	New Zealand Arbitration Reports
NZBLC	New Zealand Business Law Cases
NZCA	New Zealand Court of Appeal
NZCPR	New Zealand Conveyancing and Property Reports
NZ ConvC	New Zealand Conveyancing Cases
NZELC	New Zealand Employment Law Cases
NZHC	New Zealand High Court
NZIPR	New Zealand Intellectual Property Reports
NZ Jur	New Zealand Jurist Reports
NZLC	New Zealand Law Commission
NZLR	New Zealand Law Reports
NZ Rec Law (NS)	New Zealand Recent Law (New Series)
NZSC	New Zealand Supreme Court
NZTC	New Zealand Tax Cases
ONCA	Ontario Court of Appeal
P	President
P	Probate, Divorce and Admiralty Division
Peake NPC	Peake's Nisi Prius Cases
PD	Probate, Divorce and Admiralty Division
PPSA	Personal Property Securities Act 1999
PRNZ	Procedure Reports of New Zealand
QB	Queen's Bench
QBD	Queen's Bench Division
Qd R	Queensland Reports
RPC	Reports of Patent, Design and Trade Mark Cases
RTR	Road Traffic Reports
RSA	Returned Services Association
SA	South African Reports
SASR	South Australian State Reports
SC	Session Cases
SCR	Supreme Court Reports
SR (NSW)	State Reports (New South Wales)

List of Abbreviations

Stra	Strange
Taunt	Yaunton
TCLR	Trade and Competition Law Reports
TLR	Times Law Reports
TR	Term Reports
UKPC	United Kingdom Privy Council
Unrep.	Unreported
VR	Victorian Reports
VSC	Victoria Supreme Court
WLR	Weekly Law Reports

General Introduction

§1. General Background of the Country

I. Geography

1. New Zealand lies between the Tasman Sea and the South Pacific Ocean, about 1,600 km south-east of Australia. There are two principal islands – the North Island and the South Island – and a substantial number of smaller islands, of which the largest is Stewart Island in the far south. The total land area is approximately 267,000 sq. km.

II. History

2. New Zealand was settled by immigrants from Great Britain and other European countries early in the nineteenth century and in 1840 became a colony of Great Britain after the signing of the Treaty of Waitangi. Large-scale immigration, principally from Britain, brought the settler population to over half a million by 1900. However, the indigenous Maori population fell severely during the nineteenth century, largely as a result of epidemics. In the twentieth century the Maori population growth was very substantial, and at the same time there was further large-scale immigration. The total population of New Zealand in December 2018 was 4.93 million, of whom approximately 15% were of Maori descent.[1]

Early economic and population growth was fuelled by booms in wool, gold, and the export of frozen meat and dairy products. While primary industries of this kind remain very important, fishing, forestry products, manufacturing, and tourism now create a more balanced economy.

New Zealand acquired a well-deserved reputation in the period 1890–1940 for innovative and sometimes radical social and political innovations. Examples are the early enfranchisement of women (1893), a state-sponsored structure for conciliation and arbitration in labour disputes (1894), and the creation in the 1930s of a 'welfare state'. More recent developments include the introduction in 1962 of the first Ombudsman at common law jurisdictions,[2] and the institution of the accident compensation scheme in 1974.[3]

1. At http://www.stats.govt.nz/topics/population.
2. Parliamentary Commissioner (Ombudsman) Act 1962.
3. Accident Compensation Act 1972; *see* paras 33–48.

III. Political System

3. From 1840 to 1852 New Zealand was ruled by a governor and two appointed councils that performed executive and legislative functions. In 1852, a British statute established a bicameral local parliament (the General Assembly), and, in 1854, the colonial authorities were granted internal self-government privileges. There was a brief period of provincial government operating alongside the central legislature, but the provincial governments were abolished in 1876. After some further changes, New Zealand came to be governed by the General Assembly, constituted by the House of Representatives, the (largely moribund) Legislative Council, and the Governor-General, representing the Crown. Some residual powers to legislate for New Zealand remained with the United Kingdom (UK) Parliament, but these were removed in 1947, and, since 1950, when the Legislative Council was abolished, the House of Representatives has been the single representative body. The Governor-General must formally assent to all of its measures, but he or she exercises no political power.

There are presently 120 members of the House of Representatives. They are elected by a mixed-member proportional electoral system, whereby parties receive the same proportion of the seats in the House as their proportion of the party votes cast by electors.[4] Since the introduction of this system in 1996, New Zealand has been governed by coalitions of varying political hues. There are six seats elected on a solely Maori roll, but many other Maori exercise their right to vote through the general system.

IV. Economic and Social Values

4. New Zealand is a parliamentary democracy. Its economy is founded on private enterprise. The economic and social values of the country are those of the so-called Western model.

In recent years, the government has sought to resolve long-standing tensions arising out of the colonization of New Zealand in the nineteenth century. The Treaty of Waitangi was intended to represent a partnership between the Maori tribes already living in New Zealand and the British Crown, and to ensure the retention of Maori lands and rights. The Treaty had no formal Constitutional status and for a long time it was all but ignored in the developing legal processes and institutions of the colony. However, since about the 1980s it has come to be recognized as having very considerable political and cultural significance. New governmental initiatives commonly involve consultation with Maori interests and seek to promote the notion of a partnership between Maori and non-Maori, or 'pakeha'.[5]

The Waitangi Tribunal, set up in 1975, has been a forum for airing Maori grievances, accommodating cultural differences, and facilitating redress for historic Treaty breaches. It has helped win acceptance that the Treaty is a living instrument,

---

4. *See* the Electoral Act 1993.
5. *See* generally Joseph, *Constitutional and Administrative Law in New Zealand,* Ch. 4 (4th ed. Wellington: Brookers, 2014).

capable of adapting to developing local circumstances.[6] The Tribunal investigates claims that government legislation, policies, or practices prejudicially affected Maori, contrary to the principles of the Treaty.[7] It does not possess binding powers of decision, but may recommend to the Crown that it make reparations where a claim is upheld.[8] Most claims involve land confiscations dating from the nineteenth century. All historical claims needed to be lodged with the Tribunal by 1 September 2008.[9] Settlements generally include financial redress and a formal Crown apology for breaches of the Treaty.

New Zealand has three official languages, English, Maori, and New Zealand Sign Language.[10] English is overwhelmingly the language used, and only a small proportion of the Maori population speak Maori fluently and as a preferred language. However, various governments have taken a wide range of initiatives for the promotion of the Maori language and to foster Maori culture. There are a significant number of immigrants of various backgrounds – principally Asian, Pacific Islander, and European – and these have also been incorporated to varying extents in New Zealand culture. These immigrant communities also use various other languages, particularly Chinese and various Pacific Island languages.

§2. Legal System

I. General

5. New Zealand is a constitutional monarchy that upholds the rule of law and constitutional government.[11] It has a parliamentary system of government that is founded on the principles of representative democracy and an independent judiciary. The powers of the Crown are limited by law and are exercised either on the advice of ministers or by ministers in the name of the Crown.

There are three branches of government – the executive, the legislative, and the judiciary. The separation of powers between these three branches implies a system of checks and balances for securing the ideal of government according to law. There is no constitutional separation of the three branches, but each is separately constituted and acts as a counterbalance upon the others.

New Zealand has a parliamentary executive that is responsible for the conduct of government. Ministers are Members of Parliament and are accountable to Parliament for the discharge of their portfolios. The Prime Minister must retain the confidence of the House in order for the government to continue in office.

6. *See Te Runanga o Muriwhenua v. Te Runanganui o Te Upoko o Te Ika Association Inc* [1996] 3 NZLR 10 at 20.
7. Treaty of Waitangi Act 1975, s. 6(2).
8. *Ibid.*, s. 6(3)–(4).
9. *Ibid.*, s. 6AA.
10. Maori Language Act 1987; New Zealand Sign Language Act 2006.
11. *See* Joseph, *The Legal History and Framework of the Constitution*, in *Building the Constitution* (James ed., Wellington: Institute of Policy Studies, 2000), upon which this brief account is based.

New Zealand, it is said, has an unwritten constitution. This means only that the constitution is not contained in any one document known as 'the Constitution'. Nevertheless, the New Zealand constitution exists and has several sources: Acts of Parliament, prerogative instruments, decisions of the courts, customary international law, the law and custom of Parliament, conventions of the constitution, and the practices of executive government.

Although there is no single constitutional document, legislation provides for many critical, 'constitutional' matters. These include the Constitution Act of 1986, proclaiming New Zealand's national sovereignty; the Imperial Laws Application Act of 1988, resolving uncertainty over the inheritance of British laws in New Zealand; the New Zealand Bill of Rights Act of 1990, establishing a parliamentary Bill of Rights; the Electoral Act of 1993, redefining the electoral system; and the Supreme Court Act of 2003, establishing a final appellate court to replace the appeal to the Privy Council.

Constitutional conventions play a very important role in the working of the constitution. Conventions are binding rules of political practice, although they are not enforceable by the courts. Perhaps the cardinal convention is that which enjoins the Queen and the Governor-General to exercise their prerogative and statutory powers on ministerial advice. Most conventions operate as a restraint on the exercise of government powers.

II. Primacy of Legislation

6. Parliament is sovereign: it may legislate without restriction on any subject matter.[12] In particular, an Act of Parliament can override any rule of the common law or any decision of the courts. However, a statute that seeks to abrogate significant rights or privileges conferred by the common law needs to be expressed in very clear language. Certainly, fundamental rights cannot be overridden by general or ambiguous words.[13]

As New Zealand does not have a supreme or higher law, the judges have no power to strike down parliamentary legislation as inconsistent with any such law. The courts are required, where possible, to interpret statutes consistently with the New Zealand Bill of Rights Act of 1990,[14] but that Act does not have overriding force. So a statute that clearly is contrary to the NZ Bill of Rights Act will nevertheless be valid. However, the courts can strike down delegated legislation (statutory regulations, bylaws, and the like) where these are not in accord with the empowering legislation.[15]

As New Zealand has a unicameral parliament, the only significant legal limitation on the power of the government to legislate as it chooses is the need to ensure majority support for legislation. There is a theoretical check-in that legislation must

---

12. *See* Joseph, *Constitutional and Administrative Law in New Zealand*, Ch. 15 (4th ed., Wellington: Brookers, 2014).
13. *R v. Secretary of State for the Home Department, ex p Simms* [2000] 2 AC 115 at 131.
14. New Zealand Bill of Rights Act 1990, s. 6.
15. *See* Joseph, *Constitutional and Administrative Law in New Zealand*, Ch. 26 (4th ed., Wellington: Brookers, 2014).

receive the Royal Assent, but this is given as a matter of course by the Governor-General as the Queen's representative. Naturally, there are moral, practical, and political constraints on any unfettered use of this legislative power.

III. Position of the Judiciary

7. The courts have civil and criminal jurisdiction to resolve disputed questions of law and fact in accordance with the law laid down by the legislature and by the courts, in the decisions of the judges themselves. Their decisions are binding, subject to rights of appeal to higher courts.

Judges are normally appointed either to the High Court or to the District Court, but there have been a few instances of District Court judges being raised to the High Court bench. Judges of the Court of Appeal are usually appointed from the ranks of High Court judges, but there have been occasions of appointment direct from the ranks of the legal profession.

Judges of the High Court (including Supreme Court and Court of Appeal judges) may be removed from office only by the Governor-General, in response to a motion passed by the House of Representatives alleging misbehaviour or incapacity.[16] No address to remove a judge has ever been moved. District Court judges may be removed by the Governor-General, on the advice of the Attorney-General, on the grounds of inability or misbehaviour.[17] There have not been any recent instances of this power being used, although judges on occasion have resigned to avoid investigation. All judges are required to retire at the age of 70.[18]

IV. The Court System

A. *The Supreme Court*

8. Formerly, the highest court of the New Zealand court system was the Judicial Committee of the Privy Council, which sits in London, but, in 2003, appeals to the Privy Council were abolished and the New Zealand Supreme Court was set up as the final Court of Appeal.[19] The Court consists of the Chief Justice (CJ) and no fewer than four or more than five permanent judges.[20] It may hear appeals from the Court of Appeal or, in exceptional cases, direct from the High Court. Appellants in all cases require the leave of the Supreme Court itself, which will not be given unless the matter is of general public importance, of general commercial significance, or where there is a risk of a serious miscarriage of justice.[21]

16. Constitution Act 1986, s. 23; Senior Courts Act 2016, s. 134.
17. District Court Act 2016, s. 29.
18. Senior Courts Act 2016, s. 133; District Court Act 2016, s. 28; Te Turi Whenua Maori Act 1993, s. 12(2); Coroners Act 2006, s. 103(4).
19. Supreme Court Act 2003.
20. Senior Courts Act 2016, s. 66(2).
21. *Ibid.*, ss 73, 74.

B. The Court of Appeal

9. The Judicature Act of 1908 (now repealed) established the Court of Appeal, which presently consists of the President of the Court of Appeal and no fewer than five nor more than nine permanent judges.[22] High Court judges may also be called upon to sit where necessary. The Court of Appeal will normally sit in benches of three, although a full court of five may sometimes be assembled.[23] The Court has a very wide jurisdiction. Appeal lies to it as of right from all civil and most criminal decisions of the High Court, as well as from certain criminal matters tried in the District Court.

C. The High Court

10. The High Court consists of the CJ and a maximum of fifty-five judges.[24] The High Court is a superior court of record, and as such can hear appeals from the District Court. It has original jurisdiction in a range of civil matters, most materially those where a sum of more than NZD 350,000 is in dispute.

D. The District Court

11. The District Court is the principal workhorse of the New Zealand court system. It deals with an enormous volume of criminal and family litigation, as well as with civil cases where amounts up to NZD 350,000 are in dispute. There can be a maximum of 160 District Court judges.[25]

E. Specialist Courts

12. There are a number of inferior courts that exercise specialist statutory jurisdiction. Examples are the Family Court,[26] the Employment Court,[27] Coroners' Courts,[28] the Maori Land Court,[29] and the Maori Appellate Court.[30]

---

22. *Ibid.*, s. 45.
23. *Ibid.*, ss 50, 51.
24. *Ibid.*, ss 6, 7.
25. District Court Act 2016, s. 12.
26. Family Courts Act 1980.
27. Employment Relations Act 2000.
28. Coroners Act 2006.
29. Maori Affairs Act 1953.
30. Te Ture Whenua Maori Act 1993.

F. Disputes Tribunals

13. Small disputes are dealt with outside the formal court system by Disputes Tribunals. These have jurisdiction to deal with claims in contract and quasi-contract and with claims for property damage in tort to a maximum amount of NZD 30,000.[31] The referees who sit in the Disputes Tribunal do not have to be legally qualified (although most are) and are appointed for three-year terms with a possibility of reappointment. Unlike the judges, therefore, they have no security of tenure.

The procedure of the Tribunal is deliberately informal. Referees are required to have regard to the law but are not obliged to apply it.[32] An appeal lies to the District Court, but only on the grounds of procedural fairness.[33] There is no appeal as to the substance of any decision.

V. Distinction Between Public and Private Law

14. New Zealand law does not make a distinction between 'public' and 'private' law in the way that is found in some European countries. All tribunals (save those with a specialized jurisdiction drawing on Maori law) apply the same corpus of law. However, 'public law' is used descriptively to encompass the body of law dealing with the relations of the individual and the state. It includes the substantial body of statute and case law that governs proceedings before administrative tribunals and the procedures by which the courts may review such proceedings. Private law, on the other hand, is primarily concerned with the relationships of private individuals, and thus covers the law of contract, torts, trusts, company law, and family law. Of course, there will be many instances where private law issues arise between the government and the individual. Where the government is acting in this quasi-private character, there is no significant difference in the form of the proceedings or the manner in which cases are dealt with by the courts from that which prevails in cases between private litigants.

VI. Sources of Private Law in General and Tort Law in Particular

15. New Zealand has inherited the common law from its source in the decisions of the courts in Great Britain. Accordingly, the founding principles for the law of torts in New Zealand are based upon these decisions. Indeed, throughout much of the twentieth century, English decisions tended to be followed in this country with little debate about possible alternatives. However, since about the 1970s, the courts have taken an increasingly independent stance. Today, English decisions continue to play a significant role in the development of the law, but decisions elsewhere, and in particular those from Australia and Canada, are likely to be just as influential.

31. Disputes Tribunals Act 1988, s. 10.
32. *Ibid.*, s. 18(6).
33. *Ibid.*, s. 50.

Ultimately, the courts seek to lay down principles suitable for the local jurisdiction and local conditions, drawing upon experience in other countries where appropriate. In the following pages, many decisions from other leading common law countries are cited in addition to those in New Zealand. In its totality, the law can now fairly be described as having its own indigenous character.

§3. Functions of the Law of Torts

I. Compensating for Losses

16. Broadly speaking, the law of torts is concerned to make moral judgments about the quality of a person's behaviour. Normally, although not invariably,[34] its rules seek to make a morally blameworthy wrongdoer pay for the damage done to the victim. This idea, that tort renders an individual personally accountable for morally blameworthy behaviour, is open to various objections when one takes into account, for example, an objectively determined standard of care for negligence,[35] the imposition of vicarious liability,[36] and insurance considerations. But this is not to say that it is lacking in all credibility. The link between blameworthiness and liability may sometimes be tenuous, but a link there still is.

An award of damages accordingly performs a dual function. It imposes a sanction on a wrongdoer and it compensates the victim in respect of his or her loss. The principle that is applied in calculating the amount of the loss normally is to restore the plaintiff to his or her original position. So tort damages typically look back at a former, unharmed, plaintiff and aim to compensate for interference with or loss of something he or she already owned or possessed, such as bodily health, property, reputation, privacy, or financial prosperity.[37] Only exceptionally do they compensate for lost expectancies or bargains.[38] Of course, the amount of the plaintiff's loss has to be expressed in monetary terms, and many types of loss, such as loss of freedom or injury to reputation or any personal injury, have no precise monetary value. The courts have to do the best they can, being guided by broad tariffs and past experience.[39]

In other common law countries a primary function of the law of torts is to provide compensation in respect of personal injury and its economic consequences. A tort action can only do this where it can be shown that another person is responsible for causing the injury. If the concern really is with the need for compensation, then tort provides an uncertain and inefficient remedy. The victims of accidents causing personal injuries have needs that exist irrespective of how they suffered their accidents. These needs can be (more or less) satisfied by a tort action only in the small minority of cases in which another person can be proved to have been at fault in causing the accident and that person, or an insurer, can pay substantial damages.

34. *See* para. 427.
35. *See* para. 137.
36. *See* para. 373.
37. *See* para. 551.
38. *See* paras 117, 270.
39. *See* paras 57, 358, 559.

Parliament thus legislated to meet the need and replaced tort with an accident compensation system. As will be explained, the focus is simply on the suffering of injury and the consequences for the victim. Responsibility for causing the injury generally is not relevant.[40]

II. Encouraging Care and Deterring Wrongdoing

17. The law of torts may also serve to influence conduct, promote safety, and deter wrongful behaviour. The argument probably has some weight as regards certain instances of intentional conduct. For example, there does not seem to be much doubt that in deciding what to print, publishers are influenced by the fear of liability for damages in defamation. How far tort can be effective in deterring negligent conduct is much more uncertain. Many people know little or nothing about the civil consequences of negligent conduct. The deterrence argument presupposes that the defendant should have some such knowledge. In any event, the defendant should also have the ability to avoid running the risk. Most cases of negligence involve defendants who did not consciously decide to take a risk but who merely failed to foresee the consequences of their conduct. It is difficult to see how a person can be deterred from making a mistake. Furthermore, defendants frequently are insured, so damages do not have to be paid out of their own pockets. All this is not to say that tort liability can never deter a person from being negligent. It may sometimes discourage a person from starting a dangerous activity or getting into a situation where harm threatens in the first place. The fear of being held liable may, for example, lead an employer or professional person to devise an efficient system of working and to anticipate mishaps before they occur. Perhaps it will help create a climate of opinion in a particular profession or discipline that encourages taking care. But it seems certain that other mechanisms for maintaining standards are likely to be more effective. They include the criminal law, regulatory control, licensing of activities, education and training, disciplinary procedures by professional bodies, and peer review.

Discussion of deterrence as an objective of the law of tort leads us to consider whether the law can be evaluated on the basis of criteria of economic efficiency. The theory known as 'general deterrence' or 'market deterrence' involves the use of compensation rules to provide indirect incentives to people not to cause harm or loss to others. It says, broadly, that if the cost of the harm caused by an activity is required by law to be paid by those who engage in that activity, then they will take precautions to prevent inflicting harm, provided the cost of precautions is less than the cost of the harm (i.e., the damages they have to pay); and that in this way the optimum or efficient level of precautions (and, conversely, of harm) will be reached.[41] Of course, this assumes that the activity in question is responsive to market principles, which assumption often must be highly questionable. Again, an economically rational person takes into account the degree of likelihood that his or her conduct will result in the imposition of tort liability: yet there is only an uncertain,

40. *See* para. 33.
41. Atiyah, *Accidents, Compensation and the Law*, Ch. 18 (Cane ed., 8th ed., London: Butterworths, 2013).

and arguably minimal, chance that particular conduct will cause harm, that the victim will sue, and that he or she will recover damages. As a general proposition it is apparent that concepts of economic efficiency provide a very imperfect basis for the allocation of tort liability. However, they may have some value in institutional settings where market considerations are more likely to influence behaviour.

III. Vindicating Rights and Punishing Wrongdoing

18. The judgment of the court in a tort action may serve to vindicate a right, even where no damage has been suffered.[42] The law of torts is not generally concerned with punishing wrongdoers. This function normally is left to the criminal law. Exceptionally, however, a civil court may make an award of exemplary damages in order to make an example of the wrongdoer and to punish his or her particularly blameworthy behaviour.[43]

§4. Relationship Between Torts and Criminal Law

I. General

19. Criminal proceedings are usually brought by the state, their purpose being to punish an offender for conduct that is prejudicial to the public interest. There is a limited statutory power for a criminal court to order the offender to make reparation to the victim of the crime,[44] but the criminal law is not otherwise concerned with helping that victim or seeking to make good the damage. Proceedings in tort, on the other hand, are brought by the victim of wrongful conduct with the primary aim of gaining compensation from the person who is responsible for the wrong. If the court finds a tort has been committed, it makes an award of damages that, so far as possible, is commensurate with the plaintiff's loss. Exemplary, as opposed to compensatory, damages can only be awarded in quite exceptional cases, where the court wishes to make an example of a tortfeasor guilty of outrageous wrongdoing that is deliberate or reckless.[45]

Although their functions are quite distinct, the one act may amount to both a crime and a tort, with both criminal and civil consequences. Examples are theft and conversion, careless driving and negligence, criminal assault and battery. The criminal offence and the tort do not, however, necessarily cover exactly the same ground, for the elements of the one are found in the terms of the statute creating the offence, and the elements of the other are found in the common law. For example, the crime of assault may be committed without the victim being aware of the threatening

42. *See* paras 573, 574.
43. *See* para. 575.
44. Sentencing Act 2002, s. 32.
45. *Taylor v. Beere* [1982] 1 NZLR 81; *Couch v. Attorney-General* [2010] 3 NZLR 149; *see* para. 576.

behaviour, but knowledge is an essential part of the tort.[46] Again, there may be different defences,[47] and the standard of proof is different – proof beyond reasonable doubt in the criminal sphere, and proof on the balance of probabilities in civil actions.[48]

II. Double Jeopardy

20. The overlap between tort and crime causes no particular difficulty in circumstances where the defendant is prosecuted for the crime and the plaintiff seeks compensatory damages for the tort. The civil action is brought by a different party and for a different purpose. However, the question arises whether a civil action can be brought solely for a non-compensatory purpose, to vindicate the victim's right.[49] Furthermore, where the plaintiff seeks exemplary damages, allowing the civil action puts the defendant at risk of double jeopardy, and may place the civil court in the position of second-guessing the criminal punishment. These implications will be considered in the discussion of exemplary damages.[50]

§5. Relationship Between Contractual Responsibility and Tortious Responsibility

I. General

21. The purpose of contract damages typically is to put the promisee in the position he or she would have enjoyed had the contract been performed, and in this way to give him or her the benefit of the bargain that was struck with the promisor.[51] In this way the damages enforce performance of the contract. On the other hand, as we have seen, tort damages typically aim to restore a person to the position he or she would have been in had the tort not been committed.

Whether or how far wrongful conduct can lead to liability in both contract and tort has been a source of controversy. The question can arise both as regards third parties to contracts and as between the parties themselves. Early on, the doctrine of privity of contract was thought to bar any action in tort for negligence against a contract-breaker brought by a non-party. So B could not be liable for harm done to C as a consequence of negligence by B in carrying out a contract with A.[52] This privity theory was laid to rest in *Donoghue v. Stevenson*,[53] where the House of Lords recognized that B could also owe a duty in tort to C to take care, founded not on the

46. *R v. Kerr* [1988] 1 NZLR 270.
47. *See*, for example, paras 495, 502.
48. *See* generally *Ashley v. Chief Constable of Sussex Police* [2008] 1 AC 962.
49. *See* paras 573–574.
50. *See* para. 577.
51. *Stirling v. Poulgrain* [1980] 2 NZLR 402 at 419.
52. *Winterbottom v. Wright* (1842) 10 M & W 109; 152 ER 402.
53. [1932] AC 562.

contract with A, but on the foreseeability of harm to C, and the closeness of the relationship between B and C.[54] On this point the law is perfectly clear. However, the position as between A and B has caused greater difficulty. Furthermore, it has been recognized that the existence of a 'contractual matrix' may sometimes exclude tort.

II. Concurrent and Co-extensive Liability

22. The question has arisen whether a contracting party who acts carelessly and in breach of an express or implied contractual duty to take care must rest content with his or her contractual rights, or whether that party may seek to rely on an alternative claim in tort.[55] In *McLaren Maycroft & Co. v. Fletcher* Development *Co. Ltd*[56] the Court of Appeal held, following English authority,[57] that a claim by a land development company alleging negligence by its consulting engineers was for breach of contract and not tort. However, the ambit of this contract-only rule was not clearly defined nor was it easily supported as a matter of principle. Subsequently, in England, it was reconsidered and abandoned. In *Henderson v. Merrett Syndicates Ltd*[58] Lord Goff observed that the common law is not antipathetic to concurrent liability and that there is no sound basis for a rule that automatically restricts the claimant to either a tortious or a contractual remedy. He recognized that the result may be untidy; but, given that the tortious duty is imposed by the general law, and the contractual duty is attributable to the will of the parties, he did not find it objectionable that the claimant may be entitled to take advantage of the remedy that is most advantageous to him, subject only to ascertaining whether the tortious duty is so inconsistent with the applicable contract that, in accordance with ordinary principle, the parties must be taken to have agreed that the tortious remedy is to be limited or excluded. In similar decisions in New Zealand the Court of Appeal has affirmed that a contracting party is not confined to suing the other party in contract when a concurrent cause of action is available in negligence.[59]

While the existence of a contract between A and B does not of itself prevent A from coming under a tortious duty to B, the circumstances must still be such as to justify the imposition of the tortious duty. A duty between contracting parties co-extensive with their contractual obligations may spring up based upon an assumption of responsibility[60] or in certain other circumstances.[61]

---

54. *See* para. 75.
55. In many cases the plaintiff can rely on an action for breach of contract and nothing will turn on the point. Sometimes, however, the availability of a choice between the two will assume importance. For example, there are different rules governing both remoteness and quantum of damage (*see* paras 21, 544); the limitation period may start to run at different times (*see* para. 456); a statutory right to contribution is recoverable only from a tortfeasor, not a contract-breaker (*see* para. 588); and damages for breach of contract are not necessarily reducible on account of contributory negligence by the plaintiff (*see* para. 479).
56. [1973] 2 NZLR 100.
57. *Bagot v. Stevens Scanlan & Co.* [1966] 1 QB 197.
58. [1995] 2 AC 145.
59. *Riddelll v. Porteous* [1999] 1 NZLR 1 at 9; *Allison v. KPMG Peat Marwick* [2000] 1 NZLR 560 at 582; *Price Waterhouse v. Kwan* [2000] 3 NZLR 39 at 44.
60. *See* the discussion in *Robinson v. PE Jones (Contractors) Ltd* [2011] 3 WLR 815; and *see* para. 91.
61. For discussion of these circumstances, *see* especially paras 92–99, 102–105, 111, 117–126, 131.

Where on the facts of a particular case a cause of action in tort for negligence lies concurrently with a cause of action in contract, the further question arises as to the test to apply for determining whether any damage which is the subject of the claim should be held to be too remote. In *Wellesley Partners LLP v. Withers LLP*[62] the Court of Appeal in England held that where contractual and tortious duties to take care in carrying out instructions existed side by side, the test for recoverability of damage for economic loss should be the same, and should be the contractual one.

III. Contractual Matrices

23. The availability of a tort remedy may be qualified where it would tend to undermine the operation of the ordinary rules of contract,[63] and, more specifically, in cases involving multiple parties to a complex contractual structure. In *Price Waterhouse v. Kwan*[64] Tipping J said that there may be circumstances in which the legislative or other environment governing the relationship of the parties supports the view that the presence of a contractual right against B militates against there being a parallel tortious right against A for the same damage. This argument has prevailed in later decisions of the Court of Appeal.

In *RM Turton & Co. Ltd v. Kerslake*[65] the plaintiff builder, relying on the mechanical services specification prepared for an owner by the defendant engineers, successfully tendered for a building contract. It later turned out that the heating system would not work to the specified standard. The plaintiff undertook remedial work pursuant to its contractual obligations with the owner, and then sought to recover the cost from the engineer. A majority in the Court of Appeal held that the engineer owed no duty of care to the bidder, and an important reason in justification was that the duty contended for would cut across and be inconsistent with the overall contractual structure that defined the relations of the various parties to the work. In *Rolls-Royce New Zealand Ltd v. Carter Holt Harvey Ltd*,[66] also in the Court of Appeal, a claim by the owner of industrial plant against a subcontractor for negligence in the design and building of the plant similarly failed. The contractual context was seen to point clearly against any duty being recognized. The parties had negotiated the risk of loss in the contracts between the owner and the main contractor and between the main contractor and the subcontractor, and the court declined to disturb the agreed allocation of risk. On the other hand, in *Carter Holt Harvey Ltd v. Minister of Education*[67] the Supreme Court accepted that a manufacturer could, in principle, be liable in negligence for supplying defective material used in constructing a building, and refused to strike out the claim. O'Regan J considered that the terms of supply applying between the manufacturer and merchants and

62. [2016] 2 WLR 1351.
63. *See*, for example, *The Party Bus Co Ltd v. New Zealand Transport Agency* [2016] NZHC 413, [2017] 3 NZLR 185.
64. [2000] 3 NZLR 39 at 44; and *see Blain v. Evan Jones Construction Ltd* [2013] NZCA 680.
65. [2000] 3 NZLR 406.
66. [2005] 1 NZLR 324; and *see* further para. 122.
67. [2016] NZSC 95, [2017] 1 NZLR 78; and *see* further para. 131.

between merchants and building contractors were not likely to be seen in the same light as the carefully calibrated contractual regime that applied in *Rolls-Royce*, particularly if they were standard form contracts.

A party to a contract is free, subject to any statutory control, to restrict or exclude his or her liability to the other in tort, and a person may also give a non-contractual notice to another to the same effect.[68] So a party to a contractual matrix can make it clear to another party even without any direct contractual nexus that he or she is excluding or limiting any liability to that party. This may be done expressly, and provided reasonable notice is given to the other, then the notice operates as a non-contractual exclusion of liability and serious difficulty is avoided. It is possible that there might be an implied exclusion arising out of the particular relationship between the parties. Whether this is found is likely to turn on the scope and sophistication of the contractual dealings by the parties to the matrix, the vulnerability of the plaintiff and, conversely, that party's opportunities for self-protection. Any such limitation or exclusion should operate as a defence to the plaintiff's claim, not as a control upon the imposition of a duty of care.

IV. Pre-contractual Liability

24. Statements made during negotiations for a contract that induces the making of the contract between the representor and the representee do not give rise to any liability in tort. Rather, they are treated as if they were terms of the contract, and the representee's remedies are founded upon contract alone.[69]

§6. Protected Interests

25. The law of torts cannot protect all human interests from invasion by others, for a catalogue of these interests 'might be as long as the list of legitimate human desires'.[70] A cause of action can be given only in the case of interference with interests that are sufficiently important and sufficiently certain as to be capable of legal redress.

I. Personal Integrity

26. A primary concern of the common law of torts is with invasions of bodily integrity and, in particular, with providing a cause of action for the victims of intentionally violent or negligent conduct in respect of personal injuries and associated losses and expenses. However, the common law in New Zealand has been superseded by an accident compensation scheme, giving victims of personal injury the

68. *See* para. 516.
69. Contract and Commercial Law Act 2017, s. 35; *see* paras 96, 299.
70. Prosser & Keeton, *Handbook of the Law of Torts*, 16 (5th ed., St Paul, Minnesota: West Publishing, 1984).

right to make a claim under the scheme and barring any civil action seeking compensation for the injury.[71] Exemplary damages, which are intended to punish the wrongdoer rather than to compensate the victim, can still be sought.[72]

Compensatory damages can be claimed in the ordinary way in respect of any personal injury that is not covered by the scheme.[73] Such damages also can be claimed in respect of intentional or negligent interferences with the person causing damage not amounting to personal injury. So, for example, there can be an action for an assault causing the apprehension of injury;[74] an action for false imprisonment in the case of an invasion of the right to individual freedom;[75] and an action for malicious prosecution in the case of a wrongful criminal prosecution that threatens the liberty of the individual.[76]

II. Physical Property

27. A number of overlapping torts operate to protect a person's interest in land against various kinds of interferences by others. The law generally is as much concerned with safeguarding property as with safeguarding the person. The law of negligence applies generally as regards damage to land or premises;[77] trespass to land gives a remedy in respect of unauthorized entry on to the land;[78] nuisance protects against indirect interference with land or the use or enjoyment of land;[79] and the rule in *Rylands v. Fletcher*[80] (which is a subset of nuisance) applies where a person accumulates on his or her land something likely to do mischief if it escapes and the thing does escape and causes damage to another.[81] The invasion of the plaintiff's interest in land does not always have to be intentional or negligent. As will be seen, liability in nuisance and under the rule in *Rylands v. Fletcher* does not depend on proof of an intentional or negligent interference with the land or the use of the land.

Damage to goods may be actionable in negligence in a similar way to damage to land. Certain other torts have a role to play in protecting a person's proprietary or possessory interest in his or her goods. Thus a direct and immediate interference with another's possession is a trespass to goods;[82] an assertion of rights or dominion over goods that is inconsistent with the rights of another to possession of or control over the goods may be sued for as a conversion;[83] and retaining possession of

71. *See* para. 33.
72. *See* para. 42.
73. *See* para. 42.
74. *See* para. 52.
75. *See* paras 54–57.
76. *See* paras 316–321.
77. *See* para. 75.
78. *See* paras 163–167.
79. *See* paras 185–187.
80. (1866) LR 1 Ex 265, affirmed (1868) LR 3 HL 330.
81. *See* para. 201.
82. *See* paras 213–215.
83. *See* paras 216–238.

another's goods after the other has demanded their return is detinue.[84] Conversion and detinue are essentially concerned with the plaintiff's title to goods rather than with damage to the goods.

III. Intellectual Property

28. The law of torts has a role to play in protecting a person's rights in intellectual property – in business, trade, ideas, personality, and information – although statute governs much of the field. The common law action known as passing off accords a remedy in respect of the wrongful appropriation of trading goodwill belonging to another.[85] A cause of action founded in equity that is closely analogous to an action in tort is for breach of another's confidence.[86] Most importantly, there are statutory actions for the infringement of the intellectual property rights of copyright and design, patents and trademarks,[87] but these are outside the scope of this work.

IV. Financial Interests

29. There are any number of ways in which a person might interfere with another's financial interests, and the question whether, or to what extent, the law of torts will provide a remedy in respect of such interference is extraordinarily complex:

(1) Intentional interference with a person's advantageous business or other economic relations with others can give rise to liability on a number of different bases, namely: passing off goods or business as those of a rival so as to cash in on the rival's goodwill;[88] inducing breach of another's contract;[89] causing loss by unlawful means, including intimidatory conduct;[90] and conspiring to do an unlawful act, or a lawful act by unlawful means, for the purpose of injuring another.[91] A mere intention to inflict a business loss without more cannot be actionable, for the very purpose of trade competition is to make profits at the expense of rival traders. The courts thus look for some additional factor that is apt to give a person's conduct the character of a tort. Whether the conduct is independently unlawful, or whether two or more persons have combined to cause damage, clearly are relevant considerations. However, if a person's behaviour is otherwise lawful, even the fact that he or she acted maliciously does not render it tortious.

---

84. *See* paras 239–242.
85. *See* paras 246–254.
86. *See* paras 258–265.
87. *See* para. 245.
88. *See* paras 246–254.
89. *See* paras 270–277.
90. *See* paras 278–283.
91. *See* paras 284–291.

(2) Where a person suffers loss consequent upon conduct by a public official that is malicious or that is known to be beyond power, that loss is recoverable in the tort of misfeasance in public office.[92] The tort, broadly, is concerned with controlling the abuse of power by persons in positions of authority.
(3) A dishonest statement that induces a person to act to his or her financial detriment is actionable in deceit.[93] A dishonest statement that disparages another person's business reputation so as to cause financial loss is actionable in the tort of injurious falsehood.[94]
(4) A negligent statement that induces detrimental reliance by another may be actionable in negligence, provided that there is a close or 'special' relationship between the person making the statement and the person receiving it.[95] Negligent conduct that causes pure financial loss to another without the other having relied on it also may be actionable in negligence in certain limited categories of cases.[96]

V. Reputation and Privacy

30. An individual's personal reputation and good name can be protected by an action in defamation.[97] Injury to a person's reputation on being made subject to wrongful criminal proceedings may also be compensated, in this case by the tort of malicious prosecution.[98] Associated with reputation is an individual's interest in his or her privacy. The courts have recognized a person's right to redress for unjustifiable invasions of privacy,[99] and a right to be protected from harassment is conferred by legislation.[100]

Business reputation can be protected by defamation, by the action for passing off and, in the case of the wrongful institution of winding-up proceedings affecting a company's credit, by the action for malicious abuse of civil process.[101] A business can have no interest in personal privacy, but it does have an enforceable interest in protecting confidential information.[102]

VI. Other Interests

31. The law of torts does not standstill. Litigation is constantly testing the limits of existing torts. Furthermore, the fact that the law has not hitherto accepted that a

92. *See* paras 308–312.
93. *See* paras 292–301.
94. *See* paras 302–306.
95. *See* paras 89–99.
96. *See* paras 100–105.
97. *See* paras 330–361.
98. *See* paras 316–321.
99. *See* paras 362–366.
100. *See* para. 372.
101. *See* para. 322.
102. *See* paras 258–265.

particular interest ought to be protected does not mean that a new tort protecting that interest can never emerge. The novelty of a claim is not in itself a bar to success. So interferences with privacy only recently have been accepted as potentially tortious, whether by way of publicity given to private facts[103] or by way of intrusions into seclusion.[104] In an associated development, a claim for wrongful appropriation of another's image, or in other words for the infringement of a right of publicity, also has been recognized overseas as actionable, although it certainly remains controversial.[105] On the other hand, it has been held that there is no independent tort of spoliation of evidence by destroying or withholding evidence which is relevant to the plaintiff's case in existing or forthcoming litigation.[106] Nor is there a separate tort of wrongful interference with a body.[107]

Torts can become outmoded and fall into disuse. Various archaic torts protecting the inviolability of domestic and family relations – enticement, seduction, or harbouring of a wife or child, and negligent interferences with domestic relations – have all been abolished by statute.[108]

§7. Impact of Legislation

32. While the law of torts is to be found in the common law of New Zealand, Parliament has intervened to modify or reform the law in a wide variety of respects. Some of these legislative changes are of very considerable significance.

First, section 317 of the Accident Compensation Act of 2001 bars all causes of action in respect of personal injury (including certain instances of mental injury) suffered by the victims of accidents, of medical treatment and of occupational disease covered by the Act. These persons have instead a right to make a claim for compensation pursuant to a statutory scheme set up by the Accident Compensation Act of 1972 and governed now by the 2001 Act. The nature of the scheme and its relationship with the common law will be examined below.

Second, statute on occasion has amended or simplified the common law. The Occupiers' Liability Act of 1962 cut through a number of rather technical common law rules under which an occupier owed different duties to his or her visitors according to their particular status and the purpose of the visit, and replaced them with a common duty of care owed to all lawful visitors.[109] Another example is the Animals Law Reform Act of 1989, which abolished special rules of the common law concerning strict liability for dangerous animals and negligence in allowing domestic animals to stray on the highway, leaving ordinary principles of negligence

103. *Hosking v. Runting* [2005] 1 NZLR 1.
104. *C v. Holland* [2012] 3 NZLR 672.
105. *Douglas v. Hello! Ltd* [2006] QB 125 (on appeal *Douglas v. Hello! Ltd* [2008] 1 AC 1); *see* para. 257.
106. *Burns v. National Bank of New Zealand Ltd* [2004] 3 NZLR 289.
107. *In Re Organ Retention Group Ltd* [2005] 2 WLR 358.
108. Accident Compensation Act 1972, s. 5(2); Domestic Actions Act 1975, ss 2–4, as amended by the Family Proceedings Act 1980, s. 190.
109. *See* para. 402.

to operate.[110] As regards defences to liability, the Contributory Negligence Act of 1947 provides for the apportionment of damage where responsibility for it is attributed to both plaintiff and defendant, whereas at common law a contributorily negligent plaintiff usually failed completely.[111]

Third, Parliament has acted to fill certain gaps in the law. The general rule at common law was that the death of either party extinguished any existing cause of action in tort by one against the other.[112] This deficiency was addressed by the Law Reform Act of 1936, which provides that on the death of any person, all causes of action subsisting against or vested in him shall (save for a cause in action in defamation) survive against or for the benefit of the estate.[113] Again, at common law there is no time limit on making a claim, and the Limitation Acts of 1950 and 2010 accordingly make statutory provision for the matter.[114]

Finally, Parliament sometimes has enacted wholly new causes of action which are analogous to claims in tort. A long-standing example is the right of contribution between tortfeasors.[115] More recently, a developing consumer protection ethic led to the enactment of two important statutes, each creating new causes of action. The Fair Trading Act of 1986 governs business practices prior to the making of business or consumer transactions. In particular it prohibits conduct in trade that is misleading or deceptive or is likely to mislead or deceive, and gives persons who suffer loss or damage, caused by conduct in breach of the Act, a right to bring a civil action for compensation.[116] The Consumer Guarantees Act of 1993 is concerned with the responsibility of suppliers and manufacturers for the quality of their goods and services at the time of, and after the making of, a consumer transaction. To a considerable extent it duplicates an already available remedy of the consumer in contract founded on Part 3 of the Contract and Commercial Law Act 2017 (formerly the Sale of Goods Act of 1908), but it also gives the purchaser of consumer goods a direct action against the manufacturer notwithstanding the absence of any contractual privity between them.[117]

§8. Accident Compensation

I. Introduction

33. In most countries a primary function of the law of torts is to provide compensation to victims who suffer death or personal injury as a result of accidents caused by the wrongdoing of others. In New Zealand the law now fulfils this role

110. *See* paras 420–421.
111. *See* para. 476.
112. The rule did not apply to actions in contract or where property had been appropriated by the deceased person and added to his or her estate.
113. Law Reform Act 1936, s. 3(1); and *see* further paras 467, 580.
114. *See* para. 454.
115. Law Reform Act 1936, s. 17(1)(c); *see* paras 586–590.
116. *See* paras 444–448.
117. *See* paras 449–451.

only at the margins, for most claims for compensation for personal injury are governed exclusively by a statutory accident compensation scheme. Its importance justifies separate treatment.[118]

The scheme has its origins in the Report of the Royal Commission charged with inquiring into personal injury law in New Zealand in 1967.[119] The report highlighted multiple shortcomings of the action for damages as an efficient system for compensating accident victims. In particular, insurance considerations had caused the fault theory to develop into a legal fiction and undermined the claim that the threat of damages provided a financial incentive to be careful; the risks of litigation turned the system into a lottery; and tort was cumbersome, inefficient, and extravagant in operation to the point that the cost of administration absorbed more than 40% of the total amount of money flowing into the system. The Commission maintained that the concern should be with the needs of accident victims rather than the responsibility of alleged wrongdoers. Accordingly, it recommended that the common law should be replaced by a statutory scheme for compensating victims of personal injury by accident. After widespread debate, Parliament acted on the recommendation by passing the Accident Compensation Act 1972. From the date when this Act came into force, on 1 April 1974, most actions for damages for personal injury occurring in New Zealand were barred. The new statutory right to compensation was based not on any question of liability, but simply on the claimant coming within one of the statutory conditions for cover.

There have been four re-enactments since the 1972 Act, in the Accident Compensation Act of 1982, the Accident Rehabilitation and Compensation Insurance Act of 1992, the Accident Insurance Act of 1998 and the Accident Compensation Act of 2001. The last of these, as amended in 2005, 2008 and 2010,[120] apply today. In their totality the Acts have made various changes, some of them very significant, affecting the coverage of the scheme, the benefits it provides, the method of delivery of those benefits, and the funding of those benefits. Yet in its fundamentals, the scheme continues to operate on broadly the same basis as it did when it was first introduced. And for the time being the scheme is likely to stay in its present form, although there will be continuing debate about the ambit of coverage and the level of benefits it provides.

118. For more detailed consideration of the scheme, *see Todd on Torts* Chs 2, 3 (8th ed., Wellington: Brookers, 2019).

119. Royal Commission of Inquiry, *Compensation for Personal Injury in New Zealand* (Wellington: Government Printer, 1967).

120. Injury Prevention, Rehabilitation, and Compensation Amendment Act (No. 2) 2005; Injury Prevention, Rehabilitation, and Compensation Amendment Act 2008; Accident Compensation Amendment Act 2010. The 2001 Act originally was called the Injury Prevention, Rehabilitation, and Compensation Act, but the 2010 Act changed the name back to the Accident Compensation Act.

II. Coverage

A. Categories of Cover

34. As originally enacted, the scheme provided compensation for victims of 'personal injury by accident'. The concept was not fully defined, the courts being left to flesh out the boundaries. But Parliament intervened in 1992, following some expansive decisions,[121] and removed the judicial discretion. The main categories of personal injury attracting cover under the scheme were left unchanged in conception but were defined by the statute with considerable precision. This arrangement has been carried over into the Accident Compensation Act of 2001. There are now twelve specific categories of cover, and these fall broadly into four categories – personal injury caused by an accident, personal injury caused by treatment, personal injury caused by employment-related disease or infection, and personal injury by way of mental or nervous shock suffered as a consequence of physical injury, or by the victims of certain specified sexual offences, or which is work-related. Importantly, the scheme only covers illness or disease to the extent that this is covered in the particular case as employment-related or as falling within one of the other categories.

Persons suffering personal injury in any of the covered circumstances can make a claim to the Accident Compensation Corporation for compensation pursuant to an administrative process set up under the Act.[122] Persons suffering personal injury in other circumstances may bring an action in tort if one is or might be available, but otherwise must rely on private insurance arrangements or social security benefits.[123]

1. Personal Injury

35. Personal injury is broadly defined, and any kind of harm to the human body, including harm by mental suffering or sickness or disease, that cannot be treated as trifling or fleeting,[124] or which has some appreciable and not wholly transitory impact on the person,[125] is included.[126] Any physical injury must actually have been suffered. So there was no cover for patients who had had hip replacements involving the implantation of hip prostheses which turned out to have an unacceptably high failure rate, but whose prostheses had not in fact failed.[127]

---

121. *See* especially *ACC v. E* [1992] 2 NZLR 426 (CA); *ACC v. Mitchell* [1992] 2 NZLR 436 (CA).
122. *See* para. 44. This includes cover for New Zealand residents who suffer personal injury while abroad: Accident Compensation Act 2001, s. 22.
123. Benefits are payable under the Social Security Act 2018.
124. *Falwasser v. Attorney-General* [2010] NZAR 445 at [90], where it was held that the effects of pepper spray amounted to personal injury.
125. *Allenby v. H* [2012] 3 NZLR 425 at [56].
126. For the full statutory definition, *see* Accident Compensation Act 2001, s. 26.
127. *Sellwood v. Accident Compensation Corporation* [2017] NZHC 2604, [2017] NZAR 1593.

There can be no *compensation* for any particular form of personal injury if it falls outside the grounds for cover provided for under the Act. *Harrild v. Director of Proceedings*[128] is an exceptional case on the margins. The question here was whether a mother who suffered no direct physical injury but who gave birth to a stillborn child due to negligent medical treatment had herself suffered a personal injury. The majority held that the mother was covered for compensation. An unborn child could be part of the mother, even though the mother and foetus were biologically distinct. Although the injury suffered by the mother and the foetus was not the same, where severance of the physical link between them occurred through the death of the foetus, by that loss the mother suffered a personal injury within the meaning of the legislation. The minority said that on this view a mother and foetus were treated as a single entity, which ignored biological reality.

Another disputed, but now resolved, question is whether an unwanted pregnancy can qualify. In *ACC v. D*[129] the Court of Appeal, in a majority decision, determined that unwanted pregnancy following a failed tubal ligation was not a personal injury under the 2001 Act because it was not a 'physical injury': rather, it was a natural event that could not be seen as harm or damage. However, in *Allenby v. H*,[130] the Supreme Court held to the contrary. Tipping J said that the bodily changes during pregnancy clearly were of a physical kind, and were apt to cause a substantial degree of physical discomfort and, quite often, substantial pain and suffering. A woman who took steps to avoid a natural consequence of sexual intercourse ought to be regarded as suffering physical injuries when those natural consequences followed as a result of medical misadventure. In the same way, a woman who was raped, and became pregnant as a result, thereby suffered physical injury caused by the accident of sexual assault. But cases of consensual sexual connection leading to an unwanted pregnancy would not be covered, because there would be no 'accident' in such a case.[131]

In *Cumberland v. Accident Compensation Corporation*[132] the question in issue was whether a woman whose child was born with spina bifida, following a failure to detect that condition during an antenatal ultrasound scan, had suffered a personal injury under the 2001 Act. The court recognized that the continuation of the pregnancy following the misdiagnosis involved significant physical changes to the anatomy of the mother, and thus, applying *Allenby*, it was personal injury.

2. Personal Injury by an Accident

36. The central category of cover is personal injury by an accident.[133] 'Accident' is closely defined, its core meaning being 'a specific event, or a series of

128. [2003] 3 NZLR 289.
129. *ACC v. D* [2008] NZCA 576.
130. [2012] 3 NZLR 425.
131. On the question of 'accident', *see* para. 36. On cover for treatment injury, *see* para. 37.
132. [2014] 2 NZLR 373.
133. Accident Compensation Act 2001, s. 20(2)(a), (g).

events, other than a gradual process,[134] that involves the application of a force (including gravity), or resistance, external to the human body'. The concept also includes the inhalation or oral ingestion of certain foreign objects on a specific occasion, certain burns, and certain harm caused by exposure to the elements within a defined period of time.[135]

Strains or sprains can occur by accident, on the basis that gravity constitutes the requisite external force or resistance. The relevant 'force' refers to a significant force causative of injury, not the concept of force as used in physics. It does not cover a child suffering from foetal alcohol syndrome due to her mother having drunk alcohol during the pregnancy,[136] or a child suffering from cerebral palsy caused by an antenatal force external to the foetus but occurring within the mother,[137] or a person inhaling smoke.[138]

Idiopathic diseases, that is those that develop in a person from an unknown cause, and that are not consequential on covered events, are outside the scope of the Act.[139] Idiopathic diseases will generally be excluded because they are caused by a gradual (internal) process rather than a known external cause. Non-idiopathic diseases with physical impacts which are caused by accident may be covered, on the basis that there is personal injury as defined in the Act.[140]

In determining whether a person has suffered an 'accident', the focus is on whether the injury is accidental from the victim's point of view.[141] Whether or not another person intentionally inflicted the injury is immaterial. So, the victims of a murderous assault had suffered personal injury by an accident, and could not maintain an action for compensatory damages against the Department of Corrections for negligence by a probation officer in failing adequately to supervise their attacker.[142]

The personal injury must be caused by the accident. If preexisting degenerative changes are brought to light or become symptomatic as a consequence of an event which constitutes an accident, it can only be the injury caused by the accident and not the injury that is the continuing effects of the preexisting degenerative condition that can be covered.[143]

The definition of 'accident' applies only if the context does not otherwise require.[144] In the special case of an unwanted pregnancy, the literal meaning of the statutory definition has to be adjusted so as to exclude from its reach the application

134. As to which, *see*, for example, *Simm v. ACC* 20/12/06, Mallon J, HC, Wellington, CIV-2005-485-965; *White v. ACC* [2010] NZCA 139 at [144]–[145].
135. Accident Compensation Act 2001, s. 25(1).
136. *Winikerei v. ARCIC* 27/7/05, Fogarty J, HC Wellington CIV-1999-485-000008.
137. *Sam v. ACC* [2010] NZAR 490.
138. *Simm v. ACC* 20/12/06, Mallon J, HC Wellington CIV-2005-485-965.
139. *See* Accident Compensation Act 2001, s. 26(2).
140. *Calver v. Accident Compensation Corporation* [2019] NZHC 1591, [2019] 3 NZLR 261 esp. at [76]–[77]; for 'personal injury' *see* para. 35.
141. *Green v. Matheson* [1989] 3 NZLR 564 at 571–572.
142. *Couch v. Attorney-General* [2008] 3 NZLR 725 (but an action for exemplary damages was possible: *see* paras 42, 575).
143. *McDonald v. ARCIC* [2002] NZAR 970; *Johnston v. ACC* [2010] NZAR 673.
144. Accident Compensation Act 2001, s. 6.

of force involved in sexual intercourse to which the woman concerned truly consents. So unwanted pregnancy caused by failed contraception is not covered. Only pregnancy caused by rape is pregnancy caused by an accident.[145]

3. Treatment Injury

37. Coverage for medical injuries formerly came under the rubric of medical misadventure, but this has been transformed into treatment injury.[146] This means, broadly, personal injury that is caused by treatment, that is not a necessary part or ordinary consequence of treatment,[147] and that is not wholly or substantially caused by a person's underlying health condition.[148] It is not of itself treatment injury because desired results are not achieved.[149] In addition, there is cover for certain secondary infections, for personal injury by way of a gradual process, disease or infection that is treatment injury, and personal injury by way of a heart attack or stroke that is treatment injury. 'Treatment' is defined as including, *inter alia*, a failure to provide treatment, or to provide treatment in a timely manner, and failing to obtain a person's consent to undergo treatment.[150] Coverage for a personal injury by an accident and for medical treatment does not overlap.[151]

We have seen that, as a general rule, the scheme does not cover disease or illness. So where a person is already ill, some form of responsibility for either a failure to provide treatment or the provision of wrong treatment must be established on the balance of probabilities in order for the person to receive cover. In *Adlam v. Accident Compensation Corporation*[152] the Court of Appeal held that the injury said to be a treatment injury had to be the consequence of a departure from appropriate treatment choices and treatment actions. A failure in the sense of omitting to take a step required by an objective standard was necessary, but not a finding of negligence. Compensation would be paid for an injury if it could be assumed that an experienced specialist in the field in the circumstances would have acted differently during examination, assessment or treatment, at the time of assessment of the claim, thereby avoiding the injury.

The personal injury must be 'caused by' medical misadventure or by treatment, as the case may be. In *Atkinson v. ARCIC*[153] a child who received negligent medical

145. *Allenby v. H* [2012] 3 NZLR 425.
146. Accident Compensation Act 2001, s. 20(2)(b), (c), (d), (f), (h), (i).
147. In cases other than those involving a failure to provide medical treatment or to provide treatment in a timely manner, whether or not a treatment injury was an ordinary consequence of treatment, would involve an assessment of whether or not, in the particular facts of the case, analysed after the event and once all relevant information was known, the injury could be said to be more probable than not: *Accident Compensation Corporation v. Ng* [2018] NZHC 2848 at [102].
148. *Ibid.*, s. 32(1), (2); *see*, for example, *Accident Compensation Corporation v. Stanley* [2013] NZHC 2765.
149. Accident Compensation Act 2001, s. 32(3).
150. *Ibid.*, s. 33.
151. *Ibid.*, s. 25(2).
152. [2017] NZCA 457, [2018] 2 NZLR 102; *and see Brewster v. Accident Compensation Corporation* [2019] NZHC 1343.
153. [2002] 1 NZLR 374.

treatment in the course of surgery shortly after birth that led to hypoxia was later found to be suffering from brain damage. His claim for accident compensation failed, on the ground that the hypoxia could not be causatively linked to the brain damage. Richardson P recognized that it may have contributed to the damage, but it was not proved that it had contributed. The statute focused on outcomes, not on risk of injury or potential for injury. To accept a lesser statutory test of increased risk or to adopt a reversed onus approach would be inconsistent with the statutory language and scheme.

In *ACC v. Ambros*[154] the Court of Appeal confirmed the approach taken in *Atkinson*. Glazebrook J noted that the 1998 and 2001 Acts were passed against a background of the causation principles set out in *Atkinson*, and was satisfied that this had to be seen as legislative acceptance of those principles, and consequently, the case was correctly decided.

In *Allenby v. H*,[155] the Supreme Court held that a patient who suffered mental illness after becoming pregnant following a failed sterilization procedure had suffered 'personal injury' and was covered as being the victim of medical misadventure (and now would be covered on the basis that this was treatment injury).[156] Seemingly, however, the cover extends only to the physical effects of the unwanted pregnancy. *Allenby* did not decide that there is or could be cover for the cost of bringing up an unplanned child, and it has been held that the coverage provisions cannot be interpreted to extend so far. In *J v. Accident Compensation Corporation*[157] the court held that a claim for loss of earnings compensation for having to stay at home to look after an unplanned child should fail. The Act was concerned with the physical and mental effects of an injury. Once the mother was physically and mentally recovered from her pregnancy and the childbirth, she was not unable to work because of her pregnancy.

4. Employment-Related Disease, Heart Attacks and Strokes

38. There is a cover for disease injury where it is work-related.[158] A person suffers personal injury caused by a work-related gradual process, disease, or infection in circumstances where he or she performs an employment task or works in an environment that has a particular property or characteristic; this property or characteristic causes or contributes to the injury, and may or may not be present throughout the whole period of employment, and if the property or characteristics is present in both the person's employment tasks or environment and the person's non-employment activities or environment, it is more likely that the injury was caused

154. [2008] 1 NZLR 340; and *see Thompson v. Accident Compensation Corp* [2015] NZAR 1163.
155. [2012] 3 NZLR 425; *see* above, para. 35.
156. In *Cumberland v. Accident Compensation Corporation* [2014] 2 NZLR 373 (*see* above, para. 35) the continuation of a pregnancy following a failure to diagnose spina bifida in the foetus was 'personal injury', but cover depended on showing that the patient could have obtained a lawful termination had she been properly advised, and the case was referred back to the District Court for determination of the question.
157. [2017] NZCA 441, [2017] 3 NZLR 804.
158. Accident Compensation Act 2001, s. 20(2)(e), (j).

as a result of the former, employment, factors.[159] Work-related disease includes personal injury suffered by way of the occupational diseases listed in Schedule 2 to the Act, and in these cases specific proof that the disease is work-related is not required.[160] There is no cover where the personal injury is related to non-physical stress.[161]

A heart attack or stroke is covered for compensation where it is caused by physical effort or physical strain that is work-related and is abnormal in application or excessive in intensity for that person.[162] So a distinction must be drawn between normal exertion leading to a heart attack or stroke that happened to be suffered during employment, and activity that was abnormal or excessive for the particular claimant as compared with the effort to which the claimant was accustomed, and in that sense was caused by the employment.

5. Mental Injury

39. 'Mental injury' is defined as a clinically significant behavioural, cognitive, or psychological dysfunction.[163] There is cover for mental injury suffered 'because of' physical injury.[164] There is also cover for mental injury standing alone which is suffered by the victims of various sexual offences specified in Schedule 3 to the Act.[165] However, if the offence is not so listed, any mental harm caused by a crime is not covered.[166] Finally, there is cover for work-related mental injury caused by a single, sudden, traumatic event.[167]

---

159. *Ibid.*, s. 30(2).
160. *Ibid.*, s. 30(3), (4). The relevant diseases include pneumoconiosis caused by sclerogenic mineral dust, silico-tuberculosis, lung cancer or mesothelioma diagnosed as caused by asbestos, and various diseases of a type generally accepted by the medical profession as caused by certain specified industrial substances or their toxic compounds.
161. *Ibid.*, s. 30(5)(a).
162. *Ibid.*, s. 28(3).
163. *Ibid.*, s. 27.
164. *Ibid.*, s. 26(1)(c). The physical injury must be a cause of the mental injury. It is not enough that an accident triggers a preexisting mental injury: *Hornby v. Accident Compensation Corporation* (2010) 9 NZELC 93,476. Any physical injury is sufficient to support a claim for mental injury, even though the physical injury is not itself covered because it is a necessary part of medical treatment: *Accident Compensation Corporation v. Monk* [2013] NZAR 1. There needs to be a genuine and meaningful connection between the physical and the mental injury: *W v. Accident Compensation Corporation* [2018] NZHC 937, [2018] 3 NZLR 859.
165. *Ibid.*, ss 21, 21A, 26(1)(d).
166. In *CLM v. Accident Compensation Corporation* [2006] 3 NZLR 127 it was held that a claimant who suffered nervous shock on discovering that her partner was HIV positive, but who was not in fact infected, was not entitled to cover. The partner had pleaded guilty to criminal nuisance under s. 145 Crimes Act 1961, but this offence was not included in Schedule 3. However, in *KSB v. Accident Compensation Corporation* [2012] NZCA 82, where the facts were similar, the Court of Appeal held that the claimant's sexual partner's conduct in failing to disclose his HIV status had the consequence that the claimant's consent to sexual intercourse was vitiated by mistake as to the nature and quality of the act, and the offence of sexual violation was made out. This was an offence listed in Schedule 3, and so she was covered for compensation. The implications of the decision remain to be explored.
167. Accident Compensation Act 2001, s. 21 B.

B. Claimants

40. Persons who can claim accident compensation are all persons within New Zealand who suffer personal injury covered by the Act.[168] This includes visitors who are in New Zealand temporarily for business purposes, on holiday, or for any other reason. However, visitors are eligible only for limited benefits – primarily medical expenses and death payments. They do not qualify for earnings-related compensation as they are not taxpayers in New Zealand. There is an exception to coverage for visitors in the case of personal injury suffered while on board, embarking or disembarking from their ship or aircraft coming to, travelling around, or leaving New Zealand.[169]

The scheme also has an extraterritorial application for the benefit of New Zealand residents injured overseas in a way that would be covered for compensation if the injury had occurred in New Zealand.[170] If a New Zealand resident has a right to bring proceedings overseas, the Accident Compensation Corporation can take over the claim, or deduct the damages from the statutory entitlements, or recover entitlements already paid.[171]

III. Relationship with the Common Law

A. The Bar on Actions for Damages

41. Where cover exists, actions for damages are barred. Section 317(1) of the Accident Compensation Act 2001 provides:

> No person may bring proceedings independently of this Act, whether under any rule of law or any enactment, in any court in New Zealand, for damages arising directly or indirectly out of –
>
> a. Personal injury covered by this Act; or
> b. Personal injury covered by the former Acts.

The bar cannot be avoided by failure to make a claim or a purported denial or surrender of rights under any of the Acts or a lack of entitlement to any particular benefit.[172] Again, the source of any particular claim seeking compensation for personal injury is immaterial. All actions for damages for compensation for personal

168. *Ibid.*, s. 20(1). A 'person' includes a born-alive child seeking compensation in respect of antenatal injuries: *Harrild v. Director of Proceedings* [2003] 3 NZLR 289 at [118]–[119]. In *Abortion Supervisory Committee v. Right to Life New Zealand Inc* [2012] 1 NZLR 176 the court affirmed that an unborn child has no legal rights prior to being born alive.
169. Accident Compensation Act 2001, s. 23.
170. *Ibid.*, s. 27.
171. *Ibid.*, s. 321; *Schlaadt v. ARCIC* [2000] 2 NZLR 318; *McGougan v. DePuy International Ltd* [2018] NZCA 91, [2018] 2 NZLR 916 at [41]–[48].
172. *Ibid.*, s. 317(7).

injury covered by the Act or a former Act are barred, whether founded on tort, contract, equity, or statute.[173] Personal injury actions in New Zealand against overseas defendants equally are barred.[174]

By section 317(2), the bar does not prevent a person bringing proceedings relating to or arising from damage to property, or any express term of any contract, or the unjustifiable dismissal of any person or any other personal grievance arising out of a contract of employment. Proceedings of this kind are not in any event for damages for personal injury, and seemingly they have been singled out in order to make it clear beyond argument that the proceedings themselves are not barred insofar as they are concerned with uncovered loss. In particular, the express reference to proceedings relating to an express term of any contract confirms that a claim on, say, an insurance contract providing for additional payments to those provided under the statute in the event of injury or death, is not barred. This is a payment of an agreed amount to which a person is entitled by way of contractual performance, as opposed to damages for personal injury caused by contractual breach.[175]

B. Residual Common Law Claims

42. Where there is no cover, the right to sue remains. In *Queenstown Lakes District Council v. Palmer*[176] Thomas J noted that the exchange was frequently spoken of as a social contract or social compact. Persons covered under the Act were denied access to the courts at common law in return for the perceived advantages of the statutory scheme.

Accordingly, if a claim does not involve personal injury in any form, or if it involves personal injury but falls outside the particular categories that are covered for compensation, an action for damages, if available, can proceed in the ordinary way. For example, claims for mental injury suffered by a secondary victim of an accident, for negligent poisoning, for infection by a sexual disease, or for cancer caused by smoking, are not barred. None of these constitutes a 'personal injury by

---

173. *See*, for example, *Wilding v. Attorney-General* [2003] 3 NZLR 787, holding that the bar applied to a claim for compensation for personal injury under the New Zealand Bill of Rights Act of 1990. Further, a court making a sentence of reparation under s. 32(5) Sentencing Act 2002 must not order the making of reparation in respect of consequential loss or damage 'for which compensation has been, or is to be, paid under the Accident Compensation Act 2001'. The subsection formerly referred to loss or damage 'for which the court believes a person has entitlements under the 2001 Act', and in *Davies v. Police* [2009] 3 NZLR 189 the Supreme Court held that the inquiry should be into whether there was cover for the type of loss for which there were entitlements under the Act, not into the sums actually payable. On this basis there could be no order for reparation in respect of the 20% of lost income not paid by the Corporation in any claim for earnings-related compensation (as to which *see* para. 43). The new wording was aimed specifically at reversing the decision in *Davies*, apparently in order to make special provision for victims of crime.

174. *McGougan v. DePuy International Ltd* [2018] NZCA 91, [2018] 2 NZLR 916; and *see* generally *Todd on Torts* (8th ed, 2019) para. 2.4.06(2).

175. *Brittain v. Telecom Corporation of New Zealand Ltd* [2002] 2 NZLR 201.

176. [1999] 1 NZLR 549; and *see McGougan v. DePuy International Ltd* [2018] NZCA 91, [2018] 2 NZLR 916 at [25]–[40].

an accident' as this concept is defined in the Act.[177] Again, the treatment injury regime does not extend to personal injury caused to certain participants in clinical trials,[178] or to secondary victims suffering stress as a result of negligent medical treatment to another,[179] or to a failure to warn of a risk of medical treatment falling short of the balance of probability and that risk later eventuates.[180] It is likely that a parent who is the victim of a negligent sterilization who sues for the cost of bringing up an unplanned child is not barred. The pregnancy is covered personal injury (*see* paragraph 35) but a claim for loss of earnings is a separate claim simply for the economic consequences of the relationship between mother and child.[181]

It is possible that the Corporation may, exceptionally, be liable in a civil action at the suit of a third party for failing to provide a victim of personal injury with the statutory benefits. In *EM v. ACC*[182] the mother of a young man entitled to attendant care payments sued the Corporation for negligence and breach of statutory duty in failing to meet its obligations to make the payments, causing her to suffer significant financial losses in providing supervision and care for her son herself. The court declined to strike out the claim, on the basis that this was a loss suffered by the plaintiff for which she was not entitled to compensation under the Act. She was not the person who had sustained a covered personal injury and she was not, therefore, the object of the statutory bar. Further, the claimed loss could not be said to arise 'directly or indirectly' out of the son's covered personal injury, nor could 'personal injury covered by this Act' be said to have caused the loss. The plaintiff's argument was that, had the payments been made, she could have managed financially, whereas she effectively did the job the corporation was supposed to do. Novel common law claims for negligence and breach of statutory duty were alleged, but they were not so untenable as to warrant striking them out.

A further possible basis for an action is where the plaintiff seeks to recover exemplary, rather than compensatory, damages. In *Donselaar v. Donselaar*[183] the Court of Appeal decided that actions for exemplary damages could still be maintained.

---

177. *See* Accident Compensation Act 2001, s. 25 (definition of 'accident') and s. 26 (definition of 'personal injury'). Sometimes there may be allegedly different injuries arising out of a single event, one being covered and the other uncovered. An example is where a victim injured in a road accident suffers mental injury on account of his or her own injuries (covered) and also on account of the death or injury of another person injured in the same accident (uncovered). In such a case, if the damages are quite indivisible a common law action is barred: *P v. Attorney-General* HC, Wellington, CIV-2006-485-874, 18 Jun. 2010, at [55]; cp *Sivasubramaniam v. Yarrall* [2005] NZAR 311.
178. Accident Compensation Act 2001, ss 32(4)–(6).
179. *See*, for example, *ACC v. F* [1991] 1 NZLR 234 (husband suffered 'reactive depression' on being unable to continue sexual relations with his wife after she was injured due to medical misadventure).
180. *Accident Compensation Corporation v. Ambros* [2008] 1 NZLR 340 at [47]–[52]. However, the occurrence of an adverse event following a failure to warn is likely nonetheless to amount to treatment injury, on the basis that this is not a necessary part or ordinary consequence of the treatment, with cover accordingly.
181. *J v. Accident Compensation Corporation* [2017] NZCA 441, [2017] 3 NZLR 804, esp. at [36]–[41]. For the position at common law, *see* para. 108.
182. [2016] NZHC 2535.
183. [1982] 1 NZLR 97; and *see Couch v. Attorney-General* [2010] 3 NZLR 149 at [84]–[90].

Richardson J explained that proceedings for exemplary damages were not 'proceedings for damages arising directly or indirectly out of' a person's injury or death, where the statutory bar applied, because exemplary damages did not arise out of the plaintiff's injury and were not directed to the plaintiff's loss. A common law claim for aggravated damages, which compensate for upset and outrage arising out of the circumstances in which a tort was committed,[184] perhaps can be justified as well, on the first of these reasons.[185]

In cases where there is cover under the statutory scheme, a victim of criminal misconduct causing personal injury can still sue for exemplary damages notwithstanding any criminal proceedings that have been or might be brought against the wrongdoer, but the civil court may have regard to any criminal penalty in deciding whether to make, or the amount of, an award.[186]

IV. Statutory Benefits

43. Where there is cover there is a right to compensation. The statutory entitlements are treatment and rehabilitation, earnings-related compensation, lump sum compensation for permanent impairment, and death benefits.

The corporation is liable to pay the cost of necessary and appropriate medical treatment and of social or vocational rehabilitation.[187] The purpose of social rehabilitation is to assist in restoring a claimant's independence to the maximum extent possible, and can cover such benefits as aids and appliances, home help, child care, modifications to the home, assistance with transport and training for independent living. Vocational rehabilitation is available to persons covered by the Act who are entitled to weekly compensation. It seeks to help a claimant maintain or obtain employment, or regain or acquire vocational independence.

Earnings-related compensation is payable to claimants who were earners at the time of the personal injury and who are unable, because of their injury, to engage in their employment.[188] There are special provisions dealing with, *inter alia*, earners not in permanent employment, the self-employed, low earners and potential earners. The amount payable is 80% of the claimant's weekly earnings, as calculated in accordance with detailed statutory formulae. All calculations are subject to a maximum weekly payment that is adjustable in relation to movements in average weekly earnings.[189]

Lump sums compensate for permanent impairment, including both physical impairment and mental injury caused by a physical injury or sexual abuse, but not for pain and suffering.[190] There is a minimum impairment threshold of 10%, and a minimum payment, which was originally set at NZD 2,500. The maximum sum,

184. *Attorney-General v. Niania* [1994] 3 NZLR 106.
185. The question was left open in *P v. Attorney-General* HC, Wellington, CIV-2006-485-874, 18 Jun. 2010.
186. Accident Compensation Act 2001, s. 319; *see* para. 577.
187. *Ibid.*, ss 69(1)(a), 75–96, Sch. 1, Part 1.
188. *Ibid.*, ss 69(1)(b), (c), 100–106, Sch. 1, Part 2.
189. The minimum weekly figure in 2019-20 was NZD 566.40 and the maximum was NZD 2015.59.
190. Accident Compensation Act 2001, s. 69(1)(d), Sch. 1, Part 3.

which is payable for impairment of 80% or more, was set at NZD 100,000. These figures are adjusted annually in line with the consumers' price index.[191] The amount payable in any particular case is calibrated so that more-seriously injured claimants receive proportionately more than less-seriously injured claimants.

Lastly, the Act provides for various payments in the event of the death of a person covered by the scheme.[192] A funeral grant is payable to the personal representatives and survivors' grants to a spouse, child under the age of 18, and any other dependant. There can also be compensation for the cost of child care in certain circumstances. Weekly compensation representing loss of dependency is payable to a surviving spouse and dependent children.

A claimant who qualifies for compensation may be disentitled to relief on a number of grounds.[193] These ultimately are penal provisions, preventing payment of what would otherwise be valid claims for reasons of public policy. They include: the claimant wilfully inflicting injury on himself or herself or committing suicide;[194] the claimant seeking compensation as a spouse or dependant in circumstances where he or she has been convicted of the murder of the deceased person;[195] the claimant being in prison;[196] and the claimant being injured in the course of committing a criminal offence punishable by a maximum term of imprisonment of at least two years, unless the Minister responsible for the scheme is satisfied that there are exceptional circumstances exempting the claimant from the operation of this provision.[197]

V. Claims

A. Claims Process

44. Victims can make a claim for compensation pursuant to the statutory claims process. This provides for the lodging of claims and the making of decisions on cover and entitlements.[198] Claims for cover must be lodged within twelve months of the date when personal injury is suffered, and for an entitlement within twelve months after the need for it arose.[199] However, the corporation must not decline a late claim unless it is prejudiced in its ability to make decisions. The date of the injury is defined in certain particular cases. In particular, in the case of treatment injury it is the date when the victim first seeks or receives treatment for the

191. The minimum figure in 2019-2020 was NZD 3,506 and the maximum was NZD 140,255.
192. Accident Compensation Act 2001, s. 69(1)(e), Sch. 1, Part 4.
193. *Ibid.*, ss 118–122.
194. *Ibid.*, s. 119.
195. *Ibid.*, s. 120.
196. *Ibid.*, s. 121.
197. *Ibid.*, s. 122, 122A.
198. *Ibid.*, Part 4.
199. *Ibid.*, s. 53(1), (3).

injury,[200] and in the case of occupational disease it is the earlier of the date of treatment or the date when the injury first results in incapacity.[201]

B. *Reviews and Appeals*

45. A claimant can apply to the corporation for a review of any of its decisions on the claim.[202] The application must be in writing and be made within three months of the decision in question.[203] The corporation is obliged to engage people to carry out reviews, but a reviewer's duty is to act independently.[204] The Act lays down various requirements for the conduct of the review, persons entitled to be present and formalities in relation to the reviewer's decision.[205] The reviewer must put aside the corporation's decision and look at the matter afresh and on the basis of its substantive merits.[206]

An appeal lies from a review decision to the District Court.[207] An appeal then lies to the High Court on a question of law, with the leave of the District Court or by a special grant of leave from the High Court.[208] Similarly, a further appeal lies to the Court of Appeal on a question of law, with the leave of the High Court or by a special grant of leave from the Court of Appeal.[209] The decision of the Court of Appeal is final and there is no third appeal to the Supreme Court.

C. *Code of Claimants' Rights*

46. The Act provides for the making of a Code of Claimants' Rights. The purpose of the Code is to meet the reasonable expectations of claimants about how the corporation should deal with them, by, *inter alia*, providing for the procedure for lodging and dealing with complaints about breaches of the Code, providing for the consequences of and remedies for breaches of the Code, and explaining claimants' rights to the review of a decision about a complaint.[210]

VI. Funding

47. Since its inception, accident compensation has been funded by levies on activities where accidents tend to occur and out of general taxation. Initially there

200. *Ibid.*, s. 38(1).
201. *Ibid.*, s. 37(1).
202. *Ibid.*, s. 134.
203. *Ibid.*, s. 135.
204. *Ibid.*, ss 137–138.
205. *Ibid.*, ss 140–144.
206. *Ibid.*, s. 145(1).
207. *Ibid.*, s. 149.
208. *Ibid.*, s. 162.
209. *Ibid.*, s. 163.
210. *Ibid.*, s. 40.

were levies on employers, on the self-employed, and on motor vehicle owners. Since then their reach has been widened. Today the levies fund four accounts:[211] the Work Account (for work-related injuries of employees, private domestic workers and self-employed persons); the Motor Vehicle Account (for motor vehicle injuries); the Earners' Account (for earners' non-work injuries); and the Treatment Injury Account (for injuries caused by treatment). These accounts finance most of the costs of the scheme. In addition there is the Non-Earners' Account (for injuries to non-earners other than motor vehicle injuries or treatment injuries), funded out of general taxation.

During the 1980s and 1990s the levies for the year were set on a pay-as-you-go basis. This means that they were calculated to pay only that year's costs, including both old and new claims. However, since the Accident Insurance Act of 1998 all of the accounts save for the Non-Earners' Account have been required to be fully funded. The levies for each account must cover all the costs of claims made in any particular year, including all future costs. Formerly a separate Residual Claims Account funded the continuing cost of past claims which were unfunded on a pay-as-you-go basis, but in 2010 this account was folded into the Work Account. Full funding of these outstanding residual liabilities was achieved in 2015.[212]

The levies funding the Work Account are collected from employers, private domestic workers and the self-employed, those for the Motor Vehicle Account from vehicle registrations and from the sale of petrol, and those for the Earners' Account directly from employees' earnings. In the case of the Treatment Account a statutory power to impose levies on registered health professionals and organizations that provide treatment under the Act has never been implemented. Rather, the Account is funded from the Earners' and Non-Earners' Accounts according to the mix of earner and non-earner clients.

VII. Administration

48. The scheme is administered by the Accident Compensation Corporation, which is a body corporate with powers to hold property, to sue and be sued, to do all such things as a company may do, and to do such other things as are necessary or expedient to enable it to perform its functions and duties.[213] Its functions include determining cover, providing entitlements, managing accounts, collecting levies and administering dispute resolution procedures.[214] A primary function is to promote measures to reduce the incidence and severity of personal injury.[215]

211. *Ibid.*, Part 6.
212. Accident Compensation Corporation *Annual Report 2015* at 66.
213. Accident Compensation Act 2001, Part 7.
214. *Ibid.*, ss 165, 262.
215. *Ibid.*, s. 263.

Part I. Liability for One's Own Acts

Chapter 1. General Principles

§1. Forms of Wrongdoing

49. We have seen that the common law of torts seeks to protect various different human interests from invasion by others. These include 'personal' interests, viz. physical and mental health and well-being, freedom of movement, reputation and privacy; property interests, including intellectual property; and financial interests.[216] The extent to which an invasion of any of these interests is actionable depends ultimately on the quality of the defendant's behaviour. Broadly speaking, the plaintiff's interest may be invaded intentionally and maliciously, intentionally but without malice, negligently, or innocently. A person may be seen to act intentionally if he or she acts knowing that a certain result will very probably follow and desiring that result, or at least being reckless as to whether it might come about. Intentional conduct is also malicious where the defendant has an improper or spiteful motive for acting. A person who does not intend to cause harm nonetheless acts negligently where he or she should have foreseen and prevented the harm. Where the conduct causing the harm is neither intentional nor negligent, it may be said to be innocent.

Torts are usually committed where conduct is culpable, in the sense that the protected interest is invaded intentionally or negligently. Only rarely need it be invaded maliciously. However, liability may also be imposed for innocent conduct, and, conversely, it may be denied where harm is caused intentionally and even maliciously. Perhaps the greatest uncertainty attaches to liability for negligence. A variety of factors can bear upon the question whether the defendant was under a legally enforceable duty to take care. All this means that it is difficult to generalize both about the nature and about the degree of fault or culpability that can give rise to a liability in tort. There is no tort of intentionally or even maliciously causing harm, and while there is a general tort of negligence its ambit is limited by policy concerns in all kinds of ways.

The arrangement of the material in this and the following chapter should be understood with these points in mind. In this chapter we will consider liability for trespass to the person first, for the concern here broadly is with all intentional wrongdoing causing harm to the person. Second, we will examine the general principles of negligence, for this is the one principle of the law of torts that is avowedly

216. *See* paras 25–31.

based simply on blameworthy conduct, whatever the nature of the damage. Finally, we will consider the capacity of persons to sue or be sued. In Chapter 2, we will examine various specific cases of liability involving different standards of conduct in relation to different forms of damage. Some are founded on malicious wrongdoing (generally torts involving abuse of legal procedure and abuse of public office), some on an intention to cause harm (certain economic torts), and some on an intention to act or to speak rather than to cause harm (trespassing on land, interfering with goods, defaming a person or invading a person's privacy). Conversely, some torts involve aspects of liability without fault (nuisance and other interferences with the use of land). Permeating all these are the general principles of negligence. As may be imagined, the relevant principles of law sometimes become complex and to a degree uncertain.

The focus of both chapters in this part is on liability for one's own acts. In Part II we will consider the relevant principles governing liability for the acts of others, for property and for animals. In both Parts the concern is with common law liability. In Part III we will examine certain special heads of liability, founded on statute, where intention or negligence does not need to be shown.

§2. Intentional Wrongdoing

I. Trespass to the Person

50. There are three torts falling under the general rubric of trespass to the person, namely assault (causing the apprehension of force), battery (actually inflicting force), and false imprisonment (depriving of freedom). The function of these torts is to protect the physical safety and sanctity of the person. They retain their relevance in New Zealand notwithstanding that the accident compensation scheme bars a private remedy by way of compensation for personal injuries, for they may still serve to vindicate rights, to punish wrongdoers, and to compensate for harm not amounting to personal injury. Assault and false imprisonment are not in any event concerned with personal injury, and a common law action for battery remains possible in the case of force not causing actual injury. As regards all three torts, the award of aggravated or exemplary damages may be an option.

II. Trespass and Case

51. The earliest remedy at common law for tortious misconduct was provided by a form of writ, first issued out of the king's courts in the twelfth century, known as trespass *vi et armis et contra pacem regis* (with force and arms and against the king's peace). The writ was concerned with forcible breaches of the peace causing injury to another. However, it could not easily be adapted to give a remedy for non-violent wrongs, and eventually, in the fourteenth century, a new form of writ came to be issued omitting the allegation of force. These non-forcible trespass actions came to be known as trespass on the special case or trespass on the case.

The requirement in trespass of forcible injury corresponded quite closely in practice with harm that was *directly* inflicted. The action on the case came to provide an alternative remedy for *consequential* loss.[217] Subsequent developments show trespass becoming more closely associated with wilful injuries and cases with negligently inflicted harm. There is a paradox here, for trespass originally was regarded as prima facie wrongful, and liability was not dependent on proof of intention or negligence, although certain limited defences were recognized.[218] It was only in the late nineteenth century, after the abolition of the forms of action, that the strict approach came to be questioned and there began a move towards the assimilation of the standard of liability in trespass and in 'case' (or negligence, as 'case' was now known). The decisive step was taken in *Stanley v. Powell*,[219] where Denman J held that no action for unintended personal injury lay in the absence of fault. Even after that it was argued that the burden of proof was different. In trespass the burden was on the defendant to disprove negligence, the conduct being regarded as prima facie wrongful, whereas in negligence the burden was on the plaintiff to establish liability. However, the argument was finally rejected in *Fowler v. Lanning*.[220] In this case the plaintiff had pleaded simply that the defendant shot him and that he thereby sustained damage. Diplock J held that the statement of claim disclosed no cause of action, because in any action for trespass to the person the onus of proof as regards the defendant's intention or negligence lay on the plaintiff. The same view has been taken in New Zealand.[221]

More recent cases show trespass being founded on intention alone. In England, in *Letang v. Cooper*,[222] Lord Denning MR maintained that the distinction between trespass and case was obsolete, and that causes of action were now divided according to whether the defendant caused the injury intentionally or unintentionally. So, if the injury was inflicted unintentionally, the only cause of action was in negligence.[223] In New Zealand, in *Dehn v. Attorney-General*,[224] Tipping J similarly held that battery must involve the intentional application of force. Seemingly, the requirement that the conduct be intentional has superseded the old requirement that harm be inflicted directly.[225] Probably the position now is that trespass simply involves intentional conduct, and there is no longer any independent requirement that the harm be inflicted directly. Conversely, in the case of unintended accidents, trespass does not lie and any action must be brought in negligence.

---

217. *Reynolds v. Clarke* (1725) 1 Strange 634 at 636, 93 ER 747 at 748.
218. *Weaver v. Ward* (1616) Hob 134; 80 ER 284; *Leame v. Bray* (1803) 3 East 593; 102 ER 724; *Wakeman v. Robinson* (1823) 1 Bing 213; 130 ER 86; *Hall v. Fearnley* (1842) 3 QB 919; 114 ER 761.
219. [1891] 1 QB 86.
220. [1959] 1 QB 426.
221. *Beals v. Hayward* [1960] NZLR 131; *S v. G* [1995] 3 NZLR 641 at 687.
222. [1965] 1 QB 232; approved in *A v. Hoare* [2008] 2 WLR 311.
223. In *Stubbings v. Webb* [1993] AC 498 the House of Lords supported the converse proposition, that for an intentional direct act the only cause of action was in trespass. But the decision was widely criticized as unsound in principle and likely to lead to anomalies, and in *A v. Hoare* [2008] 2 WLR 311 it was overruled; and *see Stingel v. Clark* (2006) 80 ALJR 1339.
224. [1988] 2 NZLR 564 at 583 (on appeal [1989] 1 NZLR 320); and *see T v. H* [1995] 3 NZLR 37 at 51.
225. *Kaye v. Robertson* [1991] FSR 62 at 68–69; *Iversen v. Zendel Industries (NZ) Ltd* 8/6/93, HC Auckland CP2171/91, J. Williams.

There are a number of differences between trespass and negligence that may be significant. First, trespass is actionable per se: damage is needed in negligence.[226] An action in trespass may serve to vindicate the right to inviolability of the person even where no actual damage has been suffered. Nominal damages may be awarded in such a case.[227] Indeed, if unintentional trespass remains a possibility, it may be that damage must then be shown.[228] Second, trespass does not involve the duty of care element that exists with regard to negligence. However, in trespass the requirement of intention is a restrictive control on the ambit of liability. Third, it is still possible that the rules governing remoteness of damage may differ. Some authority holds that the test in trespass is directness rather than foreseeability.[229] The Court of Appeal has left the point open.[230] Fourth, contributory negligence probably may not be a defence in an action for trespass to the person, although the issue has not been finally determined.[231] Fifth, there may be different consequences as regards the law of limitation of actions.[232]

III. Assault

52. An assault is an overt act intentionally creating in another person an apprehension of the imminent infliction of a battery without that person's consent.[233] The question is judged objectively. The test is whether a reasonable person in the plaintiff's position would have had the necessary fear of immediate harm.[234] A common example is a threat to physically attack a person. Again, it is an assault to point a loaded gun at a person,[235] or an unloaded gun where the person reasonably believes or fears it to be loaded.[236] There is no assault if the person being threatened is not aware of the threat, as where the person is asleep,[237] although if the threat is actually carried out there will be a battery.

The defendant must create an apprehension of immediate or imminent harm. So a victim of sexual abuse was no longer assaulted during a twenty-two-year period after the abuse ended, even though she lived in continuing fear of the abuser.[238] And conduct that was no more than agitated and loud was not enough.[239] In an unusual

---

226. *Mayfair Ltd v. Pears* [1987] 1 NZLR 459 at 465; *R (Lumba) v. Secretary of State for the Home Department* [2012] 1 AC 245.
227. *Re Chase* [1989] 1 NZLR 325 at 340; *R (Lumba) v. Secretary of State for the Home Department* [2011] UKSC 12, [2012] 1 AC 245.
228. *Letang v. Cooper* [1965] 1 QB 232 at 244–245 per L.J. Diplock.
229. *Wormald v. Cole* [1954] 1 QB 614 at 625; *Wilson v. Pringle* [1987] 1 QB 237 at 247.
230. *Mayfair v. Pears* [1987] 1 NZLR 459.
231. *Standard Chartered Bank v. Pakistan National Building Corporation* [2003] 1 AC 959 at [45]; Compare *Hoebergen v. Koppens* [1974] 2 NZLR 597; *see* para. 478.
232. *See S v. Attorney-General* [2003] 3 NZLR 450 at [120]; *Murray v. Morel & Co. Ltd* [2007] 3 NZLR 721 at [49]; *see* para. 460.
233. As to consent to assault, *see* para. 495.
234. *T v. H* [1995] 3 NZLR 37 at 51.
235. *R v. Baucke* (1907) 9 GLR 317.
236. *Rixon v. Star City Pty Ltd* (2001) 53 NSWLR 98 at [56].
237. *R v. Kerr* [1988] 1 NZLR 270.
238. *T v. H* [1995] 3 NZLR 37.
239. *Outtrim v. Li* [2010] NZAR 282 at [71]–[72].

application, the President of Equatorial Guinea was not put in fear of an immediate application of force by the mounting of an attempted coup.[240] It is possible for an assault to be committed over the telephone provided the victim is put in a sufficiently immediate fear of violence.[241] However, a mere inquiry as to a person's identity did not constitute an assault, as it lacked the requisite intention to create an apprehension of imminent harm.[242]

A conditional threat can and often does constitute an assault. A threat in its very nature usually provides the person threatened with an alternative, unpleasant though it often may be. Accordingly a threat by the defendant to use a carving knife on a police constable if the constable did not get off the defendant's property was an assault on the constable.[243]

IV. Battery

53. A battery is the act of intentionally applying force to the body of another person without that person's consent[244] or other lawful justifications.[245] The act may cause actual personal injury, and where it does, the bar on actions for compensatory damages in the accident compensation legislation applies. Nevertheless, the action also provides the victim with a remedy for any contact that affronts his or her personal dignity. So, wrongful physical contact without actual injury – like spitting at another,[246] or searching a person without lawful authorization,[247] or unwanted sexual touching[248] – remains actionable. Even where personal injury is caused, an action to vindicate the victim in respect of the wrong,[249] or for exemplary damages may still be possible.[250]

There must be an application of force, although the slightest degree will suffice.[251] Ordinarily some kind of physical force is involved, but the concept may include the ability or power to control, influence or produce an effect. The delivery of an electric shock may properly be regarded as the application of force in this sense.[252]

Older authority, consistently with the origins of trespass as requiring direct injury, requires that the force be inflicted directly to the person of the plaintiff. So, for

240. *Mbasogo v. Logo Ltd* [2006] EWCA Civ 1370.
241. *R v. Ireland* [1998] AC 147.
242. *Rixon v. Star City Pty Ltd* (2001) 53 NSWLR 98.
243. *Police v. Greaves* [1964] NZLR 295.
244. As to consent to battery, *see* para. 495.
245. *P v. T* [1998] 1 NZLR 257.
246. *Moir v. Police* 10 Nov. 86, Jeffries J., HC Christchurch AP220/86.
247. *Forrest v. Attorney-General* [2012] NZAR 798.
248. Many trespass actions involve sexual abuse. For an instance *see S v. Attorney-General* [2003] 3 NZLR 450. For discussion of 'sexual grooming', *see Walsh v. Byrne* [2015] IEHC 414; *ABC v. West Heath 2000 Ltd* [2015] EWHC 2687.
249. *Ashley v. Chief Constable of Sussex Police* [2008] 1 AC 962: *see* paras 573–574.
250. *See* para. 42. For issues of double jeopardy *see* para. 577.
251. *Cole v. Turner* (1704) 6 Mod Rep 3; 86 ER 684.
252. *Kovalev. v. Police* [2010] NZAR 30.

example, it was not a battery to set a spring gun that subsequently injured a trespasser,[253] or to infect a person with venereal disease,[254] although the conduct might be actionable on some other basis.[255] Recent cases put the emphasis on the defendant's *intention*: provided the force is inflicted intentionally, the defendant is liable.[256] On this view, deliberately shining a bright light causing injury to sight[257] or exposing a person to a toxic substance[258] can qualify as batteries.

There is no liability for battery if the victim has consented to the contact.[259] Where consent is in issue, the question is whether the contact is unwanted, not whether it is in some sense hostile. A prank getting out of hand, an over-friendly slap on the back, or surgical treatment to which the patient is mistakenly thought to have consented, all may transcend the bounds of lawfulness without being characterized as hostile.[260] Certainly, a kiss can be a battery if undesired by the recipient.[261] Sometimes consent can be implied. A helpful test is whether the contact is generally acceptable in the ordinary conduct of daily life.[262] So, placing a hand on another's shoulder simply to engage her attention was generally acceptable and, accordingly, was not actionable.[263]

Battery is a crime as well as a tort,[264] and a prosecution may have implications for any civil action. First, a prior conviction may assist the plaintiff in establishing that the defendant is liable in the civil action.[265] Second, a criminal court has power to sentence an offender who causes emotional harm or property damage to make financial reparation to the victim,[266] but a sentence of this kind does not affect any right a person may have to recover in civil proceedings damages in excess of this award.[267] Third, conviction and sentencing in a criminal trial may sometimes preclude an award of exemplary damages in a subsequent civil action, on the grounds that this would constitute double punishment.[268]

---

253. *Bird v. Holbrook* (1828) 4 Bing 628; 130 ER 911.
254. *R v. Clarence* (1888) 22 QBD 23; and *see CLM v. Accident Compensation Corporation* [2006] 3 NZLR 127.
255. For example, under the rule in *Wilkinson v. Downton* [1897] 2 QB 57; *see* paras 72–73.
256. *Letang v. Cooper* [1965] 1 QB 232; *Dehn v. Attorney-General* [1988] 2 NZLR 564 at 583 (not considered on appeal [1989] 1 NZLR 320).
257. *Kaye v. Robertson* [1991] FSR 62 at 68–69.
258. *Iversen v. Zendel Industries (NZ) Ltd* 8/6/93, J. Williams, HC Auckland CP2171/91.
259. *S v. G* [1995] 3 NZLR 681 at 687.
260. *Re F* [1990] 2 AC 1, 73.
261. *Hughes v. Callaghan* [1933] GLR 330.
262. *Wainwright v. Home Office* [2004] 2 AC 406 at [9]; *Thompson v. Police* [2012] NZAR 741 at [13]–[15]; *Walker v. Commissioner of Police of the Metropolis* [2015] 1 WLR 312 at [17]–[30].
263. *Rixon v. Star City Pty Ltd* (2001) 53 NSWLR 98 at [52]–[54].
264. Crimes Act 1961, ss 188–196.
265. By s. 47(1) Evidence Act 2006, when the fact that a person has committed an offence is relevant to an issue in a civil proceeding, proof of the conviction is conclusive proof that the person committed the offence. But by s. 47(2), the judge may, exceptionally, permit a party to offer evidence tending to prove that the person did not commit the offence.
266. Sentencing Act 2002, s. 32(1).
267. *Ibid.*, s. 38(2).
268. *See* para. 577.

V. False Imprisonment

A. General

54. False imprisonment is the unlawful total restraint of the liberty of the person.[269] The restraint may be achieved by the use of physical barriers such as the four walls of a building, by physical force in circumstances amounting to the commission of a battery, or by a threat of force or assertion of authority that induces the plaintiff to submit to the will of the other.[270]

Someone who does not personally effect an imprisonment may nonetheless be liable where he or she has authorized the imprisonment, or has been active in promoting or causing it. A store detective was not liable for false imprisonment where he merely gave information to the police for them to take such action as they thought fit, and did not request, promote or encourage the plaintiff's arrest.[271] On the other hand, an arrest that was procured by a police officer who had deliberately lied to the officer making the arrest was unlawful, and the claimant accordingly had been falsely imprisoned.[272]

The restraint or detention normally will be by way of positive conduct. However, an omission to release a person from detention is actionable as a false imprisonment, at least, where the continued detention is unlawful or there is a breach of a duty to release the person. Examples are a failure to release a lawfully arrested person where there has been undue delay in bringing him or her before a court,[273] and a failure to discharge a prisoner at the end of his or her sentence.[274] But there was no liability for false imprisonment where a strike by prison officers had the indirect consequence that prisoners were left locked in their cells.[275]

In *R (Lumba) v. Secretary of State for the Home Department*[276] the UK Supreme Court affirmed that false imprisonment was a trespassory tort and was actionable per se regardless of whether the victim had suffered harm. When a claimant had proved that he was directly and intentionally imprisoned by the defendant, the burden shifted to the defendant to show that there was lawful justification for the imprisonment. In the instant case the claimants had been detained pursuant to a policy that was unlawful and in breach of public law principles, and it was not a defence to their actions for false imprisonment to show that a lawful decision to detain them could and would have been made. But, had lawful policies been applied, it was

---

269. *Willis v. Attorney-General* [1989] 3 NZLR 574 at 579.
270. *See R (Jollah) v. Secretary of State for the Home Department* [2020] UKSC 4, [2020] 2 WLR 418 at [24].
271. *Davidson v. Chief Constable of North Wales* [1994] 2 All ER 597.
272. *Copeland v. Metropolitan Police Commissioner* [2015] 3 All ER 391; and *see Barkhuysen v. Hamilton* [2018] QB 1015.
273. *Whithair v. Attorney-General* [1996] 2 NZLR 45.
274. *R v. Governor of Brockhill Prison, ex p Evans (No. 2)* [2001] 2 AC 19; *Manga v. Attorney-General* [2000] 2 NZLR 65; *see* further para. 56.
275. *Iqbal v. Prison Officers Association* [2010] 2 WLR 1054.
276. [2012] 1 AC 245; and *see R (Kambadzi) v. Secretary of State for the Home Department* [2011] 1 WLR 1299 (failure to comply with a published policy periodically to review the exercise of a statutory power of executive detention rendered the claimant's continued detention unlawful, and an action for false imprisonment could lie).

inevitable that the claimants would have been detained, and, therefore, they had suffered no loss or damage and were entitled only to nominal damages.[277]

B. Actual Restraint

55. A person who is unlawfully locked up in a room[278] or a car,[279] or who is unlawfully restrained by handcuffs,[280] or who is detained without being lawfully arrested[281] can maintain false imprisonment. However, the restraint must be total in the sense that the plaintiff is restrained in every direction. So preventing a person from walking along the public footway on one side of Hammersmith Bridge did not imprison that person because he was free to go back the way he came or to cross to the other side of the bridge.[282] But confining a person to his house in specified hours by an unlawful curfew was a sufficient restraint.[283] Where the defendant has caused the plaintiff to be detained within defined boundaries, but some means of egress is or may be available, the courts will have regard to the reasonableness of what is needed to escape. For example, a passenger who had paid to enter a ferry terminal and who could proceed on the contracted-for ferry crossing was not imprisoned where he was prevented from going back through the entrance turnstiles without making a second payment.[284]

In cases involving physical restraint, it is not necessary for the plaintiff to know of the restraint. Accordingly, an employee was falsely imprisoned when he was asked to remain in a waiting room and, unbeknownst to him, he was suspected of theft and would have been prevented from leaving had he sought to do so.[285] However, if a person is unaware that he or she has been falsely imprisoned, and has suffered no damage, he or she can normally expect to recover no more than nominal damages.[286] Sometimes the evidence may indicate that there was no detention in fact. For example, the House of Lords has taken the view that an informal mental patient who was fully compliant and who did not dissent from staying in hospital was not deprived of his liberty. The fact that staff may have had it in mind to take steps to detain the patient if he tried to leave did not mean that he was detained while he did not try to leave.[287]

Where the complaint is of a detention other than by actual physical or forcible restraint, the question is whether, in the circumstances, the plaintiff reasonably felt obliged to submit to the will of the defendant.[288] Examples are where a person was

277. *See* also *Parker v. The Chief Constable of Essex Police* [2018] EWCA 2788, [2019] 1 WLR 2238.
278. *Meering v. Grahame-White Aviation Co. Ltd* (1919) 122 LT Rep 44.
279. *Ministry of Transport v. Alexander* [1991] 2 NZLR 281; *Hicks v. Young* [2015] EWHC 1144.
280. *Hayward v. O'Keefe* [1993] 1 NZLR 181.
281. *Blundell v. A-G* [1968] NZLR 341.
282. *Bird v. Jones* (1845) 7 QB 742.
283. *R (Jollah) v. Secretary of State for the Home Department* [2020] UKSC 4, [2020] 2 WLR 418.
284. *Robinson v. Balmain New Ferry Co.* [1910] AC 295.
285. *Meering v. Grahame-White Aviation Co. Ltd* (1919) 122 LT Rep 44.
286. *Murray v. Ministry of Defence* [1988] 1 WLR 692.
287. *R v. Bournewood Trust, ex p L* [1999] 1 AC 458.
288. *Neilsen v. Attorney-General* [2001] 3 NZLR 433 at [5]–[6].

required to go to a police station and to remain there, and she reasonably considered there was no choice but to submit;[289] and where the claimant was subject to a curfew which was enforced by the wearing of an electronic tag.[290] If, however, the plaintiff acts voluntarily in complying with a request by the defendant to remain where he or she is, when under no actual or apparent compulsion to do so, there is no detention and no false imprisonment.[291]

C. Unlawful Restraint

56. There must be an intention to detain. Mere negligence in causing a person's detention where there is no such intention will not suffice to establish liability,[292] but lack of fault in wrongly believing that there is lawful authority to detain is irrelevant. So the incorrect calculation by a prison governor of a prisoner's term of imprisonment, causing her to be imprisoned for fifty-nine days longer than the period produced by the correct calculation, was a false imprisonment even though the governor had simply followed existing court decisions at a time before they had been overruled.[293] Again, a prisoner who had been detained in prison according to a calculation which had been declared correct by the Court of Appeal, but which the Supreme Court had subsequently determined was wrong, succeeded in his claim for false imprisonment in respect of the extra time he had spent in gaol.[294] On the other hand, there was no false imprisonment where the plaintiff was not released on bail after the expiry of a time limit, as the prison governor had no authority to release without a court order;[295] where a judge made a simple arithmetical mistake when handing down a ruling, and a prison governor merely followed the ruling in obeying a warrant of commitment that was on its face lawful and proper;[296] and where there was a delay in recalculating the length of the claimant's imprisonment following a change in the legal principles governing the aggregation of sentences.[297] In these cases the court took the view that there was in fact lawful authority to detain, and so there could be no false imprisonment. Again, where a prisoner was detained by an order under a statute authorizing preventive detention, and the Act was later held to be invalid, the order was treated as valid until it was set aside.[298]

289. *A-G v. Niania* [1994] 3 NZLR 106.
290. *R (Jollah) v. Secretary of State for the Home Department* [2020] UKSC 4, [2020] 2 WLR 418.
291. *MacIntosh v. Cohen* (1904) 24 NZLR 625; *A-G v. Niania* [1994] 3 NZLR 106.
292. *Thompson v. Attorney-General* [2014] NZAR 1282 (appeal dismissed on other grounds: *Thompson v. Attorney-General* [2016] NZCA 215); *see* para. 155.
293. *R v. Governor of Brockhill Prison, ex p Evans (No. 2)* [2001] 2 AC 19; and *see Roberts v. Chief Constable of the Cheshire Constabulary* [1999] 1 WLR 662 (CA); *Manga v. Attorney-General* [2000] 2 NZLR 65; cp *McCreaner v. Ministry of Justice* [2015] 1 WLR 354.
294. *Chief Executive of the Department of Corrections v. Gardiner* [2017] NZCA 608, [2018] 2 NZLR 712.
295. *Olutu v. Home Office* [1997] 1 WLR 328; and *see Percy v. Hall* [1997] QB 924.
296. *Quinland v. Governor of Swaleside Prison* [2002] 3 WLR 807.
297. *McCreaner v. Ministry of Justice* [2015] 1 WLR 354 (although a duty arose in negligence following that delay).
298. *State of New South Wales v. Kable* [2013] HCA 26.

An associated question is whether a person already lawfully detained in prison or other place of confinement can maintain false imprisonment in respect of some further, unlawful restraint within the confines of the prison. The question was considered in a joint appeal to the House of Lords in *Weldon v. Home Office* and *R v. Deputy Governor of Parkhurst Prison, ex p Hague.*[299] In *Weldon* the plaintiff alleged that while he was detained in prison certain prison officers, without good cause, dragged him from his cell, placed him in a punishment cell without clothes, and assaulted him. He argued that this unlawful mistreatment deprived him of his residual liberties within the prison and that this constituted false imprisonment. In *Hague* the plaintiff sought damages for false imprisonment and also for breach of statutory duty on the basis that he had been held in solitary confinement without lawful authority. The House of Lords held that neither action could succeed, for a prisoner had no residual liberty of which he could be deprived. Once lawfully committed to prison, a prisoner's whole life was regulated by the prison regime. Accordingly, placing Weldon in a strip cell and segregating Hague altered the conditions under which each was detained but did not deprive either of any liberty not already lost when initially confined. Again, in *Iqbal v. Prison Officers' Association*[300] Lord Neuberger MR thought that it better accorded both with principle and with practicality to limit claims by prisoners who were left locked in their cells by the inaction of prison officers to cases where the relevant prison officers were guilty of misfeasance in public office.

In *White v. Attorney-General*[301] the Court of Appeal expressed a tentative view in support of the decision in Hague. So putting an inmate in a Boy's Home in secure confinement and subjecting him to a more intrusive detention than was warranted did not amount to false imprisonment, although it might have been a breach of the Superintendent's duty of care, and also a breach of the NZ Bill of Rights Act 1990.

D. Damages

57. The plaintiff in an action for false imprisonment is entitled to recover compensatory damages for the imprisonment and for distress, humiliation, or fear.[302] In determining the measure of damages, the courts take into account, *inter alia*, the period of imprisonment[303] and circumstances of aggravation or mitigation of the damage. The conduct, character, and circumstances of the plaintiff are relevant insofar as they are concerned with the extent of the injury that he or she has suffered by

299. [1992] 1 AC 58; and *see Cullen v. Chief Constable of the Royal Ulster Constabulary* [2003] 1 WLR 1763. Compare *R (Munjaz) v. Mersey Care NHS Trust* [2006] 2 AC 148 per Lord Stein, who thought *Hague* should not be followed.

300. [2010] 2 WLR 1054.

301. [2010] NZCA 139.

302. *Willis v. A-G* [1989] 3 NZLR 574 at 579; *Innes v. Wong* [1996] 3 NZLR 238.

303. Detention of a few seconds may justify only an award of nominal damages: *Walker v. Commissioner of Police of the Metropolis* [2015] 1 WLR 312. In *Regina (Jollah) v. Secretary of State for the Home Department* [2018] EWCA Civ 1260, [2019] 1 WLR 394 at [97] the court took into account the limited degree of restraint on liberty involved in the unlawful imposition of a night-time home curfew, and in *R (Jollah) v. Secretary of State for the Home Department* [2020] UKSC 4, [2020] 2 WLR 418 the defendant's appeal on liability was dismissed.

way of shock and humiliation. For example, damages for wrongfully detaining a prisoner beyond his proper release date were reduced by the prisoner's record of recidivism,[304] whereas unlawfully imprisoning a person with no criminal record justified a substantial award.[305] The reasonableness or otherwise of the defendant's conduct may also have an impact. High-handed, intrusive, or particularly blameworthy conduct on the part of the defendant may serve to aggravate the hurt suffered by the plaintiff and consequently the damages awarded.[306] Exemplary damages may be appropriate where the defendant's conduct is so serious as to be deserving of punishment and the compensatory damages are not sufficient for this purpose.[307]

Some further guidance was provided by the Court of Appeal in *Chief Executive of the Department of Corrections v. Gardiner*,[308] where it was recognized that prisoners who had been lawfully convicted and imprisoned but detained for too long might find it difficult to prove pecuniary losses. It might be possible to establish the loss of a chance of employment or other financial gain had release been timely, but in many cases any loss would be attributable to the period of lawful imprisonment. Injury to liberty should be distinguished from emotional harm, which might be limited where the prisoner was not expecting to be released earlier. The value of liberty might vary both with the length of the sentence lawfully imposed and with the period of lawful detention. In fixing the amount the starting point should be that damages were at large and should not be assessed in a formulaic way.

As regards quantum, the cases show relatively modest sums being awarded for short periods of imprisonment, increasing for longer periods, with aggravating or mitigating factors serving to increase or decrease the total award.[309]

VI. Defences

A. *Arrest*

1. General Principles

58. The detention of a person is justified if made by way of a lawful arrest. The onus of proving that an arrest is lawful is on the person causing the arrest.[310] There is lawful authority where the arrest is made under a warrant or where a specific statutory authorization is given to arrest another without warrant. A warrant to arrest

304. *Manga v. Attorney-General* [2000] 2 NZLR 65.
305. *Spautz v. Butterworth* (1996) 41 NSWLR 1.
306. *Rowlands v. Chief Constable of the Merseyside Police* [2007] 1 WLR 1065; and *see H v. Commissioner of Police of the Metropolis* [2013] 1 WLR 3021.
307. *Carrington v. A-G* [1972] NZLR 1106; *Craig v. A-G* (1986) 2 CRNZ 551; *Hayward v. O'Keefe* [1993] 1 NZLR 181; *see Manga v. Attorney-General* [2000] 2 NZLR 65.
308. [2017] NZCA 608, [2018] 2 NZLR 712.
309. There is a list of examples in *Caie v. Attorney-General* [2005] NZAR 703 at [147] (appeal dismissed [2006] NZAR 379).
310. *Copeland v. Metropolitan Police Commissioner* [2015] 3 All ER 391 at [20].

may be issued by a District Court Judge, a Justice of the Peace, or a registrar.[311] The warrant provides authority for a duly authorized person to arrest the person named in it. Arrest without warrant is governed by section 315(1) of the Crimes Act 1961. This provides that no one shall be arrested without warrant, except under the provisions of the Crimes Act or some other enactment expressly giving power to arrest without warrant. Any arrest made under these powers, with or without a warrant, is 'justified',[312] meaning the person making the arrest is not guilty of an offence and is not liable to any civil proceedings.[313] Accordingly, no action will lie for false imprisonment, for battery or for any other tort.

The defence of lawful arrest can apply only where the defendant has purported to arrest the plaintiff. In order to make an arrest, there must be words or conduct showing an intention to detain, coupled with a claim to be acting under the authority of law.[314] Whether a person is under arrest is generally a question of fact.[315] The word 'arrest' need not be used, provided it is made clear that the person is under arrest. One test, although not necessarily exhaustive, is whether there has been physical seizure or touching of the person with a view to detention, with the intent of such seizure or touching made clear by words or otherwise; or the utterance of the words of arrest coupled with acquiescence or submission on the part of the person arrested.[316]

Detention without arrest is unlawful and actionable as false imprisonment, unless it can be justified on some other basis. The police have certain statutory powers of detention short of arrest,[317] and so do other public officers, such road enforcement officers[318] and customs officers.[319] At common law, any person, whether a police officer or not, who reasonably believes a breach of the peace is being or may be committed, is entitled to take reasonable steps, including detaining a person, in order to prevent that breach of the peace or to bring it to an end.[320] A detention also may be justified on various other bases that are considered below.

---

311. Summary Proceedings Act 1957, s. 19.
312. Crimes Act 1961, s. 26(2) and (3) (arrest with warrant), ss 31, 33 (arrest without warrant).
313. *Ibid.*, s. 2 (definition of 'justified').
314. *R v. Goodwin* [1993] 2 NZLR 153; *R v. P* [1996] 3 NZLR 132 at 136.
315. *R v. Ahmed* [2010] 1 NZLR 262 at [36]–[40].
316. *R v. Kirifi* [1992] 2 NZLR 8 at 11–12.
317. *See*, for example, the Misuse of Drugs Act 1975, s. 18(3) (a police officer may detain and search a person reasonably believed to be in the possession of controlled drugs); Arms Act 1983, s. 60 (a police officer may detain and search a person in a public place reasonably believed to be in possession of a weapon); Crimes Act 1961, s. 224 (a police officer may detain and search a person reasonably believed to be in possession of stolen goods).
318. For example, under the Land Transport Act 1998, s. 13 (road users must comply with lawful directions of enforcement officers under the Act).
319. For example, under the Customs and Excise Act 2018, ss 201–221 (a customs officer may detain and search for dutiable, restricted, uncustomed, or forfeited goods in certain circumstances).
320. *Lavin v. Albert* [1982] AC 546; *Waaka v. Police* [1987] 1 NZLR 754 at 757; *Police v. Cox* [1989] 2 NZLR 293 at 295–296; *R v. Chief Constable of Gloucestershire* [2007] 2 WLR 46; *Austin v. Metropolitan Police Commissioner* [2008] 1 All ER 564; *Regina (Hicks and others) v. Commissioner of Police of the Metropolis* [2017] UKSC 9, [2017] AC 256.

2. Arrest by a Private Citizen

59. By section 35 of the Crimes Act 1961, anyone is justified in arresting without warrant any person whom he or she finds committing an offence against the Act that is punishable by at least three years' imprisonment, or any person whom he or she finds by night committing any offence against the Act. Reasonable force may be used.[321]

For section 35 to apply, the arrested person must have been committing the offence in fact: the mere belief by the arrester (even on reasonable grounds) that the person was committing the offence does not suffice. Furthermore, the person must be 'found committing' the offence:[322] he or she must be detected during the physical perpetration of the crime or, at least, immediately on its completion or on a 'fresh pursuit'.[323] If the offence has been completed or, if it is continuing, it is punishable by less than three years' imprisonment[324] and is not committed 'by night',[325] then a private citizen has no power to make an arrest. So section 35 could not apply to an arrest by store detectives of a person who had taken a video powerpack of a value such that the maximum sentence was only one-year imprisonment.[326] In a case such as this, it is possible that an action for false imprisonment might lie at the suit of the thief. The danger is more apparent than real, and any action for damages would likely fail on the application of the common law principle of *ex turpi causa non oritur actio*.[327] Even so, a prudent course for a citizen who suspects an offence has been committed is to pass this information on to a police officer and leave the decision to arrest the suspected offender to that officer. Provided the informant does not go further and actively instigate or promote the arrest, then the arrest is the act of the officer and the informant is not liable.[328]

3. Arrest by a Police Officer

60. A police officer may arrest under a warrant, and may rely on the authority of that warrant if sued for false imprisonment.[329] In addition, by section 315(1) of the Crimes Act 1961, a police officer may arrest without a warrant pursuant to any relevant statutory power. Section 315(2) further provides that a police officer and all persons whom he calls to his assistance may arrest without a warrant (i) any person whom he finds disturbing the public peace or committing an offence punishable by imprisonment and (ii) any person whom the officer has good cause to suspect of having committed a breach of the peace or an offence punishable by imprisonment.

321. Crimes Act 1961, s. 39.
322. *See Palmer-Brown v. Police* [1985] 1 NZLR 365; *R v. Ahmed* [2010] 1 NZLR 262 at [41]–[50].
323. *Hanway v. Boultbee* (1830) 1 Moo & R 15; 174 ER 6; *Downing v. Capel* (1867) LR 2 CP 461.
324. Theft of an object worth less than NZD 1,000 carries a maximum sentence of one-year imprisonment and, if less than NZD 500, three months: Crimes Act 1961, s. 223.
325. 'Night' means between 9 p.m. and 6 a.m.: Crimes Act 1961, s. 2.
326. *R v. N* [1999] 1 NZLR 713 at 717.
327. *See* paras 486–472.
328. *Davidson v. Chief Constable of North Wales* [1994] 2 All ER 597.
329. Crimes Act 1961, s. 26(2), (3); *see* para. 58.

In addition to this, there are a large number of particular statutory provisions authorizing a police officer to arrest without a warrant.[330] By section 31 of the 1961 Act, a police officer is justified in arresting any person without warrant under any of these powers. Furthermore, by section 32, where under any enactment a police officer has power to arrest without warrant any person who has committed an offence, the police officer is justified in arresting without warrant any person whom he believes, on reasonable and probable grounds, to have committed that offence, whether or not the offence has in fact been committed, and whether or not the arrested person committed it.

Whether a police officer has good cause to suspect a person has committed an imprisonable offence (section 315(2)), or a belief on reasonable and probable grounds that a person has committed an arrestable offence (section 32) is a question of fact.[331] The ordinary standard of proof is sufficient in judging this matter. It is not necessary that sufficient cause be proved beyond reasonable doubt, or that there be prima facie proof of guilt.[332] Whether or not there was good cause is determined objectively by the court.[333] The officer's belief that there was good cause is irrelevant.[334]

In *Neilsen v. Attorney-General*[335] Richardson P recognized that the decision to arrest without warrant where the threshold requirement in section 315 of good cause to suspect is satisfied is a constrained discretion. It would be an abdication of discretion to make an arrest in every case. Rather, in deciding to arrest or detain the officer concerned should give appropriate consideration to the statutory purposes underlying section 315 and, in particular, to the values of individual liberty and public order necessarily involved in the decision. Applying these principles, a police officer's beliefs that a person suspected of a minor offence of failing to account might re-offend and that it was necessary to have his fingerprints on record were irrational and illegitimate, and the decision to arrest accordingly was unreasonable.

4. Entry on Premises of Arrested Person

61. A constable may enter a place or vehicle without warrant to search for and arrest a person if the constable has reasonable grounds to suspect that the person is unlawfully at large and to believe that the person is there.[336] A constable also may enter a place or vehicle without a warrant to search for and arrest a person where the constable has reasonable grounds: (a) to suspect that the person has committed

330. For example, *see* the Summary Offences Act 1981, s. 39 (a constable and persons assisting may arrest for a variety of offences against that Act).
331. *Police v. Anderson* [1972] NZLR 233. The protective provision of s. 32 arguably states a higher standard than the empowering provision of s. 315(2): *Thomas v. A-G* 14/8/97, CA139/96; *R v. Thompson* (1995) 13 CRNZ 546; *Niao v. A-G* (1999) 5 HRNZ 269 at 282–283.
332. *Police v. Cooper* [1975] 1 NZLR 216; *O'Hara v. Chief Constable of the RUC* [1997] AC 286.
333. *See*, for example, *Duffy v. Attorney-General* (1985) 1 CRNZ 599; *Craig v. Attorney-General* (1986) 2 CRNZ 551; and *see Hayes v. Chief Constable of Merseyside Police* [2012] 1 WLR 517.
334. *Police v. Anderson* [1972] NZLR 233; *Everitt v. Attorney-General* [2002] 1 NZLR 82 at [72].
335. [2001] 3 NZLR 433.
336. Search and Surveillance Act 2012, s. 7.

an imprisonable offence; (b) to believe that the person is there; and (c) to believe that if entry is not effected immediately the person will leave or evidential material related to the offence will be destroyed, altered, concealed or damaged.[337] An officer who is already lawfully on private premises, for example, because of an invitation to be there, or under an implied licence, may effect an arrest while on those premises.[338]

5. Use of Force

62. Section 39 of the Crimes Act 1961 provides, *inter alia*, that where a person is justified in making or assisting to make an arrest, that person is also entitled to use such force as may be necessary to overcome any force used in resisting the arrest, unless the arrest could be achieved by reasonable means in a less violent manner. There is a proviso that, except in the case of a constable or a person called upon to assist him, the section does not apply where the force used is intended or likely to cause death or grievous bodily harm.

Failure to comply with the conditions for making a valid arrest laid down in section 316(1) of the Crimes Act 1961 is relevant to an inquiry into whether reasonable force was used.[339] If the force used is excessive, the perpetrator may be held liable both in criminal proceedings[340] and also (subject to the accident compensation bar) in a civil action for battery. Again, the use of force in restraining a person without actually purporting to arrest that person cannot be justified and accordingly is a battery and a false imprisonment.[341]

6. Duty to Give Reason for Arrest

63. Section 316(1) of the Crimes Act 1961, enacting a rule of the common law,[342] provides:

> It is the duty of everyone arresting any other person to inform the person he is arresting, at the time of arrest, of the act or omission for which the person is being arrested unless it is impracticable to do so or unless the reason for the arrest is obvious in the circumstances. The act or omission need not be stated in technical or precise language and may be stated in any words sufficient to give that person notice of the true reason for his arrest.

The arrester is not required to specify a particular crime, or to give a technical definition of the crime, or to refer to his or her power of arrest. The question is

337. *Ibid.*, s. 8.
338. *Police v. Rushbrooke* [1969] NZLR 774; *Edwards v. Police* [1994] 2 NZLR 164.
339. Crimes Act 1961, s. 316(4).
340. *Ibid.*, s. 62.
341. *Edwards v. Police* [1994] 2 NZLR 164.
342. *See* generally *Christie v. Leachinsky* [1947] AC 573.

whether, having regard to all the circumstances of the particular case, the person arrested was told in simple, non-technical language that he could understand, the essential legal and factual grounds for his arrest.[343] A reason need not be given where it is impracticable to do so, for example, because the person being arrested is putting up violent resistance (although in this case, the reason for the arrest must still be given at the first reasonable opportunity),[344] or where the reason is obvious and accordingly it is unnecessary to state what it is.[345] If there are good grounds for an arrest, and the arrested person is informed of these grounds, the arrest is lawful notwithstanding that the arrester may have had a collateral motive in making the arrest.[346]

A purported arrest that fails to meet the requirements imposed by section 316(1) is unlawful from the outset, and the person who makes it may be held liable for false imprisonment. It is clear that this is so even where the arrest could have been justified if made properly.[347] However, the existence in fact of a good reason may be relevant to the assessment of damages.[348] Furthermore, an arrest that is unlawful because no reason is given becomes lawful from the moment this omission is rectified, and the plaintiff is entitled to damages only for the period of detention up to that moment.[349]

7. Search of Arrested Person

64. At common law, a personal search may be justified if it is made pursuant to the duty of an officer who lawfully has a prisoner in his or her charge to take all reasonable measures to ensure that the prisoner does not escape or assist others to escape, does not injure himself or herself or others, does not destroy or dispose of evidence, and does not commit further crime, such as malicious damage to property.[350] The search can extend only to the arrestee's person and the area within the arrestee's immediate control. What measures are reasonable in the discharge of this duty depends on the likelihood that the particular prisoner will do any of these things unless prevented. What cannot be justified is the adoption of a particular measure without having regard to all the circumstances of the particular case.[351] There may be standing procedures, including searches, which are prima facie reasonable and necessary in a particular category of case. Nevertheless, the officer having custody of a prisoner should always consider whether the special circumstances of the

343. *Taylor v. Chief Constable of Thames Valley Police* [2004] 1 WLR 3155.
344. *New South Wales v. Riley* (2003) 57 NSWLR 496 at [83].
345. *R v. Gibbons* [1997] 2 NZLR 585 (accused 'under no real misapprehension' about reason for arrest).
346. *R v. Chalkley* [1998] 2 All ER 155.
347. *Christie v. Leachinsky* [1947] AC 573; *Elder v. Evans* [1951] NZLR 801; *Kenlin v. Gardiner* [1967] 2 QB 510.
348. *Attorney-General v. Niania* [1994] 3 NZLR 106 at 110; but *see Caie v. Attorney-General* [2005] NZAR 703 (appeal dismissed [2006] NZAR 379).
349. *Lewis v. Chief Constable of the South Wales Constabulary* [1991] 1 All ER 206.
350. *Barnett & Grant v. Campbell* (1902) 21 NZLR 484; *R v. Jefferies* [1994] 1 NZLR 290.
351. *Lindley v. Rutter* [1981] QB 128.

particular case justify applying them or departing from them.[352] So, the right to search should be exercised only for good reason, and, in addition, the person being searched is entitled to be told of the reason, unless that course is impractical or the need to search is so obvious that to state a reason is unnecessary.[353]

Quite apart from common law powers, the police have a statutory power to search a person who has been taken into lawful custody, who is at a police station or in other premises or a vehicle being used for police purposes, and who is to be locked up.[354] A constable also may conduct a search of a person after the person has been locked up if the person has not already been searched, or since any search the person has been or is reasonably suspected of having been in close proximity to a person not locked up in police custody or who has not been searched, or there are reasonable grounds to believe that the person is in possession of anything that may be used to harm himself or herself or others.[355] The constable may take from the person any money or other properties found during the search.[356]

The statutory power to search is exercisable only where the person concerned is to be 'locked up' in police custody. In *Everitt v. Attorney-General*,[357] concerning the former requirement in the Police Act 1958, the Court of Appeal determined that 'locked up' meant confining the person concerned behind a closed and locked door, as typically in a cell or perhaps a communal locked-up holding area. It required confining in a separate part of the police station and could not sensibly be extended to the whole police station. It did not include the position where a person was detained briefly while formalities were completed and consideration was given to release on bail.

8. Inquiries after Arrest

65. A power of arrest on a criminal charge is given for the purpose of enabling the person arrested to be brought before a court. There is no power of arrest simply to question the suspect or to make inquiries.[358] Furthermore, section 316(5) of the Crimes Act 1961 provides that every person arrested for any offence shall be brought before a court, as soon as possible, to be dealt with according to the law. It

352. *Ibid.*
353. *Craig v. Attorney-General* (1986) 2 CRNZ 551; *R v. Jefferies* [1994] 1 NZLR 290.
354. Search and Surveillance Act 2012, s. 11(1), (2). *See also* Corrections Act 2004, s. 98 (prisoner admitted to prison may be required to undergo strip search in various circumstances). Police and prison officers also are empowered to use reasonable force in order to take identifying particulars from persons in their lawful custody: Policing Act 2008, s. 32; Corrections Act 2004, s. 41; *Moulton v. Police* [1980] 1 NZLR 443; *Keenan v. A-G* [1986] 1 NZLR 241. A personal search without an arrest having been made may sometimes be authorised by statute: *see* for example s. 210 of the Customs and Excise Act 2018.
355. Search and Surveillance Act 2012, s. 11(3).
356. *Ibid.*, s. 11(4).
357. [2002] 1 NZLR 82.
358. *Blundell v. Attorney-General* [1968] NZLR 341; *New South Wales v. Robinson* [2019] HCA 46.

has been said that this provision is at the very root of the rule of law protecting freedom of the citizen and that the courts will, therefore, be astute to ensure that its requirements are obeyed.[359]

In *R v. Alexander*[360] the Court of Appeal held that section 316(5) does not preclude a reasonable delay, objectively assessed, in bringing an arrested person before a court. Rather, the words 'as soon as possible' should be interpreted as meaning 'as soon as reasonably possible'.

There is a similar provision to section 316(5) in section 23(2) of the New Zealand Bill of Rights Act 1990. This states that everyone who is arrested for an offence who is not released shall be brought as soon as possible before a court or competent tribunal. In *R v. Te Kira*[361] Richardson J affirmed that at common law and in terms of sections 316(5) and 23(3), a police officer is not entitled to delay taking an arrested person before a court in order to facilitate a police investigation. However, Thomas J recognized that some reasonable investigatory steps involving the accused following his or her arrest were not necessarily precluded.

Whether a person has been brought before a court as soon as reasonably possible is ultimately a question of fact. Where undue delay can be established the detention is unlawful from the time the person should have been produced before a court, not from the moment of arrest.[362]

9. Impact of the New Zealand Bill of Rights Act 1990

66. In addition to the requirements of the Crimes Act 1961, a number of procedures governing arrest and detention are laid down in the New Zealand Bill of Rights Act 1990, introducing a Bill of Rights into New Zealand law.[363] The provisions of the Bill of Rights apply to acts done (a) by legislative, executive, or judicial branches of the government of New Zealand, or (b) by any person or body in the performance of any public function, power, or duty conferred or imposed by law.[364] They do not apply to acts of a private person, unless he or she is performing such public function.[365] Where action is brought against the branches of government or public persons or bodies, like the police, the requirements of the 1990 Act must be brought into account.[366]

The rights laid down in the 1990 Act concerning arrest, search, and detention are as follows:

---

359. *R v. Alexander* [1989] 3 NZLR 395 at 400.
360. [1989] 3 NZLR 395.
361. [1993] 3 NZLR 297.
362. *Whithair v. A-G* [1996] 2 NZLR 45.
363. For full discussion, *see* Rishworth, Huscroft, Optican & Mahoney, *The New Zealand Bill of Rights* (Oxford University Press, 2003).
364. New Zealand Bill of Rights Act 1990, s. 3; and *see Attorney-General v. Chapman* [2012] 1 NZLR 462, below, para. 314.
365. *R v. N* [1999] 1 NZLR 713 (Bill of Rights did not apply to arrest by private citizen).
366. The 1990 Act is not a complete statement of the rights of citizens that the law recognises in New Zealand, and rights that lie outside the Act, including common law rights, remain: *Smith v. Attorney-General* [2018] NZCA 24, [2018] 2 NZLR 899 at [47].

(1) Everyone has the right to be secure against unreasonable search or seizure of the person, property, correspondence, or otherwise.[367]
(2) Everyone has the right not to be arbitrarily arrested or detained.[368]
(3) Everyone who has been arrested and detained under any enactment (a) shall be informed at the time of the arrest or detention of the reason for it;(b) has the right to consult and instruct a lawyer without delay and to be informed of that right; and (c) has the right to have the validity of the arrest and detention determined without delay by way of habeas corpus and to be released if the arrest or detention is not lawful.[369]
(4) Everyone who is arrested for an offence has the right to be charged promptly or released.[370]
(5) Everyone who is arrested for an offence who is not released shall be brought as soon as possible before a court or competent tribunal.[371]
(6) Everyone who is arrested for an offence has the right to refrain from making any statement and to be informed of this right.[372]
(7) Everyone deprived of liberty shall be treated with humanity and with respect for the inherent dignity of the person.[373]
(8) Everyone who is charged with an offence (a) shall be informed promptly and in detail of the nature and cause of the charge; (b) shall be released on reasonable terms and conditions unless there is just cause for continued detention; (c) shall have the right to consult and instruct a lawyer; (d) shall have the right to adequate time and facilities to prepare a defence; (e) shall have the right, in certain circumstances, to trial by jury; (f) shall have the right to free legal assistance if the interests of justice so require and the person lacks the means to provide for that assistance; and (g) shall have the right if necessary to the free assistance of an interpreter.[374]

Some of these rights mirror the common law or the provisions already contained in the Crimes Act, and some lay down new or different requirements. So, for example, the question whether a search is 'unreasonable' is not the same as whether it is unlawful,[375] nor is an 'arbitrary' detention exactly coincident with an unlawful detention;[376] the rights of an arrested person of access to counsel and to be charged

367. New Zealand Bill of Rights Act 1990, s. 21.
368. *Ibid.*, s. 22.
369. *Ibid.*, s. 23(1).
370. *Ibid.*, s. 23(2).
371. *Ibid.*, s. 23(3).
372. *Ibid.*, s. 23(4).
373. *Ibid.*, s. 23(5).
374. *Ibid.*, s. 24.
375. *See* generally *R v. Williams* [2007] 3 NZLR 207; *Forrest v. Attorney-General* [2012] NZAR 798; *Hamed v. R* [2012] 2 NZLR 305.
376. *See* generally *R v. Goodwin (No. 2)* [1993] 2 NZLR 390 (CA); *Manga v. Attorney-General* [2000] 2 NZLR 65.

promptly or released add further requirements to those concerning lawful arrest contained in the Crimes Act; and the right of a person who has been deprived of liberty to be treated with humanity and respect for dignity has no direct counterpart in the common law.[377]

Where there is a breach of one or more of the provisions of the Bill of Rights, the court has a discretionary power to make an award of compensation.[378] In cases where an award of public law compensation and of damages for false imprisonment might both be made, common law damages alone normally will be regarded as adequate.[379]

A further question is whether a failure to meet any of the requirements of the Bill of Rights when a person is arrested or detained means that the continued detention of that person becomes actionable as a false imprisonment. Certainly a breach of the corresponding provisions of the Crimes Act has this result. In *Baigent's*, Gault J (who dissented on the question whether a public law action for damages ought to be recognized) took this view, but the majority expressed no opinion on the matter.

B. Execution of Sentence, Process, or Warrant

67. A ministerial officer of a court authorized to execute a lawful sentence, a prison manager of a prison, and every person lawfully assisting the officer or prison manager is justified in executing the sentence.[380] A ministerial officer of a court duly authorized to execute any lawful process or warrant and any person lawfully assisting that person is likewise justified in executing the process or warrant, and a prison manager is justified in receiving and detaining the person concerned.[381] A sentence, process, or warrant that is invalid may also afford protection in certain circumstances. Where a sentence is passed or process or warrant issued by a court or person having jurisdiction to do so, this is sufficient to justify the execution of the sentence, process, or warrant by a duly authorized person, notwithstanding that the court or person had no authority to pass the sentence, or issue the process, or had exceeded its jurisdiction as regards that sentence, process, or warrant.[382] Again, where any process has been issued out of any court or by any judge or justice, no member of the police acting in obedience to the process is responsible for any irregularity or want of jurisdiction in the issuing of the process.[383]

Any purported execution of process outside the limits of these defences may give rise to liability for battery or false imprisonment. The statutory protection extends to actions that are reasonably necessary for the execution of the process or warrant but not those going beyond that limit.[384] Accordingly, there is no immunity where

377. *See Taunoa v. Attorney-General* [2008] 1 NZLR 429.
378. *Simpson v. Attorney-General: Baigent's Case* [1994] 3 NZLR 667; *see* para. 314.
379. *Dunlea v. Attorney-General* [2000] 3 NZLR 136: *see* further para. 314.
380. Crimes Act 1961, s. 26(1); and *see* Corrections Act 2004, ss 34, 37, 38.
381. Crimes Act 1961, s. 26(2), (3).
382. *Ibid.*, s. 27.
383. Policing Act 2008, s. 44.
384. *Simpson v. Attorney-General: Baigent's Case* [1994] 3 NZLR 667 at 694.

the process is not executed in good faith, reasonably, and fairly,[385] or where the execution is known to be outside the purpose for which the warrant was issued.[386] Nevertheless, executing a lawfully issued warrant that mistakenly names the wrong person arguably is covered.[387]

C. Defence of the Person

68. A person who is sued for an assault and battery may justify the act on the ground that it was committed in his or her own defence, or in the defence of another, and that the force used was reasonable in the circumstances as that person believed them to be.[388]

D. Defence of Property

69. At common law, a person who is sued for an assault or a battery may justify the act on the ground that it was committed in defending his or her land or chattels against a person threatening to commit or committing a trespass to that property; and certain powers to defend property are also given by statute.[389]

E. Disciplinary Powers

70. At common law, a child's parents, or a schoolteacher to whom the parents have delegated their responsibility, may lawfully restrain the child within defined boundaries.[390] By statute, every parent of a child, and every person in the place of a parent, is justified in using force if the force used is reasonable in the circumstances and is for the purpose of (a) preventing or minimizing harm to the child or another person, or (b) preventing the child from engaging in criminal conduct, or (c) preventing the child from engaging in offensive or disruptive behaviour, or (d) performing the normal daily tasks that are incidental to good care and parenting.[391] However, it is provided that the use of force is not justified for the purpose of correction.[392] Schoolteachers also may not inflict force on a child by way of correction or punishment,[393] but they may still rely on the particular justifications for force available to 'every person in the place of a parent'.

385. *Ibid.*, at 673, 694, 714; *Auckland Unemployed Workers' Rights Centre Inc v. A-G* [1994] 3 NZLR 720 at 725.
386. *Simpson v. Attorney-General: Baigent's Case* [1994] 3 NZLR 667 at 688–689, 716.
387. *McGrath v. Chief Constable of the Royal Ulster Constabulary* [2001] 3 WLR 312.
388. Crimes Act 1961, s. 48; *see* para. 502.
389. *Burt v. Ross* (1886) NZLR 5 SC 161; Crimes Act 1961, s. 56; *see* para. 503.
390. *R v. Deputy Governor of Parkhurst Prison, ex p Hague* [1992] 1 AC 58 at 162.
391. Crimes Act 1961, s. 59(1).
392. *Ibid.*, s. 59(2).
393. Education Act 1989, s. 139A.

Disciplinary powers are given to the master or officer in command of a ship on a voyage, the pilot in command of an aircraft in flight, and all those obeying their orders.[394]

F. Detention and Treatment of Mentally Disordered Persons

71. Persons suffering from a mental disorder may be incarcerated against their will under the provisions of the Mental Health (Compulsory Assessment and Treatment) Act 1992, which provides authority for conduct that would otherwise be tortious and actionable. Civil actions for damages in respect of conduct that cannot be justified by the terms of the 1992 Act may be brought in the ordinary way.[395] The provisions of the mental health legislation continue to apply regardless of the New Zealand Bill of Rights Act 1990, which provides, *inter alia*, for the right to refuse to undergo any medical treatment,[396] and the right not to be arbitrarily arrested or detained.[397] The right 'everyone' has to refuse medical treatment means every person who is competent to consent. If a person is not competent, then detention or treatment under the 1992 Act or its predecessor is not in breach of the requirements of the Bill of Rights Act.[398]

VII. The Rule in *Wilkinson v. Downton*

A. Nature of the Rule

72. In *Wilkinson v. Downton*,[399] decided in 1896, Wright J laid down a form of residuary liability for intentionally inflicted harm that was not a trespass to the person. In this case the defendant, by way of a practical joke, told the plaintiff that her husband had met with a serious accident and that both his legs were broken. He intended that the plaintiff should believe what he said. The plaintiff did believe him and suffered a violent nervous shock rendering her ill. She could not sue in trespass because the damage was indirect and at that time the courts had not permitted any recovery in negligence for nervous shock. Wright J, however, formulated a new proposition of law in these terms:

> The defendant has … wilfully done an act calculated to cause physical harm to the plaintiff – that is to say, to infringe her legal right to personal safety, and has in fact thereby caused physical harm to her. That proposition without more appears to me to state a good cause of action, there being no justification alleged for the act.

394. Crimes Act 1961, s. 60; Aviation Crimes Act 1972, s. 15.
395. For example *Innes v. Wong* [1996] 3 NZLR 238 (assistance to authorized medical officer given by police acting outside terms of Act actionable as false imprisonment).
396. New Zealand Bill of Rights Act 1990, s. 11.
397. *Ibid.*, s. 22.
398. *Re M* [1992] 1 NZLR 29; *Re S* [1992] 1 NZLR 363.
399. [1897] 1 QB 57.

Applying the principle, Wright J was satisfied that an intention to harm ought to be imputed to the defendant and that the claim should succeed.

Examples of cases involving intentionally inflicted damage by shock where *Wilkinson v. Downton* has been applied include: procuring information from the plaintiff by making unlawful threats,[400] threatening to burn down the plaintiff's house,[401] and spreading a false rumour that the plaintiff's son had committed suicide.[402] Causing physical harm or the risk of physical harm is covered as well. So exposing prior criminal offending by a person appealing to the public for funds to pay for a heart transplant was calculated to or likely to cause the person's death or serious physical or emotional stress, and publication of this information accordingly could be prevented by the grant of an interlocutory injunction.[403] On the other hand, setting the plaintiff's family burial plot as the background to a scene in a horror film did not fall within the principle, for this could not foreseeably give rise to physical damage arising out of mental shock nor could any damage be said to have been intentionally inflicted.[404]

B. Future of the Rule

73. Wilkinson v. Downton has been applied in relatively few cases, partly because developments in the law of negligence concerning recovery for shock have taken over much of the ground.[405] Where intentional conduct causes physical damage, trespass seemingly can apply even though the damage is inflicted indirectly.[406] So, the question arises whether there is any need for a separate rule of liability. In *Wainwright v. Home Office*[407] the House of Lords thought that there was not. In this case the plaintiffs were strip-searched during a prison visit, and claimed that the conduct of the prison officers constituted an intentional infliction of harm within the meaning of the principle in *Wilkinson v. Downton.* In particular, they argued that damages for distress falling short of actual psychiatric injury (where a claim for negligence would fail)[408] could be recovered where there was an intention to cause harm of this kind. However, Lord Hoffmann said that to succeed on this basis, an imputed intention as in *Wilkinson v. Downton* would not do. The defendant must have acted in a way that he knew to be unjustifiable and intended to cause harm, or at least acted without caring whether he caused harm or not. The trial judge had made no finding that the prison officers intended to cause distress or realized that

400. *Janvier v. Sweeney* [1919] 2 KB 316.
401. *Stevenson v. Basham* [1922] NZLR 225.
402. *Bielitski v. Obadiak* (1922) 65 DLR 627.
403. *Tucker v. News Media Ownership* [1986] 2 NZLR 716. The injunctions were in fact discharged on the basis that maintaining them would be futile, because the plaintiff's convictions had been revealed to the public by organizations other than the defendants.
404. *Bradley v. Wingnut Films Ltd* [1993] 1 NZLR 415.
405. *See* paras 83–88.
406. *See* para. 51.
407. [2004] 2 AC 406.
408. *See* para. 84.

they were acting without justification in asking the Wainwrights to strip. Rather, they had acted in good faith. On the facts, then, the claim failed.

Even on the basis of a genuine intention to cause distress, Lord Hoffmann reserved his opinion on whether compensation should be recoverable. He observed that the Protection from Harassment Act 1997 (UK), requiring a pattern of behaviour, showed that Parliament was conscious that it might not be in the public interest to allow the law to be set in motion for one boorish incident. It might be that any development in the common law should show similar caution.[409]

The ambit of *Wilkinson v. Downton* was considered once again by the UK Supreme Court in *Rhodes v. OPO*.[410] A father proposed to publish a book describing, *inter alia*, his tormented childhood and, in particular, his suffering of sexual abuse, leading to episodes of mental illness and self-harm. The book was dedicated to his son, who suffered from Asperger's Syndrome and other vulnerabilities, but he, through his litigation friend, brought proceedings to prevent publication on the ground that it would cause him psychiatric injury and the risk of self-harm should he read it. Their Lordships held that *Wilkinson v. Downton* had three elements: a conduct element, a mental element, and a consequence element. The conduct element required words or conduct directed towards the claimant for which there was no justification or reasonable excuse. However, in the instant case, there was every justification for the publication. The father had the right to tell his story, and the law placed a very high value on freedom of speech. The mental element required an intention to cause physical harm or illness or at least to cause severe distress which in fact resulted in recognizable illness. Recklessness was not enough. But there was no evidence that the father intended to cause harm of this kind to his son, and there was no justification for imputing an intention to cause the harm on the basis of it being foreseeable. Intention was a matter of fact. It might be inferred in an appropriate case from the evidence, but it could not be imputed as a matter of law. Accordingly, there was no real prospect of establishing either the conduct element or the mental element of the tort. Third, the consequence element (which was common ground) was physical harm or recognized psychiatric injury and was not in issue. In this view, the plaintiff must show actual psychiatric injury, as in negligence, before a *Wilkinson v. Downton* claim can succeed.

Whether *Wilkinson v. Downton* still has a useful role to play in New Zealand law is rather doubtful. Where intentional conduct causes actual physical or mental harm then established torts like negligence or trespass (without the old requirement of directness) or misfeasance in a public office can give a remedy. Probably, the only circumstance where the rule could apply today where there is no other cause of action would be if the damage rule were relaxed. A tort of intentional infliction of emotional distress is well established in the United States,[411] and it remains possible, although unlikely, that the law in New Zealand will develop in this direction.

409. *See also Majrowski v. Guy's and St Thomas's NHS Trust* [2007] 1 AC 224 at [30].
410. [2015] 2 WLR 1373.
411. Dobbs, Hayden & Bublick. *The Law of Torts* §§ 385–389 (2nd ed., St Paul, MI: West Group, 2011).

An associated question is whether, or how far, the courts should seek to develop a new tort of harassment. This raises issues of privacy and is considered in that context.[412]

§3. NEGLIGENT WRONGDOING

I. Introduction

74. Giving structure to a discussion of the law of negligence is not a straightforward task, and there are many different ways of organizing the relevant material. In the arrangement that follows we will consider, first, the use that is made of the concept of the duty of care, and in particular the formulae that are employed for determining whether a duty is owed and the policy concerns that underlie the duty inquiry. Second, we will consider the differing approaches towards claims for negligently inflicted mental injury, claims in respect of negligent statements and claims in respect of negligently inflicted financial loss. These all involve the defendant's liability for his or her own conduct in causing the harm in question. Claims alleging negligent failure to prevent harm being done by others or by things are considered in Part II. Third, certain special kinds of claims will be singled out for separate treatment. Speaking broadly, they are cases where the duty question cannot, or cannot necessarily, be resolved simply by the application of a general principle, and for one reason or another require special attention. We will then turn to the issue of the standard of care expected of the defendant, or in other words, whether the duty has been broken. The further issues as to proof of cause, the remoteness of any damage and possible defences will be discussed later on.

II. Duty of Care

A. Duty Formulae

75. The potential scope of negligence as a basis for legal liability is virtually unlimited. On its face 'negligence' looks only to the quality of the defendant's conduct, and takes no account of any other implications of imposing liability in all the circumstances of the case. Thus the courts have had to devise principles to delimit the boundaries of liability. One of their solutions is found in the requirement that the person sought to be held responsible for negligent conduct must owe the victim a legal duty to take care. The language of duty provides the formula for the courts to express their conclusions as to how far the law ought to extend.

The foundation to the inquiry as to whether a person is under a legal duty to take care is the judgment of Lord Atkin in *Donoghue v. Stevenson*.[413] His Lordship said

412. *See* paras 371–372.
413. [1932] AC 562.

that there had to be some general conception of relations giving rise to a duty of which the particular cases found in the books were but instances. He went on to state the principle as follows:

> The rule that you are to love your neighbour becomes in law, you must not injure your neighbour; and the lawyer's question, Who is my neighbour? receives a restricted reply. You must take reasonable care to avoid acts or omissions which you can reasonably foresee would be likely to injure your neighbour. Who, then, in law is my neighbour? The answer seems to be – persons who are so closely and directly affected by my act that I ought reasonably to have them in contemplation as being so affected when I am directing my mind to the acts or omissions which are called in question.

Donoghue v. Stevenson itself arose out of the plaintiff allegedly having drunk ginger beer manufactured by the defendant that contained the decomposed remains of a snail. So, it was a case about physical injury caused by positive negligent conduct on the part of the defendant. In these circumstances the fact that the defendant ought to have foreseen injury to the plaintiff created a sufficiently close or proximate relationship as to give rise to a duty to take care. In cases possessing these two features, a duty of care usually will be imposed without too much difficulty. However, all kinds of different questions can arise concerning, for example, economic loss, psychiatric injury, failures to act, and the liability of public bodies acting pursuant to statute. The question is whether or how the neighbour principle or some variant of it can apply in these and many other cases.

In *Anns v. Merton London Borough Council*[414] Lord Wilberforce laid down a two-stage test of duty. This required the courts to look at the question of proximity, or neighbourhood, between the parties at stage one and at any relevant policy concerns at stage two. This approach was quickly accepted in New Zealand[415] and since then it has continued to be applied, albeit in a modified form. The favoured method of analysis is to make an 'internal' inquiry into the relationship between the parties and an 'external' inquiry into wider issues.[416] In England, by contrast, the *Anns* approach was later rejected by the House of Lords in *Caparo Industries plc v. Dickman*.[417] Lord Bridge of Harwich said that whether the courts would recognize a duty of care in any particular case depended on the foreseeability of the harm, the proximity of the relationship between the parties and, generally, considerations of fairness and reasonableness.[418]

414. [1978] AC 728 at 751–752.
415. *Scott Group Ltd v. McFarlane* [1978] 1 NZLR 553 at 565, 573–574, 583.
416. *South Pacific Manufacturing v. New Zealand Security Consultants* [1992] 2 NZLR 282 at 294, 305–306, 312, 315–316, 324–325; *Connell v. Odlum* [1993] 2 NZLR 257 at 265; *Wilson & Horton Ltd v. A-G* [1997] 2 NZLR 513 at 520; *Wellington District Law Society v. Price Waterhouse* [2002] 2 NZLR 767 at [42–44]; *A-G v. Carter* [2003] 2 NZLR 160 at [22–32].
417. [1990] 2 AC 605.
418. In *Michael v. Chief Constable of South Wales Police* [2015] AC 1732 at [106], Lord Toulson noted that paradoxically this passage in Lord Bridge's judgment had sometimes come to be treated as a blueprint for deciding cases, despite the pains which the author took to make clear that it was not intended to be any such thing.

Recently, in *Robinson v. Chief Constable of West Yorkshire Police*,[419] Lord Reed warned against misconceiving the role that should be played by the *Caparo* inquiry. In the ordinary run of cases, courts considered what had been decided previously and followed the precedents (unless it was necessary to consider whether the precedents should be departed from). In cases where the question of whether a duty of care arose had not previously been decided, the courts would consider the closest analogies in the existing law, with a view to maintaining the coherence of the law and the avoidance of inappropriate distinctions. They would also weigh up the reasons for and against imposing liability, in order to decide whether the existence of a duty of care would be just and reasonable.

In *North Shore City Council v. Attorney-General*[420] the Supreme Court gave an overview of the duty methodology. Elias CJ considered that, in the end, whether the defendant was under a duty of care to the plaintiff might be incapable of more helpful general encapsulation than the proposition that a duty of care is owed if 'a reasonable person in the defendant's position *could* have avoided damage by exercising reasonable care and was in such a relationship to the plaintiff that he or she *ought* to have acted to do so'.[421] Blanchard J said that the important insight found in New Zealand and overseas cases was that when a court was considering foreseeability and proximity, it was concerned with everything bearing upon the relationship between the parties, and that when it moved to policy features – that is, whether it was fair, just and reasonable to impose a duty – the court was concerned with externalities – the effect on non-parties and on the structure of the law and on society generally. But aspects of some matters might be required to be considered under both heads.

In most cases of negligence the existence or ambit of a duty is well established and is not a live issue. This is usually so in cases involving positive negligent conduct causing physical injury or damage to property. For example, there can be no argument about whether a driver owes a duty to other road users to take care of his or her driving. But difficulty arises in cases where existing authorities do not clearly and authoritatively point the way. In deciding these cases the courts recognize that it is desirable that the law develops incrementally, with proper use being made of the experience and reasoning to be found in existing decisions. Beyond this, the inquiry turns on issues of foreseeability and proximity and on the requirements of policy.

B. Foreseeability and Proximity

76. The courts consider first the foreseeability of damage and the proximity between the parties. The requirement of reasonable foreseeability of harm tends to

419. [2018] UKSC 4, [2018] AC 736 at [21]–[29]; and *see Darnley v. Croydon Health Services NHS Trust* [2018] UKSC 50, [2018] 3 WLR 1153 at [15].

420. *North Shore City Council v. Attorney-General* [2012] 3 NZLR 341.

421. Citing Kirby J in *Graham Barclay Oysters Pty Ltd v. Ryan* (2002) 211 CLR 540 at [240].

be undemanding. The issue is whether the law imposes or ought to impose an obligation on the defendant to avoid conduct that exposes persons in the position of the plaintiff to unreasonable risks of harm.[422] Foreseeability of harm is a necessary, but not a sufficient condition of duty.

The requirement of reasonable foreseeability of damage is not very demanding. Sometimes, however, a claim will fail at this first hurdle. For example, it was not foreseeable that a street drainage system installed by a water authority would lead to disease developing in the roots of a tree and cause the tree to fall, and thus no duty was owed to a road user who was hit by the tree.[423] Nor was it foreseeable that the purchaser of a flat for investment purposes would rely on a valuation provided for the prospective mortgagee instead of obtaining his own valuation.[424] Damage suffered by an especially sensitive plaintiff also may be unforeseeable. So a tomato grower who required water of particular purity could not complain about damaging impurities where the ordinary drinking standard was satisfied.[425] But a duty was owed by a caterer to a claimant who was allergic to eggs in circumstances where the food was served at a Sikh wedding and the claimant could reasonably expect that the food would not contain egg.[426]

Proximity involves an inquiry into factors that, in Lord Atkin's words, indicate that the defendant's act or omission closely and directly affected the plaintiff and that the parties are, in this sense, neighbours. The decision of the House of Lords in *Sutradhar v. National Environment Research Council*[427] is a clear example where proximity was lacking. It was held here that the National Environment Research Council (NERC) owed no duty of care to a citizen of Bangladesh by carrying out hydrochemical work in Bangladesh and issuing a report about the results, but failing to draw attention to the presence of arsenic in the water. The class of potential claimants was the entire population of Bangladesh, or at the very least that of the areas tested during the survey. As will be seen, the proximity issue arises frequently in claims involving mental injury, or omissions to act, or financial loss.

Furthermore, a plaintiff who happens to suffer harm as a result of a breach of the defendant's duty to another cannot succeed. If the plaintiff has a cause of action, it is because of a wrong to himself or herself. The plaintiff cannot build on a wrong to someone else.[428] So, where the defendant employer caused brain damage to the plaintiff's husband, who later assaulted the plaintiff on numerous occasions, it was held that the defendant owed a duty to the husband but there was no duty owed to the wife.[429]

422. *Tame v. NSW: Annetts v. Australian Stations Pty Ltd* (2003) 211 CLR 317 at [103].
423. *Sydney Water Corporation v. Turano* [2009] HCA 42.
424. *Scullion v. Bank of Scotland plc* [2011] 1 WLR 3213.
425. *Hamilton v. Papakura DC* [2002] 3 NZLR 308.
426. *Bhamra v. Dubb* [2010] EWCA Civ 13.
427. [2006] 4 All ER 490.
428. *Bourhill v. Young* [1943] AC 92; *Marx v. Attorney-General* [1974] 1 NZLR 164.
429. *Marx v. Attorney-General* [1974] 1 NZLR 164.

C. Guiding Policies

77. The question remains whether a duty ought to be imposed even where the parties are proximate to one another. This brings into account stage two of the *Anns* formula. On its face it is of limited value. In *South Pacific Manufacturing v. New Zealand Security Consultants*[430] Cooke P observed that formulae can help organize thinking but that they cannot provide answers. Rather, judicial judgment is needed. So it is still necessary to explore how the duty formula has been applied in the cases in order to give it real and substantial content. The question of responsibility for negligence may be argued in an almost unlimited range of circumstances, and all kinds of considerations may be taken into account in deciding how it ought to be resolved. However, this does not mean that in every case the question is at large. Underlying the inquiry in many or most cases are certain key matters of policy.[431]

1. Maintaining Individual Autonomy

78. A duty to take care should not interfere inappropriately with the autonomy of the defendant in deciding whether to act. The common law draws a very significant (although sometimes elusive) distinction between positive acts and failures to act. Imposing legal liability for omissions raises issues of freedom and autonomy. The law in a liberal democratic state seeks not unduly to constrain individual autonomy. Particular constraints are imposed only where there are good and sufficient reasons for rejecting the general rule. So any duty to take care to act positively for the benefit of one's fellow citizens should be consistent with this policy of limited interference.[432]

The cases show that before a legal duty to act can arise there should be conduct by the defendant characterized by factors such as specifically induced reliance by the plaintiff that action would be taken, positive intervention by the defendant increasing the risk of harm, the physical occupation of land creating a risk of harm, and the assumption of specific responsibility for or control over an activity or a particular danger or a particular person's behaviour. In these kinds of cases an interference with autonomy can be justified. We will examine them later in discussing liability for the acts of others and for property and things.[433]

2. Imposing an Appropriate Burden of Liability

79. The extent of the consequences of a defendant's wrongdoing can vary widely according to the nature of the harm that the plaintiff has suffered and also the way in which the harm has been inflicted. This introduces the so-called floodgates argument. A duty of care is likely to be limited or denied altogether where its

430. [1992] 2 NZLR 282 at 294.
431. *See Houghton v. Saunders* [2015] 2 NZLR 74 at [673]–[678].
432. *See* para. 392.
433. *See* Part II.

recognition would tend towards the imposition on the defendant of a potentially indeterminate liability. The justification is not simply one of practicality. Rather, it is the perception that the burden of liability would be too heavy or would be a disproportionate response to the defendant's wrongdoing. So it is a conclusion of policy that reflects a balancing of the plaintiff's moral claim to compensation for avoidable harm and the defendant's moral claim to be protected from an undue burden of legal responsibility.[434]

The application of this principle can be seen in a wide variety of contexts. Well-known examples are negligent misstatement cases[435] and claims for psychiatric injury,[436] but other types of claim, including physical damage cases, in which the issue can arise are possible. In *Attorney-General v. Strathboss Kiwifruit Ltd*,[437] the Ministry of Agriculture and Fisheries (MAF) negligently granted a permit for the import into New Zealand of a consignment of kiwifruit pollen from China without undertaking a necessary risk assessment of the pollen. The consignment introduced the Psa3 bacterium, which led to the widespread devastation of kiwifruit orchards in NZ. Strathboss, the grower plaintiff, represented approximately 200 growers, and the court recognized that a fear of indeterminate liability was a major issue. The profit to growers in the kiwifruit industry alone had been calculated at NZD 2.47 billion, and it would follow that a similar duty would apply to prospective importations of all risk goods. If liability of this magnitude was to be contemplated for biosecurity hazards, it would be better if it were introduced by legislation, in which its metes and bounds might be thoroughly examined and laid down. So in *Strathboss* the court was satisfied that imposing such wide-ranging liability on MAF, both actual and potential, had to be a matter for Parliament.

3. Recognizing an Appropriately Protective Duty

80. The courts take into account whether, or the extent to which, a plaintiff should be seen as entitled to legal protection. The principle has both a positive and a negative aspect. One concern is with protecting persons in a vulnerable position, who have no reasonably available means of protecting themselves.[438] It might be seen as a form of 'consumer' protection at common law, and to this extent it marches in step with legislative developments during the later part of the twentieth century, in New Zealand and elsewhere.[439] However, if a person is well positioned to look after him or herself a duty may be thought to be inappropriate. The focus is on the steps a person reasonably could have taken to look after his or her own interests.[440]

434. *South Pacific Manufacturing Co. Ltd v. New Zealand Security Consultants Ltd* [1992] 2 NZLR 282 at 306.
435. *See* paras 89–97.
436. *See* paras 83–88.
437. [2020] NZCA 98.
438. For example, *see* the disappointed legatee cases: para. 103.
439. Clear examples are the Fair Trading Act 1986 (*see* paras 444–448) and the Consumer Guarantees Act 1993 (*see* paras 449–451).
440. For example, the company auditor cases: *see* para. 93.

This latter argument may deny a duty in order to encourage self-protective conduct by the plaintiff or others in the future. It therefore raises the wider question as to the role of a duty of care in influencing the conduct of persons potentially subject to it. Assuming that rules of civil liability can have an impact on people's behaviour,[441] the argument as to their effect on the duty issue cuts both ways. On the one hand it can be used in favour of imposing a duty, on the basis that this will help maintain appropriate standards of conduct. On the other hand, it may be seen as putting undesirable constraints on the way in which an activity is performed and as encouraging defensive practices. The courts sometimes refer to one or other argument, but it is hard to discern any principled basis for their choice.

4. Recognizing a Duty Which Operates Coherently in the Legal System as a Whole

81. A duty of care should fit coherently into an overall scheme of rights and responsibilities or, in other words, it should be consistent with other legal rules and principles. The tort of negligence has the potential to subvert other principles of law imposing conflicting or inconsistent responsibilities on persons said to be under a duty to take care. Such other principles represent a weighing up and balancing out of varying considerations of public policy. So any rule of negligence liability ought not to interfere with these considerations without a clear understanding about and assessment of the implications of so doing. Liability for negligence may still be admitted if it is thought appropriate. Sometimes it may have a complementary role. By admitting or excluding negligence, an appropriate policy balance is struck for the law as it stands today.

Take first the relationship between negligence and contract. The argument that a duty of care would undermine the principle of privity of contract was put, and emphatically rejected, in *Donoghue v. Stevenson*.[442] However, the argument poses greater difficulty where loss is purely financial. This is a continuing source of tension in misstatement cases, where plaintiffs sue in respect of negligent words without having given any consideration in return. It is often known as the 'free rider' argument.[443]

Second, expanding negligence liability into novel areas has obvious implications for other principles of tort liability. Recognition of a duty in negligence might tend to disrupt the policy balance struck by existing principles imposing a stricter form of liability.[444]

Third, a person's liability for negligence should be consistent with any relevant statutory responsibilities.[445] The significance of the statutory context, pointing both

441. *See* para. 17.
442. [1932] AC 562; *see* para. 75.
443. For example, *Caparo Industries plc v. Dickman* [1990] 2 AC 605; *see* para. 89.
444. For example, the *South Pacific* case [1992] 2 NZLR 282; *see* para. 104.
445. For example, *Sheehan v. Watson* [2011] 1 NZLR 314.

for and against a duty, can be found in many cases involving allegations of negligence by public officers or bodies acting pursuant to statute.[446]

Finally, a postulated duty may be set in some broader legal contexts. For example, a suggested distinction in public body cases between 'policy' matters and 'operational' matters is founded ultimately on a core principle of constitutional law mandating a proper separation of powers between courts and public bodies exercising discretionary functions. This points to a duty being owed only in respect of operational or 'justiciable' matters.[447] In another example, there are public interest concerns about finality in litigation in the debate concerning the question of whether a barrister is liable for negligence in the conduct of a case in court.[448]

5. Overview

82. The preceding policies are at least of broad predictive value, and they certainly can assist in giving some content to the duty inquiry. But they are not exhaustive. Particular cases can always raise questions which cannot be covered by principles or policies of relatively general application. The decision of the UK Supreme Court in *Smith v. Ministry of Defence*[449] provides a good example. The claim was based on alleged failings by the Ministry of Defence in providing adequate equipment for service personnel engaged in military operations in Iraq. One set of claims (the Challenger claims) concerned servicemen killed or injured by 'friendly fire', it being alleged that the Ministry was in breach of its common law duty by failing to ensure that tanks were equipped with devices that would have prevented the accident. The defendants argued, *inter alia*, that the claims should be struck out under the doctrine of 'combat immunity' or on the basis that it would not be fair, just, and reasonable to impose a duty in the circumstances. However the Supreme Court held that the claims should be allowed to proceed.

Lord Hope referred to a number of authorities recognizing that there was no common law liability for negligence in respect of acts and omissions on the part of those engaged in armed combat.[450] The justification was that the interests of the state should prevail over the interests of the individual. However, his Lordship considered that at the stage when men were being trained or decisions were being made about equipment, there was time to think things through, to plan and exercise judgment. These activities were sufficiently far removed from the pressures and risks of active operations against the enemy for it not to be unreasonable to expect a duty of care to be exercised.

The alternative argument was that imposing a duty would not be fair, just, and reasonable. Lord Hope recognized, once again, that the question would depend on the circumstances and that these would vary greatly from theatre to theatre and

446. *See* para. 136.
447. *See* para. 134.
448. For example, *Lai v. Chamberlains* [2007] 2 NZLR 7; *see* paras 112–113.
449. [2014] AC 52.
450. *Shaw Savill & Albion Co Ltd v. Commonwealth* (1940) 66 CLR 344; *Groves v. Commonwealth* (1982) 150 CLR 113; *Mulcahy v. Ministry of Defence* [1966] QB 732; *Multiple Claimants v. The Ministry of Defence* [2003] EWHC 1134.

operation to operation. They could not all be grouped under a single umbrella as if they were all open to the same risk of judicializing warfare. Whether any of the claims fell within a public policy exclusion could not be properly determined without hearing evidence. It would be easier to find a breach of duty where the failure could be attributed to decisions about training or equipment taken before deployment, when there was time to assess the risks to life that had to be planned for, than where they were attributable to what was taking place in the theatre. Great care needed to be taken not to subject those responsible for decisions at any level that affected what took place on the battlefield to duties that were unrealistic or excessively burdensome.

III. Mental Injury

A. Introduction

83. As a general rule psychiatric or mental injury (the terms are interchangeable) standing alone is not covered for compensation under the accident compensation scheme, so actions for damages are possible. Claims of this kind of common law are seen as posing their own special problems of policy. A major consideration in determining the ambit of liability is the perceived risk of opening the floodgates of litigation and of imposing a burden of liability that was disproportionate to the tortious conduct involved. Accordingly, the courts view claims for such injury with caution and, certainly, they treat them differently from claims for physical injury. The duty to take care to avoid causing psychiatric harm is hedged by certain limitations beyond the mere requirement that some form of mental harm be foreseeable.

B. Actionable Injury

84. As an initial point, there must be a recognizable injury. Mere upset, grief, or distress do not give rise to any cause of action. Nor does fear from having been exposed to the risk of contracting a disease.[451] In any claim for mental harm standing alone, the shock must cause the plaintiff to suffer some medically identifiable psychiatric illness or injury.[452]

---

451. *Rothwell v. Chemical Insulating Co. Ltd* [2008] 1 AC 281.

452. *van Soest v. Residual Health Management Unit* [2000] 1 NZLR 179. In *Saadati v. Moorhead* 2017 SCC 28, [2017] 1 SCR 543 the Supreme Court of Canada rejected this requirement, holding there was no necessary relationship between reasonably foreseeable mental injury and a diagnostic classification scheme. Rather, the disturbance suffered by the claimant should be serious and prolonged and should rise above the ordinary annoyances, anxieties and fears that came with living in civil society.

There could possibly be a remedy under the so-called rule in *Wilkinson v. Downton*[453] for mental upset falling short of actual injury, where the upset is intentionally inflicted. However, the House of Lords has doubted this, although ultimately it left the point open.[454]

The requirement that there be actual psychiatric injury does not apply where the victim has been physically injured. In this case the victim can be compensated for consequential shock, upset, and the like. Internal physical change to the body without symptoms or consequences is not seen as 'damage':[455] but a pricking from a needle where there was a risk of infection was a physical injury.[456]

C. *Primary Victims*

85. A core requirement for a duty of care, laid down by Denning LJ in *King v. Phillips*,[457] is foreseeability by the defendant of injury by shock. However, in *Page v. Smith,*[458] the House of Lords held that the requirement did not apply to a victim who was put in danger by the defendant's conduct (who was called a 'primary' victim). Rather, the defendant's duty was the ordinary duty to take care not to cause personal injury, whether physical or psychiatric.[459] Once it was shown that there was a foreseeable risk of one form of personal injury, the rule that defendants take their victims as they find them applied.[460] The plaintiff was not required to be a person of 'ordinary phlegm'. Accordingly, the defendant was liable for the plaintiff's psychiatric injury resulting from a relatively minor road accident caused by the fault of the defendant, even though the plaintiff was especially susceptible to suffering such injury. However, the decision creates difficult problems of classification, and it may yet be reconsidered.[461] There is a substantial body of case law involving plaintiffs who are not secondary victims – those who suffer mental injury because of the death or injury of another person – who have been owed a duty of care in respect of psychiatric harm even though they have not been physically endangered.[462] A simple dichotomy between primary and secondary victims cannot cope with the variety of ways in which a person may become the victim of psychiatric harm.

---

453. [1897] 2 QB 57.
454. *Wainwright v. Home Office* [2004] 2 AC 406; *see* para. 73.
455. *Rothwell v. Chemical Insulating Co. Ltd* [2008] 1 AC 281; and *infra* para. 84; cp *Alcan Gove Pty Ltd v. Zabic* [2015] HCA 33.
456. *Fryers v. Belfast Health and Social Care Trust* [2009] NICA 57.
457. [1953] 1 QB 429.
458. [1996] AC 155; *see* further *Frost v. Chief Constable of South Yorkshire Police* [1999] 2 AC 455; *W v. Essex CC* [2001] 2 AC 592.
459. Mother and foetus are one and the same legal person, and the mother is a primary victim where the child is injured before birth and can sue in respect of later psychiatric injury: *YAH v. Medway NHS Foundation Trust* [2018] EWHC 2964, [2019] 1 WLR 1413.
460. *See* para. 546.
461. *See Rothwell v. Chemical Insulating Co. Ltd* [2008] 1 AC 281 at [52], [104]; *Corr v. IBC Vehicles Ltd* [2008] 1 AC 844 at [54].
462. *See* para. 88.

The problematic nature of the decision in *Page* and the anomalies to which it leads are such that the New Zealand courts are unlikely to follow it.[463] Probably, the requirement in all cases that mental injury be foreseeable continues to apply. Alternatively, *Page* would best be treated simply as laying down a special rule for cases where the plaintiff was put in danger, with no wider significance for other cases. Yet even in this view, the decision poses difficulty. In *Grieves v. F T Everard & Sons*[464] the plaintiff suffered psychiatric illness on being told that he had developed pleural plaques – localized and symptomless areas of pleural thickening – after being exposed to asbestos dust in the course of his employment. There was no evidence from which it could be deduced that his illness was reasonably foreseeable, but he argued, *inter alia*, that it was enough that his employer should have foreseen that exposure to the dust might cause him physical injury, namely an asbestos-related disease. The House of Lords rejected the argument, holding that *Page* concerned psychiatric illness caused by an accident, and it could not be extended to cover fear of a future disease. It is difficult to see why a victim of psychiatric injury caused by fear stemming from a minor traffic accident should have a cause of action, yet a victim of psychiatric injury caused by fear stemming from his exposure to the risk of contracting a fatal disease should not.

D. Secondary Victims

86. Persons who are not personally in danger who suffer mental injury from perceiving or hearing about the death or injury of another or others (sometimes called 'secondary' victims) must show that it was foreseeable by the defendant that, in the circumstances of the case, a person of ordinary susceptibility or fortitude would suffer psychiatric injury.[465] In addition, according to the House of Lords in *Alcock v. Chief Constable of South Yorkshire Police*,[466] secondary victims are subject to three particular control mechanisms, which require that the plaintiff should have a close relationship of love and affection with the primary victim, should suffer a sudden shock[467] and should be physically proximate to the accident or its immediate aftermath.[468]

In *van Soest v. Residual Health Management Unit*[469] these requirements for recovery, as laid down by the House of Lords, were considered for the first time by

463. It has been rejected in Canada: *Saadati v. Moorhead* 2017 SCC 28, [2017] 1 SCR 543.

464. [2008] 1 AC 281, sub nom *Rothwell v. Chemical Insulating Co. Ltd*; cp *Bryan v. Phillips NZ Ltd* [1995] 1 NZLR 632.

465. *Bourhill v. Young* [1943] AC 92 at 110, 117; *Jaensch v. Coffey* (1984) 155 CLR 549 at 572; and *see Tame v. New South Wales; Annetts v. Australian Stations Pty Ltd* (2003) 211 CLR 317.

466. [1992] 1 AC 310.

467. *Liverpool Women's Hospital NHS Foundation Trust v. Ronayne* [2015] EWCA Civ 588 (no 'horrifying event' where claimant's wife's appearance in hospital before and after surgery was not exceptional by objective standards).

468. In *Taylor v. A Novo (UK) Ltd* [2013] 3 WLR 989, the Court of Appeal held that the relevant event for the purpose of the proximity issue was the accident concerned, not the later consequence of the accident. So a daughter could not recover damages for the mental injury caused by seeing her mother dying at home three weeks after suffering an accident at work.

469. [2000] 1 NZLR 179.

the New Zealand Court of Appeal. The plaintiffs sought damages for mental suffering caused by the deaths of their relatives while undergoing operations in hospital, alleging negligence by the surgeon. They did not claim to have suffered actual psychiatric injury, and accordingly their actions had to fail.[470] The court went on to consider the *Alcock* requirements. Although relational proximity was not in issue, the plaintiffs all having sufficiently close relationships with the victims, Blanchard J, speaking for the majority, expressed agreement with the position taken in the House of Lords. As for the suddenness of the shock and proximity in time and space, Blanchard J reserved the position in New Zealand. His Honour considered that it might well be that the restrictions based on physical and temporal proximity to the accident should be removed or relaxed, and that *Alcock* would be seen to be unnecessarily restrictive. All that presently needed to be said was that the plaintiffs' claims were not being struck out for want of physical proximity to the relevant operation and its aftermath. Thomas J would have abandoned the whole inquiry. He pointed out the problems in defining an 'aftermath' of an accident, and maintained that there was no diagnostic or medical difference in the anxiety state caused by witnessing the accident or simply learning about it from another. In Australia, the High Court has taken the view that a duty to take care not to cause mental harm turns on whether, in all the circumstances, the defendant should reasonably have foreseen that a person in the position of the plaintiff would sustain a recognizable psychiatric injury.[471] Physical and temporal proximity, suddenness, and a close and loving relationship with a physical victim may be relevant to assessing reasonable foreseeability, causation and remoteness, but are not themselves decisive of liability. In Canada, similarly, the Supreme Court has held that the ordinary duty of care analysis should be applied, and liability for mental injury should be confined to claims which satisfied the proximity analysis within the duty of care framework and the remoteness inquiry.[472] This approach, rather than that in the UK, may well be adopted in New Zealand.

E. Rescuers

87. Claims by rescuers who suffer psychiatric injury arguably fall into a separate category. In *Frost v.* Chief *Constable of South Yorkshire Police*[473] the House of Lords, applying the preceding principles, held that police officers assisting at the scene of a disaster could not recover for psychiatric injury in their capacity as rescuers. Officers assisting at the scene who were within the range of foreseeable physical injury were primary victims who were owed a duty on the basis of the principle in *Page v. Smith*. However, rescuers who had not been exposed to the risk of physical injury or who had not reasonably believed themselves to have been so exposed were to be classified as secondary victims who were required to satisfy the

470. *See* para. 84.
471. *Tame v. New South Wales; Annetts v. Australian Stations Pty Ltd* (2003) 211 CLR 317; and *see King v. Philcox* [2015] HCA 19.
472. *Saadati v. Moorhead* 2017 SCC 28, [2017] 1 SCR 543.
473. [1999] 2 AC 455.

Alcock conditions. As they were unable to show relational proximity their claims failed. However, *Frost* may not represent the law in New Zealand. Rescuers may well suffer psychiatric injury caused by perception of or fear of physical injury or danger to others, and a rule limiting recovery by reference to personal danger seems quite arbitrary, its sole purpose being to limit the ambit of liability. If the test simply is foreseeability of mental injury, this might allow recovery where a member of the public intervenes to rescue others involved in an accident.[474] On the other hand, psychiatric injury to professional rescuers – police, fire, or ambulance officers – might be thought to be unforeseeable.

F. Other Cases

88. There are other cases, not falling within the preceding categories, where damages for negligently inflicted psychiatric illness may be available. These include claims by 'involuntary participants' – where the negligent act of the defendant has put the plaintiff in the position of being, or thinking that he is about to be or has been, the involuntary cause of another's death or injury,[475] and claims by employees against their employer for work-related stress.[476] Other, particular, instances where a duty was recognized include: solicitors negligently conducting the defence of a person charged with a criminal offence, resulting in a wrongful conviction;[477] doctors removing organs from deceased children without the parents' consent;[478] and prison authorities placing a prisoner in a cell with another prisoner known to be a suicide risk, who did in fact commit suicide.[479] None of these claims are easily classifiable as involving primary or secondary victims, and they can best be resolved by applying the test of foreseeability of mental injury.

IV. Misstatements

A. Introduction

89. Negligent words are likely to be treated in the same way as negligent positive conduct where reliance on the words leads to physical injury or damage.[480] But there are a number of reasons why the courts have proceeded with caution in relation to claims for financial loss caused by negligent words. First, damage by words may raise causation problems. The advisee suffers no damage unless he or she

---

474. *See Chadwick v. British Railways Board* [1967] 1 WLR 912.
475. *Hunter v. British Coal Corporation* [1998] QB 140; *W v. Essex CC* [2001] 2 AC 592.
476. *Attorney-General v. Gilbert* [2002] 2 NZLR 342; *Hatton v. Sutherland* [2002] 2 All ER 1 (reversed in part sub nom *Barber v. Somerset CC* [2004] 1 WLR 1089); *Dickins v. 02 Plc* [2008] EWCA Civ 1144.
477. *McLoughlin v. Jones* [2002] QB 1312.
478. *Re Organ Retention Group Litigation* [2005] 2 WLR 358.
479. *Butchart v. Home Office* [2006] 1 WLR 1155.
480. *See*, for example, *Darnley v. Croydon Health Services NHS Trust* [2018] UKSC 50, [2018] 3 WLR 1153.

chooses to rely on the information or advice that is given. So, the court must be satisfied that the advisee is not simply seeking to blame others for his or her own imprudent conduct.[481] Second, a key constraint is the courts' fear of liability 'in an indeterminate amount for an indeterminate time to an indeterminate class'.[482] In the nature of things, 'words are more volatile than deeds, they travel fast and far afield, they are used without being expended'.[483] Third, a tort duty may be seen as tending to undermine well-established principles of contract. As a matter of contract, a voluntary statement made to another without the support of any consideration is not actionable, yet an action in tort for negligence by an advisee who has not paid for the advice bypasses this rule. The courts have sought to meet these objections by recognizing a duty of specific focus and narrow ambit. In this way they have attempted to create a degree of certainty in the ambit of the duty, to counter the danger of indeterminate liability and to minimize the scope for 'free-riding' by those who have made commercial use of free advice.

There is also a statutory cause of action in respect of misleading and deceptive conduct under the Fair Trading Act 1986. This overlaps very substantially with the common law and, as we shall see, in most respects is of wider scope.[484]

B. The Rule in Hedley Byrne v. Heller

90. An action for deceit has long been available where a person has suffered loss from relying on a statement that the maker knew was false or where the maker was reckless as to its truth or falsity.[485] However, only in 1963, with the decision of the House of Lords in *Hedley Byrne & Co. Ltd v. Heller & Partners Ltd*,[486] did the courts come to give a remedy in negligence. In a groundbreaking decision, their Lordships held that there could be a duty to take care in making a statement or giving advice to another person.

The plaintiffs were advertising agents who sought a report from the defendant bank as to the creditworthiness of a client company. The defendant gave misleading assurances, the plaintiff relied on these and suffered loss when the company went into liquidation. The plaintiff's action in negligence ultimately failed, because the defendants had expressly disclaimed responsibility for the views put forward in their report.[487] But all members of the House were agreed that in certain circumstances, a duty of care in making statements was owed.

A basic requirement is that it is reasonable for the plaintiff to rely on what the defendant says. In *Hedley Byrne* itself it was recognized that no duty of care would

481. *Fleming v. Securities Commission* [1995] 2 NZLR 514 at 523–525; and *see Boyd Knight v. Purdue* [1999] 2 NZLR 278.
482. *Ultramares Corp. v. Touche* 174 NE 441 (1931) per Cardozo CJ at 444.
483. *Hedley Byrne & Co. Ltd v. Heller & Partners Ltd* [1964] AC 465 per Lord Pearce at 534, and *see also* Lord Reid at 483.
484. *See* paras 444–448.
485. *Pasley v. Freeman* (1789) 3 TR 51; 100 ER 450; *see* para. 294.
486. [1964] AC 465.
487. *See* para. 99.

be owed in the case of a casual social approach to a plaintiff's inquiry.[488] In *NRAM Ltd v. Steel*[489] a solicitor sent an email to a client that misrepresented the nature of a transaction between the client and a finance company, in circumstances where the nature and terms of the transaction were wholly within the knowledge of the company. The UK Supreme Court held that a commercial lender about to implement an agreement with a borrower referable to its security did not act reasonably if it proceeded upon no more than a description of its terms put forward by or on behalf of the borrower. It was not reasonable for the representee to rely on the representation without checking its accuracy, and it was reasonable for the representor not to foresee that he would do so. Again, a council could not reasonably rely on a report reviewing its building consent processes in reaching the conclusion that its control systems were sufficiently robust and would not expose it to the risk of claims by building owners, for that would be to ignore the cautions and criticisms expressed in the report.[490]

In some cases there may be a question about the scope of a person's duty in making a statement,[491] and the answer to it may be expressed in terms of whether reliance was reasonable in the circumstances. For example, a company could not reasonably rely on an auditor's representations which were made for a purpose that was outside the scope of what the auditor had undertaken to do.[492]

There must always be reliance by the plaintiff in fact. So purchasers of defective flats who received architects' certificates only after they had completed their purchases had no claim against the architects.[493]

Assuming there is actual and reasonable reliance, the correct basis for the duty has been expressed in different ways. One approach is to direct attention to the question of whether the maker of the statement accepted or assumed responsibility for his or her words. Another approach focuses on the closeness of the relationship between the person who gave advice and the person who acted on it, and on the purpose of the advice.

C. Assuming Responsibility for Words

91. There are a number of references in the cases to a duty of care in words being founded upon the speaker's assumption of responsibility for what he or she says. Indeed this test is found in the speeches in *Hedley Byrne* itself. Yet it is not always made clear what amounts to an assumption of responsibility and how it can be established.

---

488. [1964] AC 465 at 539.
489. [2018] UKSC 13, [2018] 1 WLR 1190.
490. *North Shore City Council v. Attorney-General* [2012] 3 NZLR 341 [*The Grange*] at [195]–[197] and [228].
491. *See Hughes-Holland v. BPE Solicitors* [2017] UKSC 21, [2018] AC 599 at [20]–[42]; *Manchester Building Society v. Grant Thornton UK LLP* [2019] EWCA Civ 40, [2019] 1 W:LR 4610.
492. *Deloitte & Touche v. Livent Inc* 2017 SCC 63, [2017] 2 SCR 795.
493. *Hunt v. Optima (Cambridge) Ltd* [2015] 1 WLR 1346.

In *NRAM Ltd v. Steel*[494] Lord Wilson maintained that the concept of an assumption of responsibility by a representor to a representee was the foundation of liability in tort for negligent misrepresentation. But in so deciding his Lordship conflated the concept with the requirement of reasonable reliance (which was held to be lacking on the facts).[495] There *may* be a duty where it is reasonable for the plaintiff to rely on the defendant's words, but there is more to the inquiry than that.

A person may agree in more or less specific terms to assume legal responsibility for what he or she says. In such a case it is reasonable to impose a duty based on an actual assumption of responsibility. But in most cases there is no such assumption, and the courts use the expression in cases where a person has chosen to speak in circumstances where the law imposes a duty to take care.[496] These circumstances are where there is a proximate or special relationship between the parties and policy supports a duty.[497] In this analysis the 'assumption of responsibility' inquiry does not stand apart from the *Caparo* approach or other similar inquiry.

This understanding has been accepted in the NZ Court of Appeal. In *Attorney-General v. Carter*[498] Tipping J recognized a difficulty with the concept of an assumption of responsibility, which suggested a voluntary act. In tort obligations were imposed, not assumed as they were in contract. But the law would deem the defendant to have assumed responsibility and find proximity accordingly if, when making the statement in question, the defendant foresaw or ought to have foreseen that the plaintiff would reasonably place reliance on what was said. This would depend on the purpose for which the statement was made and the purpose for which the plaintiff relied on it. So an 'assumption of responsibility' is more a label than a test and in itself does not provide an answer to the duty question. Again, in *Customs and Excise Commissioners v. Barclays Bank plc*,[499] Lord Bingham noted that the test was to be applied objectively; it was not answered by consideration of what the defendant thought or intended. The problem was that the further it was removed from the actions and intentions of the actual defendant, the more notional the assumption of responsibility became, and the less difference there was from the threefold, *Caparo*, test.

In similar vein, leading authority recognizes that it may sometimes be reasonable to infer an assumption of responsibility in the case of a voluntary provision of a service.[500] In a recent instance, the defendant agreed, without any contract, to provide professional services as an architect on a landscaping project for the claimants' garden, and she did in fact provide the services and was relied on by the claimants properly to perform them. In the circumstances the Court of Appeal held that she

494. [2018] UKSC 13, [2018] 1 WLR 1190.
495. Above para. 90.
496. *See*, for example, *Hedley Byrne & Co. Ltd v. Heller & Partners Ltd* [1964] AC 465 at 486; *Smith v. Eric S Bush* [1990] 1 AC 831 at 862; *Caparo Industries Plc v. Dickman* [1990] 2 AC 605 at 628, 637; *White v. Jones* [1995] 2 AC 207 at 273–274; *Phelps v. Hillingdon LBC* [2001] 2 AC 619 at 654; *Customs and Excise Commissioners v. Barclays Bank plc* [2007] 1 AC 181 at [37]–[38]; *Michael v. Chief Constable of South Wales Police* [2015] AC 1732 at [100].
497. *See* above para. 75 and below, paras 92, 93.
498. [2003] 2 NZLR 160 at [22]–[32].
499. [2007] 1 AC 181.
500. *Henderson v. Merrett Syndicates Ltd* [1995] 2 AC 145; *Customs and Excise Commissioners v. Barclays Bank Plc* [2007] 1 AC 181 per Lord Mance at [93]; and *see* per Lord Hoffmann at [35].

had assumed a responsibility and that she owed a duty of care to the claimants.[501] It is apparent that this duty was founded on a closely proximate relationship that was akin to contract, for the court recognized that there was no need to make a further inquiry into whether it would be fair, just and reasonable to impose liability. This was because such considerations would have been taken into account in determining whether there had been an assumption of responsibility.[502]

In *Poole Borough Council v. GN*[503] Lord Reed recognized that the *Hedley Byrne* assumption of responsibility did not stand apart from other iterations of the assumption principle. Accordingly, it being simply one way of giving expression to the duty inquiry, the cases show a duty being denied in the ordinary way on the grounds of a lack of proximity or of relevant considerations of policy. For example, there was no assumption of responsibility, no proximate relationship and it was not fair and reasonable to impose a duty of care on a car registration authority when it revoked the classification in the registration document of the claimant's car as a 'historic' vehicle.[504] The statutory functions of the authority were to collect tax and raise revenue for the Government and to ensure that vehicles operating on the roads in the UK were registered. There was no direct relationship between the authority and the claimant, of whom it had no knowledge, no identifiable act of assumption of responsibility, and no reliance by the claimant on the registration document for the purpose for which it had been provided.

D. The Special Relationship

92. The duty to take care in words is founded on there being a close or 'special' relationship between the parties. A core requirement is that it is reasonable for the plaintiff to rely on what the defendant says. So a statement made on a social or an informal occasion is unlikely to be actionable.[505] But foreseeable and reasonable reliance is not enough on its own. The ambit of any duty is limited in a number of additional respects. The kind of case where a duty is likely to be recognized is where a skilled person acting in a strictly business context gives misleading information or advice directly to another person, knowing the specific purpose for which the information is wanted, that that person attaches importance to, and will rely on, what he or she hears or reads, and that that person cannot reasonably be expected to make further independent inquiry about the matter.[506] The relationship here is very close and proximate, not contractual in nature but somewhat akin to it.

---

501. *Lejonvarn v. Burgess* [2017] EWCA Civ 254.
502. *Ibid.*, at [64]; and *see CGL Group Ltd v. Royal Bank of Scotland plc* [2017] EWCA Civ 1073, [2018] 1 WLR 2137 at [81].
503. [2019] UKSC 25, [2019] 2 WLR 1478 at [67]–[68].
504. *Seddon v. Driver and Vehicle Licensing Agency* [2019] EWCA Civ 14; [2019] 1 WLR 4593.
505. *Hedley Byrne & Co. Ltd v. Heller & Partners Ltd* [1964] AC 465 at 482–483; *Henderson v. Merrett Syndicates Ltd* [1995] 2 AC 145 at 180–181.
506. For example, *see Sutcliffe v. Thackrah* [1974] AC 727 (architect and building owner); *Arenson v. Casson Beckman Rutley & Co.* [1977] AC 405 (valuer and share-holder); *Hughes v. Lloyd's Bank plc* [1998] Med L Rev 368 (doctor and patient); *Arthur JS Hall & Co. v. Simons* [2002] 1 AC 615 (barrister and client); *Marlborough District Council v. Altimarloch Joint Venture Ltd* [2012] 2 NZLR 726 (council issuing LIM and prospective purchaser of land) (but there may be contributory

The position is more uncertain where, for example, the relationship between the parties is not so close, or a contractual context is seen as impacting on the duty issue, or a director gives information to a company client. Circumstances of these kinds need to be considered separately.

1. Company Auditors

93. The liability of company auditors to third parties who rely on the company audit was considered in *Caparo Industries plc v. Dickman.*[507] The House of Lords held that the auditors' duty was closely circumscribed by reference to the defendant's knowledge about the advisee and the purpose for which the advice was sought. They considered that the purpose of the statutory requirement for an audit of public companies was the making of a report to enable the body of shareholders as a whole to exercise informed control over the company,[508] and not to enable existing shareholders or members of the public at large to buy shares with a view to profit. Such persons should make their own inquiries, and could not simply appropriate the auditor's professional expertise for their own benefit. It followed that the auditors owed no duty of care to the respondents either as shareholders or as potential investors in the company.

Leading decisions in Canada[509] and Australia[510] have taken the same or a similar approach to that adopted in *Caparo*. In New Zealand, a majority in the Court of Appeal originally held that an auditor could owe a duty to persons dealing with or investing in a limited liability company.[511] However, in *Boyd Knight v. Purdue*[512] the decision in *Caparo* was accepted as an authoritative statement of the law. The defendant auditor prepared a report that was incorporated in a prospectus issued by a finance company, as required by the Securities Act 1978, certifying that the financial statements in the prospectus gave a true and fair view of the financial position of the issuer. In fact the auditors had failed to detect serious irregularities and frauds. The company collapsed and some of the investors sought to recover their losses from the auditors. The Court of Appeal accepted that the circumstances here, unlike in *Caparo*, were such as to give rise to a duty of care. The auditors must have known that the issuer was obliged to give the prospectus containing their report to potential investors, and that it would do so in order to encourage them to invest. So this was the purpose of the prospectus. Accordingly, there was the necessary closeness of relationship between the auditors and the investors. However, there was no sufficient evidence that the investors had actually read and relied upon the report, and so for this reason the claims failed.

---

negligence by the purchaser: *Johnson v. Auckland Council* [2013] NZCA 662); *Durkin v. DSG Retail Ltd* [2014] 1 WLR 1148 at [33]–[34] (bank and customer).

507. [1990] 2 AC 605.

508. *See* the Companies Act 1985, s. 236 (Eng); Companies Act 1993, ss 196, 205 (NZ).

509. *Hercules Managements Ltd v. Ernst & Young* [1997] 2 SCR 165.

510. *Esanda Finance Corporation Ltd v. Peat Marwick Hungerfords* (1997) 188 CLR 241.

511. *Scott Group Ltd v. McFarlane* [1978] 1 NZLR 576.

512. [1999] 2 NZLR 278.

Even in an audit or similar case a duty sometimes may be owed. Company reports may be prepared specifically for the purpose of being used by investors or may subsequently be shown to investors for the purpose of investment.[513]

2. Company Directors

94. Directors of companies have been accorded a special immunity from liability in negligence. In *Trevor Ivory Ltd v. Anderson*[514] the Court of Appeal decided that a director owed no duty to a client of the director's company to take care unless the director had assumed responsibility for his or her conduct. Cooke P maintained that the courts should avoid imposing on the owner of a one-man company a personal duty of care that would erode the protection of limited liability. Then in *Williams v. Natural Life Health Foods Ltd*,[515] in the House of Lords, Lord Steyn thought the question in issue was not confined to directors acting for limited liability companies. Whether the principal was a company or a natural person, someone acting on his behalf might incur personal liability in tort as well as impose vicarious or attributed liability upon his principal. Nevertheless, in order to establish personal liability under the *Hedley Byrne* principle it was not sufficient that there should have been a special relationship with the principal. There must have been an assumption of responsibility such as to create a special relationship with the director or employee himself. Lord Steyn said that this posed an objective test, the focus being on things said or done by the defendant or on his behalf in dealings with the plaintiff. The inquiry was into whether the defendant conveyed to the plaintiff, directly or indirectly, that the defendant was assuming personal responsibility.

It is not clear whether the reasoning in *Williams* can be reconciled with *Attorney-General v. Carter*,[516] where Tipping J referred to a 'deemed assumption of responsibility' where a person foreseeably and reasonably relied on words for their intended purpose. Maybe ordinary principles should apply in deciding whether a company director owes a duty of care in making statements that are relied on by company clients.[517] So, applying *Caparo*, a duty may be owed where a director makes a statement to a known person or class, to be used by that person for a known purpose without further inquiry. But there may be a *defence* available to the director, this being founded on notice having been given to the client that only the company and not the director can be liable for negligence.[518]

Whether directors will continue to receive preferential treatment pursuant to *Trevor Ivory* and *Williams* remains to be seen. The Court of Appeal has left the question open, although the majority view seemed to favour the requirement that there

513. *Allison v. KPMG Peat Marwick* [2000] 1 NZLR 560; *Price Waterhouse v. Kwan* [2000] 3 NZLR 39; cp *McNaughton (James) Paper Group Ltd v. Hicks Anderson & Co.* [1991] 2 QB 113; *Deloitte & Touche v. Livent Inc* 2017 SCC 63, [2017] 2 SCR 855.

514. [1992] 2 NZLR 517.

515. [1998] 1 WLR 830.

516. [2003] 2 NZLR 160; *see* para. 91.

517. *See Merrett v. Babb* [2001] 3 WLR 1 (employee of firm of valuers personally liable to client for negligent valuation); but cp *Bush v. Summit Advances Ltd* [2015] EWHC 665.

518. *See* para. 516.

be evidence of a personal assumption of responsibility.[519] In any view it is not necessary for a director to be shown to have assumed responsibility for an intentional tort. So a director was personally liable for fraudulent misrepresentations made by him when acting on behalf of his company.[520]

3. Tenders for Building Contracts

95. In *Edgeworth Construction Ltd v. ND Lea & Associates Ltd*[521] the Supreme Court of Canada held that an engineering firm that prepared specifications and construction drawings knowing that bidders for a construction contract would rely on it owed a duty of care to one of those bidders. The court recognized that each bidder otherwise would be obliged to do its own engineering and to conduct a thorough professional review of the engineering design and information in a very limited time. The result would be considerable duplication of time and effort, higher bid prices and greater costs. This reasoning is convincing, but in *RM Turton & Co. Ltd v. Kerslake*[522] a majority in the NZ Court of Appeal reached an opposite conclusion. The plaintiff builder, relying on the mechanical services specification prepared for an owner by the defendant engineers, successfully tendered for a building contract. It later turned out that the heating system would not work to the specified standard. The plaintiff undertook remedial work pursuant to its contractual obligations with the owner, and then sought to recover the cost from the engineer. Henry and Keith JJ held that the engineer owed no duty of care to the bidder. The duty contended for would cut across and be inconsistent with the overall contractual structure that defined the relations of the various parties to the work. There was no justification for holding that the engineer should be regarded as having voluntarily assumed responsibility to the builder.

4. Pre-contractual Representations

96. In principle a *Hedley Byrne* duty of care may attach to representations made in the course of pre-contractual negotiations. For example, a duty was owed by the vendor of a sandblasting unit to the purchaser in making a forecast of future business revenue.[523] However, the common law has been superseded by statute. By section 35 of the Contract and Commercial Law Act 2017 (formerly section 6 of the Contractual Remedies Act 1979), if a party to a contract (A) has been induced to enter into it by a misrepresentation, whether innocent or fraudulent, made to A by or on behalf of another party to that contract (B), A is entitled to damages from B in the same manner and to the same extent as if the representation were a term of

---

519. *Body Corporate 20254 v. Taylor* [2009] 2 NZLR 17; and *see Stephens v. Barron* [2014] NZCA 82. In any event an action may lie for misleading or deceptive conduct pursuant to the provisions of the Fair Trading Act 1986: *see* para. 446.
520. *Standard Chartered Bank v. Pakistan National Shipping Corp.* [2003] 1 AC 959.
521. [1993] 3 SCR 206.
522. [2000] 3 NZLR 406.
523. *Halliday v. Johnson* [1985] 2 NZLR 563.

the contract that has been broken.[524] Damages for deceit or negligence are no longer recoverable.[525] Thus, liability for pre-contractual representations is treated as a contractual matter. Such liability is dependent not on proof of negligence but simply on meeting the terms of the statute.[526]

The negligence action is still available where the person being sued is not a party to the contract but has induced the plaintiff to enter into a contract with someone else. Ordinary common law liability attaches to a misstatement by an agent inducing a contract between the representee and the principal,[527] or by an agent inducing his or her principal to contract with another party,[528] or by anyone else inducing a contract with another.[529]

If no contract ever eventuates, a duty of care owed by one negotiating party to the other is likely to be denied on account of its tendency to subvert the ordinary principles of contract.[530] The Court of Appeal has held that an attempt to use the tort of negligence to make up for the lack of a process contract should be rebuffed on policy grounds.[531]

5. Miscellaneous Cases

97. There are many examples of a duty to third parties being recognized where the requirements set out in *Caparo* are met. Thus surveyors instructed by a building society to value a house were liable to purchasers of the house who had applied to the building society for a loan and who the surveyors knew would rely on their report;[532] valuers of land owed a duty of care to prospective lenders on the security of the land;[533] managing agents at Lloyds owed a duty to names who were members of syndicates under the agents' management.[534] A council owed a duty of care

524. Contract and Commercial Law Act 2017, s. 35(1)(a).
525. *Ibid.*, s. 35(1)(b).
526. For the requirements of s. 35, *see International Encyclopaedia of Laws: Contracts (New Zealand)*, paras 103–107.
527. For example, *Wakelin v. RH & EA Jackson Ltd* (1984) 2 NZCPR 195; *ME Torbett Ltd v. Keirlor Motels Ltd* (1984) 1 NZBLC 102,079; *Tak & Co. Inc v. AEL Corporation Ltd* (1995) 5 NZBLC 99,357 (deceit).
528. *Chaudry v. Prabhakar* [1989] 1 WLR 29.
529. *Wild v. National Bank of NZ Ltd* [1991] 2 NZLR 454.
530. *See*, for example, *Design Services Ltd v. Canada* (2008) 293 DLR (4th) 437; *Daventry DC v. Daventry & District Housing Ltd* [2010] EWHC 1935 at [155]–[163] (on appeal *Daventry District Council v. Daventry & District Housing Ltd* [2012] 1 WLR 1333).
531. *Prime Commercial Ltd v. Wool Board Disestablishment Co Ltd* CA 110/05, 18 Oct. 2006.
532. *Smith v. Eric S Bush: Harris v. Wyre Forest DC* [1990] 1 AC 831; cp *Scullion v. Bank of Scotland plc* [2011] 1 WLR 3213 (surveyors owed no duty of care in respect of the claimant's purchase of a residential flat as a buy-to-let investment).
533. *Kendall Wilson Securities Ltd v. Barraclough* [1986] 1 NZLR 576.
534. *Henderson v. Merrett Syndicates Ltd* [1995] 2 AC 145.

to the purchaser of land when issuing a Land Information Memorandum (LIM) concerning the land;[535] and a manufacturer alleged to have represented that its cladding met recognized building standards arguably owed a duty of care to end-users of the cladding.[536]

In other cases, involving less close relationships, a duty has been denied. For example, directors who issued a prospectus specifically to enable shareholders to consider a rights offer owed no duty to those who relied on the prospectus for the purpose of buying shares in the market;[537] a trade association that gave the names of member companies on its website owed no duty to a customer who made a contract with one of those companies after reading the website and who suffered loss when the company failed;[538] and a bank giving a financial reference owed no duty to a casino which had used another company as a front in seeking the reference in order to preserve confidentiality for the casino's customers, because the true purpose of the reference had not been disclosed and the bank had not assumed a responsibility to the claimant or been in a special relationship with that claimant.[539]

E. Possession of Skill or Knowledge

98. In *Mutual Life and Citizens Assurance Co. Ltd v. Evatt*[540] the Privy Council held by a majority that to be accountable in words, a defendant normally had either to carry on the business of giving the advice, or otherwise let it be known to the plaintiff that he claimed skill and competence in advising. But the decision has been rejected in the High Court of Australia,[541] in the Supreme Court of Canada[542] and in the English Court of Appeal.[543] In the House of Lords it has been observed that the concept of 'special skill' must be understood broadly, certainly broadly enough to include special knowledge.[544] In New Zealand the Court of Appeal has treated *Evatt* as a case decided on its own particular facts. In *Meates v. Attorney-General*[545] Woodhouse P and Ongley J said that it did not purport to lay down an all-embracing principle. The presence or absence of a business or professional element should be regarded as but a single instance of a test in those particular situations where it had actual relevance.

---

535. *Marlborough District Council v. Altimarloch Joint Venture Ltd* [2012] 2 NZLR 726.
536. *Carter Holt Harvey Ltd v. Minister of Education* [2016] NZSC 95, [2017] 1 NZLR 78.
537. *Al-Nakib Investments (Jersey) Ltd v. Longcroft* [1990] 1 WLR 1390.
538. *Patchett v. Swimming Pool & Allied Trades Association Ltd* [2009] EWCA Civ 717.
539. *Playboy Club London Ltd v. Banca Nazionale del Lavoro SpA* [2018] UKSC 43, [2018] 1 WLR 4041.
540. [1971] AC 793.
541. *Shaddock & Associates Pty Ltd v. Parramatta CC* (1981) 150 CLR 225.
542. *Queen v. Cognos Inc* [1993] 1 SCR 87 at 117–118.
543. *Esso Petroleum Co. Ltd v. Mardon* [1976] QB 801 at 827; *Howard Marine & Dredging Co. Ltd v. A Ogden & Sons Ltd* [1978] QB 574 at 591, 600.
544. *Henderson v. Merrett Syndicates Ltd* [1995] 2 AC 145 at 180.
545. [1983] NZLR 308 at 333–334.

F. Disclaimers

99. In *Hedley Byrne* the defendants expressly disclaimed any responsibility on their part. All of their Lordships were agreed that the defendants were not liable. Lord Morris maintained that the plaintiff could not accept a reply given with a stipulation and then reject the stipulation.[546] The reason is found in the principle of notice.[547] The defendant must give reasonable notice of the disclaimer, but does not have to show that the plaintiff actually knew about it and voluntarily assumed the risk of harm.[548]

V. Financial Loss

A. Consequential Financial Loss

100. Financial loss that is consequential upon some physical harm is recoverable without special difficulty. For example, building contractors who negligently dug up a high voltage cable, causing a power failure in the plaintiff's factory, were held liable for material damage by solidification of raw material in the plaintiff's machines and also for loss of production consequent on that damage.[549] Again, plaintiffs who similarly suffered a power cut caused by the defendants' negligence were able to recover for the physical loss of a 'melt' in their furnace and for loss of profit on that melt.[550] However, they could not claim for loss of profits on another four melts that would have been put into the furnace during the period the power was off, as this loss was not consequential on the physical damage. In another context, a railway company could recover damages in respect of the sums it had to pay train operating companies for the time the track was not available after the defendants' vehicles damaged a bridge over a railway line and electrical equipment at a level crossing.[551] The claimant had suffered physical damage to its property, and the payments were demonstrably consequential upon that damage.

Some cases have taken a wide view on what qualifies as consequential loss. For example, a hotel owner could recover for loss of business profits after the defendant caused his hotel to flood, on the basis that the flooding not only made some bedrooms unavailable for a time but also deterred travellers and travel agents from making future bookings because of doubt about whether satisfactory accommodation would be available.[552]

---

546. [1964] AC 465 at 504; applied in *McKinlay Hendry Ltd v. Tonkin & Taylor Ltd* CA 81/04, 9 Dec. 2005.
547. *See* para. 516.
548. *Harris v. Wyre Forest District Council* [1988] QB 835 at 840 (on appeal [1990] 1 AC 831).
549. *SCM Ltd v. Whittal & Son Ltd* [1971] 1 QB 337.
550. *Spartan Steel & Alloys Ltd v. Martin & Co. Ltd* [1973] 1 QB 27.
551. *Network Rail Infrastructure Ltd v. Conarken Group Ltd* [2011] EWCA Civ 644.
552. *Taupo Borough Council v. Birnie* [1978] 2 NZLR 397.

B. Relational Financial Loss

101. Financial loss that occurs only because of the relationship between the immediate, physical, victim of a wrong and the plaintiff is commonly called relational financial loss. This is usually irrecoverable. Accordingly, a company could not sue a driver who negligently caused injury to its managing director,[553] nor could an employer sue a doctor who negligently treated its employee.[554] Where a tortfeasor causes the death of an earner, the dependants may have a claim only by virtue of statute, viz. the Deaths by Accidents Compensation Act 1952.[555]

The same principle applies in the case of property damage, at least in most cases. So a contractor building a tunnel on another's land was not entitled to recover from a waterworks company that caused damage to the land, rendering the building contract less profitable;[556] an insurance underwriter was held to have no direct right against a tortfeasor who damaged the underwriter's assured's property;[557] a claim by auctioneers who suffered financial loss on being unable to conduct their business following the escape of the foot and mouth disease virus from the defendant's premises was held to fail;[558] and a business which depended on the supply of kiwifruit from orchardists had no claim against the MAF for allowing the kiwifruit orchards to become infected.[559]

In England, subject to a 'joint venture' exception,[560] the rule has been consistently applied.[561] However, the High Court of Australia has taken a wider approach, allowing recovery in a case where the plaintiffs were members of a known or ascertainable class of persons, the defendants knew that its negligence would cause damage to members of that class, and the plaintiffs were vulnerable to the risk of

553. *D'Amato v. Badger* [1996] 2 SCR 1071.

554. *West Bromwich Albion Football Club Ltd v. El-Safty* [2006] EWCA Civ 1299.

555. *See* para. 560. Such claims are nearly always covered by the accident compensation scheme.

556. *Cattle v. Stockton Waterworks Co.* (1875) LR 10 QB 453.

557. *Simpson & Co. v. Thompson* (1877) 3 App Cas 279.

558. *Weller v. Foot and Mouth Disease Research Institute* [1966] 1 QB 569. In *D Pride & Partners v. Institute for Animal Health* [2009] EWHC 685 a claim by farmers who suffered loss following an escape of the virus from the same premises similarly failed. Farmers whose livestock were culled were paid statutory compensation, but here the claimants suffered loss because of the regulatory controls on the movement of livestock once infection was suspected or confirmed. The claimants argued that they had suffered physical damage to their property, in that the controls caused the animals to become older, or bigger, or fatter, or thinner, and accordingly less valuable in the market. Tugendhat J accepted that there was a real prospect of a court accepting that animal (and vegetable) produce passing the stage of its natural development at which it would be marketed was physical damage. However, the claimants could not show that they had a real prospect of establishing that a duty of care was owed to them in respect of this indirect loss. Such a duty could be owed to all farmers in Great Britain, and potentially auctioneers and many others. There was no uniquely prominent or even identifiable class that should have been within the defendants' contemplation, and the claims accordingly were dismissed.

559. *Attorney-General v. Seeka Ltd* [2020] NZCA 98. The claim by the orchardists themselves failed (as to which *see* para. 79), and the court considered that this conclusion was likewise determinative of Seeka's claim.

560. *See Morrison SS Co. v. The 'Greystoke Castle'* [1947] AC 265.

561. For further examples, *see Leigh and Sillavan Ltd v. Aliakmon Shipping Co. Ltd: The Aliakmon* [1986] AC 785; *Tate and Lyle Food and Distribution Ltd v. Greater London Council* [1983] 2 AC 409; *Esso Petroleum Co. Ltd v. Hall, Russell & Co. Ltd* [1989] AC 643.

harm.[562] In Canada, the Supreme Court has held that relational economic loss can be claimed only in exceptional cases.[563] Those identified were cases of 'transferred loss' involving claims for loss representing property damage, which the owner of the damaged property would have suffered had the loss not been transferred by contract to the plaintiff, cases where there was a joint adventure between the plaintiff and the property owner, and shipping cases involving the law of general average. The court considered that it was desirable as a general rule to exclude claims for relational economic loss. The right of action of the property owner already put pressure on the defendant to act with care; an exclusionary rule channelled to the property owner both potential liability to the plaintiff and the right of recovery against the tortfeasor, encouraging the plaintiff to make appropriate contractual arrangements with the owner; and the ripple effects of property damage causing economic loss were such that perfect compensation was almost always impossible.

In New Zealand certain first instance decisions allow relational claims on a 'proximity' analysis.[564] The Court of Appeal has not finally determined the question, but at least two decisions give some support to a transferred loss theory.[565]

C. Pure Financial Loss

102. Claims for pure financial loss come in a variety of forms which cannot easily be categorized. In each case the relevant concerns of policy and principle need to be weighed and assessed. Some examples will be given.

1. Professionals and Third Parties

103. Recognition of a tort duty owed by a professional to a third person in carrying out a contract with a client has provoked controversy, due to its potential for undermining the privity rule, ordinarily confining any action for negligence to the client. Nevertheless, such claims have been allowed in the 'disappointed legatee' cases. In *Gartside v. Sheffield, Young & Ellis*[566] a testatrix instructed solicitors to draw up a new will giving a benefit to the plaintiff, but died before the solicitors had acted on the instructions. The Court of Appeal held that the solicitors were under a duty owed to the plaintiff to carry out the instructions with care and diligence. The designated beneficiary was obviously and foreseeably likely to be closely and directly and adversely affected by any carelessness on the part of the

562. *Perre v. Apand Pty Ltd* (1999) 198 CLR 180; and *see Caltex Oil Pty Ltd v. The Dredge 'Willemstad'* (1976) 136 CLR 529; *Barclay v. Penberthy* [2012] HCA 40.
563. *Bow Valley Husky (Bermuda) Ltd v. St John Shipbuilding Ltd* [1997] 3 SCR 1210; and *see Canadian National Railway Co. v. Norsk Pacific Steamship Co. Ltd* [1992] 1 SCR 1021.
564. *NZ Forest Products Ltd v. A-G* [1986] 1 NZLR 14; *Mainguard Packaging Ltd v. Hilton Haulage Ltd* [1990] 1 NZLR 360.
565. *Williams v. Attorney-General* [1990] 1 NZLR 646; *Riddell v. Porteous* [1999] 1 NZLR 1.
566. [1983] NZLR 37.

solicitor. Recognition of a duty would compensate deserving plaintiffs, promote professional competence and enhance rather than erode the solicitor-client relationship. Similar decisions have been reached in both England[567] and Australia.[568]

It was emphasized in *Gartside* that an action would lie only at the suit of persons named in the will or identified in the testamentary instructions. The solicitor's duty cannot be extended to cover an ineffective *inter vivos* transaction where the settlor remains capable of fulfilling his or her original intention.[569] Furthermore, a solicitor is under no duty to potential beneficiaries to give positive advice to a testator as to who ought to be given a benefit under a proposed will,[570] nor to proffer unsolicited advice for their benefit about potential tax avoidance measures.[571] Again, a solicitor who is instructed to prepare a new will is not liable to beneficiaries under an earlier will who incur costs in successfully challenging the new will.[572] Where a solicitor is retained to administer an estate, and the solicitor's negligence causes a loss to the estate, an action may be brought by the executors and there is no need for an action by the beneficiaries.[573]

The *Gartside* principle is capable of application to other cases where a professional person promises to perform a service for a client and the client intends, and the professional person knows, that the service will confer a benefit on a third person if it is performed. However, the Court of Appeal has treated the legatee cases as turning on the special vulnerability of the beneficiaries, and has declined to apply a similar principle in other contexts lacking this feature. So the failure by a solicitor to give advice to the guarantor of a loan to a company, in breach of the instructions given to the solicitor by the client, was not actionable at the suit of the guarantor in circumstances where he should have taken his own financial advice.[574]

2. Reports and References

104. A particular concern in deciding whether a person owes a duty of care to another in writing a report or reference about that other is the effect of recognizing such a duty on existing principles of tort liability. In *South Pacific Manufacturing Co. Ltd v. New Zealand Security Consultants and Investigations Ltd*[575] an insurance assessor reporting to an insurer that the insured had started the fire that led to the destruction of the insured property owed no duty to the insured, partly because the suggested duty would cut across the rules governing liability for malicious prosecution and the defence of qualified privilege in defamation. A negligence duty would

---

567. *White v. Jones* [1995] 2 AC 207.
568. *Hill v. Van Erp* (1997) 188 CLR 159; and *see Graham v. Hall* [2006] NSWCA 208.
569. *Hemmens v. Wilson Browne* [1995] Ch. 223.
570. *Sutherland v. Public Trustee* [1980] 2 NZLR 536; *Clemett v. Boyce* [2005] NZFLR 785.
571. *Cancer Research Campaign v. Ernest Brown & Co.* [1997] STC 1425.
572. *Knox v. Till* [1999] 2 NZLR 753.
573. *Chappell v. Somers & Blake* [2003] 3 WLR 1233.
574. *Brownie Wills v. Shrimpton* [1998] 2 NZLR 320; and *see ORIX New Zealand Ltd v. Milne* [2007] 3 NZLR 637.
575. [1992] 2 NZLR 282.

cover the same ground yet its elements would be less stringent and liability accordingly would be easier to establish.[576] And in *Leigh v. Attorney-General*[577] the Court of Appeal struck out a claim for alleged negligent misstatement causing damage to the plaintiff's reputation, in order not to upset the balance in the law of defamation between freedom of expression and the recognition of rights to protection of reputation. Again, in *Midland Metals Overseas Pte Ltd v. The Christchurch Press Co. Ltd*,[578] the Court of Appeal held that no duty of care in negligence was owed by a newspaper publisher to persons who, or whose goods, were referred to in a news item. In the latter case, the tort of slander of goods covered the ground.[579] In England, in *Spring v. Guardian Assurance plc*,[580] a majority in the House of Lords held that an employer owed a duty to his ex-employee when writing him a reference for a new employer, notwithstanding any overlap with defamation. Their Lordships considered that defamation and negligence were not primarily directed at the same mischief, for one was concerned with loss of reputation and the other with economic loss, that the policy fear that admitting a duty in negligence would undermine the law of defamation was overstated, and that justice required that the employee should have an action. So also in Canada, in *Young v. Bella*,[581] the Supreme Court upheld a duty of care owed by a university professor to a student in reporting unfounded suspicions that the student was a child abuser to a child protection service.

In *Midland Metals* the Court of Appeal recognized the desirability of providing a remedy in *Spring's* case and accepted that such cases might justify imposing a duty of care. Accordingly, the *South Pacific* principle might not be applied in the limited context of a negligently written reference.

3. Miscellaneous Cases

105. Claims for pure financial loss come in a variety of forms that cannot easily be categorized. In every case, any relevant concerns of policy and principle need to be weighed and assessed. *Customs and Excise* Commissioners *v. Barclays Bank plc*[582] is a good example of the balancing exercise. The Customs and Excise Commissioners, wishing to recover outstanding tax liabilities from two companies, obtained freezing (or *Mareva*)[583] injunctions in respect of their assets, which included funds held by the companies in accounts with Barclays Bank. The bank was notified of the injunctions, but failed to prevent payments out of the accounts

576. Compare the requirement of malice in the tort of malicious prosecution (para. 320) and as negating the defence of qualified privilege (para. 354).
577. [2011] 2 NZLR 148 (appeal dismissed on another issue in *Attorney-General v. Leigh* [2012] 2 NZLR 713).
578. [2002] 2 NZLR 289.
579. As to which *see* paras 302–306.
580. [1995] 2 AC 296; and *see Jackson v. Liverpool Council* [2011] EWCA Civ 1068; *Sebry v. Companies House* [2015] 4 All ER 681.
581. [2006] 1 SCR 108.
582. [2007] 1 AC 181.
583. *Mareva Compania Naviera SA v. International Bulk Carriers SA* [1975] 2 Lloyd's Rep. 509.

in breach of the injunctions. The question at issue was whether the bank owed a duty to the commissioners to take reasonable care to comply with the terms of the injunction. The House of Lords recognized that a number of considerations favoured a duty: the orders were made by the court and notified to the bank to protect their interests; recognition of a duty would, in practical terms, impose no new or burdensome obligation on the bank; the rule of public policy that had first claim on the loyalty of the law was that wrongs should be remedied; there were no facts that would found a claim for effective redress for contempt, and the commissioners would otherwise be left without any remedy; a duty of care to the commissioners would not be inconsistent with the bank's duty to the court; and there would be no indeterminacy as to those to whom the duty would be owed. Nevertheless, their Lordships were unanimous in rejecting a duty. First, the *Mareva* jurisdiction had developed as one enforceable only by the court's power to punish those who broke its orders. Second, no duty was owed by the *customer* to that party. It would be a strange and anomalous outcome if an action in negligence lay against a notified party who allowed the horse to escape from the stable, but not against the owner who rode it out. Third, there was no authority holding that a non-consensual court order, without more, could give rise to a duty of care to the party obtaining the order: and one would have to ask whether a similar duty could be owed by the subject of a search order, or a witness summons, or other orders where economic loss was a foreseeable consequence of breach. Finally, it would be unjust and unreasonable that the bank should, on being notified of an order that it had no opportunity to resist, become exposed to a liability that could be very large and for which exposure it had not been in any way rewarded.

There are many more cases involving claims for financial loss apart from those already discussed. Sometimes it is seen as fair and just to impose a duty to take care. This tends to be where the defendant has assumed a specific responsibility to safeguard the economic interests of a particular person or class of persons.[584] On the other hand, relevant policy concerns – for example the effect of a contractual matrix,[585] or inconsistency with a party's assumed contractual obligations,[586] or limiting factors concerning omissions,[587] or the impact of a statutory context[588] or policy considerations relating to the conduct of litigation[589] – may tend to negate any such duty.

584. *See*, for example, *Gorham v. British Telecommunications Plc* [2000] 1 WLR 2129; *Price Waterhouse v. Kwan* [2000] 3 NZLR 39; *BNZ v. Deloitte Touche Tohmatsu* [2009] 1 NZLR 53; *The Law Society of England and Wales v. Schubert Murphy* [2017] EWCA Civ 1295.

585. *RM Turton & Co. v. Kerslake* [2000] 3 NZLR 406 (*see* para. 95); *Rolls-Royce New Zealand Ltd v. Carter Holt Harvey Ltd* [2005] 1 NZLR 324 (*see* para. 125); *Blain v. Evan Jones Construction Ltd* [2013] NZCA 680 at [63].

586. *Greenway v. Johnson Matthey plc* [2016] EWCA Civ 408, [2016] 1 WLR 4487 (reversed on another ground in *Dryden v. Johnson Matthey plc* [2018] UKSC 18, [2018] 2 WLR 1109); *CGL Group Ltd v. Royal Bank of Scotland plc* [2017] EWCA Civ 1073, [2018] 1 WLR 2137 at [98].

587. *Fleming v. Securities Commission* [1995] 2 NZLR 514 (*see* para. 400); *Wellington District Law Society v. Price Waterhouse* [2002] 2 NZLR 767 (*see* para. 397); *Poulton v. Ministry of Justice* [2010] 3 WLR 1237; *Gardiner v. Westpac New Zealand Ltd* [2015] 3 NZLR 1 at [58]–[62].

588. *Attorney-General v. Carter* [2003] 2 NZLR 160 (*see* para. 136); *Seddon v. Driver and Vehicle Licensing Agency* [2019] EWCA Civ 14; [2019] 1 WLR 4593 (*see* para. 91).

589. *James-Bowen v. Commissioner of Police of the Metropolis* [2018] UKSC 40, [2018] 1 WLR 4021.

By statute, a mortgagee exercising a power of sale of land owes a duty to the mortgagor and certain other persons, to take reasonable care to obtain the best price reasonably obtainable as at the time of sale.[590] This provision has been treated as a legislative affirmation of the scope of the duty of care in negligence by a mortgagee who has decided to sell the mortgaged property.[591]

VI. Special Duty Categories

A. *Introduction*

106. In this section we will pay particular attention to a number of special categories of duty. In each case the reason, very broadly, is that the kind of activity that is the subject of the claim, or some aspect of it, has been seen by the courts as giving rise to special, and sometimes unique, problems in deciding whether, or the extent to which, the defendant should be held to be under a duty to take care.

Three of these categories – actions against doctors, against barristers and solicitors and against judges – raise questions about professional liability, whereas the next two – actions against builders and manufacturers – are concerned more with liability in business and trade. Of course there is a good deal of overlap, as where the person being sued is an architect or engineer and the allegation is that he or she has created or contributed to the creation of a defective building or chattel. The final category brings for consideration the question of whether or the extent to which ordinary private law principles ought to apply in actions against public bodies.

The common feature of these various claims is that they are all primarily concerned with particular activities which the plaintiff alleges should give rise to negligence liability. So they are conveniently considered at this stage, following on from our consideration of the general principles of negligence. Then in Chapter 2, which concerns 'Specific Cases of Liability', we will turn to consider a series of discrete torts that are not founded on negligence and that require individual treatment.

B. *Doctors*

1. Impact of the Accident Compensation Scheme

107. There is little scope in New Zealand for tort actions against medical practitioners. This is because in nearly all cases the conduct concerned, if negligent, will constitute treatment injury and, accordingly, a tort action will be barred by the accident compensation legislation.[592] If the conduct is not negligent, then there is simply no cause of action.

---

590. Property Law Act 2007, s. 176.

591. *Apple Fields Ltd v. Damesh Holdings Ltd* [2001] 2 NZLR 586, affirmed sub nom *Newport Farm Ltd v. Damesh Holdings Ltd* [2004] 1 NZLR 721 (PC); *Gardiner v. Westpac New Zealand Ltd* [2015] 3 NZLR 1 at [83]–[91].

592. *See* paras 37, 41.

In exceptional cases medical conduct may fall outside the boundaries of the statutory scheme. A claim by a mother in respect of the physical effects of an unwanted pregnancy caused by failed medical treatment or by rape attracts cover as amounting to a 'personal injury',[593] but a claim in respect of the costs of bringing up an unplanned child does not.[594] The damage here is not the physical effect on the mother but the economic costs consequent upon the parent-child relationship. There is no cover either in the case of a claim by a child born with congenital disabilities in respect of pre-birth negligence in failing to warn the parents, as here there is neither 'personal injury' nor an 'accident'.[595] These are considered below. Other possibilities are claims for compensation in respect of wrongdoing causing only mental injury,[596] and claims for exemplary damages.[597]

2. Sterilization Cases

108. A doctor or other medical professional may have negligently performed a sterilization operation, or given negligent advice as to its efficacy. If the patient later conceives an unplanned child, the question arises whether the doctor can be liable to the patient and his or her partner for the costs of bringing up the child. Decisions overseas take opposing views.

In England, in *McFarlane v. Tayside Health Board*,[598] the House of Lords held that a mother who became pregnant following her husband's failed vasectomy could claim general damages for the pain, suffering, and inconvenience of pregnancy and childbirth and for associated expenses, but that the parents could not recover the costs of bringing up their child. The policy considerations underlying the decision included an unwillingness to regard a normal, healthy child as a financial liability or as more trouble and expense than it was worth, a recognition that the rewards that parenthood may or may not bring cannot be quantified, and a view that it would be a misallocation of public resources to award damages for such loss against the UK National Health Service. The question then arose whether the same principle should apply if the child was born with disabilities, or if the mother sought to be sterilized because she suffered from a disability making it difficult for her to bring up a child. In the former case the English Court of Appeal allowed a claim for extra expenses attributable to the disability.[599] Then in *Rees v. Darlington Memorial Hospital NHS Trust*,[600] which concerned the latter situation, the House of Lords modified *McFarlane* and held that in all failed sterilization cases the courts should make

593. *Allenby v. H* [2012] 3 NZLR 425; *see* para. 35.
594. *J v. ACC* [2017] NZCA 441, [2017] 3NZLR 804.
595. *See* paras 35–36.
596. *L v. Robinson* [2000] 3 NZLR 499; *see* para. 42.
597. *See* paras 42, 576.
598. [2000] 2 AC 59; and *see ARB v. IVF Hammersmith Ltd* [2018] EWCA Civ 2803, [2019] 2 WLR 1094 (same principle applied in a claim for breach of contract in the absence of a liquidated damages clause or any other provision which modified the legal policy of the common law).
599. *Parkinson v. St James and Seacroft University Hospital NHS Trust* [2002] QB 266; and *see Whitehead v. Searle* [2009] 1 WLR 549; *Farraj v. King's Healthcare NHS Trust* [2010] 1 WLR 2139; compare *Khan v. MNX* [2018] EWCA Civ 2609.
600. [2004] 1 AC 309.

a conventional lump sum award of GBP 15,000, in order to mark the legal wrong suffered by the mother in losing the opportunity to live her life in the way that she wished and planned.

In Australia, in *Cattanach v. Melchior*,[601] the High Court held in a four to three majority decision that a doctor who negligently failed to sterilize a patient was liable on the application of ordinary principles of negligence. It was considered, *inter alia*, that there is a distinction between the birth or existence of a child and the financial consequences of the birth, and financial loss cannot be offset against the intangible benefits of parenthood; the birth of a healthy baby is not always a benefit or blessing; and parents should not be treated as receiving a benefit when it is one they deliberately decided they did not wish to acquire. The minority view would have denied liability, on the basis, *inter alia*, that there is no legally recognizable loss or damage or that it is impossible to measure any damage, and that the claim cannot co-exist coherently with other rules affecting the parent-child relationship.

The question has been left open in New Zealand. In *J v. ACC*[602] Kos P favoured the approach taken in Australia, but Cooper and Asher JJ were not by any means certain that a claim of this kind would succeed in light of its denial in the UK, Ireland and Canada.

In Singapore, in *ACB v. Thomson Medical Pte Ltd*,[603] the Court of Appeal was required to determine liability in different, but arguably analogous, circumstances. The plaintiff and her husband sought to conceive a child through in vitro fertilization, but due to the defendant's negligence the plaintiff's ovum was fertilized using the sperm of an unknown third party. The court denied the plaintiff's claim in respect of the upkeep of the child, but recognized that the plaintiff had suffered a loss of 'genetic affinity', and that this should be an actionable head of damage.[604]

3. Wrongful Life Cases

109. Another type of claim arising out of an unplanned birth is for so-called wrongful life. This is a claim by a child who is born with a disability of some kind alleging negligence by the medical advisers of his or her mother or father in failing to diagnose or warn about the disability or risk of disability. In Australia, in *Harriton v. Stephens*,[605] the plaintiff's mother contracted rubella while she was pregnant, and as a consequence of the infection the plaintiff was born suffering from severe congenital disabilities. She sued her mother's doctor, who had failed to diagnose rubella, alleging that she had suffered damage in living her profoundly disabled life. The claim failed in the High Court of Australia, by a six to one majority. Crennan J was satisfied that the damage claimed was not amenable to being determined by the application of ordinary legal method, for had the respondent not been

601. (2003) 215 CLR 1.
602. [2017] NZCA 441, [2017] 3NZLR 804.
603. [2017] SGCA 20.
604. For an overview of the whole question, and a suggested solution, *see* Stephen Todd, 'Common Law Protection for Injury to a Person's Reproductive Autonomy' (2019) 135 LQR 635.
605. (2006) 80 ALJR 791; and *see also Waller v. James* (2006) 80 ALJR 846.

negligent the appellant would not be living at all. Damages ordinarily were measured on the basis of the compensatory principle, but a comparison between a life with disabilities and non-existence was impossible. Relevant concerns of policy also indicated that the claim should be rejected. First, there would be a conflict between the interests of the mother and the interests of the child and, indeed, the prospect of an action by a child against his or her own mother. Second, it was odious and repugnant to devalue the life of a disabled person by suggesting that such a person would have been better off not to have been born into a life with disabilities. Third, there was a lack of certainty about the degree of disability that could potentially give rise to a claim. Fourth, to allow a disabled person to claim his or her own existence as actionable damage would be inconsistent with statutes prohibiting differential treatment of the disabled and with the law's sanction of those who take a life. So the claim could not be reconciled with values expressed generally in the common law and statute. Life with disabilities, like life, was not actionable.

Wrongful life claims also have been rejected in the UK[606] and Canada,[607] on similar reasoning. And in New Zealand such a claim has been seen as contrary to public policy as a violation of the sanctity of human life.[608]

4. Professional Accountability

110. The accident compensation scheme provides for compensation in most cases, yet does not meet other functions served by civil proceedings, notably vindication, professional accountability, and deterrence. Parliament has addressed these concerns by way of the New Zealand Code of Health and Disability Services Consumers' Rights, which was adopted in 1996 pursuant to powers conferred by the Health and Disability Commissioner Act 1994.[609] The Code sets out a series of rights for 'health consumers',[610] including the right to services of an appropriate standard, the right to be fully informed about proposed treatment and the right to make an informed choice and give an informed consent to treatment. Health providers are obliged to take reasonable action to give effect to these rights. The Act lays down a procedure for making complaints to the Health and Disability Commissioner in respect of breaches of the Code. The Commissioner may investigate a

606. *McKay v. Essex Area Health Authority* [1982] QB 1166; *Whitehead v. Searle* [2009] 1 WLR 549; *A and B v. A Health and Social Services Trust* [2011] NICA 28; but compare *TBS v. Metropolitan Police Commissioner* [2017] EWHC 3094 at [37]–[40].

607. In a number of cases the defendant has caused both the injury and the birth, as where a doctor has failed to warn a mother contemplating pregnancy of the risks to a foetus posed by her medication. A duty has been denied, primarily because of the actual or potential conflict of duties which would be owed to the patient and to the child: *see Lacroix v. Dominique* (2001) 202 DLR (4th) 121; *Bovingdon v. Hergott* (2008) 290 DLR (4th) 126; *Paxton v. Ramji* (2009) 299 DLR (4th) 614.

608. *Cumberland v. Accident Compensation Corporation* [2011] NZAR 590 (on appeal [2014] 2 NZLR 373).

609. Health and Disability Commissioner Act 1994, ss 20, 74; Health and Disability Commissioner (Code of Health and Disability Services Consumers' Rights) Regulations 1996, schedule.

610. Only consumers with rights under the Code can be aggrieved persons under the 1994 Act: *Marks v. Director of Health and Disability Proceedings* [2009] 3 NZLR 108.

complaint, deliver an opinion and make recommendations for remedial action. Serious cases may be referred to the Director of Proceedings, who can institute disciplinary proceedings or civil proceedings in a Human Rights Review Tribunal.[611] The Tribunal has the power to award damages to compensate for pecuniary loss and expense, loss of any benefit, and humiliation, loss of dignity and injury to feelings, as well as to punish for any action that was in flagrant disregard of the rights of the aggrieved person.[612] However, compensatory damages for personal injury covered by the Accident Compensation Act 2001 are excluded.[613]

C. Barristers and Solicitors

1. Duty to Client

111. In New Zealand, practising lawyers are admitted as barristers and solicitors. For present purposes there is no need to draw a distinction between them.

It is now well accepted that there is no objection in principle to concurrent duties in contract and tort owed by a solicitor to his or her client. In cases of this kind, the ambit of the duties will usually be co-extensive. For example, in *Frost & Sutcliffe v. Tuiara*,[614] the defendant solicitors acted for clients in a risky conveyancing transaction, the purpose of which was to gain a quick profit for the clients, but which resulted in them losing their home. They sued the solicitors alleging, *inter alia*, breach of a duty of care in looking after their interests. It was held that on the facts the solicitors had not been negligent and, contrary to the views of the trial judge, that there was no basis for holding that the solicitor's duties differed according to whether they were founded on tort or on contract.

A solicitor also may owe a duty of care to third parties who will foreseeably suffer financial loss if the solicitor is negligent in carrying out the instructions of a client. However, the circumstances in which a duty of this kind can arise are rather uncertain.[615] Exceptionally a solicitor who is acting on behalf of a client may owe a duty to the opposite party to a transaction, as where the solicitor provides a certificate and the opposite party can reasonably rely upon and act upon the assurance the certificate contains.[616] But a duty to the other party may create an unacceptable conflict of interest, and normally the solicitor will owe a duty only to his or her own client.[617]

---

611. *Ibid.*, ss 45(f), 49(1)(a).
612. *Ibid.*, ss 52, 54, 57.
613. *Ibid.*, s. 52(2).
614. [2004] 1 NZLR 782.
615. *See* para. 103.
616. For example, *Allied Finance and Investments Ltd v. Haddow & Co* [1983] NZLR 22; *Connell v. Odlum* [1993] 2 NZLR 257; and *see Bartle v. GE Custodians* [2010] 1 NZLR 802 (duty arose from solicitor's assumption of responsibility for performance of task, irrespective of any contract of retainer) (for subsequent appeals on a different point, *see* [2010] 3 NZLR 601 (CA), [2011] 2 NZLR 31 (SC)).
617. *Radisich v. Templeton* [2009] 3 NZLR 276; *Burmeister v. O'Brien* [2010] 2 NZLR 395; *NRAM Ltd v. Steel* [2018] UKSC 13, [2018] 1 WLR 1190.

2. Abolition of Immunity from Suit

112. Special difficulties can arise where an action against a barrister or solicitor complains about work in court or about work that is related to the conduct of litigation. The question of whether the barrister or solicitor can be liable for negligence in these circumstances is controversial, and has given rise to acute differences of opinion both in New Zealand and overseas.

In *Rees v. Sinclair*[618] the Court of Appeal followed the decision of the House of Lords in *Rondel v. Worsley*[619] and held that barristers (and solicitors doing the work of a barrister) could shelter behind an immunity from suit from liability for negligence in the conduct of proceedings in court, and, extending the immunity, from liability for pre-trial work that was intimately connected with the conduct of the cause in court. Subsequently, however, in *Arthur J S Hall & Co. v. Simons*,[620] the House of Lords held that, in the light of the information available and developments since *Rondel*, it was no longer in the public interest in England that the immunity should remain. This was held unanimously as regards the conduct of civil proceedings, and by a four to three majority as regards the conduct of criminal proceedings. Then, in *D'Orta-Ekenaike v. Victoria Legal Aid*,[621] the High Court of Australia upheld the principle of barristerial immunity in both civil and criminal cases, declining even to narrow its scope. Finally, in *Lai v. Chamberlains*[622] the New Zealand Supreme Court decided unanimously to follow the House of Lords in *Hall* and, accordingly, abolished the barristers' immunity in its entirety.

In *Lai* the plaintiffs sued their solicitors for alleged negligence in advising them about an acknowledgement of liability in respect of a judgment against a company of which they were directors, which acknowledgment was incorporated in the terms of a consent order made by the court resolving the litigation. The defendants argued that they were immune from suit. Elias CJ recognized that the key issue in *D'Orta-Ekenaike* concerned the need for finality in litigation. However, she considered that the ends of finality were adequately addressed by res judicata and issue estoppel, the plea of *autrefois acquit* and convict, and the power of the court to strike-out proceedings that were an abuse of process.[623] She considered also that a claim for negligence in the conduct of civil litigation did not run counter to any public interest in the justice system, and that it made it easier to do justice between the parties to the original proceedings. Any loss suffered by one party as a result of negligence in representation could properly be addressed by claiming against the advocate without vexing the other party further. However, as regards the criminal justice system, if advocates were not immune, there might be little to inhibit irresponsible claims from clients that their deprivation of liberty was caused by the advocate. So the

618. [1974] 1 NZLR 180.
619. [1969] 1 AC 191.
620. [2002] 1 AC 615.
621. (2005) 223 CLR 1; compare *Attwells v. Jackson Lalic Lawyers Pty Ltd* (2016) 259 CLR 1 (no immunity as regards advice to settle claim); *Kendirjian v. Lepore* (2017) 259 CLR 275 (need for 'functional connection' between the work of the advocate and the determination of the case).
622. [2007] 2 NZLR 7.
623. *See* para. 113.

extent to which the public interest required redress to be obtained only, or principally, within the remedies provided by the criminal justice system itself would still need to be considered. The question should be addressed on the basis of principle rather than by blanket immunity.

A second issue was whether the immunity was cemented in legislation by section 61 of the Law Practitioners Act 1982 (now section 117 of the Lawyers and Conveyancers Act 2006), providing that 'barristers of the Court shall have the powers, privileges, duties and responsibilities that barristers have in England'. Elias CJ held that the provision applied to New Zealand barristers the common law and practice that already attached to English barristers, but left Parliament and the courts free to develop the law. Section 61 was properly to be regarded as the re-enactment of spent legislation.

Lai decides, then, that barristers and solicitors can no longer shelter behind an immunity from suit, but their former clients must still prove that there was negligence and this may not be easy to establish.[624] Again, any negligence must be proved to be a cause of the plaintiff's loss, which requirement also is likely to be difficult to overcome. The plaintiff may well be unable to show that any shortcomings in the work of his or her barrister made a material difference to the outcome about which he or she complains.

3. Abuse of Process

113. Where an action in negligence by a disappointed client against his or her former barrister or solicitor amounts to an abusive attack on the finality of the earlier court's decision, then the later court in the exercise of its inherent jurisdiction can strike it out as an abuse of process. In *Hunter v. Chief Constable of the West Midlands Police*[625] the House of Lords held that the courts normally will strike out an action where it would impugn a final decision made by another court of competent jurisdiction in previous proceedings, whether criminal or civil, in which the intending plaintiff had a full opportunity of contesting the decision in the court by which it was made. The doctrine has been applied in a number of cases involving civil actions against lawyers for alleged negligence in the conduct of litigation.[626]

In *Lai v. Chamberlains*[627] the Supreme Court agreed with the view taken in *Arthur J S Hall & Co. v. Simons*,[628] applying *Hunter*, that a collateral challenge to a subsisting conviction would usually be an abuse of process. Elias CJ said that appeal was the method of correction provided by the system. An appeal had to be allowed if a conviction was unsafe, and the conduct of counsel could be a reason for setting aside a conviction on this ground.[629] Society was in general entitled to

624. *See Moy v. Pettman Smith* [2005] 1 WLR 581; *Jung v. Templeton* [2010] 2 NZLR 255.
625. [1982] AC 529.
626. For example, *Somasundaram v. M Julius Melchior & Co.* [1988] 1 WLR 1394; *Smith v. Linskells* [1996] 1 WLR 763; cp *Walpole v. Partridge & Wilson* [1994] QB 106; *B v. Miller & Co.* [1996] 2 FLR 23.
627. [2007] 2 NZLR 7.
628. [2002] 1 AC 615.
629. *See Sungsuwan v. R* [2006] 1 NZLR 370.

treat conviction as establishing guilt against the person convicted unless the conviction was set aside on appeal. He or she could make a claim only when there was no subsisting conviction. Inconsistent court determinations on the question of guilt would be destructive of confidence in the criminal justice system. But there might be exceptions, and it would be unwise to be too definite.

As regards civil proceedings, many collateral challenges to subsisting civil judgments would not amount to abuse of process, at least where appeal rights had been exercised. But professional disciplinary proceedings, defamation proceedings and other civil proceedings (including family law proceedings) that determined matters of status might well provide examples where the administration of justice could be brought into disrepute by subsequent collateral challenge. So might a deliberate decision not to pursue an appeal. A categorical approach would be wrong. Whether proceedings were abusive could be assessed as appropriate against the principles of finality developed in *Henderson v. Henderson*[630] or against the principles developed in *Hunter* to protect public confidence in the administration of justice. These principles were sufficient and appropriate protection for the public interest in judicial process.

In *Hall*, where settlements of the parties' disputes had been embodied in consent orders approved by the judge, the claims by the plaintiffs that they would have got better terms if their solicitors had advised and acted for them with reasonable care were not manifestly unfair to the solicitors or liable to bring the administration of justice into disrepute. Allegations that different information should have been given to the judge and of bad advice did not involve any attack on the judicial process. So also in *Lai*, the plaintiffs' allegations of negligence in advising on the consent order were not seen as giving rise to a question of abuse of process.

D. Expert Witnesses

114. A long-established immunity for witnesses is founded upon considerations of policy which are similar to those which underlay the immunity from suit for advocates. In *Darker v. Chief Constable of the West Midlands Police*[631] the House of Lords identified a number of particular justifications for the immunity: (1) to protect witnesses who had given evidence in good faith from being harassed and vexed by unjustified claims; (2) to encourage honest and well-meaning persons to assist in securing that justice is done; (3) to secure that the witness will speak freely and fearlessly; and (4) to avoid a multiplicity of actions in which the value or truth of the evidence would be tried all over again. The immunity could apply generally to protect witnesses of fact, and could cover a claim brought by a litigant against his or her own expert witness[632]

630. (1843) 3 Hare 100; *see* para. 510.
631. *Darker v. Chief Constable of the West Midlands Police* [2001] 1 AC 435.
632. *Stanton v. Callaghan* [2000] QB 75 at 100–102, 108.

In the UK, in *Jones v. Kaney*,[633] the question before the Supreme Court was whether the immunity ought to be retained. Lord Phillips, giving the leading majority decision, considered that the duty owed by expert witnesses was akin to that owed by advocates. In each case the services included a paramount duty to the court and to the public, which might require the advocate or witness to act in a way which did not advance the client's case. And the suggested justifications did not support an immunity. First, his Lordship was not satisfied that if expert witnesses could be sued they would be discouraged from providing their services, noting that professional persons customarily insured against the risk of liability. Second, an immunity was not necessary to ensure that expert witnesses gave full and frank evidence to the court. An expert would be well aware of his duty to the court, and if he frankly accepted that he had changed his view it would be apparent that he was performing his duty. Third, there was the apprehension that expert witnesses might find themselves the subject of vexatious claims, yet unsupported complaints would be susceptible to a strike-out application. Finally, and for the above reasons, there was no risk of multiplicity of suits. His Lordship concluded that the immunity from suit for expert witnesses in relation to their participation in legal proceedings should be abolished. He emphasized, however, that this conclusion did not extend to the absolute privilege that they enjoyed in respect of claims in defamation.

It seems likely that *Jones* will come to be applied in New Zealand. In recent years the courts have shown an increasing reluctance to maintain policy immunities operating in favour of negligent parties, and expert witnesses probably will not be allowed to stand apart from this trend. Indeed, in *EBR Holdings Ltd (in liq) v. McLaren Guise Associates Ltd*[634] a claim against a person who arguably was an expert witness was allowed to proceed to trial. The court considered that the issues should be evaluated with the benefit of a full factual exploration and a consideration then of what principles should be applied.

E. Judges

1. Superior Courts

115. Persons exercising judicial functions in superior courts are exempt from any personal civil liability for anything said or done by them in their judicial capacity.[635] In *Nakhla v. McCarthy*[636] Woodhouse J recognized that the immunity is in no sense a private right, the judge being merely the repository of a public right designed to ensure that the administration of justice will be untrammelled by the collateral attacks of disappointed or disaffected litigants. It flows from the authority of a judge of a superior court to determine the limits of the court's own jurisdiction. Provided the judge is acting in a judicial capacity, he or she is absolutely immune

633. [2011] 2 AC 398.
634. [2016] NZCA 622, [2017] 3 NZLR 589.
635. *Nakhla v. McCarthy* [1978] 1 NZLR 291; *Harvey v. Derrick* [1995] 1 NZLR 314; *Gazley v. Lord Cooke of Thorndon* [1999] 2 NZLR 668.
636. [1978] 1 NZLR 291.

from personal liability, whether for negligence or for any other tort. Further, no public law remedy against the state by way of compensation for breach of the New Zealand Bill of Rights Act 1990 may be sought in respect of a judicial breach in circumstances where the individual judicial officer would have an immunity from suit.[637] The public policy reasons supporting personal judicial immunity justified confining Crown liability for government breaches of the 1990 Act to executive breaches.

2. Inferior Courts

116. The position in law of District Court judges formerly was different. Section 193(1) of the Summary Proceedings Act 1957 provided that 'no action shall be brought against any District Court Judge or Justice or Community Magistrate for any act done by him, unless he has exceeded his jurisdiction or acted without jurisdiction'. In *Harvey v. Derrick*[638] the Court of Appeal held that a judge of a court of limited jurisdiction was not to be treated as exceeding jurisdiction if he or she had acted in good faith and without gross negligence. Merely making a mistake as to the extent of his or her powers was not enough. However, the Law Commission took the view that the protection afforded by *Harvey* was inadequate, noting that the increased jurisdiction of the District Court often overlapped with that of the High Court.[639] The Commission accordingly recommended that the immunity of District Court judges should be expanded to equate with that of High Court judges. This was achieved by an amendment to section 193 removing District Court judges from its ambit,[640] and by the insertion of a new provision in the District Courts Act 1947 – now the District Court Act 2016 – giving them the wider immunity.[641]

There has been no change to section 193 as it affects Justices of the Peace and Community Magistrates. However, a Justice of the Peace or Community Magistrate is entitled to be indemnified where a High Court Judge certifies that, in his or her opinion, the Justice or Magistrate acted in good faith, in the belief that he had jurisdiction and ought fairly and reasonably to be excused.[642]

---

637. *Attorney-General v. Chapman* [2012] 1 NZLR 462; *Thompson v. Attorney-General* [2016] NZCA 687. *See* further para. 314 for remedies for breach of the 1990 Act.
638. [1995] 1 NZLR 314.
639. Law Commission *Crown Liability and Judicial Immunity* Report No. 37, Wellington, 1997, paras 160–171.
640. Summary Proceedings Amendment Act 2004, s. 4(1).
641. District Court Act 2016, s. 23.
642. Summary Proceedings Act 1957, s. 197(1).

F. Builders

1. Introduction

117. A builder owes an ordinary duty of care founded upon *Donoghue v. Stevenson*[643] with respect to negligent building work causing physical injury (subject to the accident compensation scheme) or physical damage to other properties. A different and much-disputed question is whether, or the extent to which, the builder, in the absence of any contract, may be liable to the owner in respect of the cost of putting right the property actually containing the defect. In this case, the owner's claim is for his or her disappointed expectations as to the true value of the property and, accordingly, is for a financial loss. This remains true irrespective of whether a defect has caused actual physical damage to the structure. Physical cracking or collapse may be a consequence of the defect, or the problem may be discovered before this happens. In either case, the owner seeks to recover the diminished value of the property or the cost of making good the defect together with, in the former case, its physical consequences.

Claims of this kind may be made against builders, developers, architects, engineers, local authorities exercising powers of inspecting the building, and any others who have contributed in some way to the construction of the building. In the case of claims against local authorities there may be further complications arising out of the fact that they have not positively caused the harm but have merely failed to prevent it,[644] and out of their status as public bodies exercising public functions.[645]

2. Origins of the Builder's Duty

118. In *Anns v. London Borough of Merton*[646] the House of Lords held that a local authority owed a duty to owners or occupiers who might suffer injury to health caused by defective foundations to take care in inspecting the foundations. Lord Wilberforce thought that the damage sustained by the plaintiff was 'material, physical damage'. What was recoverable was the amount of expenditure necessary to restore the dwelling to a condition in which there was no longer a present or imminent danger to the health or safety of persons occupying it. At about the same time the Court of Appeal came to a similar conclusion in *Bowen v. Paramount Builders (Hamilton) Ltd*,[647] holding that a builder who put up a house on inadequate foundations owed a duty of care to a subsequent purchaser of the building. Liability was founded on the builder having negligently created a hidden defect that was a source of danger to persons whom he could reasonably foresee were likely to suffer damage in the form of personal injuries or damage to property.

643. [1932] AC 562; *see* para. 75.
644. *See* paras 398–400.
645. *See* paras 132–136.
646. [1978] AC 728.
647. [1977] 1 NZLR 394; and *see Mount Albert BC v. Johnson* [1979] 2 NZLR 234.

It is apparent that *Anns* and *Bowen* both recognized a duty by a builder or inspector that was founded on physical damage to the fabric, coupled with the element of danger to the occupants. However, developments in the law in the UK and in New Zealand thereafter went in opposite directions.

3. Developments in the UK

119. The House of Lords initially was prepared to extend the *Anns* principle, holding that subcontractors who had built a defective floor in the plaintiff's factory were liable for the cost of repairing the floor notwithstanding that the defect posed no injury to health.[648] Subsequently, in two key decisions, *Anns* was comprehensively rejected.

In *D & F Estates Ltd v. Church Commissioners for England*,[649] the House of Lords held that builders could not be liable to the lessees of a flat in respect of the financial loss incurred by the lessees in renewing plasterwork incorrectly applied by subcontractors. To recognize a duty would be to impose on the builders the obligation of one who warranted the quality of the plaster as regards materials, workmanship, and fitness for purpose for the benefit of those with whom they had no contractual relationship. A claim based on breach of a warranty of quality could only be maintained by one contracting party against the other. However, two lines of argument were left open. First, their Lordships did not decide whether there could still be recovery where a defect posed a danger to health. Second, they recognized the possibility that one element of a complex structure could be regarded as distinct from another element, so that damage to one part caused by a hidden defect in another part might qualify as physical damage to 'other property'. The recoverable damages might then include the cost of making good the defect, as essential to the repair of the property which had been damaged by it.

Both questions were subsequently examined in *Murphy v. Brentwood District Council*.[650] The defendant council had approved a faulty design for the foundations of a house, with the result that the house was built with defective foundations. It later subsided and the owner, instead of repairing it, sold it for less than half its market value in an undamaged state. The House of Lords held unanimously that the owner's claim should fail, and that *Anns* should be overruled. The claim was for pure economic loss and, if allowed, would open up a very wide field of claims involving the introduction of something in the nature of an indefinitely transmissible warranty of quality. In so deciding their Lordships declined to draw a distinction between a mere defect of quality and a dangerous defect. In both cases the owner suffered a diminution in value of property, not injury to health. As for the 'complex structure' theory, this was accepted in principle but held not to apply on

648. *Junior Books Ltd v. Veitchi Co. Ltd* [1983] 1 AC 520.
649. [1989] AC 177.
650. [1991] 1 AC 398; and *see also Department of the Environment v. Thomas Bates & Son* [1991] 1 AC 499.

the facts. Where inadequate foundations led to differential settlement and cracking, the structure as a whole was seen to be defective and as it deteriorated would only damage itself.

4. Developments in Australia and Canada

120. In *Bryan v. Maloney*[651] the High Court of Australia held that the builder of a house who had negligently installed inadequate footings causing damage to the fabric owed a duty of care to a subsequent purchaser, who was entitled to recover the consequential loss measured by the decrease in the value of the house. The duty arose out of the relationship of close proximity between builder and owner. *D & F Estates* and *Murphy* were dismissed as resting upon a narrower view of the scope of the modern law of negligence and a more rigid compartmentalization of contract and tort than was acceptable in Australian law.

In Canada, in *Winnipeg Condominium Corporation No. 36 v. Bird Construction Co.*,[652] the owner of a ninety-four unit apartment building sued the builder after a large piece of concrete cladding fell from the building, necessitating the removal and replacement of the entire cladding. The Supreme Court of Canada held that where negligence in planning or constructing a building caused the building to be dangerous, the owner could recover the costs of making the building safe.

5. Developments in New Zealand

121. In *Stieller v. Porirua City Council*[653] the Court of Appeal reinterpreted *Anns* and *Bowen* and recognized that an owner's claim was for economic loss suffered through acquiring property of inferior quality. Accordingly, an inspecting council's obligations were not confined to defects affecting health and safety, nor to defects damaging or threatening to damage other parts of the structure. It was enough that they reduced the value of the premises. But *D & F Estates* and *Murphy* came after *Stieller*, and for a time it was not clear whether these decisions would also be applied in New Zealand.

The question was resolved in *Invercargill CC v. Hamlin*,[654] which upheld the New Zealand decision. The defendant council had issued a building permit for the plaintiff's house after the foundations were inspected and approved by a building inspector. The foundations were faulty and the plaintiff brought proceedings against the council, the builder having gone out of business. The Court of Appeal held that it was liable and declined to apply *D & F Estates* and *Murphy*. The court recognized, *inter alia*, that the duty of care was well established, that homeowners relied

651. (1995) 182 CLR 609.
652. [1995] 1 SCR 85; and *see City of Kamloops v. Neilsen* [1984] 2 SCR 2; *Rothfield v. Manolakos* [1989] 2 SCR 1259.
653. [1986] 1 NZLR 84; *Brown v. Heathcote CC* [1986] 1 NZLR 76, on appeal [1987] 1 NZLR 720 (PC).
654. [1994] 3 NZLR 513; [1996] 1 NZLR 513 (PC).

on local authorities to exercise reasonable care, and that to change the basis of risk allocation at this stage would have various direct and indirect economic impacts that would need first to be thoroughly explored. On the council's further appeal to the Privy Council the decision of the Court of Appeal was upheld. Their Lordships recognized that in the Court of Appeal's view, to change New Zealand law so as to make it comply with *Murphy* would have significant community implications and would require a major attitudinal shift. It would be rash for the Board to ignore these views.

More recently, a major problem in the building industry has emerged concerning the adoption of flawed building techniques that have allowed water to leak into and cause substantial damage to large numbers of new houses. In *North Shore City Council v. Body Corporate 188529 (Sunset Terraces)*; *North Shore City Council v. Body Corporate 189855 (Byron Avenue)*[655] the Supreme Court confirmed that the *Hamlin* duty can give a remedy here. Councils owed a duty of care, in their inspection role, to owners, both original and subsequent, of premises designed to be used as homes. So 'investor' owners of residential property were covered as well as private residential owners.[656]

Special statutory procedures also have been set up to deal with the problem, although they do not change the substantive law of contract and of tort.[657] However, specific provision is made for the recovery of damages for mental distress.[658]

6. Commercial Property

122. Sunset *Terraces* concerned residential property. The possibility that a duty might be owed in respect of other buildings, like schools, offices and other commercial buildings, was left open. In *Hamlin* itself Cooke P distinguished the position as regards industrial buildings, saying that the network of contractual relationships normally would provide sufficient avenues of redress without any supervening tort duties. But the point did not need to be decided.

In *Rolls-Royce New Zealand Ltd v. Carter Holt Harvey Ltd*,[659] the Court of Appeal, taking a view that was broadly similar to that adopted in Australia,[660] held that a subcontractor which had built industrial plant pursuant to a contract with the main contractor owed no duty of care to the owner. The court gave four main reasons: the parties were sophisticated commercial concerns with equality of bargaining power; the subcontractor had signified to the owner via the terms of the main

655. [2011] 2 NZLR 289.
656. The court also held (i) that a body corporate could sue for damage suffered by the common property in a multi-unit building; and (ii) that an owner could still be owed a duty notwithstanding the absence of a code compliance certificate, although the point might raise issues of causation or of contributory negligence. For the further issue of limitation, *see* para. 458.
657. Weathertight Homes Resolution Services Act 2006. However, there are statutory warranties in the Building Act 2004: *see* para. 127.
658. *Ibid.*, s. 50(1), (2).
659. [2005] 1 NZLR 325.
660. *Woolcock St Investments Ltd v. CDG Pty Ltd* (2005) 216 CLR 515.

contract and of the subcontract that its liability was limited; there was acute difficulty in setting objectively ascertainable quality standards in commercial construction contracts for specialist plant with detailed specifications; and commercial parties were normally entitled to expect that the risk they had negotiated and paid for would not be disturbed by the Courts.

Subsequent decisions in the Court of Appeal continued to deny that there could be a duty to take care.[661] But then, in *North Shore CC v. Body Corporate* 207624 (Spencer on Byron)[662] the matter came before the Supreme Court for decision. The case concerned a building with both residential and commercial uses. Six residential apartments occupied the top two levels of a 23 level building, while the remainder of the building, comprising 253 units, operated as a hotel. The building leaked and the Body Corporate, the owners of the hotel units and the owners of the apartments all sued the North Shore City Council, alleging, *inter alia*, negligence in issuing the building consents and in inspecting and approving the development. The claim was rejected in the lower courts, but in the Supreme Court it was held that the council owed all of the owners a duty to take care.

Elias CJ was satisfied that no sufficient principled basis for drawing a distinction between homeowners and owners of other buildings passed by the council as code compliant had been put forward. The Building Act 1991 set up the necessary relationship of proximity between the council and the building owners as to give rise to a duty of care: and the nature of that relationship did not differ according to the use to which the building was put. All building work was required by the Act to comply with the minimum standard of the building code, and territorial authorities were obliged to enforce its provisions. The Act made it impossible to maintain any distinction between commercial and residential buildings. It was concerned with all building work, without differentiation, and explicitly envisaged tort liability on the part of councils as well as private certifiers. Further, the risk of moisture ingress through failure to meet code standards was the very type of eventuality the Act, the code and the council checks were designed to guard against. There was no floodgates concern of indeterminate liability to an indeterminate class. Those to whom the duty was owed were owners of buildings, constructed under the supervision and certification obligations of the council.

Tipping J and Chambers and McGrath JJ (in a joint judgment) delivered opinions to a similar effect, upholding the claims. But William Young J dissented. He considered that the case was not within existing authority, proximity was not established, and uncertainties as to policy told against a duty. His Honour was sceptical about the utility of actions for negligence as a mechanism for addressing the consequences, and mitigating the risks, of defective building practices, particularly given the systemic and polycentric nature of the problem. The availability of what was at best a clumsy, uncertain and expensive remedy in negligence might have blunted a need to come up with more efficient loss-avoidance and loss-spreading mechanisms.

---

661. *Te Mata Properties Ltd v. Hastings DC* [2009] 1 NZLR 460; *Queenstown Lakes District Council v. Charterhall Trustees Ltd* [2009] 3 NZLR 786.
662. [2013] 2 NZLR 279.

7. Several Liability

123. Imposing liability on councils serves to spread the loss, which may ultimately be met by ratepayers. This arguably is an appropriate response in view of the prevalence and the systemic nature of the problem. Apart from this, there are many other potential defendants who may be held to owe a duty of care in respect of defective building construction. Fairly clearly they also are open to claims founded on *Spencer on Byron* to the extent that they negligently contribute to buildings being erected that do not comply with the building code. Chambers and McGrath JJ remarked that no one could be party to the construction of a building that did not comply with the building code, and spoke in particular of the obligations of the inspecting authority or of any supervising architect or engineer. Claims against the manufacturers of building components also may be possible.[663]

8. Standard of the Duty

124. The duty of care arises out of the builder doing the work, not out of the builder performing a contract with the original owner. The bounds of the duty are objectively determined and are not defined by reference to the terms of the original contract. In *Stieller v. Porirua City Council*[664] the Court of Appeal held that the builder's duty is to take care to build a reasonably sound structure, using good materials and workmanlike practices.[665]

The approach taken in *Stieller* was built upon in *Spencer on Byron*, where the Supreme Court determined that the touchstone was to be found in the requirements of the building code. As Tipping J remarked, the purpose of the Building Act and building code was to maintain minimum standards of construction. These standards avoided the waste, inefficiency, economic losses that might be encountered if the only control was contractual. The code standard was as clear and precise as the subject matter allowed.

That much may be clear, yet the plaintiff in a leaky building case seeking to prove that the defendant was in fact in breach of duty may face a difficult task.[666] Exactly what causes a building to leak may involve an evaluation of complex and technical issues in circumstances where relevant evidence is difficult to obtain. Sometimes the difficulties are such that apparently meritorious claims will fail.[667] Further, in litigation involving two or more defendants, it may be that one is subject to the control and instructions of another. So a builder who was obliged by tender documents to

663. *See* para. 131.
664. [1986] 1 NZLR 84 at 94.
665. The directors of building companies may be personally liable where they have exercised personal control over the work: *Body Corporate 202254 v. Taylor* [2009] 2 NZLR 17; and *see* further para. 94.
666. *See Platt v. Porirua City Council* [2012] NZHC 2445.
667. For example, *Van Huijsduijnen v. Woodley* [2012] NZHC 2685.

comply with instructions from architectural consultants was not obliged to second-guess the latter, and thus was not liable to the owner of an inadequately remediated leaky building.[668]

9. Contractual Modification of the Tort Standard

125. The tort duty owed by a builder to an owner of property can be limited or excluded by notice to or agreement with the owner, whether by contract or otherwise.[669] Without acceptance of some kind, the duty owed to a subsequent purchaser cannot be limited or excluded by reference to any term in a contract made with an earlier owner.[670] To allow the builder to rely on the contract would be to place the burden of the contract on a person who is not party to it and this is contrary to principle.[671] Even so, the High Court of Australia referred to 'evident difficulty' in holding that a builder owed a subsequent owner a duty of care to avoid economic loss if performance of that duty would have required the builder to do more or different work than the contract with the original owner required or permitted.[672] Yet it is hard to see why an agreement with another person to do work falling short of the tort standard should affect a subsequent purchaser.

Conversely, a contractor who enters into a contract with the original owner for the use of high-grade materials or special ornamental features will not be liable to subsequent purchasers for failure to meet these special standards.[673] The touchstone is in compliance with the code. So complaints about aesthetic appeal generally will not be actionable. For example, a supplier of glass pursuant to subcontract was not liable to the main contractor for failing to meet contractual specifications as to the colour of the glass.[674]

10. The Negligent Building Owner

126. A tort duty is not negated by negligence by a building owner or the owner's own experts. In *Southland Indoor Leisure Centre Charitable Trust v. Invercargill City Council*[675] the owner of a sports stadium whose contractors were responsible for creating defects in its roof, which collapsed following a heavy fall of snow, succeeded in a claim against the defendant council for issuing a building

668. *Andrews Property Services Ltd v. Body Corporate 360161* [2016] NZCA 644, [2017] 2 NZLR 772.
669. *Rolls-Royce New Zealand Ltd v. Carter Holt Harvey Ltd* [2005] 1 NZLR 324 at [109]–[113].
670. *Bowen v. Paramount Builders (Hamilton) Ltd* [1977] 1 NZLR 394 at 407, 419; *Bryan v. Maloney* (1995) 182 CLR 609 at 624–625; *Winnipeg Condominium Corporation No. 36 v. Bird Construction Co.* [1995] 1 SCR 85 at 123–124. The contractual matrix may indicate a restriction on liability: *Blain v. Evan Jones Construction Ltd* [2013] NZCA 680 at [63].
671. *See International Encyclopaedia of Laws: Contracts (New Zealand)*, para. 189.
672. *Woolcock St Investments Pty Ltd v. CDG Pty Ltd* (2005) 216 CLR 515 at [28]; and *see Rolls-Royce New Zealand Ltd v. Carter Holt Harvey Ltd* [2005] 1 NZLR 324 at [68].
673. *Winnipeg Condominium Corporation No. 36 v. Bird Construction Co.* [1995] 1 SCR 85 at 105.
674. *Simaan General Contracting Co. v. Pilkington Glass Ltd (No. 2)* [1988] QB 758.
675. [2017] NZSC 190, [2018] 1 NZLR 278.

Code Compliance Certificate. Ellen France J said that the council's functions were all directed at ensuring buildings complied with the Building Code, and this meant that the council's duty was not obviated by another party's negligence or knowledge. However, the owners were guilty of contributory negligence, because they should have followed the advice of their own expert and asked an engineer to inspect the work done on the roof.

11. The Building Act 2004

127. The Building Act 2004 lays down mandatory statutory warranties in all residential building contracts or contracts of sale of 'household units' made by or on behalf of an 'on-seller' of the units.[676] A household unit is a building or part of a building that is used or intended to be used only or mainly for residential purposes and occupied or intended to be occupied by a single household, and does not include a hostel, boarding house, or other specialized accommodations.[677] An 'on-seller' is a person who, for the purpose of on-selling the household unit, builds it or, in trade, arranges for it to be built or acquires it from a person who built it or arranged for it to be built, or acquires it in a transaction intended to defeat the purpose of the Act.[678] The warranties require, broadly, that all building work be done with reasonable care, properly and competently and in accordance with the plans and building consents; that materials used will be suitable and, unless otherwise stated, new; that household units intended to be occupied on completion of the work will be suitable for occupation; and if the contract specifies the particular purpose for which the work is required, that the work and materials will be reasonably fit for that purpose.[679] A right of action for breach of any of these warranties is not confined to the other contracting purchaser. A subsequent owner may take proceedings whether or not that person was a party to the contract.[680] Any such action is subject to the limitation defences contained in the Limitation Act 2010.[681]

The statutory warranties cannot apply in the case of complaints about defects created prior to the coming into force of the 2004 Act (30 November 2004), but such claims are now likely to be statute-barred.[682]

676. Building Act 2004, s. 362H(1).
677. *Ibid.*, s. 7.
678. *Ibid.*, s. 362H(3).
679. *Ibid.*, s. 362I.
680. *Ibid.*, s. 362J.
681. *See* para. 469.
682. Building Act 2004, s. 393; *see* para. 458.

G. Manufacturers

1. Introduction

128. Manufactured goods normally will reach the ultimate purchaser via a chain of contracts made between all or any of the manufacturer, distributor, wholesaler, retailer, and purchaser. Where loss is suffered by the purchaser because of a defect in the goods he or she may be able to sue the retailer in contract for breach of the express terms of the contract, if any are applicable, or for breach of certain terms as to fitness and quality which are implied into the contract pursuant to the provisions of Part 3 of the Contract and Commercial Law Act 2017.[683] In the particular case of a consumer contract, where the Consumer Guarantees Act 1993 applies,[684] the supplier is bound by certain statutory guarantees to similar effect.[685] Where it is available a purchaser is likely to rely on his or her remedy in contract against the supplier, for at least two reasons. First, the supplier's liability is strict whereas the manufacturer's is for negligence. Second, damages are recoverable for loss of bargain – for the fact that the product does not perform the task for which it was bought – as well as for consequential loss. The extent, if any, to which the former kind of loss is recoverable in a negligence action is uncertain.[686] But where the supplier cannot be found, or is insolvent, or has excluded liability, the purchaser may then seek to sue the manufacturer for negligence. Again, where the loss is not in any event suffered by the purchaser but by someone else not standing in contractual privity with the supplier, that person's remedy will be in tort for negligence. In addition, in cases where the Consumer Guarantees Act applies, a consumer has a statutory cause of action against the manufacturer for failure to comply with certain statutory guarantees. As will be seen, this may have advantages over the tort action.[687]

2. The Rule in *Donoghue v. Stevenson*

129. The implications for the general law of negligence of the 'neighbour' principle laid down by Lord Atkin in *Donoghue v. Stevenson* have already been examined.[688] Lord Atkin also formulated a more particular rule governing the duty of care owed by a manufacturer towards the eventual consumer of a product:[689]

> [B]y Scots and English law alike a manufacturer of products, which he sells in such a form as to show that he intends them to reach the ultimate consumer in the form in which they left him with no reasonable possibility of intermediate examination, and with the knowledge that the absence of reasonable care in the

683. *See International Encyclopaedia of Laws: Contracts (New Zealand)*, para. 304.
684. *Ibid.*, para. 313.
685. *Ibid.*, para. 314.
686. *See* para. 131.
687. *See* para. 450.
688. *See* para. 75.
689. [1932] AC 562 at 599.

preparation or putting up of the products will result in an injury to the consumer's life or property, owes a duty to the consumer to take that reasonable care.

3. Width of the Rule

130. The action is not confined to 'consumers' in the sense of purchasers or users. Any person who ought reasonably to have been foreseen as likely to be affected by the defect can maintain an action.[690] So, liability attaches not only to manufacturers but also to repairers, contractors, and anyone else who bears some degree of responsibility for the harm.[691]

The question whether goods are actually defective in such a way as to cause damage usually can be resolved without particular difficulty. Sometimes, however, the harm comes about only because the goods were being treated or used in some special fashion that was not intended by the manufacturer. In such cases it may be that the goods cannot be regarded as being defective at all.[692] Even so, products that pose special dangers may need warnings against reasonably foreseeable misuse. Again, manufacturers of products that cannot be made safer in accordance with prevailing scientific and technological standards but that pose a known risk to the consumer or user may be required to give warnings of the danger and, where appropriate, point to safety procedures.[693] Where a danger becomes known after goods have been manufactured and marketed, the manufacturer may have to cease production and recall the goods, or at least thereafter give a warning.[694]

A manufacturer may avoid liability where there was a 'reasonable possibility of intermediate examination', either by the plaintiff himself or herself or by an intermediary through whose hands the goods will pass before reaching the plaintiff. Nevertheless, a person who creates a dangerous situation cannot escape liability on the ground of expectation of intermediate examination unless the expectation is strong enough to justify that person in regarding the contemplated inspection as an adequate safeguard to persons who might otherwise suffer harm.[695] The likelihood of intermediate examination by the plaintiff will negate a duty on the part of the manufacturer only where the conduct of the plaintiff is such as to indicate consent or assumption of the risk.[696] Usually the plaintiff's lack of care will be treated simply as contributory negligence and the damages reduced accordingly.[697] In the case

---

690. *Lambert v. Lewis* [1982] AC 225.
691. For example, *Jull v. Wilson and Horton* [1968] NZLR 88 (repairer); *Perrett v. Collins* [1998] 2 Lloyd's Rep. 255 (certifier).
692. For example, *Aswan Engineering Establishment Co. v. Lupdine Ltd* [1987] 1 WLR 1.
693. *Lambert v. Lastoplex Chemicals Co.* [1972] SCR 569; *Dow Corning Corp. v. Hollis* [1995] 4 SCR 634.
694. *Rivtow Marine Ltd v. Washington Ironworks Co.* [1974] SCR 1189; cp *Thompson v. Johnson & Johnson Pty Ltd* [1991] 2 VR 449.
695. *Jull v. Wilson and Horton* [1968] NZLR 88; *Bowen v. Paramount Buildings (Hamilton) Ltd* [1977] 2 NZLR 394; *Stieller v. Porirua CC* [1986] 1 NZLR 84.
696. *Poole v. Crittal Metal Windows (NZ) Ltd* [1964] NZLR 522; *Fraser v. Jenkins* [1968] NZLR 816.
697. *See* para. 476.

of intervention by a third party, the manufacturer will be immune if he or she has given a sufficient warning to the third party, who then fails to act on it.[698]

4. Economic Loss

131. Where a defect in a chattel causes damage to other property, a duty can be recognized in the ordinary way. For example, a manufacturer of electric motors that were used to power the oxygenation pumps for the plaintiff's lobster tank was liable for loss of the lobsters when the motors cut out.[699] Where a defect simply damages the chattel itself, seemingly the owner suffers economic loss by analogy with the reasoning in the building cases.[700] Authority on whether loss of this kind can be recovered in a tort action is inconclusive. In Australia a duty has been denied,[701] but in Canada there can be a duty to repair or replace where a chattel is dangerous.[702] In New Zealand it has been held that there can be no general duty in tort to comply with contractual obligations as to quality.[703] But there may be a duty in building cases where actual damage is done by defective components to other parts of the building. In *Carter Holt Harvey Ltd v. Minister of Education*[704] the plaintiff owned schools affected by weather tightness failures, and issued proceedings alleging, *inter alia*, negligence by the manufacturer of defective cladding installed on the buildings. The defendant sought to strike out the claims, but the Supreme Court held that a duty was arguable and refused the application. The Court recognized that the Building Code requirements were not directly imposed on manufacturers, but said that they nonetheless defined the standards manufacturers were required to meet in products, so that when they were used in a building the building would be code compliant. The policy argument against a duty, that it would cut across the law of contract, creating commercial uncertainty and making the common law incoherent, would need to be fully explored at trial once the contractual relationships had been clearly established.

There is a lesser need for a remedy in tort in respect of a defective chattel as opposed to a defective building, because a purchaser who is a 'consumer' can sue the manufacturer for breach of section 27 of the Consumer Guarantees Act 1993.[705] This remedy arguably was available in *Carter Holt Harvey*, but the Supreme Court did not see the provisions of the Act as limiting any common law remedy. The question has not been finally determined and it might still be argued that the detailed statutory regime should cover the field.

---

698. *Holmes v. Ashford* [1950] 2 All ER; *Hurley v. Dyke* [1979] RTR 265.
699. *Muirhead v. Industrial Tank Specialities Ltd* [1986] QB 507; and *see Aswan Engineering Establishment Co. v. Lupdine Ltd* [1987] 1 WLR 1.
700. *See* para. 117.
701. *Minchillo v. Ford Motor Co. of Australia Ltd* [1995] 2 VR 594; *GBD Investments Pty Ltd v. Ace Ceramics Pty Ltd* (1995) Aus Torts Reps 81-359.
702. *Privest Properties Ltd v. Foundation Co. of Canada* (1995) 128 DLR (4th) 577 (appeal dismissed (1997) 143 DLR (4th) 635); *Hughes v. Sunbeam Corp.* (2003) 219 DLR 467.
703. *NZ Food Group (1992) Ltd v. Amcor Trading (NZ) Ltd* (1999) 9 TCLR 184.
704. [2016] NZSC 95, [2017] 1 NZLR 78.
705. *See* generally para. 450.

H. Public Bodies

1. Introduction

132. Negligent conduct by a public body in carrying out its statutory functions can give rise to liability in negligence at common law. The careless performance of a statutory duty or power does not in itself create such liability, although in certain relatively exceptional cases, a public body may be liable for the tort of breach of statutory duty.[706] Rather, the plaintiff has to show that the circumstances are such that there is a duty of care at common law.[707] Sometimes a statutory duty may also give rise to a common law duty of care to do or refrain from doing a particular act, and sometimes in the course of carrying out its statutory functions, the defendant may bring about such a relationship between itself and the plaintiff as to give rise to a common law duty.[708]

Key policy concerns in public body cases are whether a duty imposed by the courts would:

- trespass into a non-justiciable or political sphere; or
- interfere with the public body's autonomy in deciding whether or how to act; or
- impose on the public body a disproportionate burden of liability; or
- undermine or create inconsistency with any existing common law or statutory rules dealing with the problem in issue.

These various matters are considered below.

A common complaint against public or quasi-public bodies is of a failure to exercise supervisory or regulatory powers in a way that would have prevented the plaintiff from suffering harm. Whether there is a duty in claims of this kind can be determined by particular applications of the ordinary principles governing the liability of persons in supervisory or controlling positions in failing to prevent the harm.[709]

As we shall see, in the case of harm inflicted by a third party, normally there must be a special power of control over that party and the plaintiff must be especially vulnerable to suffering the harm.[710]

Where a public body's conduct is especially culpable such that it amounts to an abuse of power, as where a public officer maliciously causes harm to another or deliberately acts outside power, the public body or the officer concerned may be liable for the tort of misfeasance in a public office.[711]

---

706. *Attorney-General v. Carter* [2003] 2 NZLR 160 at [43]; *Hobson v. Attorney-General* [2007] 1 NZLR 374 at [37]–[43] (on appeal, *Couch v. Attorney-General* [2008] 3 NZLR 725); for breach of statutory duty *see* paras 428–441.
707. *Robinson v. Chief Constable of West Yorkshire Police* [2018] UKSC 4, [2018] AC 736 at [32]–[36].
708. *See X v. Bedfordshire County Council* [1995] 2 AC 633 at 735; *St John Poulton's Trustee in Bankruptcy v. Ministry of Justice* [2010] 3 WLR 1237 at [87]–[98].
709. *See* paras 398–400.
710. *Couch v. Attorney-General* [2008] 3 NZLR 725; *see* para. 400.
711. *See* paras 308–311.

2. Duty in Public Law

133. Some authority in England holds that a duty of care can only be owed in respect of decisions or conduct by a public body outside the ambit of a statutory discretion.[712] However, this approach has not taken root in New Zealand. In *Morrison v. Upper Hutt CC*[713] Richardson P thought that it was neither helpful nor necessary to introduce public law concepts as to the validity of a decision into the question of liability at common law for negligence. Again, in *Crimmins v. Stevedoring Industry Finance Committee*,[714] McHugh J in the High Court of Australia maintained that public law concepts of duty and private law notions of duty are informed by different rationales. The negligent exercise of a statutory power was not immune from liability simply because it was within power, nor was it actionable in negligence simply because it was ultra vires. In *A-G v. Body Corporate No. 200200*[715] Hammond J, delivering the judgment of the Court of Appeal, adopted this approach. Even in England, more recent decisions of the House of Lords indicate that the question whether a decision was within power is not determinative.[716] Common law concepts of negligence have been applied rather than public law concepts concerning the ambit of a public body's power.[717] However, where the basis for a common law duty exists, a failure in the use of a public power may also amount to a failure in fulfilling the duty of care.[718]

3. Justiciability

134. Certain decisions hold that it is necessary to distinguish between complaints against public bodies about the broad merits of a decision which is made in the exercise of a statutory power, and complaints about the manner in which a discretionary decision has been implemented in practice. A duty may be owed in respect of 'operational' matters but not in respect of 'policy' matters, which it is the function of the public body, not the court.[719]

In New Zealand a leading decision discussing this question is *Takaro Properties Ltd v. Rowling*.[720] The litigation arose out of a refusal by the Minister of Finance to give consent to a proposed injection of foreign capital into the plaintiff company.

712. *X v. Bedfordshire County Council* [1995] 2 AC 633; *Stovin v. Wise* [1996] AC 923.
713. [1998] 2 NZLR 331 at 338.
714. (1999) 200 CLR 1 at [82], [218].
715. [2007] 1 NZLR 95 at [48]–[49].
716. *Barrett v. Enfield London Borough Council* [2001] 2 AC 550; *Phelps v. Hillingdon London Borough Council* [2001] 2 AC 619; *Gorringe v. Calderdale Metropolitan Borough Council* [2004] 1 WLR 1057 at [4]–[5].
717. A public law remedy may be obtained via an application for judicial review pursuant to the Judicial Review Procedure Act 2016.
718. *Connor v. Surrey County Council* [2010] 3 WLR 1302.
719. *See*, in particular, *Anns v. London Borough of Merton* [1978] AC 728 at 754; *X (Minors) v. Bedfordshire County Council* [1995] 2 AC 633; but *see Robinson v. Chief Constable of West Yorkshire Police* [2018] UKSC 4, [2018] AC 736 at [32]–[36].
720. [1987] 2 NZLR 700; and *see Couch v. Attorney-General* [2008] 3 NZLR 725 at [59].

The minister's refusal later was held to be invalid,[721] but by that time the company had collapsed. The company sued the minister, arguing, *inter alia*, that he had a duty to take care to make a decision based upon valid considerations. After inconclusive interlocutory proceedings,[722] it was eventually held in the Privy Council that the claim should fail. Lord Keith said that the distinction between policy and operation was expressive of the need to exclude altogether those cases in which the decision under attack was of such a kind that the question whether it had been made negligently was unsuitable for judicial resolution. The minister's decision in the present case was not thought to have been of this character, but other considerations militated against the imposition of a duty. In particular, there was a danger of overkill, in that the imposition of liability might promote excessive caution in decision-making; there would be great difficulty in identifying cases where there was a duty to seek legal advice; and the legislation was enacted not for the benefit of applicants for consent to share issues but for the protection of the community as a whole.

The judgment in *Takaro* focused more on the issue of justiciability than on the distinction between policy matters and operational matters. Some recent decisions of the House of Lords also take this approach. In both *Barrett v. Enfield London Borough Council*[723] and *Phelps v. Hillingdon LBC*[724] it was considered that the ultimate question is whether the particular issue is justiciable, or whether the court should accept that it has no part to play. Whether an authority acts within its discretion and the policy/operational distinction were guides in deciding that question.

Another possible test is to ask whether a complaint involves political considerations. Decisions as to raising revenue and setting priorities in the allocation of public funds between competing claims on scarce resources, or about the extent of government regulation of private and commercial behaviour that was proper, may be regarded as essentially political and for that reason non-justiciable.[725]

4. Common Law Context

135. The common law context can have a significant influence on whether a public officer or body is under a duty of care. In *Takaro Properties Ltd v. Rowling*,[726] where the Privy Council held that there was no duty on a minister to take care to act within power, Lord Keith contemplated that it would be in the public interest for citizens to be confined to their remedy in those cases where the minister or public body had acted in bad faith. Certainly, an inquiry into the ambit of a public body's power is an inappropriate complication to the duty determination. By contrast, it is highly relevant to the question of whether a public officer or body is liable in the tort of misfeasance in a public office. Misfeasance requires a deliberate and

721. *Rowling v. Takaro Properties Ltd* [1975] 2 NZLR 62.
722. *Takaro Properties Ltd v. Rowling* [1978] 2 NZLR 314.
723. [2001] 2 AC 550.
724. [2001] 2 AC 619; *Carty v. Croydon London Borough Council* [2005] 1 WLR 2312.
725. *See Graham Barclay Oysters Pty Ltd v. Ryan* (2003) 211 CLR 540 per Gleeson CJ.
726. [1987] 2 NZLR 700; *see* para. 134; and *see Comeau's Sea Foods Ltd v. Canada (Minister of Fisheries and Oceans)* [1997] 1 SCR 12; *Holland v. Government of Saskatchewan* [2008] SCC 42.

dishonest abuse of power by a public officer.[727] Mere negligence in acting outside power is not enough for liability. So recognizing a duty of care would undercut the requirements for misfeasance. In *Northern Territory v. Mengel*[728] Brennan J observed that the state of mind of a public officer, which is a necessary element of misfeasance, defines the legal balance between the officer's duty to ascertain the functions of the office which it is his or her duty to perform, and the freedom of the individual from unauthorized interference with interests which the law protects. The balance that is struck is not to be undermined by applying a different standard of liability – namely liability in negligence – where a plaintiff's loss is purely economic and the loss is attributable solely to a public officer's failure to appreciate the absence of power required to authorize the act or omission which caused the loss.

Applying the principle, alleged negligence by a local authority in carrying out planning functions[729] or allocating social housing,[730] by a child support agency in assessing, collecting and enforcing child support payments,[731] by a government department in failing to make welfare payments,[732] by the Home Office in making a decision about applications for asylum,[733] by a registration authority in seeking an order for the cancellation of registration of a nursing home,[734] or by a local authority to protect children from harassment and abuse by third parties by rehousing them,[735] is not actionable in damages. The financial victims of unlawful decision-making can sometimes recover compensation, by bringing an action for misfeasance in a public office. By giving a remedy in damages where an officer has abused his or her power, because he or she maliciously or deliberately acted outside power, the courts are not usurping the officer's legitimate functions. Yet, where there is no abuse, it can be seen as inappropriate for a court to intervene.

The same principle can apply to limit the ambit of a duty in fields covered by other torts. A clear example is provided by cases holding that there can be no duty to take care of by police or prosecuting authorities in carrying out their investigative and prosecutorial functions.[736] This has been put broadly on the basis that a duty would have an inhibiting effect on the performance of these functions, would divert valuable resources in guarding against and defending civil actions, and would create tensions in the law and impair its coherence. Underlying these concerns is

727. *See* para. 311.
728. (1995) 185 CLR 307 at 359.
729. *Morrison v. Upper Hutt City Council* [1998] 2 NZLR 331; *Bella Vista Resort Ltd v. Western Bay of Plenty District Council* [2007] 3 NZLR 429; cp *Craig v. East Coast Bays City Council* [1986] 1 NZLR 99.
730. *Lillian Darby (Administratrix) v. Richmond upon Thames LBC* [2015] EWHC 909.
731. *Rowley v. Secretary of State for Work and Pensions* [2007] 1 WLR 2861.
732. *Murdoch v. Department for Work and Pensions* [2010] EWHC 1998.
733. *Home Office v. Mohammed* [2011] EWCA Civ 351.
734. *Jain v. Trent Strategic Health Authority* [2009] 2 WLR 248.
735. *Poole Borough Council v. GN* [2019] UKSC 25, [2019] 2 WLR 1478.
736. *Calveley v. Chief Constable of Merseyside Police* [1989] AC 1228, 1238; *Elguzouli-Daf v. Commissioner of Police of the Metropolis* [1995] QB 335; *Robinson v. Chief Constable of West Yorkshire Police* [2018] UKSC 4, [2018] AC 736 at [58]–[59]; and *see James-Bowen v. Commissioner of Police of the Metropolis* [2018] UKSC 40, [2018] 1 WLR 4021. But an action for negligence has been allowed by the Supreme Court of Canada: *Hill v. Hamilton-Wentworth Regional Police Services Board* (2007) 285 DLR (4th) 620.

the proper role of the tort of malicious prosecution. The scope of this tort is deliberately limited, in order not to create a disincentive to the prosecution of offenders. The expansion of negligence into the field would tend to undermine that general objective.

5. The Statutory Context

136. In developing the law of negligence the courts seek consistency with any relevant statutes governing the activity of the public body. Sometimes courts have called in aid the purpose of the empowering statute in deciding whether an action will lie. For example, the Supreme Court has recognized that the purpose of legislation and regulations governing the inspection of buildings is not confined to matters of health and safety and includes amenity and financial concerns.[737] But the purchasers of a ship could not recover for economic loss allegedly suffered as a result of relying on a survey certificate negligently issued by the Marine Division of the Ministry of Transport, because the statutory purpose in setting up a survey regime was to promote safety at sea rather than to safeguard the purchasers' economic interests.[738]

In other cases the question is whether a duty of care is consistent with what the statute requires or empowers the public body to do. A duty may well be imposed if it would buttress and support the legislative policy, but denied if it would be likely to cut across or discourage performance of the statutory functions. So imposing a duty to take care in issuing an LIM as to water entitlements was consistent with the recognition in the legislation providing for the issue of LIMs[739] that made it clear that applicants were entitled to rely on their accuracy.[740] But the Securities Commission owed no duty of care to individuals in relation to its power to enforce the provisions of the (former) Securities Act 1978, because a duty would interfere with the exercise of the Commission's supervisory functions.[741]

Certain child abuse cases provide clear examples of the influence of the statutory setting. In *A-G v. Prince*[742] the questions at issue were whether a social worker owed a duty of care in reporting to an adoption court about the suitability of the plaintiff's adoptive parents, and whether a social worker was under a duty to investigate a complaint that the plaintiff was being mistreated. In the former case a duty was denied, because it would cut across the finality of the adoption order, whereas in the latter a duty was recognized, because it would be consistent with proactive legislation aimed at protecting children at risk of abuse. Subsequent decisions have considered whether a duty of care may also be owed to a person suspected of abuse. In *B v. Attorney-General*[743] a father and his two daughters claimed damages in respect

737. *North Shore CC v. Body Corporate 207624 (Spencer on Byron)* [2013] 2 NZLR 297.
738. *Attorney-General v. Carter* [2003] 2 NZLR 160.
739. Local Government Official Information and Meetings Act 1987, s. 44A.
740. *Marlborough District Council v. Altimarloch Joint Venture Ltd* [2012] 2 NZLR 726.
741. *Fleming v. Securities Commission* [1995] 2 NZLR 514.
742. [1998] 1 NZLR 262.
743. [2004] 3 NZLR 145.

of the allegedly negligent way a social worker and a clinical psychologist investigated a complaint that the father had sexually abused one of the daughters. The result of the investigation was that the children were removed from the father's custody. The father was never charged with any offence, and eventually the children were returned to him. The applicable statute imposed a positive duty to arrange a prompt inquiry, which was seen by the court as necessarily comprehending a duty to arrange and conduct an adequate inquiry and to follow up such information as came to hand. Accordingly, applying *Prince*, there was a concurrent common law duty. However, the duty was owed only to the daughters and not to the father. Lord Nicholls said that in an inquiry into an abuse allegation the interests of the alleged perpetrator and of the children as the alleged victims were poles apart. Self-evidently the statutory duty in *Prince* was not imposed for the benefit of alleged perpetrators of abuse, and to utilize it in that way would be to travel far outside its rationale.

The House of Lords reached a similar conclusion in *D v. East Berkshire Community Health NHS Trust.*[744] Lord Nicholls maintained that health professionals should not be subject to potentially conflicting duties when deciding whether a child may have been abused, or when deciding whether their doubts should be communicated to others, or when deciding what further investigatory or protective steps should be taken. *Jain v. Trent Strategic Health Authority*[745] is an analogous case. It was held here that a health authority owed no duty of care to the owners of a nursing home in taking action to close it down. The purpose of the authority's statutory powers was to protect the interests of residents in nursing homes, not the economic interests of owners.

However, in *James-Bowen v. Commissioner of Police of the Metropolis*,[746] the UK Supreme Court recognized that the fact that a duty of care might give rise to conflicting interests would often be a weighty consideration against its imposition, yet pointed out that this was not, of itself, necessarily conclusive against its recognition in all situations. It was necessary to have regard to the competing underlying policy considerations, when determining whether a duty of care might be imposed notwithstanding that it might give rise to a conflict of interests.

---

744. [2005] 2 AC 373; and *see D v. Bury Metropolitan Borough Council* [2006] 1 WLR 917; *Lawrence v. Pembrokeshire County Council* [2007] 1 WLR 2991. In Australia *see Sullivan v. Moody* (2001) 207 CLR 562. In Canada, *see D(B) v. Halton Region Children's Aid Society* (2007) 284 DLR (4th) 682.
745. [2009] 1 AC 853.
746. [2018] UKSC 40, [2018] 1 WLR 4021 at [28]–[29].

VII. Breach of Duty

A. *The Standard of Care*

1. The Reasonable Person

137. The standard of care to which every defendant must conform is that of the reasonable man (as originally laid down),[747] or, today, the reasonable person. It is an objective standard that 'eliminates the personal equation and is independent of the idiosyncrasies of the particular person whose conduct is in question'.[748] So, for example, a learner driver must meet the standard of the reasonable driver, irrespective of whether he or she is capable of doing so.[749] However, the standard of reasonableness is not a counsel of perfection. It is an ordinary and not a super-human standard. Judicial descriptions include 'the man in the street', or 'the man on the Clapham omnibus', or 'the commuter on the underground'.[750] It is not an unattainable standard that guarantees against all harm in all circumstances.[751]

There is only one legal standard of care, and there are no 'high' or 'low' standards.[752] However, the degree of care needed to satisfy the standard of reasonableness is infinitely variable. Whether that standard has been attained is determined ultimately in the light of what is being done and in what particular circumstances it is being done.

2. Knowledge and Skill

138. Generally, the law imposes a standard of care employing the reasonable skill and knowledge of someone in the position of the defendant.[753] The reasonable person is credited with ordinary intelligence and perception, and with possessing the common knowledge that enables him or her to appreciate danger and take steps to guard against it. If the defendant has superior knowledge, his or her conduct is judged by the standard of the reasonable person possessing that knowledge.

In the case of the specially skilled, the standard of conduct must conform to that which ought to be attained by persons holding themselves out as possessing the relevant skills. So a competitor in a sporting contest must meet the standard of the reasonable competitor, taking into account the exigencies of the moment.[754] In the case

747. *Blyth v. Birmingham Waterworks* (1856) 11 Ex 781 at 784.
748. *Glasgow Corporation v. Muir* [1943] AC 448 at 457.
749. *Nettleship v. Weston* [1971] 2 QB 691; *Imbree v. McNeilly* [2008] HCA 40.
750. *Frost v. Chief Constable of South Yorkshire Police* [1999] 2 AC 455 at 495.
751. *Hamilton v. Papakura DC* [2000] 1 NZLR 265 at 280.
752. *Russell v. Harris* [1960] NZLR 902.
753. *Hamilton v. Papakura DC* [2000] 1 NZLR 265 at 280; *Darnley v. Croydon Health Services NHS Trust* [2018] UKSC 50, [2018] 3 WLR 1153 at [24]–[27].
754. *Wilks v. Cheltenham Car Club* [1971] 1 WLR 668 at 673–674; *Evans v. Waitemata District Pony Club* [1972] NZLR 773 at 775–776; *Vowles v. Evans* [2003] 1 WLR 1607 (referee); *Blake v. Galloway* [2004] 1 WLR 2844 (horseplay).

of a professional person, and subject to any special contractual provision, the standard required is that which ought reasonably to be attained by persons holding themselves out as possessing skill and expertise in the profession concerned, both in relation to a client with whom there is a contract and in relation to any third party to whom a duty to take care is owed. For example, architects,[755] solicitors,[756] doctors,[757] art historians[758] and engineers[759] all must exhibit the care reasonably to be expected of skilled and informed members of their respective professions, judged as at the time the work was done. Yet the obligation is to take care, not to provide a guarantee of success. The course taken by a professional may turn out to be mistaken yet if care has been taken he or she is not liable. Accordingly, there was no breach where a solicitor's professional judgment may have been erroneous but it was a judgment a competent solicitor could reasonably make.[760] So also, a barrister,[761] auditor,[762] or valuer,[763] in the exercise of his or her professional judgment, cannot be expected always to take correct action or give correct advice.

Lack of skill or experience is no defence if the task in hand demands greater knowledge or experience. Whether specialist advice or assistance is needed is a question of fact.[764] If it is, the defendant is negligent if he or she does not obtain it. As a general rule, a person who does call in a reputable expert or specialist has taken reasonable care and is not responsible for any shortcomings on the part of the expert. So a principal who has selected and instructed an independent contractor with the skill and care appropriate to the occasion generally is entitled to leave the task to the contractor without further supervision.[765] Thus a building owner was not liable for a defect in a lift, after engaging a lift engineer to inspect and maintain it.[766] In certain exceptional cases, however, commonly involving control over activities on land posing special danger to persons in vulnerable positions, the principal may be under a non-delegable duty to take care.[767]

3. Age

139. The standard of care expected of a particular child is that which should reasonably be expected of a child of his or her years.[768] So limitations upon a child's

755. *Sulco Ltd v. ES Redit & Co. Ltd* [1959] NZLR 45.
756. *Bannerman, Brydone Folster & Co. v. Murray* [1972] NZLR 411.
757. *Smith v. Auckland Hospital Board* [1965] NZLR 191.
758. *Thwaytes v. Sotheby's* [2016] 1 WLR 2143.
759. *McLaren Maycroft & Co. v. Fletcher Development Co. Ltd* [1973] 2 NZLR 100.
760. *Simperingham v. Martin* unrep., 2 Jun. 1995, CA5/96.
761. *Moy v. Pettman Smith* [2005] 1 WLR 581; *Jung v. Templeton* [2010] 2 NZLR 255.
762. *Caparo Industries plc v. Dickman* [1989] 2 WLR 316 at 331–332 (on appeal [1990] 2 AC 605 (HL)).
763. *Smith v. Eric S Bush* [1990] 1 AC 831 at 851.
764. *Lyons v. Nicholls* [1958] NZLR 409.
765. *Cashfield House Ltd v. David and Heather Sinclair Ltd* [1995] 1 NZLR 452 at 466.
766. *Haseldine v. CA Daw and Son Ltd* [1941] 2 KB 343.
767. *Cashfield House Ltd v. David and Heather Sinclair Ltd* [1995] 1 NZLR 452; *see* para. 380.
768. *Speirs v. Gorman* [1966] NZLR 897 at 905–906.

capacity for foresight or prudence can be brought into account, not as being personal to him or herself, but as being characteristic of humanity at his or her stage of development and in that sense normal.[769]

There is no particular age that, when attained, means that the standard of care of an adult has to be applied. The matter must be determined on a case-by-case basis and in the light of whatever it is that the child was doing.[770] A young person engaging in an adult activity must meet adult standards. So a 16-year old driving a car must fully conform to the standard of the reasonable driver.[771]

4. Physical and Mental Capacity

140. A person who is physically incapable of adequately carrying out a task or activity, whether by reason of old age, illness, physical disability, or the like, may be negligent in making the attempt in the first place. Thus a driver may be held liable for starting to drive with the knowledge that he or she is physically unfit to do so. There is no negligence, however, if the defendant has no reason to suspect that he or she may suffer a sudden loss of control, at least where this is due to an unexpected external force. For example, a driver was not liable for causing an accident where he was hit in the eye by a particle or insect.[772] But the position where a person has unknowingly lost the physical or mental capacity to take care is uncertain.[773]

B. Application of the Standard

141. The reasonable person test has to be applied in the light of the particular circumstances of the case in hand. In *Wyong Shire Council v. Shirt*[774] Mason J in the High Court of Australia said that the perception of the reasonable person's response to a foreseeable risk calls for a consideration of the magnitude of the risk and the degree of the probability of its occurrence along with the expense, difficulty and inconvenience of taking alleviating action and any other conflicting responsibilities which the defendant may have. In *Wilson & Horton Ltd v. A-G*[775] the Court of Appeal noted that the variables in this kind of analysis are in most cases not capable of quantitative estimate, and emphasized that the law of negligence should not lie just in a search for the cheapest loss avoider. But, even so, the approach was a useful and powerful one.

---

769. *McHale v. Watson* (1966) 115 CLR 199.
770. *See*, for example, *Gorely v. Codd* [1967] 1 WLR 19; *Mullins v. Richards* [1998] 1 WLR 1304.
771. *Tauranga Electric-Power Board v. Karora Kohu* [1939] NZLR 1040 at 1045. In *Zanner v. Zanner* [2010] NSWCA 343 an 11-year-old boy was held to be negligent in manoeuvring the family car into a carport and running over his mother.
772. *Billy Higgs & Sons Ltd v. Baddeley* [1950] NZLR 605.
773. *See* para. 160.
774. (1980) 146 CLR 40 at 47–48; and *see NSW v. Fahy* (2007) 81 ALJR 1021.
775. [1997] 2 NZLR 513 at 521.

In *Tame v. New South Wales: Annetts v. Australian Stations Pty Ltd*[776] McHugh J, in a helpful overview, said that at the breach stage it would be better to avoid any question of reasonable foreseeability of a risk. Instead, courts should see their task as that of deciding whether the defendant knew, or ought to have recognized, that he or she had created an unreasonable risk of harm to others. This was a matter for judgment, after taking into account the factors mentioned in *Wyong Shire Council.*

1. Probability of Harm

142. If there is a foreseeable risk of damage, the degree of likelihood that the damage will happen is a factor to be taken into account in deciding what, if anything, the defendant ought to do about it. A test put forward by Lord Reid is whether the risk of damage was so small that a reasonable man in the position of the defendants, considering the matter from the point of view of safety, would have thought it right to refrain from taking steps to prevent the danger.[777] Applying this test, the playing of cricket in such a way as to pose a very remote risk to passers-by of being hit by the ball was not negligent as the risk could reasonably be disregarded. On the other hand, a very small risk that oil spilled into the sea could ignite was nonetheless a real risk and was not such as would make a reasonable man think it justifiable to neglect to take steps to eliminate it.[778] The former case involved a socially valuable activity posing a risk that would have been highly burdensome to eliminate. The latter case raised neither consideration.[779] In another example, contractors digging a hole in the highway were obliged to take into account the danger this posed to the blind, even though the chance of a blind person coming was small.[780] Nevertheless, extraordinary precautions were not required, as the defendant could assume that a blind person would take reasonable steps by way of self-protection.

2. Gravity of the Risk

143. The greater the danger, the more that is expected of the defendant by way of precautionary measures.[781] A reasonable person is not called upon to take the same degree of care in pouring out a drink as in measuring a dose of medicine.[782] So a high degree of care is required, for example, as regards the possession of detonators,[783] the use of firearms,[784] or the storing of inflammable materials.[785] Even

776. (2003) 211 CLR 317 at [96]–[102].
777. *Bolton v. Stone* [1951] AC 850.
778. *Overseas Tankship (UK) Ltd v. The Miller Steamship Co. Pty Ltd: The Wagon Mound (No. 2)* [1967] 1 AC 617.
779. *See* paras 144–145.
780. *Haley v. London Electricity Board* [1965] AC 778.
781. *Read v. J Lyons & Co. Ltd* [1947] AC 156 at 173.
782. *Welch v. Dorrington* [1949] NZLR 871 at 872.
783. *McCarthy v. Wellington CC* [1966] NZLR 481.
784. *Kenealy v. Karaka* (1907) 26 NZLR 1118.
785. *Wilson & Horton Ltd v. Attorney-General* [1997] 2 NZLR 513.

serious danger can sometimes be risked if the degree of probability of the harm occurring is low and the burden of precautionary measures is high.[786]

3. Social Value of the Activity

144. Many everyday activities are inherently risky, yet they are not condemned because the risk is seen as acceptable in the light of prevailing community standards and general social benefit. In *Tomlinson v. Congleton Borough Council*[787] the House of Lords held that an occupier was not liable for injury suffered by a trespasser running and diving forward into a lake, broadly on the basis that the danger was obvious and that the occupier was not obliged to take any special steps to guard against it. Lord Hobhouse saw the arguments for the claimant as involving an attack on the liberties of the subject that should not be countenanced. They attacked the liberty of the individual to engage in dangerous, but otherwise harmless, pastimes at his own risk and the liberty of citizens as a whole fully to enjoy the variety and quality of the landscape of the country.

Sometimes a particular reason for the allegedly negligent activity needs to be brought into account. In such a case the court is required to balance the risk that is created against the end to be achieved, and certainly the question can arise in all kinds of ways.[788] In particular, saving life or limb can justify a considerable risk.[789] Many examples arise out of accidents involving emergency vehicles. For example, it was not negligent to use a left-hand drive ambulance without direction indicators in wartime, for it was essential that the ambulance service should be maintained and no other ambulances were available.[790] So also a fire authority was not liable for carrying an insecurely fastened jack on the back of a lorry when responding to an emergency call, in circumstances where the vehicle that would normally carry it was not available.[791] But breach of traffic regulations by emergency vehicles can give rise to liability for negligence where the risk is too great to warrant the incurring of the danger.[792] For example, the pursuit by the police of a car being driven by a suspected criminal for a prolonged period in breach of standing orders and in hazardous urban conditions was actionable on the ground that it posed an unacceptable risk to other road users.[793]

---

786. *Graham Barclay Oysters Pty Ltd v. Ryan* (2002) 211 CLR 540; *see* para. 142.
787. [2004] 1 AC 46; *Trustees of Portsmouth Youth Activities Committee v. Poppleton* [2008] EWCA Civ 646; *The Scout Association v. Barnes* [2010] EWCA Civ 1476.
788. *See Humphrey v. Aegis Defence Services Ltd* [2016] EWCA Civ 11, [2017] 1 WLR 2937.
789. *Watt v. Hertfordshire County Council* [1954] 1 WLR 835.
790. *Daborn v. Bath Tramways Motors* [1946] 2 All ER 333.
791. *Watt v. Hertfordshire County Council* [1954] 1 WLR 835.
792. *Ward v. London County Council* [1938] 2 All ER 341; *Gaynor v. Allen* [1959] 2 QB 403.
793. *Doern v. Phillips Estate* (1998) 43 BCLR (3d) 53; *Kurtz v. Radke* (2007) 280 DLR (4th) 647; cp *Priestman v. Colangelo and Smythson* [1959] SCR 615.

4. Burden of Precautionary Measures

145. The purpose behind the defendant's activities has to be considered in conjunction with the cost and practicability of taking measures to reduce or eliminate the risk. In Lord Reid's words in *The Wagon Mound (No. 2)*,[794] a reasonable man would not neglect a real risk of damage 'if action to eliminate it presented no difficulty, involved no disadvantage and required no expense'. In this case, spilling oil into the sea could have been avoided by simple precautions, and failure to take them was negligent. However, if an activity is beneficial and guarding against any danger is difficult then a finding of negligence is unlikely. So, a defendant was not liable for creating a small danger from playing cricket in circumstances where the danger could only be avoided by playing somewhere else.[795]

Where a danger arises on land that the landowner has not created, any liability of the landowner has to be determined in the light of his or her capacity to guard against the risk. In *Goldman v. Hargrave*[796] the Privy Council recognized that the standard of effort required of the landowner had to take account of the fact that the hazard had been thrust on him though no seeking or fault of his own. Regard should, therefore, be had to his physical capacity and financial resources. On these facts, the landowner was held liable for failing to prevent a fire started on his land by lightning from spreading on to his neighbour's land, because he could very easily have put it out. Conversely, a factory owner was not liable for failing to close down the factory when the floor became slippery after a flood and there was insufficient sawdust available to cover every part of the floor.[797] Again, an oyster grower acted reasonably in carrying out approved testing procedures, but not closing down the whole business, in response to a very slight possibility of viral contamination.[798]

C. External Standards

1. Common Practice in a Trade or Profession

146. Evidence of common practice in an industry or of accepted professional standards is relevant in determining whether a defendant has been negligent but is not decisive. The court, rather than the trade or profession concerned, ultimately must determine whether there was negligence in fact in all the circumstances of the case.[799] If it is found that a professional person did not use the degree of skill and care that the majority of his or her profession would have brought to the same task, then that is strong evidence of negligence. At the same time, the court is not bound

794. [1967] 1 AC 617 at 643–644.
795. *Bolton v. Stone* [1951] AC 850.
796. [1967] 1 AC 645; *French v. Auckland CC* [1974] 1 NZLR 340.
797. *Latimer v. AEC Ltd* [1953] AC 643.
798. *Graham Barclay Oysters Pty Ltd v. Ryan* (2002) 211 CLR 540 at [107]–[113], [187]–[204].
799. *Sulco Ltd v. ES Redit & Co. Ltd* [1959] NZLR 45 at 88.

by such evidence, for it must retain its own freedom to conclude that the general practice of a particular profession was negligent.[800]

Compliance with a clearly established practice weighs heavily in favour of the defendant, and the burden on the plaintiff of establishing negligence is not easily discharged. Furthermore, there is room for differences of opinion and practice within a trade or profession, and a court's preference for one body of opinion over another is no basis for a conclusion of negligence.[801] Even so, it might be commonplace in a competitive industry to cut corners, or a system might be convenient for those practising it, yet fail to provide sufficient protection for the public. So, evidence that a defendant adhered to a common setup in the building industry,[802] or followed a common practice in the legal profession[803] or the medical profession,[804] does not prevent a court from making a finding of negligence. In other words, deciding whether conduct was negligent ultimately is a matter for the court, not the trade or profession concerned. Furthermore, common practices must keep up with developing knowledge and technological advances.[805] For example, the question whether a blood bank or hospital was negligent in pursuing practices that failed to guard against the risk of infection by the AIDS virus was determined in the light of medical knowledge about the virus at the relevant time.[806]

In the converse case, where a defendant does not follow a common practice, this is a strong indication of want of care but, again, the court will make its own assessment. For example, police policy on car pursuits did not itself set the standard of care, but non-compliance was a very important factor in deciding whether the standard was met.[807] Yet a finding of negligence will not always follow. Failure to provide a barrier cream to protect against dermatitis, contrary to the usual practice in the industry, was not negligent where there were strong differences of opinion in the medical profession as to the value of the cream and it was not proved the cream would have prevented the damage.[808]

In *Baker v. Quantum Clothing Group Ltd*[809] the UK Supreme Court gave an overview. Employers could rely upon a recognized and established practice to exonerate themselves from liability in negligence for failing to take further steps to avoid

800. *McLaren Maycroft & Co. v. Fletcher Development Co. Ltd* [1973] 2 NZLR 100 at 107–108.
801. *Maynard v. W Midlands RHA* [1984] 1 WLR 634.
802. *Cavanagh v. Ulster Weaving Co.* [1960] AC 145.
803. *Edward Wong Finance Co. Ltd v. Johnson, Stokes & Master* [1984] AC 296; cp *Patel v. Daybells* [2001] Ll Rep PN 738, where the Court of Appeal declined to hold that the adoption by solicitors in England of the conveyancing practice condemned in *Edward Wong* was negligent.
804. *Bolitho v. City and Hackney Health Authority* [1998] AC 232, where the House of Lords maintained that the medical practice must have a 'logical basis' and be 'responsible', 'reasonable', or 'respectable'; and *see also Reibl v. Hughes* [1980] 2 SCR 880; *Rogers v. Whitaker* (1992) 175 CLR 479; *Montgomery v. Lanarkshire Health Board* [2015] AC 1430.
805. *Bussey v. 00654701 Ltd* [2018] EWCA Civ 243, [2018] 3 All ER 354 at [29]–[36].
806. For example, *Dwan v. Farquhar* [1988] 1 Qd R 234; *ter Neuzen v. Korn* [1995] 3 SCR 674; *Walker Estate v. York-Finch General Hospital* [2001] 1 SCR 647.
807. *Doern v. Phillips Estate* (1995) 2 BCLR (3d) 349 (on appeal (1998) 43 BCLR (3d) 53).
808. *Brown v. Rolls-Royce* [1960] 1 WLR 210.
809. [2011] 1 WLR 1003.

injury to their employees unless that practice was clearly bad or, in the light of developing knowledge about relevant risks, they had acquired greater than average knowledge of the risks.

Failure by a defendant to follow its own safety policy or common practices is not necessarily negligent. Whether care has been taken requires the application of an objective test, and does not turn simply on whether the defendant's internal policy has or has not been applied.[810]

2. Statutory Standards

147. Evidence of compliance or non-compliance with the standard of a duty laid down in a statute is relevant to, but not conclusive of, the question whether a common law duty of care has been broken.[811] Ultimately, whether negligence is established in respect of an activity governed by a statutory standard turns on that standard and also on all other relevant circumstances.

In most cases, compliance with a statute is likely to be treated as amounting to reasonable care. Otherwise there is a risk that the requirements of the common law will be inconsistent with a policy laid down by Parliament. An example is *Hamilton v. Papakura District Council*,[812] where the plaintiffs complained that toxic herbicide residues in the water supplied by the defendants had damaged their tomato plants and alleged, *inter alia*, that the defendants had been negligent. The defendants contended that their obligation was to supply water to the current drinking standard, which permitted certain levels of impurities, and at no time did the water depart from that standard. The Court of Appeal rejected the claim, holding that those with special needs for water of greater purity than necessary to meet all reasonable public health requirements had to accept the water at a standard suitable for domestic purposes, and carry out their own treatment to meet more specific criteria. Exceptionally, however, a statute may be seen as fixing a minimum standard of acceptable conduct but not a standard of reasonable conduct in all circumstances.[813] In *Brouwers v. Street*[814] a drainage system for carrying off storm water complied with council minimum standards, but the court thought that these standards did not purport to provide an appropriate benchmark for all conditions and that the risk of flooding was such that more than the bare minimum was required.

Non-compliance with a statute is not negligence per se but can constitute good evidence of negligence. It has been treated as raising an evidential presumption that the defendant has been negligent,[815] and normally will lead to a finding of liability.[816]

810. *Esdale v. Dover DC* [2010] EWCA Civ 407.
811. *Billy Higgs & Sons Ltd v. Baddeley* [1950] NZLR 605 at 613.
812. [2000] 1 NZLR 265 (appeal dismissed, [2002] 3 NZLR 208 (PC)).
813. *Ryan v. Victoria (City)* [1999] 1 SCR 201.
814. [2011] 1 NZLR 645.
815. *Algie v. DH Brown & Son Ltd* [1932] NZLR 779; *Dewes v. WP Martin & Co. Ltd* [1974] 2 NZLR 139.
816. For example, *Oceanview Holdings Ltd v. Clarry M O'Byrne Ltd* [1989] 1 NZLR 574.

D. *Proof of Negligence*

1. General

148. The burden rests on the plaintiff to prove on the balance of probabilities that the defendant was negligent and that the negligence caused the plaintiff's loss.[817] The quality and detail of the evidence on how the accident or event happened will vary greatly from case to case. The primary facts may be the subject of direct or merely circumstantial evidence. Witnesses may be able to provide a complete picture or there may be gaps in the chronology of events. The evidence of the witnesses must be weighed for credibility and reliability. Thus the court must, where appropriate, draw inferences, fill gaps, resolve conflicts, and ultimately, having determined the facts, evaluate them in the light of the legal standard of carefulness.

2. Province of Judge and Jury

149. The judge determines all matters of law. The jury, if there is one, determines matters of fact. Where a claim is tried before a jury the judge can withhold the case from the jury if satisfied there is no evidence of negligence. Otherwise, the judge must leave the question of whether negligence has been established to the jury. An appellate court will be prepared to upset a judge's view of the law, but will not interfere with the findings of a jury unless satisfied they are wholly unreasonable or perverse.[818]

Nowadays, negligence claims must be tried by judges alone. A party can require a jury only in the case of a proceeding for defamation, false imprisonment, or malicious prosecution.[819]

3. *Res Ipsa Loquitur*

150. The maxim '*res ipsa loquitur*', meaning 'the event speaks for itself', allows the court to draw an inference of negligence from the mere fact that an event has happened, without the benefit of detailed testimony about exactly how it happened. A leading statement of principle is by Erle CJ:[820]

817. *King v. Auckland Electric Tramway Co. Ltd* (1912) 31 NZLR 924.
818. *J M Heywood & Co. Ltd v. A-G* [1956] NZLR 668.
819. Senior Courts Act 2016, s. 16(1). If, however, the trial will involve mainly the consideration of difficult questions of law or prolonged examination of documents or accounts or investigation of difficult scientific, technical, business, or professional questions a judge may order that the proceedings be tried before a judge without a jury: s. 16(4). A proceeding for defamation, false imprisonment, or malicious prosecution that also contains other causes of action may be tried only before a High Court Judge without a jury: s. 16(5). No civil proceeding other than for defamation, false imprisonment, or malicious prosecution may be tried by a High Court Judge with a jury: s. 16(6).
820. *Scott v. London and St Katherine's Dock Co.* (1865) 3 H & C 596.

> There must be reasonable evidence of negligence. But where the thing is shown to be under the management of the defendant or his servants, and the accident is such as in the ordinary course of things does not happen if those who have the management use proper care, it affords reasonable evidence, in the absence of explanation by the defendants, that the accident arose from want of care.

This formulation makes it apparent that there are three elements to the principle: the damage must not ordinarily occur without negligence; the cause of the damage must be the responsibility of the defendant; and there must be an absence of explanation for the happening of the accident. If the circumstances are explained, then the question is simply whether they show that the defendant was negligent.

Some older authority treated *res ipsa loquitur* as laying down a rule of law under which, on proof of its elements, the defendant was presumed to have been negligent and the legal burden shifted to the defendant to disprove negligence.[821] But in *CB Norwood Distributors Ltd v. Burnetts Motors Ltd*[822] the Court of Appeal confirmed that it was for the plaintiff alleging negligence to prove it, and that the maxim did no more than raise an inference of its existence in appropriate circumstances. This is the view taken in England,[823] Australia,[824] Canada,[825] and Hong Kong.[826]

4. Criminal Convictions

151. Section 47(1) of the Evidence Act 2006 provides that when the fact that a person has committed an offence is relevant to an issue in a civil proceeding, proof of the conviction is conclusive proof that the person committed the offence. Subsection (2) then provides that, despite subsection (1), the judge may, in exceptional circumstances, permit a party to offer evidence tending to prove that the person convicted did not commit the offence, and if satisfied that it is appropriate to do so, direct that the issue whether the person committed the offence be determined without reference to that subsection.[827] Subsection (3) provides that the section applies whether or not the person convicted is a party to the proceedings and whether or not the person was convicted on a guilty plea.

821. For example, *Billy Higgs & Sons Ltd v. Baddeley* [1950] NZLR 605 at 614; *Voice v. Union Steam Ship Co. of New Zealand Ltd* [1953] NZLR 176 at 189–190; *JM Heywood & Co. Ltd v. A-G* [1956] NZLR 668.
822. Unrep., 21 Aug. 1991, CA 86/89.
823. *Ratcliffe v. Plymouth & Torbay HA* [1998] Ll Rep Med 162 at 172–173.
824. *Schellenberg v. Tunnel Holdings Pty Ltd* (2000) 200 CLR 121.
825. *Fontaine v. Loewen Estate* [1998] 1 SCR 424.
826. *Ng Chun Pui v. Lee Chuen Tat* [1988] RTR 298.
827. This qualification does not apply in the case of a proceeding for defamation based on a statement to the effect that a person has committed an offence: Evidence Act 2006, ss 47(4)(a), 48.

§4. CAPACITY

I. General

152. As a general proposition, all persons are able to sue and are liable to be sued in tort. This covers both natural and legal persons. So companies incorporated under the Companies Act 1993, societies incorporated under the Incorporated Societies Act 1908, and trade unions registered under the Employment Relations Act 2000 (a prerequisite of which is incorporation under the 1908 Act) can sue for such losses as they are capable of suffering in the same way as an individual. These may include, for example, property damage, interference with land or goods, trading losses, and loss of business reputation but not, in the nature of things, personal injury, mental injury, or wrongful detention. Again, a trading corporation, trade union, or other incorporated bodies may be sued for its own acts and for acts done on its behalf in the ordinary way.[828] So also, it may be vicariously liable for the torts of employees committed in the course of employment.[829]

On the death of any person, all causes of action subsisting against or vested in that person, except a cause of action for defamation,[830] survive against or for the benefit of the estate.[831] Actions that survive in this way are brought or defended by the personal representatives of the deceased person.[832]

In certain special cases the ordinary rules about capacity to sue or be sued need to be amplified or qualified. These are claims involving the Crown, foreign states and diplomats, bankrupt persons, minors, and persons of unsound mind.

II. The Crown

A. *Background*

153. At common law the Crown could not be proceeded against in tort. The doctrine that 'the King could do no wrong' and the principle that the monarch could not be impleaded in his or her own courts barred all actions against the sovereign, either personally or vicariously, for torts committed by servants or agents. The tortfeasor himself or herself could still be sued: but this did not help a plaintiff who could not identify the responsible individual or who obtained a judgment that was not satisfied.

---

828. A corporation is personally liable for a tort authorized by the directing mind of the corporation, for the tort is by the corporation itself acting through its alter ego: *Lennards Carrying Co. Ltd v. Asiatic Petroleum Co. Ltd* [1915] AC 705; and *see Tesco Supermarkets Ltd v. Nattrass* [1972] AC 153; *Meridian Global Funds Management Asia Ltd v. Securities Commission* [1995] 2 AC 500. It makes no difference that the tortious act was outside the statutory powers of the corporation: *Blunden v. Oxford Road District* (1901) 20 NZLR 593; *Campbell v. Paddington Corp.* [1911] 1 KB 869; *Northern Publishing Co. Ltd v. White* [1940] NZLR 75.
829. *See* paras 380–382.
830. *See Hagaman v. Little* [2017] NZCA 447, [2018] 2 NZLR 140.
831. Law Reform Act 1936, s. 3(1). But a claim for exemplary damages does not survive for the benefit of the estate of a deceased person: s. 3(2); *see* para. 580.
832. High Court Rules 2016, r 4.23; District Court Rules 2014, r 4.23.

This position was changed by the Crown Suits Act 1881, as amended, which granted the right of petition in respect of breach of any contract or of any wrong for which an action for damages would lie if the defendant was a subject of his Majesty, except:

(a) assault, false imprisonment, malicious prosecution, or erroneous judicial process;
(b) libel or slander; and
(c) any cause of action requiring a malicious motive.[833]

By this means a victim of a tort could proceed against the Crown by petition in the same manner as by a statement of claim in an ordinary action. In the UK, by contrast, the bar on actions against the Crown in tort came to be avoided by the practice of government departments putting up nominated defendants as 'whipping boys' and making ex gratia payments of compensation on being found liable. However, following the courts' condemnation of this practice as being founded on a fiction,[834] Parliament stepped in and passed the Crown Proceedings Act 1947 (UK), which brought to an end the Crown immunity in tort. This Act then became the model for the New Zealand Crown Proceedings Act 1950, which repealed the Crown Suits Acts and removed the remaining restrictions on tort actions against the Crown.[835]

B. Crown Liability in Tort

154. For the purposes of the Crown Proceedings Act 1950, 'Her Majesty' or 'the Crown' means 'Her Majesty in right of Her Government in New Zealand'.[836] The concept includes ministers of the Crown, the central government departments, and the courts of justice, all of which carry out their functions in the Queen's name and on her behalf.

By section 6(1), the Crown shall be subject to all those liabilities in tort to which, if it were a private person of full age and capacity, it would be subject in respect of:

(a) torts committed by its servants or agents;[837]
(b) any breach of the common law duties owed by an employer to his servants or agents; and

833. Crown Suits Act 1881, s. 37; Crown Suits Amendment Act 1910, ss 3–4.
834. *Adams v. Naylor* [1946] AC 543; *Royster v. Cavey* [1947] 1 KB 204.
835. For the background to the 1950 Act, *see Burrows v. New Zealand Police* [2018] NZHC 2088, [2019] 2 NZLR 652 at [39] and [44]. The Law Commission *The Crown in Court* (NZLC R 135, 2015) has recommended replacing this Act with modernised legislation.
836. Crown Proceedings Act 1950, s. 2(1).
837. A 'servant' means any servant of the Queen and includes a minister of the Crown and members of the New Zealand armed forces, but does not include the Governor-General, or any judge, District Court judge, justice of the peace, community magistrate or other judicial officer: Crown Proceedings Act 1950, s. 2(1) . An 'agent' includes an independent contractor employed by the Crown: Crown Proceedings Act 1950, s. 2(1) .

(c) the breach of the duties attaching at common law to the ownership, possession, or control of property.[838]

These provisions had the effect of removing the preexisting immunity attaching to the Crown.[839] However, even now, the Crown itself cannot do wrong, and any liability in tort must be found in the Crown's vicarious liability for wrongdoing by Crown servants or agents, or in any direct liability of Crown corporations.[840] On ordinary principles, then, the Crown is liable to third parties for torts committed by its servants in the course of their employment, and for authorized or ratified torts of independent contractors.

Section 6(2) further provides that where the Crown is bound by a statutory duty that is also binding upon persons other than the Crown and its officers, then in respect of a failure to comply with the duty, the Crown is subject to all those liabilities in tort to which it would be so subject if it were a private person of full age and capacity. The section simply explains, for the avoidance of doubt, that where there are statutory duties binding the Crown, that are also general duties binding all persons, the Crown is to be bound in the ordinary way.[841]

Proceedings by or against the Crown may be commenced, heard, and determined in the same way as in suits between subject and subjects.[842] A court may grant such orders for relief as it has power to grant in proceedings between subjects, with the proviso that the court may not grant an injunction or an order for specific performance, but may instead make an order that is declaratory of the rights of the parties.[843]

C. Discharge of Judicial Functions and Execution of Judicial Process

155. Section 6(5) of the Crown Proceedings Act provides that no proceedings may be brought against the Crown in respect of anything done or omitted to be done by any person while discharging or purporting to discharge any responsibilities of a judicial nature vested in that person, or any responsibilities that the person has in connection with the execution of judicial process. The section gives immunity only to the Crown in respect of its vicarious liability for the torts of its servants or agents. It does not give immunity to the servants or agents themselves from personal liability for their own acts.[844]

---

838. A proviso to s. 6(1) says that the Crown is not liable unless, apart from the Act, an action would have lain against the servant or agent. This preserves such special defences as act of state (as to which *see Mohammed v. Ministry of Defence* [2017] 2 WLR 287), and acting under prerogative or statutory powers.
839. *Matthews v. Ministry of Defence* [2003] 2 WLR 435 at [116].
840. *Chagos Islanders v. Attorney-General* [2004] EWCA Civ 997 at [22].
841. *Cashmere Pacific Ltd v. NZ Dairy Board* [1996] 1 NZLR 218; cp *G v. A-G* [1994] 1 NZLR 714.
842. Crown Proceedings Act 1950, s. 12(1).
843. *Ibid.*, s. 17(1); *Burrows v. New Zealand Police* [2018] NZHC 2088, [2019] 2 NZLR 652 at [41], [43] and [75] (restraining order under the Harassment Act 1997 was a form of injunction and could not be awarded against the Crown).
844. *Fyfe v. Attorney-General* [2004] NZAR 731 at [17].

Where the first limb is in issue, it is necessary to consider whether the particular function about which complaint is made involves 'responsibilities of a judicial nature'. A District Court deputy registrar who entered a person's name in the civil record book as a judgment debtor was thought to be covered;[845] but an omission by a High Court registrar, in breach of a court order, to pay money into an interest-bearing account did not involve any judicial element.[846] The responsibilities also must be 'vested in' the relevant person. So a District Court judge issuing a warrant to commit the plaintiff to prison without jurisdiction to do so was not covered, as responsibility in the matter was vested in another court and was not vested in the judge being sued.[847]

As regards the execution of 'judicial process', this covers an order or authority emanating from a judicial officer exercising judicial responsibilities.[848] The immunity covers, for example, the failure of court officials to remove a scheduled hearing from the Case Management System, resulting in the plaintiff being arrested on a warrant for non-appearance.[849] It does not apply to mere matters of administration, like a failure by a prosecuting authority to record that certain offences committed by the plaintiff had been taken into account by another court in passing sentence on him.[850] While the statutory protection extends to the unreasonable execution of process in good faith, it does not cover conduct that is malicious or in bad faith, or conduct that is outside the scope and purpose of the process.[851]

III. Foreign States and Diplomats

A. *Foreign States*

156. Foreign sovereigns and States that do not submit to the jurisdiction enjoy absolute immunity from proceedings in tort in relation to governmental matters. The immunity extends not only to the State itself and to its Heads of State personally, but also to the government and any department of government including, in the case of federal States, the government of a province of a State. However, there is no immunity in relation to commercial or other private matters.[852] So the Court of Appeal declined to apply the doctrine of sovereign immunity to the issue of tax certificates by the Cook Islands government, where the element of tax collection was

845. *Crispin v. Registrar of the District Court* [1986] 2 NZLR 246 at 254.
846. *Seatrans (Fiji) Ltd v. A-G* [1986] 2 NZLR 240.
847. *Derrick v. A-G* [1994] 1 NZLR 112, on appeal *Harvey v. Derrick* [1995] 1 NZLR 314 (CA), where the point was not discussed.
848. *Simpson v. Attorney-General: Baigent's Case* [1994] 3 NZLR 667 at 674, 689, 696, 715.
849. *Thompson v. Attorney-General* [2016] NZCA 215, [2016] 3 NZLR 206.
850. *Welsh v. Chief Constable of the Merseyside Police* [1993] 1 All ER 692.
851. *Simpson v. Attorney-General: Baigent's Case* [1994] 3 NZLR 667; *Auckland Unemployed Workers' Rights Centre Inc v. A-G* [1994] 3 NZLR 720.
852. *The Philippine Admiral* [1977] AC 373; *Marine Steel Ltd v. Government of the Marshall Islands* [1981] 2 NZLR 1; *Playa Larga v. I Congreso del Partido* [1983] 1 AC 244; *Governor of Pitcairn and Associated Islands v. Sutton* [1995] 1 NZLR 426; *Controller and Auditor General v. Sir Ronald Davison* [1996] 2 NZLR 278.

largely illusory and the activity could be seen as primarily commercial and of a private law character.[853] On the other hand, the provision within a United States military base in England of education and training was part of a State's sovereign function of maintaining its armed forces. Accordingly, the publication of an allegedly defamatory memorandum by an educational services officer about an instructor at the base attracted the immunity.[854]

B. Diplomats

157. The Diplomatic Privileges and Immunities Act 1968 brings into force in New Zealand the Vienna Convention on Diplomatic Relations of 1961. Heads of diplomatic missions and members of their staff holding diplomatic rank are immune from civil jurisdiction in respect of any tort committed by them.[855] The immunity extends to members of the household of mission heads and diplomatic staff, and to members of the administrative and technical staff of a mission and their households in respect of acts performed in the course of their duties.[856] However, there is no immunity with respect to an action relating to any professional or commercial activity exercised by a diplomatic agent outside his or her official functions.[857]

The sending State may waive diplomatic immunity, but the waiver must always be express.[858] If a person entitled to immunity initiates proceedings he or she is precluded from invoking immunity from jurisdiction in respect of any counterclaim directly connected with the principal claim.[859]

IV. Bankrupt Persons

158. Where a tort causes damage to property belonging to a bankrupt person at the commencement of the bankruptcy, or to property acquired by the bankrupt before his or her discharge, then the right to sue in respect of that tort passes to the assignee of the bankrupt's property.[860] If damage is purely personal to the bankrupt, for example damage to reputation or wrongful imprisonment, the right of action

853. *Controller and Auditor General v. Sir Ronald Davison* [1996] 2 NZLR 278.
854. *Holland v. Lampen-Wolfe* [2000] 1 WLR 1573; and *see Littrell v. United States of America (No. 2)* [1995] 1 WLR 82.
855. Diplomatic Privileges and Immunities Act 1968, s. 5, First Schedule, Art. 31, clause 1.
856. *Ibid.*, s. 5, First Schedule, Art. 37, clauses 1, 2.
857. *Ibid.*, s. 5, First Schedule, Art. 31, clause 1(c). Other exceptions are: (i) a real action relating to private immovable property not held on behalf of the sending state for the purposes of the mission; (ii) an action relating to succession in which the diplomatic agent is involved as executor, administrator, heir or legatee as a private person and not on behalf of the sending state.
858. *Ibid.*, s. 5, First Schedule, Art. 32, clauses 1, 2.
859. *Ibid.*, s. 5, First Schedule, Art. 32, clause 3.
860. Insolvency Act 2006, s. 101(1), Sch. 1(b). 'Property' means property of every kind, whether tangible or intangible, real or personal, corporeal or incorporeal, and includes rights, interests, and claims of every kind in relation to property however they arise: s. 3.

remains with the bankrupt.[861] Where conduct causes damage both to the bankrupt's property and to the bankrupt personally, so two separate causes of action arise, the assignee sues for the one and the bankrupt for the other.[862]

As for actions against a bankrupt person, a claim in tort for unliquidated damages is provable in the bankruptcy,[863] and in this case the assignee may estimate the amount of the claim.[864] An appeal lies to the High Court if the assignee rejects the claim,[865] or if the creditor is aggrieved by the estimate.[866] If the value of the bankrupt's property is estimated in this way by the assignee or the court, its amount is deemed to be a debt provable in bankruptcy and the bankrupt is not liable to be sued for the tort after his or her discharge.[867] If the proof is rejected the bankrupt's liability will continue after discharge.

V. Minors

159. An infant or minor (the terms are interchangeable) is a person who has not attained 20 years of age.[868] As a general rule, actions by or against minors are subject to no special rules.[869] Certainly, minority as such is not a defence to an action in tort. However, in torts involving malice or intention or negligence, the immaturity of the defendant is relevant to the question of whether his or her state of mind could have been malicious, or whether he or she could have intended or could have foreseen the consequences of the act under scrutiny. This is a question to be determined on the facts of the particular case. The standard of care that is required is that reasonably to be expected of a child of the particular defendant's age.[870] Apart from the child's personal liability, it is possible that the parent of a minor may be personally liable for failing to exercise proper control over his or her child.[871]

A special qualification on the tortious liability of a minor may apply where the plaintiff has entered into a contract with the minor. A long-established line of authority holds that a minor is not liable for a tort directly connected with any contract on which no action will lie on account of his or her minority.[872] The justification for

861. *Ex p Vine: Re Wilson* (1878) 8 Ch D 364 (slander); *Re Richter* [1929] NZLR 364 (action under the Deaths by Accidents Compensation Act 1908).
862. *Wilson v. United Counties Bank* [1920] AC 102.
863. Insolvency Act 2006, ss 231, 232. A plaintiff who has a right of action in tort against an insolvent estate may prove in the administration of the estate for unliquidated damages: Insolvency Act 2006, Part 6.
864. *Ibid.*, s. 251.
865. *Ibid.*, s. 239.
866. *Ibid.*, s. 252.
867. *Ibid.*, s. 304.
868. Age of Majority Act 1970, s. 4. In the case of a contract made by a minor, the age is 18: Contract and Commercial Law Act 2017, s. 85.
869. Where there is litigation involving a minor he or she is represented by his or her litigation guardian: High Court Rules 2016, r 4.31; District Court Rules 2014, r 4.31.
870. *McHale v. Watson* (1966) 115 CLR 199; *see* para. 136.
871. *Kenealy v. Karaka* (1906) 27 NZLR 1118; *Heberley v. Lash* [1922] NZLR 609; *The Bosworth Water Trust v. SSR* [2018] EWHC 444. *See* para. 396.
872. *Green v. Greenbank* (1816) 2 Marsh 485; *Stocks v. Wilson* [1913] 2 KB 235 at 246; *R Leslie Ltd v. Shiell* [1914] 3 KB 607 at 627.

this rule is that the contract cannot be enforced indirectly simply by changing the form of action. Thus a minor who hired a car for a specific journey but who then drove further away was not liable in tort for an accident that occurred during the unauthorized excursion.[873] On the other hand, the owner of a car sold to a minor on terms that property was not to pass until completion of payments for it could recover the car in an action for conversion, because the claim rested on ownership and was independent of any contract with the minor.[874]

Nowadays this line of reasoning is unlikely to be maintained. The old law as to the contractual capacity of minors has been superseded by Part 2 subpart 6 of the Contract and Commercial Law Act 2017 (formerly the Minors' Contracts Act 1969), which lays down a code replacing the rules of the common law and equity relating to minors' contracts[875] and empowers the courts to inquire into the fairness and reasonableness of the contract in question in order to determine whether or not it ought to be enforced.[876] Accordingly, the rationale for the early cases is removed, for there is no longer any question of bypassing an absolute ban on suing in contract. Furthermore, it is hard to see why a minor who does in fact commit a tort should not be sued in the ordinary way, irrespective of the existence of any contract.

VI. Persons of Unsound Mind

160. Broadly speaking, a person may be said to be of unsound mind if, by reason of demonstrable and recognized mental illness or disability, he or she is incapable of managing his or her affairs at the relevant time and in relation to the matter in hand. A person's mind may be sound for some purposes but not for others, depending upon the purpose of the inquiry, and in all cases is a matter of fact and degree.[877] But whether, or the extent to which, a person's unsoundness of mind should be taken into account in tort claims is uncertain.

A defendant who lacks capacity arguably may be absolved from the requirement of meeting an objectively determined standard of care. Decisions in Canada favour an approach based on whether there is proof of actual fault.[878] Again, in England it has been held that the standard of care expected of a driver who was involved in an accident caused by a disabling event, whether sudden or gradual, was that of a reasonably competent driver unaware that he or she was or might be suffering from a condition that impaired his or her ability to drive. So a driver who crashed into a

873. *Fawcett v. Smethurst* (1914) 84 LJKB 473.

874. *Nelson Guarantee Corp. v. Farrell* [1955] NZLR 405.

875. Contract and Commercial Law Act 2017, s. 115; *International Encyclopaedia of Laws: Contracts (New Zealand)*, para. 118.

876. Contract and Commercial Law Act 2017, ss 86–90; *see Morrow & Benjamin Ltd v. Whittington* [1989] 3 NZLR 122; *Wine Country Credit Union v. Raynor* [2008] 2 NZLR 698.

877. *T v. H* [1995] 3 NZLR 37 at 49, 60.

878. For example, *Buckley and Toronto Transportation Commission v. Smith Transport Ltd* (1946) 4 DLR 721; *Fiala v. McDonald* (2001) 201 DLR (4th) 680.

shop in circumstances where he could not function properly because, unknown to him, he suffered from malignant insulinoma, which starved the brain of glucose, was not negligent and not liable.[879]

On the other hand, a series of cases in England involving the criminal liability of drivers hold that the test is whether there was a complete loss of bodily control, so the defendant could be said to be in a state of automatism,[880] and this control test has also been applied in civil actions. So a paranoid schizophrenic who set fire to himself and in doing so seriously injured his nephew, who was trying to stop him, was held in breach of a duty to the nephew.[881] The court considered that a defendant who did not act voluntarily or was in a state of automatism was not liable. But here the uncle did something in fetching the petrol and lighting it, and his mind, although deluded, directed his actions.

An approach which looks simply at the question of culpability is difficult to reconcile with an objective standard of care. Rafferty LJ in the above decision pointed to the difficulties if partial impairment can modify the ordinary standard. Her Ladyship asked where could any line be drawn once there was introduced any qualification of 100% impairment?

There is limited authority in New Zealand on the point. It has been held that the question whether a person can be liable in battery turns on whether he or she intended to do the physical act constituting the battery.[882] As regards negligence, maybe the position is that the question of personal fault is irrelevant and that provided action is voluntary a defendant is liable if his or her conduct does not meet the objective standard of care.

879. *Mansfield v. Weetabix Ltd* [1998] 1 WLR 1263.

880. *R v. Isitt* [1978] RTR 211; *R v. Hennessey* [1989] 1 WLR 287 (CA); *Attorney-General's Reference (No 2 of 1992)* [1993] 3 WLR 982.

881. *Dunnage v. Randall* [2016] 2 WLR 839; and *see Roberts v. Ramsbottom* [1980] 1 All ER 7; *Carrier v. Bonham* [2002] 1 Qd R 474.

882. *Donaghy v. Brennan* (1901) 19 NZLR 289; *Beals v. Hayward* [1960] NZLR 131 at 138.

Chapter 2. Specific Cases of Liability

§1. Introduction

161. In Chapter 1 we considered the general principles of the law of torts under three main heads – intentional wrongdoing, negligent wrongdoing, and capacity to be sued. But discussion of general principle can only take us so far. In its totality, the law of torts is made up of a congeries of disparate heads of liability, and to these we will now turn. In this chapter, a number of related torts have been grouped together according to the different interests that they seek to protect. These are torts concerned with interferences with land, with goods, with intellectual property, and with economic interests. We will then examine the various actions that arise out of abuse of public office and abuse of legal procedure. Finally, we will consider defamation and the action for invasion of privacy, for they standalone and each deserves special attention.

Particular issues of professional, business, and public body liability for negligence were considered in Chapter 1. Our concern now is with other forms of liability in tort that are not founded on negligence.

§2. Interference with Land

I. Introduction

162. A person may interfere with another person's interest in land in a number of different ways. He or she may wrongfully enter or remain on the land, or deposit or leave something on the land, or interfere in some way with the use or enjoyment of the land, or cause actual damage to the land. These various interferences are actionable on several bases – by an action for trespass in the case of invasions onto the land, by an action for nuisance in the case of interferences with the enjoyment of land, and by an action for negligence or nuisance or under the so-called rule in *Rylands v. Fletcher*[883] in the case of damage to the land.

II. Trespass to Land

A. General

163. Trespass involves an unjustified direct interference with land that is in the possession of another.[884] A trespass to land can be committed in five ways – by unlawfully entering land, by remaining on land after the expiry of an authority or licence to be on the land, by putting an object on the land, by leaving an object on

883. (1865) 3 H & C 774, 159 ER 737 (Ex); (1866) LR 1 Exch. 265 (Exch. Ch); (1868) LR 3 HL 330 (HL).

884. *Wu v. Body Corporate 366611* [2011] 2 NZLR 837 at [74] (on appeal *Body Corporate 366611 v. Wu* [2012] NZCA 614, *Wu v. Body Corporate 366611* [2015] 1 NZLR 215 (SC)).

land after the expiry of an authority or licence for it to be there, and by interfering with an incorporeal right over the land. Where trespass is established it is actionable per se, without proof of actual damage.[885] The action may of course compensate for harm, but it may also serve to vindicate the right of a possessor of land to be free from invasion by others.[886]

'Land' includes things growing on the land, buildings or other structures fixed to the land,[887] the subsoil beneath the surface,[888] and the airspace above the land.[889] Whether there are limits to the surface occupier's rights as regards subsoil and airspace is not entirely clear. There is no case setting a depth beyond which the occupier's rights do not extend.[890] As regards airspace, it is a trespass to put up a sign,[891] erect a telegraph line,[892] fire a bullet[893] or swing the boom of a crane[894] over another's land. However, it has been held in England that there was no trespass by an aircraft flying many hundreds of feet above the plaintiff's land, on the basis that the plaintiff's rights extended only to such height as was necessary for the ordinary use and enjoyment of the land:[895] and it has been mooted that a similar approach could be applied in the case of overhanging cranes.[896]

The view that 'land' embraces the whole column of space from the centre of the earth to the heavens, as expressed in the Latin maxim cuius est solum eius est usque ad coelum et ad inferos, has been accepted in New Zealand.[897] This arguably is the better view, for limiting the landowner's interest to that which is necessary for the

885. *Mayfair Ltd v. Pears* [1987] 1 NZLR 459 at 465; *Re Chase* [1989] 1 NZLR 325 at 340.
886. *See* generally Atkin, *Trespassing on Land*, in *Todd on Torts* Ch. 9 (Todd ed., 8th ed., 2019).
887. *Lockwood Buildings Ltd v. Trust Bank Canterbury Ltd* [1995] 1 NZLR 22; *Lakes Edge Developments Ltd v. Kawarau Village Holdings Ltd* [2017] NZCA 205, [2017] 3 NZLR 336.
888. *Bulli Coal Mining Co. v. Osborne* [1891] AC 351.
889. *Kelsen v. Imperial Tobacco Co. Ltd* [1957] 2 QB 334; and *see Yeung v. Potel* [2014] EWCA Civ 481.
890. However, most minerals of value are the property of the Crown: Crown Minerals Act 1991, ss 10–11. In *Bocardo SA v. Star Energy UK Onshore Ltd* [2011] 1 AC 380 the UK Supreme Court held that trespass occurred where an oil company drilled wells at between 800 and 2,800 feet below the plaintiff's land. The court recognized there was a 'stopping point' where physical features such as pressure and temperature rendered the concept of the strata belonging to anybody so absurd as to be not worth arguing about.
891. *Kelsen v. Imperial Tobacco Co. Ltd* [1957] 2 QB 334.
892. *Board of Works for the Wandsworth district v. United Telephone Co. Ltd* (1884) 13 QBD 904.
893. *Davies v. Bennison* (1927) 22 Tas LR 52.
894. *Woollerton and Wilson Ltd v. Richard Costain Ltd* [1970] 1 WLR 411; *Concrete Properties Ltd v. Churchill Group Holdings Ltd* HC, Auckland, CP 297/8818 April 1988; *Franklin Mint Ltd v. Baxtergate Investment Co.* [1998] EWCA Civ 442.
895. *Bernstein v. Skyviews & General Ltd* [1978] QB 479.
896. *Concrete Properties Ltd v. Churchill Group Holdings Ltd* HC, Auckland, CP 297/8818 April 1988.
897. *De Richaumont Investment Co. Ltd v. OTW Advertising Ltd* [2001] 2 NZLR 831 at 840.

enjoyment of the land undermines the rule that trespass is actionable per se and confuses trespass with nuisance.[898] Special legislation has resolved the problem of overflying aircraft[899] and of building work intruding on airspace.[900]

B. Forms of Trespass

1. Entering on Land

164. Entering on land or taking possession of land without authority is a trespass. A small or short-lived intrusion, such as a temporary intrusion to steal fruit,[901] is sufficient. 'If the defendant places a part of his foot on the plaintiff's land unlawfully, it is in law as much a trespass as if the defendant had walked half a mile on it.'[902] Equally, it is a trespass unlawfully to pull down or destroy something fixed to the land, for example by dismantling a barn[903] or cutting down trees.[904]

2. Remaining on Land after Expiry of Authority or Licence

165. Where a person enters land pursuant to a licence for a fixed period of time, but remains after expiry of that time, he or she becomes a trespasser. Where the person enters pursuant to a bare licence, with no time limit, then he or she can be treated as a trespasser only after the licensor has given notice or made it clear in some other way that the licence is withdrawn, and has allowed a reasonable period for the licensee to leave.[905] A licensee who enters for a permitted purpose and who abuses the licence by acting outside the scope of the permission to enter also becomes a trespasser.[906]

---

898. In *Bocardo SA v. Star Energy UK Onshore Ltd* [2011] 1 AC 380 at [26], Lord Hope recognized that the brocard had value as encapsulating, in simple language, a proposition of law which had commanded general acceptance. It was accepted that more limitations on the maxim might apply to airspace than land and strata beneath the surface.
899. By the Civil Aviation Act 1990, s. 97(2), no action lies in respect of trespass by aircraft by reason only of the flight of aircraft over any property at a height above the ground which, having regard to wind, weather and all the circumstances of the case is reasonable, provided the conditions laid down in the Act are complied with. By s. 97(3), the owner of an aircraft is strictly liable for all material damage or loss caused to property by an aircraft in flight, taking off or landing, or by anything falling from an aircraft.
900. By the Property Law Act 2007, ss 319, 320, a court is empowered to make an order on specified terms authorizing a landowner to enter on or over neighbouring land for the purpose of erecting, repairing, altering, adding to, painting or demolishing any structure on the applicant's land, or do any other necessary or desirable thing in relation to the applicant's land: and *see De Richaumont Investment Co. Ltd v. OTW Advertising Ltd* [2001] 2 NZLR 831.
901. *Matheson v. Northcote College Board of Governors* [1975] 2 NZLR 106.
902. *Ellis v. Loftus Iron Co.* (1874) LR 10 CP 10 at 12.
903. *Shattock v. Devlin* [1990] 2 NZLR 88.
904. *Cousins v. Wilson* [1994] 1 NZLR 463.
905. *Transport Ministry v. Payn* [1977] 2 NZLR 50 at 60; *Polly v. Police* [1985] 1 NZLR 443; *Howden v. Ministry of Transport* [1987] 2 NZLR 747.
906. *Barker v. R* (1983) 153 CLR 338.

Where a licensee enters land pursuant to a contractual licence, the licensor's right to revoke the licence depends upon the terms of the contract.[907] If the licence is revocable, a period of grace to allow the licensee to leave must still be allowed.[908] Even if not revocable, the licensor can cancel the contract on account of a sufficiently serious breach of contract by the licensee.[909] If the cancellation is unjustified, the licensee remains on the land lawfully and is not a trespasser.[910]

Special rules apply where a person comes onto land as a tenant and remains after expiry of the tenancy. In the case of a residential tenancy, the landlord cannot sue in trespass: rather, he or she must seek a remedy under the statutory code laid down in the Residential Tenancies Act 1986. In the case of a commercial tenancy, a tenant who holds over becomes a tenant at sufferance. The landlord may eject the tenant or bring proceedings for possession, and in the latter case the landlord can seek damages for trespass relating back to the date of termination of the lease.[911]

Where a person enters land pursuant to statutory authority and then abuses the authority, ancient common law authority holds that the person becomes a trespasser not simply from the time of the abuse but *ab initio*, thereby increasing the amount of the damages and deterring the abuse of governmental power.[912] But it has been doubted whether the doctrine should continue to apply in New Zealand.[913]

3. Putting Object on Land

166. It is a trespass where a person causes an object directly to go on, or to intrude on, another's land. So, for example, dumping spoil,[914] parking a car,[915] throwing rubbish,[916] putting up a ladder,[917] erecting air conditioning units without permission[918] and building a wall,[919] are all trespasses of this kind.

There must be a direct invasion of the land. Where something comes onto land indirectly, the plaintiff's cause of action, if any, is for nuisance, under the rule in *Rylands v. Fletcher*, or for negligence. Often the line may be drawn according to

---

907. *Mayfield Holdings Ltd v. Moana Reef Ltd* [1973] 1 NZLR 309.
908. *Millennium Productions Ltd v. Winter Garden Theatre (London) Ltd* [1948] AC 173.
909. *Duffield v. Police* [1971] NZLR 381 (breach of implied condition requiring orderly behaviour); *see International Encyclopaedia of Laws: Contracts (New Zealand)*, Ch. 5, §1.
910. *Millennium Productions Ltd v. Winter Garden Theatre (London) Ltd* [1948] AC 173 at 189, 202; *Verrall v. Great Yarmouth Borough Council* [1980] 1 All ER 839.
911. *See* para. 172.
912. *Six Carpenters' Case* (1610) 8 Co. Rep 146A; *Clearlite Holdings Ltd v. Auckland City Corporation* [1976] 2 NZLR 729 at 734; *Cinnamond v. British Airports Authority* [1980] 1 WLR 582.
913. *Simpson v. Attorney-General (Baigent's Case)* [1994] 3 NZLR 667 at 694; *Siemer v. Spartan News Ltd* [2014] NZHC 3175 at [144]–[147].
914. *Hallenstein Bros Ltd v. Lewis & Co.* [1917] NZLR 592.
915. *Mayfair Ltd v. Pears* [1987] 1 NZLR 459.
916. *Matheson v. Northcote College Board of Governors* [1975] 2 NZLR 106.
917. *Westripp v. Baldock* [1939] 1 All ER 279.
918. *Eaton Mansions (Westminster) Ltd) v. Stinger Compania De Inversion SA* [2011] EWCA Civ 607.
919. *Burton v. Winters* [1993] 1 WLR 1077.

whether the defendant acts positively or merely allows something to happen. So putting soil on another's land is trespass,[920] but allowing soil on one's land to erode and fall onto another's land is a nuisance.[921] Again, deliberately releasing animals onto land amounts to trespass,[922] but liability for simply allowing them to stray must be based on nuisance[923] or cattle trespass.[924] Deliberately discharging storm water onto land is another instance.[925]

4. Leaving Object on Land

167. It is a trespass to leave an object on land after a landowner's permission for it to be there is determined.[926] In this case the trespass continues until the object is removed. The licensee must be allowed a reasonable time to remove the property.[927]

5. Interfering with a Profit a Prendre

168. The owner of a profit à prendre or other incorporeal right may sue in trespass for any direct interference that prevents him or her from exercising the right in question. Examples are interferences with a right to cut turf,[928] to take timber,[929] to take rabbits,[930] and to fish.[931]

6. Excluding an Owner

169. Exceptionally, there may be trespass by excluding an owner, as where one co-owner expels or excludes the other. The managers of a Body Corporate, who changed the locks and prevented owners of units in a student accommodation building from accessing the common areas in joint ownership, acted unlawfully under the Body Corporate rules and the Unit Titles Act 1972 and committed an actionable trespass.[932]

---

920. *Brown v. Dunsmuir* [1994] 3 NZLR 485 (where on the facts the defendant had a defence that he was protecting his land from the consequences of the plaintiff's illegal conduct).
921. *Leakey v. National Trust* [1978] QB 849.
922. *League against Cruel Sports Ltd v. Scott* [1986] QB 240.
923. *Farrer v. Nelson* (1885) 15 QBD 258.
924. *See* paras 424–426.
925. *Jacobs v. Waikato District Council* [2015] NZAR 1343 at [18].
926. *Cribb v. FM Custodians Ltd* [2018] NZCA 183, [2018] NZAR 1055.
927. *Pakuweka Sawmills Ltd v. Winger* [1917] NZLR 81 at 98.
928. *Coverdale v. Charlton* (1878) 4 QBD 104.
929. *Glenwood Lumber Co. Ltd v. Phillips* [1904] AC 405.
930. *Mason v. Clarke* [1955] AC 778.
931. *Nicholls v. Ely Beet Sugar Factory Ltd* [1936] Ch 343.
932. *Wu v. Body Corporate 366611* [2015] 1 NZLR 215; *BEMA Property Investments Ltd v. Body Corporate 366611* [2017] NZCA 281, [2018] 2 NZLR 514 (preventing access to an individual unit).

C. Intention or Negligence

170. The defendant must voluntarily enter the land. So a person who was thrown onto land was not liable for trespass,[933] nor was a person who had a seizure and fell onto the land.[934] But if the defendant intended to enter the land, it is no defence that he or she mistakenly thought that it was his or her own land,[935] or mistakenly believed that he or she had the permission of the owner.[936] A defendant is liable if he or she intentionally or negligently performs an act that at law constitutes a trespass, and an honest and reasonable belief that he or she had a lawful right to enter is not relevant.[937]

D. Possession or Right of Possession

1. Actual Possession

171. An action for trespass must be brought by the person in possession of the land. Actual possession is a question of fact. It consists of two elements: the intention to possess land, and the exercise of control over it to the exclusion of other persons.[938] Both elements must be shown, although intention to possess will usually be inferred from the acts that evidence actual control over the land.[939] Possession may be evidenced in various ways. For example, it may be indicated by the occupation of, or possession of a key to a building,[940] grazing cattle,[941] growing fruit trees,[942] or enclosing land with a fence.[943] Possession of the surface establishes possession of the subsoil[944] and airspace.[945] In the case of co-owners, each is entitled to be present on the land and to make normal use of it, and trespass will lie if one excludes the other.[946] In the case of a profit a prendre, the holder needs to prove the grant and the acts done in the exercise of the holder's right.[947]

The plaintiff's possession need not be lawful. It is no defence to prove that a third party has a better right to possession, unless the defendant claims that the entry was

933. *Smith v. Stone* (1647) Sty 65, 82 ER 533.
934. *Public Transport Commission v. Perry* (1977) 137 CLR 107.
935. *Conway v. George Wimpey & Co.* [1951] 2 KB 266; *Burns v. Morton* [2000] 1 WLR 347.
936. *Blenheim Borough and Wairau River Board v. British Pavements (Canterbury) Ltd* [1940] NZLR 564.
937. *Shattock v. Devlin* [1990] 2 NZLR 88.
938. *Moore v. McMillan* [1977] 2 NZLR 81 at 88; *Shattock v. Devlin* [1990] 2 NZLR 88 at 112; *Sinton Damerell Properties Ltd v. King Trounson Trustees Ltd* [2004] 2 NZLR 66 at 77.
939. *JA Pye (Oxford) Ltd v. Graham* [2003] 1 AC 419 at paras 40, 70, 79.
940. *Jewish Maternity Society's Trustees v. Garfinkle* (1926) 95 LJKB 766.
941. *JA Pye (Oxford) Ltd v. Graham* [2003] 1 AC 419.
942. *Shattock v. Devlin* [1990] 2 NZLR 88.
943. *Sinton Damerell Properties Ltd v. King Trounson Trustees Ltd* [2004] 2 NZLR 66 at 77.
944. *Mitchell v. Moseley* [1914] 1 Ch 438.
945. *Kelsen v. Imperial Tobacco Co. Ltd* [1957] 2 QB 334.
946. *Wu v. Body Corporate 366611* [2015] 1 NZLR 215; *BEMA Property Investments Ltd v. Body Corporate 366611* [2017] NZCA 281, [2018] 2 NZLR 514.
947. *Mason v. Clarke* [1955] AC 778.

made with the permission of that person.[948] But a trespasser does not gain possession simply by entering and ejecting a person already in possession.[949] On the contrary, the latter person may eject the trespasser, albeit using no more than reasonable force.[950]

Whether a person has the requisite possession at the time of the trespass is a question of fact. A bare licensee cannot bring an action, because he or she has neither the intention to possess nor the exclusive possession of the land.[951] But a contractual licensee sometimes may be entrusted with exclusive possession, and in such a case the licensee can sue.[952] In the case of a lease, the tenant has possession and, consequently, the right to sue. However, where the trespass causes permanent physical damage to the property, the landlord has an action for the injury done to his or her reversionary interest.[953] As a matter of history, this is an action on the case that is dependent on proof of damage, but in *Lockwood Buildings Ltd v. Trustbank Canterbury Ltd*[954] a majority in the Court of Appeal favoured assimilating it into the action for trespass. Furthermore, the position of a mortgagee of land was seen as analogous to that of the lessor, and the mortgagee accordingly could sue in trespass on the same basis. Further, if a lessee abandons the lease, possession reverts to the owner and physical re-entry is not needed.[955]

2. Trespass by Relation

172. A person who is not in actual possession but who has the right to immediate possession at the time of the trespass also can sue, provided he or she has entered into actual possession of the land. In such a case the proceedings are brought for a trespass committed before his or her entry, and the plaintiff's possession is deemed to relate back to the time when he or she acquired the right to possession.[956] The damages then can extend to cover all loss suffered from the date when the right of action accrued.[957] The right to immediate possession may be shown by proof of ownership or of an interest under a lease or mortgage. A mortgagee

948. *Hansard v. Tame* [1957] NZLR 542.
949. *Holder v. White* (1876) 2 NZ Jur (NS) 88.
950. *Scott v. Matthew Brown & Co. Ltd* (1884) 51 LT 746; Crimes Act 1961, s. 56(1), as to which, *see* para. 503.
951. *Moore v. McMillan* [1977] 2 NZLR 81 at 89; *Bradley v. Wingnut Films Ltd* [1993] 1 NZLR 415 at 429.
952. *Mayfield Holdings Ltd v. Moana Reef Ltd* [1973] 1 NLR 309.
953. *Blenheim Borough and Wairau River Board v. British Pavements (Canterbury) Ltd* [1940] NZLR 564 at 572; *Sinton Damerell Properties Ltd v. King Trounson Trustees Ltd* [2004] 2 NZLR 66 at 82; *Finlayson v. Clapham* [2004] NZAR 760.
954. [1995] 1 NZLR 22.
955. *BEMA Property Investments Ltd v. Body Corporate 366611* [2017] NZCA 281, [2018] 2 NZLR 514 at [40].
956. *Barnett v. Earl of Guildford* (1855) 11 Exch. 19, 196 ER 728; *Peterson v. Cowan* (1910) 13 GLR 111; *Cousins v. Wilson* [1994] 1 NZLR 463 at 466.
957. *Cribb v. FM Custodians Ltd* [2018] NZCA 183, [2018] NZAR 1055.

acquires a right to immediate possession only after the expiry of a notice under section 119 of the Property Law Act 2007 without the default being remedied.[958] However, a purchaser of land with an equitable right under the agreement for sale but with no right to immediate possession may not sue,[959] unless, by analogy with lessors and mortgagees suffering damage to their reversionary interests, there is permanent physical damage to the land.

3. Action for Recovery of Land

173. A person with the right to possession but who has not succeeded in acquiring actual possession cannot sue in trespass. However, he or she may bring an action for the recovery of land, formerly known as an action for ejectment. In this case the plaintiff must show a right to immediate possession based on the strength of his or her title.[960] The action has been described as a branch of the law of trespass.[961] It can be used in circumstances where a tenant refuses to leave and the landlord cannot re-enter the land.

The right of a third party – the *jus tertii* – is no defence to trespass,[962] but seemingly it is a good defence to an action for recovery of land.[963] Here a defendant with actual possession can show that the plaintiff has no right to oust him or her from that possession.

The plaintiff is entitled to recover damages (called mesne profits), calculated from the date when the right to immediate possession arose.[964] They can include compensation for damage to the land and for loss of use of the land during the period of wrongful occupation.[965]

E. Remedies

1. Criminal Proceedings

174. It is an offence under the Trespass Act 1980 for a person to trespass on any place and, after being warned to leave by the occupier, to neglect or refuse to do so.[966] It is also an offence for a person who has been warned by an occupier to stay off any place wilfully to trespass on the place within two years after the giving of

958. *Lockwood Buildings Ltd v. Trustbank Canterbury Ltd* [1995] 1 NZLR 22.
959. *Cousins v. Wilson* [1994] 1 NZLR 463.
960. *Asher v. Whitlock* (1865) 1 QB 1.
961. *Drury v. Secretary of State for the Environment* [2004] 2 All ER 1056 at [31].
962. *Hansard v. Tame* [1957] NZLR 542.
963. *Danford v. McAnulty* (1883) 8 App Cas 456 at 462; *Emmerson v. Maddison* [1906] AC 569 at 575.
964. *Kirkpatrick v. Hutchison* (1904) 23 NZLR 665.
965. *Southport Tramways Co. v. Gandy* [1897] 2 QB 66.
966. Trespass Act 1980, s. 3(1); *see*, for example, *Blomfield v. New Zealand Police* [2018] NZCA 180.

the warning.[967] In the latter case the warning should include an intimation of the consequences of not staying off the place.[968] In either case, if the person fails to heed the warning, he or she is liable to be arrested, removed, and prosecuted by the police.[969]

A warning may be given orally or by notice in writing delivered or sent by post in a registered letter to the person's usual place of abode in New Zealand.[970] Where there is a group of persons there is no need to give a separate warning to each member: it is enough that the terms of the warning make it plain that all members are being warned to leave.[971] Where the person giving the warning is performing a public function, he or she must act reasonably so as to comply with the New Zealand Bill of Rights Act 1990.[972]

It is a defence for the defendant to prove that the person who gave a warning to stay off is no longer an occupier of the place concerned.[973] It also is a defence for the defendant to show that it was necessary to remain in or on the place concerned or, as the case may be, to commit the trespass, for his or her own protection, or for the protection of some other person, or because of some emergency involving the property of the defendant or of some other person.[974]

2. Self-Help

175. At common law the person in possession may remove a trespasser from the land, provided he or she uses no more force than is reasonably necessary.[975] There is a statutory power to similar effect.[976]

The common law power is limited in the case of a residential tenancy. If a residential tenant refuses to leave on the expiry of the tenancy, the landlord should

---

967. Trespass Act 1980, s. 4(4). The occupier may warn anyone who is trespassing, or who has trespassed, or who the occupier has reasonable cause to suspect is likely to trespass, to stay off the trespass, to stay off the land: s. 4(1), (2). Where a person is convicted of an offence under the Act, the Court may give the warning: s. 4(3).
968. *Russell v. Police* (1981) 1 NZCPR 349.
969. In *Duffield v. Police* [1971] NZLR 381 a defendant entered as a licensee but became a trespasser on breach of the conditions of the licence, and thus could be convicted of trespass after notice to leave. In this type of case the licence should first be revoked, to make the licensee a trespasser, and then the warning should be given in terms of the statute: *Wilcox v. Police* [1994] 1 NZLR 243 at 247; *Ross v. Police* (2002) 6 HRNZ 734.
970. Trespass Act 1980, s. 5.
971. *Skold v. Police* [1982] 1 NZLR 197.
972. *Police v. Beggs* [1999] 3 NZLR 615; *Ross v. Police* (2002) 6 HRNZ 734 at [39]; *Rongonui v. Police* [2011] NZAR 128.
973. Trespass Act 1980, s. 4(5)(a).
974. *Ibid.*, ss 3(2), 4(5)(b). A trespass to prevent a lawful abortion cannot be regarded as reasonably necessary, nor can protection of 'some other person' include an unborn child: *see* generally *Wilcox v. Police* [1994] 1 NZLR 243; *Bayer v. Police* [1994] 2 NZLR 48.
975. *Burt v. Ross* (1886) NZLR 5 SC 161.
976. Crimes Act 1961, s. 56; *see* para. 503.

apply to the Tenancy Tribunal for a possession order.[977] It is an offence to enter residential premises in the occupation of a tenant without the consent of the tenant or without a possession order.[978]

A further self-help remedy is distress damage feasant – the right of an occupier to seize chattels or animals that are unlawfully on land and detain them until the owner pays compensation for any damage they have caused.[979]

3. Damages

176. Trespass is actionable per se, and the plaintiff who proves a trespass but who cannot prove damage can still succeed and is entitled to nominal damages.[980] Where damage is suffered, the measure normally is the amount by which the value of the land has been diminished.[981] But sometimes the court may award the cost of repair, at least where this is not substantially greater than the amount of the difference in value.[982]

Consequential loss also is recoverable provided the damage is not too remote. In *Mayfair Ltd v. Pears*[983] the Court of Appeal decided that damage to the plaintiff's car-parking building caused by the defendant's unlawfully parked car inexplicably catching alight was not recoverable, on the basis that the damage was unintended, unforeseeable, and indirect. The decision leaves open the question whether the test of foreseeability ought always to apply or whether direct consequences, even if unforeseeable, sometimes ought to be recoverable.[984]

Where the defendant has made use of the plaintiff's land, the plaintiff can recover damages, known as mesne profits, for loss of use of the land.[985] The measure of the loss is the sum that should reasonably be paid for the use, irrespective of whether the plaintiff could have let the land to someone else or whether the defendant derived actual benefit from the trespass.[986] If the trespasser has made improvements, a reasonable rent should be assessed on the unimproved value, but there is no set-off for the value of the improvements.[987]

977. Residential Tenancies Act 1986, s. 64.
978. *Ibid.*, s. 63.
979. *See* para. 505.
980. *Mayfair Ltd v. Pears* [1987] 1 NZLR 459 at 465; *Re Chase* [1989] 1 NZLR 325 at 340.
981. *Philips v. Ward* [1956] 1 All ER 874; *Cousins v. Wilson* [1994] 1 NZLR 463 at 467.
982. *Taylor v. Auto Trade Supply Ltd* [1972] NZLR 102; *Shattock v. Devlin* [1990] 2 NZLR 88 at 113.
983. [1987] 1 NZLR 459.
984. *See* para. 547.
985. *Baylis v. Carroll* (1908) 27 NZLR 638; *Peterson v. Cowan* (1910) 13 GLR 11; *Ramzan v. Brookwide Ltd* [2011] 2 All ER 38.
986. *Inverugie Investments Ltd v. Hackett* [1995] 1 WLR 713; *Roberts v. Rodney District Council* [2001] 2 NZLR 402; *Waugh v. Attorney-General* [2006] 2 NZLR 812.
987. *Tai Te Whetu v. Scandlyn* [1952] NZLR 30.

The plaintiff may also recover general damages for loss of enjoyment of the property[988] and for associated upset and distress.[989] Injury to feelings caused by particularly high-handed conduct can be compensated by an award of aggravated damages,[990] and where actual punishment is merited there can be an award of exemplary damages.[991]

4. Injunction

177. A landowner whose title is not in issue normally is entitled to an injunction to restrain trespass regardless of whether or not the trespass causes harm.[992] The injunction may be prohibitory, to restrain the continuance or threatened repetition of a trespass,[993] or mandatory, to remove a trespassing object on the land.[994] In the case of an encroaching building, in certain special circumstances, a court may make an order giving relief to the encroaching owner.[995] Where a trespass is threatened, and irreparable harm is likely, the court may prevent it by issuing a *quia timet* injunction.[996]

An injunction may be refused where the trespass is trifling, where damages are a sufficient remedy, or where the granting of an injunction would be oppressive.[997] Damages in addition to or in substitution for an injunction can be awarded under the Senior Courts Act 2016, section 13.[998]

F. Defences

178. Those defences that are of general application throughout the law of torts are considered later on.[999] Our concern here is with certain defences of particular relevance to claims for trespass to land.

988. *Ramsay v. Cooke* [1984] 2 NZLR 680 at 687; *Trustees Executors Agency Co. of New Zealand Ltd v. Butler* HC, Dunedin, CP 107/92, 18 Jul. 1994.
989. *Seagar v. Brady* HC, Auckland, HC 174/96, 5 May 1997.
990. *Shattock v. Devlin* [1990] 2 NZLR 88; *Jackson v. Blagojevich* (1997) 3 NZ ConvC 192,564.
991. *Mayfair Ltd v. Pears* [1987] 1 NZLR 459 at 465; *Cousins v. Wilson* [1994] 1 NZLR 463; *Ramzan v. Brookwide Ltd* [2011] 2 All ER 38; *Hikurangi Forest Farms Ltd v. Negara Developments Ltd* [2018] NZHC 607, [2018] NZAR 804; *see* para. 576.
992. *Patel v. WH Smith (Eziot) Ltd* [1987] 1 WLR 853.
993. *Beale v. Lawler* (1902) 32 NZLR 426; *Russo v. Ridgway* (1914) 33 NZLR 1495. A court may enjoin the publication of photographs and film which have been obtained during a trespass: *Bradley v. Wingnut Films Ltd* [1993] 1 NZLR 415; *TV3 Network Services Ltd v. Fahey* [1999] 2 NZLR 129.
994. *Kelsen v. Imperial Tobacco Co. Ltd* [1957] 2 QB 334.
995. *See* the Property Law Act 2007, ss 321–325; *Tram Lease Ltd v. Croad* [2003] 2 NZLR 461.
996. *Grocott v. Ayson* [1975] 2 NZLR 596; *see* para. 570.
997. *See* generally *Shelfer v. City of London Electric Lighting Co.* [1895] 1 Ch 287; *Lawrence v. Fen Tigers* [2014] AC 822; *see* para. 568.
998. *See* para. 572.
999. *See* Part IV.

1. Claim of Right

179. A defendant may of course show that he or she had a right to the possession of the land, or that he or she acted under the authority of another person having such a right.[1000] But in the absence of such authority the right of a third person is no defence in trespass, although it may be in an action for the recovery of land.[1001]

2. Licence

180. Where the plaintiff's complaint is that a licensee remained on land or left something on land after the expiry of his or her licence to be there or to leave the object there, then the onus is on the plaintiff to prove expiry or withdrawal of the licence as part of his or her cause of action.[1002] But where the plaintiff in an action for trespass alleges that the defendant unlawfully entered the land or put something on the land, the defendant can plead by way of defence that the entry was by the leave or the licence of the plaintiff.

A licence may be express[1003] or it may be implied in all the circumstances. For example, an occupier gives an implied licence to members of the public to enter land and knock at the door in order to make inquiry of the occupier for any reasonable purpose.[1004] Any such licence is likely to be implied only in relation to an entry that is made at a reasonable time.[1005] Entry for a purpose for which it is known or understood that the occupier would not give consent will be outside the ambit of the implication.[1006] A person may, of course, exclude the licence, by giving notice to this effect,[1007] or may withdraw it,[1008] and in the latter case, the licensee is not a trespasser during the reasonable time it takes to leave.[1009]

Where members of the public normally are allowed to enter land, the licence cannot be excluded by reason of any of the prohibited grounds of discrimination provided for in the Human Rights Act 1993.[1010] And where the occupier is a public

1000. *Holmes v. Newlands* (1839) 11 Ad & El 44, 113 ER 329; *Hooper v. Rawson* [1920] GLR 476.
1001. *See* para. 173.
1002. *Shattock v. Devlin* [1990] 2 NZLR 88 at 106.
1003. In *R v. Meyer* [2010] NZAR 41 an express authorization for a police officer to enter a house extended to the officer following the occupier upstairs; and *see A v. Attorney-General* [2018] NZHC 989, [2018] 3 NZLR 439.
1004. *Tararo v. R* [2012] 1 NZLR 145; and *see Robson v. Hallett* [1967] 2 QB 939; *King v. Police* [2010] NZAR 45; *Police v. McDonald* [2010] NZAR 59; cp. *O'Connor v. Police* [2010] NZAR 50; *Round v. New Zealand Police* [2020] NZHC 262 at [39]-[42].
1005. *Howden v. Ministry of Transport* [1987] 2 NZLR 747 at 754.
1006. *Hamed v. R* [2012] 2 NZLR 305 (no implied licence where police officer entered land not to communicate with the owner but for the purpose of covert surveillance).Compare *Tararo v. R* [2012] 1 NZLR 145, where the implied licence was not lost because the person entering, who was a police officer, made a record of the entry.
1007. *Ratima v. R* (1999) 17 CRNZ 227.
1008. *Attorney-General v. Hewitt* [2000] 2 NZLR 110 at 114, 118.
1009. *Transport Ministry v. Payn* [1977] 2 NZLR 50 at 60; *Polly v. Police* [1985] 1 NZLR 443; *Howden v. Ministry of Transport* [1987] 2 NZLR 747.
1010. Human Rights Act 1993, ss 21, 42.

authority or is exercising public functions, any withdrawal is conditional upon the occupier discharging its public law duties to act reasonably in the circumstances.[1011]

3. Statutory Authority

181. There are numerous statutes giving rights of entry on private land, often to the police but also to a wide variety of executive officers.[1012] However, the action for trespass provides important constitutional protection for private property, so the authority must be clear and unambiguous.[1013]

4. Execution of Process

182. Various powers to enter land in the execution of process are conferred by statute.[1014] There is also a common law power which, when it applies, constitutes a defence to a claim for trespass.[1015]

5. Distress for Rent

183. Formerly an entry could be made in the execution of a right of distress for rent,[1016] giving the landlord a good defence to an action for trespass. But the right has now been abolished.[1017]

6. Recaption of Chattels

184. In certain circumstances a person may exercise the remedy of self-help, and enter land in order to recover goods that have been wrongly taken by the occupier.[1018]

1011. *Police v. Beggs* [1999] 3 NZLR 615; *Wandsworth London Borough Council v. A* [2000] 1 WLR 1246. Where land is 'affected with a public interest', then an occupier in the absence of good reason to the contrary must make its facilities available to all at a reasonable price: *Sky City Auckland Ltd v. Wu* [2002] 3 NZLR 621.
1012. *See*, for example, Crimes Act 1961, s. 317 (*see* para. 61); Land Transport Act 1998, 119; Electricity Act 1992, s. 159; Search and Surveillance Act 2012, s. 14. For entry pursuant to an authority conferred by warrant, *see*, for example, Summary Proceedings Act 1957, s. 198; Customs and Excise Act 1996, s. 168; Commerce Act 1986, ss 98A–98F; Fair Trading Act 1986, ss 47–47F.
1013. *Choudry v. Attorney-General* [1999] 2 NZLR 582 at 592.
1014. For example, *see* the Insolvency Act 2006, s. 150.
1015. *See* generally *Southam v. Smout* [1964] 1 QB 308; *Vaughan v. McKenzie* [1969] 1 QB 557.
1016. Distress and Replevin Act 1908.
1017. Property Law Act 2007, s. 265. By s. 366(b), the Distress and Replevin Act 1908 is repealed.
1018. *See* para. 504.

III. Private Nuisance

A. Definition and Nature of Private Nuisance

185. Private nuisance is an unreasonable interference with a person's right to the use or enjoyment of land.[1019] More specifically, it involves causing an event or creating, adopting or continuing a state of affairs that threatens or brings about damage or disturbance to land, or that substantially interferes with use and enjoyment of land in the possession of the plaintiff. So the tort is based on the notion of damage, inconvenience, or annoyance, but what is a nuisance in fact may not amount to a nuisance in law. To describe something as annoying or inconvenient looks at the matter solely from the plaintiff's point of view. The courts also have to look at the conduct and interests of the defendant, the seriousness of the act, the utility of the conduct and the degree of care taken. The law of private nuisance thus involves a balancing of the interests of a landowner who wishes to use his or her land as he or she sees fit with the interests of a neighbour who wishes to be free from interferences with his or her use or enjoyment of the land.[1020] Everybody must put up with a certain amount of interference or inconvenience stemming from the activities of their neighbours. The law recognizes the principle of 'give and take, live and let live'.[1021] The conduct only becomes actionable when it is 'unreasonable' and exceeds what an ordinary person might reasonably be expected to tolerate.

B. Forms of Nuisance

186. An actionable nuisance can take various forms. There may be an interference with use or enjoyment of land by way of actual physical damage to the land or to things on the land. Examples are damage to plants growing on the land caused by poisonous fumes;[1022] the cracking of buildings caused by tree roots;[1023] radioactive contamination of the land;[1024] and excavations causing subsidence to adjoining land.[1025] Again, there may be an encroachment without physical damage, as in the

1019. For more detailed discussion *see* Atkin, *Nuisance*, in *Todd on Torts* Ch. 10 (Todd ed., 8th ed., 2019), upon which part of this account is based.

1020. *Bank of New Zealand v. Greenwood* [1984] 1 NZLR 525 at 531; *Hunter v. Canary Wharf Ltd* [1997] AC 655 at 693.

1021. *Cambridge Water Co. Ltd v. Eastern Counties Leather plc* [1994] 2 AC 264 at 299.

1022. *St Helen's Smelting Co. v. Tipping* (1865) 11 HLC 642, 11 ER 1483.

1023. *Morgan v. Khyatt* [1964] NZLR 666; *Delaware Mansions Ltd v. Westminster City Council* [2002] 1 AC 321; *Berent v. Family Mosaic Housing* [2012] EWCA Civ 961; and *see Blakesfield Ltd v. Foote* [2015] NZAR 1140 (roots affecting development of land); *Williams v. Network Rail Infrastructure Ltd* [2018] EWCA Civ 1514, [2018] 3 WLR 1105 (spread of Japanese knotweed).

1024. *Blue Circle Industries plc v. Ministry of Defence* [1999] Ch 289. But mere chemical change to the soil without more is not physical damage: *Smith v. Inco Ltd* (2011) 340 DLR (4th) 602.

1025. *Byrne v. Judd* (1908) 27 NZLR 1106; *Bognuda v. Upton & Shearer Ltd* [1972] NZLR 741; *Attorney-General v. Whangarei City Council* [1987] 2 NZLR 150; *Brouwers v. Street* [2011] 1 NZLR 645; *Cattell v. Auckland Council* [2017] NZHC 2140; cp *Blewman v. Wilkinson* [1979] 2 NZLR 208. If the land only subsides because of the extra weight of a building on it, the owner must establish that the excavator was negligent: *Bognuda v. Upton & Shearer Ltd*.

case of overhanging branches.[1026] Or there may be interference with the beneficial use of the land in ways that assail the senses. So, for example, interfering with enjoyment by causing the occupier to suffer personal discomfort from smoke,[1027] smells,[1028] reflected glare from the sun,[1029] or noise,[1030] in each case can found an action. Offensive activities on land affronting the sensibilities of neighbours exceptionally may be actionable, as where premises in a residential neighbourhood were used for the purposes of prostitution.[1031] In all of these cases the plaintiff is not being compensated for any illness or physical discomfort or inconvenience but for the diminution in the utility or amenity value of the land.[1032]

In *Wu v. Body Corporate 366611*[1033] the Supreme Court affirmed that, at least in interference with beneficial use cases, some emanation of the effect of a nuisance from a defendant's land to a plaintiff's land usually is required. Accordingly, it was hard to see the reprogramming of electronic locks to the common areas of a building, with the effect of locking out the claimant owners of units in the building, could qualify as a nuisance. Subsequently, in *BEMA Property Investments Ltd v. Body Corporate 36661*,[1034] the Court of Appeal accepted that an emanation from land was not always required, and considered that the reprogramming of the locks preventing access to individual units in the building could be an actionable nuisance.

Nuisance also extends to interference with an easement[1035] or profit à prendre.[1036] These include rights to fish, shoot, cut timber, or take crops. In *Wu* the Supreme Court suggested that an interference with a right of access to land, if substantial and unreasonable, could be a nuisance on the basis that it was an interference with a 'natural right' similar to a landowner's frontages right of access from a public highway.[1037] In this and similar cases, then, no emanation is required.

Certain interferences with enjoyment are not actionable. These include obstructing the view from land, or building a property overlooking another,[1038] or obstructing the reception of television signals by putting up a tall building.[1039] But causing interference with television reception by something emanating from land, such as electronic signals or vibrations, is actionable.[1040]

1026. *Woodnorth v. Holgate* [1955] NZLR 552; *Darroch v. Carroll* [1955] NZLR 997; *Semple v. Wilson* [2018] NZHC 992, [2018] NZAR 1025.
1027. *Ross & Glendining Ltd v. Hancock & Co.* [1929] NZLR 204.
1028. *Hawkes Bay Protein Ltd v. Davidson* [2003] 1 NZLR 536; *Barr v. Biffa Waste Services Ltd* [2012] 3 WLR 795.
1029. *Bank of New Zealand v. Greenwood* [1984] 1 NZLR 525.
1030. *Lawrence v. Fen Tigers Ltd* [2014] AC 822.
1031. *Thompson-Schab v. Costaki* [1956] 1 WLR 335.
1032. *Hunter v. Canary Wharf Ltd* [1997] AC 655 at 706; and *see Fearn v. Board of Trustees of the Tate Gallery* [2020] EWCA Civ 104, [2020] 2 WLR 1081 at [32]–[49].
1033. [2015] 1 NZLR 215; and *see* para. 194.
1034. [2017] NZCA 281, [2018] 2 NZLR 514.
1035. *Paine & Co. Ltd v. St Neots Gas & Coke Co.* [1939] 3 All ER 812.
1036. *Nicholls v. Ely Beet Sugar Factory* [1931] 2 Ch 84.
1037. [2014] NZSC 137, [2015] 1 NZLR 215 at [126]–[132].
1038. *Fearn v. Board of Trustees of the Tate Gallery* [2020] EWCA Civ 104, [2020] 2 WLR 1081 at [50]–[85].
1039. *Hunter v. Canary Wharf Ltd* [1997] AC 655.
1040. Radiocommunications Act 1989, s. 105.

Nuisance normally involves a continuing state of affairs causing or threatening interference with the plaintiff's use or enjoyment of land. Where there is a one-off escape of something harmful, and no continuing interference, the plaintiff's claim should be brought under the special rule of strict liability laid down in *Rylands v. Fletcher*,[1041] or as an ordinary action in negligence.

C. Substantial and Unreasonable Harm

187. Not every slight annoyance is actionable. The courts have to balance the right of an occupier to do with his or her land as he or she thinks fit and the right of his or her neighbour to the quiet enjoyment of his or her land. Nuisance is actionable only if there is substantial interference with the use or enjoyment of land, and the interference is found to be unreasonable in the circumstances of the case. The test is sometimes expressed in terms of whether the interference exceeds what a normal occupier in the plaintiff's position could be expected to tolerate.[1042] In nuisance, reasonable means more than taking proper care. It signifies what is legally right between the parties, taking into account all the circumstances of the case.

1. Nature and Extent of the Harm

188. The courts will find nuisance more readily on the basis of material or physical harm than personal discomfort. They accept that it is never reasonable to expect an occupier to tolerate an interference that causes physical damage to the property.[1043] But in the case of interference with comfort, the courts ask how substantial is the interference in the light of its frequency and duration and the time of day. Temporary discomfort caused for example by building work does not amount to a nuisance provided it is carried out at reasonable times and appropriate steps are taken to minimize the level of interference.[1044] But serious interference, even though intermittent, may be actionable.[1045] Yet there cannot be liability in nuisance simply because of diminished market value, as the tort is not designed to protect the value of property as an investment or financial asset.[1046]

1041. (1866) LR 1 Exch. 265; *see* para. 201.
1042. *See*, for example, *Bamford v. Turnley* (1862) 3 B & S 66, 122 ER 27; *Bloodworth v. Cormack* [1949] NZLR 1058 at 1061; *Paxhaven Holdings Ltd v. Attorney-General* [1974] 2 NZLR 185 at 188; *Bank of New Zealand v. Greenwood* [1984] 1 NZLR 525 at 531; *Hawkes Bay Protein Ltd v. Davidson* [2003] 1 NZLR 566 at [21]; *Outtrim v. Li* [2010] NZAR 282 at [29]–[31].
1043. *St Helen's Smelting Co. v. Tipping* (1865) 11 HLC 642, 11 ER 1483.
1044. *Andreae v. Selfridge & Co. Ltd* [1938] Ch 1; *Wildtree Hotels Ltd v. Harrow London Borough Council* [2001] 2 AC 1.
1045. *Bank of New Zealand v. Greenwood* [1984] 1 NZLR 525.
1046. *Williams v. Network Rail Infrastructure Ltd* [2018] EWCA Civ 1514, [2018] 3 WLR 1105 at [42], [46] and [48].

2. Character of the Neighbourhood

189. The character of the neighbourhood in which an activity is carried out cannot justify an interference that physically damages the land. So, the use of land was unreasonable where fumes from smelting works in an industrial area damaged the plaintiff's trees.[1047] But locality, or 'the established pattern of uses' in the locality,[1048] is relevant where the complaint is of interference with the enjoyment of land. Here the principle of give and take, live and let live, has most part to play.[1049] A person living in an industrial area cannot expect the same level of freedom from interferences with comfort and enjoyment as a country-dweller.[1050]

Of course, the nature of a locality may change. In *Lawrence v. Fen Tigers Ltd*[1051] the defendants obtained planning permission for, and built, a stadium and motocross track. The plaintiffs subsequently bought a house nearby and complained about the noise. The UK Supreme Court affirmed that planning permission did not provide a defence: whether an activity caused a nuisance was a question for the court, not the planning authority. However, the existence and terms of the permission were not irrelevant, and as a starting point the existence of the defendant's activities was included in the assessment of locality, but only to the extent they did not constitute a nuisance. In the instant case, on the basis of the noise levels as determined by the trial judge, a nuisance had been made out.

3. Plaintiff's Special Sensitivity

190. The test to be applied is an objective one: the court has to see what effect the respondent's activities have on the normal person of ordinary habits and sensibilities.[1052] So the plaintiff cannot rely on his or her abnormal sensitivity. He or she cannot require a higher than normal degree of freedom from outside interference.[1053]

4. Defendant's Motive

191. The fact that land is used with a good motive and for legitimate and socially valuable purposes can be relevant in determining whether the activity is unreasonable. The argument is implicit in the locality principle: reasonable people must put up with work that is a normal and necessary feature of the neighbourhood provided it is carried out at reasonable times and with reasonable precautions against undue

---

1047. *St Helen's Smelting Co. v. Tipping* (1865) 11 HLC 642, 11 ER 1483.
1048. *Lawrence v. Fen Tigers Ltd* [2014] AC 822 at [60].
1049. *Transco plc v. Stockport Metropolitan Borough Council* [2004] 2 AC 1 at 35.
1050. *Collis v. Home and Colonial Stores Ltd* [1904] AC 179 at 185.
1051. [2014] AC 822.
1052. *Bloodworth v. Cormack* [1949] NZLR 1058.
1053. *See*, for example, *Robinson v. Kilvert* (1889) 41 Ch D 88; *Eastern and South African Telegraph Co. v. Cape Town Tramways* [1902] AC 381; and see *Fearn v. Board of Trustees of the Tate Gallery* [2020] EWCA Civ 104, [2020] 2 WLR 1081 at [96]-[102].

harm. But once the relevant standard is exceeded the defendant is liable, however valuable the activity may be. The defendant cannot set up any alleged public benefit ahead of the private interests of the plaintiff.[1054]

As regards a bad motive, this does not make conduct actionable but it may be a relevant factor in difficult cases. An activity that might otherwise be judged as reasonable may be regarded as unreasonable if the defendant acted with a malicious motive.[1055] It is not reasonable to use land simply for the purpose of damaging the plaintiff.

D. Standard of Liability and Test of Remoteness

192. In claims for negligence the emphasis is on the carefulness of the defendant's conduct, and whether reasonable care has been taken is determined by the foreseeability and degree of risk created by that conduct. In nuisance, however, in cases where the defendant has created a continuing interference with the use or enjoyment of land, the court is not concerned with the degree of care taken by the defendant but with whether the level of interference caused by the activity in question is reasonable. In *Cambridge Water Co. Ltd v. Eastern Counties Leather plc*[1056] the House of Lords made it clear that if an interference is unreasonable, then the defendant is strictly liable, in the sense that evidence that he or she exercised all due care and skill and took all reasonable precautions to prevent a nuisance provides no excuse. In *Hamilton v. Papakura District Council*[1057] the Court of Appeal held that this also is the law in New Zealand. The defendant's duty is not to cause a nuisance, not merely to take care not to cause a nuisance.

However, liability extends only to the foreseeable consequences of the activity. In *Wagon Mound (No. 2)*[1058] Lord Reid, delivering the judgment of the Privy Council, said that the foreseeability test of remoteness applied to limit recovery of damages in all cases of nuisance, whether private or public. This view also was confirmed in both *Cambridge Water* and *Hamilton*. In the former case the defendants had used a toxic solvent called perchloroethene (PCE) in their tanning business, and over the years the PCE had seeped into the ground and contaminated the aquifer from which the plaintiff drew its water. It was held that the defendants were not liable because it was not reasonably foreseeable that when the PCE was being used it could at some future date contaminate the plaintiff's water. In the latter case the defendant's spraying of weeds next to its reservoir contaminated the water supply to local users, and this damaged the plaintiffs' hydroponically grown tomatoes. It was held that it was not foreseeable that weed-spray run-off would cause this damage, and the claim accordingly failed.

1054. *Bank of New Zealand v. Greenwood* [1984] 1 NZLR 525 at 535.
1055. *Christie v. Davey* [1893] 1 Ch 316; *Hollywood Silver Fox Farm Ltd v. Emmett* [1936] 2 KB 468; *Outtrim v. Li* [2010] NZAR 282 at [32].
1056. [1994] 2 AC 264.
1057. [2000] 1 NZLR 265; and *see Brouwers v. Street* [2011] 1 NZLR 645 at [137].
1058. [1967] 1 AC 617.

Where the defendant has not created a nuisance, but has simply adopted or continued a state of affairs created by someone else, then the defendant can be liable only on proof of negligence.[1059] So where the defendant is the occupier of land on which a nuisance has been created by another person or has arisen naturally, it must be shown that he or she knew or ought to have known of the condition and could reasonably have been expected to have brought it to an end.[1060] In this case, then, nuisance and negligence overlap.

E. Who Can Sue

193. The tort of nuisance seeks to provide a remedy for invasions of interests in land, and the plaintiff must, therefore, have an interest in the land.[1061] So an occupier, a tenant in possession, a licensee with exclusive possession, and even a person simply in exclusive de facto possession,[1062] all have the right to sue. Where an action lies, the occupier may recover for damage to the land even though the nuisance began before he or she acquired his or her proprietary interest in the land.[1063] But persons who have the use of the land but lack a proprietary or possessory interest – family members lacking any such interest, guests of the occupier, employees working on the land – have no right of action.

A reversioner can sue in respect of permanent damage to the land.[1064] Where the interference is of a temporary nature the person in possession should sue.

F. Who Is Liable

194. In a number of cases it has been held that the creator of a nuisance may be sued even if he or she is not the occupier of the premises from which the nuisance emanated.[1065] However, as nuisance regulates the competing uses of neighbouring land, it follows that the defendant should manage or have control over the land on which the conduct or activity occurs. So it has been held in the House of Lords that the ground of responsibility for nuisance is the possession and control of the land from which the nuisance proceeds,[1066] and this is the generally accepted approach

1059. *Sedleigh-Denfield v. O'Callaghan* [1940] AC 880.
1060. *Goldman v. Hargrave* [1967] 1 AC 645; *French v. Auckland City Corp* [1974] 1 NZLR 340; *Double J Smallwoods Ltd v. Gisborne District Council* [2017] NZHC 1284, [2017] NZAR 1167; *Williams v. Network Rail Infrastructure Ltd* [2018] EWCA Civ 1514, [2018] 3 WLR 1105.
1061. *Hunter v. Canary Wharf Ltd* [1997] AC 655; *Transco plc v. Stockport Metropolitan Borough Council* [2004] 2 AC 1.
1062. As to which *see Paxhaven Holdings Ltd v. Attorney-General* [1974] 2 NZLR 185; *Pemberton v. Southwark London Borough Council* [2000] 1 WLR 1673.
1063. *Delaware Mansions Ltd v. Westminster City Council* [2002] 1 AC 321.
1064. *Meux's Brewery Co. v. City of London Electric Lighting Co.* [1895] 1 Ch 287.
1065. For example, *Thompson v. Gibson* (1841) 7 M & W 456, 151 ER 845; *J Lyons & Sons v. Wilkins* [1899] 1 Ch 255; *Hubbard v. Pitt* [1976] QB 142.
1066. *Sedleigh-Denfield v. O'Callaghan* [1940] AC 880 at 903.

in New Zealand.[1067] Two first instance decisions hold that it is irrelevant where the interference originates and that a defendant can be liable for harm caused by activities conducted on the plaintiff's own land.[1068] These cases perhaps were wrongly decided.[1069] However, in *Wu v. Body Corporate 366611*,[1070] defendants who altered the electronic configuration of locks to a building, thereby preventing the plaintiffs from using their units, were thought to be liable in nuisance for interference with the plaintiffs' natural rights of access notwithstanding that the locked doors and lifts were on land owned by the plaintiff unit owners with others.[1071]

Wu certainly is exceptional, and in most cases nuisance will involve competing uses of land. The key requirement rendering the defendant liable seems to be a sufficient degree of control over the land in question. Examples of control falling short of a proprietary or possessory interest include: a person with a licence to excavate clay;[1072] gypsies who had paid to camp on a site,[1073] a licensee operating a speedway,[1074] a contractor carrying out building operations,[1075] and a city council maintaining grass verges along the highway.[1076]

As we have seen, the standard of liability in nuisance varies according to whether the defendant created or continued it. So an occupier who personally engages in an activity causing a nuisance will be strictly liable for that nuisance. So too, an occupier will be strictly liable in respect of a nuisance created on the land by a person under his or her control. For example, a school authority was liable for allowing children to trespass and leave rubbish on land adjoining the school,[1077] a cricket club was responsible for cricket balls hit into nearby gardens,[1078] a council that let travellers camp on its land was liable for the nuisance they caused,[1079] and a mother who let her daughter use her property was liable for her barking dog.[1080]

Furthermore, an owner not in occupation may be liable if he or she has authorized the conduct causing the nuisance. Authorization will be implied where the creation of a nuisance is the 'natural and necessary consequence' of carrying on the activity for which the premises were let.[1081] For example, the test was satisfied and a landlord was liable where it leased land for use as a go-kart track.[1082] But a landlord was not responsible where it knew that a tenant was causing a nuisance and did

---

1067. *Hamilton v. Papakura District Council* [2000] 1 NZLR 265 at 282; *Langdon v. Bailey* [2001] NZAR 120 at 127.
1068. *Paxhaven Holdings Ltd v. Attorney-General* [1974] 2 NZLR 185; *Clearlite Holdings Ltd v. Auckland City Council* [1976] 2 NZLR 729.
1069. *See Langdon v. Bailey* [2001] NZAR 120; *BP Oil New Zealand Ltd v. Ports of Auckland Ltd* [2004] 2 NZLR 208.
1070. [2015] 1 NZLR 215.
1071. The actual decision was that the defendants were liable for trespass: *see* para. 169.
1072. *White v. Jameson* (1874) LR 18 Eq 303.
1073. *Attorney-General v. Stone* (1895) 12 TLR 76.
1074. *Bloodworth v. Cormack* [1949] NZLR 1058.
1075. *Kraemers v. Attorney-General* [1966] Tas SR 113.
1076. *LE Jones Ltd v. Portsmouth City Council* [2003] 1 WLR 427.
1077. *Matheson v. Northcote College Board of Governors* [1975] 2 NZLR 106.
1078. *Miller v. Jackson* [1977] 1 QB 966.
1079. *Lippiatt v. South Gloucestershire Council* [2000] QB 51.
1080. *Cocking v. Eaton* [2016] EWCA Civ 140, [2016] QB 1080.
1081. *Harris v. James* (1876) 35 LT 240.
1082. *Tetley v. Chitty* [1986] 1 All ER 663.

not take steps to prevent this.[1083] In *Lawrence v. Fen Tigers (No 2)*,[1084] a second judgment of the UK Supreme Court in the litigation,[1085] the question in issue was the liability of the landlords of the motocross stadium for the noise created by the tenant. The Court held that the letting of the land for a stadium and race track did not fall within the 'natural or necessary consequence test' as it would have appeared possible for the planned uses of the land to be carried out without causing a nuisance. An alternative test was whether the landlord 'actively or directly participated' in the creation of the nuisance, and (by a majority) it was held that on the facts this test was not satisfied either.

In addition, an occupier may be liable for nuisance created by a trespasser or occurring naturally, if he or she adopts or continues it.[1086] In this case nuisance and negligence overlap, and the content of the duty is the same whether the claim is pleaded as nuisance or as negligence.[1087] In assessing the standard of care, the courts have taken account of the fact that the defendant has had a nuisance thrust upon him or her and without personal fault. So they have applied a subjective test and looked at the defendant's resources and capacity and what is reasonable for him or her to do in the circumstances. Examples of this subjective form of negligence include a failure to take reasonable steps to control a fire started by lightning,[1088] landslips caused by natural weathering,[1089] the proliferation and spread of weeds,[1090] or encroachment by tree roots.[1091] But there was no breach where a landowner failed to prevent an unexpected collapse of a cliff face,[1092] and where a statutory authority failed to enlarge the capacity of a sewerage system so as to remove the risk of it overflowing.[1093]

G. Defences

1. Statutory Authority

195. Statutory bodies that are authorized by empowering statutes to set up the thing creating the nuisance may seek to rely on the relevant statute as a defence, on the basis that it gives them authority to commit the nuisance. Such authority may be express, or it may be implied as a necessary consequence of the authority. So an

---

1083. *Hussain v. Lancaster City Council* [2000] QB 1.
1084. [2015] AC 106.
1085. For the first, *see* para. 189.
1086. *Sedleigh-Denfield v. O'Callaghan* [1940] AC 880; cp *Ali v. Bradford Metropolitan District Council* [2012] 1 WLR 161 (not for courts to impose liability on a highway authority for a continuing nuisance it had not created, since that would interfere with a carefully regulated statutory scheme governing obstructions on the highway).
1087. *Goldman v. Hargrave* [1967] 1 AC 645 at 657; *French v. Auckland City Council* [1974] 1 NZLR 340 at 350; *Delaware Mansions Ltd v. Westminster City Council* [2002] 1 AC 321 at 333.
1088. *Goldman v. Hargrave* [1967] 1 AC 645.
1089. *Leakey v. National Trust* [1980] QB 485.
1090. *French v. Auckland City Council* [1974] 1 NZLR 340.
1091. *Delaware Mansions Ltd v. Westminster City Council* [2002] 1 AC 321.
1092. *Holbeck Hall Hotel Ltd v. Scarborough Borough Council* [2000] QB 836.
1093. *Marcic v. Thames Water Utilities Ltd* [2004] 2 AC 42.

authority to construct an oil refinery necessarily authorized the operation of the refinery.[1094] However, the mere grant of resource consent under the Resource Management Act 1991 does not authorize a nuisance created by the permitted activity.[1095] The process is aimed at preventing nuisances, not allowing them. Even so, resource consent may lead ultimately to a change in the character of the neighbourhood, so that the activity becomes reasonable for the area and can no longer be regarded as a nuisance.[1096]

If an activity was authorized by statute, the defendant must show that the creation of a nuisance followed from the activity as its inevitable result.[1097] A nuisance is not inevitable if it could have been avoided by the taking of care and having regard for others in carrying out the activity. The onus is on the defendant to show that he or she used all reasonable care and skill, for otherwise the interference will be seen as having been caused by his or her incompetence.[1098] It is relevant to consider whether the statute confers widely permissive powers as to how, where and when to go about the work. If the statute is permissive, not mandatory, and confers a wide choice of area and method, the defendant has to exercise his or her discretion by taking due account of private rights.[1099] But if the statute prescribes where and how the activity is to be conducted, it is enough for the defendant to prove that it took all due care.[1100]

Sometimes a statute contains a 'nuisance clause', preserving liability for nuisance. Such a clause does not necessarily render the defendant strictly liable in all circumstances. If it is combined with a provision for compensation, then separate common law compensation will be treated as impliedly excluded.[1101] If the statute lays down a mandatory duty obliging the defendant to act, then the defendant is not liable in the absence of negligence.[1102]

2. Consent

196. In principle, consent may be a defence to nuisance.[1103] But an occupier does not consent merely because he or she tolerates an interference for a time without complaint.[1104] Nor is it a defence to say that the plaintiff consented to the nuisance simply on the basis that with full knowledge he or she chose to become owner

1094. *Allen v. Gulf Oil Refining Ltd* [1981] AC 1001.
1095. *Hawkes Bay Protein Ltd v. Davidson* [2003] 1 NZLR 536; *Lawrence v. Fen Tigers Ltd* [2014] AC 822.
1096. *Wheeler v. JJ Saunders Ltd* [1996] Ch 19; *Lawrence v. Fen Tigers Ltd* [2014] AC 822 at [77]–[99].
1097. *Manchester Corporation v. Farnworth* [1930] AC 171.
1098. *Allen v. Gulf Oil Refining Ltd* [1981] AC 1001; *Department of Transport v. North West Water Authority* [1984] AC 336; *Transco plc v. Stockport Metropolitan Borough Council* [2004] 2 AC 1; *Young v. Attorney-General* [2019] 3 NZLR 808 at [61]–[63].
1099. *Metropolitan Asylum District v. Hill* (1881) 6 App Cas 193.
1100. *Hammersmith & City Railway Co. v. Brand* (1869) LR 4 HL 171.
1101. *Irvine & Co. Ltd v. Dunedin City Corporation* [1939] NZLR 741.
1102. *Department of Transport v. North West Water Authority* [1984] AC 336.
1103. *Lyttelton Times Ltd v. Warners Ltd* [1907] AC 476.
1104. *Jerram v. Hood* [1954] NZLR 909.

or occupier of the land affected by it.[1105] Coming to the nuisance is no defence.[1106] It is unreasonable to allow a person to diminish the value of adjoining land without paying compensation or to expect a purchaser to refrain from buying land merely because a nuisance already exists upon it. However, a claimant who subsequently changes the use of the property may not have the same right to complain.[1107]

3. Contributory Negligence

197. Contributory negligence is no defence in cases where the defendant is strictly liable for creating a nuisance. If the activity is determined to be unreasonable and actionable, then the plaintiff is not obliged to take steps to minimize its impact or effect.[1108] But contributory negligence may be a good defence in cases where the defendant has continued or adopted a nuisance, and proof of negligence is an essential element to liability.[1109]

H. Remedies

1. Damages

198. The purpose of a damages award is to compensate the plaintiff for the diminution in the value of the land that is caused by the interference.[1110] If the land is damaged the court may award that diminution in value, or the cost of restoration if this is not disproportionate to the diminution in value.[1111] Costs incurred in preventing further damage or averting threatened damage also is recoverable.[1112] Where there is interference with the enjoyment of land, the measure is the amount by which the utility or amenity value of the land is diminished during the period in which the nuisance persisted.[1113] If the nuisance is continuing, the occupier should also seek an injunction with reasonable promptness in order to bring it to an end.[1114]

1105. *Khyatt v. Morgan* [1964] NZLR 666; *Ports of Auckland Ltd v. Auckland City Council* [1999] 1 NZLR 601.
1106. *Lawrence v. Fen Tigers Ltd* [2014] AC 822 at [51]–[52].
1107. *Lawrence v. Fen Tigers Ltd* [2014] AC 822 at [53]–[56].
1108. *Bank of New Zealand v. Greenwood* [1984] 1 NZLR 525 at 534; *Wu v. Body Corporate 366611* [2015] 1 NZLR 215.
1109. *Balloch Bros v. Jopp Bros (No. 1)* (1904) 23 NZLR 819.
1110. *Hunter v. Canary Wharf Ltd* [1997] AC 655.
1111. *Taylor v. Auto Trade Supply Ltd* [1972] NZLR 102. *Brouwers v. Street* [2011] 1 NZLR 645 (CA); *Street v. Brouwers* [2011] NZSC 17 (SC) (diminution in value of land in its improved state following loss of natural right of support rendering house uninhabitable).
1112. *Delaware Mansions Ltd v. Westminster City Council* [2002] 1 AC 321; *New Zealand Forest Products Ltd v. O'Sullivan* [1974] 2 NZLR 80.
1113. *Hawkes Bay Protein Ltd v. Davidson* [2003] 1 NZLR 536; *Outtrim v. Li* [2010] NZAR 282 at [77]; and *see Fearn v. Board of Trustees of the Tate Gallery* [2020] EWCA Civ 104, [2020] 2 WLR 1081 at [34].
1114. *Hawkes Bay Protein Ltd v. Davidson* [2003] 1 NZLR 536; *see* paras 199, 568.

The plaintiff can also recover consequential loss provided it is not too remote. The test is whether the damage is a reasonably foreseeable consequence of the activity constituting the nuisance.[1115] Recoverable losses can include damage to chattels or animals,[1116] loss of rental[1117] and loss of profits in the use of the land.[1118]

2. Injunction

199. Where an interference causes continuing harm the plaintiff is prima facie entitled to an injunction.[1119] This may specify in detail what the defendant can or cannot do,[1120] or it may simply require the defendant to refrain from causing a nuisance, in which case the defendant may be able to comply by modifying his or her activity rather than by ceasing it altogether.[1121] Equitable damages can be awarded in addition to or in substitution for an injunction.[1122] Where no damage has been suffered but the conduct, if allowed to continue, will almost certainly result in damage, the plaintiff can seek a *quia timet* injunction.[1123]

3. Abatement

200. An actionable nuisance sometimes may be dealt with by way of self-help.[1124] For example, an occupier can abate a nuisance caused by encroaching roots and branches by cutting them back to the boundary, provided at least that the occupier does not go on the other's land to do so.[1125]

IV. The Rule in *Rylands v. Fletcher*

A. Nature of the Rule

201. In Rylands *v. Fletcher*,[1126] the plaintiff owned a coal mine, and the defendant had a mill on nearby land. Rylands decided to construct a reservoir to store water for the mill, and engaged an engineer and contractors to do the work. Unbeknownst to Rylands or the contractors, there were disused mine shafts on the land where the reservoir was to be built, and below these were passages that connected

1115. *The Wagon Mound (No. 2)* [1967] 1 AC 617; *see* para. 544.
1116. *Hunter v. Canary Wharf Ltd* [1997] AC 655 at 706.
1117. *Taylor v. Auto Trade Supply Ltd* [1972] NZLR 102.
1118. *Clearlite Holdings Ltd v. Auckland City Corporation* [1976] 2 NZLR 729.
1119. *Regan v. Paul Properties DPF No. 1 Ltd* [2006] 3 WLR 1131.
1120. *McKelvey v. Invercargill Milk Supply Co. Ltd* [1928] NZLR 223.
1121. *Mayfair Ltd v. New Zealand Properties Ltd* [1940] NZLR 190.
1122. Senior Courts Act 2016, s. 13; *see* para. 572.
1123. *Darroch v. Carroll* [1955] NZLR 997; *see* para. 570.
1124. *See* para. 507.
1125. *Lemmon v. Webb* [1895] AC 1.
1126. (1865) 3 H & C 774, 159 ER 737 (Ex), (1866) LR 1 Ex 265 (Exch. Ch), (1868) LR 3 HL 330 (HL).

with Fletcher's mine. When the reservoir was built and partly filled, the water broke through and flooded Fletcher's mine. In the Court of Exchequer Chamber Blackburn J held that Rylands was liable for the damage on the basis of the following principle of law:

> We think that the true rule of law is, that the person who for his own purposes brings on his lands and collects and keeps there anything likely to do mischief if it escapes, must keep it at his peril, and, if he does not do so, is prima facie answerable for all the damage which is the natural consequence of its escape.

The case went on appeal to the House of Lords where the decision was confirmed, subject to the qualification that the rule only applied where the defendant made a non-natural use of his land.[1127]

In *Cambridge Water Co. Ltd v. Eastern Counties Leather plc*[1128] the House of Lords held that *Rylands v. Fletcher* did not create a new tort of strict liability, but was essentially an extension of the law of nuisance to cases of isolated escapes from land. Their Lordships held also that, since the recovery of damages in nuisance depended on the foreseeability of the kind of harm suffered, the same requirement of foreseeability of the damage applied in an action based on *Rylands v. Fletcher*. In *Hamilton v. Papakura District Council*[1129] the New Zealand Court of Appeal endorsed *Cambridge*, adopted the principle that *Rylands v. Fletcher* is only a 'subset' of the nuisance action, and accepted also that foreseeability of the damage needs to be shown. But liability remains strict in the sense that negligence does not have to be established. Gault J recognized that once it has been shown that the damage was foreseeable, it is irrelevant that the actual act causing the damage was not the fault of the defendant or that the defendant acted with reasonable care and skill.

Classification of the rule in *Rylands v. Fletcher* as a form of private nuisance action means that the rules relating to parties and damages should be the same for both actions. Accordingly, only a person who has a possessory or proprietary interest in land affected by the escape can sue, and the defendant must have had exclusive occupation of or control over the land from which the escape took place. So too, the basic measure of damages is the diminution in the market or amenity value of the plaintiff's interest in the land affected by the escape, together with consequential damage like physical injury to chattels and consequential economic loss.

B. Non-natural Use

202. The key difference between the rule in *Rylands v. Fletcher* and the principles of nuisance lies in the requirement for *Rylands v. Fletcher* liability there be a 'non-natural' use of land. The inquiry into reasonableness in nuisance focuses on

---

1127. *See* generally Atkin, *The Rule in Rylands v. Fletcher*, in *Todd on Torts* Ch. 11 (Todd ed., 8th ed., 2019), upon which this account is partly based.
1128. [1994] 2 AC 264; affirmed in *Transco plc v. Stockport Metropolitan Borough Council* [2004] 2 AC 1.
1129. [2000] 1 NZLR 265.

the severity of the impact of the defendant's activity on the plaintiff's land. Non-natural use is concerned with the *risk* posed by the activity. It must be some special use bringing with it increased danger to others, and not merely the ordinary use of land or such use as is proper for the general benefit of the community.[1130]

The focus here is not on whether care was taken in relation to the manner of conducting the particular use of land, but whether the risk inherent in the activity was such as to be regarded as non-natural, whatever precautions were taken. For example, the domestic use of water,[1131] fire,[1132] or electricity[1133] is treated as natural. But in each case the storage or supply of these things in bulk may create inherent danger, and the use of the land accordingly may be non-natural.[1134] Again, the storage of substantial quantities of chemicals on industrial premises was 'an almost classic case' of non-natural use.[1135] On the other hand, keeping a large stock of tyres was not an extraordinary or unusual use of land.[1136]

In *Transco plc v. Stockport Metropolitan Borough Council,*[1137] the House of Lords held that the use by a council of a water pipe servicing a block of sixty-six flats was a natural use of land. Their Lordships saw the degree of risk inherent in the activity as critical, and it was not such as to attract strict liability. The use was non-natural if the risk was so great that neighbouring occupiers could not reasonably be expected to accept it. The manner in which the defendant conducted the activity and its overall social utility, while relevant to negligence, were not considered relevant to non-natural use.[1138]

In a recent instance in New Zealand, the construction of a floodway with stop-banks that failed during heavy rain was a natural use of land.[1139] The whole point of the work was to try to defray a hazard and to benefit the community.

C. Defences

203. The defences of consent and statutory authority apply to *Rylands v. Fletcher* in the same way as they apply in nuisance. There are three further defences where the escape is caused by an intervening act or force beyond the defendant's control.

1130. *Rickards v. Lothian* [1913] AC 263 at 280.
1131. *Rickards v. Lothian* [1913] AC 263.
1132. *Sochacki v. Sas* [1947] 1 All ER 344.
1133. *Collingwood v. Home and Colonial Stores Ltd* [1936] 3 All ER 200.
1134. *See*, respectively, *Irvine & Co. Ltd v. Dunedin City Corporation* [1939] NZLR 741; *Northwestern Utilities Ltd v. London Guarantee and Accident Co. Ltd* [1936] AC 108; *Charing Cross Electricity Supply Co. Ltd v. Hydraulic Power Co.* [1914] 3 KB 772. In *Owens Transport Ltd v. Watercare Services Ltd* [2010] NZAR 568 it was seen as arguable that the bulk conveyance of water in water mains was a natural use of land.
1135. *Cambridge Water Co. Ltd v. Eastern Counties Leather plc* [1994] 2 AC 264 at 309.
1136. *Stannard v. Gore* [2014] QB 1.
1137. [2004] 2 AC 1.
1138. In *Easton Agriculture Ltd v. Manawatu-Wanganui Regional Council* [2012] 1 NZLR 120 Kós J accepted that strict liability is appropriate for a residue of cases involving 'exceptional hazard and (from the adjacent owner's perspective) unexpected outcome'.
1139. *Easton Agriculture Ltd v. Manawatu-Wanganui Regional Council* [2012] 1 NZLR 120.

1. Plaintiff's Default

204. It was expressly recognized by Blackburn J in *Rylands v. Fletcher* that if the escape is due solely to the plaintiff's default, the defendant is not liable. However, liability otherwise remains strict and the Contributory Negligence Act 1947 does not apply.

2. Act of God

205. Blackburn J also accepted that 'Act of God' could be a good defence. The defence has been applied in a case where unprecedented rainfall caused a flood that washed away the plaintiff's bridges.[1140] But in a later case the defence was rejected in similar circumstances involving flood damage.[1141] Seemingly, the operation of natural forces may provide an excuse only in the rarest of cases, where the escape is so unexpected that no reasonable human foresight could have recognized it happening even as a possibility.

3. Act of a Stranger

206. The deliberate act of a stranger constitutes a defence, as where an unknown person deliberately turned on the tap and blocked up the waste pipe on the defendant's basin, causing it to overflow.[1142] The basis of the defence is the absence of any control by the defendant over the stranger's act. So a trespasser is a stranger,[1143] but not an employee or contractor[1144] or anyone else over whom the defendant has control. Where a person is on land with the defendant's consent and deliberately causes harm, the authorities are not consistent in deciding whether there is a good defence. In one case the person was treated as a stranger, because the occupier could not reasonably have anticipated the conduct in question.[1145] But in another, the test was said to be whether the occupier had the power of control over the person's activities, and on this basis the person was not a stranger and the defence could not apply.[1146]

Where the defence is made out the defendant is not strictly liable, but may still be held liable for negligence.[1147]

1140. *Nichols v. Marsland* (1876) 2 Ex D 1.
1141. *Greenock Corporation v. Caledonian Railway Co.* [1917] AC 556.
1142. *Rickards v. Lothian* [1913] AC 263.
1143. *Perry v. Kendricks Transport Ltd* [1956] 1 WLR 85.
1144. *H N Emanuel Ltd v. Greater London Council* [1971] 2 All ER 835.
1145. *Erikson v. Clifton* [1963] NZLR 705.
1146. *Holderness v. Goslin* [1975] 2 NZLR 46 (question left open on appeal; *Dobson v. Holderness* [1975] 2 NZLR 749).
1147. *Northwestern Utilities Ltd v. London Guarantee and Accident Co. Ltd* [1936] AC 108.

D. Liability for the Escape of Fire

207. In England, the early common law imposed strict liability on an occupier for the escape of fire from his or her land. This was known as the *ignis suus* rule. To mitigate this rule, section 86 of the Fires Prevention (Metropolis) Act 1774 (which was in force in New Zealand)[1148] provided that 'no action shall be maintained against any person in whose house, chamber, stable, barn or other building or on whose estate any fire shall accidentally begin'. The Act abolished liability for fires which started and spread without anyone's negligence.[1149] A fire that 'accidentally' began meant a fire produced by chance or that could not be traced to any cause.[1150] The Act did not apply to a fire that was intentionally lit even if it escaped without negligence or if the fire started or was allowed to spread by the negligence of the occupier or someone for whom the occupier was responsible.

The 1774 Act was repealed for New Zealand by the Law of Property Act 2007.[1151] However, following the decision in *Rylands v. Fletcher*, fire was recognized as 'something likely to do mischief if it escaped' and so actions concerning the escape of fire came to be brought under this different rule. Eventually it was established that the *ignis suus* rule had been absorbed into the principle of *Rylands v. Fletcher* and, accordingly, that an action for the escape of fire was subject to the requirement that there be a non-natural use of land.[1152] So a domestic fire, even though intentionally lit, was an ordinary use that did not attract strict liability.[1153] Further, it seems that the fire itself must be brought onto land. In *Stannard v. Gore*[1154] an electrical fault caused a fire to break out at the defendant's premises, igniting a large number of tyres which the defendant had brought onto the premises. The tyres fed the ferocity of the fire, which spread to adjoining land. The English Court of Appeal held that the rule in *Rylands v. Fletcher* did not apply, because the tyres themselves had not escaped and the fire, while having escaped, had not been brought on to the defendant's land. Lewisham LJ said also that, on the supposition that fire was a dangerous thing and that *Rylands v. Fletcher* could apply, the principle was consistent only with a fire deliberately kindled.[1155] Those not deliberately kindled could give rise to liability in negligence.[1156]

Section 43(1) of the Forest and Rural Fires Act 1977 rendered a person responsible for causing a fire in a forest or rural area strictly liable for costs incurred in fighting the fire and for property damage. However, this Act was repealed by the Fire and Emergency New Zealand Act 2017, which replaced civil liability with a

1148. Imperial Laws Application Act 1988, s. 3(1).
1149. *Stannard v. Gore* [2014] QB 1.
1150. *Filliter v. Phippard* (1847) 11 QB 347, 116 ER 506.
1151. Law of Property Act 2007, s. 365(3)(a).
1152. *Boulcott Golf Club Inc v. Engelbrecht* [1945] NZLR 556; *Mason v. Levy Auto Parts Ltd* [1967] 2 QB 530; *Holderness v. Goslin* [1975] 2 NZLR 46.
1153. *Sochacki v. Sas* [1947] 1 All ER 344.
1154. [2014] QB 1.
1155. Not following the decision of the Court of Appeal in *Musgrove v. Pandelis* [1919] 2 KB 43. *Musgrove* was followed in New Zealand in *Hill v. Waimea County Council* HC, Nelson, A8/84, Heron J, 12 Mar. 1987, which decision must now be open to doubt.
1156. *Goldman v. Hargrave* [1967] 1 AC 645; *see* para. 145.

new offence and penalty regime. Civil liability at common law remains, but it is not as easy to establish as under the 1977 Act.

V. Public Nuisance

A. General

208. A public nuisance is 'a substantial interference with the comfort or convenience of the public or a significant class of the public'.[1157] The interference must, therefore, have a sufficiently significant public dimension. In *Attorney-General v. PYA Quarries Ltd*[1158] Denning LJ said that the test is whether the nuisance is so widespread in its range or indiscriminate in its effect that it would not be reasonable to expect one person to take proceedings on his own to put a stop to it, but that it should be taken on the responsibility of the community at large. The cases show that relatively small numbers of people can be treated as 'sections of the public'.[1159]

The Attorney-General has the standing to seek an injunction to restrain a public nuisance. He or she may act personally or on the relation of a private individual or public body. However, in order to prevent a proliferation of actions by affected members of the public, a private individual can bring proceedings only if he or she has suffered particular damage beyond that suffered by the affected class as a whole. The damage must be different in kind, or it must be substantial, direct and not consequential, and appreciably greater in degree than that suffered by the general public.[1160] Examples include damage to property,[1161] loss of custom,[1162] extra business expenses,[1163] and substantial delay and inconvenience.[1164] An interest in land is not required, but the damage must be of a foreseeable kind.[1165]

B. Forms of Public Nuisance

209. As with private nuisance, liability for creating a public nuisance is strict. It is no answer to say that all care was taken to minimize any interference if in fact the interference is unreasonable. Indeed, one class of public nuisance consists of widespread private nuisances that affect many members of the public at large. So

1157. *Wandsworth London Borough Council v. Railtrack plc* [2002] QB 756 at [19], [30].
1158. [1957] 2 QB 169 at 191.
1159. *Attorney-General of British Columbia, ex rel Eaton v. Haney Speedways Ltd* (1963) 39 DLR (2d) 48 (seven families near speedway); *R v. Johnson* [1997] 1 WLR 367 (thirteen women subjected to obscene phone calls); cp *R v. Madden* [1975] 1 WLR 1379 (eleven people affected by bomb hoax insufficient).
1160. *Walsh v. Ervin* [1952] VLR 361.
1161. *Halsey v. Esso Petroleum Co. Ltd* [1961] 1 WLR 683.
1162. *Amalgamated Theatres v. Charles S Luney* [1962] NZLR 226.
1163. *Tate & Lyle Industries Ltd v. Greater London Council* [1983] 2 AC 509.
1164. *Fuller v. McLeod* [1981] 1 NZLR 390 at 412.
1165. *The Wagon Mound (No. 2)* [1967] 1 AC 617.

where insanitary cattle yards caused offensive smells and plagues of flies and mosquitoes affecting the town residents, the Attorney-General brought a relator action to bring the interference to an end.[1166] Another common form of public nuisance is an unreasonable obstruction of the highway. Examples include picketing,[1167] causing long-lasting queues to block access to business premises,[1168] leaving vehicles on the highway for a sufficiently long time to amount to an obstruction,[1169] and street meetings or demonstrations.[1170] Again, obstructing a navigable waterway by causing it to silt up is a variation on this form of the tort.[1171]

Failing to abate a public nuisance created by others or by natural causes also is actionable, but here, again as with private nuisance, fault must be shown.[1172] So the owner of a railway bridge was found liable for failing to take reasonable steps to prevent pigeons from roosting under the bridge and fouling the pavement beneath.[1173]

A further form of public nuisance is that of accidents on the highway. It is clear that in this type of case it is necessary for the plaintiff to prove negligence, and reference to nuisance brings no advantage.[1174] It has been observed that 'where the law of negligence will suffice to determine liability … the less one hears of nuisance the better'.[1175]

C. Defences

210. Defences to private nuisance can apply in the same way in the case of public nuisance.[1176]

§3. Interference with Goods

I. General

A. Causes of Action

211. Broadly speaking, a person may wrongfully deprive another of his or her goods or chattels in three ways – by wrongfully taking the goods, by lawfully obtaining them but wrongfully retaining them, and by wrongfully disposing of

1166. *Attorney-General v. Abraham and Williams Ltd* [1949] NZLR 461.
1167. *Hubbard v. Pitt* [1976] QB 142.
1168. *Lyons, Sons & Co. v. Gulliver* [1914] 1 Ch 631.
1169. *Attorney-General v. Gastonia Coaches Ltd* [1977] RTR 219.
1170. *Olympic Delivery Authority v. Persons Unknown* [2012] EWHC 1012.
1171. *Tate & Lyle Industries Ltd v. Greater London Council* [1983] 2 AC 509.
1172. *Attorney-General v. Tod Heatley* [1897] 1 Ch 560.
1173. *Wandsworth London Borough Council v. Railtrack plc* [2002] QB 756.
1174. *Everitt v. Martin* [1953] NZLR 298.
1175. *Ibid.*, at 300.
1176. As to which, *see* paras 195–197.

them.[1177] The tort of conversion (and its associated remedy called trover) applies where a person has wrongfully appropriated goods, or has wrongfully deprived the owner of their use or possession, or has destroyed them or changed their quality, and accordingly the tort can be committed in any of these ways. Detinue, however, is concerned only with wrongfully failing to deliver up goods when demanded or improperly parting with their possession. Although they are tortious in form, conversion and detinue are in fact primarily concerned with the protection of proprietary interests in goods. Trespass lies where there is an unlawful taking or damaging of goods, so again there is an overlap with conversion, but trespass alone can lie in the case of an interference with goods not involving their destruction or the denial of the plaintiff's title.

B. Subject Matter

212. The subject matter of these torts must be specific personal property. Money taken or received as currency cannot be converted.[1178] However, conversion can lie in relation to specific coins or a specific cache of banknotes.[1179] There can be no conversion of a chose in action, being intangible property.[1180] But documents that constitute or evidence title to a debt can be converted, in which case the person entitled can recover damages for the face value of the document.[1181] So too, conversion lies for an undivided part of a chattel,[1182] or an undivided part of a specific quantity of money.[1183] Documents, files, artwork, and the like, having value by reason of the information or matter contained in them, may be converted,[1184] and so may the copyright in such material.[1185]

By statute, computer software is treated as 'goods' in New Zealand,[1186] and, seemingly, may be the subject matter of conversion.[1187] It has been held that internet time is 'property' and so can be the subject of theft under the Crimes Act 1961,[1188] and also that a CCTV file is 'property' within the meaning of that Act,[1189]

1177. *See* further Hawes, *Interference with Goods*, in *Todd on Torts* Ch. 12 (Todd ed., 8th ed., 2019).

1178. *Lipkin Gorman v. Karpnale Ltd* [1991] 2 AC 548; *Officeserve Technologies Ltd v. Annabel's (Berkeley Square) Ltd* [2018] 3 WLR 1568; and *see Money World New Zealand 2000 Ltd v. KVB Kunlun New Zealand Ltd* [2006] 1 NZLR 381.

1179. *R v. Collis* [1990] 2 NZLR 287; *Tamworth Industries Ltd v. Attorney-General* [1991] 3 NZLR 316.

1180. *OBG Ltd v. Allan* [2008] 1 AC 1 at [97]–[107], [271], [321]; cp at [220]–[241], [308]–[318].

1181. *Lipkin Gorman v. Karpnale Ltd* [1991] 2 AC 548; *Central Acceptance Ltd v. Smith Hughes & Robertson* [1992] 3 NZLR 413.

1182. *Coleman v. Harvey* [1989] 1 NZLR 723.

1183. *Jackson v. Anderson* (1811) 4 Taunt 24, 128 ER 235.

1184. *SSC & B: Lintas New Zealand Ltd v. Murphy* [1986] 2 NZLR 436.

1185. Copyright Act 1994, s. 120(2) (all remedies for property available to copyright owner); *Pacific Software Technology Ltd v. Perry Group Ltd* [2004] 1 NZLR 164.

1186. Contract and Commercial Law Act 2017, s. 119; Fair Trading Act 1986, s. 2(1); Consumer Guarantees Act 1993, s. 2(1).

1187. This is the law in Canada: *see Unisys Canada Inc v. Imperial Optical Co.* (2000) 49 CCLT 2d 237; cp *Thunder Air Ltd v. Hilmarsson* [2008] EWHC 355 (Ch); *Your Response Ltd v. Datateam Business Media Ltd* [2015] QB 41.

1188. *Davies v. Police* [2008] 1 NZLR 638 (HC).

but neither decision determines the question of conversion. In the United States it has been held that an Internet domain name can be converted,[1190] but Australian authority is to the contrary.[1191]

Conversion does not lie in respect of land and fixtures permanently attached to the land, but it does lie for fixtures, crops, timber, minerals, and the like once they have been severed from the land. Examples are shingle excavated from land,[1192] joinery detached from a building,[1193] and a whole barn not fixed to the land.[1194]

The general rule of the common law is that there can be no property in the human body or body parts.[1195] So the parents of deceased children upon whom post-mortems had been conducted and whose organs had been removed and disposed of without their consent could not maintain actions for wrongful interference with their children's bodies.[1196] However, the rule is not absolute, and it is possible that an action can lie in respect of a body or parts that have acquired different attributes by virtue of the application of skill or labour, such as the preserved stillborn body of a foetus.[1197] It is clear also that recent developments in medical science may require a re-evaluation of the law. So, in a UK case, six plaintiffs who stored samples of semen with the defendants before undergoing courses of chemotherapy were held to have ownership of the semen, and accordingly they had an action as bailors when the defendants allowed the semen to thaw and the sperm within it to perish.[1198] But a recent decision in New Zealand determined that the rule that there could be no property in a human body still applied, and that a widow's application for the use of her deceased husband's sperm should be dealt with by the Ethics Committee under the Human Assisted Reproductive Technology Act 2004.[1199]

II. Trespass to Goods

A. *Nature of Trespass*

213. Trespass to goods is an act committed without lawful justification that directly and immediately interferes with goods in the possession of another person.[1200] This interference can take a number of forms. It is a trespass wrongfully to

1189. *Dixon v. R* [2015] NZSC 147.
1190. *Kremen v. Cohen* 337 F 3d 1024 (9th Cir 2003). Other cases from the United States that deal with the tangibility or otherwise of software are described in *Dixon v. R* [2015] NZSC 147.
1191. *Hoath v. Connect Internet Services Pty Ltd* (2006) 229 ALR 566.
1192. *Blenheim Borough and Wairau River Board v. British Pavements (Canterbury) Ltd* [1940] NZLR 564.
1193. *Whenuapai Joinery (1988) Ltd v. Trust Bank Central Ltd* [1994] 1 NZLR 406.
1194. *Shattock v. Devlin* [1990] 2 NZLR 88.
1195. *R v. Kelly* [1999] QB 621 at 630.
1196. *In re Organ Retention Group Litigation* [2005] 2 WLR 358.
1197. *Doodeward v. Spence* (1908) 6 CLR 406.
1198. *Yearworth v. North Bristol NHS Trust* [2009] 3 WLR 118; and *see Re Edwards* [2011] NSWSC 478; *Holdich v. Lothian Health Board* 2014 SLT 495.
1199. *Re Lee* [2017] NZHC 3263, [2018] 2 NZLR 731.
1200. *Aitken Agencies v. Richardson* [1967] NZLR 65 at 66.

destroy goods or to damage them,[1201] to seize them,[1202] to move them from one place to another,[1203] to use them,[1204] or to immobilize them, at least where physical contact is involved.[1205] Whether it is trespass to touch goods without damaging them or immobilizing them is uncertain.[1206]

B. Intention or Negligence

214. It is possible that trespass can lie in the case of an unintentional but negligent act causing damage to the goods.[1207] But the better view, consistently with developments in relation to trespass to the person, is that trespass to goods is an intentional tort. So, negligent conduct damaging goods cannot be sued for as a trespass.[1208] The plaintiff's remedy in such a case is to bring an action in the ordinary way for negligence. However, the intention that must be shown is an intention to interfere with the goods in the requisite way, and it is immaterial that there is no intention to act wrongfully or culpably. So a tow truck driver who acted in good faith in towing away a car and delivering it to an unknown person following a hoax phone call was liable to the true owner for trespass.[1209] Tipping J said that tow truck operators, like auctioneers, dealt with the goods of others at their peril, and that the driver's absence of fault and his honest belief that the conduct was lawful were no defence.

C. Possession or Right to Possession

215. Trespass is a wrong to possession rather than to ownership. As a general rule the plaintiff must show that at the time of the wrongful act he or she had actual possession of the goods,[1210] although when possession is doubtful it is attached by law to the title.[1211] Possession involves two elements, namely an intention to possess the goods and the exercise of control over them to the exclusion of others.

1201. *Fouldes v. Willoughby* (1841) 8 M & W 540.
1202. *Jamieson's Tow and Salvage v. Murray* [1984] 2 NZLR 144.
1203. *Wilson v. New Brighton Panelbeaters Ltd* [1989] 1 NZLR 74.
1204. *Penfold Wines Pty Ltd v. Elliott* (1946) 74 CLR 204 at 214.
1205. *Police v. Krupinski* [1994] DCR 12 (wheel clamp on car).
1206. *Everitt v. Martin* [1953] NZLR 298; and *see Wilson v. New Brighton Panelbeaters Ltd* [1989] 1 NZLR 74 at 77.
1207. *Everitt v. Martin* [1953] NZLR 298 at 303 (no action for accidental contact where no damage, not decided whether action would lie on proof of damage); *Mayfair Ltd v. Pears* [1987] 1 NZLR 459 at 465.
1208. *National Coal Board v. J E Evans & Co. (Cardiff) Ltd* [1951] 2 KB 861.
1209. *Wilson v. New Brighton Panelbeaters Ltd* [1989] 1 NZLR 74. He was also liable for conversion: *see* para. 221.
1210. *Wilson v. New Brighton Panelbeaters Ltd* [1989] 1 NZLR 74 at 77.
1211. *Koppel v. Koppel* [1966] 1 WLR 802.

Accordingly, a person without possession of goods but with a right to possession cannot normally sue. In *Penfold Wines Pty Ltd v. Elliott*[1212] the appellant winemaker, who had sold wine to customers but had retained ownership of the bottles containing the wine, sought an injunction to prevent the respondent hotelkeeper from selling wine to buyers from his bulk supply by filling the appellant's bottles. The High Court of Australia held that an injunction should be refused. The appellant was not actually in possession of the bottles and could not maintain an action for trespass.

In certain exceptional cases a person with a right to possession may bring an action for trespass if goods are interfered with before the person takes possession. These include:

(1) a personal representative, where the interference occurs before probate or letters of administration are granted;[1213]
(2) a trustee of goods still in actual possession of the beneficiary;[1214] or
(3) the owner of a franchise, for example to take a wreck, who has yet to seize the goods.[1215]

In the case of a bailment of goods at will, the bailor is entitled to immediate possession, and both bailor and bailee may sue.[1216] But in the case of a bailment for consideration the bailee has the right to exclusive possession and must bring the action.[1217] The bailor may sue for damage to his or her reversionary proprietary interest, if any, but this is not an action for trespass.[1218]

III. Conversion

A. Nature of Conversion

216. The conversion of goods is conduct by the defendant that denies the plaintiff's possessory interest in or title to the goods. It has been said to have three essential features:

(1) the defendant's conduct is inconsistent with the rights of the owner or other person entitled to possession;
(2) the conduct is deliberate; and
(3) the conduct is so extensive an encroachment on the rights of the owner or other person as to exclude him or her from use and possession of the goods.[1219]

1212. (1946) 74 CLR 204.
1213. *Thorpe v. Stallwood* (1843) 5 Man & G 760, 134 ER 766.
1214. *White v. Morris* (1852) 11 CB 1015, 138 ER 778.
1215. *Bailiffs of Dunwich v. Sterry* (1831) 1 B & Ad 831, 109 ER 995.
1216. *Ward v. Macauley* (1789) 4 Term Rep 489, 100 ER 1135.
1217. *Ibid.*
1218. *East West Corporation v. DKBS AF 1912 A/S* [2003] 3 WLR 916.
1219. *Kuwait Airways Corporation v. Iraqi Airways Co. (Nos 4 & 5)* [2002] 2 AC 883 at 1084; *Glenmorgan Farm Ltd v. New Zealand Bloodstock Leasing Ltd* [2012] 1 NZLR 555 at [26]–[28].

The defendant must intend to do the act that is inconsistent with the plaintiff's right of possession, but there need not be knowledge by that person that the goods belong to someone else[1220] nor a positive intention to challenge the true owner's rights.[1221] It does not matter that a defendant acts in the honest belief that he or she has a right to the goods if, in fact, the defendant deals with them in a way that violates the plaintiff's rights. So there may be successive and independent conversions by a chain of innocent buyers and sellers, none of whom are aware of the true owner's rights.[1222] A physical taking of the goods is not necessary: it is a conversion to sign an order wrongfully authorizing the delivery of goods to another,[1223] or to make an invalid appointment of a receiver to deal with a debtor company's assets.[1224]

Conversion may take various, sometimes overlapping, forms. There may be conversion by taking possession of goods, by dealing with them, by detaining them, by misusing them, by disposing of them to another, and by receiving them.

1. Taking Possession

217. Taking possession of another's goods is conversion where the taking amounts to an assertion of dominion over them in a way that infringes the plaintiff's rights in relation to the goods.[1225] The defendant need not intend to keep the goods or to claim ownership: an intention to assert a right to temporary dominion where no such right exists may suffice. For example, the taking of a car for a joyride is conversion,[1226] as is the unjustified taking and holding of a vehicle until storage charges and removal costs are paid.[1227] But taking or dealing with goods without any assertion of dominion over them does not constitute conversion, as where the defendant merely put horses ashore from a ferry without making any claim to their possession.[1228] So too, no tort is committed by taking possession of found goods for safekeeping.[1229]

Taking possession of premises may be regarded as taking possession of goods on the premises if there was an intention to deprive the plaintiff of the right to possession or a substantial interference with that right.[1230] Refusing to allow the owner of

1220. *Wilson v. New Brighton Panelbeaters Ltd* [1989] 1 NZLR 74; *Central Acceptance Ltd v. Smith, Hughes and Robertson* [1992] 3 NZLR 413.
1221. *Blenheim Borough and Wairau River Board v. British Pavements (Canterbury) Ltd* [1940] NZLR 564; *Helson v. McKenzies (Cuba Street) Ltd* [1950] NZLR 878.
1222. *Elwin v. O'Regan & Maxwell* [1971] NZLR 1124.
1223. *Union Credit Bank v. Mersey Docks & Harbour Board* [1899] 2 QB 205.
1224. *Royal Bank of Canada v. W Got & Associates Electric Ltd* [1999] 3 SCR 408.
1225. *Cuff v. Broadlands Finance Ltd* [1987] 2 NZLR 343.
1226. *Aitken Agencies Ltd v. Richardson* [1967] NZLR 65.
1227. *Wellington City v. Singh* [1971] NZLR 1025.
1228. *Fouldes v. Willoughby* (1841) 8 M & W 540, 151 ER 1153; and *see Marshall v. Dibble* [1920] NZLR 497; *McKaskell v. Benseman* [1989] 3 NZLR 75 at 89.
1229. *Helson v. McKenzies (Cuba Street) Ltd* [1950] NZLR 878.
1230. *Oakley v. Lister* [1931] 1 KB 148.

goods to enter land to retrieve them can be a taking if the occupier is setting up for himself or herself a right in respect of the goods or denying the right of the plaintiff.[1231]

2. Dealing

218. Physical possession of goods or physical dealing with goods is not necessary. There can be conversion by dealing with goods as owner without actual possession. Examples are: a wrongful sale to a purchaser already in possession;[1232] signing an order authorizing the delivery of goods to another;[1233] and selling and taking a sale back of hired goods remaining in the possession of the hirer.[1234]

3. Detaining

219. The wrongful detention of goods gives rise to an action for detinue.[1235] But conversion also is committed by detaining goods in such a way as to amount to a denial of the plaintiff's right to immediate possession.[1236] Merely having custody of goods is not sufficient: there must be some act amounting to an assertion of dominion that is inconsistent with the plaintiff's rights. The normal method of establishing a wrongful detention of goods is to show that the defendant refused a demand for their return. However, at the time of refusal the party must have it in his or her power to deliver up the chattel, and there is no conversion if a bailee cannot deliver because he or she has allowed goods to be lost or destroyed in breach of duty to the bailor.[1237] If the bailee has intentionally disposed of the goods to another then he or she is liable for that earlier disposal.[1238]

It is not necessarily unlawful to refuse to hand over goods immediately that a demand is made. The person detaining the goods is entitled to inquire into the right of the person claiming them. In this case the person withholding the goods is not denying the plaintiff's interest, but is seeking to ascertain that the plaintiff is justified in demanding them.[1239] Again, goods that have been lawfully seized by the police may be retained for the time necessary for any relevant investigation or prosecution, but must be returned once that time has expired.[1240]

1231. *Oakley v. Lister* [1931] 1 KB 148; *Howard E Perry & Co. Ltd v. British Railways Board* [1980] 1 WLR 1375.
1232. *Van Oppen & Co. Ltd v. Tredegars Ltd* (1921) 37 TLR 504.
1233. *Union Credit Bank v. Mersey Docks and Harbour Board* [1899] 2 QB 205.
1234. *Douglas Valley Finance Co. Ltd v. S Hughes (Hirers) Ltd* [1969] 1 QB 738.
1235. *See* para. 239.
1236. *Cuff v. Broadlands Finance Ltd* [1987] 2 NZLR 343 at 346.
1237. *Alicia Hosiery Ltd v. Brown Shipley & Co. Ltd* [1970] 1 QB 195.
1238. *General and Finance Facilities Ltd v. Cooks Cars (Romford) Ltd* [1963] 1 WLR 644 at 649.
1239. *EE McCurdy Ltd v. Postmaster-General* [1959] NZLR 553.
1240. *Webb v. Chief Constable of Merseyside* [2000] 1 All ER 209; *Costello v. Chief Constable of Derbyshire Constabulary* [2001] 2 Lloyd's Rep. 216.

4. Destroying or Misusing

220. The wilful destruction of goods is conversion, because the plaintiff can no longer possess the goods or exercise his or her rights over them, and so is abusing the possession of goods leading to their loss in some other way.[1241] It is conversion to change the quality of goods so that they cannot be restored to the plaintiff in their original form, such as by adding water to wine.[1242] Misusing goods may sometimes be conversion, where the conduct is calculated to impair the plaintiff's right of possession. For example, a majority in the High Court of Australia thought that the defendant filling the plaintiff's bottles with his own wine was conversion, although in all the circumstances the remedy of an injunction was refused.[1243] A wilful act that damages goods without destroying them is actionable as a trespass, and a negligent act that destroys or damages goods is actionable in negligence.

5. Disposing to Another

221. Whether a disposal or purported disposal of the plaintiff's goods to another amounts to conversion depends upon the effect of the transaction on the plaintiff's interest. Delivering the plaintiff's goods to a person who is not entitled to them is conversion, for this denies the plaintiff's right of dominion over the goods. So a shop that handed over a customer's bag to a stranger without checking the stranger's right to it was liable,[1244] and so was a towing firm that innocently delivered a car to a thief.[1245] However, an innocent transferor who merely acts ministerially is excused.[1246] For example, a warehouseman was not liable for restoring goods to a depositor,[1247] nor a carrier for delivering them to the consignee.[1248] Auctioneers who effect a contract of sale are liable;[1249] but, in a borderline case, auctioneers who innocently took possession of a stolen painting, tried to sell it and then returned it to the person who supplied it were acting simply as ministerial agents.[1250]

A mere agreement to sell the plaintiff's goods that is not accompanied by delivery is not normally conversion because the agreement passes no property in the goods and the plaintiff's right of possession is unaffected. But if the purported sale is accompanied by delivery of the goods, then there is an interference with the plaintiff's right of possession and both seller and buyer are liable.[1251] A similar rule can apply if the defendant allows a third person to gain possession of the plaintiff's

1241. *Moorgate Mercantile Co. Ltd v. Finch* [1962] 1 QB 701 (car carrying smuggled watches forfeited by customs).
1242. *Richardson v. Atkinson* (1723) 1 Stra 576, 93 ER 710.
1243. *Penfold Wines Pty Ltd v. Elliott* (1946) 74 CLR 204.
1244. *Helson v. McKenzies (Cuba Street) Ltd* [1950] NZLR 878.
1245. *Wilson v. New Brighton Panelbeaters Ltd* [1989] 1 NZLR 74.
1246. *Hollins v. Fowler* (1875) LR 7 HL 757.
1247. *Ibid.*
1248. *Re Samuel (No. 2)* [1945] Ch 408.
1249. *RH Willis & Son v. British Car Auctions* [1978] 1 WLR 438.
1250. *Marcq v. Christie Manson & Woods Ltd* [2003] 3 All ER 561.
1251. *Coleman v. Harvey* [1989] 1 NZLR 723 at 729.

goods. So an occupier that purported to sell property on its land belonging to the plaintiff, and then allowed the third-party purchaser to remove it, was liable for converting the property.[1252]

Furthermore, an agreement to sell without delivery may give rise to liability for conversion if the buyer obtains a good title, for then the owner's right of possession is impaired. Normally the maxim *nemo dat quod non habet* applies – the unauthorized seller cannot transfer a title where he or she has no title to transfer, so the original owner's rights prevail over those of any innocent transferee.[1253] But there are a number of statutory exceptions to the *nemo dat* rule, when the innocent third party obtains a good title to the goods.[1254] In this case the seller is liable, but not the buyer.[1255]

6. Receiving

222. Receiving another's goods is conversion where the receiving amounts to an assumption of dominion over the goods that is inconsistent with that of the true owner. Knowledge of the plaintiff's interest is not necessary so long as the act in question amounts to a denial of that interest. So an innocent transferee who gives value may be liable for conversion at the suit of the owner.[1256] But, again, the innocent purchaser is not liable if one of the exceptions to the maxim *nemo dat quod non habet* applies, and he or she gets a good title to the goods.

Innocently finding goods is not conversion if there is no assertion of a right contrary to that of the owner. There must be a demand and a refusal to return or some other act inconsistent with the owner's rights.[1257] Seemingly, a finder should at least take reasonable steps to inform the true owner of the finding.[1258]

Involuntary receipt of goods is not conversion. In the case of unsolicited goods, the recipient is not bound to pay for them unless he or she causes their loss or damage by a deliberate act.[1259] Indeed, the recipient acquires the rights of ownership and immunity from claims by the sender after the goods have remained in the recipient's possession for ten days, or the sender has failed to inform the recipient of the recipient's statutory rights and obligations in relation to the goods.[1260]

1252. *Smith v. Bridgend County Borough Council* [2002] 1 AC 336.
1253. *Elwin v. O'Regan & Maxwell* [1971] NZLR 1124.
1254. *See* para. 224.
1255. *Coleman v. Harvey* [1989] 1 NZLR 723 at 729.
1256. *Nash v. Barnes* [1922] NZLR 303.
1257. *Spackman v. Foster* (1883) 11 QBD 99; *Miller v. O'Dell* [1891] 1 QB 468.
1258. *Tamworth Industries Ltd v. Attorney-General* [1991] 3 NZLR 616.
1259. Fair Trading Act 1986, s. 21A.
1260. *Ibid.*

B. The Nemo Dat *Rule*

1. General

223. The principle that a person who receives another's goods is guilty of conversion even where the person's conduct is quite innocent reflects the operation of the maxim *nemo dat quod non habet* – no one may give what he or she does not possess. This is a 'fundamental principle' of the common law relating to the transfer of property in chattels.[1261] So, on the application of this principle, an unauthorized disposition of goods is of no effect, and a purchaser cannot take a title the vendor does not possess. But there are a number of statutory exceptions to the *nemo dat* rule, and where one of these exceptions applies the original owner loses his or her title, and a good title is vested in the innocent third party. These exceptions are founded on the premise that in cases where an owner has done something to give the appearance that the seller was entitled to sell them, the innocent third party ought to be protected. So in these circumstances the person receiving the goods is not guilty of conversion.

2. Exceptions to the Rule

224. The exceptions to the *nemo dat* rule are as follows.

a. Estoppel

225. The true owner may be precluded from denying the seller's authority to sell.[1262] The basis for this exception is estoppel. For example, the owner may represent to a third party, expressly or impliedly, that another has the right to deal with the goods.[1263] However, mere inaction or silence will not usually constitute conduct that can give rise to an estoppel.[1264]

b. Sale by Mercantile Agent

226. A sale in the ordinary course of business of a mercantile agent who is in possession of goods with the consent of the owner confers a good title on a purchaser who takes in good faith without notice of any lack of authority of the agent.[1265]

1261. *GE Capital Bank Ltd v. Rushton* [2006] 1 WLR 899 at 901.
1262. Contract and Commercial Law Act 2017, s. 149(2).
1263. *New Zealand Securities and Finance Ltd v. Wrightcars Ltd* [1976] 1 NZLR 77.
1264. *Moorgate Mercantile Co. Ltd v. Twitchings* [1977] AC 890.
1265. Contract and Commercial Law Act 2017, s. 297. By s. 296, a mercantile agent is an agent having in the ordinary course of the agent's business as an agent authority either to sell goods, or to consign goods for the purpose of sale, or to buy goods, or to raise money on the security of goods. By s. 298, if the goods are subject to a perfected security interest under the Personal Property

c. Sale under a Voidable Title

227. Where a seller of goods has a voidable title, but the title has not been avoided at the time of sale, the buyer acquires a good title to the goods, provided the buyer buys them in good faith and without notice of the seller's defect of title.[1266] So where a contract is voidable for fraud, but the fraudulent buyer resells the goods before the original owner avoids the sale, the innocent buyer gets a good title.[1267]

Many of the cases involve fraudulent buyers who either give a fictitious identity or impersonate another, real, person. Where the seller intends to deal with the particular buyer with whom he or she is dealing, whoever he or she may be, a voidable contract comes into existence notwithstanding the seller's fraudulently induced mistake about the buyer's creditworthiness.[1268] Conversely, where the seller intends to deal only with the person who the fraudulent party purported to be, so there is a mistake as to the identity of the purchaser, the original sale is void *ab initio* and a later innocent purchaser stands in no better position than the fraudster.[1269]

d. Seller in Possession

228. A seller who continues in possession of goods after selling them can pass a good title to a second purchaser who takes in good faith without notice of the previous sale.[1270] The exception can apply even where the seller in possession sells the goods in circumstances amounting to theft from the first buyer.[1271]

e. Buyer in Possession

229. Where a seller retains property in goods, but a buyer obtains possession of the goods with the consent of the seller, then a sale to an innocent third person who takes without notice of the original seller's rights has the same effect as if the person making the delivery or transfer were a mercantile agent in possession of the goods with the consent of the owner.[1272] This exception operates to validate a sale as if the buyer in possession were a mercantile agent: it does not require that his

---

Securities Act 1999, the person taking under the disposition is deemed to have notice of the mercantile agent's lack of authority, unless it is proved that the authority did exist; and *see* further para. 231.

1266. Contract and Commercial Law Act 2017, s. 151.

1267. *Jeffcott v. Andrew Motors* [1960] NZLR 721. An owner who cannot communicate with a fraudulent party must take all reasonable steps to avoid the sale: *Car and Universal Finance Co. Ltd v. Caldwell* [1965] 1 QB 525.

1268. *Lewis v. Averay* [1972] 1 QB 198.

1269. *Shogun Finance Ltd v. Hudson* [2004] 1 AC 919.

1270. Contract and Commercial Law Act 2017, s. 153(1) and (2). The rule does not apply to the delivery of goods by a person who has possession with the consent of the holder of a security interest in the goods which has been perfected under the Personal Property Securities Act 1999; s. 153(3); and *see* further para. 231.

1271. *Sigglekow v. Gibbs* [1990] 3 NZLR 503.

1272. Contract and Commercial Law Act 2017, s. 154(1) and (2). The rule does not apply in the case of a delivery of goods by a person who has possession of them with the consent of the holder of a perfected security interest; s. 154(4); and *see* further para. 231.

conduct be that of a mercantile agent.[1273] The words 'consent of the owner' have been interpreted as meaning 'consent of the seller', for otherwise a title could come into existence as goods passed along a chain of buyers even though no title passed at the time of the first sale.[1274]

f. Special Powers of Sale

230. Nothing in the Contract and Commercial Law Act 2017 affects the validity of any sale under a special common law or statutory power of sale or the order of a Court of competent jurisdiction.[1275] There are many statutes conferring powers of sale on persons such as District Court registrars and bailiffs, sheriffs, pawnbrokers, and others.

3. Personal Property Securities Act 1999

231. The exceptions to the *nemo dat* regime do not apply to goods that are subject to a perfected security interest under the Personal Property Securities Act 1999 (PPSA). This Act creates a broad and comprehensive system relating to security interests in personal property, including the creation and enforceability of security interests, the determination of priority among security interests and between security interests and other interests and the enforcement of security interests (other than in consumer goods). The PPSA provides for the creation of an electronic register of security interests and deals with the method and effect of registration of those interests. The result is a scheme of uniform rules for all security interests in personal property. The details are beyond the scope of this work.[1276]

C. Possession or Right of Possession

1. General

232. An action for conversion lies at the suit of one who has actual possession or the right of possession of the goods at the time of the act of conversion.[1277] Frequently, of course, the person with a proprietary right to goods also has possession of them. But an owner out of possession and with no right to possession cannot sue. For example, a seller who wrongfully repossessed goods that were taken on hire

---

1273. *Jeffcot v. Andrew Motors Ltd* [1960] NZLR 721.
1274. *Elwin v. O'Regan and Maxwell* [1971] NZLR 1124; *National Employers Mutual General Insurance Association Ltd v. Jones* [1990] AC 24.
1275. Contract and Commercial Law Act 2017, s. 149(4)(b).
1276. *See* further Holderness (ed.), *Introduction to Commercial Law in New Zealand* (5th ed., Wellington: LexisNexis, 2016), Chs 25, 26 (by Scragg).
1277. *Clayton v. Morrison* (1873) 1 NZ Jur 15 at 18; *Whenuapai Joinery (1988) Ltd v. Trust Bank Central Ltd* [1994] 1 NZLR 406.

purchase was liable in conversion to the buyer;[1278] a seller of joinery fitted on mortgaged property who had retained title to the joinery under a *Romalpa* clause[1279] was liable to the mortgagee for removing the joinery from the property, for the mortgagee had the right to immediate possession;[1280] and an unpaid seller with a lien over goods had the right to possession and therefore the right to exclude the buyer from possession until payment was made.[1281]

An owner without possession has a separate action for damage to his or her reversionary proprietary interest in goods.[1282] But where a bailee repaired a bailor's goods, the bailor's claim against the person who damaged them failed because there had been no permanent damage to the bailor's reversionary proprietary interest.[1283]

2. Finders

233. A person who finds goods that are not in the possession of another acquires a possessory right that is good against all save the true owner.[1284] But sometimes the occupier of land where a chattel is found may be regarded as the possessor, as where the chattel is buried in or attached to the land,[1285] or the occupier has clearly manifested an intention to exercise control over things in or on the land.[1286] The occupier also has a better right as against a finder who is trespassing or acting with dishonest intent.[1287]

3. Bailed Goods

234. In the case of a gratuitous bailment either bailor or bailee can sue, for the one has the right to possession and the other the actual possession;[1288] but where the bailment is for a fixed term that has not expired, only the bailee can sue, and can recover full damages as if he or she were the owner.[1289] If the bailee recovers more than represents his or her own interest in the goods bailed, he or she holds the surplus as trustee for the bailor.[1290]

1278. *Harris v. Lombard New Zealand Ltd* [1974] 2 NZLR 161.
1279. *Aluminium Industrie Vaasen BV v. Romalpa Aluminium Ltd* [1976] 1 WLR 676.
1280. *Whenuapai Joinery (1988) Ltd v. Trust Bank Central Ltd* [1994] 1 NZLR 406.
1281. *Coxhead v. Dwyer* [2015] NZAR 1335.
1282. *Checker Taxicab Co. Ltd v. Stone* [1930] NZLR 169; *East West Corporation v. DKBS AF 1912 A/S* [2003] 3 WLR 916.
1283. *HSBC Rail (UK) Ltd v. Network Rail Infrastructure Ltd* [2006] 1 WLR 643.
1284. *Helson v. McKenzies (Cuba Street) Ltd* [1950] NZLR 878.
1285. *Elwes v. Brigg Gas Co.* (1886) 33 Ch D 562.
1286. *Parker v. British Airways Board* [1982] QB 1004; *Tamworth Industries Ltd v. Attorney-General* [1991] 3 NZLR 616.
1287. *Parker v. British Airways Board* [1982] QB 1004.
1288. *Manders v. Williams* (1949) 4 Exch. 339, 154 ER 1242.
1289. *The Winkfield* [1902] P 42.
1290. *NZ Securities & Finance Ltd v. Wrightcars Ltd* [1976] 1 NZLR 77.

4. Co-owners

235. A co-owner can bring an action for the whole value of the goods. Where it is another co-owner who is guilty of conversion, he or she may be sued by the innocent co-owner.[1291]

5. Owner's Wrongdoing

236. Seemingly a person who acquires property as a result of unlawful conduct may still maintain a claim for conversion, relying on his or proprietary interest and right to possession of the property. So in the absence of a statutory power of forfeiture, a person who acquired money as a result of illegal contracts for the sale of drugs could assert a proprietary right to the money.[1292] Again, the possessor of a stolen car the true owner of which was unknown could recover it from the police, who had lawfully seized it, on the ground that the 'frail' possessory title was still deserving of protection.[1293] However, where the sole basis of a claim is previous possession by a dishonest claimant, it is strongly arguable that police in actual possession of goods after an honest taking have the better right.[1294]

The above principles apply subject to the statutory powers of the police to seize and detain stolen goods or goods used in connection with the commission of a criminal offence.[1295] No action for conversion or detinue will lie where goods are detained pursuant to these powers.

D. Remedies

1. Damages

237. The purpose of the action for conversion is to provide just compensation for the loss that has been suffered. The principles to be applied were discussed by the House of Lords in *Kuwait Airways Corporation v. Iraqi Airways Co. (Nos 4 & 5)*,[1296] where Lord Nicholls maintained that the plaintiff should recover his or her 'true loss'. A twofold inquiry was necessary. The first question was whether the defendant's wrongful conduct contributed to the loss. Normally the 'but for' test should be applied, but this could be over-exclusionary in cases where more than one wrongdoer was involved.[1297] Where there were successive conversions, as in the instant case, the test called for a comparison between the owner's position had he

1291. *Coleman v. Harvey* [1989] 1 NZLR 723.

1292. *R v. Collis* [1990] 2 NZLR 287; *Tamworth Industries Ltd v. Attorney-General* [1991] 3 NZLR 616; *Webb v. Chief Constable of Merseyside* [2000] 1 All ER 209.

1293. *Costello v. Chief Constable of Derbyside Constabulary* [2001] 2 Lloyd's Rep. 216.

1294. *Buckley v. Gross* (1863) 3 B & S 566.

1295. *See*, in particular, the Summary Proceedings Act 1957, s. 199; Proceeds of Crime Act 1991, ss 36–37.

1296. [2002] 2 AC 883.

1297. *See* para. 524.

or she retained the goods and the position he or she was in, as a result of being deprived by the defendant of the goods. So, loss that would have been suffered had the owner retained the goods would not be caused by the conversion.[1298] The second question was the extent of the loss for which the defendant ought to be liable. The normal measure of damages was the value of the goods at the date when they were converted. But the measure of damages ultimately is a question of fact. In *Gardiner v. Metcalfe*[1299] the Court of Appeal recognized that there is no universally applicable rule, and the court seeks to determine what is the actual loss suffered by the plaintiff.

Where the normal measure applies, the 'value' of the goods is determined by reference to their market value at the time and place of their conversion.[1300] Changes in market value after the date of the conversion normally are not taken into account. The plaintiff must take reasonable steps in mitigation of the loss. If the plaintiff knew or should have known that the conversion had occurred or was about to occur, he or she should act to prevent it or should promptly make his or her claim.[1301]

Where the defendant makes improvements to converted goods, he or she is entitled to the value of the improvements, whether they were made before or after the conversion and whether the defendant is the original converter or an innocent purchaser.[1302] So the owner of a converted car could recover only its value at the date of conversion, not its increased value consequent upon work done by an innocent purchaser.[1303] And where a purchaser adds accessories to converted goods, he or she is entitled to their return or compensation for their value, unless the added items are mixed inextricably with the goods and cannot be detached from them.[1304]

Consequential damage that is not too remote also is recoverable. In the *Kuwait Airways* case, Lord Nicholls noted that conversion could be committed either dishonestly or innocently, and it was inappropriate to treat all defendants alike. Foreseeability of the damage was the appropriate test in cases where the defendant acted in good faith, while consequences that were direct and natural could be recovered where the defendant was guilty of dishonesty. Whether the courts in New Zealand will take this approach has not been determined.[1305]

Assuming the test of remoteness is satisfied, the plaintiff can recover general damages for detention, inconvenience, and annoyance.[1306] Special damage also may be recoverable, such as the cost of hiring a substitute for the goods during the period

1298. *See also Glenmorgan Farm Ltd v. New Zealand Bloodstock Leasing Ltd* [2012] 1 NZLR 555 (seizure of stallion by creditor from lessee, even if unlawful, did not cause loss as a default by the lessee and a sale by the receiver was inevitable).

1299. [1994] 2 NZLR 8 at 12.

1300. *Gardiner v. Metcalfe* [1994] 2 NZLR 8; *Campbell v. Dominion Breweries Ltd* [1994] 3 NZLR 559.

1301. *Sachs v. Miklos* [1948] 2 KB 23.

1302. *Nash v. Barnes* [1922] NZLR 303.

1303. *Ibid.*

1304. *Thomas v. Robinson* [1977] 1 NZLR 385.

1305. There is some support for foreseeability in *Gardiner v. Metcalfe* [1994] 2 NZLR 8 at 10; and *see* further para. 547.

1306. *Harris v. Lombard New Zealand Ltd* [1974] 2 NZLR 161 at 169–170; *Jamieson's Tow & Salvage Ltd v. Murray* [1984] 2 NZLR 144.

of detention.[1307] If the plaintiff used the goods for the purposes of trade then the defendant may be liable for loss of profits.[1308] And where the plaintiff cannot show actual loss of earnings, he or she may still recover general damages for loss of use of a commercial asset.[1309] The damages are for being deprived of the goods, and it is irrelevant that the plaintiff did not in fact use or intend to use them.[1310] If the wrongdoer has obtained a benefit from their use, damages may be assessed by reference to the benefit irrespective of whether the owner has suffered financial loss.[1311]

A person in possession but with only a limited interest in goods can recover their full value.[1312] However, where the person being sued also has an interest in the goods, the plaintiff with a limited interest may recover only the value of his or her interest.[1313]

Where goods are restored to the owner when a claim for conversion is brought, the owner must give credit for their value.[1314] However, the plaintiff is not obliged to accept them unless they are in the same condition in which they were converted.[1315]

2. Restitution

238. Specific restitution of goods is a remedy that is available at the discretion of the court in the case of an action in detinue.[1316] Seemingly, it also is available in the case of an action for conversion. If there is no order for restitution, once an order for damages is satisfied, the title to the goods vests in the defendant.[1317]

IV. Detinue

A. Nature of Detinue

239. The essence of the cause of action in detinue is a wrongful detention consciously adverse to the rights of the owner.[1318] It is not detinue merely to keep possession of another's goods, as where a finder takes possession or a bailee holds over

---

1307. *Aitken Agencies Ltd v. Richardson* [1967] NZLR 65; *Kuwait Airways Corporation v. Iraqi Airways Co. (Nos 4 & 5)* [2002] 2 AC 883.
1308. *Mrs Eaton's Car Sales Ltd v. Thomasen* [1973] 2 NZLR 686.
1309. *Greig v. Tasman Rental Cars Ltd* [1982] 2 NZLR 171; *Newmans Coach Lines Ltd v. Robertshawe* [1984] 1 NZLR 53; *see* further para. 555.
1310. *The Mediana* [1900] AC 113 at 117.
1311. *Kuwait Airways Corporation v. Iraqi Airways Co. (Nos 4 & 5)* [2002] 2 AC 883 at 1094.
1312. *The Winkfield* [1902] P 42.
1313. *Campbell v. Dominion Breweries Ltd* [1994] 3 NZLR 559.
1314. *Aitken Agencies Ltd v. Richardson* [1967] NZLR 65 at 67.
1315. *Moon v. Raphael* (1835) 2 Bing NC 310, 132 ER 122.
1316. *See* para. 242.
1317. Ex parte *Drake, re Ware* (1877) 5 Ch D 866.
1318. *E E McCurdy Ltd v. Postmaster-General* [1959] NZLR 553 at 556.

after the period of the bailment has expired.[1319] Rather, the possessor must in some way manifest an intention to exclude the owner. This can be established by proof that the person entitled to the goods made a demand for their return, and the person in possession refused or failed to comply with the demand.[1320] The demand should be specific and its refusal categorical and unqualified. The person in possession of the goods does not necessarily act unlawfully in refusing immediately to return them. For example, in cases where there are conflicting claims, the possessor is entitled to adequate time to inquire into the rights of the claimants.[1321] But a refusal is wrongful where the possessor refuses to deliver on the ground of an unsubstantiated claim of right by another.[1322]

A demand and refusal arguably is a condition precedent to an action in detinue.[1323] But in nearly every case, the conduct will also amount to conversion, which can be established by evidence showing the defendant's intent to retain the goods as against the person rightfully entitled. A demand and a refusal to comply is the usual, but not the only, way of showing that intent.[1324]

B. Possession or Right of Possession

240. A claim in conversion depends on the plaintiff having possession or the right to possession of goods. However, there is authority that, as regards a claim for detinue, the person with a right to possession must also have had a right of property in the goods.[1325] Yet there is no decision actually denying a claim in detinue by a plaintiff with only a possessory right, nor does there seem to be any compelling reason why the rule in detinue should differ from that in conversion. In any event, it is clear that the plaintiff's property need not be absolute, and an immediate right of possession arising from some special property in the goods can suffice. So, for example, a co-owner,[1326] a bailee,[1327] a finder,[1328] and a person with a lien over goods,[1329] can all sue both for conversion and for detinue.

1319. *Central Acceptance Ltd v. Smith Hughes & Robertson* [1992] 3 NZLR 413 at 416.
1320. *E E McCurdy Ltd v. Postmaster-General* [1959] NZLR 553 at 556.
1321. *E E McCurdy Ltd v. Postmaster-General* [1959] NZLR 553; *Central Acceptance Ltd v. Smith Hughes & Robertson* [1992] 3 NZLR 413 at 416.
1322. *Redler Grain Silos Ltd v. BICC Ltd* [1982] 1 Lloyd's Rep. 435.
1323. *Clayton v. Le Roy* [1911] 2 KB 1031 at 1048.
1324. *Cuff v. Broadlands Finance Ltd* [1987] 2 NZLR 343.
1325. *Harris v. Lombard New Zealand Ltd* [1974] 2 NZLR 161 at 166; *Berg v. Anglo Pacific International (1988) Ltd* (1988) 1 PRNZ 713 at 716.
1326. *Coleman v. Harvey* [1989] 1 NZLR 723; *Coxhead v. Dwyer* [2015] NZAR 1335.
1327. *Jarvis v. Williams* [1955] 1 WLR 71.
1328. *Kowal v. Ellis* (1977) 76 DLR (3d) 546.
1329. *Rogers v. Kennay* (1846) 9 QB 592, 115 ER 1401.

C. *Remedies*

1. Damages

241. The cause of action in detinue accrues at the date of the wrongful refusal to deliver up the goods and continues to accrue until the goods are delivered up or judgment is obtained. The normal measure of *damages* is the value of the goods together with damages for additional loss caused by their detention. They may include the cost of hiring a substitute, and profits that would have been earned from the goods.[1330] If the goods have been returned, the plaintiff must give credit for their value, including any added value from improvements.[1331] Damages for the detention itself will be nominal if the plaintiff has suffered nothing except the bare denial of a right that is sufficiently vindicated by success in the action.[1332]

2. Restitution

242. An owner has no absolute right to recover possession of the goods. Rather, the court has a discretionary equitable jurisdiction to decree the specific restitution of a chattel.[1333] An order is unlikely to be made if the chattel is an ordinary article of commerce that can easily be replaced in the market, where damages will constitute an adequate remedy.[1334] Again, no order will be made where this would cause injustice to the defendant, as where an innocent defendant had spent a lot of money on improving the goods.[1335] Generally, in cases where goods have been altered or mixed together, the court awards possession to the person who in justice is thought to be entitled, and awards compensation in money to the other.[1336]

V. Defences

A. *General*

243. Certain self-help remedies can operate as defences to claims for interference with goods. These include defence of property,[1337] recaption of chattels,[1338] distress damage feasant,[1339] and impounding of straying stock.[1340]

1330. *Gaba Formwork Contractors Pty Ltd v. Turner* (1993) 32 NSWLR 175.
1331. *Thomas v. Robinson* [1977] 1 NZLR 385.
1332. *Williams v. The Peel River Land and Mineral Co. Ltd* (1886) 55 LT 689.
1333. *Nash v. Barnes* [1922] NZLR 303 at 309.
1334. *Cohen v. Roche* [1927] 1 KB 169; *Howard E Perry & Co. Ltd v. British Railways Board* [1980] 1 WLR 1375.
1335. *Nash v. Barnes* [1922] NZLR 303.
1336. *Ibid.*, at 308.
1337. *See* para. 503.
1338. *See* para. 504.
1339. *See* para. 505.
1340. *See* para. 506.

It is a defence to show that the plaintiff consented to the defendant taking the goods,[1341] or, perhaps, was guilty of contributory negligence.[1342] Goods also may be seized and detained pursuant to powers conferred by statute. Examples are where goods are seized by the police on the authority of a search warrant or other court order,[1343] or, in certain circumstances, by customs officers carrying out a lawful search.[1344]

B. Jus Tertii

244. The defendant may not set up as a defence to a claim that the title to the goods is in some third party. In other words, the defendant cannot claim the *jus tertii*, the right of a third person, in answer to a claim brought by the person in or entitled to possession.[1345] That right generally is not a concern of the defendant where the plaintiff is asserting a right to retain possession as against the defendant.[1346] However, an exception, based on ordinary agency principles, is where the defendant acted with the authority of the true owner in committing the act in question or defending the action. Again, while a bailee generally cannot deny the bailor's title, the bailee nonetheless can defend on behalf of, or with the authority of the true owner,[1347] or by showing that he or she has been evicted by the true owner.[1348]

§4. Interference with Intellectual Property

I. Introduction

245. A person's rights in intellectual property are protected both by the principles of common law and equity and, very significantly, by statute. At common law the tort of passing off gives a remedy in respect of wrongful interference with business goodwill. Such interference may also give rise to an action for misleading or deceptive conduct in breach of the Fair Trading Act 1986, which overlaps very considerably with the common law action. A further action requiring mention in this context is the action (founded in equity) that gives protection in respect of misuse or misappropriation of the plaintiff's confidential information.

In addition to the position at common law and in equity, a number of statutes confer and protect rights in some form of intellectual property. Such rights include

1341. *Fielding Loan and Investment Co. Ltd v. Kelly* [1931] GLR 298; and *see ParkingEye Ltd v. Beavis* [2016] AC 1172 (consent by parking on land with knowledge of a notice that warns of the risk of a charge for overstaying).
1342. *Helson v. McKenzies (Cuba Street) Ltd* [1950] NZLR 878; but cp *Standard Chartered Bank v. Pakistan National Shipping Corporation* [2003] 1 AC 959; *see* para. 478.
1343. Summary Proceedings Act 1957, s. 199.
1344. Customs and Excise Act 1966, s. 166.
1345. *Knight v. National Mortgage and Agency Co.* [1920] NZLR 748 at 759; *Hansard v. Tame* [1957] NZLR 542.
1346. *Berg v. Anglo Pacific International (1988) Ltd* (1988) 1 PRNZ 713 at 716.
1347. *Berg v. Anglo Pacific International (1988) Ltd* (1988) 1 PRNZ 713.
1348. *Wilson v. Lombank Ltd* [1963] 1 WLR 1294.

copyright in various forms of works (Copyright Act 1994); designs, by registration, provided they relate to the appearance and not function of an article (Designs Act 1953); patents, again by registration, for inventions (Patents Act 1953); and, by registration, trademarks relating to goods and services (Trade Marks Act 2002).[1349] In all these areas, infringement of the proprietor's property rights created by the statute gives rise to a right of action for that proprietor that is in many respects akin to an action for passing off, and on the facts of individual cases will often overlap with, and be pleaded in the alternative to, such an action. Such overlap is particularly likely to occur with an action for infringement under the Trade Marks Act.

II. Passing Off

A. General

246. In *Erven Warnink BV v. J Townend & Sons (Hull) Ltd* (the *Advocaat*),[1350] Lord Diplock identified the elements that need to be established to give rise to a cause of action for passing off as:

> (1) a misrepresentation, (2) made by a trader in the course of trade, (3) to prospective customers of his or ultimate consumers of goods or services supplied by him, (4) which is calculated to injure the business or goodwill of another trader (in the sense that this is a reasonably foreseeable consequence), and (5) which causes actual damage to a business or goodwill of the trader by whom the action is brought or (in a quia timet action) will probably do so.

These requirements have been recognized in a number of cases in New Zealand as describing the elements necessary for establishing liability in the modern form of the action.[1351]

Broadly speaking, there is passing off where the defendant claims that his or her goods or services are those of the plaintiff, and in this way seeks improperly to appropriate and to benefit from the plaintiff's goodwill.[1352] Examples include: copying a business name[1353] or Internet domain name,[1354] copying the name of a

1349. *See* generally Frankel, *Intellectual Property in New Zealand* (2nd ed., Wellington: LexisNexis, 2011); *Intellectual Property in New Zealand: Copyright and Design* (Wellington: LexisNexis) (looseleaf).

1350. [1979] AC 731.

1351. *Dominion Rent A Car Ltd v. Budget Rent A Car Systems (1970) Ltd* [1987] 2 NZLR 395; *Klissers Farmhouse Bakeries Ltd v. Harvest Bakeries Ltd (No. 2)* [1985] 2 NZLR 143; *Taylor Bros Ltd v. Taylors Group Ltd* [1988] 2 NZLR 1.

1352. There may also be 'reverse' passing off, where the defendant claims that the plaintiff's goods are his: *Holdfast New Zealand Ltd v. Mechanical Plastics Corporation* [2013] NZCA 335.

1353. For example, *Patience & Nicholson (NZ) Ltd v. Cyclone Hardware Pty Ltd* [2001] 3 NZLR 490 (HC & CA), and *Resene Paints Ltd v. Orica New Zealand Ltd* [2003] 3 NZLR 709. Registration of company name under the Companies Act 1993, s. 22, does not preclude a civil action by another for passing off: *see The Paint Factory Ltd v. Registrar of Companies* [2000] 3 NZLR 220.

1354. For example, *British Telecommunications plc v. One in a Million Ltd* [1999] 1 WLR 903; *Containerlift Services Ltd v. Maxwell Rotors Ltd* (2003) 10 TCLR 807; *Tesco Stores Ltd v. Elogicom Ltd* [2007] FSR 83.

professional association[1355] or of a charity,[1356] copying the name of an author or an artist,[1357] copying the get-up of the goods of another,[1358] claiming special characteristics or attributes of the good of another,[1359] making false associations with another's business,[1360] and enabling the deception of ultimate consumers via intermediaries.[1361] These various cases well illustrate the truth of Lord Diplock's statement in *Erven Warnink*, that passing off is the 'most protean' of the forms that actionable unfair trading can take in English (or, semble, New Zealand) law.[1362]

B. Plaintiff's Protectable Interest

247. The plaintiff is entitled to protect his or her intangible right of property in the business or goodwill likely to be injured by the misrepresentation.[1363] 'Goodwill' is a concept akin to, but wider than, reputation since it denotes also some activity, or at least recognition, in the marketplace. It has been defined as 'the benefit and advantage of the good name, reputation and connection of a business. It is the attractive force which brings in custom'.[1364]

In order to establish a protectable right, the plaintiff must show some distinctive feature in his or her goods or services that is recognized in the market as being linked with the goods or services.[1365] As regards names, the requirement usually can be satisfied where the name has been made up (save where a name is so widely adopted it passes into common speech). But distinctiveness is hard to show where a name uses ordinary or descriptive words. The more a name is generally descriptive of a commercial activity, the less likely it is that the public will associate the name with a particular source, or that the courts will protect the words.[1366] Certainly,

---

1355. For example, *Law Society of England and Wales v. Society of Lawyers* [1996] FSR 739.

1356. For example, *British Diabetic Association v. Diabetic Society Ltd* [1995] 4 All ER 812.

1357. For example, *Clark v. Associated Newspapers Ltd* [1998] 1 WLR 1558; In addition, s. 102 Copyright Act 1994 gives a person the right not to have a literary or similar work falsely attributed to him or her as author.

1358. For example, *Reckitt & Colman Products Ltd v. Borden Inc* [1990] 1 WLR 491; *Tui Foods Ltd v. New Zealand Milk Corporation Ltd* [1997] 2 NZLR 214.

1359. For example, *Wineworths Group Ltd v. Comité Interprofessionel du Vin de Champagne* [1992] 2 NZLR 327.

1360. For example, *Irvine v. Talksport Ltd* [2002] 1 WLR 2355 (appeal on liability dismissed [2003] FSR 619); *Fenty v. Arcadia Group Brands Ltd* [2015] 1 WLR 3291. On appropriation of personality, *see* para. 257.

1361. For example, *Draper v. Trist & Tristbestos Brake Linings Ltd* (1939) 56 RPC 429.

1362. [1979] AC 731 at 741.

1363. *Spalding v. Gamage Ltd* (1915) 32 RPC 273 at 274 per Lord Parker.

1364. *IRC v. Muller Co.'s Margarine Ltd* [1901] AC 217 at 223–224.

1365. *Cadbury Schweppes Pty Ltd v. Pub Squash Pty Ltd* [1981] 1 All ER 213 at 218.

1366. *See* generally *Dominion Rent A Car Ltd v. Budget Rent A Car Systems (1970) Ltd* [1987] 2 NZLR 395; *NZ Tax Refunds Ltd v. Brooks Homes Ltd* [2013] NZCA 90; *Intercity Group (NZ) Ltd v. Nakedbus NZ Ltd* [2014] 3 NZLR 177.

minor variations are likely to be seen as sufficiently distinguishing one business from another.[1367] In the end it is the overall picture given by the name, how it is presented and, sometimes, any associated get-up, which determines whether a case of passing off can be shown.

Passing off may be committed by the defendant imitating the appearance or get-up of the plaintiff's goods. The get-up is protectable, but only if the plaintiff can establish sufficient distinctiveness and that there is a probability of confusion as a result of the defendant's misrepresentation of the source of the goods.[1368] A key question is whether features such as design, shape, colour, or pattern are functional or capricious. Features are capricious if they are dictated not by the purpose for which goods are made but by, for example, whim, aesthetics, or a desire to be distinctive. The cases show, broadly, that protection can be given only to non-functional features or functional features in a capricious form.[1369]

A question of 'product goodwill' can arise where a particular region has acquired a reputation for goods of a particular kind, and the defendant misrepresents its goods as having that origin. A producer can succeed in a passing off action where it has the necessary reputation or goodwill, whether individually or as a member of an identifiable group, in a product of that region.[1370] So, French producers could restrain the use of the word 'Champagne' as describing sparkling wine imported into New Zealand from Australia;[1371] and Scotch whisky producers could sue in respect of 'Scotch whisky' adulterated by other products.[1372] A similar principle has been applied to protect the name of a product of a particular character or composition that has been marketed under a descriptive name, and under that name has gained a public reputation that distinguishes it from competing products of a different composition.[1373] So, the protectable goodwill is not restricted to the special qualities of a product that are related to geographical provenance.

1367. *National Mini Storage Ltd v. National Storage Ltd* [2018] NZCA 45 at [22].

1368. *See* generally *Klissers Farmhouse Bakeries Ltd v. Harvest Bakeries Ltd* [1985] 2 NZLR 143 (HC); [1988] 1 NZLR 16 (CA).

1369. *See* generally *Reckitt & Colman Products Ltd v. Borden Inc* [1990] 1 WLR 491; *Tot Toys Ltd v. Mitchell* [1993] 1 NZLR 325 at 344; *Kirkbi AG v. Ritvik Holdings Ltd* [2005] 3 SCR 302.

1370. The Geographical Indications (Wine and Spirits) Registration Act 2006 provides for a system of registration of a geographical indication that identifies the geographical origin of a wine or spirit. By s. 34, wrongful use of a registered geographical indication is a breach of s. 9 of the Fair Trading Act 1986, and the provisions of that Act apply accordingly: *see* para. 447.

1371. *Wineworths Group Ltd v. Comité Interprofessionel du Vin de Champagne* [1992] 2 NZLR 327; and *see Bollinger v. Costa Brava Wine Co. Ltd* [1960] Ch 262 (Spanish champagne), and *Taittinger v. Allbev Ltd* [1994] 4 All ER 75 (CA) (elderflower champagne).

1372. *John Walker & Sons Ltd v. Henry Ost & Co. Ltd* [1970] 1 WLR 917.

1373. *Erven Warnink BV v. J Townend & Sons (Hull) Ltd* [1979] AC 731 (producers of egg and spirit drink known as 'advocaat' could restrain use of name for drink with different ingredients).

C. Plaintiff's Claim to the Goodwill

248. The plaintiff must show that he or she is entitled to the goodwill attaching to the business. There must be a public association of the plaintiff with the product or service. The goodwill may be within a particular town or city or area or throughout the country as a whole. Where an international corporation is not actually trading in New Zealand but has an international reputation extending to New Zealand, not much in the way of activity within the jurisdiction is required to establish goodwill. The reputation of the corporation may be almost tantamount to goodwill, activity having importance in localizing that reputation in New Zealand.[1374] But the UK Supreme Court has affirmed that claimants had to show goodwill in the form of customers within the jurisdiction and that a mere reputation was not enough.[1375]

Some authorities suggest that in certain circumstances a person may trade in his or her own name notwithstanding that there is a trader in the field with a similar name.[1376] But there is no such exception in claims under the Fair Trading Act 1986,[1377] and it is unlikely that there is any longer an own name exception in the New Zealand common law.[1378]

On any view, there is no room for an 'own name' defence where a person has sold a business together with the goodwill associated with his or her name. The vendor cannot derogate from that goodwill.[1379]

Sometimes, more than one person may claim to have established a protectable right in a name or mark, as where, for example, there is concurrent entry into the market, or acquiescence by the person with rights to goodwill to entry into the market by another. In this kind of case, the solution may be to allow concurrent use of the name or mark by two or more persons.[1380]

D. Deception Causing Confusion

249. The existence of a misrepresentation is essential to the cause of action in passing off. The misrepresentation must deceive or be likely to deceive consumers as to the source or characteristics of the product, causing them to be confused about what they are getting. There is no passing off where the consumer is confused, but not by deception.[1381] Fraud or intentional deception is not required.[1382] The conduct must be likely to injure the business or goodwill of another, in the sense that this is

1374. *Dominion Rent A Car Ltd v. Budget Rent A Car Systems (1970) Ltd* [1987] 2 NZLR 395; *Midas International Corporation v. Midas Autocare Ltd* (1987) 2 TCLR 491.
1375. *Starbucks (HK) Ltd v. British Sky Broadcasting Group (No 2)* [2015] 1 WLR 2682.
1376. *See* especially *Joseph Rodgers & Sons Ltd v. W N Rodgers & Co.* (1924) 41 RPC 277; *New Zealand Farmers' Co-op Association of Canterbury Ltd v. Farmers Trading Co. Ltd (No. 1)* (1979) 1 NZIPR 212, 230–232; *Taylor Bros Ltd v. Taylors Group Ltd* [1988] 2 NZLR 1, 22–24 (HC & CA).
1377. *See* para. 255.
1378. *Neumegen v. Neumegen and Co.* [1998] 3 NZLR 310 at 317.
1379. *I N Newman Ltd v. Richard T Adlem* [2006] FSR 253.
1380. *See Dominion Rent A Car Ltd v. Budget Rent A Car Systems (1970) Ltd* [1987] 2 NZLR 395.
1381. *Reckitt & Colman Products Ltd v. Borden Inc* [1990] 1 WLR 491 at 510.
1382. *Anheuser-Busch Inc v. Budweiser Budvar National Corporation* [2001] 3 NZLR 666 at [133].

a reasonably foreseeable consequence.[1383] However, proof of fraudulent intent will assist the court in deducing that deception occurred, since it will be ready to infer that defendants were successful in what they set out to achieve.[1384]

Whether deception leads to confusion by the public is a question of fact in each case. In *Tot Toys Ltd v. Mitchell*[1385] Fisher J emphasized that close regard must be paid to the circumstances in which a product will be sold to the public. Relevant considerations include:

(1) whether the product is of a type and cost likely to prompt inquiry over source;
(2) whether the product will be sold with packaging or labelling that would serve to distinguish;
(3) whether the anticipated type of buyer is likely to be discerning; and
(4) whether retailers would be likely to present and represent the product in a way that would distinguish or confuse.

In modern circumstances the likelihood of confusion often may be assessed by reference to what consumers may find on searches of the internet. In a recent example, after considering evidence of this kind, the Court of Appeal was not persuaded that a significant number of consumers were likely to be confused, or misled or deceived.[1386]

A defendant may seek to negate the risk of confusion by issuing a disclaimer saying something to the effect that the goods are not those of the plaintiff. In principle this is possible and may be effective, but the disclaimer must be sufficiently clear and prominent to destroy any link with the plaintiff that would otherwise be suggested, so consumers are not confused.[1387]

Market surveys can be an important source of evidence tending to establish (or to deny) confusion. In determining the weight to be given to such evidence, relevant factors include the way the survey was conducted (e.g., the size of the sample, whether the interviewees represented a relevant cross-section of the public, and the form of the questions), whether the instructions to the interviewers as to how to carry out their survey were disclosed, and whether the other side had an opportunity to check the accuracy and honesty of the survey.[1388]

1383. *Erven Warnink BV v. J Townend & Sons (Hull) Ltd* [1979] AC 731 at 742.

1384. *UPL Group Ltd v. Dux Engineers Ltd* [1989] 3 NZLR 135 at 146.

1385. [1993] 1 NZLR 325 at 354.

1386. *National Mini Storage Ltd v. National Storage Ltd* [2018] NZCA 45, (2018) 131 IPR 538 at [34]–[73].

1387. *See*, for example *Music Productions Ltd v. Tansing* (1993) 27 IPR 640; cp *Miller v. Britt Allcroft (Thomas) LLC* (2002) 52 IPR 419.

1388. For discussion of this issue *see* in particular *Customglass Boats Ltd v. Salthouse Bros Ltd* [1976] 1 NZLR 36, *Patience & Nicholson (NZ) Ltd v. Cyclone Hardware Pty Ltd* [2001] 3 NZLR 490 at [80]–[96] (HC), [39] (CA); *Anheuser-Busch Inc v. Budweiser Budvar National Corporation* [2001] 3 NZLR 666 at [99]–[105] (HC), [2003] 1 NZLR 472 at [134] (CA).

E. Damage

250. An essential element of passing off is that there be damage or, in the context of injunctive relief, a likelihood of damage to the goodwill of the plaintiff.[1389] A common form of damage is diversion of custom from the plaintiff's to the defendant's business. The plaintiff must prove source motivation – that customers were motivated by the defendant's deception to purchase the product in the belief that it was the plaintiff's product. Seemingly this normally can be presumed on proof of passing off. Where the attributes or qualities of the product are 'transparent', so the customer can clearly see what he or she is getting, proof that the source of the product did influence customers may be needed. There is no diversion of custom if the origin of a product is a matter of indifference to the customer.[1390] But even where goods are transparent, customers may still seek to buy from a particular source on its reputation for quality. There is damage in this case where passing off can be shown.

A plaintiff may also suffer damage to reputation caused by the passing off by another of inferior goods or services.[1391] Again, unauthorized use of a name associated with the plaintiff may cause injury through the dilution of the value of the name, for example by the reduction or loss of the resale value of the goodwill or by a loss of licensing value.[1392] The reasoning that allows recovery for this form of damage tends to change the basis of passing off from an action to protect trade and business to an action to protect a property right in a name.

F. Remedies

251. The remedies in an action for passing off include an interim or permanent injunction, damages, an account of profits, and delivery up or destruction of offending articles.

1. Injunction

252. In *American Cyanamid Co. v. Ethicon Ltd*[1393] the House of Lords held that a plaintiff seeking an interim injunction must first establish a serious question to be tried, after which the court will assess the balance of convenience as between the parties.[1394] An important factor in passing off cases is the adequacy of damages as compensation to the plaintiff if the injunction is refused and he or she is successful at the trial. Sometimes compensation may be not only difficult to quantify but also

1389. *Erven Warnink BV v. J Townend & Sons (Hull) Ltd* [1979] AC 731, 742, 755–756; *Dominion Rent A Car Ltd v. Budget Rent A Car Systems (1970) Ltd* [1987] 2 NZLR 395 at 405, 420.

1390. *Tot Toys Ltd v. Mitchell* [1993] 1 NZLR 325 at 351–352.

1391. *See* the discussion in *Taylor Bros Ltd v. Taylors Group Ltd* [1988] 2 NZLR 1 at 15, 20, 37.

1392. *Ibid.*

1393. [1975] AC 396.

1394. *See* generally para. 571.

inadequate, as coming too late to save the situation.[1395] Or there may be particular detriment to the defendant if an injunction is granted and the defendant ultimately is successful in cases where there is a question about the ability of the plaintiff to pay damages.[1396] It is also relevant to consider whether the defendant entered the situation with his or her eyes open.[1397] And where an injunction is granted the court may need to take care to limit its terms to the minimum necessary to maintain the status quo.[1398]

The most effective remedy for passing off will usually be a permanent injunction. The injunction will often be in absolute terms, for example, restraining the use of a particular name or mark in circumstances where there is no real possibility of using the mark in question in a manner that will differentiate the defendant's goods or business from that of the plaintiff's.[1399] In circumstances where it may be possible for the defendant to use the name or mark in some way without passing off, the injunction may be qualified or limited, for example by the use of the formula 'without clearly distinguishing its trade or business from the trade or business of the plaintiff'.

2. Damages

253. Where passing off is proved, damage may be inferred by the court and general damages awarded. The measure of damages is largely a question of fact in each case, but in general the plaintiff is entitled to damages for all loss, which is the natural and direct consequence of the defendant's wrongful acts.[1400]

3. Other Remedies

254. If the court allows, the plaintiff may elect to seek an account of profits in lieu of damages.[1401] The purpose of an account is to prevent unjust enrichment, not to punish the defendant.[1402] It will not be ordered if the defendant is innocent, and

1395. *See*, for example, *Shotover Gorge Jet Boats Ltd v. Marine Enterprises Ltd* [1984] 2 NZLR 154 at 161; *Klissers Farmhouse Bakeries Ltd v. Harvest Bakeries Ltd* [1985] 2 NZLR 129 at 139, 141; *Resene Paints Ltd v. Orica New Zealand Ltd* [2003] 3 NZLR 709.
1396. *See*, for example, *Gallagher Electronics Ltd v. Livewire Products Ltd* (1987) 2 TCLR 457.
1397. *Klissers Farmhouse Bakeries Ltd v. Harvest Bakeries Ltd* [1985] 2 NZLR 129 at 139.
1398. *Shotover Gorge Jet Boats Ltd v. Marine Enterprises Ltd* [1984] 2 NZLR 154 at 161–162; *Prudential Building & Investment Soc of Canterbury v. Prudential Assurance Co. of NZ Ltd* [1988] 2 NZLR 653. For difficulties if the injunction becomes too elaborate *see Taylor Bros Ltd v. Taylors Group Ltd* [1988] 2 NZLR 1 at 34–35, 41.
1399. For example, *NZ Insurance Co. Ltd v. NZ Insurance Brokers Ltd* [1976] 2 NZLR 40; *Taylor Bros Ltd v. Taylors Group Ltd* [1988] 2 NZLR 1 at 4, 31–32.
1400. *Spalding v. Gamage Ltd* (1918) 35 RPC 101 at 117.
1401. For example *Noel Leeming Television Ltd v. Noel's Appliances* (1985) 5 IPR 249; *see International Property Development Corporation Pty Ltd v. Primary Distributors NZ Ltd* [2010] 2 NZLR 729 for discussion of the remedy in the context of an action for trademark infringement.
1402. *Apand Pty Ltd v. Kettle Chip Co. Pty Ltd* (1999) 43 IPR 225.

is limited to the period when the defendant had knowledge of the plaintiff's rights. The defendant is liable to pay over the profits that are directly attributable to the passing of.[1403]

Other remedies may be available in appropriate circumstances. These may include delivery up or destruction of articles,[1404] or removal of the offending name or mark where this is possible.[1405]

III. Fair Trading Act 1986

A. *Misleading or Deceptive Conduct*

255. The aim of the Fair Trading Act 1986 is primarily to prohibit unfair practices in the marketplace from the point of view of consumers or the general public.[1406] To this end, section 9 provides:

> No person shall, in trade, engage in conduct that is misleading or deceptive or likely to mislead or deceive.[1407]

This provision, which is considered in more detail later on,[1408] is not concerned solely with consumer protection or with conduct directed at consumers. It can also apply to disputes between businesses and, in particular, to those involving the principles of passing off. To establish misleading or deceptive conduct under the Act in a case akin to passing off, the plaintiff must prove that the goods or services supplied in trade have an existing reputation that in the minds of customers is associated with a particular name, mark or get-up, and the defendant's conduct caused or is likely to cause customers to be misled or deceived over the implications of that name, mark or get-up.[1409]

The words of the Fair Trading Act are not hedged by the restrictions of the common law. In *Tot Toys Ltd v. Mitchell*[1410] Fisher J pointed to five respects in which it would seem easier to establish a cause of action for misleading or deceptive conduct than for passing off. First, the statutory words 'conduct that is misleading or deceptive' are unqualified and so any deception can qualify. Second, there is no need to show injury to obtain relief: damage is not an essential element of the cause of action. Third, source motivation is not an essential element of the cause of action even where the plaintiff complains of a diversion of trade. The test is purely whether

---

1403. *See* generally *My Kinda Town Ltd v. Soll* [1983] RPC 15.
1404. *Hansells (NZ) Ltd v. Baillie* [1967] 2 NZLR 774 at 784.
1405. *Slazenger & Sons Ltd v. Feltham & Co.* (1889) 6 RPC 531.
1406. *See* generally *Taylor Bros Ltd v. Taylors Group Ltd* [1988] 2 NZLR 1, 39.
1407. *See also* s. 10 (misleading conduct in relation to goods), s. 11 (misleading conduct in relation to services), s. 13 (certain false representations).
1408. *See* paras 444–448.
1409. *See* generally *Tot Toys Ltd v. Mitchell* [1993] 1 NZLR 325 at 367; *Bonz Group Pty Ltd v. Cooke* (1996) 5 NZBLC 104,188.
1410. [1993] 1 NZLR 325 at 376–378.

customers will be misled or deceived, and so a plaintiff need not go on to demonstrate the adverse consequences of the deception. Fourth, there is no requirement that the reputation with which the defendant is being confused be that of the plaintiff. Fifth, deception at any time constitutes a breach of the Act. If there is initial deception, correction at the point of sale will be too late retrospectively to nullify the breach of section 9 that will already have occurred.

It is difficult to contemplate that there might be conduct amounting to passing off which is not also a breach of the Act. Indeed, traders alleging interference with business goodwill ordinarily allege both passing off and breach of section 9,[1411] or, it may be, breach of section 9 alone.[1412]

B. Remedies

256. Contravention of many of the provisions of the Fair Trading Act amounts to a criminal offence and can result in financial penalties.[1413] Contravention of section 9 is not criminal, but it does give rise to civil liability. Both an injunction[1414] and an order for compensation[1415] can be granted at the suit of any private individual. In deciding whether a private remedy ought to be granted, the focus is not the same as at common law. Whereas damages are available as of right, remedies under the Act are discretionary.[1416] In exercising the discretion, the most important question is whether the misleading and deceptive conduct is likely to have a sufficiently serious impact upon customers rather than trade competitors.[1417]

IV. Misappropriation of Personality

257. Unauthorized use of a person's image to make false allegations of endorsement or sponsorship that cause him or her to lose custom or revenue can amount to passing off[1418] or can be a breach of the Fair Trading Act 1986.[1419] Yet in many unauthorized character merchandising cases there may be neither deception nor damage. In *Tot Toys Ltd v. Mitchell*[1420] Fisher J observed that the point may be to

1411. There are many examples. Both claims succeeded in *Patience & Nicholson (NZ) Ltd v. Cyclone Hardware Pty Ltd* [2001] 3 NZLR 490. Both failed in *National Mini Storage Ltd v. National Storage Ltd* [2018] NZCA 45, where the plaintiff treated passing off as something of an afterthought (at [77]).
1412. For example, *Neumegen v. Neumegen and Co.* [1998] 3 NZLR 310.
1413. Fair Trading Act 1986, s. 40.
1414. *Ibid.*, s. 41.
1415. *Ibid.*, s. 43(3)(f).
1416. *See* further para. 447.
1417. *Taylor Bros Ltd v. Taylors Group Ltd* [1988] 2 NZLR 1, 40 (HC & CA); *Tot Toys Ltd v. Mitchell* [1993] 1 NZLR 325 at 368.
1418. *Tony Blain Pty Ltd v. Splain* [1993] 3 NZLR 185; *Irvine v. Talksport Ltd* [2002] 1 WLR 2355 (appeal on liability dismissed [2003] FSR 619); *Fenty v. Arcadia Group Brands Ltd* [2015] 1 WLR 3291. In some cases there may be a remedy under the Major Events Management Act 2007.
1419. *Talmax Pty Ltd v. Telstra Corp. Ltd* (1996) 36 IPR 46.
1420. [1993] 1 NZLR 325 at 359–366.

project an association with the beneficial image per se, not a commercial connection with the persons responsible for creating or licensing it. There is no inherent deception in showing a product in juxtaposition with a popular man-made image, any more than there would be in juxtaposing it with an image drawn from nature. As to damage, the problem may be that frequently the only damage is the loss of the right to exploit exclusive character merchandising rights, the very existence of which is the subject under inquiry. So to point to the loss of a fee as damage is circular. Unless there is some other damage then an action for passing off should fail on this ground.

In many of the passing off cases the plaintiff's complaint has really been about misappropriation, not misrepresentation. There is some support overseas for recognizing conduct of this kind as a tort in its own right. It appears that the tort is committed where there has been a wrongful appropriation of a person's personality or image causing damage to that person. First, a misappropriation involves an unauthorized use of the plaintiff's name or image or other indicia of his or her persona.[1421] A technical or incidental publication, as where the plaintiff is a face in a crowd, is not enough.[1422] Second, the action protects the goodwill actually or potentially generated by the personality rather than the name or image per se. The damage is the diverted goodwill and the damages are calculated by reference to the value of the goodwill. So the plaintiff can recover, for example, for the value of the endorsement, as being equivalent to a licence fee or lost user fee.[1423] However, it would seem that private persons with no commercial goodwill can sue, if at all, only for an invasion of privacy.[1424] Third, there is a defence of public interest. The use of a personality's identity is immune if the defendant's purpose is informational or cultural or newsworthy. But if it is primarily commercial, to exploit the personality, there is no defence.[1425]

In *Tot Toys*, Fisher J considered that there might be a case for giving a cause of action for appropriation of personality and/or breach of rights of privacy and publicity. As regards artificial images, however, there was already considerable protection from trademarks, registered designs, patents, the Fair Trading Act, and copyright. Before proceeding further there would need to be close scrutiny of the competing policy considerations and, if further protection was warranted, a careful formula to achieve the right balance between them. However, in *Hosking v. Runting*[1426] Gault and Blanchard JJ said that they did not consider that there was a cause of action in New Zealand law directed to unauthorized representation of a person's image. Again, in *Douglas v. Hello! Ltd* in the Court of Appeal the celebrity plaintiffs recovered damages in respect of unauthorized photographs of their wedding.[1427] However, the House of Lords treated the photos in the same way as any

1421. *Athans v. Canadian Adventure Camps Ltd* (1977) 80 DLR (3d) 583.
1422. *Krouse v. Chrysler Canada Ltd* (1973) 40 DLR (3d) 15.
1423. *Krouse v. Chrysler Canada Ltd, ibid.*; *Athans v. Canadian Adventure Camps Ltd* (1977) 80 DLR (3d) 583.
1424. *See* para. 363.
1425. *Midler v. Ford Motor Co.* 849 F 2d 401 (1988).
1426. [2005] 1 NZLR 1 at [171]; and *see X v. Attorney-General (No 2)* [2017] NZHC 1136, [2017] NZAR 1365 at [32].
1427. [2006] QB 125.

other information of commercial value. In so deciding, Lord Hoffmann remarked that there was no question of the decision creating an 'image right' or any other unorthodox form of intellectual property.[1428] The position has not been finally determined, both in the UK and in New Zealand, and it requires at least some further consideration.

V. Breach of Confidence

A. *Introduction*

258. A further action that may provide assistance to a trader seeking to protect his or her intangible interests in trade is the action for breach of confidence or misuse of confidential information. Sometimes the basis for the action may be found in a contract between the parties, but quite apart from any contractual remedy there is a well-established right of action for breach of confidence that is founded ultimately on equitable principles.[1429] The right of action is at least analogous to a tort, and in some cases it has been referred to as a tort.[1430] Debate about the jurisdictional basis of the action has been linked to the availability of certain remedies, particularly of damages, should the jurisdiction be based solely in equity, and to the availability of remedies against third parties. The Court of Appeal has favoured flexibility on this issue and has made it clear that the full range of remedies is available.[1431] In a recent discussion the action has been regarded as sui generis.[1432]

B. *Elements of the Cause of Action*

259. The elements of an action for breach of confidence were conveniently set out by Megarry J in *Coco v. A N Clark (Engineers) Ltd*:[1433]

(1) The information itself must have the necessary quality of confidence about it.
(2) The information must have been communicated in circumstances importing an obligation of confidence.
(3) There must have been an unauthorized use of that information to the detriment of the person communicating it [that is, the person who is entitled to the benefit of the confidence].

1428. [2008] 1 AC 1 at [124].
1429. *AB Consolidated Ltd v. Europe Strength Food Co. Pty Ltd* [1978] 2 NZLR 515; *Aquaculture Corporation v. New Zealand Green Mussel Co. Ltd* [1990] 3 NZLR 299; *Skids Programme Management Ltd v. McNeill* [2013] 1 NZLR 1; *Vidal-Hall v. Google Inc* [2015] 3 WLR 409.
1430. For example *Malone v. Metropolitan Police Commissioner* [1979] Ch 344 at 360; *McKaskell v. Benseman* [1989] 3 NZLR 75 at 88; *Stepping Stones Nursery Ltd v. Attorney-General* [2002] 3 NZLR 414 at [19], [20].
1431. *Aquaculture Corporation v. New Zealand Green Mussel Co. Ltd* [1990] 3 NZLR 299.
1432. *Hunt v. A* [2008] 1 NZLR 368 at [64].
1433. [1969] RPC 41 at 47–48.

The analysis in this case has been adopted and relied on in New Zealand decisions.[1434] Accordingly, in determining whether an action for breach of confidence will lie, the three requirements identified by Megarry J must be satisfied.

1. Confidential Information

260. The origins of the action for breach of confidence lie in cases involving the protection of commercial secrets, and this remains the focus of the bulk of the cases. Often the need for protection arises in or at the ending of an employment relationship, both in relation to the (ex) employee and to third parties to whom the information may be divulged. But the action for breach of confidence in a commercial setting is not confined to the employment relationship; it may also arise in connection with other types of contracts, for example licensing arrangements or business sales, or in circumstances where no contractual relationship is concluded.

It has been said that what makes information confidential is the fact that the maker 'has used his brain and thus produced a result which can only be used by somebody who goes through the same process'.[1435] It will have the requisite characteristic of confidence if it is the product of thought and work.[1436] The information may relate to any subject matter – business, financial, scientific, literary. But it must be identifiable, in the sense that it is not part of a generalized know-how. This qualification is of particular importance in the employment context, where the courts have been at pains to distinguish trade secrets, particularly in the sense of secret processes, recipes, designs, and formulae, from the general body of information that can be acquired in a job and that workers must be free to use for their own advantage, and especially to take to fresh employment.[1437]

Recent developments show the action for breach of confidence being used outside the commercial sphere to protect personal confidences, in which context it may

1434. For example, *AB Consolidated Ltd v. Europe Strength Food Co. Pty Ltd* [1978] 2 NZLR 515 at 520; *Attorney-General (UK) v. Wellington Newspapers Ltd* [1988] 1 NZLR 129 at 141; *Norbrook Laboratories Ltd v. Bomac Laboratories Ltd* [2004] 3 NZLR 49 at [22] (appeal allowed [2006] UKPC 25); *A v. Hunt* [2008] 1 NZLR 368; *Earthquake Commission v. Krieger* [2014] 2 NZLR 547 at [27]; *Karum Group LLC v. Fisher & Paykel Financial Services Ltd* [2014] 3 NZLR 421 at [182]; *Henderson v. Walker* [2019] NZHC 2184 at [144]–[198].

1435. *Saltman Engineering Co. v. Campbell Engineering Co.* [1963] 3 All ER 413n at 415 per Lord Greene MR.

1436. *Skids Programme Management Ltd v. McNeill* [2013] 1 NZLR 1 at [82].

1437. For protected information *see*, for example, *New Zealand Needle Manufacturers Ltd v. Taylor* [1975] 2 NZLR 33 (workings of machine); *SSC & B: Lintas New Zealand Ltd v. Murphy* [1986] 2 NZLR 436 (specialized knowledge of plaintiff's activities in relation to client's affairs); *Peninsular Real Estate Ltd v. Harris* [1992] 2 NZLR 216 (business records); *Skids Programme Management Ltd v. McNeill* [2013] 1 NZLR 1 (childcare policies and procedures manual). For unprotected information *see*, for example, *Faccenda Chicken Ltd v. Fowler* [1987] Ch 117 (sales information); *Bendon Industries Ltd v. Presslok Industries Ltd* (1982) 1 TCLR 61 (client lists and pricing information); *Laser Alignment (NZ) 1984 Ltd v. Scholz* [1993] 2 ERNZ 250 (service manuals); *Karum Group LLC v. Fisher & Paykel Financial Services* [2014] 3 NZLR 421 (computer codes in credit management software system).

well overlap with the action for invasion of privacy.[1438] Examples are a breach of confidence in disclosing intimate marital secrets,[1439] information relevant to a financial settlement in pending divorce proceedings,[1440] a lesbian relationship,[1441] details of drug addiction,[1442] wedding photographs,[1443] and personal thoughts and impressions in the private journal of a public figure.[1444] Sometimes it may be that a person's identity is confidential. So there was protection for an AIDS victim,[1445] the natural parent of an adopted child,[1446] an undercover police officer,[1447] a party to a confidential settlement of a harassment complaint,[1448] two persons convicted of a notorious murder on being released from jail,[1449] and even a married claimant alleging that disclosure would be detrimental to the interests of his teenage children.[1450]

The action for breach of confidence also may be invoked in the context of disputes concerning the disclosure of government secrets. For example, the so-called *Spycatcher* case concerned the (largely unsuccessful) attempts by the UK government to prevent the publication of the memoirs of an ex-employee of the UK secret service in various countries throughout the world.[1451]

2. The Obligation of Confidence

261. The obligation of confidence commonly arises out of a relationship between the parties in which one has imparted information to the other on the basis that the other is to make use of the information only for the limited purpose for which it was given. Such an obligation can arise in various kinds of business or similar relationships. Frequently the relationship will be contractual, but it may also arise in a variety of other circumstances, like pre-contractual bargaining during negotiations for a licensing agreement[1452] or dealings with the police concerning

1438. In *Vidal-Hall v. Google Inc* [2015] 3 WLR 409 the Court of Appeal in England took the view that it was only in cases involving personal privacy that a claim could be seen as clearly tortious: and *see* para. 367.
1439. *Argyll v. Argyll* [1967] Ch 302.
1440. *Imerman v. Tchenguiz* [2011] 2 WLR 592.
1441. *Stephens v. Avery* [1988] 2 WLR 1280.
1442. *Campbell v. MGN Ltd* [2004] 2 AC 457.
1443. *Douglas v. Hello! Ltd* [2008] 1 AC 1, sub nom *OBG Ltd v. Allan*, recognizing both a personal claim by the parties to the marriage and a commercial claim by the purchaser of exclusive rights to the photographs.
1444. *HRH Prince of Wales v. Associated Newspapers Ltd* [2008] Ch 57.
1445. *X v. Y* [1988] 2 All ER 648.
1446. *G v. Attorney-General* [1994] 1 NZLR 714.
1447. *X v. Attorney-General* [1997] 2 NZLR 623.
1448. *M v. Independent Newspapers Ltd* [1992] 1 ERNZ 202.
1449. *Venables v. News Group Newspapers Ltd* [2001] 2 WLR 1038.
1450. *K v. News Group Newspapers Ltd* [2011] 1 WLR 1827; cp *Donald v. Ntuli* [2011] 1 WLR 294.
1451. *Attorney-General (UK) v. Heinemann Publishers (Australia) Pty Ltd* (1988) 165 CLR 30 (Australia); *Attorney-General (UK) v. Wellington Newspapers Ltd* [1988] 1 NZLR 129 (New Zealand); *Attorney-General v. Guardian Newspapers Ltd (No. 2)* [1990] 1 AC 109 (UK).
1452. *AB Consolidated Ltd v. Europe Strength Food Co. Pty Ltd* [1978] 2 NZLR 515.

sensitive commercial information.[1453] So too, personal information may be disclosed in confidence to another, such as a professional person,[1454] a friend, or relative.[1455] But there was no confidentiality in a Law Society report on a complaint about the conduct of the plaintiff solicitor.[1456]

The question of whether a *relationship* of confidence is always necessary is controversial. Certainly it is clear that a third party (often a newspaper) receiving information in circumstances where that party knows or ought to know that it has been divulged in breach of an obligation of confidence owed to another is bound to respect the confidence.[1457] Again, an action may lie where a person has acquired information by surreptitious or other improper means, such as obtaining the plaintiff's privileged letters by a trick,[1458] unlawfully tapping the plaintiff's telephone,[1459] and surreptitiously taking films or photographs.[1460] The most satisfactory principle to proceed on may be to ask whether a third-party recipient of confidential information has acted unconscionably in relation to the acquisition of the information or in the way it has been employed.[1461]

In *Attorney-General v. Guardian Newspapers Ltd (No. 2)*[1462] Lord Goff contemplated that the action can be extended to include cases where 'obviously confidential' information is acquired innocently, as where it is simply lost or sent to another by mistake.[1463] His Lordship thought that the critical factor was the defendant's knowledge that information was confidential, so it would be just that he should be precluded from disclosing the information to others. Apparently, no prior relationship between plaintiff and defendant needs to be shown. And certainly a remedy for breach of confidence will equally be available in New Zealand.[1464]

1453. *Stepping Stones Nursery Ltd v. Attorney-General* [2002] 3 NZLR 414.
1454. *McKaskell v. Benseman* [1989] 3 NZLR 75.
1455. *Stephens v. Avery* [1988] Ch 449.
1456. *Napier v. Pressdram Ltd* [2010] 1 WLR 934.
1457. *See*, for example, *T v. Attorney-General* (1988) 4 FRNZ 582; *M v. Independent Newspapers Ltd* [1992] 1 ERNZ 202; *Douglas v. Hello! Ltd* [2008] 1 AC 1.
1458. *Lord Ashburton v. Pape* [1913] 2 Ch 469.
1459. *Francome v. Mirror Group Newspapers Ltd* [1984] 1 WLR 892; *see Malone v. Metropolitan Police Commissioner* [1979] Ch 344.
1460. *Hellewell v. Chief Constable of Derbyshire* [1995] 1 WLR 804, 807; *Shelley Films Ltd v. Rex Features Ltd* [1994] EMLR 134; *Creation Records Ltd v. News Group Newspapers Ltd* (1998) 39 IPR 1.
1461. *A v. Hunt* [2008] 1 NZLR 368 at [92]. In *Vestergaard Frandsen A/S v. Bestnet Europe Ltd* [2013] 1 WLR 1556 the UK Supreme Court held that a defendant could not be liable for breach of confidence as a party to a common design where she did not know that the product had been developed using the claimant's trade secrets.
1462. [1990] 1 AC 109 at 281.
1463. *See*, for example, *ANZ Bank New Zealand Ltd v. Blum Global Prestige Brands Ltd* [2014] NZHC 640.
1464. *R v. X* [2010] 2 NZLR 181.

The UK courts have built upon this foundation in order to give a remedy for breach of confidence in personal information cases where the obligation of confidence arises out of the confidential nature of the information, irrespective of the circumstances in which the information was obtained.[1465] However, in New Zealand, the law of confidence has not been developed in this way. In *Hosking v. Runting*[1466] the Court of Appeal accepted in a majority decision that an invasion of privacy is actionable as a new tort, and in so deciding preferred to recognize breaches of confidence and invasions of privacy as separate causes of action. Even so, in personal information cases where a confidential relationship does exist, the concepts of confidence and privacy will overlap. *Hosking* makes it clear that where there is no such relationship, only the law of privacy will apply.[1467] By contrast, in commercial cases, where the law of confidence continues to apply, a confidential relationship normally is needed. But in exceptional cases, as in Lord Goff's example where commercial information that is 'obviously confidential' is acquired innocently, an action for breach of confidence may still lie.

3. Unauthorized Use

262. The defendant must have made, or be about to make, unauthorized disclosure or use of the confidential information. If misuse of the information cannot be established then an action for damages fails.[1468] In *Norbrook Laboratories Ltd v. Bomac Laboratories Ltd*[1469] the Court of Appeal maintained that the purpose of protecting confidences was to prevent disclosure and misuse, not to stifle competition. In cases where proof of misuse depended on the drawing of an inference from the similarity between products, there should be proof that knowledge of confidential information caused the person with that knowledge to do or omit to do something, normally by avoiding having to undertake some part of the process required to develop the product. In the instant case the defendant had developed an equivalent product to that of the plaintiff and had taken comfort from knowledge of the plaintiff's confidential information, but it had not been shown that the defendant had done or omitted to do anything based on that comfort. On appeal, however, the Privy Council disagreed,[1470] holding that the defendant, although acting in good faith, had deliberately disclosed and used what was known to be confidential information.

It appears that little is needed to satisfy the requirement of detriment. In commercial cases normally there will in fact be actual or potential financial loss,[1471] but proof of such loss is not necessary. It is sufficient that confidential information has

1465. *Campbell v. MGN Ltd* [2004] 2 AC 457; *Re S* [2005] EMLR 11. In *Ash v. McKennitt* [2008] QB 73 Buxton LJ at [8] referred to a 'feeling of discomfort' in using the action for breach of confidence without a preexisting relationship, and thought the action should be for the tort of misuse of private information: *see* further para. 370.
1466. [2005] 1 NZLR 1.
1467. *See* para. 370.
1468. *Arklow Investments Ltd v. Maclean* [2000] 2 NZLR 1.
1469. [2004] 3 NZLR 49.
1470. [2006] UKPC 25.
1471. But *see Fisher & Paykel Financial Services Ltd v. Karum Group LLC* [2013] 2 NZLR 266.

been or is to be disclosed to persons whom the plaintiff would prefer not to know of it, even though the disclosure is not or would not be harmful in any positive way.[1472] Seemingly, the consequences of misuse merely go to the issue of quantification of the damage.

A special rule applies in the case of government secrets, where public detriment has to be shown. The government is required to establish not only that information is confidential and disclosure is unauthorized but also that publication would cause harm to the public interest.[1473] The public must be allowed to discuss, review, and criticize government action unless this is inimical to the public interest.[1474]

C. Defences

1. Information in the Public Domain

263. It is a good defence to an action for breach of confidence that information that was initially confidential has come into the public domain. The information then is no longer confidential and disclosure causes no further damage. Whether there has been sufficient publication to establish the defence is a matter of degree. It will not necessarily be decisive against the plaintiff if, say, there has been only limited publication in early editions of newspapers,[1475] or limited and impermanent disclosure on television.[1476] Again, an action lay in respect of the publication of unauthorized wedding photographs even after the publication of the authorized photographs: the unauthorized photographs did not enter the public domain merely because they resembled other pictures that had entered it.[1477] However, an injunction to prevent publication is likely to be refused if at the time of the hearing the confidential information has in fact been widely disseminated by others.[1478]

If it is the defendant who has wrongfully placed confidential information in the public domain, then he or she may not be released from the duty of confidence in respect of further publication.[1479] Otherwise, a defendant could profit from his or her own wrong. Similarly, under what has been called the 'springboard' doctrine, a

1472. *Attorney-General v. Guardian Newspapers Ltd (No. 2)* [1990] 1 AC 109, 256.
1473. *Ibid.*, at 257, 270, 283.
1474. *Commonwealth of Australia v. John Fairfax & Sons Ltd* (1980) 147 CLR 39 at 52.
1475. *European Pacific Banking Corporation v. Fourth Estate Publications Ltd* [1993] 1 NZLR 559 at 565.
1476. *G v. Day* [1982] 1 NSWLR 24 at 37–41.
1477. *Douglas v. Hello! Ltd* [2008] 1 AC 1, sub nom *OBG Ltd v. Allan*.
1478. *Attorney-General v. Guardian Newspapers Ltd (No. 2)* [1990] 1 AC 109; *Attorney-General (UK) v. Wellington Newspapers Ltd* [1988] 1 NZLR 129; and *see Attorney-General v. Times Newspapers Ltd* [2001] 1 WLR 885.
1479. *Attorney-General v. Guardian Newspapers Ltd (No. 2)* [1990] 1 AC 109 at 259, 266, 271, 286–289; *Attorney-General (UK) v. Wellington Newspapers Ltd* [1988] 1 NZLR 129 at 176, 179; *European Pacific Banking Corporation v. Fourth Estate Publications Ltd* [1993] 1 NZLR 559 at 565.

person who has obtained commercial information in confidence cannot use it to get a head start over others, even though the information has since come into the public domain.[1480]

2. Public Interest in Publication

264. A second defence is public interest in publication. One instance is the public interest in the disclosure of iniquity.[1481] The concept of iniquity includes crimes and frauds and perhaps other civil wrongs.[1482] Where information raises only a suspicion or risk of criminal wrongdoing, it may be disclosed if it is reasonably necessary to do so for the purpose of preventing or detecting crime and the information is distributed only to persons having reasonable need to make use of it.[1483] But a wrongful taking of information cannot be justified by the fear that a spouse may seek to conceal his assets in proceedings for ancillary relief on divorce.[1484] Information concerning unethical or oppressive conduct, even though not illegal, sometimes may not be protected.[1485] But the disclosure of matters of personal morality is likely to fall on the other side of the line,[1486] unless perhaps the plaintiff has courted publicity.[1487]

The public interest defence also may be invoked in cases concerning confidential information casting doubt on the efficacy or safety or reliability of goods or services that are made available to or that affect the public. Examples include information concerning the safety of aircraft,[1488] failings in the security system of an allied country,[1489] dangerous pseudo-scientific nonsense propagated to the public,[1490] and transactions enabling foreign companies to avoid or circumvent New

1480. *Terrapin Ltd v. Builders Supply Co. (Hayes) Ltd* [1967] RPC 375 at 391; *see*, for example, *Aquaculture Corporation v. New Zealand Green Mussel Co. Ltd* (1985) 5 IPR 353, on appeal on the question of damages [1990] 3 NZLR 299; *Stepping Stones Nursery Ltd v. Attorney-General* [2002] 3 NZLR 414 at [72]–[73].

1481. *Gartside v. Outram* (1857) 26 LJ Ch (NS) 113.

1482. *See*, for example, *Jockey Club v. Buffham* [2003] QB 462 (corruption); *ISTIL Group Inc v. Zahoor* [2003] 2 All ER 252 (fraud); *LNS v. Persons Unknown* [2010] EWHC 119 at [104] (possible examples included insider dealing, archaeological purloining and exploitation of weaker persons by more powerful people).

1483. For example, *Malone v. Metropolitan Police Commissioner* [1979] Ch 344 (telephone tapping by police of criminal suspect justified); *R v. Metropolitan Police Commissioner* [2005] EMLR 29 (publicity to anti-social behaviour order justified).

1484. *Imerman v. Tchenguiz* [2011] 2 WLR 592.

1485. For example, *Initial Services v. Putterill* [1967] 3 All ER 145 (employer's misleading conduct), and *Imutran Ltd v. Uncaged Campaigns Ltd* [2002] FSR 20 (issues relating to animal welfare); *see British Steel Corporation v. Granada Television Ltd* [1980] 3 WLR 114 (mere mismanagement).

1486. *Stephens v. Avery* [1988] Ch 449 at 454; *see Woodward v. Hutchins* [1977] 1 WLR 760 (disclosure justified where plaintiffs had otherwise encouraged publicity about their personal lives); *Maccaba v. Lichtenstein* [2005] EMLR 109 (unsolicited love letters from married man to married woman not protected).

1487. *Woodward v. Hutchins* [1977] 1 WLR 760.

1488. *New Zealand Air Line Pilots Association v. Air New Zealand Ltd* [1992] 2 NZLR 656 at 663.

1489. *Attorney-General (UK) v. Wellington Newspapers Ltd* [1988] 1 NZLR 129.

1490. *Church of Scientology of California v. Kaufman* [1973] RPC 627.

Zealand tax legislation.[1491] On the other hand, the public interest in maintaining confidentiality of hospital records outweighed the public interest in knowing the identities of doctors who had contracted AIDS;[1492] the disclosure of information by the police to a commercial rival in the course of a criminal investigation into allegations of theft was remote from the purpose of preventing crime and was inimical to the public interest defence;[1493] and the confidentiality of the private journals of the Prince of Wales prevailed over the 'minimal' public interest in their publication.[1494]

In some cases the public interest may favour publication, but not necessarily to the world at large. Often disclosure to an authority competent to deal with the matter or to a person with a special interest in the information will be sufficient, in which case wider publication will be a breach of confidence. So, disclosure of alleged financial wrongdoing solely to the Inland Revenue Department (IRD),[1495] of photographs of a habitual shoplifter to local shopkeepers,[1496] of convictions for paedophilia of caravan dwellers to the site owner,[1497] and of statements by a registered nurse to the police when under caution to the regulatory body for nursing,[1498] in each case was permissible.

D. Remedies

265. The remedies in an action for breach of confidence include an interim or permanent injunction, damages or an account of profits, and additional orders such as delivery up of articles or destruction of materials.[1499] A full range of remedies is available, whether of equitable or common law origin.[1500]

§5. Interference with Economic Interests

I. Introduction

A. General

266. The primary concern of the torts discussed in this section is with intentional interferences in the trade or business of another person, causing him or her to suffer economic loss. The bases for imposing liability for loss of this kind have been

1491. *European Pacific Banking Corporation v. Fourth Estate Publications Ltd* [1993] 1 NZLR 559.
1492. *X v. Y* [1988] 2 All ER 648; *H v. Associated Newspapers Ltd* [2002] EMLR 425.
1493. *Stepping Stones Nursery Ltd v. Attorney-General* [2002] 3 NZLR 414.
1494. *HRH Prince of Wales v. Associated Newspapers Ltd* [2008] Ch. 57.
1495. *Re a Company's Application* [1989] Ch 477.
1496. *Hellewell v. Chief Constable of Derbyshire* [1995] 1 WLR 804.
1497. *R v. Chief Constable of the North Wales Police, ex p Thorpe* [1999] QB 396.
1498. *Woolgar v. Chief Constable of the Sussex Police* [2000] 1 WLR 25.
1499. *See* paras 252–254 for discussion of these remedies in the context of the tort of passing off.
1500. *AB Consolidated Ltd v. Europe Strength Food Co. Pty Ltd* [1978] 2 NZLR 515; *A v. Hunt* [2008] 1 NZLR 368; and *see Skids Programme Management Ltd v. McNeill* [2013] 1 NZLR 1.

disputed, but in light of an authoritative survey in the House of Lords[1501] we can say that that there are three, core, heads of claim: inducing breach of contract, causing loss by unlawful means, and conspiracy. Whether or how the common law should set the boundaries of conduct of a trader who wants to damage his competitor in order to make his own business more profitable is a contentious matter.[1502]

In addition, we shall examine the torts of deceit and of malicious falsehood. These two torts, which are concerned with deliberately false representations, usually arise and are asserted in a business context, although they can operate in other contexts as well.

Various torts considered elsewhere also may give a remedy for business losses. Passing off is concerned with the wrongful appropriation of business goodwill. Claims of this kind can also be made under the Fair Trading Act 1986. The action for breach of confidence similarly gives a remedy for wrongful use of confidential information. So these actions focus on interferences with intangible property, usually, but not invariably, in a commercial setting. The tort of misfeasance in a public office, discussed later on, can protect businesses from the consequences of the deliberate misuse of statutory or regulatory powers, and the focus here is on abusive conduct by public officers.

B. Industrial Law Context

267. The question whether the torts of inducing breach of contract, causing loss by unlawful means and conspiracy have been committed arises frequently in an industrial law context. Disputes are likely to involve strikes, lockouts and picketing, and the lawfulness of these activities to some extent is regulated by statute. Accordingly, the common law principles that are discussed below operate subject to this statutory regime.

First, there is the question of jurisdiction. By the Employment Relations Act 2000, the Employment Court has full and exclusive jurisdiction to hear and determine proceedings founded on tort issued against a party to a strike or lockout that is threatened, or is occurring, or has occurred, or issued against any person in respect of picketing related to a strike or lockout.[1503] The Court also has full and exclusive jurisdiction to hear and determine proceedings issued for the grant of an injunction to stop a strike or lockout that is occurring or to prevent a threatened strike or lockout, or to stop any picketing or threatened picketing related to a strike or lockout.[1504] The Court does not possess jurisdiction in tort outside the context of strikes and lockouts. All other disputes are resolved in the ordinary way by the District Court or High Court.

1501. *OBG Ltd v. Allan* [2008] 1 AC 1.

1502. *See* generally *Wagner v. Gill* [2015] 3 NZLR 157; *AI Enterprises Ltd v. Bram Enterprises Ltd* [2014] 1 SCR 177; *British Airways plc v. Emerald Supplies Ltd* [2015] EWCA Civ 1024.

1503. Employment Relations Act 2000, s. 99(1).

1504. *Ibid.*, s. 100(1).

1. Strikes and Lockouts

268. Strikes are designated as lawful (1) if the strike is not designated as independently unlawful (as to which *see* below), and relates to bargaining for a collective agreement,[1505] or (2) if the employees who strike have reasonable grounds for believing that the strike is justified on the grounds of safety or health.[1506] Such strikes are not to give rise to proceedings founded on tort.[1507] Again, the Employment Court cannot entertain proceedings for an injunction based upon a lawful strike, actual or threatened.[1508] There are parallel provisions applying to lockouts.

Strikes designated as unlawful are those that occur while a collective agreement binding the striking employees is in force; strikes that occur during bargaining for a proposed collective agreement unless a forty-day strike-free period has been observed; strikes that relate to a personal grievance, and in certain other limited circumstances.[1509] Anyone who suffers adversely can bring a civil action for an injunction, damages, or a compliance order. However, some forms of strikes, like political or sympathy strikes, are not designated either as lawful or unlawful. It seems likely that the listed strikes are the only strikes that are lawful, so outside these the ordinary common law can apply.

2. Picketing

269. There is no statutory recognition in the Employment Relations Act 2000 of any right or freedom to picket. However, picketing that is peaceful and simply to provide information is perfectly lawful at common law.[1510] But the picketing must not involve the commission of an independent tort, such as inducement of breach of contract,[1511] causing loss by unlawful threats amounting to intimidation,[1512] nuisance,[1513] or trespass.[1514] Picketing also may constitute a breach of the criminal law. For example, a person commits an offence who, with intent to frighten or intimidate or knowing his or her conduct is likely to frighten or intimidate, stops, confronts or accosts another person in any public place, or forcibly prevents or hinders any person from carrying out his or her work.[1515] Such a breach may be relevant in determining whether there is liability for causing loss by unlawful means or for conspiracy using unlawful means.[1516]

1505. *Ibid.*, s. 83.
1506. *Ibid.*, s. 84.
1507. *Ibid.*, s. 85(1)(a).
1508. *Ibid.*, s. 85(1)(b).
1509. *Ibid.*, s. 86.
1510. *Hubbard v. Pitt* [1976] QB 142.
1511. *Port of Timaru Ltd v. New Zealand Waterfron Workers Union* [1991] 2 ERNZ 787; *Cook Islands National Line Ltd v. New Zealand Seafarers IUW* [1991] 3 ERNZ 358; *International Stevedoring Operations Ltd v. New Zealand Waterfront Workers Union* [2001] ERNZ 321.
1512. As to which *see Rookes v. Barnard* [1964] AC 1129; *see* para. 280.
1513. *News Group Newspapers Ltd v. SOGAT 82 (No. 2)* [1987] ICR 181.
1514. *See* para. 164.
1515. Summary Offences Act 1981, s. 21; *Ihaia v. Police* [1982] 2 NZLR 211.
1516. *See* paras 280–281, 291.

II. Inducing Breach of Contract

A. Elements

270. The modern form of the tort of inducing a breach of contract originates with the decision in *Lumley v. Gye*.[1517] The defendant impresario induced a singer to break her contract with the plaintiff, a rival, and to perform for the defendant instead. The defendant was held liable to pay damages to the rival, on the basis that he had interfered with the plaintiff's legitimate expectation that others would not interfere with his contractual rights.

In subsequent decisions the ambit of the decision was widened, from inducing a breach of a contract to interference with a contract without necessarily causing a breach. In *Jiao v. Barge*[1518] the Court of Appeal accepted that there was a tort of interference with contractual relations, and that its essential elements were: (1) a legally enforceable contract; (2) a deliberate intention to interfere with the contract in order to harm or bring pressure to bear on the plaintiff; (3) direct persuasion or indirect interference by unlawful means; (4) interference without lawful justification; and (5) interference causing loss to the plaintiff. These elements represented the common understanding of the law at the time of the decision, but since then the House of Lords, in *OBG Ltd v. Allan*,[1519] has rejected the wider version of the tort and restored the founding principles of *Lumley v. Gye*. On this basis the elements to liability are: (1) conduct that in fact induces a breach of contract; (2) knowledge that the conduct would induce a breach; (3) an intention to induce a breach; and (4) damage caused by the inducing conduct. In exceptional cases there is (5) a defence of justification.

The decision of their Lordships in *OBG* has been applied in the Court of Appeal, albeit without the court definitively accepting the recasting of the law in that case.[1520] In the examination of the law that follows we will assume that *OBG* will be fully accepted and applied.

B. Conduct Inducing a Breach of Contract

1. Accessory Liability

271. In *OBG Ltd v. Allan*[1521] Lord Hoffmann said that the important point to bear in mind about *Lumley v. Gye* was that the person procuring the breach of contract was held liable as accessory to the liability of the contracting party. Liability depended upon the contracting party having committed an actionable wrong. This

---

1517. (1853) 2 El & B 216; 118 ER 749.
1518. CA 236/05, 19 Jul. 2006.
1519. [2008] 1 AC 1.
1520. *Diver v. Loktronic Industries Ltd* [2012] 2 NZLR 388. The decision has been applied in a number of High Court cases: *see*, for example, *Onyx Bar & Café (Cambridge) Ltd v. Jans* [2012] NZHC 948; *Philip Moore & Co Ltd v. Surridge* [2018] NZHC 562 at [202].
1521. [2008] 1 AC 1 at [5]; and *see* the judgment of Lord Nicholls at [172]; *One Money Mail Ltd v. RIA Financial Services* [2015] EWCA Civ 1084 at [28].

was contrasted with the tort of causing loss by unlawful means, which imposed primary liability on a defendant for his own conduct, irrespective of whether anyone else was liable either in contract or tort.

In some cases a defendant has been held liable in this tort for disabling or preventing a party to a contract from performing it.[1522] But in prevention cases the defendant does not join with the contracting party in a wrong but acts independently of that party. There is no question of accessory liability. So the defendant is liable, if at all, for the tort of causing loss by unlawful means.[1523]

2. Inducing Conduct

272. There is inducing conduct where the breaking of the contract is fairly attributable to any pressure, persuasion, or procuration on the part of the defendant.[1524] This may be contrasted with the mere giving of information or advice, which is not actionable.[1525] The issue really is one of causation. The plaintiff must establish more than advice simpliciter concerning possible dangers arising from the continuance of contractual relations, but must prove actual inducement, procurement, or coercion.[1526] The principle is the same as that on which a person is liable for the act of another in committing a tort.[1527]

3. Inducing Breach

273. Formerly, the courts held that a defendant could be liable for indirectly interfering with a contract provided the means used were unlawful. In *DC Thomson & Co. Ltd v. Deakin*[1528] the Court of Appeal in England held that *Lumley v. Gye* extended to all interference with contractual relations by unlawful means. Direct procurement of a breach of contract was regarded as a wrongful act in itself and was the 'primary form' of the tort. But other forms of interference with contracts by unlawful means were seen as coming within the same tort. This unified theory

1522. For example, *GWK Ltd v. Dunlop Rubber Co. Ltd* (1926) 42 TLR 376; and *see Merkur Island Shipping Corporation v. Laughton* [1983] 2 AC 570 at 581.
1523. *OBG Ltd v. Allan* [2008] 1 AC 1, espec at [174]–[180].
1524. *Pete's Towing Services Ltd v. Northern Industrial Union of Workers* [1970] NZLR 32.
1525. *Pete's Towing Services Ltd v. Northern Industrial Union of Workers* [1970] NZLR 32 at 47; *New Zealand Baking Trades Employees Industrial Union v. General Foods Corporation (NZ) Ltd* [1985] 2 NZLR 110.
1526. *Northern Road Transport Union v. Kawau Island Ferries Ltd* [1974] 2 NZLR 617.
1527. *See CBS Songs Ltd v. Amstrad Consumer Electronics plc* [1988] AC 1013; *Unilever plc v. Chefaro Proprietaries* [1994] FSR 135.
1528. [1952] Ch 646; and *see Merkur Island Shipping Corporation v. Laughton* [1983] 2 AC 570.

treated procuring breach of contract as one species of a more general tort of actionable interference with contractual rights. It has been accepted in a number of decisions in New Zealand.[1529] But in *OBG Ltd v. Allan*[1530] the House of Lords saw this theory as a source of confusion. Lord Hoffmann said that it distracted attention from the real question, which was whether the defendant's acts of encouragement, threat, persuasion, and so forth had a sufficient causal connection with the breach by the contracting party to attract accessory liability. The direct/indirect distinction also had the further disadvantage that it suggested that the two forms of the tort were mutually exclusive. But there was no reason why the same act should not create both accessory liability for procuring breach of contract and primary liability for causing loss by unlawful means. The distinction was unsatisfactory, and the two torts should be restored to the independent status that they originally enjoyed.

Accordingly, there can be no liability for inducing breach of contract if the defendant acts lawfully and prevents or hinders performance without causing any breach, as where the contract contains a 'force majeure' clause. There can be no secondary liability without primary liability. In *OBG Ltd v. Allan*[1531] Lord Nicholls thought that the force majeure point could hardly arise in inducement cases, on the basis that an exemption clause could scarcely apply to a contracting party who chose to default. In unlawful interference cases, the existence of an exemption clause would be neither here nor there. The question always would be: how much loss did this interference cause the claimant?

In *OBG* itself, the invalidly appointed receivers of the claimant company, acting in good faith, terminated the contracts of the majority of the claimants' subcontractors and settled claims under contracts made by the claimants. The claim for inducing breach of contract failed, for there had been no breach or non-performance of any contract, and therefore there was no wrong to which accessory liability for breach of contract could attach.

C. Knowledge That the Conduct Would Induce a Breach of the Contract

274. The defendant must intend to interfere with the contract. In order to hold this intention, the defendant must know of the existence of the contract, but need not know its exact terms.[1532] Generalized knowledge about a contractual situation or business practice in a particular field can suffice. For example, seamen's unions

---

1529. *Pete's Towing Services Ltd v. Northern Industrial Union of Workers* [1970] NZLR 32 at 46–47; *Ports of Auckland Ltd v. New Zealand Seafarers Union* HC, Auckland, CL 40/97, J. Laurenson, 26 Nov. 1998; *International Stevedoring Operations Ltd v. New Zealand Waterfront Workers Union* [2001] ERNZ 321.

1530. [2008] 1 AC 1 at [34]–[38].

1531. [2008] 1 AC 1 at [181]–[190], disapproving *Torquay Hotel Co. Ltd v. Cousins* [1969] 2 Ch 106 and *Merkur Island Shipping Corporation v. Laughton* [1983] 2 AC 570 at 608; and *see* per Lord Hoffmann at [44].

1532. *Pete's Towing Services Ltd v. Northern Industrial IUW* [1970] NZLR 32, 46; *Northern Drivers' Union v. Kawau Island Ferries Ltd* [1974] 2 NZLR 617 at 622; *McIntyre v. Bianchi* [1992] 3 ERNZ 1057.

and officials will be taken to understand that charterparties, hiring of ships and the like are founded on binding contracts.[1533]

A person who has the means of knowledge of a contract or the terms of a contract but deliberately disregards them, or in other words turns a blind eye, can be treated as having knowledge of the contract or of those terms. In Lord Denning's words, 'it is unlawful for a third person to procure a breach of contract knowingly, or recklessly, indifferent whether it is a breach or not'.[1534] This accords with the general principle of law that a conscious decision not to inquire into a fact is in many cases treated as equivalent to knowledge of that fact.[1535]

Ellen France J in the Court of Appeal has said that the required state of knowledge involves a suspicion of sufficient strength that a contract exists and a deliberate choice not to make inquiries. The fact that the existence of a contract should have been obvious is not sufficient as that is negligence. A subjective approach is required, this according with the fact that liability is for an intentional tort.[1536]

D. Intention to Induce a Breach of the Contract

275. The defendant must intend to procure a breach of contract, and in *Jiao v. Barge*[1537] the Court of Appeal thought that he or she must do this in order to harm or bring pressure to bear on the plaintiff. But *OBG Ltd v. Allan*[1538] the House of Lords rejected this second element. Lord Hoffmann said that it was necessary to distinguish between ends, means, and consequences. If someone knowingly caused a breach of contract, it did not normally matter that it was the means by which he intended to achieve some further aim. People seldom knowingly caused loss by unlawful means out of simple disinterested malice. It was usually to achieve the further end of securing an economic advantage to themselves. But if the breach was neither an end in itself nor the means to an end, but merely a foreseeable consequence, then it could not for this purpose be said to have been intended. That was what judges and writers meant when they said that the claimant must have been 'targeted' or 'aimed at'.[1539] Lord Nicholls said that the defendant was liable if he induced the contracting party to act in a way he knew was a breach of that party's obligations under the contract. But a desire to injure the claimant was not an essential ingredient of the tort.[1540]

1533. *International Stevedoring Operations Ltd v. New Zealand Waterfront Workers Union* [2001] ERNZ 321.
1534. *Emerald Construction Co. Ltd v. Lowthian* [1966] 1 WLR 691 at 700–701.
1535. *OBG Ltd v. Allan* [2008] 1 AC 1 at [41].
1536. *Diver v. Loktronic Industries Ltd* [2012] 2 NZLR 388 at [47]; and *see British Industrial Plastics Ltd v. Ferguson* [1940] 1 All ER 479; *OBG Ltd v. Allan* [2008] 1 AC 1 at [39]–[41].
1537. CA 236/05, 19 Jul. 2006.
1538. [2008] 1 AC 1.
1539. *Ibid.*, at [42]–[43].
1540. *Ibid.*, at [192]; *see*, for example, *Sar Petroleum Inc v. Peace Hills Trust Co* (2010) 318 DLR (4th) 70; *Barber v. Vrozos* (2010) 322 DLR (4th) 577.

In *Mainstream Properties Ltd v. Young*, decided together with *OBG*, two employees of the claimant property development company, acting in breach of their contracts of employment, diverted a development opportunity to a joint venture in which they were interested. The defendant, knowing of the employees' duties towards the claimant but believing, wrongly, that there was no conflict of interest and that the employees would not be acting in breach of contract, provided the finance for the project. So the defendant had acted honestly, he had not been indifferent as to whether there was a breach, nor had he consciously made the decision not to inquire or to shut his eyes in case he discovered a disagreeable truth. Accordingly, he had not intended to cause a breach of the employment contracts.

A defendant who honestly believed that the act he was procuring would not amount to a breach of contract was not liable, even if that belief was mistaken in law, and it did not matter whether the defendant's erroneous belief was caused by his own ignorance or by incorrect advice received from his lawyers.[1541]

E. Justification

276. Inducing a breach of contract sometimes may be justified, as where the defendant acts in the exercise of an equal or superior right of his own.[1542] However, the limits to the defence have not been precisely defined. Relevant factors may include the nature of the contract broken; the position of the parties to the contract; the grounds for the breach; the means employed to procure the breach; the relation of the person procuring the breach to the person who breaks the contract; and the object of the person procuring the breach.[1543]

A person is justified in insisting on the performance of another inconsistent contract made previously between him or her and the third person,[1544] or in acting in accordance with a statutory right.[1545] It has also been held that inducing a breach is justified where this is done in performance of a particularly compelling moral duty. Examples are where the defendant induced breaches of the plaintiff's contracts with theatre proprietors in order to force him to pay higher wages to chorus girls who had been compelled to resort to prostitution;[1546] and where the defendant acted to protect the public from the 'absolutely nonsensical mumbo-jumbo' of the plaintiff Scientologists.[1547] There is also support for the view, at least in New Zealand, that a union may sometimes be justified in inducing a breach of contract where this is done in pursuance of its duty to protect the interests of its members.[1548] However,

1541. *Allen v. Pollock* [2020] EWCA Civ 258, [2020] 2 WLR 1070.
1542. *OBG Ltd v. Allan* [2008] 1 AC 1 at [193].
1543. *Glamorgan Coal Co. Ltd v. South Wales Miners' Federation* [1903] 2 KB 545 at 574.
1544. *State Insurance Ltd v. New Zealand Motor Body Builders' Association Inc* (1992) 5 TCLR 12.
1545. *Stott v. Gamble* [1916] 2 KB 504.
1546. *Brimelow v. Casson* [1924] 1 Ch 302.
1547. *Church of Scientology of California v. Kaufman* [1973] RPC 627.
1548. *Pete's Towing Services Ltd v. Northern Industrial IUW* [1970] NZLR 32, 46; *Northern Drivers' Union v. Kawau Island Ferries Ltd* [1974] 2 NZLR 617 at 622; *McIntyre v. Bianchi* [1992] 3 ERNZ 1057; cp *Ports of Auckland Ltd v. New Zealand Seafarers Union* HC, Auckland, CL 40/97, J. Laurenson, 26 Nov. 1998.

it is no defence that the defendant did not act maliciously, or that he or she was motivated by self-interest, or, normally, that he or she acted for impersonal or altruistic motives.

F. Damage

277. Actual damage must be shown: it is the gist of the action.[1549] Particular damage need not be shown if the defendant has induced a breach that must in the ordinary course of business cause damage to the plaintiff.[1550] As regards the question of remoteness, the plaintiff can recover for damage that was intended,[1551] or that was a reasonably foreseeable consequence of the defendant's conduct.[1552]

III. Causing Loss by Unlawful Means

A. Elements

278. It is a tort to intentionally cause loss to another by the use of unlawful means. This is a tort of primary liability, which does not require a wrongful act by anyone else. Its origins are found in the long-standing decisions in *Garret v. Taylor*[1553] and *Tarleton v. M'Gawley*.[1554] In *Garret*, the defendant was held liable because he drove away the plaintiff's customers by threatening them with mayhem and vexatious suits. In *Tarleton*, the defendant was similarly liable for depriving a rivalship of trade, by firing at African traders approaching the ship by canoe in order to scare them away.

In *Van Camp Chocolates Ltd v. Aulsebrooks Ltd*,[1555] the Court of Appeal accepted that the tort was part of New Zealand law. More recently, in *Diver v. Loktronic Industries Ltd*,[1556] the Court of Appeal accepted as correct the relevant applicable principles as stated by the House of Lords in *OBG Ltd v. Allan*.

1549. *Exchange Telegraph Co. Ltd v. Gregory & Co.* [1896] 1 QB 147.
1550. *Ibid.*
1551. *Quinn v. Leathem* [1901] AC 495 at 537.
1552. *Nauru Local Government Council v. New Zealand Seamen's Industrial Union of Workers* [1986] 1 NZLR 466 at 481.
1553. (1620) Cro Jac 567.
1554. (1790) 1 Peake NPC 270.
1555. [1984] 1 NZLR 354. For earlier recognition of the tort *see Fairburn Wright & Co. Ltd v. Levin & Co. Ltd* (1914) 34 NZLR 1; *Coleman v. Myers* [1977] 2 NZLR 225 at 294.
1556. *Diver v. Loktronic Industries Ltd* [2012] 2 NZLR 388 at [100]. The paragraphs in this case that deal with unlawful means ([100]–[126]) have been omitted in the NZLR report.

It is clear that this tort may be committed in circumstances not covered by other existing torts, as where no contract is broken and there is no element of combination. Its essence, as described by Lord Lindley in *Quinn v. Leathem*[1557] and confirmed by Lord Hoffmann and Lord Nicholls in *OBG Ltd v. Allan*[1558] is:

(1) a wrongful interference with the actions of a third party in which the claimant has an economic interest;
(2) an intention thereby to cause loss to the claimant; and
(3) actual damage suffered by the claimant.

It is possible that there could, exceptionally, be a defence of justification, but there is little authority on the point.

There is no reason why the same facts should not give rise both to accessory liability for inducing breach of contract and primary liability for using unlawful means. The areas of liability under the two torts may be intersecting circles that cover common ground.[1559]

B. Unlawful Means

1. Nature of the Unlawful Means

279. There has been some uncertainty in the cases as to what should count as unlawful means, but the law has been clarified in *OBG Ltd v. Allan.*[1560] Lord Hoffmann considered that acts against a third party counted as unlawful means only if they were actionable by that party, or would have been actionable if the third party had suffered loss. So the requisite unlawful means consisted of acts intended to cause loss to the claimant by interfering with the freedom of a third party in a way that was unlawful as against that third party and that was intended to cause loss to the claimant. It did not include acts that might be unlawful against a third party but that did not affect his freedom to deal with the claimant.[1561] The common law had traditionally been reluctant to become involved in devising rules of fair competition, and the courts should be similarly cautious in extending a tort that was designed only to enforce basic standards of civilized behaviour in economic competition. Otherwise there was a danger that it would provide a cause of action based on acts that were wrongful only in the irrelevant sense that a third party had the right to complain if he chose to do so. It would be arbitrary and illogical to make liability

1557. [1901] AC 495.
1558. [2008] 1 AC 1 at [56]–[57], [143]–[144]. The analysis has been accepted in New Zealand: *Diver v. Loktronic Industries Ltd* [2012] 2 NZLR 388 at [100]; *Philip Moore & Co Ltd v. Surridge* [2018] NZHC 562.
1559. *OBG Ltd v. Allan* [2008] 1 AC 1 at [21].
1560. [2008] 1 AC 1.
1561. This analysis was accepted in *Diver v. Loktronic Industries Ltd* [2012] 2 NZLR 388 at [101]; and *see Secretary of State for Health v. Servier Laboratories Ltd* [2019] EWCA Civ 1160, [2019] 3 WLR 938.

depend upon whether the defendant had done something that was wrongful for reasons that had nothing to do with the damage inflicted on the claimant.

Lord Nicholls took a wider view. He thought that all conduct rendered unlawful by the civil or the criminal law was included, on the ground that the law should curb clearly excessive conduct. But Lord Hoffmann's views were supported by Lord Walker, Baroness Hale, and Lord Brown and are likely to prevail in New Zealand.[1562]

2. Actionable Unlawful Conduct

280. The unlawful conduct may be the committing of a crime, a tort, a breach of contract, or a breach of a statute. But the unlawful conduct must be actionable by the third party, or potentially actionable if the third party had suffered damage. Examples include: intentionally causing loss to the plaintiff by fraudulently inducing a third party to act to the plaintiff's detriment,[1563] interfering with the plaintiff's livelihood by defaming her and conspiring to injure her by breaking a contract with a third party,[1564] committing a trespass to the goods of a third party with the aim of damaging the plaintiff,[1565] preventing performance of a contract by destroying necessary tools or machinery,[1566] physically detaining a party to a contract with the plaintiff so that that party is unable to perform the contract,[1567] and threatening a contracting party with assault unless he breaks his contract with the plaintiff.[1568]

The final example indicates that the tort may be committed where unlawful threats are used to intimidate a third party in order to cause loss to the plaintiff. This right of action for intimidation was upheld by the House of Lords in *Rookes v. Barnard*,[1569] where it was confirmed that the threat of unlawful conduct can include a threat to break a contract. In *OBG*, their Lordships recognized that intimidation can be understood simply as a variant of the broader tort.[1570] However, Lord Hoffmann, while recognizing this, added a footnote by saying that he was concerned only with interference with the actions of a third party in relation to the plaintiff, and was not deciding whether a claimant who had been compelled by unlawful intimidation to act to his own detriment could sue for his loss. Such a case raised altogether different issues. The concept of 'two-party intimidation' has been accepted in England[1571] and in several New Zealand cases.[1572] However, allowing the claim

---

1562. In *Diver v. Loktronic Industries Ltd* [2012] 2 NZLR 388 the Court of Appeal adopted the narrower view, but the point was not in issue in that case and there was no debate about it.
1563. *National Phonograph Co. Ltd v. Edison-Bell Consolidated Phonograph Co. Ltd* [1908] 1 Ch 335; *Lonrho plc v. Fayed* [1990] 2 QB 479.
1564. *Alleslev-Krofchak v. Valcom Ltd* (2010) 322 DLR (4th) 193.
1565. *GWK Ltd v. Dunlop Rubber Co. Ltd* (1926) 42 TLR 376.
1566. *DC Thomson & Co. Ltd v. Deakin* [1952] Ch 646 at 696, 702.
1567. *DC Thomson & Co. Ltd v. Deakin* [1952] Ch 646 at 677–678.
1568. *OBG Ltd v. Allan* [2008] 1 AC 1 at [21].
1569. [1964] AC 1129.
1570. [2008] 1 AC 1 at [7].
1571. *See Kolmar Group AG v. Traxpo Enterprises Ltd* [2010] 2 Lloyd's Rep. 653; *Berezovsky v. Abramovich* [2011] 1 WLR 2290 (implied threat can suffice).
1572. *See*, for example, *Huljich v. Hall* [1973] 2 NZLR 279; *O'Boyle v. Liggett* HC Christchurch, A174/81, J. Roper, 18 May 1984; *Broadlands Finance Ltd v. Leland* HC Auckland, A249/80, J. Thorp,

tends to convert the element of duress from a factor that vitiates the plaintiff's consent to a transaction into a cause of action for damages. In the common case where the threat is to break a contract with the plaintiff, it means that the threat becomes actionable independently of the remedy for breach of contract should the threat be carried into execution.[1573]

3. Non-actionable Unlawful Conduct

281. Unlawful conduct that does not interfere with the third party's liberty of action in relation to the plaintiff, even if actionable by that party, does not give rise to a claim by the plaintiff for the loss that the conduct may have caused. So a claim by the exclusive licensee of a registered design that the defendant had intentionally caused him loss by unlawful means, by selling goods that infringed the rights of the registered owner, was rejected, on the ground that the exploitation of the licence may not have been so successful commercially by reason of the infringement, but the contractual relations between the owner and the licensee were unaffected.[1574]

It is clear that conduct that is alleged to be a criminal offence but that is not actionable by anyone cannot found a claim. In *Lonrho Ltd v. Shell Petroleum Co. Ltd (No. 2)*,[1575] the plaintiff alleged that the defendant had supplied oil in breach of a statute prescribing sanctions on trading with the unlawful regime in Rhodesia that this had prolonged the period during which sanctions were imposed, and that the plaintiff suffered loss while its refinery and pipeline in Rhodesia stood idle. The House of Lords held that the illegality gave rise to no cause of action on which the plaintiff could rely. The defendant did not interfere with any third party's dealings with the plaintiff, and even if it had done so, its actions were not wrongful in the sense of being actionable by such third party. In *OBG Ltd v. Allan*[1576] Lord Hoffmann said that in a case like *Lonrho* it was not for the courts to create a cause of action out of a regulatory or criminal statute that Parliament did not intend to be actionable in private law.[1577]

In *Van Camp Chocolates Ltd v. Aulsebrooks Ltd*,[1578] the Court of Appeal emphasized the need for a link between the unlawful means and the plaintiff, and recognized in light of *Lonrho* that early New Zealand cases relying on breach of statute as unlawful means might have to be reconsidered. This approach is consistent with

7 Sep. 1983. In *Outtrim v. Li* [2010] NZAR 282 at [70], it was held that mere threats to register a caveat over land were not capable of giving rise to the tort of intentionally causing loss by unlawful means or any subsidiary tort of intimidation.

1573. *See* generally *International Encyclopaedia of Laws: Contracts (New Zealand)*, para. 136.

1574. *Isaac Oren v. red Box Toy Factory Ltd* [1999] FSR 785; and *see RCA Corporation v. Pollard* [1983] Ch 135 (selling bootleg records in breach of a statute).

1575. [1982] AC 173.

1576. [2008] 1 AC 1 at [57].

1577. However, in *Revenue and Customs Commissioners v. Total Network SL* [2008] 1 AC 1174 Lord Walker thought that the focus in *Lonrho* was on the absence of any intent to injure: *see* para. 291.

1578. [1984] 1 NZLR 354 at 359.

that in *OBG*, but the question as to what unlawful conduct should be treated as actionable has not been finally determined.

C. Intention to Cause Harm

282. The defendant must have the intention to cause harm to the plaintiff. The nature of this intention was considered by the Court of Appeal in *Van Camp Chocolates Ltd v. Aulsebrooks Ltd.*[1579] An Australian company (E) that manufactured health food bars entered negotiations with a New Zealand company (ABC) concerning a possible licensing agreement, but these were abandoned. ABC then began manufacturing bars in New Zealand, and made use of confidential information that E had disclosed during the negotiations. E obtained an injunction and an account of profits,[1580] and following this the plaintiff, a licensee of E, sought damages from the defendant, the legal successor of ABC, for causing loss by unlawful means. The claim was rejected, on the ground that any intention of causing loss to the plaintiff 'could have been no more than superadded and inessential'. The court expressed the governing principles in this way:

> In principle, as we see it, an intent to harm a plaintiff's economic interests should not transmute the defendant's conduct into a tort actionable by the plaintiff unless that intent is a cause of his conduct. If the defendant would have used the unlawful means in question without that intent and if that intent alone would not have led him to act as he did, the mere existence of the purely collateral and extraneous malicious motive should not make all the difference. The essence of the tort is deliberate interference with the plaintiff's interests by unlawful means. If the reasons which actuate the defendant to use unlawful means are wholly independent of a wish to interfere with the plaintiff's business, such interference being no more than an incidental consequence foreseen by and gratifying to the defendant, we think that to impose liability would be to stretch the tort too far.

So, on this view, an intention to harm the plaintiff need not be the defendant's only or primary purpose, but it must at least be a concurrent and activating purpose. However, the distinction between an activating purpose and a causative but merely incidental purpose may not be easy to draw.[1581]

In *OBG Ltd v. Allan*[1582] the House of Lords once again has provided some clarification. Lord Hoffmann said that in the *Lumley* tort there had to be an intention to procure a breach of contract. In the unlawful means tort there had to be an intention to cause loss. But the concept of intention was in both cases the same. A person would intend to cause loss even though it was the means by which he or she achieved the end of enriching himself or herself. On the other hand, a person was

1579. [1984] 1 NZLR 354.
1580. *See AB Consolidated Ltd v. Europe Strength Food Co. Pty Ltd* [1978] 2 NZLR 515.
1581. *See McIntyre v. Bianchi* [1992] 3 ERNZ 1057 at 1105.
1582. [2008] 1 AC 1.

not liable for loss that was neither a desired end nor a means of attaining it but merely a foreseeable consequence of his or her actions. However, Lord Nicholls, expressing a minority view, required a highly specific intention that 'targeted' the plaintiff. But this would include a case where the defendant sought to advance his own interests by conduct necessarily injurious to the claimant – where loss to the claimant was the other side of the coin from gain to the defendant.

On the facts of *OBG v. Allan*,[1583] the receivers were not liable as they had acted in good faith, they had not employed unlawful means, and they had not intended to cause any loss to the claimant. Again, in *Mainstream Properties Ltd v. Young*,[1584] the defendant had not intended to cause a breach of contract nor had he caused loss by unlawful means.

The approach of the Court in *Van Camp* and the distinction between an intended end and unintended consequences were accepted as correct in principle by the Court of Appeal in *Diver v. Loktronic Industries Ltd.*[1585] The plaintiff's loss must therefore be either the desired end itself or the intended means of obtaining it.

D. Damage

283. Damage must be shown,[1586] which normally will be financial. The damage may be interference with a contract without causing actual breach, or interference with the creation of a contract,[1587] or, more broadly, loss of profitable business opportunities,[1588] but there must always be the requisite intention to harm and the use of unlawful means. The tort might also extend to interference with non-pecuniary interests, such as the interest of an occupier in having visitors to his or her house.[1589]

IV. Conspiracy

284. There are two forms of actionable conspiracy. One is a conspiracy with an unlawful purpose and the other is a conspiracy using unlawful means.[1590]

1583. *See* para. 273.
1584. *See* para. 275.
1585. *Diver v. Loktronic Industries Ltd* [2012] 2 NZLR 388 at [100]; *Philip Moore & Co Ltd v. Surridge* [2018] NZHC 562.
1586. *Van Camp Chocolates Ltd v. Aulsebrooks Ltd* [1984] 1 NZLR 354; *Philip Moore & Co Ltd v. Surridge* [2018] NZHC 562.
1587. *JT Stratford & Son Ltd v. Lindley* [1965] AC 269 at 324; *Merkur Island Shipping Corporation Laughton* [1983] 2 AC 570 at 609.
1588. *Van Camp Chocolates Ltd v. Aulsebrooks Ltd* [1984] 1 NZLR 354 (loss of profits caused by the defendant's use of the plaintiff's confidential information).
1589. *Allen v. Flood* [1898] AC 1 at 137.
1590. The development of the tort of conspiracy is discussed by the UK Supreme Court in *JSC BTA Bank v. Ablyazov (No 14)* [2018] UKSC 19, [2018] 2 WLR 1125.

A. Conspiracy with an Unlawful Purpose

285. The elements necessary to establish liability for conspiracy with an unlawful purpose, or 'simple' conspiracy, were identified in *Crofter Hand Woven Harris Tweed Co. Ltd v. Veitch.*[1591] The House of Lords held that there must be:

(1) a combination of two or more persons;
(2) made with the dominant purpose of injuring another and not of legitimate self-interest; and
(3) causing damage to the other person.

Here the defendant union officials combined with mill owners to hinder the supply of yarn by a competitor to small wool producers, their object being to reduce competition against the mill owners who employed their members. It was held that they were justified in their actions. The mill owners were acting in self-interest to protect their trade, and the union officials were seeking to improve conditions for their members, having negotiated increased wages and a closed shop with the mill owners.

The difficulty in establishing the elements to liability means that the tort was virtually strangled at its birth. Indeed, the tort is widely regarded as anomalous,[1592] on the basis that it makes conduct unlawful in circumstances where it is not unlawful when done by one person alone. Even so, it has been accepted as applying in New Zealand on a number of occasions.[1593]

1. The Combination

286. It is the 'magic of plurality' to achieve ends that, if brought about by a sole actor, would not be tortious, which constitutes the cause of action.[1594] Accordingly, it is essential that there is shown to be a combination followed by action taken pursuant to a common design, since the same conduct by an individual, without any combination, would not be actionable. So evidence must be adduced as to the interests, objects, and actions of the alleged combiners.[1595] Normally the plaintiff will seek to draw inferences from overt acts and to show community of purpose from coincidental behaviour.[1596]

1591. [1942] AC 435.

1592. *See* especially *Lonrho Ltd v. Shell Petroleum Co. Ltd (No. 2)* [1982] AC 173 at 188; *Lonrho plc v. Fayed* [1992] 1 AC 448.

1593. *See*, in particular, *PTY Homes Ltd v. Shand* [1968] NZLR 105 at 109; *Pete's Towing Services Ltd v. Northern IUW* [1970] NZLR 32 at 55; *SSC & B: Lintas New Zealand Ltd v. Murphy* [1986] 2 NZLR 436 at 460.

1594. *Pete's Towing Services Ltd v. Northern IUW* [1970] NZLR 32 at 55.

1595. *PTY Homes Ltd v. Shand* [1968] NZLR 105 at 110. Union officials and members can combine to injure, but if union officials are acting as agents of the union in carrying out its policy, they might not be liable as conspiring with each other or the union: *Nauru Local Government Council v. New Zealand Seamen's IUW*, HC Wellington, A 583/78, Ongley J, 27 Jul. 1982. An employee who is simply carrying out the business of the employer is not normally to be regarded as conspiring with the employer: *PTY Homes* at 113.

1596. *McIntyre v. Bianchi* [1992] 3 ERNZ 1057 at 1099.

2. Intention

287. The purpose of the combination must have been to injure the plaintiff, for it is this purpose that makes the combination unlawful. It is not enough that harm to the plaintiff may have been foreseeable, or even inevitable: 'It is not consequence that matters, but purpose.'[1597] Furthermore, injury to the plaintiff must have been the predominant purpose rather than a secondary or incidental purpose.[1598] If the defendant acts with a legitimate purpose, and this includes acting out of simple self-interest, then he or she is excused. Furthermore, the onus lies on the plaintiff to prove the absence of a legitimating purpose as an element in establishing the tort rather than on the defendant to prove its existence by way of a defence.[1599] All this means that liability for the tort is likely to be established only very rarely.

Crofter confirmed the early decisions,[1600] that legitimate self-interest could justify a conspiracy as regards both trade interests and union activity. Examples of both can be found in New Zealand law. As regards the first, an allegation of conspiracy to injure the plaintiff's car hire business was rejected, on the ground that the defendant's purpose was to promote the success of their own business.[1601] Again, a defendant's 'asset stripping' was held not to have been dominantly directed at the plaintiff creditor, but was done for other business purposes, including protecting assets and settling with other creditors.[1602] As regards the second, union officials were justified in acting to prevent industrial discord and financial harm to the union.[1603] Furthermore, the notion of self-interest has been interpreted widely, and certainly is not confined to economic self-interest. It has included a desire to break a so-called colour bar,[1604] a belief in the need for union solidarity and mutual support,[1605] and a good faith performance of a public duty in settling a contentious industrial dispute.[1606]

On the other hand, where the real or predominant purpose of the defendants is to injure or punish the plaintiff, or to demonstrate the power of the conspirators, or to exact revenge, this is illegitimate and actionable.[1607]

1597. *Crofter Hand Woven Harris Tweed Co. Ltd v. Veitch* [1942] AC 435 at 445.

1598. *Crofter Hand Woven Harris Tweed Co. Ltd v. Veitch* [1942] AC 435 at 444; *Pete's Towing Services Ltd v. Northern IUW* [1970] NZLR 32 at 56; *Lonrho Ltd v. Shell Petroleum Co. Ltd* [1982] AC 173 at 189; *SSC & B: Lintas New Zealand Ltd v. Murphy* [1986] 2 NZLR 436 at 460; *Hadmor Productions Ltd v. Hamilton* [1983] 1 AC 191 at 228.

1599. *Sorrell v. Smith* [1925] AC 700; *PTY Homes Ltd v. Shand* [1968] NZLR 105 at 110; *Pete's Towing Services Ltd v. Northern IUW* [1970] NZLR 32 at 56; *Dellabarca v. Northern Storemen and Packers Union* [1989] 2 NZLR 734.

1600. *See* in particular *Mogul Steamship Co. v. McGregor Gow & Co.* [1892] AC 25; *Quinn v. Leathem* [1901] AC 495; *Sorrell v. Smith* [1925] AC 700.

1601. *Dominion Rent A Car Ltd v. Budget Rent A Car Systems (1970) Ltd* [1987] 2 NZLR 395.

1602. *Wagner v. Gill* [2013] NZHC 1304. There was no appeal against this aspect of the decision in *Wagner v. Gill* [2015] 3 NZLR 157.

1603. *Pete's Towing Services Ltd v. Northern IUW* [1970] NZLR 32 at 56.

1604. *Scala Ballroom (Wolverhampton) Ltd v. Ratcliffe* [1958] 1 WLR 1057.

1605. *Nauru Local Government Council v. New Zealand Seamen's IUW*, HC Wellington, A 583/78, J. Ongley, 27 Jul. 1982 (on appeal [1986] 1 NZLR 466).

1606. *PTY Homes Ltd v. Shand* [1968] NZLR 105.

1607. *Huntley v. Thornton* [1957] 1 WLR 321; *O'Boyle v. Liggett* HC, Christchurch, A 174/81, J. Roper, 18 May 1984; *Gulf Oil (Great Britain) Ltd v. Page* [1987] Ch 327.

The essence of the tort being the *combination* to injure, it follows that the wrongful purpose must be shared by the other members of the combination. If one has the purpose of injuring the plaintiff and the others do not, there is no unlawful purpose conspiracy and no liability.[1608]

3. Damage

288. Damage is the gist of the action.[1609] The loss that was intended by the defendants is recoverable and so is the other loss that is not too remote. This can include, for example, loss of business profits,[1610] and expenses incurred by the plaintiff in investigating and counteracting the conduct of the defendants.[1611] Aggravated and exemplary damages can be recovered in appropriate cases.[1612]

B. Conspiracy by Unlawful Means

289. An 'unlawful means conspiracy' is a combination of persons who act in concert so as to intentionally injure the plaintiff in his trade or other legitimate interests by an act that is independently unlawful.[1613] The elements of combination, overt act, and damage must be established in the same way as with unlawful purpose conspiracy for there to be liability under this head. However, we must look separately at the defendants' intention and at the element of unlawful means.

1. Intention

290. There must be a combination whose object is to injure the plaintiff. It is not enough that the defendants combine to do an unlawful act that causes damage to the plaintiff. However, in *Lonrho plc v. Fayed*[1614] the House of Lords held that in the case of a conspiracy by unlawful means, unlike in the case of a *Crofter* conspiracy, the object to injure need not be the defendants' predominant purpose. So the necessary mental element is an intention to inflict damage as an end in itself, or to inflict it as a means to some other end. The intention to injure is at least a concurrent or subsidiary purpose.

1608. *Nauru Local Government Council v. New Zealand Seamen's IUW*, HC Wellington, A 583/78, J. Ongley, 27 Jul. 1982 (on appeal [1986] 1 NZLR 466); *Ballard v. Multiplex Ltd* [2012] NSWSC 426 at [72].
1609. *Crofter Hand Woven Harris Tweed Co. Ltd v. Veitch* [1942] AC 435 at 439; *Wagner v. Gill* [2015] 3 NZLR 157.
1610. *SSC & B: Lintas New Zealand Ltd v. Murphy* [1986] 2 NZLR 436.
1611. *BMTA v. Salvadori* [1949] Ch 556.
1612. *O'Boyle v. Liggett* HC, Christchurch, A 174/81, Roper J, 18 May 1984; *SSC & B: Lintas New Zealand Ltd v. Murphy* [1986] 2 NZLR 436; *McIntyre v. Bianchi* [1992] 3 ERNZ 1057.
1613. *SSC & B: Lintas New Zealand Ltd v. Murphy* [1986] 2 NZLR 436 at 461.
1614. [1992] 1 AC 448.

In *Revenue and Customs Commissioners v. Total Network SL*[1615] the House of Lords held that a conspiracy to defraud the public revenue was actionable by the claimant commissioners; although the conspirators intended primarily to enrich themselves by their scheme, their conduct was aimed at causing harm to the claimants. But damage that was simply an incidental result did not satisfy this requirement, even if it was foreseeable.[1616]

This seemingly is the position in New Zealand as well. The Court of Appeal in *Wagner v. Gill*,[1617] whilst acknowledging that the distinction between means and foreseeable consequences was a narrow one, indicated its preference for a requirement that the conduct must be directed at the plaintiff.

2. Unlawful Means

291. There is a mass of case law concerning the definition of 'unlawful means' for the purpose of the tort of conspiracy. Perhaps the sharp end of the problem was whether a conspiracy to commit a crime was actionable by a person who suffered damage as a consequence of the conduct. Many authorities upheld the victim's claim, provided that there was also an intention to injure that victim.[1618] On this view an independently unlawful element to the conduct was sufficient. But other authorities required that the unlawful means should be actionable at the suit of the plaintiff,[1619] which meant that the element of conspiracy was only of secondary importance. Furthermore, in *Lonrho Ltd v. Shell Petroleum Co. Ltd*[1620] the House of Lords held that allegedly criminal conduct that was not actionable by anyone could not found a claim in private law.

The requirement that the unlawful conduct should be independently actionable was confirmed by the House of Lords in *OBG Ltd v. Allan*[1621] for the purposes of the unlawful means tort. But in *Revenue and Customs Commissioners v. Total Network SL*[1622] the House of Lords held that the requirement was not the same in the case of a conspiracy using unlawful means. Lord Walker considered that criminal conduct engaged in by conspirators as a means of inflicting harm on a claimant was actionable, whether or not conduct on the part of a single individual would be

1615. [2008] 1 AC 1174.
1616. *See also Meretz Investments NV v. ACP Ltd* [2008] 2 WLR 904 at [146]; *W H Newson Holding Ltd v. IMI plc* [2014] 1 All ER 1132; *British Airways plc v. Emerald Supplies Ltd* [2015] EWCA Civ 1024; *JSC BTA Bank v. Ablyazov (No 14)* [2018] UKSC 19, [2018] 2 WLR 1125 at [14].
1617. [2015] 3 NZLR 157.
1618. For example, *Blanche v. McGinlay* (1912) 31 NZLR 807; *Ruddock v. Sinclair* [1925] NZLR 677; *Harder v. New Zealand Tramways Employees Union* [1977] 2 NZLR 162. *SSC & B: Lintas New Zealand Ltd v. Murphy* [1986] 2 NZLR 436.
1619. For example, *Yukong Line Ltd of Korea v. Rendsburg Investments Corporation of Liberia* [1998] 1 WLR 294; *Powell v. Boladz* [1998] Ll Rep Med 116; *Michaels v. Taylor Woodrow Developments Ltd* [2001] Ch 493.
1620. [1982] AC 173; *see* para. 281.
1621. [2008] 1 AC 1; *see* para. 279.
1622. [2008] 1 AC 1174; and *see Mbasogo v. Logo Ltd* [2006] EWCA Civ 1370; *Alleslev-Krofchak v. Valcom Ltd* (2010) 322 DLR (4th) 193 at [72].

actionable as some other torts. To hold otherwise would deprive the tort of conspiracy of any real content, since the conspirators would be joint tortfeasors in any event. The situation in *OBG* was different, for the tort of causing loss by unlawful means was generally concerned with unlawful acts directed at a third party. But the gist of conspiracy was damage intentionally inflicted on the plaintiff by persons who combined for that purpose. So 'unlawful means' had a wider meaning in the tort of conspiracy than in the intentional harm tort. As for *Lonrho v. Shell*, the emphasis was on the absence of an intent to injure, and not on the need for an independently actionable wrong.

On the facts it was held that a conspiracy to defraud the Commissioners of Customs & Excise of tax revenue was actionable on the above basis. Lord Walker said that 'unlawful' certainly covered crimes and torts, provided they were the means by which harm was intentionally inflicted on the claimant rather than being merely incidental to it.[1623] Beyond that, the scope of the concept might sometimes extend to breach of contract, breach of fiduciary duty and perhaps even matters making a contract unenforceable.[1624]

In *Wagner v. Gill*,[1625] the Court of Appeal accepted *Total Network* as authority for the correct approach. The plaintiff, Ms Wagner, contended that the first defendant had conspired with others to transfer a contract away from a company under his control to another, thereby rendering her unable to recover debts owed to her by the first company. The alleged unlawful means was breach of fiduciary duty owed by the defendant to that company. The Court of Appeal held that this, in principle, did not preclude the plaintiff's action, and the unlawful means did not need to be tortious conduct or actionable at the suit of the plaintiff. However, it was held that for policy reasons the particular breach of fiduciary duty did not constitute unlawful means for the purposes of unlawful means conspiracy. These included the fact that the fiduciary duty owed by the defendant was not to the plaintiff, but to his company; that the plaintiff could have protected herself by obtaining a personal guarantee from the defendant; that a breach of a director's obligation to act in good faith and in the interests of the company was not actionable by a creditor; and that there were alternative statutory remedies available to the plaintiff and there was no gap in the law that needed to be filled. The Court also noted that even in the criminal context a defendant's conduct might not qualify as unlawful means unless the statute creating the offence was intended to protect the plaintiff.

In *JSC BTA Bank v. Ablyazov (No 14)*[1626] the question was whether contempt of court could constitute the necessary unlawful means for conspiracy. Conspiracy being a tort of primary liability, the UK Supreme Court considered that 'the real test' could not depend upon whether the unlawful means adopted would give rise to a cause of action independent of conspiracy. Rather, the test was whether there was a just cause or excuse for combining to use unlawful means. The answer would

---

1623. *See*, for example, *Racing Partnership Ltd v. Done Bros (Cash Betting) Ltd* [2019] EWHC 1156, [2019] 3 WLR 779.

1624. *See*, further, *JSC BTA Bank v. Ablyazov (No 14)* [2018] UKSC 19, [2018] 2 WLR 1125; *Axa Insurance UK plc v. Financial Claims Solutions Ltd* [2018] EWCA Civ 1330; *Racing Partnership Ltd v. Done Bros (Cash Betting) Ltd* [2019] EWHC 1156, [2019] 3 WLR 779.(breach of confidence).

1625. [2015] 3 NZLR 157.

1626. [2018] UKSC 19, [2018] 2 WLR 1125.

depend upon, first, the nature of the unlawfulness and, second, its relationship with the resultant damage to the claimant. Unlawful conduct that resulted in purely incidental harm to the claimant would not constitute conspiracy, because the unlawful actions were not the means by which the defendant intended the harm to the claimant.

V. Deceit

A. *Introduction*

292. The development of the tort of deceit dates from the famous case of *Pasley v. Freeman*,[1627,1628] decided in 1789. It was held here that a false affirmation made by the defendant concerning the creditworthiness of a third person, with intent to defraud the plaintiff and that caused the plaintiff damage, was the ground of an action on the case in the nature of deceit.

In *Amaltal Corporation Ltd v. Maruha Corporation*[1629] the Court of Appeal held that the tort of deceit involves: a false representation as to a past or existing fact made by a defendant who knew it to be untrue or who had no belief in its truth or who was reckless as to its truth; intention that the claimant should have acted on the representation; and action by the defendant in reliance on the representation.[1630] In addition, the plaintiff must suffer damage as a result of relying upon the representation.

It is apparent that fraud or dishonesty by the defendant lies at the heart of the tort. But fraudulent conduct is not a tort in its own right.[1631] Rather, the fraud may be a means by which the tort of deceit is committed. For example, bribery by an agent may not induce any reliance by the principal or cause the principal any loss. But where a bribed agent procures a contract between the briber and the briber's principal, the briber may have assisted the agent to induce the principal to give a higher price than the principal would have done if he or she had known the truth, or the agent's advice to the principal may at least convey a representation that the advice is disinterested. In this case there is a deliberately false representation of fact causing loss, and there is a remedy in damages for deceit.[1632] Again, fraudulent conduct may be a means of committing other torts, such as inducement of breach of contract or intentionally causing loss by unlawful means.[1633]

1627. For more detailed discussion, *see* Todd (ed.), *Todd on Torts* Ch. 15 (8th ed., 2019).
1628. (1789) 3 TR 51; 100 ER 450.
1629. [2007] 1 NZLR 608 at [46], [55] (on appeal [2007] 3 NZLR 192, where deceit was not in issue).
1630. There is no separate requirement that there be an 'intention to deceive'. The phrase is merely another way of describing the mental element of the tort – a compendious description of the knowledge and the reliance elements: *Eco3 Capital Ltd v. Ludsin Overseas Ltd* [2013] EWCA Civ 413 at [78].
1631. *Armitage v. Nurse* [1998] Ch 241 at 250.
1632. *Mahesan v. Malaysia Government Officers' Co-op Housing Soc Ltd* [1979] AC 374 at 381–383.
1633. *See* paras 270, 278.

The action for deceit is commonly asserted in a commercial context. It is not formally limited in this way,[1634] but in *Magill v. Magill*[1635] the High Court of Australia declined to apply the tort in a domestic context. The question here was whether a wife could be liable in respect of statements made to her husband concerning the paternity of children born during the marriage. A key reason for denying the claim was that conduct that constituted a breach of promise of sexual fidelity, and any consequential false representation about paternity, occurring within a personal, private, and intimate relationship, could not be justly or appropriately assessed by reference to bargaining transactions with which the tort of deceit was typically associated. There was a mantle of privacy over such conduct that protected it from scrutiny by the law.

In *A v. Attorney-General*[1636] Ellis J considered that no commercial/non-commercial divide could be gleaned from the cases and held that a claim against the police should succeed where the plaintiff suffered financial loss as a result of false statements made in the course of an unlawful undercover operation. Further, it was difficult to see why the claim could not properly be regarded as 'commercial', when what the plaintiff was claiming for was loss suffered by him in the course of operating his business.

The availability of the action for deceit has been limited by statute in certain cases, in particular in the case of pre-contract representations.[1637]

B. Representation of Fact

293. It is essential that the defendant makes a misrepresentation of fact. The representation may be expressed or implied from conduct,[1638] and may be of a continuing nature.[1639] We need to consider how this requirement might be satisfied in a case where the defendant makes a statement of intention, gives an opinion, or keeps silent.

1. Statements of Intention

294. A statement of intention is not a representation as to whatever is said to be intended, for whether the intention is carried into effect lies in the future and is not a matter of present or past fact. The statement may, however, involve a representation as to the existence of the intention: in the much-quoted words of Bowen LJ,

1634. *Clayton v. Currie* [2018] NZHC 1898 at [153], but in the particular case it was held that there was no principled basis for extending the tort into the public law arena.
1635. (2007) 226 CLR 551. *See also PP v. DD* [2017] ONCA 180 (no damages for 'involuntary parenthood' where the parties engaged in unprotected sexual intercourse following false statement by defendant that she was taking a contraceptive pill).
1636. [2018] NZHC 986, [2018] 3 NZLR 439.
1637. *See* para. 299.
1638. *Amaltal Corporation Ltd v. Maruha Corporation* [2007] 1 NZLR 608.
1639. *Cramaso LLP v. Ogilvie-Grant* [2014] AC 1093.

the state of a man's mind is as much a fact as the state of his digestion.[1640] So there was deceit where company directors stated in a prospectus that a loan secured by debentures would be used for the purpose of building up the assets of the company, when the intention was to use it for paying off debts;[1641] where the owner of a company making a take-over bid represented to shareholders of the offeree company that he intended to keep certain property of the offeree company, whereas in fact he intended to sell the property, and that cash would be committed to another company in which the offeree company owned a 50% share, whereas in fact it was available for capital dividends;[1642] where the vendor of a hairdressing business falsely stated that he would not be working in another salon in the same area;[1643] and where a representor who made a representation that property would be placed in a secure family trust in fact intended to transfer the property to another trust in which the representees had no interest.[1644]

2. Opinions

295. A mere statement of opinion is not a statement of fact, but, once again, it may be if the defendant did not hold the opinion and misrepresents his or her state of mind. For example, the vendor of a business who falsely told the purchaser that he did not know that any competitor was likely to open in the area was liable for deceit.[1645] Again, a statement of opinion may imply a state of fact that justifies the opinion. So a statement that a kiwifruit orchard would produce in two years' time was a misrepresentation because it implied the present state of the orchard was such as to justify the opinion;[1646] and a budget forecast for a company implied a factual statement about the existing financial state of the company.[1647]

3. Non-disclosure of Information

296. Saying nothing is not normally a misrepresentation of fact. In principle, a person dealing with another who knows that the other has a wrong impression of a matter material to their dealings is at liberty to acquiesce in the other's ignorance or self-deception.[1648] So a vendor of property is not obliged to disclose defects to a prospective purchaser: the principle of caveat emptor applies. But there may be a duty to disclose in 'half-truth' cases – where a failure to speak distorts the truth of

1640. *Edgington v. Fitzmaurice* (1885) 15 Ch D 459 at 483.
1641. *Ibid.*
1642. *Coleman v. Myers* [1977] 2 NZLR 225.
1643. *East v. Maurer* [1991] 1 WLR 461.
1644. *Burmeister v. O'Brien* [2010] 2 NZLR 395.
1645. *Newbrook v. Marshall* [2002] 2 NZLR 606.
1646. *Ware v. Johnson* [1984] 2 NZLR 518.
1647. *NZ Motor Bodies Ltd v. Emslie* [1985] 2 NZLR 569.
1648. *Banque Keyser Ullmann SA v. Skandia (UK) Insurance Co. Ltd* [1991] 2 AC 249.

what a person has already said.[1649] For example, there was actionable non-disclosure where the vendor of an orchard gave the purchaser an incomplete list of herbicides after the purchaser had inquired whether any deleterious sprays had been used.[1650] Again, there is an exception to the normal rule where there is active concealment, or where a true representation is rendered false by a subsequent change of circumstances.[1651] Thus the vendor of leases in a shopping arcade who provided the purchaser with a brochure containing information about the sublease rentals, which was correct when the brochure was prepared, was obliged to inform the purchaser of a subsequent arrangement for some of the tenants to pay only half the rentals.[1652]

A duty to speak or to disclose information may arise in certain special categories of case. The obligation may be founded on a fiduciary relationship, like that existing between solicitor and client or principal and agent, for breach of which compensation in equity may be awarded.[1653] There is a duty of pre-contract disclosure in the case of contracts based on the utmost good faith, such as contracts of insurance. Breach of this duty entitles rescission of the contract but arguably it does not sound in damages, because it is not a tort or a breach of contract or a breach of fiduciary duty.[1654] Lastly, a duty to give information may be imposed by statute. For example, the Financial Services Management Act 2013 provides that an offer of financial products for issue should disclose all information that is required by regulation.[1655] There is a right of redress for non-compliance with the Act.[1656]

C. Knowledge of Falsity

297. In *Derry v. Peek*[1657] Lord Herschell held that fraud is proved when it is shown that a false representation has been made knowingly, or without belief in its truth, or recklessly, careless whether it be true or false.

In essence, then, the plaintiff must show that the defendant lacked an actual and honest belief in the truth of his or her representation.[1658] If the defendant knows the statement to be untrue, the defendant will be responsible, irrespective of his or her motives. If deceit is established, it is immaterial that there was no intention to cheat or injure the person to whom the false statement was made.[1659]

1649. *Amaltal Corporation Ltd v. Maruha Corporation* [2007] 1 NZLR 608 at [47].
1650. *Ware v. Johnson* [1984] 2 NZLR 518.
1651. *Amaltal Corporation Ltd v. Maruha Corporation* [2007] 1 NZLR 608 at [47].
1652. *Awaroa Holdings Ltd v. Commercial Securities & Finance Ltd* [1976] 1 NZLR 19.
1653. *Day v. Mead* [1987] 2 NZLR 443; *Watson v. Dolmark Industries Ltd* [1992] 3 NZLR 311.
1654. *Agnew v. Länsförsäkringsbolagens AB* [2001] 1 AC 223 at 265. The question was left open in *Scales Trading Ltd v. Far Eastern Shipping Co. Public Ltd* [1999] 3 NZLR 26 (on appeal [2001] 1 NZLR 513).
1655. Financial Services Management Act 2013, Part 3.
1656. *See* para. 443.
1657. (1889) 14 App Cas 337 at 374.
1658. *Klingenstein v. Walters* (1885) 3 NZLR 18; *Newark Engineering (NZ) Ltd v. Jenkin* [1980] 1 NZLR 504; *Gloken Holdings Ltd v. The CDE Co. Ltd* (1997) 8 TCLR 278; *Amaltal Corporation Ltd v. Maruha Corporation* [2007] 1 NZLR 608 at [50].
1659. *Amaltal Corporation Ltd v. Maruha Corporation* [2007] 1 NZLR 608 at [49].

In determining whether fraud is established, the standard of proof applicable is the civil standard of balance of probability and not the criminal standard of proof beyond reasonable doubt. However, the degree of probability must be commensurate with the occasion and proportionate to the subject matter,[1660] and a claim accordingly needs to be supported by clear and cogent evidence.[1661] It has been said that the more serious the allegation, the less likely it is that the event occurred and, hence, the stronger should be the evidence before the court concludes that the allegation is established on the balance of probability.[1662] So, on the one hand, the conduct of a vendor of land in failing to notify the plaintiff that a survey report disclosed problems as to access on to the land fell short of the actual conscious intention to deceive that was necessary to establish the vendor's liability for deceit.[1663] On the other hand, an inference of dishonesty was drawn where the defendant concealed from its partner in a joint venture the tax advantages it had gained from an agreement with the Inland Revenue.[1664]

D. Reliance

298. The defendant's statement does not have to be made to the plaintiff personally or be aimed at the plaintiff individually. It may be made to a particular person, or a class of persons, or the world at large. However, it must be made with the intention that it should be relied on by the plaintiff. In *Peek v. Gurney*[1665] it was held that a company prospectus was prepared in order to induce investors to apply to the company for shares, and was not directed at persons buying already issued shares in the market. A claim by a purchaser in the latter category accordingly failed.[1666]

A plaintiff must also show that he or she did in fact rely on the defendant's statement, but need not establish that it was the only reason or cause for acting, or that without it he or she would have acted differently.[1667] Seemingly there is no requirement that a representation should be 'material', in the sense that it is one that would induce a reasonable person to act.[1668] It does not matter that the plaintiff had the

1660. *Hornal v. Neuberger Products Ltd* [1957] 1 QB 247; *Fenton v. Kenny* [1971] NZLR 1 (CA); *Felton v. Thomas* (2000) Aust Torts Reps 81-559.

1661. *Coleman v. Myers* [1977] 2 NZLR 225 at 320; *Newark Engineering (NZ) Ltd v. Jenkin* [1980] 1 NZLR 504; *Back v. National Insurance Co. of NZ Ltd* [1996] 3 NZLR 363.

1662. *Re H (Minors)* [1996] AC 563, quoted with approval in *Amaltal Corporation Ltd v. Maruha Corporation* [2007] 1 NZLR 608 at [71].

1663. *Hughes v. Huppert* [1991] 1 NZLR 474.

1664. *Amaltal Corporation Ltd v. Maruha Corporation* [2007] 1 NZLR 608 (on appeal *Amaltal Corporation Ltd v. Maruha Corporation* [2007] 3 NZLR 192, where deceit was not in issue).

1665. (1873) LR 6 HL 377.

1666. There may be a remedy in this kind of case under the Financial Services Management Act 2013; *see* para. 443.

1667. *Coleman v. Myers* [1977] 2 NZLR 225 at 322, 369; and *see BV Nederlandse Industrie van Eiprodukten v. Rembrandt Enterprises Inc* [2019] EWCA Civ 596, [2019] 4 All ER 561.

1668. *Savill v. NZI Finance Ltd* [1990] 3 NZLR 135.

means of checking the truth of the representation but did not do so.[1669] It follows from this that in an action for deceit contributory negligence is no defence.[1670]

Usually, if the plaintiff knows that a representation is false or does not believe that it is true, he or she cannot then complain about it.[1671] But it is not necessary as a matter of law for a plaintiff to believe that a representation was true. In *Zurich Insurance Co plc v. Hayward*[1672] the claimant insurers suspected that the defendant was exaggerating the extent of the injuries he had suffered at work for the purposes of his claim against his employer, but they could not find sufficient evidence to prove this and so they settled the claim. The insurers later received proof that the defendant had recovered from his injuries before the settlement, and succeeded in recovering what they had paid to him. The question was not what view the employer or its insurer took but what view the court might take in due course, because the defendant might be believed by the judge at the trial and the views of the judge would determine the amount of damages awarded.

E. Damage

1. General

299. Deceit is actionable only on proof of damage. In principle there may be damages for personal injury,[1673] but the accident compensation bar almost invariably will apply.[1674] So claims in deceit will be for property damage or, normally, for financial loss. Common forms of the latter are loss arising out of entry into an unprofitable contract[1675] and, generally, loss of income.[1676] Damages for associated worry, strain, and stress not amounting to personal injury also may be awarded.[1677]

In the case of pre-contractual representations, section 35 of the Contract and Commercial Law Act 2017 may apply, and if it does the actions for deceit and for negligence are abolished.[1678] In this case, where the representor and the representee proceed to enter a contract, damages are for breach of contract rather than for tort.[1679] But where the plaintiff's loss is incurred other than through entering into a

1669. *Central Railway Co. of Venezuela v. Kisch* (1867) LR 2 HL 99.
1670. *Standard Chartered Bank v. Pakistan National Shipping Corporation* [2003] 1 AC 959; *ASB Securities Ltd v. Guerts* [2005] 1 NZLR 484; *Amaltal Corporation Ltd v. Maruha Corporation* [2007] 3 NZLR 192 at [23]; *see* further para. 478.
1671. *Wasteneys v. Wasteneys* [1900] AC 446.
1672. [2016] UKSC 48, [2016] 3 WLR 637.
1673. *Langridge v. Levy* (1837) 2 M & W 519, 150 ER 863.
1674. *See* para. 41.
1675. *Foster v. Public Trustee* [1975] 1 NZLR 26; *Clemance v. Hollis* [1987] 2 NZLR 471.
1676. *East v. Maurer* [1991] 1 WLR 461.
1677. *Ibid.*
1678. *See* para. 96.
1679. *Walsh v. Kerr* [1989] 1 NZLR 490; *Crump v. Wala* [1994] 2 NZLR 331.

contract with the defendant being sued, as where the plaintiff sues the agent who induces the contract as opposed to his or her principal,[1680] the action for deceit remains available.[1681]

The primary object of contract damages is to give the benefit of the bargain, whereas an action for damages in deceit seeks to restore the plaintiff to the position he or she would have been in had the tort not been committed.[1682] In the context of an action for deceit, the measure is an award that puts the claimant in a position he or she would have been in had the representation not been made.[1683] It is apparent, then, that there may be a different measure of damages in cases where section 35 applies and in those where it does not.

2. Date of Assessment

300. In the case of a sale, damages are usually assessed at the time of purchase, whether under section 35 or in deceit, but the court may choose a later date when it is just to do so.[1684] For example, the measure of damages in respect of a misrepresentation about the pedigree of a yearling colt was the difference between the purchase price and the value of the colt when the misrepresentation was discovered;[1685] and purchasers fraudulently induced to buy an unviable business could recover their capital loss as at the date when they discovered that they had been misled and had an opportunity to avoid further loss.[1686]

In *Smith New Court Securities Ltd v. Scrimgeour Vickers (Asset Management) Ltd*,[1687] the House of Lords affirmed that a plaintiff who has been induced to purchase property by fraud must give credit for any benefits he or she has received as a result of the transaction, that the general rule is that the benefits include the market value of the property as at the date of acquisition, but that such general rule is not to be inflexibly applied where to do so would prevent the plaintiff from obtaining full compensation for the wrong suffered. Accordingly, damages for fraudulently inducing the purchase of shares were assessed not by reference to the shares' current market value at the time of acquisition, but by taking into account an unconnected and then undiscovered fraud which, if known about, would have considerably reduced their value.

1680. The principal may still be liable for the agent's tort under s. 35, on the basis that the agent's representation was within his or her express or ostensible authority.

1681. *See Shing v. Ashcroft* [1987] 2 NZLR 154; *Wild v. National Bank of NZ Ltd* [1991] 2 NZLR 454; *Tak & Co. Inc v. AEL Corp. Ltd* (1995) 5 NZBLC 103,887.

1682. *See* para. 551.

1683. *Amaltal Corporation Ltd v. Maruha Corporation* [2007] 1 NZLR 608 at [56].

1684. *See* generally the discussion in *Clemance v. Hollis* [1987] 2 NZLR 471.

1685. *Naughton v. O'Callaghan* [1990] 3 All ER 191.

1686. *Downs v. Chappell* [1997] 1 WLR 426.

1687. [1997] AC 254; and *see OMV Petrom SA v. Glencore International AG* [2016] EWCA Civ 778, [2017] 3 All ER 157.

3. Consequential Loss

301. Consequential loss is recoverable provided it is not too remote. In the *Smith New Court Securities decision*[1688] it was held by the House of Lords that the test of remoteness in an action for deceit is whether the damage flows directly from the fraudulent inducement.[1689]

Recoverable damage may include expenses reasonably incurred by the plaintiff in trying to run a business fraudulently sold to him,[1690] and interest on loans taken out in order to buy the property that is the subject of the representation.[1691] But Cooke J has said that to allow the plaintiff in an action in deceit to recover profits or gains that he would have made from the property purchased would be to treat him as if he were a buyer suing for breach of contract, and that is not normally permissible.[1692] On this basis, a plaintiff fraudulently induced to buy a defective tractor could not recover the cost of employing contractors to clear scrub that the plaintiff himself would have cleared with the tractor, nor loss of farming profits that would have been achieved had the land been cleared as originally intended. However, while the plaintiff may not be entitled to the profits of the business as represented, he or she may still be able to recover profits foregone or other loss of income caused by the inducement.[1693] Loss of this kind tends to be equated with loss of profit, and certainly a broad-brush assessment is likely to be required.[1694]

VI. Injurious Falsehood

A. Introduction

302. Where a deliberately false representation is made to and acted on by the plaintiff, then the defendant may be held liable in the tort of deceit. Where it is made to a third person and that person acts so as to cause loss to the plaintiff, then the defendant's liability is in the tort of injurious falsehood. This latter tort originally was known as 'slander of title' and protected the owner of land in respect of aspersions on his title hindering his disposal of the land.[1695] It was later extended to statements disparaging the plaintiff's goods,[1696] and later again to aspersions as to the quality of, as distinct from the title to, property. The tort has widened even further and now covers any false statement that affects the defendant's pecuniary interests.

1688. [1997] AC 254. Affirming the decision of the English Court of Appeal in *Doyle v. Olby (Ironmongers) Ltd* [1969] 2 QB 158.
1689. In cases governed by s. 35 of the Contract and Commercial Law Act 2017 (*see* para. 299) the contract test applies, as to which *see* para. 21.
1690. *East v. Maurer* [1991] 1 WLR 461; *A v. Attorney-General* [2018] NZHC 986, [2018] 3 NZLR 439 (expenses caused by deceitful phone call).
1691. *Archer v. Brown* [1985] QB 401.
1692. *Foster v. Public Trustee* [1975] 1 NZLR 26.
1693. *Felton v. Johnson* (2000) Aus Torts Reps 81-559, appeal dismissed CA 32/00, 13 Dec. 2000; *East v. Maurer* [1991] 1 WLR 461; *Parabola Investments Ltd v. Browallia Cal Ltd* [2011] QB 477.
1694. For example, *see Newbrook v. Marshall* [2002] 2 NZLR 608.
1695. *Atkins v. Perrin* (1862) 3 F & F 179, 176 ER 81.
1696. *Healy v. Heenan* (1874) 1 NZ Jur 189.

Examples include statements that the plaintiff had gone out of business;[1697] that the plaintiff had been guilty of stealing confidential letters from her employer;[1698] and that a well-known actor had consented to give an interview with the defendant, a scurrilous newspaper, while in hospital recovering from a serious accident when in fact he was too ill to give a genuine consent.[1699]

It is apparent from these examples that injurious falsehood may overlap with other torts, and in particular with the tort of defamation. However, it is both wider and narrower than defamation: wider because the statement need not reflect upon the reputation of the plaintiff, and narrower because a defamation plaintiff does not have to prove falsity, malice, or damage. Again, there might, exceptionally, be an overlap with passing off.[1700] Furthermore, the tort of negligence has expanded to cover various kinds of claims for financial loss,[1701] and potentially could provide a remedy as well. However, the Court of Appeal has held that negligence should not be allowed to intrude into areas that are properly the province of injurious falsehood.[1702] A duty of care in negligence would undermine the need to show malice in an action for injurious falsehood and change the balance that is achieved in this tort between protecting the plaintiff's goods or reputation and protecting the defendant's freedom of speech.[1703]

To establish injurious falsehood, the plaintiff must prove that there has been a false statement, that that statement was published to a third person, that the statement was published maliciously, and that damage resulted.[1704]

B. A False Statement

303. There must be a false statement of fact, whether made expressly or implied from all the circumstances. As was discussed in relation to the tort of deceit,[1705] the actionable statement may arise out of conduct, a half-truth, or an opinion that is not honestly held.

Cases involving disputes between businesses where one makes unfavourable comparisons about the other's goods may fall outside the ambit of the tort, on the basis that the statements concerned amount to no more than advertising puffery and will be treated by the public with scepticism. 'The courts will do what any ordinary reasonable man would do, namely, take it with a large pinch of salt.'[1706] But when the statement goes beyond mere puffery and denigrates the rival's goods then it may become actionable. A useful test is 'whether a reasonable man would take the claim

1697. *Ratcliffe v. Evans* [1892] 2 QB 524.
1698. *Joyce v. Sengupta* [1993] 1 WLR 337.
1699. *Kaye v. Robertson* [1991] FSR 62.
1700. *See* para. 246.
1701. *See* paras 102–105.
1702. *Bell-Booth Group Ltd v. Attorney-General* [1989] 3 NZLR 148; *Midland Metals Overseas Pte Ltd v. The Christchurch Press Co. Ltd* [2002] 2 NZLR 289.
1703. *See* further para. 104.
1704. *Palmer Bruyn & Parker Pty Ltd v. Parsons* (2001) 208 CLR 388 at 404.
1705. *See* paras 293–296.
1706. *De Beers Abrasive Products Ltd v. International General Electric Co. of New York Ltd* [1975] 1 WLR 972 at 978 per J. Walton.

being made as being a serious claim or not'.[1707] It was held, applying this test, that a claim was actionable when it purported to rely on detailed scientific criteria to reach the conclusion that the plaintiff's product was superior to those of its rival.

The 'single meaning rule' in defamation, which states that the words complained of are deemed to bear only one natural and ordinary meaning,[1708] does not apply to the tort of malicious falsehood.[1709] Where the meanings which reasonable consumers might put on words included both the damaging and the innocuous, the law should move on to proof of malice in relation to the damaging meaning and, if malice were proved, to the consequential damage, without artificially pruning the facts so as to presume a single meaning.[1710]

C. Publication

304. As in the tort of defamation, the false statement must be published to a third person. So in a case concerning the venue for a trial, it was held that the plaintiff could bring proceedings in the place where the letters sent by the defendant, a business rival, were received by the plaintiff's potential customers.[1711]

D. Malice

305. The requirement of malice is satisfied if the defendant knew that the statement was false, or was reckless whether it was true or false.[1712] In *Alexander v. Clegg*[1713] the Court of Appeal accepted the conclusion of the trial judge that the defendant had made the statements in question with a genuine belief in their accuracy, and that they had not been made recklessly or with the motive of injuring the plaintiffs. It was argued that the defendant must have been reckless because he had no evidence to support his allegations and took no steps to check their accuracy. But recklessness in the case of injurious falsehood had the implication of not knowing whether a fact is true or false and not caring. A genuine belief that facts were true might reflect carelessness but not recklessness.

There is a question as to how the requirement of malice should be applied in circumstances where words have more than one meaning. It has been held that a defendant should only be liable for malicious falsehood if the falsehood represented one of the possible correct meanings of the defendant's words and the defendant intended to convey that falsehood.[1714]

1707. *Ibid.*

1708. *See* para. 332.

1709. *Ajinomoto Sweeteners Europe SA v. Asda Stores Ltd* [2011] 2 WLR 91; *Cruddas v. Calvert* [2015] EWCA Civ 171 at [95].

1710. *Ajinomoto Sweeteners Europe SA v. Asda Stores Ltd* [2011] 2 WLR 91.

1711. *Ravensdown Fertiliser Co.-Operative Ltd v. Balance Agri-Nutrients Ltd* (2002) 16 PRNZ 516.

1712. *Shapiro v. La Morta* (1923) 40 TLR 201; *Joyce v. Motor Surveys Ltd* [1948] Ch 242; and *see Customglass Boats Ltd v. Salthouse Bros Ltd* [1976] 1 NZLR 36 at 49.

1713. [2004] 3 NZLR 586.

1714. *Cruddas v. Calvert* [2015] EWCA Civ 171.

Even if the defendant does believe the untrue statement, there will still be malice if he is actuated by some indirect or improper motive. This covers the case where the defendant has the dominant purpose of injuring the plaintiff rather than defending his own interests.[1715]

E. Damage

306. At common law it was necessary for the plaintiff to prove special damage. In other words, damage could not be presumed, and actual pecuniary damage had to be proved. But the requirement was relaxed by section 5 of the Defamation Act 1992. This provides:

> In proceedings for slander of title, slander of goods, or other malicious falsehood, it is not necessary to allege or prove special damage if the publication of the matter that is the subject of the proceedings is likely to cause pecuniary loss to the plaintiff.

The section is designed to provide a remedy in cases where actual loss is difficult to prove, as where it is impossible to identify potential customers who have declined to deal with the plaintiff because of the defendant's false statement. In one case, concerning a false statement that a party had designed a product that was in fact designed by another, the judge was satisfied that there was a risk of loss of trade to that other.[1716] In another, where it was falsely alleged that the plaintiff was involved in providing telephone sex services, the court gave damages representing the plaintiff's loss of potential earning capacity as a school teacher, and also aggravated damages for injury to feelings.[1717]

Where the plaintiff cannot prove that the statement was 'likely to cause pecuniary loss', he or she may still seek to satisfy the requirement at common law of proof of special damage. Seemingly this may be satisfied by proof of a general loss of business, which is the natural result of the statement and where from the nature of the case particular instances of loss cannot be specified.[1718]

§6. Abuse of Public Office

I. Introduction

307. Misfeasance in a public office is the single common law tort that applies only to a public rather than a private defendant. Misfeasance may have a role to play in cases where a claim for negligence fails because there was not a duty to take care.

1715. *Dunlop v. Maison Talbot* (1904) 20 TLR 579; *Wilts United Dairies Ltd v. Thomas Robinson Sons & Co. Ltd* [1957] RPC 220.
1716. *Customglass Boats Ltd v. Salthouse Bros Ltd* [1976] 1 NZLR 36.
1717. *Khodaparast v. Shad* [2000] 1 All ER 545.
1718. *Taupo Borough Council v. Birnie* [1978] 2 NZLR 397 at 404.

There may be no sufficiently proximate relationship for a negligence action, yet the greater culpability required for success in misfeasance can justify the imposition of liability. Conversely, in cases involving abusive conduct by a public body acting outside power, which is the stuff of misfeasance, a remedy in negligence is unlikely to be recognized.[1719]

In addition to the principles of the common law, there may be a civil right of action against the state for compensation for interference with the human rights and freedoms that are protected by the New Zealand Bill of Rights Act 1990. This is commonly known as a *Baigent* action, after the name of the plaintiff in the seminal case recognizing the right of action.[1720] It overlaps very substantially with the tort of misfeasance.

II. Misfeasance in a Public Office

308. The tort of misfeasance in a public office is based upon the need to prevent the wrongful use of power by public officers charged with the exercise of public functions. It requires a deliberate and dishonest abuse of power by a public officer, by acting with the object of injuring the plaintiff or knowingly acting outside power with actual foresight that this would cause harm to the plaintiff or a class including the plaintiff.[1721] These elements to the cause of action will be examined separately.

A. Public Officer

309. The defendant must be a 'public officer'. A public officer is one who is paid out of public funds and who, in the discharge of his or her public duty 'owes duties to members of the public as to how the office shall be exercised'.[1722] Examples include ministers,[1723] police officers,[1724] prison officers,[1725] probation officers[1726] and local authority councillors,[1727] but not a Law Society President,[1728] an independent barrister briefed for a prosecution[1729] or a private legal practitioner acting for the IRD.[1730]

1719. *See* para. 135.
1720. *Simpson v. A-G [Baigent's Case]* [1994] 3 NZLR 667.
1721. *Northern Territory v. Mengel* (1995) 185 CLR 307; *Garrett v. A-G* [1997] 2 NZLR 332; *Three Rivers DC v. Governor and Company of the Bank of England (No. 3)* [2000] 2 WLR 1220; *New Zealand Defence Force v. Berryman* [2008] NZCA 392 at [62]; *Commissioner of Inland Revenue v. Chesterfields* [2013] 2 NZLR 679 at [38].
1722. *Tampion v. Anderson* [1973] VR 715 at 720.
1723. *Takaro Properties Ltd v. Rowling* [1978] 2 NZLR 314.
1724. *Garrett v. A-G* [1997] 2 NZLR 332.
1725. *Racz v. Home Office* [1994] 2 AC 45.
1726. *Hobson v. Attorney-General* [2007] 1 NZLR 374.
1727. *Jones v. Swansea City Council* [1990] 1 WLR 1453.
1728. *Henderson v. McCafferty* [2002] 1 Qd R 170.
1729. *Cannon v. Tahche* (2002) 5 VR 317; *Leerdam v. Noori* [2009] NSWCA 90.
1730. *Commissioner of Inland Revenue v. Chesterfields Preschools Ltd* [2013] 2 NZLR 679 at [70]–[82].

There was some doubt about the position of judicial officers, but when the issue arose for decision the Court of Appeal held that they were included.[1731] The position of a Crown Prosecutor was discussed in *Currie v. Clayton*.[1732] In this case the trial judge thought that in any trial the prosecutor played the role of advocate like any other practitioner and was not in this respect a public officer.[1733] However, the Court of Appeal held that a Crown Prosecutor had a ministerial function involving the exercise of public powers and that a claim in respect of conduct in court was arguable.

B. Conduct in the Exercise of the Public Office

310. The public officer must act 'in the exercise or purported exercise of some power or authority with which he is clothed by virtue of the office he holds' and not in some other capacity.[1734] However, this does not preclude a public officer being liable in this tort where he or she is exercising a power that could also be exercised by a private person. So a council acting as a landlord and exercising a power conferred by contract in circumstances in which, according to private law, no cause of action based on malice would lie, could still be liable for misfeasance in a public office.[1735]

There is first instance authority in New Zealand to the effect that conduct by a public officer in relation to matters internal to a public body may not amount to conduct in the exercise of a public office.[1736] But it has been accepted in the High Court of Australia that the decision by a Minister in the Norfolk Island Legislative Assembly to dismiss a government employee could fall within the ambit of the tort.[1737] The better view is that there can be an abuse of office in relation to any person who is vulnerable to the exercise of the public officer's power.

A public body as well as its individual officers can be directly liable in this tort.[1738] In addition, a public officer's employer can be vicariously liable on the application of ordinary principles.[1739] It is a question of fact and degree whether an officer is engaged in a misguided and unauthorized method of performing authorized duties, or is engaged in what is tantamount to a personal frolic outside the ambit of and unconnected with those duties.[1740]

1731. *Rawlinson v. Rice* [1998] 1 NZLR 454 (CA).
1732. [2015] 2 NZLR 195.
1733. *See Clayton v. Currie* [2013] 1 NZLR 263.
1734. *Calveley v. Chief Constable of Merseyside* [1989] AC 1228 at 1240.
1735. *Jones v. Swansea City Council* [1990] 1 WLR 54 at 70–71, 85, on appeal [1990] 1 WLR 1453 at 1458 (HL).
1736. *McKenzie v. McLachlan* [1979] 1 NZLR 670.
1737. *Sanders v. Snell* (1998) 196 CLR 329.
1738. *Jones v. Swansea City Council* [1990] 1 WLR 1453.
1739. *See* para. 373.
1740. *Racz v. Home Office* [1994] 2 AC 45 at 53.

C. State of Mind of the Defendant

311. One basis for liability for misfeasance is a malicious state of mind. It has to be shown that the defendant exercised his or her power with a wrongful or improper motive. A clear instance of a wrongful motive is spite or ill will towards the particular plaintiff.[1741] Any other improper motive, that is, one that is foreign to the reasons for which the office and the power are conferred, will also suffice. For example, evidence that police officers continued to search a house pursuant to warrant without believing that they had the right address would constitute bad faith and would render them liable in this tort.[1742]

Even where the defendant acts without malice, the plaintiff may still succeed on proof that the defendant purported to exercise authority knowing that he or she had no power to do the act complained of,[1743] or with reckless indifference as to the illegality of the act or the extent of his or her power.[1744] So there was a good cause of action where it was alleged that a minister had withdrawn the plaintiff's licence to import goods into the UK on grounds that were known to be unlawful under European Community law.[1745]

The defendant's state of mind also relates to his or her knowledge or foresight of consequences. In *Garrett v. Attorney-General*[1746] the Court of Appeal held that simple foreseeability of damage was not enough for liability. Blanchard J maintained that the plaintiff must prove that the official had an actual appreciation of the consequences for the plaintiff, or people in the general position of the plaintiff, of the disregard of duty or that the official was recklessly indifferent to the consequences and thus could be taken to have been content for them to happen as they would. On the particular facts, the claim failed. The allegation was that the police had failed properly to follow up the plaintiff's complaint that she had been raped by a police officer. Blanchard J considered that there was nothing in the evidence suggesting that the officer knew that by failing to report he was likely to cause harm of the kind alleged. It was neither foreseen nor bound to occur.

The approach taken in *Garrett* was accepted in the House of Lords in *Three Rivers DC v. Governor and Company of the Bank of England (No. 3)*.[1747] It was held that the tort of misfeasance arose when a public officer exercised his power specifically intending to injure the plaintiff or when he acted in the knowledge of, or with reckless indifference to, the illegality of his act and the probability of causing injury to the plaintiff or to persons of a class of which the plaintiff was a member.

1741. *Roncarelli v. Duplessis* (1959) 16 DLR (2d) 689 at 706; *Clayton v. Currie* [2018] NZHC 1898 at [131]–[144].
1742. *Simpson v. A-G [Baigent's Case]* [1994] 3 NZLR 667 at 675.
1743. *Bourgoin SA v. Ministry of Agriculture, Fisheries and Food* [1986] QB 716.
1744. *Northern Territory v. Mengel* (1995) 185 CLR 307; *Three Rivers District Council v. Governor and Company of the Bank of England (No. 3)* [2003] 2 AC 1.
1745. *Bourgoin SA v. Ministry of Agriculture, Fisheries and Food* [1986] QB 716.
1746. [1997] 2 NZLR 332; and *see Rawlinson v. Rice* [1997] 2 NZLR 651; *Ministry of Fisheries v. Pranfield Holdings Ltd* [2008] NZCA 216 at [121], *Commissioner of Inland Revenue v. Chesterfields* [2013] 2 NZLR 679 at [41]; *Currie v. Clayton* [2015] 2 NZLR 195.
1747. [2003] 2 AC 1; and *see Odhavji Estate v. Woodhouse* [2003] 3 SCR 263.

In some cases a defendant will not know who in particular might suffer harm. In *Akenzua v. Home* Secretary[1748] the allegation was that a violent and dangerous criminal committed murder after employees of the defendant, acting recklessly as to the risk at which this put the potential victims of the criminal's violent proclivities, unlawfully set him at liberty. The predictable victim was neither an identifiable individual nor an identifiable group of individuals, yet the English Court of Appeal held that misfeasance could still lie. Sedley LJ said that Lord Steyn's reference to a class was simply a practical means in some kinds of cases, including *Three Rivers*, of relating and restricting liability to effects in the direct contemplation of the wrongdoer. It was an expansive rather than a restrictive element of the tort, allowing the action to be maintained where the identities of the eventual victims were not known at the time when the tort was committed. So what mattered was not the predictability of the criminal killing the deceased but the predictability of his killing someone.

On the other hand, in *Hobson v. Attorney-General*[1749] the failure by a probation officer adequately to supervise a convicted criminal who had been released on parole did not give rise to liability. Applying *Akenzua*, it would be sufficient for the claimant to show that injury to her as a member of the public was foreseen by the Department as the probable consequence of its alleged dereliction of duty. But, at most, the probation officer, if she had thought about non-enforcement, might have accepted that there was a possibility that the risk that the criminal would act with violence again was enhanced to an unknown degree, and that was not enough.

D. Damage

312. Damage is an ingredient of the cause of action. This usually will take the form of economic loss, for example loss of bank deposits[1750] or of employment[1751] or of the opportunity to import goods.[1752] Damage also may take other forms, such as loss of reputation,[1753] mental illness,[1754] or loss of liberty, including loss of residual liberties of a person already lawfully confined to prison.[1755] Upset, anxiety

1748. [2003] 1 WLR 741.
1749. [2007] 1 NZLR 374. An appeal to the Supreme Court by the second plaintiff on an issue of negligence succeeded; *see Couch v. Attorney-General* [2008] 3 NZLR 725; *see* para. 400.
1750. *Three Rivers District Council v. Governor and Company of the Bank of England (No. 3)* [2003] 2 AC 1.
1751. *Sanders v. Snell* (1998) 196 CLR 329.
1752. *Bourgoin SA v. Ministry of Agriculture* [1986] QB 716.
1753. *Garrett v. Attorney-General* [1997] 2 NZLR 332.
1754. *Niao v. Attorney-General* (1999) 5 HRNZ 269.
1755. *Karagozlu v. Commissioner of Police of the Metropolis* [2007] 1 WLR 1881.

and distress on their own are not enough,[1756] although they may aggravate actionable damage.[1757] Exemplary damages are recoverable in an appropriate case,[1758] but only from the actual wrongdoer. Normally there can be no vicarious liability to pay exemplary damages.[1759]

Whether damage must always be shown has been debated. In *Watkins v. Secretary of State for the Home Department*[1760] it was held by the House of Lords that there was no category of claim involving a right that might be identified as a 'constitutional right' where there could be an action for infringement without proof of special damage. In the particular case, three prison officers had acted in bad faith when dealing with the claimant prisoner's legally privileged correspondence, but this had not caused actual damage. Lord Bingham noted that none of the existing authorities lent support to the proposition that misfeasance was actionable per se. As for the policy of the matter, there were a number of reasons why the House should not change the long-established law. Some of these were: that it would open the door to argument whether other rights less obviously fundamental, basic, or constitutional than the right to vote or to the confidentiality of legal correspondence were sufficiently close or analogous to be treated in the same way; that it would introduce by judicial decision, a change in the law that the consultation and research conducted by the Law Commission might show to be an unsatisfactory solution; and that legal remedies, other than an action in tort were available to a claimant who had suffered a wrong without having suffered material damage, such as judicial review and disciplinary or criminal proceedings against the wrongdoer.

III. Public Law Compensation

A. The New Zealand Bill of Rights Act 1990

313. The purpose of the New Zealand Bill of Rights Act 1990 is to affirm, protect, and promote human rights and fundamental freedoms in New Zealand and to affirm New Zealand's commitment to the International Covenant on Civil and Political Rights.[1761] It contains a Bill of Rights that protects life and security of the person,[1762] democratic and civil rights,[1763] non-discrimination and minority

1756. *Hobson v. Attorney-General* [2007] 1 NZLR 374 (appeal by second plaintiff allowed: *Couch v. Attorney-General* [2008] 3 NZLR 725).
1757. *Garrett v. Attorney-General* [1993] 3 NZLR 600 at 608 (on appeal [1997] 2 NZLR 332 (CA)).
1758. *Garrett v. Attorney-General* [1997] 2 NZLR 332.
1759. *S v. Attorney-General* [2003] 3 NZLR 450; *see* para. 578.
1760. [2006] 2 AC 395.
1761. New Zealand Bill of Rights Act 1990, Long Title. *See* generally Rishworth, Huscroft, Optican & Mahoney, *The New Zealand Bill of Rights* (Melbourne: Oxford University Press, 2003).
1762. *Ibid.*, s. 8 (the right not to be deprived of life); s. 9 (the right not to be subjected to torture or cruel treatment); s. 10 (the right not to be subjected to medical or scientific experimentation); and s. 11 (the right to refuse to undergo medical treatment).
1763. *Ibid.*, s. 12 (electoral rights); s. 13 (the right to freedom of thought, conscience and religion); s. 14 (the right to freedom of expression); s. 15 (the right to freedom of manifestation of religion and belief); s. 16 (the right to freedom of peaceful assembly); s. 17 (the right to freedom of association); and s. 18 (the right to freedom of movement).

rights,[1764] and rights of individuals with regards to arrest, search, and detention.[1765] This charter of rights applies to acts done by the legislative, executive, and judicial branches of the government of New Zealand.[1766] It also applies to acts done by any person or body in the performance of any public function, power or duty conferred or imposed on that person or body by or pursuant to law.[1767] Accordingly, the Bill of Rights is concerned with acts of an essentially public character. It does not apply to acts of private persons.[1768] A remedy under the Act lies against the state independent of the Crown Proceedings Act 1950,[1769] and the Attorney-General as the first law officer of the Crown is the appropriate defendant.[1770]

The New Zealand Bill of Rights Act has the same status as any other Act. Its provisions have no special constitutional force. In particular, the Act itself provides that in relation to any enactment, whether passed before or after the 1990 Act, no court shall hold any provision of the enactment to be impliedly repealed or revoked, or to be in any way invalid or ineffective, by reason only that it is inconsistent with any provision of the Bill of Rights.[1771] But wherever an enactment can be given a meaning that is consistent with the rights and freedoms contained in the Bill of Rights, that meaning is to be preferred to any other.[1772] Generally, the rights and freedoms contained in the Bill of Rights may be subject only to such reasonable limits prescribed by law as can be demonstrably justified in a free and democratic society.[1773]

Certain of the protected rights concerning search, arrest, and detention stipulate a standard of conduct, such as the right to be secure against unreasonable search or seizure in section 21 and the right not to be arbitrarily arrested or detained in section 22. Otherwise, for a derogation from a protected right to have occurred, there is no general requirement that the defendant must fail to attain a particular standard of conduct or should have a guilty state of mind. Eichelbaum CJ has rejected the argument that a claim alleging breach of the provisions of the Bill of Rights Act should lie only where there had been conscious or reckless indifference to the plaintiff's rights.[1774] His Honour could see no principled basis for circumscribing the words of the Act with some additional requirement.

1764. *Ibid.*, s. 19 (the right to freedom from discrimination pursuant to the provisions of the Human Rights Act 1993); and s. 20 (community rights of ethnic, religious, or linguistic minorities).
1765. *Ibid.*, s. 21 (the right to be secure against unreasonable search or seizure); s. 22 (the right not to be arbitrarily arrested or detained); s. 23 (the rights of persons arrested or detained); s. 24 (the rights of persons charged); s. 25 (minimum standards of criminal procedure); s. 26 (prohibitions on retroactive penalties and double jeopardy); and s. 27 (the right to natural justice); *see* para. 66.
1766. *Ibid.*, s. 3(a). But as regards the judicial branch, *infra* para. 314.
1767. *Ibid.*, s. 3(b). *See Low Volume Vehicle Technical Association Inc v. Brett* [2019] NZCA 67, [2019] 2 NZLR 49.at [23]-[29].
1768. In *R v. N* [1999] 1 NZLR 713 the Court of Appeal held that a statutory *immunity* from liability given to a private citizen did not amount to the conferment of a public function, power or duty, so the Act did not apply to the conduct of the citizen.
1769. *See* para. 154.
1770. *Attorney-General v. Chapman* [2012] 1 NZLR 462.
1771. New Zealand Bill of Rights Act 1990, s. 4.
1772. *Ibid.*, s. 6.
1773. *Ibid.*, s. 5. For consideration of ss 4, 5 and 6 *see Ministry of Transport v. Noort* [1992] 3 NZLR 610; *Moonen v. Film and Literature Board of Review* [2000] 2 NZLR 9.
1774. *Whithair v. Attorney-General* [1996] 2 NZLR 45 at 56–57.

B. Remedies

314. The 1990 Act itself does not provide for any remedies for breach, but in *Baigent*[1775] the Court of Appeal developed a remedial jurisdiction. It was held here that a breach of the Bill of Rights gives rise to a direct liability of the state in public law as guarantor of the statutorily affirmed rights and freedoms, and that in an action for such breach the court has unrestricted remedial power. The governing principle was simply that the remedy should be that which is appropriate and effective in all the circumstances of the particular case, including monetary compensation.

Unlike tort damages, the remedy of monetary compensation is not available as of right. Rather, compensation is awarded only in the discretion of the court.[1776] Other forms of relief may afford adequate redress. Where compensation is thought appropriate, a relevant consideration is the availability or otherwise of concurrent causes of action. The Bill of Rights remedy frequently will overlap with other causes of action in tort, and these have to be taken into account when deciding whether to award damages or when assessing how much compensation to award. In *Dunlea v. Attorney-General*[1777] a majority in the Court of Appeal considered that there were strong reasons for taking a similar approach to compensation for breach of the Bill of Rights and compensation for tort. There might be occasional gaps, but the existing law of tort had continued to meet the need to compensate persons adversely affected by the wrongful acts of others exercising public powers. The common law courts also had long recognized that breaches of important rights by officers of the state should be marked by appropriate awards of damages. On this view the normal measure of damages in tort will provide a sufficient remedy.

In *Attorney-General v. Van Essen*[1778] Stevens J said that the focus of an inquiry into the appropriateness of an award of public law damages was on what order or package of relief was necessary to provide an effective remedy for breach of the right concerned. The question of remedy first required consideration of the non-monetary relief that could be or had been given. The court would assess whether that was enough to redress the breach and any relevant injury. An award of damages would be considered necessary only if the breach required something more to vindicate it. The quantum of those damages did not necessarily proceed on the basis of any equivalence with quantum of awards in tort.

Where there are concurrent claims, then compensation or damages may sometimes be awarded both under Baigent and in tort, or there may be an award of damages alone.[1779]

1775. *Simpson v. A-G [Baigent's Case]* [1994] 3 NZLR 667; *Auckland Unemployed Workers' Rights Centre Inc v. A-G* [1994] 3 NZLR 720.
1776. *Link Technology 2000 Ltd v. Attorney-General* [2006] 1 NZLR 1 at [34]–[39]; *Taunoa v. Attorney-General* [2008] 1 NZLR 429 at [253]–[257].
1777. [2000] 3 NZLR 136; and *see Manga v. Attorney-General* [2000] 2 NZLR 65; *Attorney-General v. Hewitt* [2000] 2 NZLR 110.
1778. [2015] NZCA 22.
1779. For examples *see Niao v. Attorney-General* (1999) 5 HRNZ 269; *Manga v. Attorney-General* [2000] 2 NZLR 65; *Dunlea v. Attorney-General* [2000] 3 NZLR 136; *Small v. Attorney-General* (2000) 6 HRNZ 218; *Neilson v. Attorney-General* [2001] 3 NZLR 433.

The position where there is no right to damages at common law was considered by the Court of Appeal in *Brown v. Attorney-General*.[1780] The plaintiff sought compensation for breach of his rights to a fair trial under section 25 of the 1990 Act, but failed on the ground that on the facts no breach had been established. However, William Young J went on to express doubt about giving compensation as a remedy for unfair trial processes even on proof of breach. The costs to litigants and the community of such a discretionary head of jurisdiction would be grossly disproportionate to the value of the few, if any, awards likely to be made and to any other public benefits likely to be derived from the litigation. In *Currie v. Clayton*,[1781] the Court of Appeal held that the cause of action was not plainly unarguable and should not be struck out, but at the trial it was held that damages were not available, and that even if they were the case was not exceptional and involved no egregious behaviour that would justify an award.[1782]

In *Taunoa v. Attorney-General*[1783] the plaintiffs claimed that while confined to prison they were subject to a special behaviour management regime that, *inter alia*, failed to treat them with humanity and respect for dignity as required by section 23(5) of the Bill of Rights Act.[1784] The Supreme Court held that the plaintiffs had established serious breaches of section 23(5), and while declaratory relief might in some cases be sufficient to vindicate a breach, here damages were the only practicable effective remedy. As for their measure, the court was to begin with the nature of the right and the nature of the breach. Any sum awarded should reflect any relevant intention behind the conduct, the duration of the breach and the ways in which the state had acknowledged the wrongdoing. The court was not to proceed on the basis of any equivalence with the quantum of awards in tort. The sum had to be enough to provide an incentive to the state not to repeat the infringing conduct and to ensure that the plaintiff did not reasonably feel that the award trivialized the breach, but was not to be influenced significantly by the character of the particular plaintiff, or by the fact that the case exemplified systemic failures. As regards the amounts of the awards thought to be appropriate, these were relatively modest, ranging from NZD 4,000 to NZD 35,000.[1785]

Whether or in what circumstances damages may be available for breach of section 27(1) of the Act – the right to natural justice – has been considered in a number of recent cases. Any such breach is not actionable as a tort,[1786] and in *Attorney-General v. Udompun*[1787] the Court of Appeal counselled caution, taking the view that it should not lightly be assumed that the Bill of Rights had overtaken the existing law on administrative damages. Then in *Combined Beneficiaries Union Inc v.*

1780. [2005] 2 NZLR 405; for similar caution *see Attorney-General v. Udompun* [2005] 3 NZLR 204.
1781. [2015] 2 NZLR 195.
1782. *Clayton v. Currie* [2018] NZHC 1898 at [195]–[238].
1783. [2008] 1 NZLR 429; and *see Forrest v. Attorney-General* [2012] NZAR 798; *Vogel v. Attorney-General* [2012] NZAR 154.
1784. Claims by prisoners are subject to the provisions of the Prisoners' and Victims' Claims Act 2005; *see Forrest v. Attorney-General* [2012] NZCA 125, [2012] NZAR 798; *Chief Executive of the Department of Corrections v. Gardner* [2017] NZCA 608, [2018] 2 NZLR 712.
1785. *See also Attorney-General v. Udompun* [2005] 3 NZLR 204 (NZD 4,000 for breach of s. 23(5)).
1786. *Peters v. Davison* [1999] 2 NZLR 164, 208.
1787. [2005] 3 NZLR 204.

Auckland City COGS Committee[1788] the question whether Bill of Rights damages were ever available for breaches of natural justice was left open. Applying *Taunoa*, there would at least need to be something more than a bare breach of the right, such as an affront to dignity or an unwarranted intrusion into personal integrity or perhaps a major incursion into the integrity of property.

There is also the very significant control laid down by the majority decision of the Supreme Court in *Attorney-General v. Chapman*,[1789] holding that the Crown could not be liable to pay public law damages in the case of breaches of the Act by the judicial arm of government. In light of the judicial immunity from suit conferred by the common law and by statute,[1790] any Crown liability for government breaches of the Act should be confined to executive breaches. The desirability of finality in litigation, public confidence in judicial independence, and effective protection against judicial breaches provided by the criminal appeal process and an ex gratia compensation system was strongly unfavourable to extending the availability of public law damages. Taking any such step ultimately would be destructive of the administration of justice and human rights protection in New Zealand.

§7. Abuse of Legal Procedure

I. Introduction

315. Wrongful use of legal proceedings can give rise to a liability in tort on a number of different grounds. Liability for malicious prosecution arises, broadly, where the plaintiff has been the victim of ill-founded criminal proceedings brought by a malicious defendant. The tort of malicious civil proceedings imposes a similar liability in the case of wrongfully instituted civil actions. Malicious process covers maliciously procuring the issue of legal process, such as a warrant to arrest the plaintiff or to search his or her property. In addition, the tort of abuse of process involves the use of legal process in its proper form and, it may be, on good or arguable grounds, but for an improper or collateral purpose. Finally, maintenance and champerty are torts directed at those who assist in promoting civil actions between others and in this way wrongfully stir up litigation in which they are not concerned.

The courts are unlikely to recognize new heads of tort liability in relation to the bringing of legal proceedings. In *Burns v. National Bank of New Zealand Ltd*[1791] the Court of Appeal declined to uphold a new tort of spoliation of evidence, because alternative remedies are available, including procedural sanctions and disciplinary and criminal proceedings, the fact of damage often will be irreducibly uncertain, the tort is potentially inconsistent with the policy favouring final judgments, and lawyers may be placed in a position of conflict by owing duties both to their client and to an opposing party.

1788. [2009] 2 NZLR 56.
1789. [2012] 1 NZLR 462; applied in *Thompson v. Attorney-General* [2016] NZCA 215.
1790. *See* paras 115, 116.
1791. [2004] 3 NZLR 280.

II. Malicious Prosecution

A. Elements

316. A person who has been the victim of unsuccessful criminal proceedings may be able to sue his or her prosecutor for malicious prosecution. There are five elements to the tort:

(1) a prosecution by the defendant of the plaintiff on a criminal charge;
(2) termination of the proceedings in favour of the plaintiff or, at least, without the plaintiff being incriminated;
(3) no reasonable and probable cause for the defendant to bring the proceedings;
(4) malice by the defendant; and
(5) damage suffered by the plaintiff.

B. Prosecution of the Plaintiff

317. Generally a person is treated as prosecuted where the matter in question has been brought before a court. So a plaintiff was prosecuted where a magistrate had considered the allegations against the plaintiff and proceeded no further because the informant asked to withdraw the information.[1792] The essence of the matter was whether the magistrate had taken cognizance of a complaint within the magistrate's jurisdiction. At that point the informant had done all he could to launch the criminal proceedings against the accused.

A person who has been the subject of disciplinary proceedings is not 'prosecuted' for the purpose of this tort. In *Gregory v. Portsmouth CC*[1793] Lord Steyn noted that there is a great diversity of statutory and extra-statutory disciplinary proceedings, from the formalized procedures of professional bodies to proceedings by social and sporting clubs, with varying purposes. Leaving it to the courts to decide what proceedings could ground the tort would plunge this area of law into uncertainty. His Lordship thought also that a number of other torts – defamation, malicious falsehood, conspiracy, and misfeasance – could be capable of providing an alternative remedy.

Sometimes there is difficulty in determining who is the prosecutor. Criminal proceedings usually are started by a police officer signing the information, although there are exceptions such as where, for example, a private individual brings a private prosecution. It is clear that the police officer, or anyone else formally involved in the bringing of charges, may be sued for malicious prosecution.[1794] In addition, a person who did not personally instigate or conduct the criminal proceedings, but who gave information or advice to the police on the basis of which the police decided to prosecute, may also be sued where that person intended to bring about a

1792. *Casey v. Automobiles Renault Canada Ltd* [1965] SCR 607.
1793. [2000] 1 AC 419.
1794. *Commercial Union Assurance Co. of New Zealand Ltd v. Lamont* [1989] 3 NZLR 187, 207; *Martin v. Watson* [1996] AC 74, 84–85.

prosecution and did in fact procure it. In *Commercial Union Assurance Co. of New Zealand Ltd v. Lamont*[1795] Richardson J recognized that simply furnishing information was insufficient, and that to incur liability the defendant must have played a sufficient role in the institution of proceedings as to be regarded as setting them in motion. For example, in *Martin v. Watson*,[1796] where the defendant had falsely accused the plaintiff of indecent exposure, the facts relating to the alleged offence were solely within the complainant's knowledge, the police officer to whom the complaint was made could not have exercised any independent discretion in making the decision to prosecute, and deliberate procurement accordingly was established.[1797]

C. Non-incriminating Termination of the Criminal Proceedings

318. The conventional expression of the second element in establishing liability for malicious prosecution is that the prior criminal proceedings must have terminated in favour of the plaintiff.[1798] However, in *Van Heeren v. Cooper*[1799] the Court of Appeal preferred to ask whether the proceedings had terminated in a way that did not incriminate the plaintiff. The plaintiff alleged that the defendant had made false complaints to the police of demanding with menaces and intimidation. The police had investigated the matter and offered the plaintiff the opportunity of diversion, which he had accepted.[1800] He also signed documents admitting guilt and wrote a letter apologizing to the defendant. The charge of intimidation was then dismissed and the charge of demanding money with menaces withdrawn. Fisher J held that there was no plea or finding of guilt in either case, and accordingly there was a non-incriminating termination of the prosecution. The plaintiff's admission to the police was not part of a formal court process and was not a bar, although it was likely to figure prominently in the evidence given at the malicious prosecution hearing if actual guilt were to be run as a defence.

1795. [1989] 3 NZLR 187.

1796. [1996] 1 AC 74.

1797. For further examples, *see Marley v. Mitchell* [2006] NZAR 181; *Copeland v. Metropolitan Police Commissioner* [2015] 3 All ER 391 at [24]–[33].

1798. *Abrath v. North Eastern Railway Co.* (1883) 11 QBD 440, 455, affirmed (1886) 11 App Cas 247.

1799. [1999] 1 NZLR 731.

1800. Diversion is a non-statutory scheme under which the police, in the exercise of their discretion whether to prosecute and within certain guidelines, offer the defendant the opportunity to pay reparation or carry out some community activity. No formal plea is entered but an intimation of guilt and, in many cases, the consent of the victim is required. Provided the requirements of the diversion are satisfied the charge is then withdrawn.

D. Want of Reasonable and Probable Cause

319. The plaintiff must prove that the criminal proceedings were instituted without reasonable and probable cause.[1801] In *Hicks v. Faulkner*[1802] Hawkins J defined reasonable and probable cause as:

> an honest belief in the guilt of the accused based upon a full conviction, founded upon reasonable grounds, of the existence of a state of circumstances which, assuming them to be true, would reasonably lead any ordinarily prudent and cautious man, placed in the position of the accuser, to the conclusion that the person charged was probably guilty of the crime imputed.

This classic statement on the meaning of reasonable and probable cause for a prosecution raises two distinct questions. The first is whether the defendant genuinely believed he or she had reasonable and probable cause (the subjective aspect), and the second is whether, on the facts known by the defendant, such cause actually existed (the objective aspect). The plaintiff must be able to establish that at least one of these elements is absent.[1803]

Taking first the question of the defendant's belief, it is not necessary that the defendant should think that the accused was actually guilty of the offence charged. What is required is that the defendant should be satisfied that there was a proper case to lay before the court.[1804] If he or she does not have a genuine belief that the prosecution is justified, then as a general rule it is immaterial that sufficient grounds may exist in fact.[1805] An exception is where it is proved at the trial of the civil action that the plaintiff had actually committed the offence, in which circumstances the defendant's belief seemingly is immaterial.[1806]

Even if the defendant acted with the necessary belief, the plaintiff may still seek to show that a person of ordinary prudence and caution would have taken the view that a prosecution was not justified. Provided the defendant has made sufficient inquiry the question is whether, on the basis of the facts honestly believed by the defendant, there were, objectively, sufficient grounds for taking action.[1807] The defendant cannot rely on grounds that were not known to him or her at the time.[1808] It is relevant to ask whether the defendant took reasonable steps to find out the true state of the case, fully considered the matter upon admissible evidence only, and in all but the plainest cases laid the facts fully and fairly before counsel of standing

---

1801. The jury determines the facts upon which the question of reasonable and probable cause depends, but the judge must decide whether those facts in truth amount to such cause: *Marley v. Mitchell* [2006] NZAR 181; *Attorney-General v. Withey* 20 Jul. 1999, CA211/98.

1802. (1878) 8 QBD 167, 171.

1803. *Attorney-General v. Withey* 20/7/99, CA211/98.

1804. *Glinski v. McIver* [1962] AC 726, 758; *Marley v. Mitchell* [2006] NZAR 181; *Miazga v. Kvello Estate* [2009] 3 SCR 339 (the inquiry is not concerned with a Crown prosecutor's personal views as to the accused's guilt but his or her professional assessment of the legal strength of the case).

1805. *Harcourt v. Aiken* (1903) 22 NZLR 389, 402; *Van Heeren v. Cooper* [1999] 1 NZLR 731, 738.

1806. *McLeod v. Reeves* (1883) 1 NZLR 50, 53; *Harcourt v. Aiken* (1903) 22 NZLR 389 at 402–404; *Van Heeren v. Cooper* [1999] 1 NZLR 731.

1807. *Glinski v. McIver* [1962] AC 726, 768; *Marley v. Mitchell* [2006] NZAR 181.

1808. *Van Heeren v. Cooper* [1999] 1 NZLR 731 at 738.

and experience in the relevant branch of the law, and received the advice that a prosecution was justified.[1809] As regards the last of these, the opinion of counsel based upon full information and instructions is in practice a very important factor in deciding whether there was reasonable and probable cause for a prosecution.[1810] Conversely, a want of cause may easily be shown where the defendant has failed to take advice, certainly if the question whether in law any offence had been committed was hotly disputed.[1811]

There may be reasonable and probable cause for a prosecution if the plaintiff was convicted at first instance, even though the conviction was subsequently quashed on appeal.[1812] But the conviction is not conclusive. For example, it might have been procured by the prosecutor's fraud or concealment of material evidence.[1813]

E. Malice

320. A plaintiff also must prove, separately from want of reasonable and probable cause, that the defendant acted with malice. This means more than spite, ill will and the like and includes 'any motive other than that of simply instituting a prosecution for the purpose of bringing a person to justice'.[1814] It can be proved either by showing what the motive was and that it was wrong, or by showing that the circumstances were such that the prosecution can only be accounted for by imputing some wrong or indirect motive to the prosecutor.[1815] Where motives are mixed the court will consider whether the dominant motive was something other than the vindication of the law.

While the absence of a subjective belief in reasonable and probable cause is relevant to the malice inquiry, it does not equate with malice and does not dispense with the requirement of proof of an improper purpose. By requiring proof of an improper purpose, the malice element ensures that liability will not be imposed in cases where a prosecutor proceeds, absent reasonable and probable grounds, by reason of incompetence, inexperience, honest mistake, negligence, or even gross negligence.[1816] However, evidence that the defendant lacked a genuine belief in the accusation may be adduced to establish both want of reasonable and probable cause and malice.[1817] Conversely, proof that the defendant had a genuine belief in the

---

1809. *Abbott v. Refuge Assurance Co. Ltd* [1962] 1 QB 432 at 454.
1810. *Glinski v. McIver* [1962] AC 726 at 744–745.
1811. *See*, for example, *Marley v. Mitchell* [2006] NZAR 181.
1812. *Riches v. Director of Public Prosecutions* [1973] 1 WLR 1019 at 1022.
1813. *Herniman v. Smith* [1938] AC 305.
1814. *Commercial Union Assurance Co. of New Zealand Ltd v. Lamont* [1989] 3 NZLR 187 at 202; *Attorney-General v. Hewitt* [2000] 2 NZLR 110 at 125.
1815. *Brown v. Hawkes* [1891] 2 QB 718 at 722; *Rawlinson v. Purnell Jenkison & Roscoe* [1999] 1 NZLR 479 at 489.
1816. *Miazga v. Kvello Estate* [2009] 3 SCR 339.
1817. *Harcourt v. Aiken* (1903) 22 NZLR 389; *Glinski v. McIver* [1962] AC 726 at 743–744; *Moulton v. Chief Constable of West Midlands* [2010] EWCA Civ 524 at [52].

plaintiff's guilt that was based on unreasonably insufficient grounds affords no evidence of malice.[1818] Yet evidence showing that the defendant instituted the proceedings in the complete absence of any information pointing to guilt might justify an inference of malice in a particular case.[1819]

F. Damage

321. 'Damage' in the context of an action for malicious prosecution has a special and restricted meaning. In *Savile v. Roberts*,[1820] Sir John Holt CJ classified the necessary damage as being of three kinds:

(1) damage to reputation, as where the matter of which the plaintiff is accused is scandalous;
(2) damage to the person, as where the plaintiff's life, limb, or liberty is endangered; and
(3) damage to property and pecuniary loss, as where the plaintiff is put to expense in acquitting himself of the crime of which he is charged.

In the case of damage to reputation, seemingly the charge should be necessarily and naturally defamatory of the plaintiff.[1821] A relevant consideration in determining the question is whether the offence charged is punishable by imprisonment. There may be no sufficient moral stigma attaching to the charge if the proceedings are substantially civil in their nature. But a claim that an architect was deliberately flouting town planning laws (which conduct carried very substantial penalties) did suggest moral turpitude by the architect.[1822] As regards damage to the person, a likely instance is actual loss of liberty. Arguably, the mere risk of imprisonment can suffice, so there is damage if the crime is punishable by imprisonment even though the plaintiff had not in fact been imprisoned.[1823] As for pecuniary loss, this may be shown for example in the difference between the costs awarded in the criminal proceedings and those actually incurred in defending them.[1824] Once one of these heads of damage is proved, damages are at large and may include compensation for loss of reputation and injured feelings.[1825]

1818. In such a case there can be no alternative claim in negligence: *Desmond v. Chief Constable of Nottinghamshire* [2011] EWCA Civ 3; and *see* further para. 135.
1819. *See Oniel v. Metropolitan Toronto Police Force* (2001) 195 DLR (4th) 59.
1820. (1698) 1 Ld Raym 374; 91 ER 1147.
1821. *Wiffen v. Bailey and Romford Urban District Council* [1915] 1 KB 600; *Calix v. Attorney-General of Trinidad and Tobago* [2013] 1 WLR 328 (eccentric behaviour in withdrawing from society did not diminish the value of the claimant's character).
1822. *Marley v. Mitchell* [2006] NZAR 181.
1823. *Wiffen v. Bailey and Romford Urban District Council* [1915] 1 KB 600.
1824. *Berry v. British Transport Commission* [1962] 1 QB 306 (CA); *Marley v. Mitchell* [2006] NZAR 181.
1825. *Wershof v. Commissioner of Police for the Metropolis* [1978] 3 All ER 540; and *see Rawlinson v. Purnell Jenkison & Roscoe* [1999] 1 NZLR 479. For (English) guidance on the level of awards *see Thompson v. Commissioner of Police of the Metropolis* [1998] QB 498; *see* further para. 57.

III. Malicious Civil Proceedings

322. Whether malicious civil proceedings are or should be actionable in the same way as malicious criminal proceedings is controversial. In one established category it is clear that an action does lie, namely civil proceedings that attack the credit of the person sued, like bankruptcy proceedings or a winding-up petition against a company.[1826] But in other cases the courts have in the past denied a remedy, even in the case of civil claims making serious allegations of fraud or immorality.[1827] In England, in *Gregory v. Portsmouth City Council*,[1828] Lord Steyn thought that the extension of the tort to civil proceedings generally had not been shown to be necessary because adequate protection was afforded by other related torts. By contrast, in *Crawford Adjusters (Cayman) Ltd v. Sagicor General Insurance (Cayman) Ltd*[1829] the Privy Council favoured recognition of the tort. Lord Wilson JSC considered that the tort could be supported by justifications similar to those underlying malicious prosecution and that control of abuse of legal proceedings was particularly well-suited to developments in judge-made law. Then in *Willers v. Joyce*[1830] the UK Supreme Court, by a 5-4 majority, favoured the view taken in *Crawford.* Lord Toulson recognized that there were various counter-arguments – for example, a fear of vindictive claims, the need to avoid satellite litigation and the duplication of remedies, alleged inconsistency with the principle of witness immunity, whether there would also be a reciprocal action for maliciously instituted defence – but these had not disallowed the action for malicious prosecution and/or were not ultimately convincing. They were not sufficient to outweigh the argument that simple justice dictated a remedy.[1831]

In New Zealand there has been a degree of support for the action[1832] but no final appellate decision in favour. The likelihood is that the action will in due course be confirmed as part of New Zealand Law.

1826. *Johnson v. Emerson* (1871) LR 6 Ex 329; *Quartz Hill Consolidated Gold Mining Co. v. Eyre* (1883) 11 QBD 674; *Cross v. The Commercial Agency Ltd* (1900) 18 NZLR 153; *Jones v. Foreman* [1917] NZLR 798.

1827. *Jones v. Foreman* [1917] NZLR 798 (malicious paternity proceedings).

1828. [2000] 1 AC 419, 432; and *see Metall und Rohstoff AG v. Donaldson Lufkin & Jenrette Inc* [1990] 1 QB 391 at 471.

1829. [2014] AC 366.

1830. [2016] 3 WLR 477.

1831. Compare *Lee Tat Development Pte Ltd v. Management Corporation of Grange Heights Strata Title Plan No 301* [2018] SGCA 50, which strongly supports the minority view in *Willers.*

1832. *New Zealand Social Credit Political League Inc v. O'Brien* [1984] 1 NZLR 84; *Rawlinson v. Purnell Jenkison & Roscoe* [1999] 1 NZLR 479; *Robinson v. Whangarei Heads Enterprises Ltd* [2015] 3 NZLR 734.

IV. Abuse of Process

A. General

323. The tort of abuse of process is committed where a person brings proceedings to achieve an ulterior purpose or collateral advantage or where a person maliciously procures the issue of a warrant or other legal process. A court may stay a proceeding for abuse of process, but its power to do so is not limited to cases where the tort has been committed.[1833] The court may issue a stay in the exercise of its inherent power to prevent misuse of its procedure which would be manifestly unfair to a party to litigation before it or would otherwise bring the administration of justice into disrepute.[1834]

B. Improper Purpose

324. It is an abuse of process that is actionable in damages as a tort to use the legal process in its proper form in order to accomplish an ulterior purpose that is outside the ambit of the legal claim upon which the court is asked to adjudicate. So, proceedings are an abuse where they are used as a means of obtaining some advantage for which they are not designed or some collateral advantage beyond what the law offers.[1835] Possibly the mere commencement of the proceedings without more can amount to use of them for an improper purpose,[1836] although most authority holds that some separate manifestation of the defendant's intent is needed.[1837] This usually is found in the form of an overt act, such as a demand that identifies the true collateral purpose. Furthermore, the improper purpose need not be the sole purpose, so long as it is a predominant purpose.[1838] The objection to the conduct is the same whether or not the process is well founded, for the abuse of the process to effect the improper purpose is the true basis for liability.

1833. *Waterhouse v. Contractors Bonding Ltd* [2014] 1 NZLR 91 at [30].

1834. *Hunter v. Chief Constable of the West Midlands Police* [1982] AC 529 at 536; *Lai v. Chamberlains* [2007] 2 NZLR 7 at [61], [165]; and *see Jeffery & Katauskas Pty Ltd v. SST Consulting Pty Ltd* (2009) 239 CLR 75 at [27].

1835. *Grainger v. Hill* (1838) 4 Bing NC 212, 132 ER 769; *Gordon v. Treadwell Stacey Smith* [1996] 3 NZLR 281; *see also Metall und Rohstoff AG v. Donaldson Lufkin & Jenrette Inc* [1990] 1 QB 391 at 469; *Williams v. Spautz* (1992) 174 CLR 509; *Crawford Adjusters (Cayman) Ltd v. Sagicor General Insurance (Cayman) Ltd* [2013] 3 WLR 927. The tort has been rejected in Singapore: *Lee Tat Development Pte Ltd v. Management Corporation of Grange Heights Strata Title Plan No 301* [2018] SGCA 50.

1836. *Williams v. Spautz* (1992) 174 CLR 509 at 527–529.

1837. *See*, for example, *Hanrahan v. Ainsworth* (1990) 22 NSWLR 73 at 121–122; *United Tele-casters Sydney Ltd v. Hardy* (1991) 23 NSWLR 323 at 343; *Brown v. Durham Regional Police Force* (1996) 134 DLR (4th) 177; *Butler v. Simmonds Crowley and Calvin* [2000] 2 Qd R 252.

1838. *Goldsmith v. Sperrings Ltd* [1977] 1 WLR 478 at 496; *Metall und Rohstoff AG v. Donaldson Lufkin & Jenrette Inc* [1990] 1 QB 391 at 469; *Williams v. Spautz* (1992) 174 CLR 509 at 529.

In *Grainger v. Hill*,[1839] the leading case, it was an abuse for the mortgagee of a vessel to have the owner arrested, ostensibly for non-payment of a debt, but in reality in order to compel him to surrender the register of the vessel. Further examples include the laying of information against the officers of a former employer in order to exert pressure on the employer to reinstate the plaintiff or to agree to a favourable settlement of his action for wrongful dismissal;[1840] and conducting the defence to an action as part of a plan to discredit the plaintiff through publicity and to exert pressure to settle proceedings between the plaintiff and another person.[1841] On the other hand, the purpose of avoiding liability in respect of an allegedly negligent misrepresentation that land was not contaminated, by later issuing an order requiring remediation by the occupier, was an acceptable purpose, and there was no abuse in issuing the order.[1842] Again, solicitors did not act abusively in threatening and bringing proceedings against a council for judicial review of the grant of planning permission for a site opposite their offices.[1843] The claimants had an economic interest in the quashing of the grant, and the court affirmed that the tort is not committed by a person who instituted proceedings with a genuine interest in, and an intention to secure, their successful outcome, even if the claimant's motives were mixed and they hoped that they might also achieve a commercially advantageous objective not itself within the scope of the proceedings.

This requirement of an ulterior purpose distinguishes the tort of abuse of process from the tort of malicious prosecution or malicious institution of civil proceedings, where the defendant may have acted with a corrupt motive but nonetheless has used the law for its assigned rather than an ulterior purpose. The distinction is between corruptly trying to win a case and corruptly using it for a collateral purpose.[1844] This explains why the tort does not extend to a person who dishonestly presents a false case for the purpose of advancing or sustaining his or her claim or defence in civil proceedings, or who gives perjured evidence in a criminal action. So the bringing of a counterclaim to an action for wrongfully lodging a caveat, whether or not the sum claimed was truly owing, was not an abuse of process. The proceedings were not being used as a means to extort from another some collateral advantage.[1845] Again, the Court of Appeal has rejected spoliation of evidence as a new tort, partly because spoliation is simply a form of presenting a false case and this is not ordinarily actionable in damages.[1846]

1839. (1838) 4 Bing NC 212, 132 ER 769.
1840. *Williams v. Spautz* (1992) 174 CLR 509.
1841. *Hamer-Mathew v. Gulabrai (No. 2)* (1995) Aust Torts Reps 81–334.
1842. *Border Enterprises Ltd v. Beazer East, Inc* (2002) 216 DLR (4th) 107.
1843. *Land Securities Plc v. Fladgate Fielder* [2010] 2 WLR 1265.
1844. *Burns v. National Bank of New Zealand Ltd* [2004] 3 NZLR 289.
1845. *Gordon v. Treadwell Stacey Smith* [1996] 3 NZLR 281; and *see Crawford Adjusters (Cayman) Ltd v. Sagicor General Insurance (Cayman) Ltd* [2013] 3 WLR 927.
1846. *Burns v. National Bank of New Zealand Ltd* [2004] 3 NZLR 289.

C. Malicious Process

325. It is a tort for a person maliciously and without reasonable and probable cause to procure the issue of a warrant to arrest the plaintiff.[1847] The arrest itself constitutes damage,[1848] although special and exemplary damages may also be awarded. In a case where the procurement takes the form of evidence given in court, the plaintiff's claim will not be defeated on the ground that witnesses have immunity from suit. This is because the plaintiff is suing not in respect of the evidence itself but on the basis that the defendant procured the plaintiff's arrest by means of judicial process.[1849]

Second, it is a tort maliciously and without reasonable and probable cause to procure the issue of a warrant to search the plaintiff's house.[1850] What amounts to reasonable cause depends upon the statutory conditions for the grant of the warrant. It must be shown that the defendant lacked any bona fide belief that he or she was placing before the issuing judge material sufficient to meet the necessary conditions. This encompasses the subjective belief in good faith that material grounds for suspicion exist and the objective requirement that the belief is reasonably held. Malice includes improper motive, which in this case is shown by proof of intent to use the process for a purpose other than to search in the permitted circumstances. There is a presumption that the judge issuing the warrant acted properly, but that establishes neither the accuracy of the matters presented to the judge or the state of mind of the defendant. Generally, any damage will arise from execution rather than issue of the warrant, but there may be special circumstances in which it can be shown that the issue of the warrant causes harm.[1851]

Lastly, it is also an actionable wrong maliciously and without reasonable and probable cause to procure execution to be levied on the plaintiff's goods.[1852] Again, an action will lie against a person who maliciously and without reasonable cause procures the arrest of a ship, even without proof of special damage.[1853]

V. Maintenance and Champerty

A. Introduction

1. General

326. The tort of maintenance is committed where a person, without lawful justification, assists a party to a civil action to bring or to defend the action, thereby causing damage to the other party. Champerty is that form of maintenance in which

1847. *Meikle v. The Wellington Loan Co. Ltd* (1911) 31 NZLR 217; *Roy v. Prior* [1971] AC 470.
1848. *Roy v. Prior ibid.*
1849. *Roy v. Prior ibid.* at 479–480. Compare *Crawford v. Jenkins* [2015] 3 WLR 843.
1850. *Evans v. Crawford* (1884) 2 NZLR 407; *Gibbs v. Rea* [1998] AC 786; *Keegan v. Chief Constable of Merseyside Police* [2003] 1 WLR 2187.
1851. On all these points, *see Gibbs v. Rea, ibid.*, at 797–798.
1852. *Churchill v. Siggers* (1854) E & B 929; 118 ER 1389; *Gilding v. Eyre* (1861) 10 CB (NS) 592.
1853. *The Collingrove; The Numida* (1885) 10 PD 158; *The Walter D Wallet* [1893] P 202.

the person giving the assistance does so in consideration of his or her receiving a share of anything that may be gained as a result of the proceedings. The law of maintenance and champerty seeks to prevent wanton and officious interfering with the disputes of others in which the intervener has no interest and where the assistance is without justification or excuse.[1854] Champerty has been especially condemned because giving assistance with a view to division of the spoils has been regarded as a particularly obnoxious form of maintenance.[1855]

Maintenance and champerty as torts have been abolished in England and in some Australian states, on the grounds that they had become outdated and no longer fulfilled any useful purpose. In New Zealand, the Law Commission has favoured their retention, being concerned about 'unruly corporations' employing ruthlessly aggressive litigious processes, hiding behind nominal litigants if need be, about cases where the opponent of a maintained party suffered loss other than costs, and about situations where the opponent faced procedural difficulties in proving the role of the maintainer unaided by the processes of discovery. Furthermore, no great simplification of the law would be achieved by following the English and Australian precedents, which abolished the torts but preserved the underlying public policy issues in their application to contract legality.[1856]

Judicial comment has been mixed. In *Auckland CC as Assignee of Body Corporate 16113 v. Auckland CC*[1857] Heath J remarked that access to justice and the desirability of promoting settlement of litigation were reasons for reconsideration of the public policy-based rules. He thought that if the old rules continued to have any place in modern society, it was to protect the vulnerable from exploitation by those with means to take over their legitimate claims. But the court had ample jurisdiction to prevent abuse of its processes without recourse to ancient remedies, and he would favour letting maintenance and champerty fall into disuse.

In *Saunders v. Houghton*[1858] the Court of Appeal did not go so far. Examination of experience elsewhere, especially in the United States, showed that there was still force in the concerns underlying maintenance and champerty as torts. Subjection to litigation could be a heavy burden for any defendant and the resulting cost and anxiety could exact a heavy toll. But the court recognized that the common law in other jurisdictions, in particular Australia[1859] and Canada,[1860] allowed such claims, and access to justice and comity with other states meant that New Zealand should follow. Again, in *Body Corporate 160361 (Fleetwood Apartments) v. BC 2004 Ltd and*

1854. *Giles v. Thompson* [1994] 1 AC 142 at 161; *see* generally *Campbells Cash and Carry Pty Ltd v. Fostif Pty Ltd* (2006) 80 ALJR 1441 at [66]–[82].
1855. *First City Corporation Ltd v. Downsview Nominees Ltd* [1989] 3 NZLR 710 at 754, on appeal [1990] 3 NZLR 265 (CA); [1993] 1 NZLR 513 (PC).
1856. Law Commission, *Subsidising Litigation*, Report No. 72, Wellington, 2001.
1857. [2008] 1 NZLR 838 at [17], [45]–[46].
1858. [2010] 3 NZLR 331.
1859. *Fostif Pty Ltd v. Campbells Cash & Carry Pty Ltd* (2006) 229 ALR 58; *Jeffery & Katauskas Pty Limited v. SST Consulting Pty Limited* (2009) 260 ALR 34.
1860. *Western Canadian Shopping Centres Inc v. Dutton* [2001] 2 SCR 534.

BC 2009 Ltd,[1861] Fogarty J noted that the law tolerated some relief from the strictures imposed by maintenance and champerty when there were good reasons in the public interest to do so, but otherwise the policy objections to trading in causes of action applied.

B. Wrongful Assistance

327. Providing a litigant with encouragement or moral support is unobjectionable. The assistance given by the defendant in promoting someone else's action must take some tangible form. Usually maintenance or champerty is committed by giving or lending money, or bearing the whole or part of the expense of an action. The assistance must be wrongful, in that it is wanton and officious and lacks lawful justification. In *Giles v. Thompson*[1862] Lord Mustill said that all aspects of the transaction should be taken together for the purpose of considering whether officious intermeddling without any justification or excuse had occurred.

In *Saunders v. Houghton*[1863] the Court of Appeal examined the lawfulness of litigation funding arrangements. The court held that it was preferable to h the courts in New Zealand should refrain from condemning maintenance and champerty as tortious and unlawful where (a) the court was satisfied that there was an arguable case for rights that warranted vindicating, (b) there was no abuse of process, and (c) the proposed funding arrangement was approved by the court.[1864] However, in *Waterhouse v. Contractors Bonding Ltd*[1865] the Supreme Court was careful to emphasize that it was not the role of the courts to act as general regulators of funding arrangements. However, on application for a stay on the grounds of abuse of process the courts might order disclosure of the agreement, subject to redactions relating to confidentiality and privilege. The stay should only be granted where there was an abuse of process on traditional grounds[1866] or where the funding arrangement effectively constituted the assignment of a cause of action to a third party in circumstances where such an assignment was not permissible.[1867]

Affording assistance to the poor for reasons of charity is well established as a justifying circumstance.[1868] For example, funding a party to a custody dispute out of charity and religious sympathy did not constitute maintenance.[1869] The principle has particular relevance to the lawfulness of contingency fees. A lawyer may make a 'conditional fee agreement', which means an agreement under which a lawyer agrees with a client that some or all of the lawyer's fees and expenses are payable

---

1861. [2014] 3 NZLR 758.
1862. [1994] 1 AC 142.
1863. [2010] 3 NZLR 331.
1864. The funding arrangement in the particular case was subsequently approved by the Court of Appeal in *Saunders v. Houghton* [2013] 2 NZLR 652 (appeal on other issues dismissed in *Credit Suisse Private Equity LLC v. Houghton* [2014] 1 NZLR 541).
1865. [2014] 1 NZLR 91.
1866. *See* para. 323.
1867. *See* para. 329.
1868. *Harris v. Brisco* (1886) 17 QBD 504.
1869. *Young v. Young* [1993] 4 SCR 3.

only if the outcome of the client's case is successful, provided the remuneration is either a normal fee or a normal fee plus a premium.[1870] The common law permits similar arrangements.[1871] But contingency fees going beyond these limits are void and may also give rise to liability in tort. An example is an agreement providing for payment of disbursements plus a fee of two-thirds of any sum recovered in the action.[1872]

A person is also justified in supporting an action brought by another if he or she has an interest recognized by law in the subject matter of the action. So co-owners of property may maintain one another in defence of their common interests.[1873] Even if there is no legal interest, a common commercial or similar interest may suffice, such as the interest of an insurer in assisting and meeting the costs of actions by or against their insured. Other examples of a common interest include: an anglers' association supporting proceedings by some of its members against a factory that was alleged to have polluted a river;[1874] an unsatisfied vendor of land helping his immediate purchaser prosecute an action against a second purchaser;[1875] and a car dealer supporting claims by customers against the administrator and insurer of service contracts sold to the customers by the dealer.[1876] But it is difficult to show a relevant interest where the action is in respect of an essentially personal wrong, such as defamation or malicious prosecution.[1877]

Justification for maintenance may sometimes be found even without any commercial interest flowing from the relationship, such as, fairly obviously, a family or domestic relationship. So too, trade unions can support claims by or against their members, and employers can assist their employees.[1878] But whether a defendant can rely on a notion of public duty as justifying the maintenance of another's action is not certain.[1879]

1870. Lawyers and Conveyancers Act 2006, s. 334. 'Premium' means remuneration that: (1) is payable only if the outcome is successful; (2) is expressly provided for in the agreement; (3) compensates the lawyer for the risk of not being paid and for the disadvantages of not receiving payments on account; and (4) is not calculated as a proportion of the amount recovered.
1871. *Sievwright v. Ward* [1935] NZLR 43; *Thai Trading Co. v. Taylor* [1998] QB 781; *Sibthorpe v. Southwark London Borough Council* [2011] 1 WLR 2111; *Kain v. Wynn Williams & Co* [2013] 1 NZLR 498.
1872. *Mills v. Rogers* (1899) 18 NZLR 291.
1873. *Alabaster v. Harness* [1894] 2 QB 897 at 902.
1874. *Martell v. Consett Iron Co. Ltd* [1955] Ch 363.
1875. *Brett Wotton Properties Ltd v. Cameron* 29 Jul. 1986, Bisson J, HC Rotorua A3/83, on appeal 11 Aug. 1987, CA221/86.
1876. *American Home Assurance Co. v. Brett Pontiac Buick GMC Ltd* (1993) 96 DLR (4th) 485.
1877. *Alabaster v. Harness* [1895] 1 QB 339; cp *Hill v. Archbold* [1968] 1 QB 686.
1878. *Hill v. Archbold* [1968] 1 QB 686.
1879. In *Bradlaugh v. Newdegate* (1883) 11 QBD 1 the public interest in seeing that the law of the land was respected and obeyed was held not to be a justifying circumstance.

C. Damage

328. The plaintiff in an action for maintenance must prove that he or she has suffered damage. This may include any costs incurred in defending the maintained proceedings.[1880] Seemingly, the action should succeed only where the assisted proceedings ended in failure, for it is difficult to identify any special damage in a case where the maintained claim succeeded. A plaintiff cannot sensibly be seen to have suffered a legal wrong in being compelled to discharge his or her legal obligations.[1881] Certainly, no action will lie against the maintainer of successful proceedings if the only damages alleged are the expenses incurred in paying the amount of the judgment, costs awarded, and costs incurred in defending the action.[1882] The position is the same if the maintained action ends by a settlement under which money is paid to the person bringing the action.[1883]

D. Assignment of Causes of Action

329. The common law rule condemning maintenance has implications for the law governing assignments. It provides the basis for the rule that a purported assignment of a bare cause of action in tort to a person without any other interest in the subject matter is without effect.[1884] But an assignment of a right to sue for breach of contract may validly be made where the assignee has a genuine commercial interest in the subject matter of the proceedings,[1885] and the same principle has been recognized as applying in the case of a right of action in tort.[1886] Thus, a debenture holder's causes of action in tort were assignable along with the debenture, as they were ancillary to the assignment of the debenture and the new debenture holder clearly had an interest in protecting the value of the security.[1887] A cause of action may also be assigned, even where the assignee has no such property interest, provided that the assignee's interest goes beyond a mere personal interest in profiting from the outcome of the proceedings and extends to an interest in the assignor or its business affairs, or activities that the assignment may in some way protect. So an owner of defective property can assign its cause of action to a subsequent

1880. *Hill v. Archbold* [1968] 1 QB 686 at 694–695.

1881. However, in *Neville v. London 'Express' Newspaper Ltd* [1919] AC 368, in a decision which is difficult to understand, the House of Lords held that the plaintiff was not prevented from succeeding by virtue of the success of the assisted action against him.

1882. *Sievwright v. Ward* [1935] NZLR 43 at 50.

1883. *Ibid.*

1884. *Trendtex Trading Corp. v. Credit Suisse* [1982] AC 679; *PricewaterhouseCoopers v. Walker* [2017] NZSC 151, [2018] 1 NZLR 735. If a funding arrangement amounts to an assignment of a cause of action to a third-party funder in circumstances where this is not permissible, then this will be an abuse of process; *Waterhouse v. Contractors Bonding Ltd* [2014] 1 NZLR 91 at [57].

1885. *Trendtex Trading Corp. v. Credit Suisse* [1982] AC 679.

1886. *Trendtex Trading Corp. v. Credit Suisse* [1980] QB 629 at 656, 670–671; *Fredrickson v. Insurance Corp. of British Columbia* (1986) 28 DLR (4th) 414 (appeal dismissed [1988] 1 SCR 1089); *Frucor Beverages Ltd v. Blumberg* [2019] NZCA 547, [2020] 2 NZLR 51 at [55].

1887. *First City Corp. Ltd v. Downsview Nominees Ltd* [1989] 3 NZLR 710, on appeal [1990] 3 NZLR 265 (CA), [1993] 1 NZLR 513 (PC), where the issue was not discussed.

owner.[1888] In a leaky building case, purchasers who acquired units in a large building knowing of defects, and taking assignments from the vendor of the right to pursue claims in respect of those defects, were held to be acquiring enforceable property rights, with the assigned causes of action being incidental to those rights.[1889] They were not buying their units to acquire a cause of action.

Two instances in New Zealand may be contrasted. On the one hand, a council which settled a claim against it for negligence in approving the construction of a defective residential complex, and which took an assignment of the original plaintiffs' causes of action against the remaining defendants, had a 'genuine commercial interest' in taking the assignment. Heath J considered that no rule of public policy should prevent a genuine settlement of that type.[1890] On the other hand, in a case raising the same issue, Fogarty J insisted that the preexisting commercial interest should be in matters separate from the litigation itself, which criterion was not met. If the assignment stood, there was nothing to stop any defendant entering into a bargain to purchase the plaintiff's causes of action as part of a settlement in order to sue the other defendants.[1891]

There can be no assignment of purely personal tort claims, like a claim for defamation[1892] or for damages for personal injury.[1893] There is no objection to assigning the damages to be recovered in an action, as opposed to the cause of action itself.[1894] The assignment of a debt is perfectly valid.[1895] What is contrary to public policy is an agreement which has maintenance or champerty as its object.

§8. Injury to Reputation

I. Introduction

330. The tort of defamation protects the interest of a person in his or her reputation.[1896] Very broadly, it gives a cause of action to the victim of an attack upon his or her good name. At common law defamation was divided into two classes – libel, which required publication in a permanent form and that was actionable per se (i.e., without proof of special damage or loss that can be estimated in money terms), and slander, which involved publication in a non-permanent form and was actionable,

1888. *Darlington Borough Council v. Wiltshier Northern Ltd* [1995] 1 WLR 68.
1889. *Body Corporate 326421 v. Auckland Council* [2015] NZHC 862 at [272]–[286].
1890. *Auckland CC as Assignee of Body Corporate 16113 v. Auckland CC* [2008] 1 NZLR 838.
1891. *Body Corporate 160361 (Fleetwood Apartments) v. BC 2004 Ltd and BC 2009 Ltd* [2014] 3 NZLR 758.
1892. *Trendtex Trading Corp. v. Credit Suisse* [1980] QB 629 at 656 (CA); *Fredrickson v. Insurance Corp. of British Columbia* (1986) 28 DLR (4th) 414 at 421 (appeal dismissed [1988] 1 SCR 1089).
1893. *Simpson v. Norfolk & Norwich University Hospital NHS Trust* [2012] 1 All ER 1423.
1894. *Camdex International Ltd v. Bank of Zambia* [1998] QB 22 at 33.
1895. *Camdex International Ltd v. Bank of Zambia* [1998] QB 22 (CA) at 40; *PricewaterhouseCoopers v. Walker* [2017] NZSC 151, [2018] 1 NZLR 735 at [78]–[79].
1896. For detailed treatment *see* Cheer, *Defamation*, in *Todd on Torts*, Ch. 16, (Todd ed., 8th ed., Wellington: Thomson Reuters, 2019).

in most cases, only on proof of special damage. The significance of this distinction has been removed by statute,[1897] and so the rules are the same whatever the form of the defamation.

How far the law of defamation ought to extend is controversial, because of its tendency to inhibit freedom of expression. The courts seek to achieve a balance between the protection of individual reputation and free speech. Many commentators have doubted whether the balance has been struck at the right point and have taken the view that the law is too heavily weighted in favour of plaintiffs. So, for example, the plaintiff need show only that words are defamatory and not that they are false, upon which the onus shifts to the defendant to show by way of defence that they are true,[1898] a plaintiff can succeed even though there was no intention to defame or even to refer to the plaintiff,[1899] and where there is republication of the same material by multiple defendants, the plaintiff can sue in respect of each and every publication.[1900] However, recent developments have tended to reduce somewhat the stringency of the law and to give greater emphasis to the importance of freedom of expression. This change has been prompted in part by section 14 of the New Zealand Bill of Rights Act 1990, which provides that everyone has the right to freedom of expression, including the freedom to seek, receive, and impart information and opinions of any kind in any form. It is manifested in a newly recognized defence, which attaches qualified privilege to responsible communications on matters of public interest.[1901]

II. Who Can Sue?

331. As a matter of general principle any person with a reputation to protect, whether a natural person or an artificial person, such as a company, can sue in defamation. So a trading corporation can bring proceedings to protect its commercial reputation.[1902] However, proceedings by a body corporate must fail unless that body proves that the publication of the defamatory matter had caused or was likely to cause pecuniary loss.[1903]

In *Derbyshire County Council v. Times Newspapers Ltd*[1904] the House of Lords held that a local authority could not protect its 'governing reputation' by an action for defamation because a government body should be open to uninhibited public criticism, and the threat of civil action would have an inhibiting effect on freedom of speech. On similar reasoning a claim by a political party also has been rejected.[1905] But individual members of such bodies subject to personal attack may be able to sue.

1897. Defamation Act 1954, s. 4(1); Defamation Act 1992, s. 4.
1898. *See* para. 339.
1899. *See* para. 334.
1900. *See* para. 336.
1901. *Durie v. Gardiner* [2018] NZCA 278, [2018] 3 NZLR 131; *see* para. 352.
1902. *Jameel v. Wall Street Journal Europe Sprl* [2007] 1 AC 359.
1903. Defamation Act 1992, s. 6: *Chinese Herald Ltd v. New Times Media Ltd* [2004] 2 NZLR 749.
1904. [1993] AC 534.
1905. *Goldsmith v. Bhoyrul* [1997] 4 All ER 268.

III. Elements of Defamation

A. Defamatory Statement

332. The judges have not adopted any single definition of defamation, yet a composite definition drawn from three leading cases is possible. A defamatory statement is a statement that reflects upon a person's reputation by tending to lower him or her in the estimation of right-thinking members of society generally,[1906] or that exposes him or her to hatred, contempt or ridicule,[1907] or that causes him or her to be shunned or avoided by others.[1908] The statement must be defamatory in the sense that it has the tendency to have one or more of these consequences, for example to lower the plaintiff in the eyes of right-thinking people generally: it need not be proven to have had that effect. The words complained of must be construed in their natural and ordinary meaning.

If the trial is before a judge and jury,[1909] the judge decides whether the words are capable of bearing a defamatory meaning. The test is objective – whether a reasonable person could regard them as defamatory.[1910] If they are capable of being so regarded then the jury decides whether the words do in fact bear that meaning.[1911]

Examples of defamatory statements are limitless. Some (random) instances include: imputations of criminality,[1912] of dishonesty,[1913] or of anti-social behaviour,[1914] holding a person up to ridicule,[1915] alleging that a person was hideously ugly or repulsive,[1916] implying that a person was homosexual,[1917] alleging that a person was insane[1918] or diseased,[1919] or even that she had been raped,[1920] and imputing unfitness or incompetence in a person's trade or profession.[1921] On the

1906. *Sim v. Stretch* [1936] 2 All ER 1237 at 1240.
1907. *Parmiter v. Coupland* (1840) 6 M & W 105 at 109; 151 ER 340 at 342.
1908. *Youssoupoff v. Metro-Goldwyn-Mayer* (1934) 50 TLR 581 at 587.
1909. There can be a jury trial in civil proceedings only in the case of a proceeding for defamation, false imprisonment or malicious prosecution: Senior Courts Act 2016, s. 16(6).
1910. For the 'reasonable person' test, *see Young v. Television New Zealand Ltd* [2014] NZCA 50.
1911. *Morgan v. Odhams Press Ltd* [1971] 1 WLR 1239 at 1251.
1912. *Lewis v. Daily Telegraph* [1964] AC 234. In the case of imputations of misconduct, the Supreme Court in *APN New Zealand Ltd v. Simunovich Fisheries Ltd* [2010] 1 NZLR 315 has accepted the 'tiered meaning' approach in England as a convenient means of describing different forms of meaning. A 'tier one' meaning suggests actual misconduct, a 'tier two' meaning suggests that there are grounds to suspect the plaintiff is guilty of misconduct, and a 'tier three' meaning suggests that there are grounds for investigating whether the plaintiff is guilty of misconduct. For use of this classification, *see*, for example, *Peters v. Television New Zealand* [2012] 2 NZLR 466.
1913. *Lloyd v. David Syme Ltd* [1986] AC 350; *Cairns v. Modi* [2013] 1 WLR 1015 (fixing cricket matches).
1914. *John v. MGN Ltd* [1996] 2 All ER 35.
1915. *Burton v. Crowell Publishing Co.* (1936) 83 F 2d 154.
1916. *Berkoff v. Burchill* [1996] 4 All ER 1008.
1917. *Liberace v. Daily Mirror* The Times, 18 Jun. 1959; but *see Trimingham v. Associated Newspapers Ltd* [2012] 4 All ER 717 at [255]. Context is crucial: *Gluyas v. Canby* [2015] VSC 11 at [42]–[45].
1918. *Pearce v. Symes* (1909) 28 NZLR 562.
1919. *Villers v. Monsley* (1769) 95 ER 886.
1920. *Youssoupoff v. Metro-Goldwyn-Mayer* (1934) 50 TLR 581.
1921. *Truth (NZ) Ltd v. Holloway* [1961] NZLR 22.

other hand, mere abuse or invective that is not taken literally is not defamatory.[1922] Trivial claims are excluded, and the words must attain a minimum threshold of seriousness.[1923] There can be no defamation of a dead person.[1924]

Whether words are defamatory must be determined in the particular context. It is assumed that a reasonable reader will judge a publication in the context as a whole, and will form an opinion as to the one true meaning of the publication.[1925] So photos suggesting that the plaintiffs participated in the making of a pornographic film were potentially defamatory, but an accompanying story explained that the pictures had been taken from a computer game in which the plaintiffs' likenesses had been juxtaposed upon the bodies of other persons. The bane was neutralized by the antidote, and the defendant newspaper was not liable.[1926] Again, the casual reader of a Facebook posting would conclude that the words 'he [the defendant's husband] tried to strangle me' meant that the husband grasped his wife by the throat and applied force to her neck rather than that he had tried deliberately to kill her.[1927]

B. Innuendo

333. Words may be defamatory on their face or they may imply something defamatory. A reasonable person will 'read between the lines' and draw reasonable inferences from what has been said. These are known as innuendoes, and they come in two forms.

First, there is the 'popular' or 'false' innuendo. This arises where a reasonable person can draw the inference from the matter read as a whole. It is simply an aspect of the natural and ordinary meaning of the words. For example, an article may give rise to suspicion about a person's conduct, on the basis that there is no smoke without fire.[1928] So where a magazine article contained a denial that the plaintiff had had a lesbian affair with another woman, the court was not persuaded that the denial necessarily removed the sting of the defamatory words.[1929] Again, innocent words or material may assume a defamatory connotation from the context of the publication.

1922. *Parkins v. Scott* (1862) 158 ER 839.
1923. *CPA Australia Ltd v. NZ Institute of Chartered Accountants* [2015] NZHC 1854; *Sellman v. Slater* [2017] NZHC 2392, [2018] 2 NZLR 218 at [64]–[69]. *See also Lachaux v. Independent Print Ltd* [2019] UKSC 27, [2019] 3 WLR 18, considering the seriousness requirement laid down by statute in England.
1924. *Hagaman v. Little* [2017] NZCA 447, [2018] 2 NZLR 140. A defamatory statement during a person's lifetime cannot be continued by the person's personal representatives after his or her death: Law Reform Act 1936, s. 3(1).
1925. *Charleston v. News Group Newspapers Ltd* [1995] 2 AC 65; *Stocker v. Stocker* [2019] UKSC 17, [2019] 2 WLR 1033 at [32]–[38].
1926. *Charleston v. News Group Newspapers Ltd* [1995] 2 AC 65; and *see Hockey v. Fairfax Media Publications Ltd* [2015] FCA 652.
1927. *Stocker v. Stocker* [2019] UKSC 17, [2019] 2 WLR 1033.
1928. *See Leigh v. Attorney-General* [2011] 2 NZLR 148 (appeal dismissed: *Attorney-General v. Leigh* [2012] 2 NZLR 713).
1929. *New Zealand Magazines Ltd v. Hadlee* [2005] NZAR 621.

For example, the positioning of the plaintiff's waxwork likeness alongside that of a murderer and at the entrance to a 'Chamber of Horrors' gave rise to the inference that the plaintiff too was a murderer.[1930]

Second, there can be a true or 'legal' innuendo. This is where a defamatory implication can be drawn only by those with special knowledge about the matter in question. So a statement that a man was seen entering a certain house may be defamatory in relation to persons who live nearby and know that the house is a brothel.[1931] And a report in a newspaper about C and his fiancée was defamatory of C's wife, because it suggested to those who knew that she claimed to be married to C that she was passing herself off as being married to C.[1932] In cases such as these, the plaintiff must prove that the words were published to persons who possessed the special knowledge that enabled them to draw the defamatory inference.

In any proceedings for defamation, the plaintiff must give particulars specifying the meanings the plaintiff alleges the matter bears, unless it is evident from the matter itself. If the plaintiff alleges a meaning other than the ordinary and natural meaning, then he or she must give full particulars of the supporting circumstances.[1933]

C. Intention of the Defendant

334. In determining whether words are defamatory the defendant's intention is irrelevant. The concern is not with what the defendant intended to say, or convey, but with what he or she did in fact say or convey to a reasonable reader or listener.[1934] For example, words written about a fictitious person defamed a real person of the same name, even though the writer knew nothing of that person.[1935] So too, true words about a real person defamed another person of the same name.[1936] The onus was on the defendant to identify the person referred to with sufficient particularity as to avoid the risk of such a coincidence.[1937]

1930. *Monson v. Tussauds Ltd* [1894] 1 QB 671.
1931. *Lewis v. Daily Telegraph* [1964] AC 234 at 278.
1932. *Cassidy v. Daily Mirror Newspapers Ltd* [1929] 2 KB 331.
1933. Defamation Act 1992, s. 37.
1934. *Hulton v. Co. Ltd v. Jones* [1910] AC 20 at 23.
1935. *Hulton v. Co. Ltd v. Jones* [1910] AC 20.
1936. *Newstead v. London Express Newspaper Ltd* [1940] 1 KB 377.
1937. The Defamation Act 1954, s. 6 formerly provided for a special defence in cases of unintentional defamation, but the 1954 Act was repealed by the Defamation Act 1992, which contains no similar provision.

D. Identification of the Plaintiff

335. The defamatory material must identify the plaintiff, whether by express words, by description, or by reasonable inference. The core requirement is that reasonable persons should reasonably believe that the words referred to the plaintiff.[1938] The test was held to be satisfied in a case where the defendant made statements that could reasonably be read as implying that the plaintiff, who was the leader of a certain religious sect in Christchurch, was linked with the oppressive practices of the same sect in another town that had driven one of its former members to suicide.[1939]

It is not necessary that the plaintiff actually be named. For example, a poster advertising a skifield in an objectionable and tasteless manner defamed the owners of the skifield, even though not named, on the basis that readers would assume that they had authorized the poster.[1940] Similarly, where the plaintiff is identifiable only by persons having extrinsic information, the plaintiff may still succeed by proving the existence of extrinsic facts that would allow a reasonable person knowing those facts to connect the statement with the plaintiff. An example is where a newspaper article stated that M had been kidnapped by a dog doping gang, and at the time M was staying voluntarily in the plaintiff's flat. It was held in the House of Lords that the plaintiff had established that he was sufficiently referred to, on the basis that he had called witnesses who knew of these facts and who said that they thought that the article referred to the plaintiff as being one of the kidnappers.[1941]

Where a statement is defamatory of a class of persons, the courts must determine whether a reasonable person would regard the statement as referring to the plaintiff personally. Sweeping statements about a large class – 'all lawyers are thieves'[1942] – are not actionable because ordinary readers would understand them as exaggerations and not as referring to any particular individual or group of individuals. But sometimes the words may go beyond mere generalization and may reflect upon a particular member. On the one hand, certain statements about a wartime political party with about 2,000 members in all and twenty-four in Britain were held not to be actionable at the suit of the leader of the British branch, even though readers might have known of him as the leader.[1943] But, on the other, an article about a worldwide religious group was held, on the facts, to refer sufficiently to its leader in Britain.[1944] Furthermore, at least where the group is small, a statement may be read as directed to every member of it. An example is where the words referred to a so-called Gang of Twenty as being engaged in corrupt practices.[1945]

1938. *Hyams v. Peterson* [1991] 3 NZLR 648 at 654; *Television New Zealand Ltd v. Keith* [1994] 2 NZLR 84.
1939. *Christchurch Press Co. Ltd v. McGaveston* [1986] 1 NZLR 610.
1940. *Mt Cook Group Ltd v. Johnstone Motors Ltd* [1990] 2 NZLR 488.
1941. *Morgan v. Odhams Press Ltd* [1971] 1 WLR 1239.
1942. *Eastwood v. Holmes* (1858) 175 ER 758 at 759.
1943. *Knupffer v. London Express Newspaper Ltd* [1944] AC 116.
1944. *Orme v. Associated Group Newspapers Ltd*, The Times, 28 Jan. 1980.
1945. *Hyams v. Peterson* [1991] 3 NZLR 648 at 654–655; *Opai v. Culpan* [2016] NZHC 30 at [38]-[39].

It is possible for two statements made by the same person, but published at different times, to be aggregated for the purpose of giving rise to a completed cause of action in defamation. There needs to be created in the mind of the reasonable reader a sufficient nexus, connection or association between them, so that, where one is defamatory and the other identifies the subject, there comes a moment in time at which, in the mind of that reader, the claimant is identified as the subject of the defamatory accusation. That moment will generally be the time of publication of the second statement.[1946]

E. Publication

1. General

336. There can be no action in defamation unless the defamatory material is published to a person other than the plaintiff. Publication is the essence of defamation because the wrong is to the plaintiff's reputation, which is what others think about the plaintiff. A private communication to the plaintiff alone that would be defamatory in the eyes of others is not actionable, for the damage, if any, is only to the plaintiff's dignity, feelings, or self-esteem.

A person may actively publish defamatory material by saying, writing, or printing something that is published to another. Sometimes, there will be a series of publications, as where an informant passes information to a newspaper reporter, who publishes it to an editor, who publishes to a printer, who publishes to the general public. Here, each publisher can be jointly liable with the others.[1947] Generally, in the case of publications by newspapers, magazines, television, radio, and the like, there is a separate publication every time the offending words are read or heard.

The same principle applies to publications on the Internet: there is a publication on each occasion when a statement is downloaded and read.[1948] Even an Internet Service Provider (ISP) can be liable, depending on the circumstances of the publication. An ISP whose role was entirely passive and who had not been notified of the presence of defamatory material was not treated as a publisher.[1949] But an ISP was held to have published defamatory material where, knowing of the material, it failed to remove it from its server.[1950] In *Tamiz v. Google Inc*,[1951] a decision in England, Google provided a service called Blogger that allowed any internet user to create an independent blog, including the use of Uniform Resource Locators (URLs) to host their blogs. Richards LJ was satisfied that Google's role was not purely passive, and that by the provision of the service it facilitated publication of the blogs, including

1946. *Simon v. Lyder* [2019] UKPC 38, [2019] 3 WLR 537.
1947. *Cutler v. McPhail* [1962] 2 QB 292.
1948. *Loutchansky v. Times Newspapers Ltd (No. 2)* [2002] 1 All ER 652; *Dow Jones Ltd v. Gutnick* (2002) 194 ALR 433; *Sellman v. Slater* [2017] NZHC 2392, [2018] 2 NZLR 218 at [22]–[28], [35]–[40]. Tweeters can be liable: *Cairns v. Modi* [2013] 1 WLR 1015; *The Lord McAlpine of West Green v. Bercow* [2013] EWHC 1342.
1949. *Bunt v. Tilley* [2007] 1 WLR 1243.
1950. *Godfrey v. Demon Internet Ltd* [1999] 4 All ER 342.
1951. [2013] 1 WLR 2151; and *see Davison v. Habeeb* [2011] EWHC 3031.

comments posted on them. The blog was likened to a notice board for users to post notices which the provider could take down if pointed out to it. Again, in *Trkulja v. Google LLC*,[1952] the High Court of Australia considered that it was strongly arguable that Google's intentional participation in the communication of allegedly defamatory results to Google search engine users supported a finding that Google published those results.

In New Zealand, in *Murray v. Wishart*,[1953] the question in issue was whether a Facebook host could be liable for allegedly defamatory comments posted on his Facebook page by anonymous users. The Court of Appeal held that the publisher should have actual knowledge of the offending material and fail to remove it within a reasonable time, so that it could be inferred that the publisher was taking responsibility for the statement.

Hyperlinking also is problematic. It has been held in Canada that publication on the internet containing a hyperlink to another website was not a publication of the content to which the hyperlink referred. When a person followed a hyperlink to a secondary source that contained defamatory words, the actual creator or poster of the defamatory words in the secondary material was the person who was publishing the libel. Only when a hyperlinker presented content from the hyperlinked material in a way that actually repeated the defamatory content, should that content be considered to be 'published' by the hyperlinker.[1954] But a New Zealand court might not inevitably follow this authority.[1955] It may be that, say, a hyperlink automatically connecting to a website containing defamatory material will amount to publication of that material.

It is not necessary that the defendant should have intended that the material be published. So where an email that is sent to the plaintiff is mistakenly forwarded to others, where the defendant speaks to the plaintiff too loudly and is overheard, or where material is written on a postcard or is sent by fax so that it may be read by others in the course of transmission, then in each case there is publication to a third person. But the defendant must either intend the words to be published or at least be negligent in allowing this to happen. There was no publication where an unauthorized person opened a sealed envelope,[1956] or where stored material was stolen and published by another.[1957]

2. Repetition

337. Every repetition of a defamatory statement amounts to a fresh publication and creates a fresh cause of action, so each publisher can be individually liable. For example, every newspaper that repeats the defamatory words of another can be

1952. [2018] HCA 25.
1953. [2014] 3 NZLR 722.
1954. *Crookes v. Newton* [2011] SCC 47.
1955. *Karam v. Parker* [2014] NZHC 737, where the court rejected an application for separate consideration of the question of publication arising from hyperlinks; and *see Sellman v. Slater* [2017] NZHC 2392, [2018] 2 NZLR 218 at [41].
1956. *Huth v. Huth* [1915] 3 KB 32.
1957. *Coulthard v. State of South Australia* [1995] Aus Torts Reps 81-326.

sued,[1958] although multiple claims against different newspapers in respect of the same defamatory material are subject to certain special rules concerning time limits and the consolidation of the claims in the one action.[1959]

The original maker of a defamatory statement also may be liable for its repetition by others. Prima facie, the court will treat the unauthorized repetition of a libel as a *novus actus interveniens* that breaks the chain of causation between the original publication and the damage suffered by the injured party. But the originator may be liable where it was the natural and foreseeable result of the publication that it would be repeated.[1960] For example, it was held arguable that the natural and foreseeable consequence of the publication of defamatory material in a film was that the material would be repeated in reviews of the film.[1961]

3. Innocent Dissemination

338. By section 21 of the Defamation Act 1992, a person who has published matter solely in the capacity of, or as the employee or agent of, a 'processor or distributor' has a defence if able to prove that the:

(1) person did not know that the matter contained the material that is alleged to be defamatory; and
(2) person did not know that the matter was of a character likely to contain material of a defamatory nature; and
(3) person's lack of knowledge was not due to any negligence on that person's part.

The defence is available to printers, distributors and sellers of books, magazines, newspapers, and the like, and seemingly can also extend to, for example, radio broadcasters and ISPs. Of course it does not apply to the original author, editor, or publisher. In deciding whether there was negligence, regard may be had to the extent of the defendant's responsibility for the decision to publish, the nature or circumstances of the publication, and the previous conduct of the author or publisher. So an ISP playing a purely passive instrumental role may be able to rely on the defence, but not, for example, if it has chosen to receive and store the offending material and has refused to remove it.[1962]

1958. *Television New Zealand Ltd v. Ah Koy* [2002] 2 NZLR 616; *Simunovich Fisheries Ltd v. Television New Zealand Ltd* [2008] NZCA 350 at [74].
1959. Defamation Act 1992, ss 46–48.
1960. *Slipper v. BBC* [1991] 1 QB 283; *McManus v. Beckham* [2002] 4 All ER 497.
1961. *Slipper v. BBC* [1991] 1 QB 283.
1962. *See* para. 336.

IV. Defences

A. Truth

339. The plaintiff does not have to prove that defamatory matter is false. Rather, the law assumes this, and the onus is on the defendant to prove by way of defence that the matter is true. The matter must be true in fact, and it is not enough that the defendant honestly and reasonably believes it to be true. If a statement carries an innuendo, the defendant must prove the truth of the innuendo. So if a true statement that the plaintiff is being investigated by the police carries the implication for reasonable readers that there are grounds for suspecting criminal activity, then the defendant must prove that these grounds exist, although not that the defendant is actually guilty of criminality.[1963] Again, defendants arguing that that there were reasonable grounds to suspect a plaintiff of particular conduct cannot prove the truth of the proposition simply by repeating the claims of others, but must prove the primary facts supporting the proposition.[1964]

The defendant need not prove that every detail is true, but only that the substance is true or not materially different from the truth.[1965] It is the 'sting' of the charge that must be proved to be true. For example, a statement that a car dealer had wound back the odometers of cars he was selling was justified as true in substance on proof that the dealer had sold cars known to have had their odometers rewound.[1966]

1. Several Allegations

340. At common law, where there were several charges or allegations, the defendant had to prove the truth of every charge. And if the plaintiff chose to sue on only one of them, the defendant could not justify this libel by proving the truth of another. In *Templeton v. Jones*,[1967] the defendant had said of the plaintiff that he was a man who 'despised bureaucrats, civil servants, politicians, women, Jews and professionals'. The plaintiff sued only in respect of the allegation that he despised Jews. The Court of Appeal held that this allegation alone was relevant, and the defendant was not allowed to prove the truth of the other allegations. But the rule applied only where there were two or more distinct defamatory allegations. If several allegations had a common sting, then the defendant could justify the sting by proving the truth of the allegations about which the plaintiff did not complain. So certain allegations about the plaintiff's business activities could be justified by proving other allegations of a similar kind.[1968]

1963. *Lewis v. Daily Telegraph* [1964] AC 234.
1964. *APN New Zealand Ltd v. Simunovich Fisheries Ltd* [2010] 1 NZLR 315.
1965. Defamation Act 1992, s. 8(3)(a). A defendant who proves truth under s. 8(3)(a) cannot set up alternative meanings and prove the truth of those meanings: *Television New Zealand Ltd v. Haines* [2006] 2 NZLR 433; *Simunovich Fisheries Ltd v. Television New Zealand Ltd* [2008] NZCA 350 at [51]; *APN New Zealand Ltd v. Simunovich Fisheries Ltd* [2010] 1 NZLR 315 at [41]–[43] (SC).
1966. *Pepi Holdings Ltd v. BMW New Zealand Ltd* 25/8/97, CA 21/97.
1967. [1984] 1 NZLR 448.
1968. *Polly Peck Holdings plc v. Trelford* [1986] 2 All ER 84.

The position at common law has been modified by section 8(2) of the Defamation Act 1992. This provides that in proceedings for defamation based on only some of the matter contained in a publication, the defendant may allege and prove any facts contained in the whole of the publication. Section 8(3)(b) goes on to provide that where proceedings are based on all or any of the matter contained in a publication, the defence of truth shall succeed where the defendant proves that the publication taken as a whole was in substance true or was in substance not materially different from the truth.

Section 8(2) would allow the defendant in *Templeton* to prove the truth of the other allegations,[1969] but seemingly this at most would affect the level of the damages. The defence of truth still would not succeed, for the publication as a whole could not be seen to be substantially true in accordance with section 8(3)(b) if the allegation that the defendant despised Jews, a serious and separate allegation, could not be proved to be true.[1970]

2. Different Meanings

341. Where there is doubt as to the natural and ordinary meaning of words, the plaintiff must give particulars of the meaning or meanings that the plaintiff alleges that they bear.[1971] The Court of Appeal has held that in this case the defendant may only plead the truth of the publication in the sense complained of by the plaintiff.[1972] In England, by contrast, the courts have allowed the defendant to plead that the words have a different meaning to that alleged and to prove the truth of that meaning.[1973]

B. Honest Opinion

342. At common law it is a defence to a claim for defamation that the defamatory matter was fair comment on a matter of public interest. In New Zealand, the defence is founded upon section 9 of the Defamation Act 1992 and is called 'honest opinion'.[1974] The statute has made little change in the substance of the defence. It has been said that the whole point about a defence of fair comment is that it is to allow citizens to express hard hitting opinions on matters of public interest honestly without fear of being brought before the courts.[1975]

1969. *Manning v. TV3 Network Services Ltd* [2003] NZAR 328 at [40].
1970. For discussion of the ambit of s. 8(3)(b), *see Television New Zealand Ltd v. Haines* [2006] 2 NZLR 433; *Simunovich Fisheries Ltd v. Television New Zealand Ltd* [2008] NZCA 350 at [45]–[53].
1971. Defamation Act 1992, s. 37(2).
1972. *Broadcasting Corporation of New Zealand v. Crush* [1988] 2 NZLR 234; *Television New Zealand Ltd v. Haines* [2006] 2 NZLR 433.
1973. *Polly Peck Holdings plc v. Trelford* [1986] 2 All ER 84; *Williams v. Reason* [1988] 1 All ER 262; *Lucas-Box v. News Group Newspapers Ltd* [1986] 1 WLR 147.
1974. In England, in *Spiller v. Joseph* [2010] 3 WLR 1791 at [117], the Supreme Court has held that the defence of fair comment should be renamed 'honest comment'.
1975. *Branson v. Bower* [2002] 2 WLR 452.

The elements to the defence are that the opinion must be:

(1) based on true facts;
(2) recognizable as opinion; and
(3) genuine.

The requirement at common law that the comment should concern a matter of public interest is not included and appears to have been abandoned.[1976]

1. Opinion Based on True Facts

343. The person giving the opinion needs to give some indication of the facts on which he or she is commenting.[1977] The requirement is easily satisfied if the facts are well known. For example, a headline 'Lower than Kemsley' was capable of being comment, as members of the public generally would know about the newspapers published by Lord Kemsley.[1978] Again, a comment that the claimants were unprofessional and demonstrated a contemptuous and cavalier approach to their contractual obligations could be supported by evidence of a contractual breach which was sufficiently identified as part of the subject matter of the comment, albeit that the breach was not particularised.[1979] But whether statements in a letter commenting on an article were fact or opinion had to be judged in terms of the letter alone, as many readers would not have read the article.[1980]

Normally, the facts upon which the comment is made must be true. So criticism of a play described as 'based on a hackneyed theme involving adultery' could not be fair comment where the play did not involve adultery at all.[1981] But the 'true facts' rule does not apply where opinion is expressed about privileged facts.[1982] Nor does it apply where facts not proved to be true are irrelevant to the opinion. Section 11 of the Defamation Act 1992 provides:

> In proceedings for defamation in respect of matter that consists partly of statements of fact and partly of statements of opinion, a defence of honest opinion shall not fail merely because the defendant does not prove the truth of every statement of fact if the opinion is shown to be genuine opinion having regard to:

1976. The cases take the view that it is not a requirement under the statute: *see*, for example, *Awa v. Independent News Auckland Ltd* [1997] 3 NZLR 590 at 595; *Lange v. Atkinson* [1998] 3 NZLR 424 at 436; *Mitchell v. Sprott* [2002] 1 NZLR 766.
1977. The defendant must give particulars specifying the statements he or she alleges are statements of fact, and the facts and circumstances in support of the allegation that the statements are true: Defamation Act 1992, s. 38; discussed in *Simunovich Fisheries Ltd v. Television New Zealand* [2008] NZCA 350 at [126]–[127].
1978. *Kemsley v. Foot* [1952] AC 345.
1979. *Joseph v. Spiller* [2010] 3 WLR 1791; and *see Karam v. Parker* [2014] NZHC 737.
1980. *Telnikoff v. Matusevich* [1992] 2 AC 343.
1981. *Merivale v. Carson* (1887) 20 QBD 275.
1982. *APN New Zealand Ltd v. Simunovich Fisheries Ltd* [2010] 1 NZLR 315; and *see* paras 346, 349.

a. those facts (being facts that are alleged or referred to in the publication containing the matter that is the subject of the proceedings) that are proved to be true, or not materially different from the truth; or
b. any other facts that were generally known at the time of the publication and are proved to be true.

2. Opinion Recognizable as Opinion

344. The defendant's statement must be recognizable as a statement of opinion rather than of fact.[1983] The statement may be a value judgment, as where a critic gives his or her view on whether a book or play or television programme is good or bad. But a bare assertion unaccompanied by supporting facts may itself be treated as a statement of fact. Cases on the borderline tend to be those where a person draws an inference of fact from primary facts. Depending on how it is presented, this may be treated as opinion. For example, the writer of an article containing much factual information about the debate concerning cot death concluded that the plaintiff doctor's tactics 'were aimed at preventing that debate', and this was held to be recognizable by a reasonable reader as a statement of opinion.[1984] The claims that there was not 'one jot of evidence' that chiropractic methods helped treatments and that a chiropractic association 'happily promotes bogus treatments' were held to be expressions of opinion rather than allegations of fact.[1985] But an assertion that the plaintiff was part of what appeared to be a plot to force the closure of a play after the leading actors gave notice was not comment, for it stated as a fact that there was a plot.[1986]

3. Genuine Opinion

345. The common law requirement that comment be 'fair' is a little misleading, for the test is not the objective fairness of the comment. Rather (i) it must be possible to say that the comment could have been made by an honest person, and (ii) the defendant must not have been actuated by malice. The first requirement poses an objective test. The comment need not be reasonable, but it must be a comment that 'any fair man, however prejudiced he may be, however exaggerated or obstinate his views' could have made.[1987] If the test is satisfied, the plaintiff must rebut the defence by proving malice or other improper motives of the defendant in making the statement.

1983. *Television New Zealand Ltd v. Haines* [2006] 2 NZLR 433; *Du Claire v. Palmer* [2012] NZHC 934.
1984. *Mitchell v. Sprott* [2002] 1 NZLR 766.
1985. *British Chiropractic Association v. Singh* [2011] 1 WLR 133.
1986. *London Artists Ltd v. Littler* [1969] 2 QB 375; compare *Newton v. Dunn* [2017] NZHC 2083 at [221]–[223].
1987. *Merivale v. Carson* (1887) 20 QBD 275; *Channel Seven Adelaide Pty Ltd v. Manock* (2008) 82 ALJR 303 at [3].

Section 10(1) of the Defamation Act 1992 replaces the two limbs of the common law with the requirement that the defendant prove that 'the opinion expressed was the defendant's genuine opinion'. Accordingly, the onus is on the defendant to prove that the opinion is genuine, not on the plaintiff to prove it is not. Unthinking, prejudiced, irrational, or even malicious views may still be genuine. Indeed, section 10(3) provides that the defence of honest opinion will not fail because the defendant was motivated by malice. Furthermore, by section 12, the defence can apply in the ordinary way in cases where the matter that is the subject of proceedings attributes to the plaintiff a dishonourable, corrupt, or base motive.[1988]

Difficulty can arise where the defendant being sued is not the author of the opinion, as where a defendant newspaper has published an article or letter written by someone else. Section 10(2)(a) provides that in the case where the author was the employee or agent of the defendant, the defence of honest opinion shall fail, unless the defendant proves that:

(1) the opinion, in its context and in the circumstances of the publication of the matter that is the subject of the proceedings, did not purport to be the opinion of the defendant; and
(2) the defendant believed that the opinion was the genuine opinion of the author of the matter containing the opinion.

Presumably the belief of the defendant in this context means the belief of an editor, managing director, or other person whose belief can be attributable to a corporate defendant and thus treated as that of the defendant.[1989] Provided that a defendant employer has this belief, then it can rely on the defence of honest opinion, notwithstanding any malice by its employee. Of course the employee in such a case could be personally liable.

A different rule applies where the author is not an employee or agent of the defendant but, for example, a freelance journalist, a writer of a letter to the editor, or a caller to a radio talkback show. Section 10(2)(b) provides that the defence of honest opinion shall fail unless the defendant proves that:

(1) the opinion, in its context and in the circumstances of the publication of the matter that is the subject of the proceedings, did not purport to be the opinion of the defendant or of any employee or agent of the defendant; and
(2) the defendant had no reasonable cause to believe that the opinion was not the genuine opinion of the author of the matter containing the opinion.

Here, the defendant (or, strictly, a person whose opinion can be attributed to the defendant) need not positively believe that the opinion is genuine: it is sufficient that

1988. Section 12 changes the rule at common law laid down in *Campbell v. Spottiswoode* (1863) 122 ER 288, which treated assertions of corrupt motives as a special case and required that they be 'warranted by the facts'.

1989. For discussion of the rules of attribution, *see Meridian Global Funds Management Asia Ltd v. Securities Commission* [1995] 2 AC 500.

the defendant has no reasonable cause to believe that it is not genuine.[1990] The tone of the opinion and whether the language is extravagant are likely to be relevant.[1991]

In other cases involving joint responsibility for a publication, one defendant's defence of honest opinion does not fail merely because another defendant did not genuinely hold the opinion.[1992]

C. Absolute Privilege

346. In certain kinds of situations the law holds that persons should have complete freedom to speak without fear of being sued for defamation. The two main categories are statements made in parliamentary proceedings and statements made in judicial proceedings.[1993] Such statements are protected by absolute privilege, which means that they cannot be called into question whatever the defendant's state of mind and however dishonest or malicious he or she may be. The privilege exists to protect freedom of communication and to encourage those entitled to the privilege to speak without inhibition or fear of consequences.

1. Parliamentary Proceedings

347. The origin of the privilege attaching to parliamentary proceedings is in the words of Article 9 of the Bill of Rights of 1688:

> The freedom of speech and debates or proceedings in Parliament ought not to be impeached or questioned in any court or place out of Parliament.

Section 13(1) of the Defamation Act 1992 provides that proceedings in the House of Representatives are protected by absolute privilege. This covers debate in Parliament and all matters that are part of the proceedings of Parliament, such as proceedings before parliamentary committees.[1994] By section 13(2), the privilege extends to any live broadcasts of parliamentary proceedings and, by section 13(3), to matters published under the authority of Parliament. The privilege does not extend to statements made by MPs which are not part of proceedings of Parliament.[1995]

1990. Cp *Chernesky v. Armadale Publishers Ltd* (1978) 90 DLR (3d) 321, where the Supreme Court of Canada held that the editor of a newspaper who published a reader's letter could not rely on the defence of fair comment as the editor did not honestly hold the opinion in the letter.

1991. *See Karam v. Fairfax New Zealand Ltd* [2012] NZHC 887.

1992. Defamation Act 1992, s. 20(1).

1993. Statements made between officers of state also are protected: *see*, for example, *Peerless Bakery Ltd v. Watts* [1955] NZLR 339 (statement by minister to civil servant).

1994. *Giffins v. Donnelly* (1881) 6 QBD 307. It does not extend to the preparation of materials for the purpose of answering a Parliamentary Question: *Leigh v. Attorney-General* [2011] 2 NZLR 148.

1995. *Brooks v. Muldoon* [1973] 1 NZLR 1.

The privilege may operate to prevent a defendant from relying on the plaintiff's words by way of defence. So in *Prebble v. Television New Zealand Ltd*[1996] the defendant could not rely on statements made by the defendant in Parliament to establish that the allegations about which the plaintiff was suing were true. But the court accepted that, exceptionally, the defamation proceedings might be stayed, on the ground that it would be unfair to the defendant to allow them to continue.

Privilege does not extend to statements made by Members of Parliament outside Parliament. It was held in *Jennings v. Buchanan*[1997] that if a member effectively repeated outside Parliament what was originally said within it, the statement was not protected. The defendant MP made a defamatory statement about the plaintiff in Parliament, and later in a newspaper interview he said he 'did not resile from' his statement. It was held in the Privy Council that the defendant had effectively repeated the allegation and, accordingly, that the plaintiff could sue. The meaning of his later words could only be ascertained by referring to the words in Parliament, but this was not to question those words, but merely to prove that they were uttered: the cause of action was still based upon what was said outside Parliament.[1998]

Jennings was a controversial decision. So was *Attorney-General v. Leigh*,[1999] involving a claim arising from civil servants giving advice to a minister for the purpose of replying to questions for oral answer in the House. The Supreme Court held that absolute privilege must be truly necessary for the proper and effective functioning of Parliament and that it was not necessary to protect civil servants from defamation claims absolutely. The proper functioning of the House required that those communicating with ministers to be strongly discouraged from acting on improper motives, and the advisory function would not be chilled because a limited qualified privilege defence was still available.

Following these decisions, an inquiry by the Privileges Committee of Parliament led to the law being amended by the Parliamentary Privilege Act 2014. Section 10(1) and (2) provide:

> (1) Proceedings in Parliament, for the purposes of Article 9 of the Bill of Rights 1688, and for the purposes of this Act, means all words spoken and acts done in the course of, or for purposes of or incidental to, the transacting of the business of the House or of a committee.
> (2) The definition in subsection (1) must be taken to include the following:
>   a. the giving of evidence (and the evidence so given) before the House or a committee:
>   b. the presentation or submission of a document to the House or a committee:

1996. [1994] 3 NZLR 1.
1997. [2005] 1 AC 115.
1998. *See also Hyams v. Peterson* [1991] 3 NZLR 648; cp *Peters v. Cushing* [1999] NZAR 241 (defamatory words in Parliament explaining earlier statement outside Parliament protected); *Peters v. Television New Zealand* [2012] 2 NZLR 466 (reporter saying of a person who had sworn an affidavit referred to in the House that 'she still stands by her claims in the affidavit' did not amount to adoption by TVNZ).
1999. [2012] 2 NZLR 713.

c. the preparation of a document for purposes of or incidental to the transacting of any business of the House or of a committee:
d. the formulation, making, or communication of a document, under the House's or a committee's authority (and the document so formulated, made, or communicated):
e. any proceedings deemed by an enactment to be (or a thing said or produced, or information supplied, in an inquiry or proceedings, if an enactment provides the thing or information is privileged in the same way as if the inquiry or proceedings were) for those purposes proceedings in Parliament.

It is apparent that this section alters the law in the *Leigh* decision[2000] and that material prepared for the purposes of or incidental to the business of the House is a proceeding in Parliament and protected accordingly.

Further, by section 11, in proceedings in a court or tribunal, evidence must not be offered or received, and questions must not be asked or statements made, concerning proceedings in Parliament, by way of (a) questioning or relying on the truth, motive, intention, or good faith of anything forming part of those proceedings, (b) determining the credibility, motive, intention, or good faith of any person, (c) drawing inferences from those proceedings, (d) proving or disproving any fact necessary for, or incidental to, establishing any liability, (e) resolving any matter arising in the court or proceedings. This provision certainly overturns the *Jennings* decision.[2001]

Part 3 of the Act deals with the communication of proceedings in Parliament. Subpart 1 provides a process whereby a person can seek a stay of civil or criminal proceedings based on communication by that person of proceedings in Parliament or of a document relating to those proceedings, or communication of an authorized parliamentary communication. Subpart 2 provides for a form of qualified immunity from civil or criminal liability for certain communications. The immunity defence is not available if the defendant abused the opportunity to communicate the information by acting in bad faith or with a predominant motive of ill will or both. This form of qualified immunity is available for delayed communication to the public of proceedings in Parliament, fair and accurate reports of proceedings in Parliament, fair and accurate extracts from or summaries of documents communicated under the House's or a Committee's authority and documents relating to proceedings in Parliament.

2. Judicial Proceedings

348. Absolute privilege attaches to anything said, written or done by the judge, jury, counsel, parties, and witnesses in the course of judicial proceedings.[2002] The

2000. This is confirmed by s. 3(2)(c) and s. 10(7).
2001. This is confirmed by s. 3(2)(d).
2002. *Royal Aquarium and Summer and Winter Garden Society v. Parkinson* [1892] 1 QB 423.

privilege extends to include proceedings before all courts or tribunals or other authorities having a duty to act judicially.[2003]

The privilege is not confined to the actual conduct of the hearing before the court or tribunal. It covers everything that is done from the inception of the proceedings, including all pleadings, briefs of evidence, and words spoken during interviews of potential witnesses.[2004] Communications between solicitor or barrister and client for the purpose of enabling the client to seek or obtain legal advice, or between solicitor and barrister for the purpose of enabling legal advice to be provided, are fully protected as well.[2005]

D. Qualified Privilege

349. The public interest in promoting freedom of speech favours special protection being given to statements made in a far wider range of circumstances than those covered by absolute privilege. In these wider circumstances the privilege is said to be qualified, that is, it is defeated if the plaintiff proves that the defendant was motivated by ill will or otherwise took improper advantage of the occasion of privilege. The circumstances giving rise to the privilege are founded in the occasion giving rise to the privilege.[2006] They are found both in the common law and in statute.

1. Common Law Qualified Privilege

350. In *Adam v. Ward*[2007] Lord Atkinson in the House of Lords said that a qualified occasion exists where a person who makes a communication has an interest or a duty, legal, social, or moral, to make it to a person who has a corresponding interest or duty to receive it. His Lordship affirmed that the essence of this type of privilege is that there is reciprocity between maker and recipient constituted by the duty or interest in question. Examples include: a letter by the overseas manager of a company to the Chairman of the Board about the conduct of an employee (but not a similar letter to the employee's wife),[2008] a police report about an incident to a superior officer,[2009] a reference about an employee provided by a former employer to a prospective employer,[2010] a circular sent to distributors of a company about the activities of a competing company,[2011] and letters and an email from the Deputy Solicitor-General to the IRD and the Serious Fraud Office commenting negatively

2003. Defamation Act 1992, s. 14(1).
2004. *Teletax Consultants Ltd v. Williams* [1989] 1 NZLR 698.
2005. Defamation Act 1992, s. 14(2).
2006. *Craig v. Williams* [2019] NZSC 38, [2019] 1 NZLR 457 at [24].
2007. [1917] AC 309 at 334.
2008. *Watt v. Longsdon* [1930] 1 KB 130.
2009. *Dehn v. Attorney-General* [1989] 1 NZLR 320.
2010. *Spring v. Guardian Assurance plc* [1995] 2 AC 296. It was held in this case that the employee had a cause of action for negligence, to which the defence of privilege did not apply, if the reference contained negligent errors: *see* para. 104.
2011. *Alexander v. Clegg* [2004] 3 NZLR 586.

on the conduct of an IRD litigation lawyer involved in a public litigation matter.[2012] Again, a qualified privilege attaches to communications made in self-defence,. So a film-maker could defend himself against criticism by attacking the critic's competence.[2013] Similarly, a politician could defend himself against accusations of sexual impropriety in a nationwide attack by communicating what he believed to be true in a nationwide response. However, whether he did in fact know that the attack had been justified required the plaintiff to show that the person attacked had acted outside the privilege.[2014] But where a newspaper promoting corporal punishment was accused by a Member of Parliament of acting for private advantage rather than the public good, and responded by making new accusations against the MP unconnected with the original attack, then the privilege was lost.[2015]

Publication beyond those who have an interest or duty to receive the information is publication in excess of the privilege and is not protected. For a long time this meant that publications in newspapers were likely to fall outside the ambit of the privilege, on the basis that there could be no privilege to publish defamatory statements about an individual merely because the topic was of some general public interest.[2016] But in some limited circumstances the courts recognized that there could be a duty on the media to communicate information to readers with an interest in receiving it, as in the case of reports of certain official proceedings,[2017] and even in other cases where the interest of the public in receiving the information was particularly strong.[2018] These latter indications for a time remained undeveloped, but recent cases in the UK, New Zealand, Australia, and Canada have grappled with the question whether a special privilege ought to be accorded in the case of debate about matters of public interest or concern.

2. Public Interest Privilege

351. The decision of the House of Lords in *Reynolds v. Times Newspapers Ltd*[2019] sought to apply the classical duty/interest privilege to publication to the world where this was in the public interest. The defendant newspaper had alleged that the plaintiff, a former Irish Prime Minister, had lied to parliament. Their Lordships held that there was no 'generic' privilege for political statements, but that generally published statements may sometimes attract privilege. The test was whether there was a duty to publish and an interest in the public to receive the material. That depended on the circumstances of each individual case. Lord Nicholls listed ten illustrative, non-exhaustive factors to be taken into account. These were:

(1) the seriousness of the allegation;

2012. *Du Claire v. Palmer* [2012] NZHC 934.
2013. *Turner v. Metro-Goldwyn-Mayer* [1950] 1 All ER 449.
2014. *Craig v. Williams* [2019] NZSC 38, [2019] 1 NZLR 457. For abuse of privilege, *see* para. 354.
2015. *News Media Ownership v. Finlay* [1970] NZLR 1089.
2016. *Truth (NZ) Ltd v. Holloway* [1960] NZLR 69, judgment affirmed [1961] NZLR 22 (PC).
2017. *See* now the Defamation Act 1992, s. 16, Sch. 1; *see* para. 355.
2018. *See*, in particular, *R Lucas & Son (Nelson Mail) Ltd v. O'Brien* [1978] 2 NZLR 289.
2019. [2001] 2 AC 127.

(2) the nature of the information, and how far it was of public concern;
(3) the source of the information;
(4) the steps taken to verify the information;
(5) the status of the information;
(6) the urgency of publication;
(7) whether comment was sought from plaintiff;
(8) whether the article contained the gist of the plaintiff's side of the story;
(9) the tone of the article; and
(10) the circumstances of publication, including the timing.

Lord Nicholls emphasized that the weight of the various factors would vary. He noted that a paper's unwillingness to disclose its sources should not weigh against it, cautioned against the use of hindsight to judge conduct, and exhorted the courts to have particular regard to free expression. On the facts the defence failed, as the newspaper had failed to give the plaintiff's explanation of the allegations.

The *Reynolds* privilege seems to attach more to the publication itself than to the occasion of publication. Only Lord Nicholls' first two factors relate to the occasion of privilege, and the other factors are mainly concerned with the defendant's behaviour. This means that factors that would normally be relevant to abuse of privilege are treated as going to the prior issue of whether a privileged occasion has arisen in the first place. The focus on reasonable behaviour as creating the privilege transfers decision-making power on factual issues from the jury to the judge and largely obliterates the jury's role. It also transfers the burden of proof on important issues from claimant to defendant. The defendant has the burden of proving qualified privilege including factors such as lack of abuse. Normally, the *plaintiff* must prove malice or abuse. Accordingly, the privilege is sui generis and does not operate in the same way as the ordinary duty/interest privilege.

Reynolds may be seen as conferring a privilege upon 'responsible journalism'. The privilege extends to publications made by any person who publishes material of public interest in any medium, so long as the conditions applicable to responsible journalism are satisfied.[2020] Its application is highly fact-specific.[2021] Some decisions tend to reassert primacy in the protection of reputation and to curtail investigative reporting.[2022] But others support the emergence of a 'neutral reporting' doctrine, allowing publication notwithstanding the lack of a belief that the allegations are true, and indicate an unwillingness to impose a single, rigid view of what a responsible journalist would report.[2023] *Jameel v. Wall Street Journal Europe Sprl*[2024] indicates that this is now the dominant view. Here the defendant newspaper had asserted that the plaintiffs' bank accounts were being monitored to prevent their use for channelling funds to terrorist organizations. Although the defendant had

2020. *Seaga v. Harper* [2008] 1 All ER 965.
2021. *See* generally *Loutchansky v. Times Newspapers Ltd* [2002] QB 783; *Charman v. Orion Publishing Group Ltd* [2008] 1 All ER 750; *Flood v. Times Newspapers Ltd* [2012] 2 WLR 760.
2022. *Galloway v. Telegraph Group Ltd* [2006] EWCA Civ 17.
2023. *Al-Fagih v. HH Saudi Research and Marketing (UK) Ltd* [2002] EMLR 215; *Roberts v. Gable* [2008] 2 WLR 129.
2024. [2007] 1 AC 359.

failed to obtain the plaintiffs' response, the subject matter was of considerable public importance, the inclusion of names was necessary, and the article had been written by an experienced and specialized reporter and approved by senior staff who had sought to verify its contents. In these circumstances the defence of qualified privilege was held to succeed.[2025]

3. Responsible Communication on a Matter of Public Interest

352. The law in New Zealand has developed rather differently. In *Lange v. Atkinson*[2026] the defendant journalist published an article that was highly critical of the then Prime Minister, David Lange. Mr Lange sued for defamation, and in response the defendant pleaded a qualified privilege for 'political discussion'. The Court of Appeal upheld the defence, and in this and a second decision[2027] laid down a number of principles to determine when it might apply,[2028] However, the law has moved on and these can be put to one side, for later cases contemplated that a wider, public interest, defence might be developing. Eventually, in *Durie v. Gardiner*[2029] in 2018, the Court of Appeal, following developments in Canada,[2030] laid down a new defence of responsible communication on a matter of public interest.

It is apparent that there are two limbs to the new defence. French and Winkelmann JJ, giving a joint judgment, said that in determining the question of public interest the judge should step back and look at the thrust of the publication as a whole.[2031] It was not necessary to find a separate public interest justification for each item of information. And public interest was not confined to publications on political matters. Nor was it necessary that the plaintiff be a public figure. However, defining what was a matter of public interest in the abstract with any precision was a notoriously difficult exercise. On the approach taken in Canada,[2032] the subject matter should be one inviting public attention, or about which the public or a segment of the public had some substantial concern because it affected the welfare of citizens, or one to which considerable public notoriety or controversy had attached.

As for when a communication was responsible, there should be regard to all the relevant circumstances of the publication.[2033] Such circumstances might include:

2025. In the UK the *Reynolds* defence was abolished by the Defamation Act 2013 (UK), s. 4(6), and replaced by the defence that the statement complained of was on a matter of public interest, and the defendant reasonably believed that publishing the statement was in the public interest: Defamation Act 2013 (UK), s. 4(1). On the question of reasonable belief, *see Economou v. de Freitas* [2018] EWCA Civ 2591.

2026. [1998] 3 NZLR 424.

2027. *Lange v. Atkinson* [2000] 3 NZLR 385.

2028. A political discussion privilege also was recognised in Australia: *Lange v. Australian Broadcasting Corporation* (1997) 71 ALJR 818.

2029. [2018] NZCA 278, [2018] 3 NZLR 131.

2030. *Grant v. Torstar Corp* 2009 SCC 61, [2009] 3 SCR 640.

2031. [2018] NZCA 278, [2018] 3 NZLR 131 at [64]-[65].

2032. *Grant v. Torstar Corp* 2009 SCC 61, [2009] 3 SCR 640 at [99]-[106].

2033. [2018] NZCA 278, [2018] 3 NZLR 131 at [67]-[68].

(a) The seriousness of the allegation – the more serious the allegation, the greater the degree of diligence to verify it.
(b) The degree of public importance.
(c) The urgency of the matter – did the public's need to know require the defendant to publish when it did, taking into account that news was often a perishable commodity.
(d) The reliability of any source.
(e) Whether comment was sought from the plaintiff and accurately reported. In most cases it was inherently unfair to publish defamatory allegations of fact without giving the target an opportunity to respond. Failure to do so also heightened the risk of inaccuracy. The target might be able to offer relevant information beyond bare denial.
(f) The tone of the publication.
(g) The inclusion of defamatory statements which were not necessary to communicate on the matter of public interest.

This list of factors was not exhaustive, and not all factors would be relevant in all cases. In some cases, publishing defamatory allegations from an unidentified source might not be responsible. In others it might be responsible if for example the publisher had good reason to consider the source reliable and the article made it clear it was relying on a confidential source. The factors had to be applied in a practical and flexible manner, taking into account the practical realities. Appropriate deference should be paid to the editorial judgment of the publisher, particularly where professional editors and journalists were involved.[2034]

Their Honours also decided that both the question of the public interest and the question whether a communication was responsible should be determined by the judge. The process involved mixed questions of fact and law, a highly evaluative exercise better suited to judicial assessment. So where a case was tried by a jury, the trial judge should determine whether the two elements of the defence were established, based on the primary facts as found by the jury.

4. Reportage

353. It is apparent that the factors bearing upon responsible communication cover much the same ground as those indentified in *Reynolds*. They include the neutral reporting of the fact that a statement was made – so-called reportage – which was protected in the UK on a broad view of *Reynolds*,[2035] and which then came to be treated by statute as part of the public interest defence.[2036] In *Durie v. Gardiner* French and Winkelmann JJ similarly recognized that reportage should be treated as

2034. For examples of applications of the defence *see Craig v. Slater* [2018] NZHC 2712 at [342]–[356]; *Lee v. Lee* [2018] NZHC 3136; and *see Low Volume Vehicle Technical Association Inc v. Brett* [2019] NZCA 67, [2019] 2 NZLR 49 at [79].
2035. *Roberts v. Gable* [2008] 2 WLR 129; *supra* para. 351.
2036. Defamation Act 2013 (UK), s. 4(3).

a special form of the new defence in New Zealand.[2037] The court should consider whether, viewing the publication as a whole, the publishers had made it clear they did not subscribe to any belief in the truth of the allegation and had not adopted it as their own. Relevant considerations would include whether the source of the information was disclosed in the publication and the tone of the publication, including whether the allegations had been embellished. Timing might also be relevant. If, for example, the allegation or its context was stale or there was some other ulterior reason for the timing of the publication, then reportage might not be available even if the report was otherwise full, fair and neutral. However, unlike in the UK and Canada, no dispute needed to be shown. There was no reason why a public interest defence could not in an appropriate case protect the disinterested repetition of a unilateral allegation.[2038]

Their Honours considered that reportage would only be available in circumstances where the public interest in the fact of the allegation was overwhelming and so compelling on its own that urgent reporting of it was justified without further investigation. The stakes for publishers – mainstream or otherwise – who did not attempt to verify the truth of the defamatory allegation were high. They were likely to do so at their peril and accordingly the incentive to make the attempt remained high.

5. Abuse of Privilege

354. At common law, qualified privilege is defeated by proof of malice. The meaning of this concept was considered by the House of Lords in *Horrocks v. Lowe*.[2039] There is malice where a person publishes words without a positive or honest belief in their truth, or publishes recklessly, without caring whether they are true or false. But indifference to the truth is not to be equated with carelessness, impulsiveness, or irrationality in arriving at a positive belief that words are true. Exceptionally, even where words are believed to be true, they may be shown to be published for an improper purpose such as a desire to injure the plaintiff.

In New Zealand, the common law has been replaced by section 19 of the Defamation Act 1992. This provides:

(1) In any proceedings for defamation, a defence of qualified privilege shall fail if the plaintiff proves that, in publishing the matter that is the subject of the proceedings, the defendant was predominantly motivated by ill will towards the plaintiff, or otherwise took improper advantage of the occasion of publication.
(2) Subject to subsection (1) of this section, a defence of qualified privilege shall not fail because the defendant was motivated by malice.

2037. [2018] NZCA 278, [2018] 3 NZLR 131 at [69]-[81]. Brown J differed on this point and was nor prepared to recognise a reportage defence in NZ law, at least until a case arose where the issues were squarely engaged.

2038. So the rule that repetition of a defamatory statement is a fresh publication and independently actionable (*supra* para. 337) does not apply in the circumstances covered by the public interest defence.

2039. *Horrocks v. Lowe* [1975] AC 135.

The statutory definition covers much the same ground as the common law. But in *Lange* 2000[2040] the Court of Appeal considered that the concept of 'improper advantage' could go beyond the traditional meaning. When considering whether an occasion of privilege had been misused, it was useful to ask whether the defendant had exercised the degree of responsibility that the occasion required, and this was influenced by the circumstances in which the allegations were made.[2041]

The whole question was examined afresh in the Supreme Court in *Craig v. Williams*.[2042] The court held that section 19 was concerned with improper purpose, being a purpose outside the occasion of the privilege. The reference to ill will was an example of using the occasion for an improper purpose, and the presence of malice or animosity was not material provided that the defendant had not been predominantly motivated by an improper purpose. In the circumstances, improper purpose could be found if the defendant had known that the allegations of sexual harassment which he had sought to rebut had in fact been true, so he had no belief in what he had said. The trial judge had misdirected the jury on the key question of the defendant's knowledge, so a retrial as to both liability and damages was ordered.[2043]

6. Statutory Qualified Privilege

355. A number of statutes confer qualified privilege on statements made by various public officials.[2044] In particular, the various reports, proceedings, and matters listed in the Defamation Act 1992 are privileged[2045] unless (as with the common law privilege) the plaintiff proves that the defendant was predominantly motivated by ill will towards the plaintiff or otherwise took improper advantage of the occasion of privilege.[2046] There are two categories of privilege. In one, the statements are privileged without explanation or contradiction, and in the other the opportunity for explanation or contradiction must have been given.

Four types of reports are privileged without explanation or contradiction:[2047]

(1) The publication, in any proceedings before a tribunal or statutory authority not protected by absolute privilege, of any matter by a member of the tribunal or authority or by a party, representative or witness.
(2) The publication of a fair and accurate report of the pleadings of the parties in any proceedings before any court in New Zealand.

2040. [2000] 3 NZLR 385 at 399.
2041. *Ibid.*, at 401.
2042. [2019] NZSC 38, [2019] 1 NZLR 457.
2043. As to the damages, *see* para.358.
2044. For example, the Ombudsmen Act 1975 s. 26; Local Government Official Information and Meetings Act 1987, s. 52.
2045. The public interest behind this privilege relates to the location where the statement was made, not the fact that it was made: *Durie v. Gardiner* [2018] NZCA 278, [2018] 3 NZLR 131 at [78].
2046. Defamation Act 1992, s. 16, Sch. 1. The Schedule originally contained seven clauses. The first three have been repealed and replaced in the Parliamentary Privilege Act 2014: *see* para. 342.
2047. *Ibid.*, s. 16(1), Sch. 1, Part 1.

(3) The publication of a fair and accurate report of the proceedings of any Court in New Zealand or of the result of those proceedings.
(4) The publication of a fair and accurate translation of words from one language to another where the publication is by the person who made the translation and in his or her capacity as translator.

Certain other types of reports and matters are privileged subject to explanation or contradiction.[2048] In cases in this category, the privilege does not apply unless, at the time of publication, the report or matter is a matter of public interest in any place at which the publication occurs,[2049] and is lost if it is proved that a newspaper or broadcaster has been requested to publish a reasonable letter or statement by way of explanation or contradiction of the defamatory publication, and the defendant has refused or failed to comply with the request or has complied in a manner that is inadequate or unreasonable.[2050] There are fifteen types of reports or matters covered by the privilege:

(1) A fair and accurate report of the proceedings of a legislature of a territory outside New Zealand.
(2) A fair and accurate report of the proceedings of a Court outside New Zealand or of the result of those proceedings.
(3) A fair and accurate report of the proceedings of a government commission of inquiry in New Zealand or overseas.
(4) A fair and accurate report of the proceedings of an international organization of countries or legislatures or governments, or an international conference at which governments are represented.
(5) A fair and accurate report of the proceedings of a meeting or sitting of a local authority or other statutory body.
(6) A fair and accurate report of the proceedings of an inquiry relating to a member of an association promoting (a) any sport, game, or pastime, or (b) any trade, business, industry, or profession, or (c) an interest in any art, science, religion, or learning.
(7) A fair and accurate report of the proceedings in an inquiry by an association formed for the purpose of promoting and safeguarding the standards of the New Zealand press.
(8) A fair and accurate report of the proceedings of a bona fide and lawful public meeting held in New Zealand for the furtherance or discussion of any matter of public concern.
(9) A fair and accurate report of the proceedings at meetings of a public company, incorporated society, and other body corporate.
(10) A fair and accurate report of the proceedings at a press conference of anybody whose proceedings are privileged subject to explanation or contradiction under the present head.

2048. *Ibid.*, s. 16(2), Sch. 1, Part 2.
2049. *Ibid.*, s. 18(1).
2050. *Ibid.*, s. 18(2).

(11) A fair and accurate report of a publication issued under the authority of a foreign legislature or state.
(12) A fair and accurate copy or extract from the companies register, the district land register, and any other New Zealand public register.
(13) A notice or advertisement published by or under the authority of any court.
(14) A notice or advertisement published for the purpose of complying with a New Zealand Act.
(15) A copy or a fair and accurate report or summary of a statement or notice issued for the information of the public by the government or any local authority.

The privilege may be lost by the addition of extraneous, non-privileged material. This may depend on the amount of such material, whether the typical reader would be able to distinguish the reportage from the unprivileged material, and the extent to which the material was connected with the privileged reportage.[2051]

E. Consent

356. It is a defence to proceedings for defamation if the defendant proves that the plaintiff consented to the publication of the matter that is the subject of the proceedings.[2052] Whether the plaintiff's consent extends to all the circumstances of the publication is a question of fact. A person who tells a story against himself in the presence of friends may not consent to the story being published in a newspaper.[2053] Again, an author who gives consent to a publishing company to advertise and promote a book does not normally consent to defamatory words about him in the advertising material.[2054]

V. Remedies

357. The remedies available in an action for defamation include damages, an injunction, a declaration, and correction of the defamatory matter.

A. Damages

358. An award of damages will include general damages for loss of reputation, injury to feelings and, where appropriate, special damages for material loss capable of being estimated in money. The level of the general damages will be influenced by factors such as the nature and seriousness of the allegation, the nature of the

2051. *Curistan v. Times Newspapers Ltd* [2008] 1 WLR 126.
2052. Defamation Act 1992, s. 22.
2053. *Cook v. Ward* (1830) 130 ER 1338.
2054. *Mihaka v. Wellington Publishing Co. (1972) Ltd* [1975] 1 NZLR 10.

defendant's behaviour and state of mind, and how widely the words have been published. For example, insulting or high-handed behaviour or persistence in maintaining an unjustified attack may aggravate the hurt to the plaintiff's feelings. So may an allegation of a particularly serious kind,[2055] and in rare cases exemplary damages may be justified.[2056] Words published to the world at large are likely to cause greater harm to reputation than words published to an individual or small group of persons. But a reduced award may be appropriate where a defendant publishes without malice and in the belief that the words are true.

On the one hand, damages sometimes may include an element of vindication.[2057] On the other hand, damages may be reduced, sometimes to a nominal sum, where defamatory words cause little further damage in light of what is proved to be true,[2058] or where the plaintiff already has a bad reputation.[2059] As regards the latter, the defendant is entitled to adduce evidence of particular instances of misconduct in order to establish that the plaintiff is a person whose reputation is generally bad in the aspect to which the proceedings relate.[2060] But other contemporaneous defamatory publications do not amount to evidence of generally bad reputation or provide admissible evidence of specific instances of misconduct.[2061] Evidence of the plaintiff's misconduct in aspects or ways unconnected with the defamatory allegation is irrelevant and inadmissible.[2062]

The damages also may be mitigated by the defendant publishing an apology or a statement of explanation or rebuttal,[2063] by the terms of any injunction or declaration that the Court proposes to make,[2064] by the plaintiff's delay in bringing proceedings,[2065] and by the plaintiff recovering damages or bringing other proceedings against the defendant or any other person in respect of substantially the same matter.[2066]

The quantum of damages that may be awarded in defamation cases can vary a good deal, and certainly a number of very high awards have been made in recent times.[2067] However, an award may be overturned on appeal if it is seen to be excessive. It has been observed in the Supreme Court of Appeal that judges should feel free to indicate the appropriate boundaries of an award while exercising care not to

2055. *See*, for example, *Siemer v. Stiassny* [2011] NZCA 106.
2056. *Williams v. Craig* [2018] 3 NZLR 1 (CA) at [34] (not mentioned on appeal in *Craig v. Williams* [2019] 1 NZLR 457 (SC)).
2057. *Purnell v. Business Fi Magazine Ltd* [2008] 1 WLR 1.
2058. *Grobbelaar v. News Group Newspapers Ltd* [2002] 4 All ER 732.
2059. *Goody v. Odhams Press Ltd* [1976] QB 333.
2060. Defamation Act 1992, s. 30.
2061. *Television New Zealand Ltd v. Ah Koy* [2002] 2 NZLR 616.
2062. *Jorgensen v. New Zealand Newspapers Ltd* [1974] 2 NZLR 45.
2063. Defamation Act 1992, s. 29(a), (b).
2064. *Ibid.*, s. 29(c).
2065. *Ibid.*, s. 29(d).
2066. *Ibid.*, s. 31.
2067. For example, *Idour v. INL Publications Ltd* HC Wellington CIV-2003-485-968, 2 August 2004 (NZD 780,000); *Korda Mentha v. Siemer* HC Auckland CIV-2005-404-1808, 23 December 2008 (NZD 825,000); *Karam v. Parker* [2014] NZHC 737 (NZD 525,000).

usurp the jury's function, particularly where the judge had concluded that the plaintiff's counsel had been extravagant in pitching the damages claim.[2068]

B. Injunction

359. Whether an interlocutory injunction ought to be granted normally is determined by the courts asking whether there is a serious question to be tried, and then considering the balance of convenience as between the plaintiff and the defendant.[2069] But the courts are very cautious about awarding an interlocutory injunction to prevent the publication of defamatory matter, because of the need to preserve freedom of speech and expression. In this context, the more restrictive rule in *Bonnard v. Perryman*[2070] applies. This states that an interlocutory injunction will not be granted if there is any doubt whether words are defamatory, or if the defendant intends to plead a recognized defence and the court is not satisfied that the defence will fail. The Court of Appeal has affirmed that the rule applies in New Zealand,[2071] and that the jurisdiction to prevent publication should be exercised only in the clearest of cases.[2072]

The reluctance of the courts to grant injunctions against the media is reinforced by section 14 of the New Zealand Bill of Rights Act 1990. This provides that everyone has the right to freedom of expression, including the freedom to seek, receive and impart information and opinions of any kind and in any form. Seemingly, since the courts are public bodies, the development of the common law is subject to the Bill of Rights and should proceed in accordance with it.[2073]

C. Declaration

360. A plaintiff may be more concerned about restoring his or her reputation than about money. In such a case the plaintiff may seek a declaration that the defendant is liable to the plaintiff in defamation.[2074] Special provisions apply as to costs.[2075]

2068. *Craig v. Williams* [2019] NZSC 38, [2019] 1 NZLR 457 at [80], [161] (where a jury award of NZD 1.2m was quashed and a retrial of both the liability and the damages issue was ordered).

2069. *American Cyanamid Co. v. Ethicon Ltd* [1975] AC 396.

2070. [1891] 2 Ch 269.

2071. *New Zealand Mortgage Guarantee Co. Ltd v. Wellington Newspapers Ltd* [1989] 1 NZLR 4; *Ron West Motors Ltd v. Broadcasting Corporation of New Zealand Ltd (No. 2)* [1989] 3 NZLR 520.

2072. *TV3 Network Services Ltd v. Fahey* [1999] 2 NZLR 129.

2073. *See*, for example, *Auckland Area Health Board v. Television New Zealand Ltd* [1992] 3 NZLR 406; *TV3 Network Services Ltd v. Fahey* [1999] 2 NZLR 129.

2074. Defamation Act 1992, s. 24(1); *see*, for example, *Willy v. Fairfax New Zealand Ltd* HC, Wellington, CIV-2008-085-1429, 22 Jul. 09.

2075. Defamation Act 1992, s. 24(2).

D. Correction

361. The plaintiff may seek a recommendation from the court that the defendant publish a correction of the matter that is the subject of the proceedings.[2076] Any such recommendation may include matters relating to the content, time of publication and prominence of the correction.[2077] If the defendant publishes a correction in accordance with the order, then the plaintiff is entitled to costs but no other relief or remedy and the proceedings are deemed to be finally determined.[2078] If the defendant fails to publish the correction then, if the court gives final judgment in favour of the plaintiff, the failure is taken into account in the assessment of the damages and normally the plaintiff is entitled to costs.[2079]

§9. INVASION OF PRIVACY

I. Introduction

362. It may be said that a person's interest in privacy is invaded where, without that person's consent, others see or hear or read about what he does or says, or what others say or do comes unwillingly to his attention.[2080] Of course, this means that any 'right' to privacy amounts to no more than the right to be left alone, and in this very broad sense, the right is not and cannot be protected by way of an action in tort. Indeed, in *Wainwright v. Home Office*[2081] Lord Hoffmann said that English law was unable to formulate any high-level principle of privacy, but also recognized that aspects of privacy may be protected at a lower, more specific, level via a number of common law and statutory remedies. In this case, their Lordships rejected a claim that mental injury caused by a strip search at a prison amounted to an actionable invasion of privacy. A remedy, if any, had to be found in existing and accepted principles of law, guided by privacy as an important underlying value.

Established torts that may indirectly protect a person's privacy include trespass, nuisance, defamation, and malicious falsehood, but until recently there was no cause of action giving protection to any form of privacy interest standing alone. This stance has now come to be abandoned, with the courts recognizing a new action that protects a person's interest in the privacy of personal information. In New Zealand, the action has been developed as a new tort, whereas in England it has emerged via the existing action in equity for breach of confidence. In another development, the courts in England began to explore the idea of protecting a right to seclusion via an action in tort for harassment, but then, in both England and New Zealand, Parliament stepped in to provide a statutory remedy.[2082]

2076. *Ibid.*, s. 26(1); *Newton v. Dunn* [2017] NZHC 2083, at [269]-[273].
2077. *Ibid.*, s. 27(1).
2078. *Ibid.*, s. 27(2).
2079. *Ibid.*, s. 27(3).
2080. *See* generally *Privacy: Concepts and Issues* LC Study Paper (Wellington, 2008).
2081. [2004] 2 AC 406.
2082. *See* paras 371, 372.

New Zealand also provides statutory protection for privacy in certain other circumstances. For example, the Broadcasting Act 1989 requires broadcasters to maintain standards that are consistent with the privacy of the individual.[2083] This is enforced by complaint to the Broadcasting Standards Authority, which has developed a set of privacy principles. These have the approval of the High Court,[2084] and they can help inform the development of the common law.[2085] The Privacy Act 1993 is a data protection statute that lays down principles prescribing how personal information is to be obtained, stored, and used. Breaches can be the subject of complaint to the Privacy Commissioner and the Human Rights Review Tribunal, but the principles are not generally enforceable in court proceedings. A court may order a director or former director of a company to provide a liquidator with such information about the business accounts or affairs of the company as the liquidator requests.[2086] The relevant provisions have been interpreted as not authorizing liquidators to obtain private financial information from a director for the purpose of ascertaining whether he could meet any money judgment obtained against him. The gravity of such intrusion into a director's private affairs had to weigh in a jurisdictional assessment by reference to New Zealand's developing privacy jurisprudence.[2087]

II. Misuse of Private Information

A. General

363. Following a number of expressions of support in first instance decisions,[2088] a majority in the Court of Appeal in *Hosking v. Runting*[2089] accepted that in New Zealand there is a tort of invasion of privacy by the unauthorized publication of personal or private information. Gault P and Blanchard J considered that the two fundamental requirements were (1) the existence of facts in respect of which there was a reasonable expectation of privacy, and (2) publicity given to those facts that would be considered highly offensive to an objective reasonable person. Tipping J preferred to say that the level of intrusiveness should be taken into account in assessing whether or not there was a reasonable expectation of privacy. There was a defence if the information or material constituted a matter of legitimate public concern justifying publication in the public interest. On the facts, the claim was not made out. The plaintiffs, a so-called celebrity couple who had separated following the birth of their twin daughters, sought to prevent the publication of photographs of the twins being pushed in a stroller in the street by their mother. It was held that there was no reasonable expectation of privacy in the photographs, which were

2083. Broadcasting Act 1989, s. 4.
2084. *TV3 Network Services Ltd v. Broadcasting Standards Authority* [1995] 2 NZLR 720.
2085. *See* generally J. Burrows & U. Cheer, *Media Law in New Zealand* Ch. 6 (7th ed., LexisNexis, 2015).
2086. Companies Act 1993, ss 261 and 266.
2087. *Finnigan v. Ellis* [2017] NZCA 488, [2018] 2 NZLR 123 at [44]–[46].
2088. *See*, in particular, *Tucker v. News Media Ownership* [1986] 2 NZLR 716; *Bradley v. Wingnut Films Ltd* [1993] 1 NZLR 415; *P v. D* [2000] 2 NZLR 591.
2089. [2005] 1 NZLR 1.

taken in a public place and that posed no risk to the children. Nor could it reasonably be said that publication should be regarded as likely to cause substantial offence or other harm to a person of reasonable sensibility.

In *Rogers v. Television New Zealand Ltd*[2090] Elias CJ and Anderson J, in dissenting judgments, did not accept that the limits to the tort of privacy were necessarily those stated in the majority opinions in *Hosking*. Elias CJ in particular, questioned whether the 'highly offensive' test should be required, and pointed to unanswered questions, such as the time at which the reasonable expectation of privacy should be assessed. However, the majority (Blanchard, Tipping, and McGrath JJ) were content to accept *Hosking* and to determine that on the facts the plaintiff's claim to privacy should be rejected. The plaintiff had confessed at a police interview to killing a woman. The videotape of the confession was excluded from the evidence at his trial, as it was obtained in breach of the New Zealand Bill of Rights Act 1990, and the plaintiff was acquitted. TVNZ obtained a copy of the videotape and proposed to broadcast it. The plaintiff sought an injunction to prevent this, but the majority held that his application failed. Having elected to make a statement to the police, he could not claim to have a reasonable expectation of privacy concerning the occasion. Furthermore, his confession was already in the public arena, so his privacy interest could only relate to the circumstances in which the confession was made. While his demeanour could be a private fact, his interest was relatively slender when balanced against freedom of information concepts in section 14 of the New Zealand Bill of Rights Act 1990.[2091]

B. Elements to Liability

364. The elements to this new tort will require further exploration. In particular, there will be much room for disagreement in identifying facts in respect of which there is a reasonable expectation of privacy – sometimes expressed as 'private facts'. The contents of the Prince of Wales' diary were private even though the Prince disclosed them to a number of friends and acquaintances.[2092] And personal and private matters disclosed by a former friend could be protected even though some of them were untrue.[2093] But the writer of a blog on the internet had no right to remain anonymous, because blogging was a public activity.[2094]

A difficult question is whether there can ever be an expectation of privacy in respect of something that happens in a public place. Probably, a case of this kind is rare but not impossible. For example, the European Court of Human Rights has held that the publication of a film taken in a street of the claimant attempting to commit suicide was an invasion of the claimant's privacy in breach of Article 8 of the European Convention on Human Rights.[2095] In England, a photograph of the plaintiff in

2090. [2008] 2 NZLR 277.
2091. *See* para. 359.
2092. *HRH The Prince of Wales v. Associated Newspapers Ltd* [2008] Ch 57.
2093. *Ash v. McKennitt* [2008] QB 73.
2094. *The Author of a Blog v. Times Newspapers Ltd* [2009] EWHC 1358.
2095. *Peck v. UK* [2003] EMLR 287.

the street was treated as part of an intrusion into the plaintiff's private life.[2096] In New Zealand, it has been held that the conversations between a husband and wife while being extracted from a crashed car after an accident were private facts.[2097] Another imponderable is whether or when a 'public' fact can become 'private'. In dicta in a decision preceding *Hosking*, it was thought to be arguable that the plaintiff's criminal convictions had, by the passage of time, receded into the realm of private facts.[2098] In the case of public figures there will be a lesser expectation of privacy, but it has been recognized that celebrities are still entitled to privacy about intimate personal matters.[2099]

What about the privacy rights of children? In *Hosking*, as already noted, the claim failed as the photograph was taken in the street, but it is nonetheless clear that children may need to be protected by this tort.[2100] In *PJS v. News Group Newspapers Ltd*[2101] the UK Supreme Court granted an interim injunction restraining the defendant from publishing a story in one of its newspapers about his alleged extramarital sexual activities, on the basis that disclosure of the material would be likely to add greatly and on a potentially enduring basis to the intrusiveness and distress felt by the claimant, his partner and their children. Baroness Hale said that it was simply not good enough to dismiss the interests of any children likely to be affected by the publication of private information about their parents by the bland statement that 'these cannot be a trump card'. They had privacy interests of their own and a right to respect for their family life with their parents. At trial, the court would have to consider carefully the nature and extent of the likely harm to the children from publication of the material in the short, medium and longer terms.

The requirement that the publicity be highly offensive to a reasonable person is concerned with publicity that is truly humiliating or distressful. So the disclosure of a person's mental illness without the person's consent was thought to be offensive and actionable.[2102] But publicity about a domestic incident involving a school principal would be embarrassing and distressing to the plaintiff but could not be described as offensive or objectionable.[2103] Further, the especially sensitive who complain about publicity given to harmless or neutral facts have no redress. In the car crash case, it was held that there was nothing in what the husband and wife said to each other that could be treated as highly offensive: their words were neither humiliating nor embarrassing.

2096. *Campbell v. MGN Ltd* [2004] 2 AC 457; *see* para. 367.
2097. *See Andrews v. Television New Zealand Ltd* [2009] 1 NZLR 220.
2098. *Tucker v. News Media Ownership* [1986] 2 NZLR 716.
2099. *A v. B plc* [2003] QB 195; *McKennitt v. Ash* [2007] 3 WLR 194.
2100. *Murray v. Express Newspapers plc* [2008] 3 WLR 360 (claim in respect of photographs of children allowed to go to trial); *Weller v. Associated Newspapers Ltd* [2016] 1 WLR 1541 (damages awarded).
2101. [2016] UKSC 26, [2016] AC 1081. However, the behaviour of parents can reduce a child's reasonable expectation of privacy by 'giving it away': *AAA v. Associated Newspapers Ltd* [2013] EWCA Civ 554.
2102. *P v. D* [2000] 2 NZLR 591.
2103. *Clague v. APN News and Media Ltd* [2013] NZAR 99.

C. Public Concern

365. The defence of legitimate public concern seeks to reconcile an individual's right to privacy with the guarantee of freedom of expression in the New Zealand Bill of Rights Act 1990. Applying section 5, any limits on that freedom must be reasonable and justifiable in a free and democratic society. The issue here is whether publication is justified in the public interest, not whether it is justified because it is newsworthy. The courts must strike a balance between the free dissemination of news and the proper protection of private interests. In *PJS v. News Group Newspapers Ltd*[2104] the UK Supreme Court distinguished between reporting facts capable of contributing to a debate of general public interest in a democratic society and making tawdry allegations about an individual's private life. In *Hosking*, it was recognized that the greater the intrusion into privacy, the greater the degree of public concern that needs to be shown.[2105] In *Rogers*, the majority were satisfied that public concern about how the law had operated in that case together with considerations of open justice carried more weight than the plaintiff's privacy interests.[2106]

III. Intrusion into Seclusion

366. Hosking involves the wrongful publication of information. Intrusion into seclusion, by contrast, involves an invasion of the victim's private space. The question whether this could be actionable arose in *C v. Holland*.[2107] C was an occupant in a house owned by her boyfriend and H, the defendant. H surreptitiously installed a recording device in the roof cavity above the shower and toilet and videoed C while she was showering. The videos were never published but C discovered them and was deeply upset. She brought an action against H alleging that his conduct constituted an invasion of her privacy. Whata J upheld the claim and recognized for the first time in New Zealand that an intrusion into seclusion was a tort in its own right.

Whata J was satisfied that an intrusion tort would give effect to a recognized value in protecting privacy and would be a compatible with, and a logical adjunct to, the decision in *Hosking v. Runting*. His Honour considered that the plaintiff had to show (a) an intentional and unauthorized intrusion, (b) into seclusion (namely intimate personal activity, space or affairs); (c) involving infringement of a reasonable expectation of privacy; and (d) that was highly offensive to a reasonable person. 'Intentional' connoted an affirmative act, not an unwitting or simply careless intrusion. 'Unauthorized' excluded consensual and/or lawfully authorized intrusions. Further, not every intrusion into a private matter was actionable. The reference to intimate personal activity acknowledged the need to establish intrusion into matters that most directly impinged on personal autonomy. As for the last two elements, these replicated the *Hosking* requirements and the tort thus remained consonant with existing privacy law. Only private matters were protected, and a right

2104. [2016] UKSC 26, [2016] AC 1081 at [21]–[24].
2105. [2005] 1 NZLR 1 at [257].
2106. [2008] 2 NZLR 277 at [75].
2107. [2012] 3 NZLR 672.

of action only arose in respect of an intrusion that was objectively determined, due to its extent and nature, to be offensive by causing real hurt or harm. Lastly, a legitimate public concern in the information might provide a defence to the privacy claim.

The ambit of this new tort will need to be fleshed out. Examples overseas of an intrusion tort include unauthorized prying into the plaintiff's private bank account;[2108] telephone tapping without disclosing the information to others;[2109] and highly personal questions and demands by a person in authority.[2110] It may be that the tort can be committed in a public place, such as by intrusive questioning or photographing of an accident victim.[2111]

IV. Breach of Confidence

367. It is a well-recognized principle of equity that an action for breach of confidence lies where information has a quality of confidence, the information is communicated to another in circumstances importing an obligation of confidence, and there is unauthorized use or disclosure of the information causing detriment to the person entitled to the benefit of the confidence.[2112] The origins of the action lie in cases involving the protection of commercial secrets that had been imparted in confidence by one person to another. However, developments in England show the action being extended (1) by using it to protect personal information,[2113] and (2) by abandoning the requirement of a relationship giving rise to an obligation of confidence.[2114] In this context the action can be seen as founded in tort rather than in equity.[2115]

The leading decision is *Campbell v. MGN Ltd*,[2116] where the House of Lords confirmed that that breach of confidence could cover complaints about the publication of private information in circumstances where there was no relationship of confidence. Baroness Hale saw the first question as being whether in respect of the disclosed information, the person in question had a reasonable expectation of privacy. Once the threshold test was satisfied and the information was identified as private, the court should balance the claimant's interest in keeping the information private against the countervailing interest of the recipient in publishing it. The exercise was influenced by Article 8 of the European Convention on Human Rights (right to respect for private and family life) and Article 10 (right to freedom of expression), because the court, as a public authority, was required by section 6 of the Human Rights Act 1998 (UK) not to act in a way that was incompatible with a Convention

2108. *Jones v. Tsige* (2012) 108 OR (3d) 241.
2109. *Fowler v. Southern Bell Telephone and Telegraph Co* 343 F 2d 150 (1965).
2110. *McSurely v. McLellan* 753 F 2d 88 (1985).
2111. *See Andrews v. Television New Zealand Ltd* [2009] 1 NZLR 220.
2112. *Coco v. A N Clark (Engineers) Ltd* [1969] RPC 41 at 47.
2113. For example, *Argyll v. Argyll* [1967] Ch 302; *Stephens v. Avery* [1998] Ch 449; *see* para. 260.
2114. *See* para. 261.
2115. *See Vidal-Hall v. Google Inc* [2015] 3 WLR 409.
2116. [2004] 2 AC 457.

right. Neither right should take precedence over the other, the balancing exercise being determined by considerations of proportionality.

The claimant, a famous fashion model, gave information to the media about her private life and maintained publicly, but untruthfully, that she did not take drugs. The defendant newspaper subsequently reported that the claimant was in fact addicted to drugs, gave details of her receiving therapy at meetings of Narcotics Anonymous, and showed photographs of her in a street as she was leaving a meeting. It was common ground that information about a person's health and treatment ordinarily would be confidential or private, but the defendant argued that it was justified in publishing the information in the public interest in the light of the claimant's earlier denials. Their Lordships decided by a majority that the defendant's report went beyond that which was necessary to correct the claimant's lies. The fact that the claimant was addicted to drugs and was receiving treatment could be published, but the details of her therapy and the accompanying photographs constituted private information that was outside the journalistic margin of appreciation allowed to a free press. The claimant's right to respect for her private life outweighed the newspaper's right to freedom of expression and, accordingly, the claimant was entitled to damages.

Many decisions show the balancing exercise recognized in *Campbell* in operation. In a high profile case already noted,[2117] the Prince of Wales was entitled to summary judgment against a newspaper that had published extracts from his private travel journals after these had been supplied to the paper in breach of confidence by the plaintiff's employee.[2118] In other well-known applications, the celebrity plaintiffs were entitled to damages from the defendant magazine for infringing their right to privacy by publishing unauthorized photographs of their wedding;[2119] and a public figure recovered damages for newspaper articles exposing his sadomasochistic activities with a number of prostitutes.[2120]

V. Remedies

A. *Injunction*

368. As in cases of defamation,[2121] interim injunctions to restrain publication are not readily granted. In *Hosking v. Runting*,[2122] Tipping J said that prior restraint by injunction should be confined to cases that were severe in likely effect and clear in likely outcome. Certainly, in cases involving celebrities seeking to prevent disclosure of extramarital sexual activity, an injunction often has been refused.[2123] On the

2117. Above para. 364.
2118. *HRH Prince of Wales v. Associated Newspapers Ltd* [2008] Ch 57.
2119. *Douglas v. Hello! Ltd* [2003] 3 All ER 996, affirmed [2008] 1 AC 1, sub nom *OBG Ltd v. Allan*.
2120. *Mosley v. News Group Newspapers Ltd* [2008] EWHC 1777.
2121. *See* para. 359.
2122. [2005] 1 NZLR 1 at [258].
2123. For example, *Theakston v. MGN Ltd* [2002] EMLR 398; *A v. B plc* [2003] QB 195; *Giggs v. News Group Newspapers Ltd* [2012] EWHC 431. But *see PJS v. News Group Newspapers Ltd* [2016]

other hand, in *Douglas v. Hello! Ltd*[2124] the English Court of Appeal considered that the earlier refusal, also by the Court of Appeal,[2125] of an injunction to restrain publication of unauthorized photographs of the plaintiffs' wedding was wrong and a strong disincentive to respect for private life.

In a number of recent cases the courts have been asked to make orders granting anonymity to claimants seeking to prevent the publication of material alleged to be an invasion of their right to privacy. In *JIH v. News Group Newspapers Ltd*[2126] it was recognized that an order for anonymity derogated from the principle of open justice and interfered with the rights of the public at large. So courts should only make such orders after very close scrutiny of the application. In the instant case it was concluded that the applicant should continue to remain anonymous, but that details of the claim revealed in the judgments could nonetheless be revealed.

B. Damages

369. Damages can be awarded for humiliation, hurt feelings, loss of dignity, and loss of the right to control the use of the information.[2127] It has been said that the damages should be kept at a modest level,[2128] but substantial awards can nonetheless be made.[2129] Seemingly, damages also can be awarded for injury to reputation. In *Khuja v. Times Newspapers Ltd*[2130] the UK Supreme Court recognized that the protection of reputation was the primary function of the law of defamation, and that while the ambit of the right of privacy was wider, it provided an alternative means of protecting reputation which was available even when the matters published were true. In a recent High Court decision in England Mann J said that it was obvious that reputational harm could arise from matters of fact which were true but which were within the scope of a privacy right. In any event, that loss of reputation had an impact on the feelings of the wronged individual and would inevitably come into that extent in any event.[2131]

UKSC 26, [2016] AC 1081, where the UK Supreme Court granted an interim injunction preventing disclosure of the claimant's sexual activities notwithstanding that the story and the names of those involved had been published overseas, on the internet and in social media.

2124. [2005] 3 WLR 884. For the decision of the House of Lords on the damages to be awarded to the purchaser, *see* [2008] 1 AC 1.

2125. *Douglas v. Hello! Ltd* [2001] QB 967.

2126. [2011] EWCA Civ 42; and *see Donald v. Ntuli* [2011] 1 WLR 294.

2127. *Gulati v. MGN Ltd* [2016] 2 WLR 1217.

2128. *Archer v. Williams* [2003] EMLR 869 at 889.

2129. For example, *Gulati v. MGN Ltd* [2016] 2 WLR 1217 (awards to eight claimants totalling GBP 1.2 million for egregious hacking of the claimants' telephones); *Richard v. British Broadcasting Corp* [2018] EWHC 1837, [2018] 3 WLR 171 (GBP 210,000 for identifying famous claimant as being the subject of a police investigation into allegations of sexual abuse).

2130. *Khuja v. Times Newspapers Ltd* [2017] UKSC 49, [2017] 3 WLR 351 at [21] and [34].

2131. *Richard v. British Broadcasting Corp* [2018] EWHC 1837 (Ch), [2018] 3 WLR 1715 at [345].

VI. Privacy or Confidence?

370. The decisions in England clearly can assist the development of the law of privacy in New Zealand. *Campbell* recognizes a cause of action for interference with privacy by way of publication of private facts, although the action is called breach of confidence. The action is also treated as a tort, notwithstanding its origins in equity, for their Lordships accepted that it is founded on the private nature of the information, rather than the conscience of the person sued. Lord Nicholls, in particular, thought the essence of the tort was better encapsulated as misuse of private information. In *Hosking*, the Court of Appeal preferred to recognize breaches of confidence and invasions of privacy as separate causes of action, and this is the better view. Sometimes there may be a breach of confidence in the traditional sense in relation to personal information, as where the recipient of a private letter publishes it in breach of an obligation of confidence imposed by the sender. The concepts of confidence and of privacy frequently overlap. But only the law of confidence can apply in commercial cases. On the other hand, where there is no relationship importing an obligation of confidence, and the complaint is about the publication of personal information, then the action is best understood as an action for invasion of privacy.[2132] In *R v. X*[2133] Hammond J in the Court of Appeal recognized that the law of confidence had experienced a shift which had removed the requirement for a distinct relational context, with the result that information will be protected as confidential where the complainant has a reasonable expectation of confidentiality or privacy and the defendant has agreed to keep the information confidential or has notice of its confidentiality. In such cases, then, either privacy or breach of confidence seemingly can apply.

VII. Harassment

A. Common Law

371. A person's interest in privacy also is invaded where he or she is subject to harassing conduct. Instances of stalking, phone ringing, persistent unwanted attention, and the like are distressing to the victim and call for redress. Yet the common law has had difficulty in dealing with the problem, for the conduct concerned may not fit easily within the ambit of an existing tort. Where harassing conduct causes physical or psychiatric harm, then negligence can provide a remedy.[2134] Where there is a threat of violence, this can constitute an assault. Where the harassment affects the plaintiff in the use and enjoyment of his or her land, there may be a remedy in nuisance. But the conduct may not cause or threaten actual injury and may have nothing to do with the enjoyment of land. However, decisions of the Court of Appeal in England give a degree of support for recognizing harassing conduct as a

2132. *See also Ash v. McKennitt* [2008] QB 73 at [8]; *Mosley v. News Group Newspapers Ltd* [2008] EWHC 1777 at [7].
2133. [2010] 2 NZLR 181.
2134. *Waters v. Commissioner of Police of the Metropolis* [2000] 1 WLR 1607.

tort in its own right. In one case, the plaintiff obtained an interlocutory injunction forbidding the defendant, a former friend, from using violence to harass her, or harassing or pestering her with telephone calls at her parents' home.[2135] In another, the plaintiff obtained an interlocutory injunction following threats and harassment, restraining the defendant from assaulting, threatening or harassing her or communicating with her, and prohibiting him from coming within 250 yards of her house.[2136] Seemingly, for the tort to be committed, there needs to be unwanted harassing conduct of such a degree of seriousness and persistence that an ordinary person should not reasonably be expected to endure it.

In *Wainwright v. Home Office*[2137] Lord Hoffmann noted that following these cases a remedy for harassment was provided by the Protection from Harassment Act 1997 (UK), which gives the courts extensive powers to protect the victim, to make orders preventing harassment from occurring, and to give damages for anxiety.[2138] Further development of the common law in the UK accordingly is unlikely. In New Zealand, the Harassment Act 1997 gives wide-ranging injunctive powers to the courts to prevent harassment, but no right to the victim to seek damages. As regards the latter, he or she must rely on a tort action, whether for harassment or, if this is not accepted, for an established tort like assault or nuisance.

B. Harassment Act 1997

372. Usually, the victim of harassment wants protection from the conduct in the future. The Harassment Act makes the most serious types of harassment criminal offences, empowers the court to make orders to protect victims who are not covered by domestic violence legislation,[2139] and provides effective sanctions for breaches of the criminal and civil law relating to harassment.[2140] The Act provides that a person harasses another person if he or she engages in a pattern of behaviour that is directed at that other person, being a pattern of behaviour that includes doing any specified harassing acts to the other person, on at least two occasions, within a period of twelve months.[2141] The harassment is criminal where the first person intends to cause the other person to fear for his or her, or a family member's, safety,

2135. *Khorasandjian v. Bush* [1993] QB 727 (overruled by *Hunter v. Canary Wharf Ltd* [1997] AC 655 (HL) insofar as it held that an action for nuisance can lie at the suit of a mere licensee without an interest in land).

2136. *Burris v. Adazani* [1995] 1 WLR 1372.

2137. [2004] 2 AC 406.

2138. *See*, for example, *Daiichi Pharmaceuticals UK Ltd v. Stop Huntingdon Animal Cruelty* [2004] 1 WLR 1503.

2139. As to which, *see* the Domestic Violence Act 1995.

2140. Harassment Act 1997, s. 6.

2141. *Ibid.*, s. 3(1). The specified acts are defined widely in s. 4. They include watching or loitering near a person's place of residence, business or employment; following, stopping, accosting or making contact with the person; and giving offensive material to the person. In *Majrowski v. Guy's and St Thomas's NHS Trust* [2007] 1 AC 224 at [30] Lord Hoffmann said that there is a boundary between conduct which is unattractive, even unreasonable, and conduct which is oppressive and unacceptable. Examples include: publishing racist criticism (*Thomas v. News Group Newspapers Ltd* [2009] EWCA Civ 1288); workplace bullying (*Veakins v. Kier Islington Ltd* [2009] EWCA

or the first person knows that the harassment is likely to cause the other person, in his or her particular circumstances, such fear.[2142] The remedy of the victim in civil law, whether or not the harassment is a criminal offence, is to apply to the District Court for a restraining order.[2143] Broadly, the court may make such an order if it is satisfied that this is justified in all the circumstances by the degree of distress caused or threatened, and making an order is necessary to protect the applicant from further harassment.[2144] Probably, the remedy can be invoked only by natural persons, not by corporate claimants.[2145]

There is no harassment if the respondent proves that a specified act was done for a lawful purpose.[2146] This undefined defence may exempt such activities as inquiries by journalists and protesters exercising the right of public protest, provided, at least, that the conduct is not directed at individual victims.

Civ 1288); letters threatening civil action for alleged non-payment of a gas bill (*Ferguson v. British Gas Trading Ltd* [2010] 1 WLR 785); an irrational and obsessive campaign against a former employer (*Hayes v. Willoughby* [2013] 1 WLR 935); assault, threat to kill, and following a neighbour (*Xu v. Mayes* [2014] NZHC 349); conduct motivated by continuing grudge against former police officer (*Clarke v. Watts* [2014] NZHC 822). Examples where harassment was not established include: a series of domestic disagreements (*R v. Curtis* [2010] 1 WLR 2770); articles about an affair with a politician (*Trimingham v. Associated Newspapers Ltd* [2012] 4 All ER 717).

2142. Harassment Act 1997, s. 8. As to knowledge of consequences *see P v. D* [2000] 2 NZLR 641.

2143. *Ibid.*, s. 9(1).

2144. *Ibid.*, s. 16(1).

2145. *Daiichi Pharmaceuticals UK Ltd v. Stop Huntingdon Animal Cruelty* [2004] 1 WLR 1503 ('person' for the purpose of the Protection from Harassment Act 1997 (Eng) does not embrace a corporate entity).

2146. Harassment Act 1997, s. 17.

Part II. Liability for the Acts of Others, for Property and for Things

Chapter 1. Vicarious Liability

§1. Introduction

I. Nature of Vicarious Liability

373. The common law doctrine of vicarious liability imposes liability on one person in respect of a tort or other civil wrong committed by another.[2147] Accordingly, it is a form of strict liability: the person being held liable is not personally blameworthy. Three questions must be asked in determining whether the doctrine can apply. First, what is the relationship between the person who is sought to be made liable and the person who has committed the wrong? Second, what kind of wrongs can import vicarious liability? Third, what is the connection between the wrongful conduct and the relationship in question? As regards the first question, the relationship must be in the nature of that between an employer and an employee[2148] or which is akin to such relationship[2149] or, in certain circumstances, that between a principal and an agent.[2150] As regards the second question, the concern normally is with tortious wrongdoing, but vicarious liability also can apply to breach of a statutory obligation sounding in damages unless the statute expressly or impliedly excludes such liability,[2151] and to breach of an equitable obligation.[2152] As regards the third question, the tort or other civil wrong must be shown to have been committed in the course of the employment or agency,[2153] or to have been closely connected with the employment or relationship analogous to employment.[2154]

An employer's vicarious liability, normally founded on tortious misconduct by an employee, should be distinguished from the employer's *personal* liability, for example in failing to provide competent fellow workers or in choosing an independent contractor, where the employer's own conduct is in issue.

2147. For further discussion *see Todd on Torts* Ch. 22 (Todd ed., 8th ed., 2019).
2148. *See* paras 375–381.
2149. *See* para. 379.
2150. *See* paras 388–390.
2151. *Majrowski v. Guy's and St Thomas's NHS Trust* [2007] 1 AC 224.
2152. *Ibid.*, at [30].
2153. *See* paras 380–382.
2154. *See* paras 383, 384.

Imposition of vicarious liability on an employer or principal does not affect the legal position of the tortfeasor. He or she remains personally liable in respect of his or her own tort. The employer or similar person does not commit the tort but in law is held responsible for it.[2155] That person and the actual wrongdoer are joint tortfeasors.[2156] However, the employer or principal being innocent of blame, he or she can claim an indemnity from the wrongdoer, although this right is rarely exercised.[2157]

II. Policy Considerations

374. The doctrine of vicarious liability lacks any firm basis in theory or principle.[2158] Promoting fairness by linking the benefits of an enterprise with a corresponding liability for losses incurred in the course of the enterprise, distributing losses, ensuring tort victims are compensated, deterring wrongdoing, encouraging care, all can play a part.[2159] In *Majrowski v. Guy's and St Thomas's NHS Trust*[2160] Lord Nicholls recognized that a combination of policy factors provides its rationale. All forms of economic activity carried a risk of harm, and fairness required that those responsible should be liable to those suffering loss from wrongs committed in the conduct of the enterprise. This was fair, because it meant that injured persons could look for recompense to a source better placed financially than individual wrongdoers. It also meant that loss could be spread more widely, by liability insurance and higher prices. In addition, imposing strict liability encouraged employers to maintain standards of good practice by their employees.

The consideration that persons injured in the course of business enterprises should not go uncompensated now has little weight in New Zealand, because personal injury is covered by the accident compensation scheme and tort claims are barred.[2161] However, the rules governing vicarious liability are well established and continue to apply to other forms of loss.

Vicarious liability is concerned with compensation for losses, not punishment of wrongdoers. Accordingly it does not extend to an award of exemplary damages, the purpose of which is to punish and deter wrongdoers who are guilty of egregious misconduct.[2162]

2155. *Majrowski v. Guy's and St Thomas's NHS Trust* [2007] 1 AC 224 at [15].
2156. *Coleman v. Harvey* [1989] 1 NZLR 723; *Brooks v. NZ Guardian Trust Co. Ltd* [1994] 2 NZLR 134, on appeal [1995] 1 WLR 96 (PC); *Cashfield House Ltd v. David & Heather Sinclair Ltd* [1995] 1 NZLR 452.
2157. *See Lister v. Romford Ice and Cold Storage Co. Ltd* [1957] AC 555 concerning the right of a vicariously liable employer, and by subrogation its insurer, to claim an indemnity from a negligent employee.
2158. *See ICI Ltd v. Shatwell* [1965] AC 656 at 685.
2159. For comprehensive discussion *see Bazley v. Curry* [1999] 2 SCR 534.
2160. [2007] 1 AC 224 at [9]; and *see Various Claimants v. Catholic Child Welfare Society* [2013] 2 AC 1 at [34]–[35], [47]; *Cox v. Ministry of Justice* [2016] AC 660 at [20]–[24].
2161. *See* para. 41.
2162. *S v. Attorney-General* [2003] 3 NZLR 450; *see* para. 578.

§2. EMPLOYERS AND EMPLOYEES

375. A contract creating the relationship of employer and employee (often called a contract of service), upon which a vicarious liability is very commonly founded, should be distinguished from a contract creating the relationship between a principal and an independent contractor (often called a contract for services). The question is whether the person concerned has engaged himself or herself to perform services in business on his or her own account. If the answer to that question is 'yes' then the contract is a contract for services and the person performing the work is an independent contractor. If the answer is 'no' then the contract is a contract of service and the person concerned is an employee.[2163]

I. The Test of Control

376. The most important and, in most cases, decisive criterion is that of control. The question is not whether the employer exercises actual control over how work is done but whether the employer exercises ultimate managerial authority or control. It is the employer's right of control over the employee so far as there is scope for control, not the exercise of a power of command.[2164] Particular factors that may be relevant include whether the person performing the services provides his own equipment, whether he hires his own helpers, what degree of financial risks he takes, what degree of responsibility for investment in management he has, and whether and how far he has an opportunity to profit from sound management in the performance of the work.[2165] Another, related, way of looking at the question is to examine whether the person concerned is an integral part of the employer's business or is only accessory to it.[2166] The court asks whether the worker is genuinely in business on his own account or whether he is 'part and parcel of' – or 'integrated into' – the enterprise of the person or organization for whom the work is performed.[2167]

Where the terms of a contract are fully set out in writing which is not a sham, the true nature of the contract depends on an analysis of the rights and obligations so defined at the time of its execution.[2168] The contractual description given to the relationship by the parties themselves is relevant but is not decisive.[2169]

2163. *Market Investigations Ltd v. Minister of Social Security* [1969] 2 QB 173 at 184–185.
2164. *Challenge Realty Ltd v. Commissioner of Inland Revenue* [1990] 3 NZLR 42 at 62.
2165. *Market Investigations Ltd v. Minister of Social Security* [1969] 2 QB 173 at 184–185; *TNT Worldwide Express (NZ) Ltd v. Cunningham* [1993] 3 NZLR 681 at 700.
2166. *Stevenson, Jordan and Harrison Ltd v. MacDonald and Evans* [1952] 1 TLR 101.
2167. *Challenge Realty Ltd v. Commissioner of Inland Revenue* [1990] 3 NZLR 42 at 65.
2168. *TNT Worldwide Express (NZ) Ltd v. Cunningham* [1993] 3 NZLR 681 at 686.
2169. *See* Employment Relations Act 2000, s. 6(3); *Ferguson v. Dawson Partners Ltd* [1976] 1 WLR 1213; *Challenge Realty Ltd v. Commissioner of Inland Revenue* [1990] 3 NZLR 42 at 59–60; *Bryson v. Three Foot Six Ltd* [2005] 3 NZLR 721.

II. Borrowed Employees

377. Sometimes an employee continues to be employed by one employer but carries out work for another. In this case the question of vicarious liability for the employee's torts is determined on the basis of the right to control not merely what is done, but how it is to be done.[2170] So where an employer supplied a crane and driver to another employer, the first employer was vicariously liable for the negligence of the driver.[2171] The hirer could direct the driver what cargo to move, but not how he should manage the crane. Indeed, it is rare for a court to find that there has been a shifting of liability to the second employer. However, exceptional circumstances were shown in a case where the purchaser of a helicopter and associated business employed the pilot, but the vendor continued to operate the business.[2172] The vendor maintained complete operational control over the pilot and was held to be vicariously liable for the pilot's negligence.

Sometimes, in appropriate cases, there may be dual vicarious liability. This approach concentrates on the relevant negligent act and asks whose responsibility it was to prevent it. So where there were two employers each obliged to control the employee's negligent act, there could be joint vicarious liability.[2173]

III. Employee Directors

378. It has been held by the Privy Council that an employer who appointed two employees as directors of a subsidiary company was not liable for the employee/directors' negligence.[2174] The ordinary principles of vicarious liability were seen as impliedly excluded by the role of the employees as officers of the company in question. But the Court of Appeal later expressed doubt about the decision, on the ground that it was not consistent with commercial reality.[2175]

§3. Relationships Analogous to Employment

379. Recent decisions in England and in Canada have imposed vicarious liability in the case of relationships that are analogous to employment. These developments have been driven by cases involving child abuse committed by priests in circumstances where the defendant being sued is not their employer.

2170. *Mersey Docks and Harbour Board v. Coggins and Griffith (Liverpool) Ltd* [1947] AC 1; *Steel Structures Ltd v. Rangitikei County* [1974] 2 NZLR 306.

2171. *Mersey Docks and Harbour Board v. Coggins and Griffith (Liverpool) Ltd* [1947] AC 1.

2172. *Airwork (NZ) Ltd v. Vertical Flight Management Ltd* [1999] 1 NZLR 641.

2173. *Viasystems (Tyneside) Ltd v. Thermal Transfer (Northern) Ltd* [2006] QB 510; approved in the UK Supreme Court in *Various Claimants v. Catholic Child Welfare Association* [2013] 2 AC 1; *see* below para. 379.

2174. *Kuwait Asia Bank EC v. National Mutual Life Nominees Ltd* [1991] 1 AC 187.

2175. *ANZ Banking Group (NZ) Ltd v. Dairy Containers Ltd* unrep., CA 156/92, 17 Dec. 1992; and *see Nimmo v. Westpac Banking Corporation* [1994] 1 NZLR 472; *Dairy Containers Ltd v. NZI Bank Ltd* [1995] 2 NZLR 30.

The leading decision is *Various Claimants v. Catholic Child Welfare Association.*[2176] The question here was whether the Institute of the Brothers of the Christian Schools (the Institute), founded by Jean-Baptiste De La Salle in 1680, was responsible for sexual and physical abuse of children committed by its brothers at a residential institute for boys (St William's) who were in need of care and protection. Claims had been brought by the victims against two groups of defendants. The first (called the Middlesbrough Defendants), who were the managers of the school and the employers of the brother teachers, were held at first instance to be vicariously liable in respect of abuse by those teachers. The second (the De La Salle Defendants) were found not to be vicariously liable, on the basis that the Institute did not employ the brothers at St William's. Rather, it sent its brothers to teach there. The Court of Appeal upheld the judge's decision and the Middlesbrough Defendants appealed, on the ground that the Institute should share joint vicarious liability for the acts of its brother members. The UK Supreme Court was unanimous in upholding this contention.

Lord Phillips said that where the defendant and the tortfeasor were not bound by a contract of employment, but their relationship had the same incidents, that relationship could properly give rise to vicarious liability on the ground that it was 'akin to that between an employer and an employee'. In the instant case the relationship between the teaching brothers and the Institute had all the essential elements of the relationship between employer and employee: the Institute was subdivided into a hierarchical structure and conducted its activities as if it were a corporate body; the teaching activity of the brothers was undertaken because the provincial head directed the brothers to undertake it; the teaching activity undertaken by the brothers also was in furtherance of the objective, or mission, of the Institute; and the manner in which the brother teachers were obliged to conduct themselves as teachers was dictated by the Institute's rules. The relationship between the teacher brothers and the Institute differed from that of the relationship between employer and employee in that the brothers were bound to the Institute not by contract, but by their vows, and the brothers entered into deeds under which they were obliged to transfer all their earnings to the Institute, but neither difference was material. Indeed, they rendered the relationship closer than that of an employer and its employees.

Various Claimants was applied by the Supreme Court in *Cox v. Ministry of Justice.*[2177] It was held here that the UK Ministry of Justice could be held vicariously liable for the negligence of a prisoner assisting with work in the prison kitchen who dropped a heavy bag of rice onto the prison catering manager and injured her. Lord Reed affirmed that the general approach in *Christian Brothers* was not confined to some special category of cases, such as the sexual abuse of children. By focusing upon the business activities carried on by the defendant and their attendant risks, it directed attention to the issues which were likely to be relevant in the context of modern workplaces.

2176. [2013] 2 AC 1; and *see Maga v. Archbishop of Birmingham* [2010] 1 WLR 1441; *E v. English Province of Our Lady of Charity* [2013] 2 WLR 958. In Canada *see John Doe v. Bennett* [2004] 1 SCR 436.

2177. [2016] AC 660.

This expansive trend was continued in *Armes v. Nottinghamshire County Council.*[2178] In this case the Supreme Court held that a local authority which had placed a child with foster parents was vicariously liable for the abuse of a child by those parents. Lord Reed said that the picture as a whole pointed towards the conclusion that the foster parents provided care to the child as an integral part of the local authority's organization of its childcare services. It could properly be said that the torts committed against the claimant were committed by the foster parents in the course of an activity carried on for the benefit of the local authority.

On the other hand, in *Barclays Bank plc v. Various Claimants*,[2179] the Supreme Court held that the defendant bank was not vicariously liable in respect of alleged sexual assaults to which they were subjected by a doctor to whom the bank referred them for medical assessments prior to their employment. The bank argued that the doctor was an independent contractor, and the court accepted that there was nothing in the preceding trilogy of cases to suggest that the classic distinction between employment and relationships akin or analogous to employment, on the one hand, and the relationship with an independent contractor, on the other hand, had been eroded.

§4. The Connection Between the Relationship and the Wrong

I. The Course of Employment

A. *General*

380. An employer is vicariously liable for the tort of an employee only where the tort is committed in the course of employment. The test that is commonly applied, derived from *Salmond on Torts*,[2180] a leading text, has two limbs. It must be asked whether the employee's act is a wrongful act authorized by the employer, or is a wrongful and unauthorized mode of doing some act authorized by the master. The first limb of this test is not really about vicarious liability, as where a wrongful act is authorized, the employer is personally liable. The second limb raises the problem of deciding whether conduct is an unauthorized mode of doing something or is simply not authorized at all. It is a question of fact and degree whether a tortious act is so much within the scope of employment that it was generally authorized, albeit tortiously carried out.[2181]

If an employee is pursuing personal ends unrelated to the employment, the employer is not liable. It is not enough that a tort was committed during working hours, nor that the employment gave the opportunity to the employee to commit it. An old decision asks whether the employee was 'on a frolic of his own'.[2182]

2178. [2017] UKSC 60, [2018] AC 355.
2179. [2020] UKSC 13, [2020] 2 WLR 960.
2180. *Salmond on Torts* (1907) at 83–84.
2181. *Commercial Union Assurance Co. of NZ Ltd v. Lamont* [1989] 3 NZLR 187 at 212.
2182. *Joel v. Morrison* (1834) 172 ER 1338 at 1339.

Another, more recent, decision asks whether the act was 'incidental' to the employment.[2183] These tests restate the problem in different words. Decisions on whether conduct is an unauthorized mode of carrying out the employment, or falls right outside it, turn very much on their facts. In a leading example, an employer was vicariously liable where a lorry driver dropped a lighted match while delivering petrol, which caused an explosion.[2184] The driver was employed to deliver petrol and was doing this, but in a negligent way. On the other hand, firefighters involved in an industrial dispute with their employer who deliberately drove slowly when called to a fire, with the result that the plaintiff's premises were destroyed before they got there, were acting for their own purposes unconnected with the employer's business.[2185]

B. Prohibitions

381. A prohibition on certain conduct may limit the scope of the employee's employment or merely regulate the employee's conduct within the sphere. In the former case the employer will not be liable, in the latter he will.[2186] The question frequently arises in cases where employees were employed as drivers. For example, allowing an unauthorized person to take the wheel contrary to instructions was within the course of employment, as the driver was employed not only to drive the vehicle but also to be in charge of it.[2187] Again, where an employee employed to drive a milk float wrongly allowed a child to ride on it, who assisted the employee in his work, the employer was vicariously liable when the child was injured, because the employee's act was performed for the employer's business.[2188] But an employer was not liable to a hitch-hiker to whom a driver, in breach of a prohibition, had given a lift, as the provision of the lift was not part of the job the employee was employed to do.[2189] In another context, an employee who had been told not to carry out valuations for a client who had failed to pay its bills, but who nonetheless made further valuations, was acting in 'total' departure from the scope of the employment.[2190]

C. Wilful Wrongdoing

382. In principle, employers may be liable for their employees' wilful, as well as negligent, wrongdoing. It may be harder to see such conduct as a wrongful mode of carrying out authorized work, but sometimes a connection can be made. For example, a bar attendant charged with keeping order in the bar was acting in the

2183. *Smith v. Stages* [1989] 1 AC 928 at 936.
2184. *Century Insurance Co. Ltd v. Northern Ireland Road Transport Board* [1942] AC 509.
2185. *General Engineering Services Ltd v. Kingston & St Andrew Corporation* [1988] 3 All ER 867.
2186. *Attorney-General v. Hartley* [1964] NZLR 785 at 801.
2187. *Ilkiw v. Samuels* [1963] 2 All ER 879.
2188. *Rose v. Plenty* [1976] 1 WLR 140.
2189. *Conway v. George Wimpey & Co. Ltd* [1951] 2 KB 266.
2190. *Kooragang Investments Pty Ltd v. Richardson & Wrench Ltd* [1982] AC 462.

course of employment when an intoxicated customer threw a glass at him and he threw it back, injuring another customer.[2191] But other cases hold that employers are not liable for harm resulting from personal disputes. So an employee whose responsibilities included an obligation to see that 'the job ran sweetly', who killed another employee following a dispute about alleged inefficiency, was not doing authorized work in any way at all.[2192] Nor was a club manager who told a patron to leave the premises and who attacked him after an altercation when he was starting to walk away.[2193]

II. The Close Connection Test

A. *Sexual Abuse Cases*

383. A rather different approach to vicarious liability has been taken or considered in recent leading cases in Canada, England, Australia, and New Zealand, all of them being concerned with the question of vicarious liability for sexual abuse. In *Bazley v. Curry*[2194] McLachlin J in the Supreme Court of Canada maintained that vicarious liability was generally appropriate where there was a significant connection between the creation or enhancement of a risk and the wrongful act, even if unrelated to the employer's desires. Relevant factors might include the opportunity that the enterprise afforded the employee to abuse his or her power; the extent to which the wrongful act may have furthered the employer's aims (and hence be more likely to have been committed by the employee); the extent to which the wrongful act was related to friction, confrontation, or intimacy inherent in the employer's enterprise; the extent of power conferred on the employee in relation to the victim; and the vulnerability of potential victims to wrongful exercise of the employee's power. Applying these principles, a foundation operating residential care facilities for troubled children was vicariously liable for paedophilic assaults by a caregiving employee. His duties included general supervision and also intimate activities like bathing and putting the children to bed, and in these circumstances the employer was seen as having created or enhanced the risk of his sexual wrongdoing. By contrast, in *Jacobi v. Griffiths*[2195] it was held in a majority decision that a children's club was not vicariously liable for sexual abuse by an employee away from the club premises and outside working hours. The employment gave the opportunity to commit the assaults, but the employee was not placed in a special position of trust and the actual work created no special risk of wrongdoing.

2191. *Pettersson v. Royal Oak Hotel Ltd* [1948] NZLR 136; and *see Mattis v. Pollock* [2003] 1 WLR 2158.

2192. *Rutherford v. Hawke's Bay Hospital Board* [1949] NZLR 400.

2193. *Auckland Workingmen's Club and Mechanics Institute v. Rennie* [1976] 1 NZLR 278.

2194. [1999] 2 SCR 534; and *see Blackwater v. Plint* [2005] 3 SCR 3.

2195. [1999] 2 SCR 570; and *see B v. Order of the Oblates of Mary Immaculate* [2005] 3 SCR 45; *Reference re: Broome v. Price Edward Island* (2010) 317 DLR (4th) 218 (no sufficiently close connection between provincial government and privately managed children's home as to give rise to vicarious liability).

The same question arose in *Lister v. Hesley Hall*,[2196] where the House of Lords imposed vicarious liability on the employer of a warden of a boarding house for boys with emotional and behavioural difficulties who systematically sexually abused the boys. The majority of their Lordships took a similar approach as in *Bazley*, seeing the discussion in that case as a clarification of the second limb of the Salmond test. Accordingly they focused attention on the closeness of the connection between the employee's acts and the duties of the employment. Merely providing the opportunity for the abuse was not enough.

In *Various Claimants v. Catholic Child Welfare Association*[2197] the UK Supreme Court confirmed that there needed to be proof that the defendant caused a material increase in the risk that abuse would occur, and held that on the facts this was established. The relationship between the Institute and the brothers enabled the Institute to place the brothers in teaching positions. Living cloistered on the school premises were boys who were vulnerable because they were children in the school, because they were virtually prisoners, and because their personal histories made it very unlikely that if they attempted to disclose what was happening to them they would be believed. The brother teachers were placed in the school to care for the educational and religious needs of these pupils. Abusing the boys in their care was diametrically opposed to those objectives but, paradoxically, that very fact was one of the factors that provided the necessary close connection between the abuse and the relationship between the brothers and the Institute. In *S v. Attorney-General*[2198] the close connection test was accepted by the Court of Appeal as part of New Zealand law. Applying it, the Crown was held to be vicariously liable for sexual abuse by foster parents of a child placed with the parents by the Department of Social Welfare.[2199] Blanchard J was satisfied that the abuse was sufficiently connected with the purpose of parenting for which the placement was made. The Department, by placing children in private homes where they were vulnerable to a wrongful exercise of power and where their condition necessarily was not able to be monitored as regularly and fully as in an institution, had created or increased a risk of child abuse.

The High Court of Australia initially declined to endorse *Bazley*,[2200] but in *Prince Alfred College Inc v. ADC*[2201] it adopted a test which, although expressed differently, is consistent with developments elsewhere. In the High Court's view, vicarious liability could arise where the employment provided the 'occasion' for the wrongful act and the fact that the act was a criminal offence did not preclude the possibility of liability. In determining the question, relevant features included

---

2196. [2002] 1 AC 215; applied in *Maga v. Archbishop of Birmingham* [2010] 1 WLR 1441; *Various Claimants v. The Catholic Child Welfare Society* [2010] EWCA Civ 1106; *E v. English Province of Our Lady of Charity* [2012] 2 WLR 709.

2197. [2013] 2 AC 1; *see* above para. 379.

2198. [2003] 3 NZLR 450.

2199. The foster parents were seen as agents of the DSW, as to which *see* para. 390.

2200. *New South Wales v. Lepore* (2003) 212 CLR 511.

2201. [2016] HCA 37.

authority, power, trust, control, and the ability to achieve intimacy with the victim.[2202] In so deciding, the High Court certainly recognized that employment-created risk was the focus of the inquiry, apparently seeing this as inherent in its favoured test.

B. Other Cases

384. The decisions applying the close connection test have brought into account the existence of a prior relationship between the employer and the plaintiff involving the employer's care of or control over the plaintiff. Certain fraud cases are somewhat similar in principle. Where an agent commits a fraud for his or her own benefit while working for the principal, the conferral by the principal of power and authority in the agent in relation to the victim is such as to render the principal vicariously liable for the fraud.[2203] So in both the sexual abuse cases and the fraud cases the courts have imposed vicarious liability notwithstanding that the wrongdoers acted entirely on their own account in, respectively, committing sexual offences or seeking the benefit of the fraud. It is apparent that these are exceptional cases.[2204] While the close connection test also applies in other cases of deliberate wrongdoing, with the focus being on the closeness of the connection between the deliberate wrongdoing in the employment and the nature of the risk created by the employment, the normal rule in such cases is that the employee was in some sense purporting to act for the employer rather than for purely personal purposes.

Mohamud v. Wm Morrison Supermarkets plc[2205] can be explained on this basis. The claimant, who was of Somali origin, inquired at the defendant's petrol station about printing documents from a USB stick, but the defendant's employee, who worked in the kiosk, abused him using foul, racist and threatening language. He then followed him to his car, ordered him never to come back to the petrol station and subjected him to a violent assault. The claimant sued the defendant employer, seeking damages in respect of this unprovoked assault. The UK Supreme Court held that the claim succeeded. It was the employee's job to attend to customers and to respond to their inquiries. His conduct in answering the claimant's request in a foul-mouthed way and ordering him to leave and never to come back was inexcusable, but he was purporting to act about his employer's business. It was within the 'field of activities' assigned to him and part of an unbroken sequence of events.[2206]

2202. The claim concerned sexual abuse by a school housemaster, but was held to be statute barred.

2203. *Lloyd v. Grace, Smith & Co* [1912] AC 716; *Nathan v. Dollars & Sense Ltd* [2008] NZSC 20, [2008] 2 NZLR 557.

2204. In *Various Claimants v. WM Morrison Supermarkets plc* [2020] UKSC 12, [2020] 2 WLR 941 at [23] Lord Reed observed that in the sexual abuse cases the courts had emphasised the importance of criteria that were particularly relevant to that form of wrongdoing, such as the employer's conferral of authority on the employee over the victims which he had abused.

2205. [2016] AC 677.

2206. See also *Bellman v. Northampton Recruitment Ltd* [2018] EWCA Civ 2214 (violent assault committed by the employer's managing director on another employee at a voluntary gathering for late-night drinking in a hotel following the work Christmas party, the assault occurring after the employee had challenged a managerial decision of the managing director); *Wallbank v. Wallbank*

On the other hand, in *Various Claimants v. WM Morrison Supermarkets plc*[2207] an employer was held not to be vicariously liable for the criminal actions of a rogue employee, a senior IT auditor, in disclosing personal information about the claimant co-employees on the web when motivated by a work-related grudge. It was abundantly clear that the employee was not engaged in furthering his employer's business when he committed the wrongdoing in question. On the contrary, he was pursuing a personal vendetta – 'a frolic of his own'[2208] – seeking vengeance for disciplinary proceedings against him some months earlier, and his wrongful conduct was not closely connected with acts which he was authorized to do. In further examples, an assault on a work manager motivated simply by personal resentment lacked any sufficient link with the employment,[2209] and nor did the act of an employee who murdered a co-employee while he was at work.[2210]

§5. Independent Contractors

I. General

385. The generally accepted view is that a person who employs an independent contractor is not vicariously liable for the contractor's negligence in the course of the work. As has been seen, the imposition of vicarious liability seeks to channel liability to defendants who are in a good position to prevent the loss or to bear it and to make their business arrangements accordingly. But in the case of independent contractors, considerations such as these point away from the liability of the employer and towards the liability of the contractor. He or she is in the best position to take precautions against causing harm and can build in liability costs in the charge for the work. Accordingly, the UK Supreme Court has confirmed that an employer is not vicariously liable for the tort of an independent contractor.[2211] Rather, any liability of the employer can be founded either on a primary personal liability or on a non-delegable duty to take care. This was the approach taken in *Cashfield House Ltd v. David & Heather Sinclair Ltd*,[2212] where Tipping J laid down the following three propositions:

(1) A principal has no vicarious, that is, secondary, liability for the negligence of an independent contractor on the basis that the activity involved is a particularly hazardous one, or on any other basis.
(2) The principal may nevertheless in some circumstances owe a primary non-delegable duty of care and thus be liable to those to whom the independent contractor is liable if the independent contractor is negligent.

Fox Designs Ltd [2012] EWCA Civ 25 (deliberate assault committed on an employee by another employee in response to criticism of the latter's work).

2207. [2020] UKSC 12, [2020] 2 WLR 941.
2208. Citing *Joel v Morison* (1834) 6 C & P 501, 503.
2209. *Weddall v. Barchester Health Care Ltd* [2012] EWCA Civ 25.
2210. *Vaickuviene v. J Sainsbury plc* [2013] CSIH 67.
2211. *Barclays Bank plc v. Various Claimants* [2020] UKSC 13, [2020] 2 WLR 960; *supra* para. 379.
2212. [1995] 1 NZLR 452 at 465–466.

(3) The principal may well also owe a primary duty of care to those who could foreseeably be damaged by the acts or omissions of the independent contractor.

II. Personal Duties

386. In the *Cashfield House* decision, Tipping J said that the principal's primary duty may include a duty to select, instruct and sometimes to supervise the independent contractor with reasonable care. The greater the expertise of the contractor and the more specialized the task, the less call there may be for the involvement of the principal beyond selection and instruction. If the principal has selected and instructed the independent contractor with the skill and care appropriate to the occasion, the principal should generally be entitled to leave the task to the independent contractor without further supervision.

Examples where a principal may be in breach of this primary duty of care include: hiring an independent contractor to do a tortious act; failing to take care in choosing a reputable and careful contractor;[2213] hiring an independent contractor who lacks the expertise for the work involved;[2214] finding a contractor carrying out work in a defective and foreseeably dangerous way and condoning it;[2215] and failing to warn or to supervise in respect of work involving a special danger of harm to others that was known to the principal.[2216]

III. Non-delegable Duties

387. In certain limited circumstances, a person may be under a special responsibility or duty not simply to take reasonable care, but to ensure that reasonable care is taken. In such cases a defendant who engages an independent contractor to carry out a task may be personally liable if the contractor is negligent. In *Woodland v. Swimming Teachers' Association*,[2217] Lord Sumption identified two broad categories of case in which a non-delegable duty may be owed. The first, said to be anomalous, concerned inherently dangerous activities performed by a contractor on the defendant's land.[2218] The second concerned the assumption of a protective relationship with the plaintiff, founded on five particular factors:[2219]

(1) The claimant is especially vulnerable or dependent on the protection of the defendant against the risk of injury.

2213. *Ferguson v. Welsh* [1987] 1 WLR 1553 (HL).
2214. *Wells v. Cooper* [1958] 2 QB 265.
2215. *D & F Estates Ltd v. Church Commissioners for England* [1989] AC 177 at 209.
2216. *Attorney-General v. Geothermal Produce Ltd* [1987] 2 NZLR 348.
2217. [2014] AC 537.
2218. *Black v. Christchurch Finance Co Ltd* [1894] AC 48; *Burnie Port Authority v. General Jones Pty Ltd* (1994) 179 CLR 520.
2219. [2014] AC 537 at [23].

(2) There is an antecedent relationship between the claimant and the defendant (i) which places the claimant in the actual custody, charge or care of the defendant, and (ii) from which it is possible to impute to the defendant the assumption of a positive duty to protect the claimant from harm.
(3) The claimant has no control over how the defendant chooses to perform those obligations.
(4) The defendant has delegated to a third party some function which is an integral part of the positive duty which he has assumed towards the claimant; and the third party is exercising the defendant's custody or care of the claimant and the element of control that goes with it.
(5) The third party has been negligent in the performance of the very function assumed by the defendant and delegated by the defendant to him.

In the instant case a school authority was held liable for injury suffered by a schoolchild during a school swimming lesson supervised by an independent contractor to whom the school authority had delegated its control over the child. Other examples include the non-delegable duty of an employer to maintain a safe system of work[2220] and the non-delegable duty owed by a hospital to its patients to ensure that they are treated with skill and care.[2221]

A controversial question is whether a fostering authority might owe a non-delegable duty in respect of abuse committed by foster parents on a foster child placed with the parents by the authority. In New Zealand a local authority has been held to be vicariously liable in such a case,[2222] but the relationship is hardly analogous to employment, and a better solution might be to impose a non-delegable duty. However, in the UK such a duty has been denied, broadly on the basis that imposing such a duty was inconsistent with the statutory context in which the authority operated.[2223]

However, the concept of the non-delegable duty has been applied in New Zealand in the case of financial loss caused by the defective construction of buildings. In *Mount Albert Borough Council v. Johnson*[2224] a development company that had acquired and subdivided land was held to be under a non-delegable duty to see that care was used in the building of houses on the land. The policy was to ensure there was a remedy for a purchaser should the builder be unable to pay the damages. But this decision has been heavily criticized in the House of Lords,[2225] where Lord Bridge said that the social policy might be entirely admirable, but he could see no basis on which it was open to the court to embody the policy in law without the assistance of the legislature.[2226]

2220. *McDermid v. Nash Dredging and Reclamation Co. Ltd* [1987] AC 906.
2221. *X (Minors) v. Bedfordshire County Council* [1995] 2 AC 633 at 740. The duty does not extend to activities not amounting to treatment, like carrying out tests on samples which are provided by a person who is a patient: *Farraj v. King's Healthcare NHS Trust* [2010] 1 WLR 2139.
2222. *S v. Attorney-General* [2003] 3 NZLR 450.
2223. *Armes v. Nottinghamshire County Council* [2017] UKSC 60, [2018] AC 355.
2224. [1979] 2 NZLR 234.
2225. *D & F Estates Ltd v. Church Commissioners for England* [1989] AC 177 at 210.
2226. Such assistance has been supplied in the case of defective houses: Building Act 2004, ss 362H–362J; *see* para. 127.

§6. AGENTS

I. General

388. In the law of contract, an agent is a person who is engaged for the purpose of bringing his or her principal into contractual relations with third parties.[2227] In the law of torts the concept of agency sometimes is used in a wider sense, an agent simply being a person who is authorized to act on behalf of another person, called the principal. Accordingly, it is apparent that there is no general rule that a principal is vicariously liable for the tort of an agent committed in the course of the agency, for this would subsume all the law about employees and independent contractors. An independent contractor is an agent in this wide sense and, as has been noted, a principal is not vicariously liable for an independent contractor. Nor is there any general rule suggesting that a principal is vicariously liable for a tort whenever it is committed by a person acting on the principal's behalf, whether by contract or otherwise.

An agency relationship can bring about a liability in tort of the principal in circumstances where the principal has actually or ostensibly authorized the agent to commit the tort. Actual authority can be express or implied. Where there is actual authority, the liability is personal, not vicarious. Again, a principal will be personally liable if the principal ratifies the agent's tort.[2228] As for ostensible authority, this requires a holding out of the agent, giving the appearance of authority. The question is whether the agent acted within the scope of authority which the principal led the plaintiff to believe that the agent possessed. So the principal's liability will tend to arise in a context where the agent is acting in a transaction involving the principal and the plaintiff, and has been clothed with ostensible authority to do the tortious act. Usually it will involve fraud or deceit.

In a recent instance in England the court held, applying leading authority,[2229] that in a case of deceit the essential ingredients for vicarious liability were a holding out or representation by the principal to the claimant, intended to be and in fact acted upon by the claimant, that the agent had authority to do what he or she did, including acts falling within the usual scope of the agent's ostensible authority.[2230] Accordingly, where the requisite authority or holding out exists, there is a relationship upon which a claim for vicarious liability may be founded. However, there remains the second limb to the inquiry, that is, whether the wrongdoing is sufficiently connected with the agency relationship.

In *Nathan v. Dollars & Sense Ltd*[2231] the NZ Supreme Court held that the test for the scope of an agency in the context of vicarious liability was whether the tortious act had a sufficiently close connection with the task so that the commission of the tort could be regarded as the manifestation of the risk inherent in that task. In this

2227. *International Encyclopaedia of Laws: Contracts (New Zealand)*, para. 257.
2228. *McIntyre v. Bianchi* [1992] 3 ERNZ 1057.
2229. *Armagas Ltd v. Mundogas SA* [1986] AC 717.
2230. *Hockley Mint Ltd v. Ramsden* [2018] EWCA Civ 2480, [2019] 1 WLR 1617.
2231. [2008] 2 NZLR 577.

case a borrower had been asked by the lender to secure a loan by obtaining signatures from his parents to a mortgage document over their property. He forged his mother's signature and later defaulted on the loan. When the lender attempted to exercise its power of sale over the property, the borrower's mother argued that the fraud was attributable to the lender as mortgagee, for whom the borrower had acted as agent when 'obtaining' signatures. The court resolved the question by asking whether the act in question was sufficiently connected with an authorized act such that it could be treated as a mode of performing it and therefore done within the agency. An act could have the necessary 'close connection' even if of a criminal character and done with fraudulent intent by an agent for his or her exclusive benefit, and even more so if done for the benefit of the principal also. In *Nathan* itself this analysis led the court to conclude that the forgery was committed in the course of the borrower's agency for the lender.

It is clear that a principal can be vicariously liable for an agent who is authorized to act in relation to the principal's clients. So where a principal held out an agent as having authority to carry out conveyancing operations, and the agent induced the plaintiff to execute documents that she thought were necessary to sell her property to others, the principal was held vicariously liable for the agent's fraud in conveying the property to himself.[2232]

II. Vehicle Owners and Drivers

389. A vehicle owner who allows another person to drive may sometimes come under a personal duty of care, founded on the owner's control over and responsibility for the car and how it is driven.[2233] An example is where an owner permitted an inexperienced young woman, with whom he had been drinking, to take over the driving, knowing that it was dangerous for her to do so.[2234] But, apart from any possible primary liability, it has been held that a car owner may be vicariously liable as a principal for negligence by a person driving as his or her agent.[2235] In this exceptional case the 'agent' is simply a person who is authorized to carry out an activity on behalf of a principal rather than a contractual agent. The rule is not easy to justify as a matter of principle.

There is no presumption of agency simply from the fact that a person is driving another's car. The onus is on the plaintiff to show that the driver is driving for the owner's purposes as his or her agent, and not merely for the driver's own benefit and on his or her own concerns.[2236] There must be an express or implied authorization to drive the vehicle,[2237] and the driving must be for the owner's purposes under delegation of a task or duty.[2238]

2232. *Lloyd v. Grace, Smith & Co.* [1912] AC 716.
2233. *See* generally para. 400.
2234. *Rongonui v. Sirett* unrep., CA 52/76, 10 Dec. 1976; cp *Harris v. Van Spijk* [1986] 1 NZLR 275 at 278–279.
2235. *Manawatu County v. Rowe* [1956] NZLR 78; *Morgans v. Launchbury* [1973] AC 127.
2236. *Manawatu County v. Rowe* [1956] NZLR 78.
2237. *Ansin v. R & D Evans Ltd* [1982] 1 NZLR 184.
2238. *Morgans v. Launchbury* [1973] AC 127 at 135.

In *Morgans v. Launchbury*[2239] a husband used his wife's car to go to work, and in the evening went out drinking. At some stage he realized that he was intoxicated and asked a friend to drive. Later there was an accident caused by the negligence of the friend. The wife was not vicariously liable for the negligent driving, as the friend was not acting as the wife's agent. Her interest in or concern for the safety of the car and its occupants was not sufficient to bring about an agency relationship. By contrast, an owner was held to be vicariously liable for an accident that occurred after he permitted an intoxicated companion to drive for the purpose of getting them, and the vehicle, to their destination.[2240] He had delegated the task of driving to the companion for their mutual benefit.

III. Other Special Cases

390. Vicarious liability for agents may also be imposed in certain other exceptional cases. For example, in *S v. Attorney-General*[2241] the Court of Appeal held that the Crown was vicariously liable for sexual abuse amounting to assault and battery by foster parents on their foster child. Blanchard J, giving the majority view, recognized that the court was concerned with a statutory enterprise involving the placement of children by the Department of Social Welfare with suitable persons as foster parents. This relationship was appropriately characterized as one of agency, albeit that the agency was of an unusual, indeed unique, nature. His Honour also was satisfied that the abuse occurred in the course of the agency duties of the foster parents, it being sufficiently connected with the purpose of parenting for which the placement were made. On the other hand, Tipping J preferred to regard the relationship as sui generis, and was satisfied that as a matter of policy and analogy vicarious liability ought to be found to exist. It may be, however, that the protective relationship points more towards the imposition of a non-delegable duty.[2242]

§7. Partners

391. A partnership is liable for the tort of a partner where the tort was committed while acting in the ordinary course of the firm's business, or if outside the ordinary course of business, was authorized by co-partners.[2243] In *Proceedings Commissioner v. Ali Hatem*[2244] a partner sexually harassed existing and prospective employees, thereby committing a statutory tort.[2245] The Court of Appeal said that,

2239. [1973] AC 127.

2240. *Harris v. Van Spijk* [1986] 1 NZLR 275.

2241. [2003] 3 NZLR 450; cp *B v. British Columbia* [2003] 2 SCR 534, where the Supreme Court of Canada held that foster parents were not acting as agents of the relevant government department in fostering children.

2242. *See* para. 387.

2243. Partnership Act 1908, s. 13.

2244. [1999] 1 NZLR 305.

2245. The conduct was in breach of s. 15 of the Human Rights Commission Act 1977 (since replaced by the Human Rights Act 1993).

this being wilful misconduct, the question was whether the partner was acting within the general scope of the authority created by the firm's business, although the particular conduct was tortious. The concept of the ordinary course of employment in an employer/employee relationship was seen as sufficiently analogous to the ordinary course of business of a firm to be helpful. On the facts the harassment had occurred when the partner was dealing with staff members in the work environment, and it was held that he thereby tortiously did something that he was generally authorized to do.

Chapter 2. Liability of Persons in Supervisory Positions

§1. Personal Responsibility for Others

I. General Principles

392. Where vicarious liability is imposed, the defendant is liable for someone else's conduct by reason of the particular relationship between the defendant and the other person and the connection between that relationship and the other person's tortious conduct. A defendant may also be personally liable for failing to prevent tortious conduct by others. But such liability arises only in limited circumstances, for the common law recognizes no duty to act as a good Samaritan.[2246] As a general rule, applying *Donoghue v. Stevenson*,[2247] a person is under a duty to take care not to positively inflict physical damage on another. However, a person is not normally bound to take action to prevent injury to, or otherwise confer a benefit on, that other.[2248] There is a distinction to be drawn between the way an activity is being conducted and not carrying on any relevant activity.[2249]

Imposing legal liability for a failure to prevent harm brings into account core issues relating to the desirability of maintaining, within reasonable limits, the freedom and autonomy of individuals to act as they wish, the need not to undermine ordinary principles of contract whereby purely gratuitous undertakings are not actionable, practical difficulties in determining who might be fixed with a duty to aid others, and the danger of opening up a wide and quite uncertain area of responsibility. But, sometimes, the impact of these considerations can be limited or negated and a duty to act can be recognized. This tends to be where the defendant has specifically induced the plaintiff to rely on action being taken, has positively intervened in the plaintiff's affairs in such a way as to increase the risk of harm, or has assumed specific responsibility for or control over an activity, a particular danger, or a particular person's behaviour.[2250] A positive duty to act also can be founded on the physical occupation of land creating a risk of harm, which will be considered in Chapter 3 below.

II. Causal Issues

393. How far a mere omission to prevent harm can be said to be a cause of the harm can also be problematic. Where there is an existing risk or danger to which the defendant fails to respond, arguably the risk or danger alone is the cause of the harm which ensues. The defendant has not contributed to the risk, which simply continues to operate without interference on the part of the defendant, or anyone

2246. *Home Office v. Dorset Yacht Co. Ltd* [1970] AC 1004 at 1060 per Lord Diplock.

2247. [1932] AC 562.

2248. *Brownie Wills v. Shrimpton* [1998] 2 NZLR 320 at 327.

2249. *See Robinson v. Chief Constable of West Yorkshire Police* [2018] UKSC 4, [2018] AC 736 at [69.4]–[69.6].

2250. For an overview *see Mitchell v. Glasgow City Council* [2009] 1 AC 874 at [23] per Lord Hope; and *see Michael v. Chief Constable of South Wales Police* [2015] AC 1732 at [97]–[101].

else. However, if the circumstances are such as to give rise to a positive duty to act, on one of the bases mentioned above, then a failure to act is treated as a cause of action would have prevented the harm.[2251] There would otherwise be little point in recognizing the duty. Greater uncertainty surrounds the case where a basis for a duty to act exists, but the circumstances are such that whether action by the defendant would have averted the plaintiff's loss is inherently unpredictable. One solution is for the court to evaluate the chance that the damage would have been avoided and give damages based on the value of that chance, provided that it was a real or more than minimal chance.[2252]

§2. Induced Reliance

394. The mere fact that a person was in a position to warn another of danger is no sufficient reason for imposing a legal duty to warn. Otherwise there would be liability in negligence on the part of one who sees another about to walk over a cliff and fails to shout a warning.[2253] For example, the insurer of a car who cancelled the policy in accordance with its terms by giving notice to the insured was not obliged to give notice to a finance company with an interest in the car.[2254] So also, insurers conducting pre-contractual negotiations with a bank who knew that the bank's insurance broker had been acting fraudulently, were not obliged to give warning to the bank.[2255] But there may be a duty to act if one has undertaken to do so, or induced a person to rely upon one doing so.[2256] So liability was imposed on an ambulance service that had undertaken to assist a patient but that had delayed in doing so, and as a result other possible means of transporting the patient to hospital were abandoned;[2257] a personnel officer who induced an employee to believe that he could rely on her in handling the financial arrangements in transferring to a new job came under a duty to take care in making the arrangements;[2258] strike-breaking workers at a mine reasonably relied on the security firm guarding the mine to protect them from violence by the striking miners;[2259] and a parent company owed a duty of care to an employee of its subsidiary where the parent knew or ought to have foreseen that the subsidiary or its employees would rely on its using that superior knowledge for the employees' protection.[2260]

An undertaking inducing reliance should be distinguished from a mere failure to fulfil a promise, for in the latter case the rule in contract is that promise can be

---

2251. *Reeves v. Commissioner of Police of the Metropolis* [1999] 3 WLR 363 at 368.
2252. *See* para. 531.
2253. *Yuen Kun Yeu v. A-G of Hong Kong* [1988] AC 175 at 192.
2254. *Cooper Henderson Finance Ltd v. Colonial Mutual General Insurance Co. Ltd* [1990] 1 NZLR 1.
2255. *Banque Keyser Ullmann SA v. Skandia (UK) Insurance Co. Ltd* [1990] 1 QB 665, affirmed [1991] 2 AC 249 (HL).
2256. *Stovin v. Wise* [1996] AC 923 at 944.
2257. *Kent v. Griffiths* [2000] 2 WLR 1158 at 1162.
2258. *Lennon v. Metropolitan Police Commissioner* [2004] 2 All ER 266.
2259. *Fullowka v. Pinkerton's of Canada Ltd* [2010] 1 SCR 132.
2260. *Chandler v. Cape plc* [2012] 1 WLR 3111; and *see James Hardie Industries plc v. White* [2018] NZCA 580, [2019] 2 NZLR 49; *Lungowe v. Vedante Resources plc* [2019] UKSC 20, [2019] 2 WLR 1051.

enforced only where it is supported by consideration. In *Meates v. A-G*,[2261] the Court of Appeal imposed liability on a government minister for negligently undertaking to give support to a fledgling industry in financial trouble, in reliance upon which the owner refrained from putting the company into liquidation and rescuing what he could from the venture. Cooke J maintained that a speaker who had promised to give assistance to another was bound to do what was reasonably within his power to bring about that result. This was not an absolute duty or guarantee, which belonged to the realm of contract. It depended simply on what a reasonable man would regard as his duty to his neighbour. The status of this decision is uncertain, for, in a judgment of the Privy Council in further litigation arising out of the same events, Lord Oliver observed that their Lordships had considerable difficulty in grasping the concept of a duty in tort to take reasonable care to pay or procure payment of a sum that nobody was under any contractual obligation to pay.[2262] However, an alternative remedy in cases of this kind might be to rely on the doctrine of promissory estoppel.[2263]

§3. Assumption of Responsibility for Other Persons

I. Duty to the Other Person

395. A person may come under a legal duty to act because, in one way or another, he or she has taken on responsibility for the welfare of another. Sometimes this may induce reliance by the other, constituting an alternative reason for imposing a duty to act, but liability may arise independently of any question of reliance. A classic instance is the duty owed by a parent or person in *loco parentis* to a child.[2264] In *A v. Roman Catholic Archdiocese of Wellington*[2265] William Young P explained that damages for bad parenting will not be entertained, for reasons associated with parental autonomy and a sense that the issues would not be practicably justifiable. But there could be a duty as to children's physical and psychiatric health and this would encompass emotional abuse. Provided it did not extend to anything approaching a duty to maximize or enhance the emotional well-being of children, it should be reasonably manageable. The case at hand involved a claim against an orphanage and a voluntary social service provider, and on the facts the plaintiff's allegations in respect of any actionable harm were not made out.

2261. [1983] NZLR 308.

2262. *Meates v. Westpac Banking Corp Ltd* [1991] 3 NZLR 385 at 403.

2263. *See International Encyclopaedia of Laws: Contracts (New Zealand)*, paras 87–89.

2264. Parents: *McCallion v. Dodd* [1966] NZLR 710; *Tweed SC v. Howarth* [2009] Aust Torts Reps 82-101. Local authority: *Barrett v. Enfield LBC* [2001] 2 AC 550. School: *Barnes v. Hants CC* [1969] 1 WLR 1563; *Commonwealth v. Introvigne* (1982) 150 CLR 258; *Myers v. Peel County Board of Education* [1981] 2 SCR 21.

2265. [2008] 3 NZLR 289; applied in *White v. Attorney-General* [2010] NZCA 139.

There are many instances of a duty being founded on an assumption of responsibility for another person. Thus, a prison authority may be obliged to protect a prisoner[2266] or to release him in due time,[2267] a doctor to treat a patient in hospital,[2268] a competition organizer not to endanger an intoxicated competitor,[2269] a nightclub owner or hotel proprietor to protect a guest,[2270] and, arguably, a police commissioner in the position of an employer to protect a police officer from being victimized by fellow officers.[2271] But the licensee of a club was not liable to a patron who became drunk and who suffered injury in a road accident, for the patron could make up his own mind in deciding whether or how much to drink.[2272] A mental health authority was not liable to a patient who, shortly after his release, attacked and killed his father and was then detained as suffering from a psychotic disorder.[2273] There was no duty to detain the plaintiff against his wishes in circumstances where there was no statutory power to do so. Again, police officers owed no duty to prevent the driver of a parked car who was contemplating suicide from driving away to talk to his wife, and were not liable when the driver did in fact commit suicide later that day.[2274] The officers had not assumed responsibility for the driver, and were in no different position to any passer-by who could have intervened but who decided not to do so. Nor is there any general duty of care owed by police officers to individual members of the public who might suffer injury through a criminal's activities to identify and apprehend the criminal.[2275]

There must be a close and direct relationship between the supervisor and the person supervised. So members of the International Rugby Football Board owed no duty to rugby players to alter or amend rules to minimize the risk of injury to the players.[2276] But a rugby referee was held to owe a duty to a player in the game under his control.[2277]

In principle, a person may also assume responsibility for another's economic welfare. But issues as to the other's autonomy may come into play. So a club owed no duty to take care to protect a member who was a problem gambler against financial

2266. *Morgan v. A-G* [1965] NZLR 134; *Reeves v. Commissioner of Police of the Metropolis* [2000] 1 AC 360; *NSW v. Budjiso* (2005) 227 CLR 1.
2267. *McCreaner v. Ministry of Justice* [2015] 1 WLR 354.
2268. *Barnett v. Chelsea Hospital* [1969] 1 QBD 428; and *see Lowns v. Woods* (1995) Aust Torts Reps 81-376.
2269. *Crocker v. Sundance Northwest Resorts Ltd* [1988] 1 SCR 1186.
2270. *Everett v. Comojo* [2012] 1 WLR 150 (no breach); *Al-Najar v. Cumberland Hotel (London) Ltd* [2019] EWHC 1593, [2019] 1 WLR 5953 (no breach).
2271. *Waters v. Commissioner of Police of the Metropolis* [2000] 1 WLR 1607.
2272. *Cole v. South Tweed Heads Rugby League Football Club Ltd* (2004) 78 ALJR 933; and *see CAL No 14 Pty Ltd v. Scott* (2009) 239 CLR 390; cp *Jordan House Ltd v. Menow* [1974] SCR 239.
2273. *Ellis v. Counties Manukau District Health Board* [2007] 1 NZLR 196; *Hunter Area Health Service v. Presland* (2005) 63 NSWLR 22.
2274. *Stuart v. Kirkland-Veenstra* (2009) 237 CLR 215.
2275. *Hill v. Chief Constable of West Yorkshire Police* [1989] AC 53; *Smith v. Chief Constable of Sussex Police* [2009] 1 AC 225 (reported sub nom *Van Colle v. Chief Constable of the Hertfordshire Police*); *Michael v. Chief Constable of South Wales Police* [2015] AC 1732.
2276. *Agar v. Hyde* (2000) 201 CLR 552.
2277. *Vowles v. Evans* [2003] 1 WLR 1607; and *see Watson v. British Boxing Board of Control* [2001] QB 1134.

loss from gambling.[2278] By contrast, a bookmaker did assume a responsibility for a problem gambler by promising, but failing, to close his telephone account: but the breach did not cause loss because the gambler would nonetheless have gambled away his money with someone else.[2279]

II. Duty to a Third Party

396. A duty of care also may be owed to third parties who might reasonably be expected to suffer harm caused by persons under the defendant's control. In *Home Office v. Dorset Yacht Co. Ltd*,[2280] a leading decision, a prison authority owed a duty of care to property owners in the vicinity when prisoners in the custody of the authority were negligently allowed to escape and cause damage to the plaintiff's yacht. Applying the principle, parents may be under a duty to take such precautionary measures as are appropriate to their supervisory position over their children. Accordingly, a father was held liable for not preventing his 10-year-old son of known reckless disposition from taking a rifle out of the house and shooting the plaintiff.[2281] On similar reasoning, a school authority was held to be responsible for allowing a small child to go through an unlocked gate into the road and so cause an accident.[2282] Again, a parent company which has sufficiently intervened in the activities of a subsidiary may owe a duty of care to persons affected by those activities.[2283] So there was a serious issue to be tried where a holding company was alleged to have exercised control over a subsidiary in its production of defective building products which were used in the construction of the plaintiffs' buildings.[2284]

Where control or the right to control exists there must also be a reasonably close and immediate link between the failure to exercise control and the damage that is suffered. A duty cannot be extended to remote victims of another's wrongdoing. On the one hand, an application to strike out a claim for exemplary damages against a Health Board for its failure to protect the plaintiff as a vulnerable psychiatric patient from rape by a male patient was rejected.[2285] Young J said that it was 'pretty obvious' that the defendant should take reasonable precautions to protect women outpatients who were or might be brought into contact with potentially dangerous sexual offenders. On the other hand, where a health authority negligently released a person committed for compulsory in-treatment as a psychiatric patient, the relatives of a woman with whom the patient formed a relationship after his release, whom he

2278. *Reynolds v. Katoomba RSL All Services Club Ltd* (2001) 53 NSWLR 43; *Politarkis v. Westpac plc* (2009) Aust Torts Reps 82-010; *Ritz Hotel Casino Ltd v. Al Daher* [2015] 4 All ER 222; *Sinclair v. New Zealand Racing Board* [2015] NZHC 2067.

2279. *Calvert v. William Hill Credit Ltd* [2009] Ch 330.

2280. [1970] AC 1004; cp *NSW v. Godfrey & Godfrey* [2004] NSWCA 113.

2281. *Kenealy v. Karaka* (1906) 26 NZLR 1118; *The Bosworth Water Trust v. SSR* [2018] EWHC 444.

2282. *Carmarthen CC v. Lewis* [1955] AC 549.

2283. *Lungowe v. Vedante Resources plc* [2019] UKSC 20, [2019] 2 WLR 1051; compare *Okpabi v. Royal Dutch Shell Plc* [2018] EWCA Civ 191 (permission to appeal to the Supreme Court granted).

2284. *James Hardie Industries plc v. White* [2018] NZCA 580, [2019] 2 NZLR 49.

2285. *S v. Midcentral District Health Board* [2004] NZAR 342.

subsequently killed, failed in a claim for injury by shock.[2286] The deceased victim was not under threat at the time of the release, and it was impossible to distinguish the plaintiffs from the public at large.

Many of the cases where plaintiffs allege a duty by the defendant to prevent harm being done by others involve public bodies, which frequently are in supervisory or controlling positions. And a number of recent claims against public officers or bodies well illustrate the just-discussed principles of liability in operation. We will consider these cases below in the particular context of claims against public bodies.[2287]

In principle it is possible for those in supervisory or controlling positions to be held responsible for the acts of intoxicated persons. For example, it was held by the Supreme Court of Canada that a commercial vendor of alcohol owed a duty to persons who might foreseeably be injured by an intoxicated patron.[2288] Clearly it is very relevant in this type of case that the defendant has actually contributed to the danger by supplying the alcohol. However, the Supreme Court declined to impose a similar duty on a social host in respect of injury caused by a drunken guest, but left open the possibility that the host might be liable if he or she continued to serve alcohol to a visibly inebriated guest who was known to be going to drive.[2289] In New Zealand there is no decision concerning either a commercial or a social host. The issue could arise in relation to a claim for property damage or for exemplary damages, in which case the Canadian cases no doubt would be influential.

The reach of any potential duty to warn third parties of danger or to take care to safeguard them from harm was potentially extended in *ABC v. St George's Healthcare NHS Trust*,[2290] where there was no failure in the defendant's supervision of or control over another person. In this case the Court of Appeal in England held that it was arguable that a clinician owed a duty to inform the pregnant daughter of his patient about the patient's diagnosis of Huntington's disease, which condition was inherited, progressive and fatal.

§4. Assumption of Responsibility for a Task

397. A duty of positive action may exist where a person has taken on a particular task and in that way has assumed responsibility to carry out the task with due care. Merely assuming an office or status and having the ability to help is not usually seen as enough. However, taking on or starting on a task can give rise to a duty to persons who are sufficiently closely and proximately affected by a failure properly to carry it out. In other words, there must be an assumed responsibility for a particular activity or task in relation to a particular person or class. It is a similar inquiry to that undertaken in the case of a person who assumes responsibility to give information or advice to another.[2291]

2286. *Maulolo v. Hutt Valley Health Corporation Ltd* [2002] NZAR 375. In Australia, *see Hunter and New England Local Health District v. McKenna* [2014] HCA 44.

2287. *See* para. 400.

2288. *Stewart v. Pettie* [1995] 1 SCR 131. In these circumstances there was no breach of the duty.

2289. *Childs v. Desormeaux* [2006] 1 SCR 643.

2290. [2017] EWCA Civ 336.

2291. *See* generally the discussion *supra*, para. 91.

The duty of a person taking on a responsibility for performing a task does not extend to a duty to protect the public at large.[2292] So a Law Society with supervisory responsibilities over solicitors was not responsible for losses suffered by a client as a result of a fraud that the Society's inspector had not detected.[2293] The Court of Appeal noted that any duty necessarily would be to all clients of the firm and would require investigation of all matters that might bear upon their affairs. Such wide and indeterminate duties should not readily be imposed upon a regulatory (but not closely controlling) body, which received no fees from solicitors' clients, had limited resources, and had no links with solicitors' clients similar to those of professional service providers such as valuers, surveyors and auditors. But it was arguable that NZ Exchange Ltd, in carrying out an annual inspection of its members as part of its responsibility to regulate the stock exchange, owed a duty of care to the clients of a member broker that was placed in liquidation following fraud by one of its officers.[2294]

Another example is the decision of the House of Lords in *White v. Jones*.[2295] A testator instructed the defendant solicitors to prepare a will leaving certain legacies to the plaintiffs, yet two months later the testator died without a new will having been executed. A majority of their Lordships held that the defendants owed a duty of care to the intended beneficiaries. Lord Browne-Wilkinson said that the defendants' assumption of responsibility for the task in hand created a special relationship with the plaintiff, in relation to which the law attached a duty to carry out carefully the task so assumed.[2296] Again, a person who voluntarily agreed to provide landscape gardening services to her neighbour owed a duty to act with care.[2297] On the other hand, in *Brownie Wills v. Shrimpton*,[2298] a solicitor, in breach of contract with a client bank, failed to give advice to a non-client director of a company about the effect of signing a guarantee for a loan to the company, and was held to owe no duty to the director. The Court of Appeal considered that the solicitor had not assumed any responsibility towards the director, who was not aware of the client's instruction and who could not expect that the solicitor would look after his interests without giving any indication of that to the solicitor.

2292. *See Sutradhar v. National Environment Research Council* [2006] 4 All ER 490, discussed at para. 76.

2293. *Wellington District Law Society v. Price Waterhouse* [2002] 2 NZLR 767.

2294. *Bank of New Zealand v. NZ Exchange Ltd* [2008] NZCA 25; and *see Price Waterhouse v. Kwan* [2000] 3 NZLR 39 (auditor of solicitor's accounts arguably owed duty to solicitor's clients).

2295. [1995] 2 AC 207.

2296. *Gartside v. Sheffield Young & Ellis* [1983] NZLR 37 is a similar decision in New Zealand but was explained simply in terms of the close proximity between the solicitor and the intended beneficiaries. *See also Hawkins v. Clayton* (1988) 164 CLR 539 (HCA); *Hill v. Van Erp* (1997) 188 CLR 159.

2297. *Lejonvarn v. Burgess* [2017] EWCA Civ 254; *supra* para. 91.

2298. [1998] 2 NZLR 320. *See also*, for example, *Thorburn Consultants (NZ) Ltd. v. Air Action Installation Ltd* [2011] NZCA 317.

§5. Assumption of Responsibility by Public Bodies

I. General

398. Some of the cases concerning failure to prevent harm that have been mentioned already involve failures by public bodies. Certainly, the preceding principles can be seen in operation in a large number of decisions involving public or quasi-public bodies charged with exercising regulatory or supervisory responsibilities. It is clear that the mere assumption of a public office or position, coupled with a power to intervene, is no sufficient basis for a duty to take care in private law.[2299] Rather, consistently with general principle, there needs to be close control over, or a specific assumption of responsibility in relation to, the particular risk of harm that eventuated in circumstances where the defendant body knew or ought to have known of the risk in relation to a specific, known plaintiff or a specific class including the plaintiff.

In *Poole Borough Council v. GN*[2300] Lord Reed recognized that an assumption of responsibility might arise out of conduct undertaken in the performance of an obligation, or the operation of a statutory scheme. The point was illustrated by the assumption of responsibility arising out of a local authority's functions under child care legislation, or the provision of medical or educational services, or the custody of prisoners. The operation of a statutory scheme did not automatically generate such an assumption, but it might have that effect if the defendant's conduct pursuant to the scheme met the criteria in such cases as *Hedley Byrne*[2301] and *Spring v. Guardian Assurance plc.*[2302] In the instant case the claimants alleged that the defendant council was under a duty to protect them from abusive neighbours, in particular, by rehousing them, but the Supreme Court held that no duty was owed. The council had not provided a service on which the claimants or their mother could be expected to rely, nor could it be said that they had entrusted their safety to the council or that the council had accepted that responsibility.[2303]

II. Control

399. An example of a position of control is where action is brought against a local authority for negligence in its enforcement of building regulations. Local councils assume responsibility by instituting and requiring adherence to building and planning regulations and exercise control over the work of the builder. Building

2299. *See* generally *Gorringe v. Calderdale Metropolitan Borough Council* [2004] 1 WLR 1057, especially at [17], [70], [88], [102]–[103].
2300. [2019] UKSC 25, [2019] 2 WLR 1478 at [73].
2301. *Supra*, para. 90.
2302. *Supra*, para. 104.
2303. *See* also *Seddon v. Driver and Vehicle Licensing Agency* [2019] EWCA Civ 14; [2019] 1 WLR 4593; *supra* para. 91.

bylaws require notification to and approval by the council of building work at particular stages, creating a continuing supervisory role for that body. This has commonly been seen as providing the foundation for a duty to take care to inspect the building work.[2304]

By contrast, in an Australian case, it was held that the state of New South Wales and a Local Council were under no duty to take steps which might have reduced the risk of contamination of oysters being grown commercially in a lake.[2305] The element of control was seen as of fundamental importance: if it was remote, in a legal and practical sense, it would not suffice to found a duty of care. Between the Council and the consumers stood an entire oyster-growing industry, with many intervening levels of decision-making. As regards the state, the Executive Government of New South Wales had made a political decision to enlist shellfish industry participants in a system of industry-funded self-regulation, rather than to impose on that industry a publicly funded regulatory regime. So in neither case was there close or day-to-day control over the oyster-growing industry.

III. Proximity

400. An associated question focuses on the proximity of the relationship between the public body and the person bringing the action. There needs to be an assumed responsibility that brings about a special, proximate, relationship between the defendant body and the person affected by its failure to act. The requisite relationship cannot be established in the case of actions against regulatory bodies for not preventing financial loss from being suffered by members of the public.[2306] Accordingly, while local authority inspectors owe a duty of care in inspecting houses in the course of construction, the Court of Appeal held in *Attorney-General v. Body Corporate No. 200200 (Sacramento)*[2307] that the New Zealand Building Industry Authority (BIA) owed no duty to building owners to exercise its powers under the Building Act 1991 (NZ) and the Building Code by taking steps to warn about and to prevent poor building practices leading to leaky building syndrome. There was no sufficient proximity between the BIA and property owners, responsibility rested far more directly on developers, designers, builders and certifiers, the

2304. *Mt Albert City Council v. New Zealand Municipalities Co-op Insurance Co. Ltd* [1983] NZLR 190, 196; *Stieller v. Porirua City Council* [1986] 1 NZLR 84, 94; *Invercargill City Council v. Hamlin* [1994] 3 NZLR 513 at 519, 525–526, 530 (CA); [1996] 1 NZLR 513 at 516, 518 (PC); *North Shore City Council v. Body Corporate 188529 (Sunset Terraces)* [2011] 2 NZLR 289 at [48]; cp *McNamara v. Auckland City Council* [2012] 3 NZLR 701; (no backstop duty owed by council where owner elected to obtain a code compliance certificate issued by an independent building certifier rather than the council).

2305. *Graham Barclay Oysters Pty Ltd v. Ryan* (2003) 211 CLR 540.

2306. *Fleming v. Securities Commission* [1995] 2 NZLR 514 (Securities Commission owed no duty to members of public to prevent publication of advertisements breaching the Securities Act 1978); and *see Yuen Kun Yeu v. Attorney-General of Hong Kong* [1988] AC 175; *Davis v. Radcliffe* [1990] 1 WLR 821.

2307. [2007] 1 NZLR 95; and *see North Shore City Council v. Attorney-General (The Grange)* [2012] 3 NZLR 341 (no duty owed by BIA to council in reviewing performance of council's technical operations).

BIA exercised quasi-legislative or quasi-judicial functions where no duty of care could arise, a duty of general superintendence would require the courts to review the reasonableness of resources allocated to the BIA, and the policy of the 1991 Act was not to produce official over-vigilance but to place responsibility on building certifiers.

Again, in physical injury cases there must be a foreseeable risk to a specific individual or class of individuals including the plaintiff. So a highway authority did not owe an individual user of the road a common law duty to prevent injury allegedly due to its failure to put up a sign warning of danger.[2308] And nor did the police owe a duty of care to protect members of the public from the attacks of a murderer.[2309] Indeed, the UK Supreme Court has rejected any duty owed by the police to protect a victim from a crime, even where the victim had phoned the police at a time when she was at immediate risk of being murdered by a known and identified person.[2310] However, in several decisions in New Zealand a duty has been recognized where a particular person or class has been put at risk of harm. For example, the Department of Social Welfare was under a duty to investigate a complaint concerning a particular child's mistreatment,[2311] and to take steps to protect a child with whom it was dealing from suffering abuse.[2312]

In *Couch v. Attorney-General*[2313] the Supreme Court declined to strike out a claim against the Probation Service brought by the victim of a violent assault committed by a criminal while on parole. Any claim for compensatory damages was barred by the accident compensation scheme.[2314] However, the plaintiff sought exemplary damages for what she alleged was grossly deficient supervision of the criminal. The assault on the plaintiff, and the murder of three colleagues, took place at the Returned Services Association (RSA) premises where the victims worked. The criminal had been placed at the RSA for work experience, and he returned there to commit his crimes. In these circumstances the plaintiff's claim was thought to be arguable. The criminal had a known alcohol addiction, he had been allowed to work at premises where significant cash was likely to be present, and he could find out about the security system. This might make the RSA a predictable target, so anyone present there was at greater risk than the general public, and would be particularly vulnerable because of the criminal's known tendency to random violence.

2308. *Gorringe v. Calderdale Metropolitan Borough Council* [2004] 1 WLR 1057; *Sumner v. Colborne* [2018] EWCA Civ 1006, [2018] 3 All ER 1049; cp *Yetkin v. Mahmood* [2011] 2 WLR 1173 (highway authority liable for creating danger by planting shrubbery obscuring pedestrian's view of traffic, although damages reduced for contributory negligence).

2309. *Hill v. West Yorkshire Police* [1995] 2 AC 663; and *see Brooks v. Commissioner of Police for the Metropolis* [2005] 1 WLR 1495.

2310. *Michael v. Chief Constable of South Wales Police* [2015] AC 1732.

2311. *Attorney-General v. Prince and Gardner* [1998] 1 NZLR 262.

2312. *B v. Attorney-General* [2004] 3 NZLR 145.

2313. [2008] 3 NZLR 725.

2314. *See* para. 41.

It has been held in England that an ambulance service was under a duty to respond promptly to a call for assistance.[2315] But no similar duty was imposed on the fire service.[2316]

2315. *Kent v. Griffiths* [2001] 1 QB 36.

2316. *Capital & Counties plc v. Hampshire County Council* [1997] QB 1007; cp *The Wembridge Claimants v. Winter* [2013] EWHC 2331.

Chapter 3. Liability for Property

§1. OCCUPIERS OF LAND

401. The question of whether an occupier of land can be liable to a visitor or a trespasser usually arises in the context of a claim for personal injury. Accordingly, there have been few occupiers' liability claims in New Zealand since the introduction of the accident compensation scheme.[2317] However, the legal principles remain relevant in the case of claims for property damage, which can still be maintained.

I. Liability to Visitors

A. *Introduction*

402. At common law, the courts recognized a number of particularised duties that were owed to persons coming on to land, the content of the duty varying according to the status of the entrant. It was thought appropriate that more protection should be given to those whose entry was of some benefit to the occupier, as opposed to those whose entry was merely tolerated or even was not permitted. On this basis entrants were divided into four main categories and these, in descending order according to the degree of care required of the occupier, were persons entering by virtue of a contract, invitees (where the occupier had a material interest in the purpose of the visit), licensees (where there was simply permission to enter), and trespassers.

The categorization of entrants in this way created a number of problems. Many cases could not easily be fitted into an appropriate pigeonhole; it became increasingly difficult to draw distinctions between the content of the different duties; and, after *Donoghue v. Stevenson*, the complexity of the law contrasted unfavourably with an 'activity' duty founded simply on reasonable foreseeability of damage. Accordingly, by the Occupiers' Liability Act 1962, following statutory reform in England,[2318] the old distinctions were abolished and a 'common duty of care' was imposed on occupiers in relation to all lawful visitors.[2319] The Act does not cover trespassers, whose position continues to be governed by the common law.[2320]

B. *Occupiers*

403. The Act preserves common law principles as to the meaning of 'occupier'.[2321] These were restated by the House of Lords in *Wheat v. E Lacon & Co.*

2317. *See* para. 33.
2318. Occupiers' Liability Act 1957 (Eng).
2319. Occupiers' Liability Act 1962, s. 4(2).
2320. *See* para. 414.
2321. Occupiers' Liability Act 1962, s. 3(2).

Ltd[2322] where it was confirmed that an occupier is a person who has a sufficient degree of control over premises to come under a duty of care to those who come lawfully on to the premises. In this case the owners of an inn were held to be occupiers of the upper part of the building, as well as the licensee and his wife, because they still had some control over the whole inn: the licensee was not a tenant and would have to quit in the event of his ceasing to hold office; the licensee's wife could only take in guests by permission of the owners; and the owners had a right to enter the upper part of the inn to do repairs.

Wheat makes it clear that ownership may be quite separate from occupation, and that more than one person can be an occupier of premises, for the control need not be entire or exclusive. However, a landlord who lets premises to a tenant is treated as parting with all control, even if he or she has undertaken to repair, and the landlord is not, therefore, an occupier.[2323] But the landlord may remain the occupier of the common parts of the building.[2324]

C. Premises

404. The rules set out in the 1962 Act apply in consequence of a person's occupation or control of 'premises' or of a 'fixed or movable structure'.[2325] 'Premises' includes land and 'structure' includes any vessel, vehicle, or aircraft.[2326] The occupancy duty thus applies not only to houses and buildings but also, for example, to a hotel fire escape,[2327] a diving board,[2328] a ship,[2329] scaffolding,[2330] and a ladder.[2331]

The Act does not to apply to the obligations of any person under or by virtue of any contract for the hire of, or for the carriage for reward of persons or goods in, any vehicle, vessel or aircraft, or other means of transport, or under or by virtue of any contract of bailment.[2332] In these types of contract a term is implied that the chattel is as fit for the purpose for which it is hired or bailed as reasonable care and skill can make it.[2333]

2322. [1966] AC 552.
2323. *Ibid.*, at 579.
2324. *Connor v. Nelson, Moate & Co.* [1925] NZLR 123.
2325. Occupiers' Liability Act 1962, ss 3(1), 3(3).
2326. *Ibid.*, s. 2.
2327. *Horne v. Speed* [1946] NZLR 164.
2328. *Perkowski v. Wellington City Corporation* [1959] NZLR 1.
2329. *Hartwell v. Grayson Rollo and Clover Docks Ltd* [1947] KB 901.
2330. *Kealey v. Heard* [1983] 1 WLR 573.
2331. *Wheeler v. Copas* [1981] 3 All ER 405.
2332. Occupiers' Liability Act 1962, s. 9.
2333. *Hyman v. Nye* (1881) 6 QBD 685.

D. Visitors

405. The occupier's duty is owed to lawful visitors. Persons who initially enter premises as visitors retain that status only while using them for a permitted purpose,[2334] staying within authorized areas[2335] and not remaining after the expiry of any authorized time.[2336] If they step outside such boundaries they become trespassers. Persons crossing land by virtue of a right of way are not formally visitors.[2337] In this case the occupier can be liable for misfeasance in creating a danger, but not for mere non-feasance in failing to repair.[2338]

The existence or scope of any licence to enter land depends upon an analysis of any invitation or permission, express or implied, by the occupier in each case. For example, a householder gives an implied licence for persons to come to his or her door[2339] unless permission is withheld by a sufficiently prominent notice[2340] or it has been made clear that the licence has been revoked,[2341] or the entry is not for the purpose of communicating with the occupier but for some alien purpose.[2342] In some older cases, a licence to enter was implied in the case of children allowed by the occupier repeatedly to enter land, especially when alluring objects were present on the land, in order to avoid categorizing them as trespassers.[2343] However, the formerly harsh treatment of trespassers has been relaxed,[2344] and any need to discover a fictional licence has disappeared.

E. The Common Duty of Care

406. The common duty of care owed by an occupier of premises to visitors arises in respect of dangers due to the state of the premises or to things done or omitted to be done on them.[2345] This 'occupancy' duty can be compared with the 'activity' duty at common law, which arises out of negligent conduct and has no necessary link with the state of the premises.[2346] In substance they are the same, and nothing is likely to turn on the distinction.

2334. Occupiers' Liability Act 1962, s. 4(2).
2335. *Eagle v. NZ Picture Supplies Ltd* [1924] GLR 78.
2336. *Stone v. Taffe* [1974] 1 WLR 1575.
2337. *McGeown v. Northern Ireland Housing Executive* [1995] 1 AC 233.
2338. *Ibid.*
2339. *Robson v. Hallett* [1967] 2 QB 939.
2340. *Christian v. Johannesson* [1956] NZLR 664.
2341. *Dehn v. A-G* [1988] 2 NZLR 564 (on appeal [1989] 1 NZLR 320).
2342. *TV3 Network Services Ltd v. The Broadcasting Standards Authority* [1995] 2 NZLR 720.
2343. *Glasgow Corporation v. Taylor* [1922] 1 AC 44; *Reardon v. A-G* [1954] NZLR 978; *Matheson v. A-G* [1956] NZLR 849.
2344. *See* para. 414.
2345. Occupiers' Liability Act 1962, s. 3(1).
2346. *See Perkowski v. Wellington City Corporation* [1959] NZLR 1; *Percival v. Hope Gibbons Ltd* [1959] NZLR 642; *Spittal v. Wellington City Corporation* [1959] NZLR 1095; *Heard v. NZ Forest Products Ltd* [1960] NZLR 329.

In *Tomlinson v. Congleton Borough Council*[2347] the House of Lords drew an important distinction between danger due to the state of premises and danger due to a person's own conduct on premises. In this case, the plaintiff suffered serious injury on running into a lake, diving forward in the shallow water and hitting his head on the bottom. The risk was that the claimant might not execute his dive properly, and this could not be attributed to the state of the premises. Rather, the water was perfectly safe for normal activities. Accordingly there was no risk of a kind that gave rise to a duty under the UK Act, and the claim failed in limine.

The common duty of care is defined as 'a duty to take such care as in all the circumstances of the case is reasonable to see that the visitor will be reasonably safe in using the premises for the purposes for which he is invited or permitted to be there'.[2348] The Act makes it clear that the duty is also owed with regard to damage to property on the premises, whether owned by the visitor or someone else.[2349] For example, an occupier of premises used for a spray-painting business who negligently allowed inflammable materials to accumulate in a rubbish bin was liable to the owners of vehicles that were on the premises, pursuant to contracts of bailment when the vehicles were damaged in a fire starting in the bin.[2350]

In determining whether an occupier has discharged the common duty of care, regard is to be had to all the circumstances.[2351] Whether what was done was reasonable and sufficient to render visitors or their property reasonably safe is ultimately a question of fact. However, the Act itself sets out certain guidelines drawn from previous case law, which are considered below. They direct attention to the care expected of the visitor, the effect of a warning, and the use made of independent contractors. The courts may have regard to these factors and to any others that may be relevant, such as the purpose of the visit, whether the danger is obvious or unexpected,[2352] the stringency of any systems of inspection,[2353] and the degree of control the occupier could exercise to guard against the risk.[2354]

1. Reasonable Steps by Way of Self-Protection

407. A visitor can be expected to take reasonable steps by way of self-protection. The Act accordingly provides that it is relevant to take into account the degree of care, and of want of care, which would ordinarily be looked for in the particular visitor.[2355] So, for example, an occupier should be prepared for children to be less careful than adults. Relevant considerations are whether the occupier could

---

2347. [2004] 1 AC 46; *Vairy v. Wyong Shire Council* (2005) 223 CLR 422; *Keown v. Coventry Healthcare NHS Trust* [2006] 1 WLR 153.
2348. Occupiers' Liability Act 1962, s. 4(2).
2349. *Ibid.*, ss 3(3)(b), 7(1).
2350. *Oceanview Holdings Ltd v. Clarry M O'Byrne Ltd* [1989] 1 NZLR 574.
2351. Occupiers' Liability Act 1962, s. 4(4).
2352. *Tomlinson v. Congleton BC* [2004] 1 AC 46; *Mulligan v. Coffs Harbour CC* (2005) 223 CLR 422.
2353. *Dulhunty v. JB Young* (1975) 7 ALR 409; *Ward v. Tesco Stores* [1976] 1 WLR 810; *Maguire v. Sefton Metropolitan Borough Council* [2006] 1 WLR 2550.
2354. *Evans v. Waitemata District Pony Club* [1972] NZLR 773, affirmed [1974] 1 NZLR 28.
2355. Occupiers' Liability Act 1962, s. 4(3).

reasonably expect the child to be accompanied by a responsible adult,[2356] whether the danger amounted to a hidden trap or allurement,[2357] and, conversely, whether any danger was obvious or presented no special danger even to those of tender years.[2358] Again, a specialist visitor can be expected to guard against preventable risks ordinarily incident to his or her calling.[2359] But a duty still is owed in respect of the inherent risks posed by the particular occupation, and is qualified only insofar as the knowledge or skill of the visitor could reasonably have been expected to have prevented the harm.[2360] The occupier also is responsible for the risks posed by the state of the premises which are not ordinarily incidental to the plaintiff's calling, such as, for example, the stairs giving access to the place of work.[2361]

2. Warnings

408. A warning does not absolve an occupier from liability unless in all the circumstances it was enough to enable the visitor to be reasonably safe.[2362] The question is whether a visitor with knowledge of the danger reasonably incurred it.[2363] Where two chimney sweeps disregarded warnings from the occupier about fumes in the flue they had come to clean, climbed up the flue when no one else was present and died from inhaling the fumes, the court decided that the warnings were in the particular circumstances sufficient to absolve the occupier.[2364] Further, a failure to warn will not necessarily give rise to liability, at least where the danger is self-evident. So an occupier was not obliged to warn players of indoor cricket of the risk of being hit by the ball,[2365] or to warn against swimming in a lake where there was no special or unusual danger.[2366]

3. Independent Contractors

409. Where damage is caused to a visitor by a danger due to the faulty execution of any work of construction, reconstruction, demolition, maintenance, repair, or other like operation by an independent contractor employed by the occupier, the occupier is not to be treated without more as answerable for the danger if, in all the circumstances, he had acted reasonably in entrusting the work to an independent

2356. *Phipps v. Rochester Corporation* [1955] 1 QB 450.
2357. *Reardon v. A-G* [1954] NZLR 978 (CA); *Matheson v. A-G* [1956] NZLR 849 (CA).
2358. *Dyer v. Ilfracombe UDC* [1956] 1 WLR 218.
2359. *Roles v. Nathan* [1963] 1 WLR 1117.
2360. *Ogwo v. Taylor* [1988] AC 431; cp *Christmas v. General Cleaning Contractors* [1952] 1 KB 141 (affirmed [1953] AC 180).
2361. *Bates v. Parker* [1953] 2 QB 231.
2362. Occupiers' Liability Act 1962, s. 4(5).
2363. *Bunker v. Charles Brand & Son Ltd* [1969] 2 QB 480 at 489.
2364. *Roles v. Nathan* [1963] 1 WLR 1117.
2365. *Woods v. Multi-Sport Holdings Pty Ltd* (2002) 208 CLR 560.
2366. *Tomlinson v. Congleton BC* [2004] 1 AC 46.

contractor and had taken such steps (if any) as he reasonably ought in order to satisfy himself that the contractor was competent and that the work had been properly done.[2367]

As regards the choice of contractor, the occupier must initially take care in choosing a reputable and careful contractor.[2368] The occupier may also be under an obligation to inquire into an independent contractor's insurance position, in order to confirm that the contractor could properly meet any potential liability that might occur.[2369]

As for whether there is an obligation to check or to supervise, this turns largely on whether the work entails special expertise. The occupier cannot attribute all blame to the contractor if no special skill was needed to discover and guard against the danger. So liability was imposed on a school authority for an icy and dangerous step left in that condition by a cleaner.[2370] But if the work calls for technical skill and the occupier, not being competent to exercise it, employs suitably qualified and experienced contractors, then he or she will not be responsible for the contractors' neglect. Indeed, it would be negligent for the occupier to attempt to do the work himself or herself. Thus, a landlord was not liable for negligence by lift engineers in repairing his lift,[2371] nor an office tenant for faulty wiring installed by electrical contractors.[2372] Exceptionally, however, an occupier may be under a non-delegable duty to take care.[2373]

F. Contractual Duties and Third Parties

410. The Act provides that where an occupier of premises is bound by contract to permit persons who are strangers to the contract to enter or use the premises, the common duty of care that he owes to them as his visitors cannot be restricted or excluded by that contract, but (subject to any provision of the contract to the contrary) shall include the duty to perform his obligations under the contract, whether undertaken for their protection or not, so far as those obligations go beyond the obligations otherwise involved in the common duty of care.[2374] In addition, whereby the terms or conditions governing any tenancy (including a statutory tenancy that does not in law amount to a tenancy) either the landlord or the tenant is bound, though not by contract, to permit persons to enter or use premises of which he is the occupier, the section applies as if the tenancy were a contract between the landlord and tenant.[2375]

2367. *Ferguson v. Welsh* [1987] 1 WLR 1553.
2368. Occupiers' Liability Act 1962, s. 4(6).
2369. *Gwilliam v. West Hertfordshire Hospitals NHS Trust* [2002] 3 WLR 1425; but compare *Glaister v. Appleby-in-Westmoreland Town Council* [2009] EWCA Civ 1325.
2370. *Woodward v. Mayor of Hastings* [1945] KB 174.
2371. *Haseldine v. Daw & Son Ltd* [1941] 2 KB 343.
2372. *Green v. Fibreglass Ltd* [1958] 2 QB 245.
2373. *See* para. 387.
2374. Occupiers' Liability Act 1962, s. 5(1).
2375. *Ibid.*, s. 5(4).

As regards the burden of the contract, the effect is that an occupier cannot contract out of his or her statutory obligation of care so far as strangers to the contract are concerned. But, having taken reasonable care, the occupier is not liable (unless the contract expressly provides otherwise) for faulty work of construction and the like by persons other than himself or herself, his or her servants and persons acting under his or her direction and control.[2376] As regards the benefit of the contract, the third person can sue for breach even of a strict contractual duty.

G. Defences

1. Contributory Negligence

411. The Act provides that where the occupier fails or neglects to discharge the common duty of care to a visitor, and the visitor suffers damage as the result partly of that fault and partly of his own fault, the provisions of the Contributory Negligence Act 1947 shall apply.[2377]

2. Assumption of Risk

412. The common duty of care does not impose on an occupier any obligation to a visitor in respect of risks willingly accepted as his by the visitor.[2378]

3. Exclusion of Liability

413. An occupier owes the common duty of care to all visitors 'except so far as he is free to and does extend, restrict, modify or exclude his duty to any visitor or visitors by agreement or otherwise'.[2379] Liability as regards the condition of the premises or the occupier's activities on the premises may be limited or excluded either by contract with the visitor,[2380] or by giving reasonable notice to the visitor of the terms upon which he or she may enter the premises.[2381]

The occupier can only modify the common duty of care 'so far as he is free to' do so. Of course, liability in respect of personal injuries cannot arise in the first place.[2382] There are no broad statutory restrictions or prohibitions affecting the ability of occupiers (and others) to exclude their liability in respect of property damage.

2376. *Ibid.*, s. 5(2).
2377. *Ibid.*, s. 4(8); *Heard v. NZ Forest Products Ltd* [1960] NZLR 329.
2378. *Ibid.*, s. 4(7); *Heard v. NZ Forest Products Ltd* [1960] NZLR 329.
2379. *Ibid.*, s. 4(1).
2380. *Ibid.*, s. 7(1).
2381. *Ashdown v. Williams & Sons Ltd* [1957] 1 QB 409; *see* para. 516.
2382. *See* para. 41.

II. Liability to Trespassers

414. At one time, an occupier was only liable in respect of an act intended to injure the trespasser or done with reckless disregard of the presence of the trespasser.[2383] However, in *British Railways Board v. Herrington*[2384] the House of Lords thought this test to be unduly harsh. It was recognized that an occupier's relationship with a trespasser was forced on the occupier, and so it was inappropriate to impose upon the occupier a common or ordinary duty of care. Rather, the nature and extent of the occupier's duty had to be based on considerations of common humanity. Applying this principle, the defendants were liable to a child injured by touching an electrified rail. They had created a lethal danger, they knew that children played in the area and they could easily have taken steps to keep them off their land.

It is apparent from *Herrington* that the humanitarian duty differs from the duty of care in at least two respects. First, it is not enough that the presence of a trespasser is foreseeable: the occupier must know that there is a 'substantial probability' of a trespasser coming on the land. Second, the humanitarian duty is essentially *subjective*. A duty of care may be broken regardless of the defendant's inability to prevent breach due to lack of skill or resources. Negligence lies in permitting the dangerous situation to occur in the first place. However, the capabilities and resources of the occupier are clearly of relevance as regards obligations to trespassers. As trespassers come uninvited then, in Lord Reid's words in *Herrington*, 'they must take the occupier as they find him'.

Seemingly the humanitarian duty is concerned primarily with trespassers suffering personal injury. Even so, an occupier might be liable for a trespasser's property damage – for, say, harm to animals or to property carried or left on the land – on the application of a similar kind of approach. In the only modern case on the point, an occupier sprayed his crop of oilseed rape with an insecticide without warning and at an inappropriate time, killing the plaintiff's bees that were working the crop. It was held that the occupier either owed a common duty of care or, if the bees were to be treated as analogous to trespassers, the occupier was required to take precautions that equated precisely with what the law of negligence would expect.[2385] This indicates that the subjective aspect of the occupier's duty is unlikely to have substantial impact in the context of damage to property.

III. Liability to Neighbours

415. Where damage is done to visitors by a danger on land, the Occupiers' Liability Act 1962 applies. In the case of damage occurring off the premises, common law principles apply. If the occupier actually creates a danger on the premises

2383. *Robert Addie & Sons Ltd v. Dumbreck* [1929] AC 358.
2384. [1972] AC 877; and *see Southern Portland Cement Ltd v. Cooper* [1974] AC 623.
2385. *Tutton v. AD Walter Ltd* [1986] QB 61.

that spreads elsewhere, he or she may be held liable on a straightforward application of *Donoghue v. Stevenson*.[2386] Where a danger arises on land that the occupier has not created, the occupier comes under a duty of care founded on his or her control over the land. However, the obligations imposed by the duty are essentially subjective. In *Goldman v. Hargrave*[2387] the Privy Council held that an occupier was under a duty to take steps that were reasonable in the light of the resources that were available to him to prevent a fire on his land, which had been started by a bolt of lightning, from encroaching onto nearby property. So also, an occupier was liable for letting variegated thistle seed proliferate on his land and failing to prevent it from spreading,[2388] for allowing the slipping of earth and debris from his land on to adjoining property,[2389] and for failing to pigeon-proof a bridge in order to prevent pigeons roosting in the bridge and fouling the pavement below.[2390] On an analogous principle, an owner of inflammable goods was liable to a warehouse owner for having stored the goods in the warehouse in a way that made firefighting difficult after an unexplained fire broke out.[2391]

The *Goldman* principle can apply where an occupier allows intruders to create a danger on his or her land that then causes damage to others. But the occupier must know or have means of knowledge of the particular risk. So in *Smith v. Littlewoods Organization Ltd* the owners of a derelict cinema owed no duty to an adjoining owner in circumstances where vandals started a fire that damaged the adjoining property, because they had not known of any previous acts of vandalism involving fire or a risk of fire.[2392] Lord Goff said that a duty also could arise where premises or a chattel were a special source of danger and it was reasonably foreseeable that a third party might interfere and spark off the danger. But here an empty cinema could not be described as an unusual danger in the nature of a fire hazard.

A 'special danger' principle can be seen as underlying a number of cases involving third parties causing harm by using someone else's property. For example, the owner of a quarry was liable when the quarry safe was left in an accessible place, some children retrieved detonators from it by driving the rod out from the hinges, passed them on to a friend and one exploded when being used as a plaything by the friend's small brother.[2393] On the other hand, a motor vehicle cannot be regarded as posing a special danger such that the owner is obliged to take care to prevent someone else from using it. So the owner of a car was not liable when a thief stole it and later ran down and killed a pedestrian.[2394]

2386. [1932] AC 562; *see* para. 75.
2387. [1967] AC 645.
2388. *French v. Auckland CC* [1974] 1 NZLR 340; and *see Double J Smallwoods Ltd v. Gisborne District Council* [2017] NZHC 1284.
2389. *Leakey v. National Trust* [1980] QB 485; *Coope v. Ward* [2015] EWCA Civ 30.
2390. *Wandsworth London Borough Council v. Railtrack plc* [2002] 2 WLR 512.
2391. *Wilson & Horton Ltd v. Attorney-General* [1997] 2 NZLR 513.
2392. *Smith v. Littlewoods Organization Ltd* [1987] AC 241; and *see Modbury Triangle Shopping Centre Pty Ltd v. Anzil* (2000) 205 CLR 254.
2393. *McCarthy v. Wellington CC* [1966] NZLR 481.
2394. *Topp v. London Country Bus (South West) Ltd* [1993] 1 WLR 976; *Rankin (Rankin's Garage & Sales) v. JJ* 2018 SCC 19.

Another approach to the problem, put forward by Lord Mackay in *Smith*, is to base the defendant's liability on proof of a high degree of likelihood of harm. However, in *Mitchell v. Glasgow CC*[2395] Lord Hope said that it was not easy to reconcile an approach relying generally on the likelihood of harm with the rule that a person is under no general duty to protect another from harm. He favoured Lord Goff's approach, which depended on showing that the particular situation was one where it was readily understandable that the law should regard the defender as under a responsibility to take care.

§2. Vendors and Lessors

I. Creating a Defect

416. Vendors or lessors of property who have created a defect in the property owe a duty of care to those who suffer physical harm caused by the defect. The duty is founded on *Donoghue v. Stevenson* in the ordinary way.

Claims by owners for their economic loss are more controversial. Builders and on-sellers in trade of 'household units' are bound by mandatory statutory warranties of quality that are enforceable by an original or subsequent purchaser.[2396] The builder also owes a duty in tort to an original or subsequent purchaser to take reasonable care in building a house or other property.[2397]

Where a private vendor of a house has personally done building work, the better view is that the vendor owes a duty of care to subsequent purchasers of the house on the same basis as any other builder.[2398] However, it has been held, not very convincingly, that a private owner who did his own renovations owed no duty to purchasers in respect of the diminished value of the house, on the basis (i) that the purchasers were capable of looking after themselves by inspection, by questioning the quality of workmanship and by negotiating protective contract terms, and (ii) that the do-it-yourself tradition was part of the New Zealand social fabric.[2399]

II. Letting or Selling with a Defect

417. The question remains whether an owner who lets or sells premises containing a known defect that he or she did not create owes a duty in tort to third persons who suffer harm caused by the defect. The common law formerly granted an immunity to lessors or vendors who let or sold property without warning of a dangerous defect.[2400] But recognizing a duty of care in letting or selling property in respect of dangers created by others that pose a risk of physical injury or harm to property arguably is supportable in principle, in light of developments in negligence since

2395. [2009] 1 AC 874.
2396. Building Act 2004, ss 362H-362J; *see* para. 127.
2397. *See* paras 121, 122.
2398. *Chase v. de Groot* [1994] 1 NZLR 613.
2399. *Willis v. Castelein* [1993] 3 NZLR 103.
2400. *Robbins v. Jones* (1863) 15 CB (NS) 221; [1861-73] All ER Rep 544.

Donoghue v. Stevenson and the significance attached to property holding in giving rise to a duty to take positive action or to warn. In *Northern Sandblasting Pty Ltd v. Harris*[2401] in Australia the High Court held, in a four to three decision, that a landlord who let property containing a dangerous defect created by an independent contractor was liable to a child of the tenants who was injured by the defect. Two majority judges (Brennan CJ and Gaudron J) held that the landlord was in breach of duty in letting out the premises in an unsafe condition that could reasonably have been discovered. The other two majority judges (Toohey and McHugh JJ) held that the landlord was under a non-delegable duty to ensure that the independent contractor took care in carrying out the repairs in question. There is no clear ratio to this case, nor any relevant decision in New Zealand.

A subsequent purchaser may complain not about physical damage done by a defect to persons or other property but, rather, the diminished value of the property itself. In *Mount Albert Borough Council v. Johnson*[2402] the Court of Appeal held that a building developer had a duty to take care to see that proper care and skill was exercised in building a block of flats, which duty could not be avoided by delegation to an independent contractor. So the developer was liable to a purchaser even though it had not created the defect in the flats and was not personally at fault. The decision was later condemned in the House of Lords,[2403] although it remains the law in the New Zealand. However, on-sellers in trade of household units may be liable pursuant to statute.[2404] Private vendors who have not created a defect owe no similar duty. Caveat emptor remains the basic rule.

2401. (1997) 188 CLR 313.
2402. [1979] 2 NZLR 234.
2403. *D & F Estates Ltd v. Church Commissioners for England* [1989] AC 177 at 209–210; *see* para. 387.
2404. *See* para. 127.

Chapter 4. Liability for Animals

§1. Introduction

418. Control over an animal, like control over other forms of property, imposes responsibilities on the owner or keeper. He or she may be held liable for damage done by the animal on the application of a number of common law and statutory rules. Statute has abolished certain strict common law rules concerning damage done by dangerous animals, and the position now is that ordinary principles of negligence apply across the board. However, these have been modified by statute in the cases of straying stock and damage done by dogs. In addition, damage done by animals may attract liability under the principles of nuisance and trespass. As regards the latter, the ancient action for cattle trespass continues to apply.

§2. Negligence

I. General Principles

419. An action in negligence against the keeper is available to the victim of damage caused by an animal.[2405] Examples of negligence liability include: keeping bees in unreasonable numbers and with appreciable danger to a neighbour;[2406] taking animals onto the highway without exercising proper control over them;[2407] and organizing a pony club gymkhana without providing an adequate supply of hitching rails.[2408] But an owner was not liable for letting a large dog off a lead where there was no reason for the owner to anticipate injury to another by coming into contact with the dog.[2409]

In the particular case of straying stock, an adjoining occupier is under a statutory obligation to maintain an adequate fence in order to keep stock out, and cannot recover damages if he or she fails to do this.[2410]

II. Stock Straying Onto the Highway

420. Under an old common law rule, affirmed by the House of Lords in *Searle v. Wallbank*,[2411] an owner or occupier of land owed no duty to persons using the

2405. *Paterson v. Fleming* (1904) 23 NZLR 636.
2406. *Robins v. Kennedy and Columb* [1931] NZLR 1134.
2407. *Lynsar v. Binnie* (1904) 25 NZLR 241; *Paul v. Rowe* (1905) 24 NZLR 641; *Barrett v. Hardie and Thompson Ltd* [1924] NZLR 228; *Griffith v. Turner* [1955] NZLR 1035; *Purdon v. Scott* [1968] NZLR 83; cp *Allen v. Borough of St. Kilda* (1912) 31 NZLR 265; *George Graham (1960) Ltd v. Crawford* [1964] NZLR 668.
2408. *Evans v. Waitemata District Pony Club* [1972] NZLR 773, affirmed [1974] 1 NZLR 28.
2409. *Whippey v. Jones* [2009] EWCA Civ 452.
2410. Impounding Act 1955, s. 26(1); *Grainger v. Rossendale Holdings Ltd* [1989] 2 NZLR 389 at 394. *See* para. 426.
2411. [1947] AC 341.

highway to take care to prevent his or her animals from straying onto the highway. The rule developed in England at the time of the open field system, when new roads were dedicated by adjoining landowners and when there was no motorized traffic. Even so, as recently as 1970 it was held to be part of New Zealand law.[2412] However, the law was changed by section 5 of the Animals Law Reform Act 1989. Section 5(1) abolished the immunity, opening the way to an action in negligence against the landowner. Section 5(2) provides that in deciding whether the landowner was negligent, it is relevant to take into account (a) the common practice in the locality in relation to fencing or other measures to prevent animals from straying, and (b) any measures taken to warn highway users of the likely presence of animals. Examples of conduct by a landowner adjoining a highway which have been held to be negligent include the use of a deer netting fence to contain cattle,[2413] and a failure promptly to repair a fence after a tree fell on it.[2414]

III. Dangerous Animals

421. At common law the keeper of an animal which was normally dangerous (*ferae naturae*), or an animal which was normally harmless (*mansuetae naturae*) with a known dangerous propensity, was liable without proof of negligence for all harm done by the animal. Animals were classified under one or other of these heads according to whether they were a danger to mankind. This rule of strict liability was known as the scienter action, the scienter being a keeper's presumed or proved knowledge of an animal's dangerous propensity. However, the action became outmoded following the introduction of the accident compensation scheme, and, by section 4 of the Animals Law Reform Act 1989, Parliament intervened to abolish it. So liability for dangerous animals is determined under ordinary principles of negligence.

Negligence formerly was available as an alternative cause of action where a plaintiff was unable to show that a keeper of a normally harmless animal knew of a dangerous propensity.[2415] Now, in the case of property damage, in deciding whether the keeper of a dangerous animal was negligent the court can impose a duty which is commensurate with the risk. The dangerous nature of the particular animal and the circumstances generally will be taken into account.

§3. Liability for Dogs

422. There is a special statutory liability in the case of damage done by dogs. Section 63(3) of the Dog Control Act 1996 provides:

2412. *Ross v. McCarthy* [1970] NZLR 449.
2413. *O'Dwyer v. Dalgliesh* [1993] DCR 986.
2414. *Brown v. Toohey* (1994) 35 NSWLR 417.
2415. *Draper v. Hodder* [1972] 2 QB 556.

> The owner of a dog shall be liable in damages for damage done by the dog, and it shall not be necessary for the person seeking damages to show a previous mischievous propensity in the dog, or the owner's knowledge of any such mischievous propensity, or that the damage was attributable to neglect on the part of the owner of the dog.[2416]

The 'owner' who can be liable under this section is the person who owns or possesses the dog, or the parent or guardian of a person under the age of 16 who is the owner or possessor.[2417]

Certain decisions interpreting previous legislation expressed in similar terms suggest that the section merely shifts the onus of proof of negligence. For example, where an owner visiting a friend secured his dog by a short chain, and the dog sprang at but could not reach another visitor, who fell back and was injured, it was held that the owner was not liable on the ground, *inter alia*, that the injury was due to an accident and not to any negligence on his part.[2418] Again, where a dog wandered into the road and was hit by the plaintiff's car, the defendant owner was held to have established the defence of accident.[2419] However, the onus cannot be discharged simply by the owner showing lack of knowledge that a dog had a propensity to cause harm. So where the defendant's dog bit the plaintiff's mare, the defendant could not avoid liability by showing that the dog had never before attacked anything or demonstrated any aggressive tendency. The owner had to start with the assumption that the propensity or vice existed and take appropriate precautions.[2420] Indeed, in Australia, in relation to similar legislation, it has been held that lack of negligence alone is not a defence.[2421]

A further argument raises for consideration the meaning of 'damage done by the dog'. It has been held that these words connote something of an active nature, and not mere passivity on the part of the dog.[2422] Applying this principle, damage to the plaintiff's car from hitting a dog in the road was thought not to be damage 'done by' the dog.[2423]

The defences which were formerly available in the scienter action – violent, contributory negligence, the injured person being a trespasser and, perhaps, escape caused by a stranger and no escape by the animal from control – are available for actions under the Dog Control Act.[2424]

2416. The rule does not apply in respect of damage done by a dog kept by the police or various government departments or ministries while the dog is lawfully being used to carry out any function, duty or power of one of these bodies if, had the section not been enacted, there could be no claim for damage against them: Dog Control Act 1996, s. 63(2).
2417. *Ibid.*, s. 2.
2418. *Chittenden v. Hale* [1933] NZLR 836.
2419. *Knowlson v. Solomon* [1969] NZLR 686.
2420. *Glenie v. Mowat* [1983] NZ Rec Law 40.
2421. *Martignoni v. Harris* [1971] 2 NSWLR 102; *Irving v. Slevin* (1982) 30 SASR 66.
2422. *Knowlson v. Solomon* [1969] NZLR 686.
2423. *Ibid.*
2424. *Chittenden v. Hale* [1933] NZLR 836; *Christian v. Johannesson* [1956] NZLR 664; *Knowlson v. Solomon* [1969] NZLR 686.

§4. Nuisance

423. The principles of nuisance govern the liability of an occupier of land in respect of unreasonable interferences with a neighbour's right to the use or enjoyment of his or her land.[2425] These principles can apply to interferences created by animals in the ordinary way. For example, keeping animals in such a fashion as to cause a substantial and unreasonable annoyance to a neighbour from smells[2426] or noise,[2427] or using land in a way that encourages flies or vermin,[2428] may all constitute actionable nuisances.

§5. Cattle Trespass

I. General Principles

424. Under the old common law action for cattle trespass, a keeper is strictly liable where cattle trespass onto land of another and cause damage.[2429] 'Cattle' means, broadly, domestic or farmyard livestock, including poultry.[2430] The common law meaning is synonymous with the definition of 'stock' in the Impounding Act 1955 as including 'any horse, cattle, deer, ass, mule, sheep, pig or goat', and of 'poultry' as including 'turkeys, geese, ducks, and domestic fowls of all descriptions'.[2431] As with the ordinary action for trespass to land, the person who can sue is the person in possession of the land.[2432] The person who can be sued is the possessor or keeper of the cattle. Where a remedy is claimed under the Impounding Act 1955,[2433] the owner is liable as well.[2434]

The rule of strict liability does not apply where cattle stray from the highway onto adjoining land. The occupier is deemed to accept the normal risks incidental to cattle passing along the highway, and so the keeper is liable only on proof of negligence.[2435]

2425. *See* para. 185.
2426. *Wright v. New Zealand Co-operative Dairy Ltd* [1924] GLR 478; *A-G v. Abraham and Williams Ltd* [1949] NZLR 461; *Wheeler v. JJ Saunders Ltd* [1995] 3 WLR 466.
2427. *Leeman v. Montagu* [1936] 2 All ER 1677.
2428. *A-G v. Abraham and Williams Ltd* [1949] NZLR 461; cp *Stearn v. Prentice Bros* [1919] 1 KB 394.
2429. *Redfern & Son Ltd v. Storey* [1969] NZLR 945 at 948; *Mayfair Ltd v. Pears* [1987] 1 NZLR 459 at 466. *See* Williams, *Liability for Animals* Ch. 8 (CUP 1939).
2430. Williams, *ibid.*, Ch. 9.
2431. Impounding Act 1955, s. 2.
2432. *McKenzie v. Risk* [1974] 2 NZLR 214; *Grainger v. Rossendale Holdings Ltd* [1989] 2 NZLR 389.
2433. *See* para. 426.
2434. Impounding Act 1955, s. 26(2).
2435. *Gayler & Pope Ltd v. Davies* [1924] 2 KB 75.

II. Defences

425. Consent to livestock coming onto land or contributory negligence in allowing them to enter can be raised by way of defence.[2436] It appears that proof that the trespass was caused by an act of a stranger for whom the defendant was not responsible or by an 'act of God' may also be good defences.[2437]

III. Remedies

426. Where livestock trespass onto land and cause damage, the occupier can seek to recover damages. However, there is a restriction on recovery in the Impounding Act 1955. This provides, in substance, that the occupier cannot recover unless the land in question was adequately fenced or, if it was not, the lack of fencing did not cause or contribute to the trespass.[2438] The policy of this provision is that occupiers have the responsibility of keeping out straying stock rather than a duty to keep their own stock in.[2439] If there is no adequate fence, the remedy of an occupier is to serve a notice on his or her neighbour under the Fencing Act 1978, which provides a mechanism for sharing the cost between adjoining landowners. Seemingly an occupier cannot avoid these requirements by seeking an injunction requiring the neighbour to keep out trespassing stock.

The precondition to recovery under the Impounding Act is that the fence should be 'adequate', which means a fence that is 'reasonably satisfactory for the purpose that it serves or is intended to serve'.[2440] So where a fence was erected to keep in horses, and the defendant landowner later put sheep against it, which broke through the fence and ate the plaintiffs' vegetables, the plaintiffs' claim could succeed.[2441] The fence was adequate for its original purpose, and the defendant could not make it inadequate and then invoke the Impounding Act by changing its purpose. The defendant should have given a notice under the Fencing Act or himself have modified the fence.

Where an action for damages can be maintained, the plaintiff can recover for damage caused by trespassing animals which is ordinarily within their nature to commit.[2442] This includes damage to the land itself and to crops growing on it,[2443] damage to other animals, and damage to chattels. In certain limited circumstances the occupier also can destroy the trespassing stock.[2444]

2436. *See* paras 476, 493, respectively.
2437. *Grainger v. Rossendale Holdings Ltd* [1989] 2 NZLR 389.
2438. Impounding Act 1955, s. 26(1).
2439. *Grainger v. Rossendale Holdings Ltd* [1989] 2 NZLR 389 at 392.
2440. Impounding Act 1955, s. 2; Fencing Act 1978, s. 2.
2441. *Grainger v. Rossendale Holdings Ltd* [1989] 2 NZLR 389.
2442. *Ibid.*, at 391.
2443. *Gardiner v. Metcalf* [1994] 2 NZLR 8.
2444. *See* the Impounding Act 1955, s. 31(2).

An occupier also has a statutory right to seize and impound trespassing stock in a public pound. The owner can recover the stock on paying certain charges and trespass rates fixed by regulation.[2445] An occupier can elect to receive trespass rates or can claim damages, but cannot claim both.

2445. Impounding Act 1955, ss 14–16. Trespass rates are set in the Impounding Regulations of 1981.

Part III. Forms of Strict Liability

Chapter 1. General Principles

427. In certain circumstances a person may be liable in tort without proof of fault for causing harm to another. Such liability may be absolute, that is, the defendant may be held liable simply on proof that his or her conduct caused the harm, and there are no defences upon which he or she may rely. Or the defendant may be strictly liable, in the sense that it is no defence to show that all reasonable precautions were taken, or that all proper care and skill was employed to prevent the harm. However, in this case there may still be certain defences to liability.

There is no rule of absolute liability in New Zealand tort law. However, there are a number of possible actions where strict liability is imposed. One is the action for breach of statutory duty, which is discussed immediately below. Other torts which impose forms of strict liability are discussed elsewhere. They include: an action for nuisance, where the defendant interferes with the plaintiff's use and enjoyment of land;[2446] an action based on the rule in *Rylands v. Fletcher*,[2447] seemingly a particular form of nuisance, where the defendant accumulates a dangerous thing on land and it escapes and causes damage to a neighbour;[2448] an action for the conversion or detention of goods, which does not depend on the converter's moral blameworthiness;[2449] and an action for defamation, where the defendant causes injury to the plaintiff's reputation.[2450] The common law also imposed strict liability for damage done by a dangerous animal, known as the scienter action, but this was abolished by legislation in 1989.[2451] In addition to these heads of claim, the imposition of liability without personal fault also is found in the principle of vicarious liability[2452] and in the idea of a non-delegable duty to take care.[2453]

It is difficult to discern any compelling themes or considerations of principle which underlie the preceding instances of liability. Probably the most we can say is that, as between two innocent parties, the fact that one has created a particular or special danger sometimes can be recognized as a reason for requiring him or her to bear the risk of harm, even without intentional or negligent misconduct. Beyond this

2446. *See* para. 192.
2447. (1866) LR 1 Exch. 265.
2448. *See* para. 201.
2449. *See* para. 216.
2450. *See* paras 330–334.
2451. Animals Law Reform Act 1989, s. 4; *see* para. 421.
2452. *See* para. 373.
2453. *See* para. 387.

we struggle to find much in the way of coherent justification for the present state of the law. Why exactly should a person's interest in land receive greater protection than his or her interest in being free from bodily harm? What is it about defamation that justifies us in disregarding the defendant's lack of culpability in publishing defamatory words? The reality is that the rules of liability in the torts concerned have varied histories and have evolved in ways that have sought to take into account many different and sometimes competing matters of policy, such as deterrence of harm-producing activity, security of property, commercial convenience, the practicality of any particular rule of liability, the economic implications of the rule, certainty in the law, and, generally, considerations of fairness and justice.

The disparate forms of strict liability, the haphazard protection of the different interests and the differing degrees of strictness that are imposed all mean that the various heads of liability are better considered separately and on their own merits. There is little here by way of unifying principle.

In addition to the various forms of strict liability at common law, the legislature has created a number of causes of action for damages which are analogous to common law actions for damages in tort. Two important instances are an action under the Fair Trading Act 1986 alleging misleading or deceptive conduct by a trader in the course of trade, and an action under the Consumer Guarantees Act 1993 against a manufacturer of consumer goods alleging that the goods fail to comply with certain statutory guarantees as to their quality. These and certain other instances will be considered below.[2454] Again, there is an action for damages in public law for conduct which is in breach of the New Zealand Bill of Rights Act 1990, which is considered in the context of possible actions for abuses of public office.[2455]

2454. *See* paras 443–45347.
2455. *See* paras 313–314.

Chapter 2. Breach of Statutory Duty

§1. Introduction

428. Our concern in this section is with the common law tort of breach of statutory duty. Sometimes the breach of a statute or of a statutory regulation amounts to a tort in itself, and the plaintiff can bring an action for breach of statutory duty.[2456] Liability in such a case is based on showing that the requirements of the statute have not been complied with. If the duty imposed by the statute is strict or absolute, then the defendant is liable because he or she has not complied with the statute in question. As Lord Wright has remarked, if the liability imposed by the statute is strict, then the defendant's negligence or lack of it is immaterial.[2457]

In some American states the violation of a statute is conclusive evidence of negligence in a civil action, or, in other words, is negligence per se. On this view, the source of the liability is not the statute but the common law duty of care, and the statute merely gives a precise and predictable form to what constitutes breach of that duty. But there is no support for this view in New Zealand law. Rather, the courts have favoured the view that breach of statutory duty is a nominate tort distinct from negligence, and they have also made clear that there is no intermediate tort of careless performance of a statutory duty.[2458] As regards liability for negligence, breach of a statute may be good evidence of negligent conduct, but whether negligence is established depends ultimately on all the circumstances, including the existence of the particular statutory standard.[2459]

In overseas jurisdictions the availability of an action for breach of statutory duty tends to be most commonly recognized in the context of actions by employees alleging that their employers' breach of industrial safety legislation has caused them to suffer personal injury. In New Zealand such claims are barred by the accident compensation legislation,[2460] and the scope of the action in this country accordingly has been reduced. However, it may still apply, relatively exceptionally, to claims for property damage and for economic loss, and possibly for other forms of damage.

§2. Elements to Liability

429. It is not every breach of a penal statute that will give rise to a civil action for damages. On the contrary, an action has been held to lie only in very limited

2456. The right of action for breach of statutory duty is distinct from the right of action for breach of a duty of care in exercising a statutory power, discussed at paras 132–136.

2457. *London Passenger Transport Board v. Upson* [1949] AC 155 at 168 per Lord Wright.

2458. *Attorney-General v. Carter* [2003] 2 NZLR 160 at [43]; *Hobson v. Attorney-General* [2007] 1 NZLR 374 at [40] (appeal by second plaintiff allowed: *Couch v. Attorney-General* [2008] 3 NZLR 725). Of course, there may be concurrent liability under both heads: *Ashley v. Chief Constable of Sussex Police* [2008] 1 AC 962 at [56].

2459. *See* para. 147.

2460. Accident Compensation Act 2001, s. 317; *see* para. 41.

circumstances. While it is not especially difficult to identify the necessary elements to liability, there is considerable uncertainty in determining when they can be seen to be satisfied.

The essential elements to an action for breach of statutory duty are fourfold:

(1) the statute must create a duty that is enforceable by way of a civil action for damages;
(2) the damage must be of a kind which the statute was designed to prevent;
(3) there must be a breach of the relevant duty; and
(4) there must be a causal link between the damage and breach of duty.[2461]

It is the first of these requirements – the existence of an enforceable duty – that creates particular difficulty and that is the focus of the discussion below.

§3. The Existence of an Enforceable Duty

430. Whether an individual can bring a civil action for breach of a statute is said to depend, in the final analysis, on the intention of the legislature.[2462] In *Cutler v. Wandsworth Stadium Ltd*[2463] Lord Symonds has stated, in influential words, that the only rule that in all circumstances is valid is that the answer must depend on a consideration of the whole act and the circumstances, including the preexisting law, in which it was enacted. Accordingly, each statute must be approached individually, and the question asked whether it was Parliament's intention that a duty should be owed to the individual as well as to the public at large. Sometimes an Act will provide expressly for a remedy in damages for a person suffering harm caused by a breach,[2464] but in such cases the cause of action is statutory. The action for breach of statutory duty is founded on the common law.

In determining whether an action lies, it is relevant to look at all the circumstances bearing upon a question of statutory interpretation, and in particular the wording of the statute, its purpose and scope, the evil it was intended to remedy, and the context in which it was passed.[2465] Relevant guidelines include: whether the statute was passed for the benefit of an ascertainable class of persons; whether the statute makes provision for an alternative mode of enforcement, whether the common law grants a remedy, the type of damage caused by the breach; and whether

2461. For detailed treatment *see* Todd (ed.), *Todd on Torts* Ch. 8 (8th ed., 2019).

2462. *Atkinson v. Newcastle Waterworks Co.* (1877) 2 Ex D 441; *Dominion Air Lines Ltd v. Strand* [1933] NZLR 1.

2463. [1949] AC 398 at 407.

2464. *See* para. 432.

2465. *See*, for example, *Fairbairn Wright & Co. v. Levin & Co. Ltd* (1914) 34 NZLR 1; *Dominion Air Lines Ltd v. Strand* [1933] NZLR 1; *MacEachern v. Pukekohe Borough* [1965] NZLR 330; *Rowan v. Attorney-General* [1997] 2 NZLR 559; *Gauld v. Waimakariri District Council* [2012] NZAR 391.

the duty is defined with reasonable clarity and precision. However, none of the 'tests' of intent are conclusive, and nor are they reliable predictors.[2466]

I. Class of Persons Protected

431. A test that is frequently relied upon is whether the statute was passed for the benefit of an ascertainable class of persons, for this is some indication that members of that class are intended to have a right of action.[2467] Examples are aircraft passengers,[2468] factory workers,[2469] gas consumers,[2470] hirers of chattels,[2471] property owners,[2472] former property owners holding options to acquire back their land,[2473] purchasers of houses acquiring a LIM,[2474] and family members of an injured person entitled to accident compensation payments.[2475] On the other hand, where legislation is passed for the benefit of the public at large, it will not usually be construed as giving a right of action to any individual member of the public. So, for example, breaches of a statutory scheme of social welfare,[2476] road traffic legislation,[2477] town and country planning legislation,[2478] or of mental health legislation,[2479] do not give rise to a private right of action for damages. Further, the obligation must be placed on the person sought to be made liable: the 'class' exception does not permit a person to be made indirectly liable for breach of an obligation placed on someone else.[2480]

The 'class' test is open to a number of objections. First, it is difficult to define with any degree of certainty what is meant by a 'class' of persons who are intended to benefit from a statute. So, comparing some of the examples given above, why are factory workers and other employees treated as a class, but motorists are treated as members of the public at large? Again, why should certain property owners have an action, but not those in the neighbourhood of a building that infringes town planning regulations? Second, there is frequently no obvious answer to the question whether a particular class was intended to benefit from the legislation or whether it

2466. *Select 2000 Ltd v. ENZA Ltd* [2002] 2 NZLR 367 at 374; *St John Poulton's Trustee in Bankruptcy v. Ministry of Justice* [2010] 3 WLR 1237.

2467. *Lonrho Ltd v. Shell Petroleum Co Ltd (No 2)* [1982] AC 173, 185; *Campbell v. Peter Gordon Joiners Ltd* [2016] 3 WLR 294 at [7], [12].

2468. *Dominion Air Lines Ltd v. Strand* [1933] NZLR 1.

2469. *Jackson v. De Havilland Aircraft Co. of NZ Ltd* [1945] NZLR 250; *Howell v. Caxton Printing Works Ltd* [1971] NZLR 1068.

2470. *Morton Eltham Borough* [1961] NZLR 1; *Pease v. Eltham Borough* [1962] NZLR 437.

2471. *Harris v. Lombard NZ Ltd* [1974] 2 NZLR 161.

2472. *Small v. Buller DC* [1998] 1 NZLR 190.

2473. *Rowan v. Attorney-General* [1997] 2 NZLR 559.

2474. *Altimarloch Joint Venture Ltd v. Moorhouse* HC Blenheim CIV-2005-406-91, 3 Jul. 2008. This finding was not in issue on appeal: *Marlborough District Council v. Altimarloch Joint Venture Ltd* [2012] 2 NZLR 726 at [14].

2475. *EM v. Accident Compensation Corporation* [2016] NZHC 2535.

2476. *X (Minors) v. Bedfordshire County Council* [1995] 2 AC 633.

2477. *Gardiner v. McManus* [1971] NZLR 475.

2478. *Attorney-General v. Birkenhead Borough* [1968] NZLR 383.

2479. *Ellis v. Counties Manukau District Health Board* [2007] 1 NZLR 196 at [198]–[207].

2480. *Campbell v. Peter Gordon Joiners Ltd* [2016] 3 WLR 294 at [13].

had some other purpose. For example, should the requirement that a car be sold with a warrant of fitness be characterized as concerned with the safety of the public or the protection of a class of purchasers?[2481] Third, the very basis for the test is suspect, for it 'would be strange if a less important duty, which is not owed to a section of the public, may be enforced by an action, while a more important duty owed to the public at large cannot'.[2482] However, notwithstanding criticisms such as these, the courts continue to treat the 'class' test as an important indicator of the statutory purpose.[2483]

II. Alternative Modes of Enforcement

432. If a statute does not provide expressly for a penalty or a remedy for breach, a court may treat this as pointing in favour of an action for damages. In *X (Minors) v. Bedfordshire County Council.*[2484] Lord Browne-Wilkinson observed that if the statute provides no other remedy for its breach and an intention to protect a limited class is shown, that indicates that there may be a private right of action, since otherwise there is no method of securing the protection the statute was intended to confer. So the courts may take the view that if there is no private remedy, the statutory duty would otherwise amount to little more than a pious aspiration.[2485]

The converse proposition is that provision for enforcement of a statutory duty other than by a damages action is an indication that no such action was intended. Accordingly, if an Act provides its own method of enforcement, a court may treat this as the only method and thus as precluding an action for damages.[2486] However, the fact that a statute renders a breach a criminal offence punishable by fine or imprisonment is an uncertain indicator that only a criminal sanction was intended. In a number of decisions, the courts have reached the opposite conclusion, that a breach was intended to confer a civil remedy in addition to the criminal penalty.[2487]

2481. *See Fenton v. Scotty's Car Sales Ltd* [1968] NZLR 929, which favoured the former option.

2482. *Phillips v. Britannia Hygienic Laundry Co. Ltd* [1923] 2 KB 832 at 841.

2483. For a recent affirmation, *see Hobson v. Attorney-General* [2007] 1 NZLR 374 at [43] (appeal by second plaintiff allowed: *Couch v. Attorney-General* [2008] 3 NZLR 725).

2484. [1995] 2 AC 633 at 731.

2485. *See*, for example, *Morton Eltham Borough* [1961] NZLR 1; *Pease v. Eltham Borough* [1962] NZLR 437 (bare duty to supply gas under the Gas Supply Act 1908); *Harris v. Lombard NZ Ltd* [1974] 2 NZLR 161 (no other remedy for breach of Hire Purchase Agreements Act 1939 causing loss of equity of redemption); *G v. Attorney-General* [1994] 1 NZLR 714 (no provision for enforcement of Adult Adoption Information Act 1985); *EM v. Accident Compensation Corporation* [2016] NZHC 2535 (no alternative remedy for carer of injured person under the accident compensation scheme).

2486. *See*, for example, *Askin v. Knox* [1989] 1 NZLR 248 (breach of building bylaws remediable by way of injunction and pulling down of contravening works); *Feary v. Commissioner of Crown Lands* [2001] 1 NZLR 704 (statutory right of appeal from administrative decision); *Select 2000 Ltd v. ENZA Ltd* [2002] 2 NZLR 367 (breach of statutory regulations governing export licences enforceable by criminal penalties and revocation of licence).

2487. The older cases concerning breach of industrial safety legislation all reach this conclusion; *see*, for example, *Jackson v. De Havilland Aircraft Co. of NZ Ltd* [1945] NZLR 250; *Dickson v. Kamo Collieries Ltd* [1948] NZLR 397; *Hibberds Foundry Ltd v. Hardy* [1953] NZLR 14; *Howell v. Caxton Printing Works Ltd* [1971] NZLR 1068.

An argument to this effect will be strengthened if the provision in question is clearly for the benefit or protection of a limited class of persons.[2488] Again, there can be an action if the statute creates a public right and a particular member suffers particular, direct, and substantial damage, other and different from that which was common to the rest of the public.[2489]

III. Common Law Remedy

433. There is authority for the proposition that where a statutory provision lays down a specific duty in a matter where the defendant is already bound to take reasonable care under the common law of negligence, the statutory duty will more readily be held to give rise to an action for breach of statutory duty.[2490] But the converse also has been asserted, that the existence of a common law remedy indicates that no additional civil remedy was intended.[2491] Nowadays, the courts seem more inclined to take the latter view.

IV. Nature of the Duty

434. Where a statutory duty is expressed in wide and general terms, this can indicate that a private remedy for breach was not intended. So no enforceable right of action arose from: the breach by a State-owned enterprise of a statutory obligation to act in a 'socially responsible manner';[2492] a failure by the Inland Revenue to use its 'best endeavours to preserve the integrity of the tax system';[2493] a failure by an education body to provide a statutory right to an education;[2494] a breach of duty by a local authority in failing to promote the welfare of children and to provide 'a range and level of service appropriate to those children's needs';[2495] and an alleged failure by a mental health authority in invoking processes under mental health legislation.[2496]

V. Nature of the Damage

435. In proceedings for breach of statutory duty, the damage of which the plaintiff complains must be of a type or kind that the law regards as remediable by way

2488. *Lonrho Ltd v. Shell Petroleum Co. Ltd (No. 2)* [1982] AC 173 at 185.
2489. *Ibid.*
2490. *O'Connor v. S P Bray Ltd* (1937) 56 CLR 464 at 478; *M A Paterson Ltd v. Robertson* [1960] NZLR 1160 at 1166.
2491. *Phillips v. Britannia Hygienic Laundry Co. Ltd* [1923] 2 KB 832 at 842; *McCall v. Abelesz* [1976] QB 585 at 594.
2492. *Auckland Electric Power Board v. Electricity Corporation of New Zealand* [1994] 1 NZLR 551.
2493. *Russell v. Taxation Review Authority* (2002) 20 NZTC 17,832.
2494. *Attorney-General v. Daniels* [2003] 2 NZLR 742.
2495. *R(A) v. Lambeth LBC* [2004] 1 All ER 97.
2496. *Ellis v. Counties Manukau District Health Board* [2007] 1 NZLR 196 at [198]–[207].

of damages. In *Pickering v. Liverpool Daily Post and Echo Newspapers Plc*,[2497] Lord Bridge said that he knew of no authority where a statute had been held to give a cause of action for breach of statutory duty where when the nature of the statutory obligation or prohibition was not such as to cause personal injury, injury to property or economic loss. So in the instant case, which concerned publication of unauthorized information about proceedings on a patient's application for discharge to a mental health review tribunal, it was held that the breach of duty was incapable of causing actionable loss to the patient.

There being a bar on claims for personal injury in New Zealand imposed by the accident compensation legislation, any claims for breach of statutory duty must be for other forms of damage. There are indeed many cases where recovery has been allowed for property damage or economic loss: and as regards the latter, unlike in cases involving the tort of negligence, it has not been suggested that the nature of the damage should by itself be a reason for limiting or denying the action.[2498] Indeed, notwithstanding Lord Bridge's words, new and different forms of damage may come to be accepted in actions for breach of statutory duty in the same way as for actions in negligence.

§4. Damage of a Kind That the Statute Was Intended to Prevent

436. The injury or damage must be of a kind that the statute was intended to prevent. So once again it is necessary to examine the statutory purpose. In *Gorris v. Scott*[2499] a shipowner failed, in breach of a statute, to provide pens for cattle carried on his ship. The plaintiff's sheep were lost overboard in a storm and the plaintiff sued for their loss, but the action failed. The statute required that pens be used in order to prevent the spread of disease, so the loss suffered was not of the kind at which the statute was directed. In another example, a remedy for breach of an obligation to maintain a highway was concerned with the protection of the legal rights of the public to use the highway, not with the safety of the condition of the highway.[2500]

2497. [1991] 2 AC 370.

2498. Examples of cases where claims for economic loss caused by a breach of statutory duty have succeeded include *Harris v. Lombard New Zealand Ltd* [1974] 2 NZLR 161; *Cashmere Pacific Ltd v. New Zealand Dairy Board* [1966] 1 NZLR 218; *Rowan v. Attorney-General* [1997] 2 NZLR 559; *Small v. Buller DC* [1998] 1 NZLR 190. Examples where such claims have failed include *Fenton v. Scotty's Car Sales Ltd* [1968] NZLR 929; *Emms v. Brad Lovett Ltd* [1973] 1 NZLR 282; *Craig v. East Coast Bays City Council* [1986] 1 NZLR 99 at 105 (and on the negligence aspect of the decision, *see* now *Bella Vista Resort Ltd v. Western Bay of Plenty DC* [2007] 3 NZLR 429); *Gregory v. Rangitikei District Council* [1995] 2 NZLR 208.

2499. (1874) LR 9 Exch. 125.

2500. *Ali v. Bradford Metropolitan District Council* [2012] 1 WLR 161; and *see Wentworth v. Wiltshire CC* [1993] QB 654.

§5. Breach of Duty

437. The standard of conduct required of the defendant depends upon the terms of the Act. Sometimes the duty may be absolute, and all that is necessary to prove a breach is to show that the statutory requirements have not in fact been complied with. In such cases the defendant can be liable irrespective of whether there is negligence.[2501] Or the duty may be qualified, for example by requiring steps that are 'reasonably practicable' or by requiring reasonable care. If there is no express provision then it is a matter of construction of the particular statute whether there is a defence that the defendant could not avoid a breach by the exercise of reasonable care.[2502]

§6. Causation

438. In an action for breach of statutory duty, the ordinary rules of causation apply. So the burden is on the plaintiff to prove that the defendant's breach caused the loss or materially contributed to it. In *Dominion Air Lines Ltd v. Strand*[2503] the pilot of an aircraft that crashed did not have the licence required by statutory regulations, but an action by a victim of the crash for breach of statutory duty failed on the ground that it was not shown that the breach was a cause of the damage.

Sometimes proof of causation can be difficult to establish, and the courts have modified the ordinary rules by requiring only that the plaintiff prove that the defendant contributed to a risk or chance of harm.[2504] The circumstances in which the courts will take this kind of approach are considered in the discussion of causation.[2505]

Where cause is established, such authority as there is holds that the damages recoverable are those that are contemplated by the statute and are the natural consequences of the breach.[2506] However, the courts may prefer to apply the well-established test in *The Wagon Mound (No. 2)*,[2507] and ask whether the damages were a reasonably foreseeable consequence of the breach.[2508]

2501. This view was taken in a number of cases involving industrial safety legislation: *see*, for example, *Dickson v. Kamo Collieries Ltd* [1948] NZLR 397; *Slater v. Glen Afton Collieries Ltd* [1951] NZLR 971; *McAuliffe v. Fletcher Construction Co. Ltd* [1970] NZLR 680.
2502. *Hammond v. Vestry of St Pancras* (1874) LR 9 CP 316 at 322.
2503. [1933] NZLR 1.
2504. *See*, in particular, *McGhee v. National Coal Board* [1973] 1 WLR 1.
2505. *See* paras 531–534.
2506. *Harris v. Lombard New Zealand Ltd* [1974] 2 NZLR 161.
2507. [1967] 1 AC 617.
2508. *See* para. 544.

§7. Defences

I. Statutory Defence in Criminal Proceedings

439. Whether a defence provided by statute to criminal liability applies also to civil liability is a question of construction of the statute.[2509] Certainly a defence that is open in criminal proceedings is not necessarily a defence to an action in tort.[2510] Lord Porter has observed that the legislature might well be unwilling to convict an owner who failed to carry out an absolute statutory duty of a crime with which he was not directly concerned, but still be ready to leave the civil liability untouched.[2511]

II. Consent

440. Consent is unlikely to be accepted as a defence to an action for breach of statutory duty, for reasons of public policy. Certainly a person cannot contract out of the terms of a statute creating criminal or regulatory offences. In *Smythe v. Bayley's Real Estate Ltd*,[2512] concerning the Fair Trading Act 1986, Thomas J observed that in enacting the legislation Parliament sought to protect the consumer from unfair trading, and it would be inconsistent with that objective to permit a person engaged in trade to exempt himself or herself from liability under the Act. So it will generally follow that the other person's consent cannot be a defence where there is a breach of a statute. However, a defence might possibly succeed in the case of a breach of statute not involving any question of public right or public policy.[2513] But identifying cases where no wider element of public policy is involved is likely to be a difficult and uncertain exercise.

III. Contributory Negligence

441. Contributory negligence can be a good defence, even where the duty that is broken is absolute.[2514] So where both parties are at fault, the amount of the damages will be apportioned between them on the basis of what is a just and equitable division.[2515]

2509. *Yelland v. Powell Duffryn Associated Collieries Ltd* [1941] 1 KB 154.
2510. *Sovar v. Henry Lane Pty Ltd* (1967) 116 CLR 397.
2511. *Potts v. Reid* [1943] AC 1 at 31.
2512. (1993) 5 TCLR 454 at 472.
2513. *Connell v. Phoenix Aerated Water Co. Ltd* (1915) 34 NZLR 666 at 676; *Re Tollison* [1924] NZLR 860.
2514. *Dunne v. New Zealand Refrigerating Co. Ltd* [1932] NZLR 1040; *Ralph v. Henderson & Pollard Ltd* [1968] NZLR 759; *Howell v. Caxton Printing Works Ltd* [1971] NZLR 1068.
2515. *See* para. 482.

Chapter 3. Statutory Torts

§1. Introduction

442. Torts are civil wrongs created by the decisions of the courts. They are creatures of the common law. But sometimes the legislature has stepped in and created new causes of action that are similar in nature to common law torts, in that there is a statutory wrong and statutory provision for victims to make claims for compensation from the wrongdoer. Important instances are claims under the Financial Markets Conduct Act 2013, the Fair Trading Act 1986, the Consumer Guarantees Act 1993, the Human Rights Act 1993, and the Privacy Act 1993. Further examples are statutes that confer rights of action in respect of interferences with certain forms of intellectual property, including copyright, designs, patents, and trademarks, but detailed consideration of matters of this kind is outside the scope of a treatise on the principles of tort.

§2. Financial Markets Conduct Act 2013

443. The Financial Markets Conduct Act 2013, replacing the Securities Act 1978, provides, *inter alia*, for: (i) prohibiting misleading or deceptive conduct and false or misleading representations in connection with financial products and financial services; (ii) disclosure to investors and regulating advertisements in relation to certain offers of financial products; (iii) the governance of debt securities and of managed investment products; (iv) prohibiting insider trading and market manipulation; (v) the licensing of certain financial market service providers and imposing conduct obligations on providers of discretionary investment management services; (vi) financial reporting obligations; and (vii) enforcement and liability matters.[2516] Civil liability orders are available for a contravention, or involvement in a contravention, of a civil liability provision,[2517] including (a) a declaration of contravention; (b) a pecuniary penalty order (on application by the Financial Markets Authority (FMA) only); (c) a compensatory order.[2518] As regards the last of these, the court may make a compensatory order, on application by the FMA or any other person, if the court is satisfied that: (a) there is a contravention of a civil liability provision; and (b) a person (the aggrieved person) has suffered, or is likely to suffer, loss or damage because of the contravention.[2519] The court may make any order it thinks just to compensate an aggrieved person in whole or in part for the loss or damage, or to prevent or reduce the loss or damage.[2520] This may include an order

2516. Financial Markets Conduct Act 2013, s. 5.

2517. A civil liability provision is defined as: (a) a Part 2 fair dealing provision; (b) a Part 3 offer provision; (c) a Part 4 governance provision; (d) a Part 5 market provision; (e) an unsolicited offer provision; (f) a Part 6 services provision; (g) a Part 7 financial reporting provisional; (h) failing to comply with the FMA's orders; (i) certain transitional requirements: *Ibid*., s. 485.

2518. *Ibid*., s. 484.

2519. *Ibid*., s. 494.

2520. *Ibid*., s. 495(1).

to direct any person in contravention to pay to the aggrieved person the amount of the loss or damage (in whole or in part).[2521]

§3. Fair Trading Act 1986

444. Section 9 of the Fair Trading Act 1986 prohibits conduct in trade that is misleading or deceptive or is likely to mislead or deceive. Sections 10, 11, and 12 are more specific and prohibit misleading or deceptive conduct in relation to, respectively, goods, services, and employment. Breach of these provisions can give rise to a remedy in damages.[2522] Accordingly, the common law rules governing misstatements are supplemented by this statutory cause of action.[2523]

I. Trade

445. The misleading conduct must be in 'trade'. This means any trade, business, industry, profession, occupation, activity of commerce, or undertaking relating to the supply or acquisition of goods or services or to the disposition or acquisition of any interest in land.[2524] 'Business' is further defined as any undertaking that is carried on whether for gain or reward or not, or in the course of which goods or services are acquired or supplied, or any interest in land is acquired or disposed of, whether free of charge or not.[2525]

Both parties may be in trade. Conduct in trade is not limited to conduct that is directed to consumers,[2526] and section 9 is commonly invoked in disputes between businesses. Regularity in dealing is not essential. Thus, the sale of an asset or of a whole business on a one-off basis can constitute conduct in trade.[2527] On the other hand, conduct that is essentially of a private character is not included.[2528]

Conduct engaged in on behalf of a corporate body by a director, servant, or agent acting within the scope of his or her actual or apparent authority is deemed to have been engaged in also by the body corporate.[2529] So, directors who participate in negotiations on behalf of a company are likely to be regarded as acting in trade,[2530] notwithstanding duty restrictions at common law requiring an assumption of responsibility to a company client.[2531] For example, a director who made a misleading representation about the turnover of a business was personally liable under the

2521. *Ibid.*, s. 495(2)–(4).
2522. *See* para. 447.
2523. *See* further the discussion of passing off, where the Fair Trading Act has particular significance: paras 255–256.
2524. Fair Trading Act 1986, s. 2(1).
2525. *Ibid.*
2526. *Concrete Constructions (NSW) Pty Ltd v. Nelson* (1990) 169 CLR 594.
2527. *Artifakts Design Group Ltd v. NP Rigg Ltd* [1993] 1 NZLR 196 at 223–224; *Gloken Holdings Ltd v. The CDE Co. Ltd* (1997) 8 TCLR 278.
2528. *Council of the Municipality of Woollahra v. Sved* (1996) Aust Torts Reps 81-398.
2529. Fair Trading Act 1986, s. 45(2).
2530. *Magavitamins Laboratories (NZ) Ltd and Stewart v. Commerce Commission* (1995) 6 TCLR 231.
2531. *See* para. 94.

statute.[2532] The decision was criticized, and an indication was given by the Court of Appeal that it might be reconsidered,[2533] but the Court later decided to affirm it.[2534]

II. Misleading or Deceptive Conduct

446. Whether the conduct of the defendant in any particular case is misleading or deceptive is essentially a matter of fact. The question is determined objectively in relation to the section of the public to which any representations or conducts have been directed.[2535] There must be conduct that gives rise to a real, and not a remote, chance that it will mislead or deceive when encountered by reasonable members of a significant section of the public.[2536] In *AMP Finance NZ Ltd v. Heaven*[2537] Tipping J said that there were three steps in determining whether there was a breach of section 9 – whether the conduct was capable of being misleading, whether the plaintiff was in fact misled by the conduct, and whether, objectively, it was in all the circumstances reasonable for the plaintiff to have been misled.[2538] However, in *Red Eagle Corporation Ltd v. Ellis*,[2539] Blanchard J said that the court in *Heaven* had not intended its formulation to apply in every situation and that it was undesirable for the methodology to be too prescriptive. The approach to be taken would vary from case to case. In a simple case the court should ask whether the conduct objectively had the capacity to mislead or deceive the hypothetical reasonable person. It was not necessary to show it did actually mislead or deceive the particular plaintiff. With breach proved, the court should see if the claimant had suffered loss or damage 'by' the conduct of the defendant.[2540] This posed a common law practical or common sense test of causation. The court should ask if the claimant was actually misled and if the defendant's conduct was an operating cause. It need not be the sole cause but should be an effective case. The claimant's own carelessness might also be an operating cause, in which case the court could apportion the loss.[2541]

Conduct can be misleading or deceptive irrespective of the defendant's state of mind. The plaintiff does not have to show an intention to commit a breach of section 9 or knowledge that a breach was likely or negligence in relation to a

2532. *Kinsman v. Cornfields Ltd* (2001) 10 TCLR 342.; and *see Wellington City Council v. Dallas* [2014] NZCA 631.
2533. *Newport v. Coburn* (2006) 11 TCLR 831 at [54]–[56].
2534. *Body Corporate 20254 v. Taylor* [2009] 2 NZLR 17.
2535. *Savill v. NZI Finance Ltd* [1990] 3 NZLR 135 at 146.
2536. *Bonz Group Pty Ltd v. Cooke* (1996) 5 NZBLC 104,188 at 104,194; and *see Godfrey Hirst NZ Ltd v. Cavalier Bremworth Ltd* [2014] 3 NZLR 611.
2537. (1998) 6 NZBLC 102,414 at 102,420.
2538. In *Janus Nominees Ltd v. Fairhall* [2009] 3 NZLR 757 the Court of Appeal emphasized that s. 9 does not provide a guarantee to purchasers who fail to look after their own interests. The instant case concerned a transaction between sophisticated parties who were independently advised, and to impose liability under s. 9 would cut deeply into the principle of caveat emptor.
2539. [2010] 2 NZLR 492.
2540. Fair Trading Act 1986, s. 43(1); *see* para. 447.
2541. *See* para. 447.

breach.[2542] The defendant may be liable even though he or she acted quite innocently. But normally there must at least be a misrepresentation in the sense understood at common law.[2543] The expression of an opinion that subsequently turns out to be incorrect does not, of itself, give rise to liability for misleading or deceptive conduct under section 9. However, the person expressing the opinion represents that he or she honestly holds it, and also (in some cases at least) that he or she has a reasonable basis for the opinion.[2544] Mere non-disclosure will not render a party liable under section 9 unless that party knew the information that had not been disclosed.[2545] Yet innocent half-truths are not simply representations by silence, and the need for deliberate non-disclosure might not be applicable in this case.[2546]

III. Remedies

447. If a person (person A) has suffered, or is likely to suffer, loss or damage by conduct of another person (person B), the court may make an order directing person B to pay to person A the amount of the loss or damage.[2547] In assessing the measure of the compensation, a claim under the statute is treated like a claim in tort. Accordingly, the court makes a comparison between what the position of the plaintiff was or would have been without the contravention and what it was because of the contravention.[2548] In other words, the remedy is for loss resulting from the misleading representation, and the damages are not based on what the position would have been had the representation been true.[2549] Consequential loss is recoverable, and this may include wasted expenditure and trading losses in appropriate cases.[2550] Damages may be reduced if the plaintiff's own culpable conduct or the conduct of others has contributed to the loss.[2551] So the rule of liability in solidum at common law[2552] does not apply to claims under the statute.

2542. *Goldsbro v. Walker* [1993] 1 NZLR 394 at 401; *Bonz Group Pty Ltd v. Cooke* (1996) 5 NZBLC 104,188 at 104,193; *McAlister v. Lai* [2018] NZCA 141 at [26].
2543. *Supra* paras 293–296.
2544. *Premium Real Estate Ltd v. Stevens* [2009] 1 NZLR 148 at [50]–[55]; *David v. TFAC Ltd* [2009] 3 NZLR 239 at [43].
2545. *Des Forges v. Wright* [1996] 2 NZLR 758; *Ladstone Holdings Ltd v. Leonora Holdings Ltd* [2006] 1 NZLR 211.
2546. *Clarkson v. Whangamata Metal Supplies Ltd* HC, Auckland, CIV-2003-404-6869, 8 Jun. 2006.
2547. Fair Trading Act 1986, s. 43(1), (3)(f).
2548. *Cox & Coxon Ltd v. Leipst* [1999] 2 NZLR 15; *Harvey Corporation Ltd v. Baker* [2002] 2 NZLR 213.
2549. *Gavigan v. Eichelbaum* [2017] NZCA 412, [2018] 2 NZLR 530.
2550. *Cox & Coxon Ltd v. Leipst* [1999] 2 NZLR 15 at 28.
2551. *Goldsbro v. Walker* [1993] 1 NZLR 394; *Red Eagle Corporation Ltd v. Ellis* [2010] 2 NZLR 492 at [30]–[31].
2552. *See* para. 581.

IV. Defences

448. The limitation period for claims under the Act is three years from the date on which the loss or damage, or the likelihood of loss or damage, was discovered or should have been discovered.[2553] There is a special defence for business advertisers who publish an advertisement without knowing or having reason to suspect that it contravenes the Act.[2554]

The provisions of the Act have effect despite anything to the contrary in any agreement, and a provision of an agreement that has the effect of overriding a provision of the Act (whether directly or indirectly) is unenforceable.[2555] Before 2014 the Act did not deal specifically with exclusion clauses, but the courts nonetheless recognized that it lays down mandatory standards and that these cannot be avoided by contract or notice. Thomas J has stated that a court cannot allow anyone simply to opt out of a statute decreeing fair trading in the public interest.[2556] However, it has been observed in the Court of Appeal that while that justification has force in relation to consumer transactions, it has less force in the context of commercial transactions involving substantial independently advised parties negotiating from positions of equality.[2557] At all events, an appropriately worded disclaimer may be material to the nature of the alleged misleading and deceptive conduct. For example, if it was made clear that an agent was merely acting as a conduit for someone else's information, then a court might conclude that the agent's conduct was not itself misleading.[2558] Again, a recommendation to take independent advice might be effective in preventing any breach of the Act. In *David v. TFAC Ltd*[2559] the vendor of a franchise in Australia required that the purchasers take advice about its prospects for success in New Zealand, where it was a new venture. The vendor was willing to provide information but did not want to give such advice himself. In these circumstances the court thought it unreasonable for the purchasers simply to rely on assurances they thought they had been given rather than on independent advice from someone experienced in franchising. It is apparent that the kind of argument seen in these cases – in essence that there has been no breach of the Act to begin with – can still be made notwithstanding the new provision preventing contracting out of the Act.

2553. Fair Trading Act 1986, s. 43A. An applicant is not required to have become aware of actual loss or damage as ultimately established; knowledge that some more than minimal loss or damage was likely to have resulted from a probable contravention is sufficient: *Commerce Commission v. Carter Holt Harvey Ltd* [2010] 1 NZLR 370.

2554. *Ibid.*, s. 44(4).

2555. *Ibid.*, s. 5C. There is a limited exception to this rule in the case of parties in trade: s. 5D.

2556. *Smythe v. Bayley's Real Estate Ltd* (1993) 5 TCLR 454 at 471–472; and *see Phyllis Gale Ltd v. Ellicott* (1998) 6 NZBLC 102,445.

2557. *David v. TFAC Ltd* [2009] 2 NZLR 239 at [61].

2558. *Body Corporate 202254 v. Taylor* [2009] 2 NZLR 17; and *see Butcher v. Lachlan Elder Realty Pty Ltd* (2004) 218 CLR 592 at [50]–[51] *McAlister v. Lai* [2018] NZCA 141 at [29].

2559. [2009] 2 NZLR 239; and *see PAE (New Zealand) Ltd v. Brosnahan* (2009) 10 TCLR 626.

§4. Consumer Guarantees Act 1993

I. Application of the Act

449. The normal rules of privity of contract prevent the ultimate purchaser of a defective product from suing the manufacturer simply for breach of a warranty of quality. But, in 1993, Parliament accepted that the common law rules were too restrictive, by passing the Consumer Guarantees Act. Apart from conferring new rights of action on consumers against suppliers,[2560] the Act also gives consumers a direct right of action against manufacturers where their goods fail to measure up to certain statutory guarantees. This right of action is more in the nature of a claim on a non-contractual warranty than a claim in tort.

A 'manufacturer' is a person that carries on the business of assembling, producing, or processing goods, and can include the importer or distributor of the goods.[2561] A 'consumer', broadly, is a person who acquires goods of a kind ordinarily acquired for personal, domestic, or household use or consumption and not for the purposes of trade.[2562] 'Goods' include goods attached to, or incorporated in, real property.[2563] In *Nesbit v. Porter*[2564] the evidence showed 80% use of a multi-use four-wheel-drive utility vehicle for business purposes and 20% use for private purposes. The court held that the majority or dominant purpose was not determinative, and it was necessary to ask whether there was a personal use as a matter of regular practice or in the ordinary or usual course of events or things. It was a question of fact and degree whether goods were ordinarily acquired for personal use when only a proportionately small number was acquired for that purpose, and, on the facts, the Act was held to apply.

II. Right of Redress Against Manufacturers

450. There is a right of redress by a consumer against a manufacturer for failure of the guarantee of acceptable quality[2565] and of correspondence with description where the description was applied by or on behalf of the manufacturer or with the express or implied consent of the manufacturer,[2566] and in certain other cases.[2567] Subject to two qualifications,[2568] the consumer has a remedy in damages. They are calculated by reference to the reduction in value below the price paid or payable by

---

2560. *See International Encyclopaedia of Laws: Contracts (New Zealand)*, paras 314–317.
2561. For the full definition, *see* Consumer Guarantees Act 1993, s. 2.
2562. *Ibid.*
2563. *Ibid.*
2564. [2000] 2 NZLR 465.
2565. Consumer Guarantees Act 1993, ss 6, 25(a).
2566. *Ibid.*, ss 9, 25(b).
2567. *Ibid.*, ss 12, 25(c) (guarantee as to repairs and parts), ss 14, 25(d) (express guarantees in a document in respect of goods).
2568. *Ibid.*, s. 26(a)(i), (ii), 26(b) (failure to comply due to cause occurring after goods have left the control of the manufacturer), s. 26(a)(iii) (failure to comply due to price being higher than manufacturer's recommended retail price or average retail price).

the consumer or below the average retail price of the goods at the time of the supply, whichever is the lower.[2569] The consumer may also recover consequential loss where it was reasonably foreseeable as liable to result from the failure to comply with the guarantee.[2570] The test is similar to that applied in determining the remoteness of damage issue in negligence claims at common law.[2571]

The right of action against the manufacturer is not confined to the consumer who first acquires the goods from the supplier, but extends to any person who later acquires the goods from or through the consumer.[2572] This covers anyone who obtains the goods by way of gift, purchase, or exchange, or takes them on lease, hire, or hire purchase.[2573] However, the remedy does not apply to a person who acquires goods from or through a consumer unless that person also is a 'consumer' within the meaning of the Act.[2574]

It is apparent that the 1993 Act gives a consumer a cause of action against the manufacturer in respect of the diminished value of the chattel. It thus removes any need to resort to the so-called complex structure argument,[2575] whereby a distinction must be drawn between compensation for the defectiveness of a chattel, which is not recoverable in tort, and compensation for damage done by a chattel to separate property in the same structure, which may be. Both can be sued for under the Act. The Act also goes further than the common law in imposing strict liability, where negligence or fault is not a necessary ingredient of the right of action.

As under the Fair Trading Act, damages may be reduced to take account of other contributory causes. The court's power to award the full loss is discretionary, carrying with it the power to award less. Consumers should protect their own interests, and must ensure that their acts or omissions do not contribute to the failure of relevant guarantees. But where a guarantee under the Act is breached and damage results, the consumer is likely to recover his or her reasonably foreseeable losses in full unless the retailer can point to evidence of another contributing cause.[2576]

It is possible that there could be a remedy under the 1993 Act against a manufacturer of the component parts of a building in the case of a claim by the owner or purchaser of a leaky building. In *Carter Holt Harvey Ltd v. Minister of Education* the Court of Appeal[2577] considered that it was not untenable to propose that allegedly defective building cladding was supplied by the manufacturer in a manner bringing it within the ambit of the Act,[2578] and that it was a good to which the Act applied,[2579] and refused to strike out the claim. The plaintiff appealed to the

2569. *Ibid.*, s. 27(1)(a).
2570. *Ibid.*, s. 27(1)(b).
2571. *See* para. 544.
2572. Consumer Guarantees Act 1993, s. 27(1).
2573. *Ibid.*, s. 2.
2574. *Ibid.*, s. 27(3).
2575. *See* para. 119.
2576. *Contact Energy Ltd v. Jones* [2009] 2 NZLR 830 at [129]–[137].
2577. [2015] NZCA 321.
2578. On the basis that the owner was acquiring the cladding for personal use and not for trade or similar purposes: *see* para. 449.
2579. On the basis that the cladding was a good attached to, or incorporated in, real property: *see* para. 449.

Supreme Court but only on the concurrent common law claim,[2580] so the question of the application of the Act awaits final determination.

III. Contracting Out

451. The general rule with manufacturers, as with suppliers, is that any agreement purporting to contract out of the provisions of the Act is ineffective.[2581] However, two parties in trade may agree in writing to contract out of the provisions of the Act, and provided that such agreement is fair and reasonable they are bound by it.[2582] In this case the benefit of the exclusion is available to the manufacturer as well.[2583]

§5. Human Rights Act 1993

452. A person who has made a complaint of unlawful discrimination under the Human Rights Act 1993 may bring civil proceedings before the Human Rights Tribunal, and may seek relief by way of a number of remedies, including a declaration, a restraining order, and damages.[2584] As regards damages, the tribunal may award compensation for pecuniary loss and expenses caused by the breach, the loss of any benefit, whether or not of a monetary kind, that the complainant might reasonably have been expected to obtain but for the breach, and humiliation, loss of dignity, and injury to the feelings of the complainant.[2585]

§6. Privacy Act 1993

453. An aggrieved individual may bring proceedings before the Human Rights Tribunal against an 'agency'[2586] alleging breach of certain information privacy principles concerning, broadly, the collection, storage and security of personal information as laid down by the Privacy Act 1993.[2587] If satisfied that any action of the defendant is an interference with the privacy of an individual, the tribunal may grant a declaration, a restraining order or damages, or require remedial action.[2588] As with complaints of discrimination, the tribunal may award compensation for pecuniary

2580. [2016] NZSC 95, [2017] 1 NZLR 78; *see* para. 131.
2581. *Ibid.*, s. 43(1).
2582. *Ibid.*, s. 43(2).
2583. *Ibid.*, s. 43(5).
2584. Human Rights Act 1993, s. 92B, 92I.
2585. *Ibid.*, s. 92M.
2586. An 'agency' means any person or body of persons, whether corporate or unincorporated, and whether in the public or private sector, but subject to certain exceptions: Privacy Act 1993, s. 2(1)(a), (b) (definition of 'agency'). For exemptions *see* ss 54–57.
2587. *Ibid.*, s. 83. The twelve information privacy principles are set out in s. 6. The Privacy Act 1993 is shortly to be repealed and replaced by the Privacy Act 2020. The new Act comes into force on 1 Dec. 2020: Privacy Act 2020, s. 2(2).
2588. *Ibid.*, s. 85.

loss and expenses caused by the breach, the loss of any benefit, whether or not of a monetary kind, that the complainant might reasonably have been expected to obtain but for the breach, and humiliation, loss of dignity, and injury to the feelings of the aggrieved person.[2589]

2589. *Ibid.*, s. 88.

Part IV. Defences

Chapter 1. Limitation of Actions

§1. Introduction: The Limitation Act 1950

454. The Limitation Act 1950 lays down the time limits for the bringing of civil actions in New Zealand. In particular, section 4(1) provides that an action in tort shall not be brought after the expiration of six years from the date on which the cause of action accrued. The general rule is qualified where the plaintiff is under a disability[2590] or where the right of action has been concealed by fraud on the part of the defendant.[2591] In addition, some particular types of proceedings have special rules of their own.[2592]

Limitation principles embody a tension between competing policies of (1) finality in civil litigation and that defendants should have the opportunity to avoid meeting stale claims, and (2) justice being done in the individual case, which is secured by the facility for extension or postponement of the limitation periods.[2593] However, the 1950 Act can be criticized for failing to achieve an appropriate balance between these objectives. In particular, as will be seen, the impact of the Act is uncertain in some critical aspects, and is capable of causing serious injustice. Following calls for parliamentary intervention,[2594] wide-ranging reform was achieved with the passing of the Limitation Act 2010.[2595] The Act came into force on 1 January 2011.[2596] However, the 1950 Act continues to apply to claims based on acts or omissions before that date, but these must be brought by the later of fifteen years

2590. *See* para. 462.
2591. *See* para. 463.
2592. *See* paras 464–466.
2593. *Amaltal Corporation Ltd v. Maruha Corporation* [2007] 1 NZLR 608 at [147] (on appeal [2007] 3 NZLR 192 (SC)).
2594. *See*, in particular, *Murray v. Morel & Co Ltd* [2007] 3 NZLR 721 at [76].
2595. The Act is based substantially on the recommendations of the NZ Law Commission; *see Limitation Defences in Civil Proceedings*, NZLC R6 (1988); *Tidying the Limitation Act* NZLC R 61 (2000); *Limitation Defenses in Civil Cases: Update Report for the Law Commission* NZLC MP 16 (2007).
2596. Limitation Act 2010, s. 2.

after the date of the relevant act or omission or five years after the date of commencement of the new Act.[2597] So the 1950 Act and the 2010 Act are going to be operating side by side for up to fifteen years (and, it may be, in some exceptional cases for even longer). Accordingly, in the discussion below, we will look first at the existing law under the 1950 Act, and then at the provisions of the 2010 Act.

Under both Acts, and save in one particular case,[2598] the limitation defence bars the remedy but does not affect substantive rights. Accordingly, an action may be brought after the prescribed period and can (subject to the merits) succeed unless the defendant establishes the defence.[2599] The principle that he who alleges must prove applies, so the onus is on the defendant to show that the limitation period has expired.[2600] The defendant may seek to have the action struck out, by showing that the cause of action is so clearly statute barred that the plaintiff's claim can properly be regarded as frivolous, vexatious or an abuse of process. However, the plaintiff may be able to show that there is an arguable case for extension of the ordinary limitation period or postponement of that period (on bases to be considered) which would bring the claim back within time,[2601] but preliminary determination of the issue is not normally favoured. The Court of Appeal has held that, unless clear cut, limitation defences are best determined at trial on full evidence and that, if leave is required, it should be given in doubtful cases but without prejudice to the limitation point being raised at trial.[2602]

§2. Conversion and Detinue

455. The expiry of the limitation period can affect substantive rights in the case of claims for conversion or detinue. A cause of action for conversion accrues from the date of the conversion irrespective of whether the owner knows the identity of the converter,[2603] and in detinue from the date of the refusal of a lawful demand for the chattel.[2604] However, once the cause of action for conversion or detention has accrued, then unless the owner has first recovered possession of the chattel no fresh action can be brought for any further conversion after the expiry of six years from the accrual of the original cause of action.[2605] Furthermore, where the six-year period in respect of the original cause of action, and of any such further conversion or detention, has expired without any action having been commenced, the owner's title is extinguished.[2606] These provisions may operate to protect even a thief or a person who takes in bad faith. However, where goods have been stolen and the

2597. *Ibid.*, s. 23B.
2598. *See* para. 455.
2599. *AMP Finance NZ Ltd v. Heaven* (1997) 8 TCLR 144 at 154.
2600. *Humphrey v. Fairweather* [1993] 3 NZLR 91.
2601. *Matai Industries Ltd v. Jensen* [1989] 1 NZLR 525; *Murray v. Morel & Co. Ltd* [2007] 3 NZLR 721 at [33].
2602. *W v. Attorney-General* [1999] 2 NZLR 709.
2603. *White v. Taupo Totara Timber Co.* [1960] NZLR 547 at 550.
2604. *Miller v. Dell* [1891] 1 QB 468.
2605. Limitation Act 1950, s. 5(1).
2606. *Ibid.*, s. 5(2).

offender is prosecuted to a conviction, the property in the goods revests in the person who was the owner, notwithstanding any intermediate dealing with them.[2607] A criminal court also has a general power to make an order for the restitution of stolen property.[2608] Furthermore, and quite apart from any criminal proceedings, the prescribed period of limitation may be extended where the plaintiff's action is based on the defendant's fraud or the right of action is concealed by fraud.[2609]

§3. Accrual of the Cause of Action

I. General

456. The period of limitation runs from the date on which the cause of action accrued. This has been said to be when every fact exists that it would be necessary for the plaintiff to prove in order to support his or her right to the judgment of the court.[2610] In an action for breach of contract,[2611] and in an action for a tort that is actionable per se, like trespass to the person,[2612] a long-standing view is that the cause of action accrues at the moment when the wrongful act is committed. The time that any damage occurs is not material. However, where a tort is actionable only on proof of damage, as in negligence and nuisance, the date of the wrongful act is not material and the general rule is that time runs from the date of that damage.[2613] Whether actual damage has happened is a question of fact in each case.

Cases involving building defects, or damage by way of physical or mental injury, on the face of it take a different approach. In these, the courts have developed rules that require that the plaintiff knows or ought to know of the facts necessary to establish his or her cause of action. Drawing on these cases, some first instance decisions accepted that knowledge or reasonable discoverability of the facts was necessary in all other circumstances before a cause of action was deemed to accrue.[2614] However, in *Murray v. Morel & Co.*[2615] the Supreme Court rejected this view, holding that the building defects cases could be justified on ordinary principle,[2616] and that physical or mental injury cases were in a category of their own.[2617] Tipping J noted

2607. Contract and Commercial Law Act 2017, s. 152(1). Property does not revest in the person who was the owner where the goods were obtained by fraud or other wrongful means not amounting to theft: s. 152(2).

2608. Crimes Act 1961, s. 404(1).

2609. *See* para. 463.

2610. *Williams v. A-G* [1990] 1 NZLR 646 at 678; *Hunt v. New Plymouth District Council* [2011] NZCA 406 at [72].

2611. *White v. Taupo Totara Timber Co.* [1960] NZLR 547; *Stuart v. Australian Guarantee Corporation (NZ) Ltd* (2002) 16 PRNZ 139.

2612. *Buxton v. McKenzie* [1960] NZLR 732 at 735; *T v. H* [1995] 3 NZLR 37 at 45.

2613. *Byrne v. Judd* (1908) 27 NZLR 1106; *T v. H ibid.*

2614. *BP Oil New Zealand Ltd v. Ports of Auckland Ltd* [2004] 2 NZLR 208; *Bomac Laboratories Ltd v. F Hoffman-La-Roche Ltd* (2002) 7 NZBLC 103,627 at [172]; cp *Saunders & Co. v. Bank of New Zealand* [2002] 2 NZLR 270; *Stuart v. Australian Guarantee Corporation (NZ) Ltd* (2002) 16 PRNZ 139.

2615. [2007] 3 NZLR 721.

2616. *See* para. 458.

2617. *See* paras 459–460.

that the long-established meaning of accrual related to the occurrence of all material facts rather than knowledge of them. The Limitation Act as a whole was structured around that fundamental starting point. Time limits were imposed from accrual, and circumstances of postponement of accrual or extension of time for suing, as in the case of fraud and mistake, were then engrafted. Some considerable straining of the core concept had occurred to cope with what the courts had regarded as particularly necessitous individual circumstances. But the introduction of discoverability as a general principle would be to alter in a substantial way the balance that Parliament had struck between the interests of plaintiffs and defendants.

II. Date of the Damage

457. In cases involving loss of or physical damage to property, the limitation period starts to run from the time when that loss or damage actually happens. This may be the time of the defendant's conduct or some later time. For example, where a pipe in a chemicals factory cracked for an unknown reason, was repaired and later cracked again resulting in an explosion damaging the plant, it was held that the cause of action accrued at the time of the explosion rather than the initial cracking.[2618] Again, where there is continuing conduct causing physical damage, each fresh continuance gives rise to a fresh cause of action. So too, if distinct damage occurs on different occasions, a fresh cause of action arises each time damage occurs. Applying the principle, a defendant who has withdrawn support from the plaintiff's land is liable on a fresh cause of action each time a slip thereafter happens.[2619] Where damage to a building is caused by the original building work, and the owner's claim in respect of this work is statute barred, and concurrent damage is caused by later prevention work, and a claim for this work is not barred, the owner can seek to establish how much of the total loss is properly to be attributed to the failure of the prevention work.[2620]

In claims for economic loss the same principle applies, but determining exactly when financial damage happens may not be easy. In the case of a negligent statement, it may be the date when the plaintiff relies on the words to his or her detriment.[2621] But many of the cases involve a notional or potential loss, or a contingency that may or may not happen. Some English decisions hold, in effect, that the plaintiff suffers loss when he or she is put at risk of a loss. For example, a client who acted on a solicitor's allegedly negligent advice by executing a mortgage as surety for her son's debts suffered damage and had a cause of action at that time, even though she was not required to pay the debts for another two years.[2622] But

2618. *Nitrigin Eireann Teoranta v. Inco Alloys Ltd* [1992] 1 WLR 498.

2619. *Darley Main Colliery Co. v. Mitchell* (1856) 11 App Cas 127; *Bowen v. Paramount Builders (Hamilton) Ltd* [1977] 1 NZLR 394 at 424; *Mount Albert Borough Council v. Johnson* [1979] 2 NZLR 234.

2620. *Johnson v. Watson* [2003] 1 NZLR 626.

2621. *Hunt v. New Plymouth District Council* HC, New Plymouth, CIV-2006-043-435, 26/10/10, J. Mallon (date of alleged over-payment for property).

2622. *Forster v. Outred & Co.* [1982] 1 WLR 86; *DW Moore & Co. Ltd v. Ferrier* [1988] 1 WLR 267; *Bell v. Peter Browne & Co.* [1990] 2 QB 495; *Islander Trucking Ltd v. Hogg Robinson Gardner*

other cases point to the need for the plaintiff to have suffered actual loss. For example, a negligent valuation on the basis of which a lender entered into a loan transaction could not be said to have caused loss while there were means of recouping the loan, so a writ issued within six years of the end of that period, although more than six years from the date of the advance, was within time.[2623] Again, negligence by accountants in certifying a solicitor's fraudulent accounts put the Law Society at risk of a liability to make payments to defrauded clients out of the Solicitors' Compensation Fund, but until a claim was actually made no loss or damage was sustained by the Fund.[2624]

Some first instance decisions in New Zealand favour the second approach.[2625] In *Gilbert v. Shanahan*[2626] the Court of Appeal examined the question and drew a distinction between present and contingent liabilities.[2627] Tipping J, delivering the judgment of the court, said that if a liability is subject to a condition or contingency that may or may not be fulfilled, it appeared more satisfactory for limitation purposes to say that the debtor had suffered no loss or damage unless and until an event occurred that converted the liability from a potential to an actual liability. On the other hand, if there was a present liability there would be loss or damage when it was incurred, notwithstanding that it might not be dischargeable until a future date. In the instant case, a client sued a solicitor for negligent advice allowing him to sign a guarantee of his company's obligations. The guarantee rendered the client a principal debtor, so the liabilities assumed on signing were present rather than prospective and the cause of action accrued at that time.

The distinction between an actual and a potential or contingent loss is well illustrated by the decision of the Supreme Court in *Thom v. Davys Burton*.[2628] It was held here that the plaintiff suffered immediate loss through the negligence of his solicitor when he married his wife without the protection of a valid agreement contracting out of the shared property provisions of the Matrimonial Property Act 1976. He did not get what he should have got, and his assets were diminished by an existing liability through the attachment of the matrimonial property regime.

Mountain (Marine) Ltd [1990] 1 All ER 826; *Iron Trade Mutual Insurance Co. Ltd v. JK Buckenham Ltd* [1990] 1 All ER 808; *Axa Insurance Ltd v. Akther & Darby Solicitors* [2010] 1 WLR 1662.

2623. *First National Commercial Bank plc v. Humberts* [1995] 2 All ER 673.

2624. *Law Society v. Sephton & Co.* [2006] 2 WLR 1091.

2625. *Broadcasting Corporation of New Zealand v. Progeni International Ltd* [1990] 1 NZLR 109; *Matthews Corporation Ltd v. Edward Lumley & Sons (NZ) Ltd* (1995) 8 PRNZ 388; *Rabadan v. Gale* [1996] 3 NZLR 220.

2626. [1998] 3 NZLR 528; and *see Stratford v. Phillips Shayle-George* (2001) 15 PRNZ 573.

2627. *See also* the distinction drawn by the Privy Council in *Maharaj v. Johnson* [2015] UKPC 28 between 'flawed transaction' cases and 'no transaction' cases.

2628. [2009] 1 NZLR 437; and *see Roose v. Duthie* [2016] NZCA 600. In nearly all of the decisions there has been immediate loss of some kind: *see*, for example, *Lane v. Cullens Solicitors* [2012] QB 693; *Green v. Eadie* [2012] Ch 363; *Edehomo v. Edehomo* [2011] 1 WLR 2217; *Axa Insurance Ltd v. Akther & Darby* [2010] 1 WLR 1662; *Frucor Beverages Ltd v. Blumberg* [2019] NZCA 547, [2020] 2 NZLR 51 at [46]-[51].

III. Latent Defects in Property

458. The uncertainties involved in determining the date when damage is suffered are well illustrated in cases involving claims by purchasers against builders or local authorities in respect of latent defects in property. In England, the House of Lords held initially that time ran from the date of physical damage to the property. So a claim against engineers in respect of the negligent design of a chimney was barred in circumstances where physical cracking to the chimney had started at some time outside the six-year period, even though not discovered at that time.[2629] But this decision overlooked the true nature of the damage. In *Invercargill City Council v. Hamlin*,[2630] a New Zealand case taken on appeal to the Privy Council, Lord Lloyd drew attention to *Murphy v. Brentwood DC*,[2631] where the House of Lords held that the owner of a house that was found to contain defects sued not for physical damage to the house or foundations but for a financial loss.[2632] His Lordship said that once this point was appreciated the difficulties surrounding the limitation question fell away. The plaintiff's loss occurred when the market value of the house was depreciated by reason of the defective foundations. If he or she resold the house at full value before the defect was discovered, he or she suffered no loss. Thus, in the common case, the occurrence of the loss and the discovery of the loss would coincide. The plaintiff could not postpone the start of the limitation period by shutting his or her eyes to the obvious. The cause of action accrued when the cracks become so bad, or the defects so obvious, that any reasonable homeowner would call in an expert. Accordingly, in this type of case, the date of discoverability is also the date of the damage.

Suppose now that a house is sold after a defect is discoverable, yet the purchaser does not in fact discover it and pays the house's undamaged value. In several decisions it was held that the cause of action accrued only to the owner when the damage appeared or was reasonably discoverable.[2633] On this view the purchaser's cause of action, if any, would be against the vendor, yet caveat emptor probably would apply unless, perhaps, there was deliberate concealment by the vendor amounting to a deceitful misrepresentation.[2634] However, in *Sunset Terraces*[2635] the Supreme Court held that there was no reason to absolve a negligent council from its liability to a subsequent owner simply because the owner's predecessor was also able to sue. A complete bar as a result of the first owner having an accrued right of action was seen as too draconian and blunt an approach to resolving the problem. So the court recognized a duty owed by the council which is owed to the owner for the time

2629. *Pirelli General Cable Works Ltd v. Oscar Faber & Partners* [1983] 2 AC 1.
2630. [1996] 1 NZLR 513.
2631. [1991] 1 AC 398.
2632. *See* para. 119.
2633. *See* in particular *Sparham-Souter v. Town and Country Developments (Essex) Ltd* [1976] QB 858 at 868; *Mount Albert BC v. Johnson* [1979] 2 NZLR 234 at 242.
2634. *Gordon v. Selico* (1986) 18 HLR 219; *Sutherland v. Kao* HC, Auckland, CIV-2006-404-5990, 8-8-08.
2635. [2011] 2 NZLR 289; *see* para. 121.

being even after a defect is discoverable or has actually been discovered by the previous owner. However, the decision can lead to difficulties, for it means that a new limitation period might commence on every sale.

Applying a discoverability principle also can open the way to claims being made against builders or local authorities long after their work has been completed. However, a longstop period has been imposed by statute. Section 393(2) of the Building Act 2004 (re-enacting section 91(2) of the Building Act 1991) provides that civil proceedings relating to any building work[2636] may not be brought against any person after ten years or more from the date of the act or omission on which the proceedings are based. This time limit is neither extended by a discoverability principle nor by the fraud and concealment provisions in section 28 of the Limitation Act.[2637] Section 393(2) is a statutory bar that is self-contained, both as to the commencement of the period allowed and its duration.[2638]

The date of the act or omission from which time starts to run is not necessarily the date of negligent building work. So where a vendor warranted that work on a house was carried out in compliance with the 1991 Act, the basis of the proceeding was the act of warranting that previous building work was compliant, not the building work itself. Entry into the sale and purchase agreement gave rise to a contractual relationship between the parties, and the limitation period and the longstop period commenced to run at the same point in time.[2639]

The ten-year long stop means that questions as to the date of accrual of the cause of action under the Limitation Act 1950 in building cases can no longer arise from 1 January 2021, as the different principles in the Limitation Act 2010 apply to all relevant acts or omissions from 1 January 2011.[2640]

IV. Personal Injuries

459. Claims for personal injuries are ordinarily covered by the Accident Compensation Act 2001 and accordingly they cannot be litigated at common law. Yet actions may still be brought in respect of, *inter alia*, injury by disease, mental injury, heart attacks and strokes, as well as where the plaintiff seeks exemplary damages.[2641] In these cases it is still necessary to determine the date on which the cause of action accrued.

Initially the 'date of damage' rule was applied. In England, in *Cartledge v. E Jopling & Sons Ltd*,[2642] a cause of action for injury by pneumoconiosis accrued

---

2636. This means work associated with an *individual* building: *North Shore City Council v. Attorney-General* [2012] NZSC 49, [2012] 3 NZLR 341 [*The Grange*] at [205]–[210]. It does not cover defective building materials: *Carter Holt Harvey Ltd v. Minister of Education* [2016] NZSC 95, [2017] 1 NZLR 78 at [86]-[103].

2637. As to which *see* para. 463.

2638. *Johnson v. Watson* [2003] 1 NZLR 626. The section applies to claims for contribution (as to which *see* para. 454); *Body Corporate 88863 v. Pimento Holdings Ltd* [2012] NZHC 2225 at [21].

2639. *Gedye v. South* [2010] 3 NZLR 271.

2640. *See* para. 454. For the principles of the Limitation Act 2010, *see* paras 469-474.

2641. *See* para. 42.

2642. [1963] AC 758.

when damage by scarring of the lung tissue from inhaling silica dust must have occurred, although the plaintiff did not find out about the injury until much later. Unlike in the defective property cases, this damage existed even though it had not been discovered. The plaintiff's action was commenced more than six years after the date of the unknown damage and accordingly was held to be barred.

Cartledge well illustrates the injustice that the date of damage rule can cause. In England, the decision was quickly reversed by legislation bringing into account the plaintiff's date of knowledge of an injury and its cause. In New Zealand, a discoverability principle was introduced by judicial decision. In *G D Searle & Co. v. Gunn*,[2643] the plaintiff sued the manufacturer and distributor of an intrauterine device, alleging that it had caused her to contract pelvic inflammatory disease and to become infertile. Proceedings were filed shortly after the plaintiff became aware that the disease may have been caused by the IUD, but more than ten years after its onset. The Court of Appeal held that the cause of action accrued when bodily injury of the kind complained of was discovered or was reasonably discoverable as having been caused by the acts or omissions of the defendant. To hold that a plaintiff who had not discovered that a bodily injury was attributable to the wrongful action of another, and who could not reasonably have discovered that fact, was barred from suit if the injury in fact occurred outside the statutory period would be effectively to deny that person a right of action.

V. Sexual Abuse Cases

460. The discoverability principle also has been applied and refined in a series of decisions involving sexual abuse. This development started in the decision of the Court of Appeal in *S v. G*,[2644] where Gault J held that where damage was an element of the cause of action the reasonable discoverability of the link between psychological harm and past sexual abuse might be employed to determine the accrual of the cause of action. The question as to the extent to which this test can take account of the subjective characteristics of the particular plaintiff was subsequently considered by the Court of Appeal in *W v. Attorney-General.*[2645] Tipping J concluded that the correct approach was to ask when the intending plaintiff did in fact make the link between the abuse and the harm and then, if it was asserted that the link should have been made earlier, to examine the circumstances of the intending plaintiff and to ask whether in those circumstances the link should have been made earlier, and, if so, when. Salmon J thought similarly, whereas Thomas J, in a minority view, favoured an essentially subjective approach, simply asking when the victim did in fact make the connection.

In the case of torts that are actionable per se, like assault and battery, the cause of action accrues at a different time. In *S v. G* Gault J considered that if a principle of reasonable discoverability was to be applied, the relevant time was when the victim should reasonably have recognized that she lacked true consent to the conduct.

2643. [1996] 2 NZLR 129.
2644. [1995] 3 NZLR 681.
2645. [1999] 2 NZLR 709.

Subsequently, in *P v. T*,[2646] the Court of Appeal affirmed that knowledge of lack of consent was the appropriate test. So where a victim of sexual abuse remained for many years unable fully to confront and address his experience of child abuse, but he remembered what had been done to him and knew that it was wrong and that he had not consented to it, his cause of action accrued when he must have been aware that he had always had a right not to consent. It was irrelevant that he may have had no appreciation of the damage thereby caused to him.[2647] Again, any continuing damage is irrelevant. So a cause of action accrued to a plaintiff who was fully aware that sexual abuse during childhood had caused her continuing psychological problems, but who had refrained from suing for more than twenty years after the abuse had ended through fear of the abuser.[2648]

In *Murray v. Morel & Co. Ltd*[2649] the majority view in the Supreme Court was that *Searle* and *S v. G* were exceptional cases that were designed to deal with special problems in personal injury litigation. They should be given no wider significance.

VI. Contribution Between Tortfeasors

461. A cause of action in respect of a claim for contribution is deemed to have accrued at the first point in time when everything has happened that would have to be proved to enable judgment to be obtained for a sum of money in respect of the claim.[2650] This is the date on which the liability of the defendant making the contribution claim has been ascertained, either by judgment in or by settlement of the action against that defendant.[2651] He or she then has six years in which to make a claim against any other tortfeasor liable in respect of the same damage. It is immaterial whether a separate action by the plaintiff against that tortfeasor is or might be statute barred when the contribution proceedings are commenced. This is because the statutory liability to make contribution arises where that tortfeasor 'is, or would if sued in time have been, liable in respect of the same damage'.[2652] The words 'if sued in time' mean that the supposed action must be treated as having been brought within time, whether or not some limitation as to time might otherwise apply.[2653]

§4. Plaintiff's Disability

462. Where a claim is brought by a person under a disability, section 24 of the Limitation Act 1950 provides that his or her right of action is deemed to accrue only

2646. [1998] 1 NZLR 257.
2647. *S v. Attorney-General* [2003] 3 NZLR 450. *See* para. 462 for the further question as to whether the period could be extended on the ground of the plaintiff's disability.
2648. *T v. H* [1995] 3 NZLR 37.
2649. [2007] 3 NZLR 721.
2650. Limitation Act 1950, s. 14.
2651. *Maloney v. Mullan* [1963] NZLR 865; *Steele v. LF Grey Ltd* [1972] NZLR 498.
2652. Law Reform Act 1936, s. 17(1)(c); *see* para. 586.
2653. *Campbell v. Jenkins* [1974] 1 NZLR 578 at 582.

when he or she ceased to be under a disability or died, whichever event first occurred. It is apparent that where this provision applies, the period of limitation may be subject to long or, in the case of unsoundness of mind, indefinite extension. Indeed, the person under a disability can bring his or her action at any time within the extended period, however great the delay and whatever the reason for it.[2654]

A person is deemed to be 'under a disability' while he or she is an infant or of unsound mind.[2655] An infant is a person who has not attained the age of 20.[2656] A person is conclusively presumed to be of unsound mind while he or she is detained under any provision of the Mental Health (Compulsory Assessment and Treatment) Act 1992.[2657] The Limitation Act does not purport to give an exhaustive definition of disability, but in *T v. H*[2658] Hardie Boys J thought that it was unlikely that it went beyond the two deemed circumstances. Thus it did not extend to physical disability, or mental incapacity short of unsoundness of mind. This view is commonly accepted, but in *W v. Attorney-General*[2659] Thomas J took a broader approach. His Honour questioned why it was necessary to conclude that infancy and unsoundness of mind were the only circumstances covered by a 'disability'. The wording of the Act did not require that construction. He thought that it should be enough that the plaintiff was a person who for a clearly established psychological reason was disabled from instructing a solicitor and commencing proceedings.

In *T v. H*[2660] Hardie Boys J thought that the test for when a person was of unsound mind was whether the person was capable of managing his or her affairs at the relevant time. His Honour favoured a compartmentalized approach to the question, so a person who was capable of managing his or her affairs in some respects, but for a recognized psychiatric or psychological cause was incapable of managing them in other relevant respects, could be regarded as of unsound mind for the purposes of the Act in the latter respects. Tipping J, who was of a similar view, stressed that the plaintiff must show a demonstrable and recognized mental illness or disability rather than just an inability to face up to the process of suing.

The decisions of the Court of Appeal in *S v. Attorney-General*[2661] and *W v. Attorney-General*[2662] fall on either side of the line. In *S* the victim of sexual abuse that had caused post-traumatic stress disorder possessed skills that enabled him to function, somewhat erratically, in employment and to pass some exams. But the evidence showed that such a person could function well in areas of life that did not require the person to face the abuse, and it was held that he was nonetheless suffering from a disability. In *W*, on the other hand, the court concluded that it had not been shown that the plaintiff, another victim of sexual abuse, was suffering from a disability that prevented her from bringing a claim for assault and battery. She may

---

2654. *See Tolley v. Morris* [1979] 1 WLR 592.
2655. Limitation Act 1950, s. 2(2).
2656. Age of Majority Act 1970, s. 4. In the case of contracts made by minors, the age is 18: Contract and Commercial Law Act 2017, s. 85.
2657. Limitation Act 1950, s. 2(3).
2658. [1995] 3 NZLR 37 at 47–50; *P v. T* [1998] 1 NZLR 257 at 260.
2659. [1999] 2 NZLR 709 at 731.
2660. [1995] 3 NZLR 37 at 47–50.
2661. [2003] 3 NZLR 450.
2662. CA 227/02, 15 Jul. 2003.

have been inhibited to an extent that would have made it difficult for her to pursue litigation, but that was not enough to disable her from suing.

§5. Fraud and Concealment

463. The running of time is postponed in cases of fraud and concealment. Section 28 of the Limitation Act 1950 provides, *inter alia*, that (a) where an action is based upon the fraud of the defendant or his agent, or (b) the right of action is concealed by the fraud of the defendant or his agent, the period of limitation shall not begin to run until the plaintiff has discovered the fraud or could with reasonable diligence have discovered it.[2663] The onus of proof is on the plaintiff to show that the accrual of the cause of action ought to be extended to within the period.[2664]

Paragraph (a) covers the tort of deceit.[2665] Paragraph (b) covers causes of action other than fraud but where the right of action has been 'concealed by fraud'. In this context 'fraud' covers deliberate or reckless concealment of a cause of action. Examples are a builder knowingly laying defective foundations and then deliberately covering the work up so that the defect is hidden,[2666] or a person sexually abusing a child but concealing the abusive nature of the conduct.[2667] But there is no deliberate concealment where an actor fails to disclose a negligent breach of duty that he was not aware of committing.[2668] A right of action also may be concealed by 'equitable fraud'. In *Inca Ltd v. Autoscript (New Zealand) Ltd*,[2669] Mahon J held that this covered wilful non-disclosure in breach of either a fiduciary duty or a special duty of disclosure inherent in the contract made by the parties or in some other legal relationship to which they had become committed. In other cases, where there was no actual fraud and no special duty, non-disclosure of a cause of action, no matter how 'unconscionable', would not stop the statute running.

Where section 28 applies, the running of the limitation period is postponed until the plaintiff has discovered the fraud or could with 'reasonable diligence' have discovered it. In *Paragon Finance plc v. DB Thakerar & Co.*,[2670] a commercial fraud case, the Court of Appeal in England held that the test was how a person carrying on a business of the relevant kind would act if he had adequate but not unlimited staff and resources and was motivated by a reasonable but not excessive sense of

2663. The running of time in an action to recover property is not suspended as against a bona fide purchaser for value where the property has been converted by a tortfeasor guilty of concealed fraud: Limitation Act 1950, s. 28(d).

2664. *Johnson v. Watson* [2003] 1 NZLR 626.

2665. *Amaltal Corporation Ltd v. Maruha Corporation* [2007] 1 NZLR 608 at [149] (on appeal [2007] 3 NZLR 192 (SC)).

2666. *Inca Ltd v. Autoscript (New Zealand) Ltd* [1979] 2 NZLR 700 at 707.

2667. *S v. G* [1995] 3 NZLR 681.

2668. *Cave v. Robinson, Jarvis & Rolf* [2003] 1 AC 384, interpreting 'deliberate concealment' in the context of limitation legislation in England.

2669. [1979] 2 NZLR 700; *Official Assignee of Collier v. Creighton* [1993] 2 NZLR 534 (CA) (appeal dismissed (1996) 3 NZ ConvC 192, 355 (PC)).; *Brinsdon v. Beazley* [2019] NZHC 808 at [36]-[65].

2670. [1999] 1 All ER 400.

urgency. In *Amaltal Corporation Ltd v. Maruha Corporation*[2671] Hammond J confirmed that what is required is reasonable diligence – not exceptional diligence – and that the *Paragon* test was simply an articulation of the 'reasonableness' standard.

A problem arises with the wording of the statute where a defendant conceals a cause of action not at the outset but at some time after it has accrued. It can be argued that the provision that the period 'shall not begin to run' shows that paragraph (b) is not intended to apply once the period of limitation has already started to run, and hence time will continue to run. On this view a concealment occurring at any time after the accrual of the cause of action results in the plaintiff gaining no protection from section 28. However, in *Sheldon v. RHM Outhwaite Ltd*[2672] the House of Lords held by a majority that the concealment provisions in similar legislation in England were not restricted to concealment contemporaneous with the cause of action. The provision that time 'shall not begin to run' could apply literally in relation to a subsequent concealment, so time started to run only when the concealment was or should have been discovered by the plaintiff. On this view the defendant is deprived of the benefit of time that has already run in his or her favour before any concealment.

§6. Special Periods of Limitation

464. The normal six-year period for actions in tort applies 'except as otherwise provided in [the] Act'.[2673] The period is modified in the case of claims in respect of personal injuries and for defamation. The Limitation Act as a whole does not apply to any action for which a period of limitation is prescribed by any other enactment.[2674] There are a number of statutory causes of action equivalent to proceedings in tort which are subject to special time limits.[2675] In these latter cases, any qualifications on the running of time contained in the 1950 Act are excluded and the relevant rules must be found only in the statute in question.

I. Claims for Personal Injuries

465. Where a claim at common law is still possible, notwithstanding the accident compensation legislation, section 4(7) of the Limitation Act 1950 applies. This provides that actions in respect of bodily injury must be brought within two years of the date on which the cause of action accrued, unless the intended defendant consents to it being brought within six years from that date. However, application may be made to the court, after notice to the intended defendant, for leave to bring the

2671. [2007] 1 NZLR 608 at [155]–[161] (on appeal [2007] 3 NZLR 192 (SC)).
2672. [1996] 1 AC 102. This also is the law in New Zealand: *Roose v. Duthie* [2016] NZCA 600 at [58].
2673. Limitation Act 1950, s. 4(1).
2674. *Ibid.*, s. 33.
2675. *See*, for example, the Fair Trading Act 1986, s. 43(A); Maritime Transport Act 1994, ss 97, 361; Civil Aviation Act 1990, ss. 91I, 91ZL; Contract and Commercial Law Act 2017, ss 278–280 (carriage of Goods).

action at any time within six years from the date when the cause of action accrued, and the court may, if it thinks it just to do so, grant leave accordingly where it considers the delay was caused by mistake of fact or law or by any other reasonable cause or that the intended defendant was not materially prejudiced by the delay. A similar scheme applies to actions in respect of the death of another under the (largely obsolete) Deaths by Accidents Compensation Act 1952.[2676] Insofar as a burden of proof is involved, the onus falls on the plaintiff bringing the application to satisfy the court that it would be just to grant it.[2677]

'Bodily injury' is not defined in the Limitation Act, but it is probably interchangeable with 'personal injury' and clearly it includes actual psychiatric injury.[2678] The question is whether an action, however framed, is in respect of bodily injury.[2679] The proceedings need not be solely concerned with the injury. So proceedings involving bodily injury but founded in part on trespass (which is actionable per se) and breach of fiduciary duty must still meet the section 4(7) requirements.[2680] Equally, a claim for exemplary damages is a claim to a remedy, not a cause of action. Where the damage alleged is bodily injury, the subsection applies.[2681]

Once one of the criteria for the exercise of the discretion has been satisfied, a court should take into account all of the circumstances bearing upon the justice of allowing the claim to be brought by the proposed plaintiff against the proposed defendant out of time.[2682] These circumstances may include the length of and the reasons for the delay and the conduct of the parties. Once there has been delay after the limitation period has expired, the court can take into account the whole of the time since the accrual of the cause of action in deciding whether to exercise its discretion.[2683] Leave may be refused even where no prejudice has been caused to the defendant if the delay is substantial and there is no reasonable excuse for it.[2684] Leave also will be refused if there is no prospect of the claim succeeding.[2685]

In cases where the cause of action for personal injury accrues only when the damage and its cause is reasonably discoverable,[2686] the plaintiff should reasonably be expected to act promptly once the right of action is recognized. So where there is further delay beyond the two-year period, there should be good reason to obtain further benefit in the court's discretion.[2687]

2676. Deaths by Accidents Compensation Act 1952, s. 10(2).
2677. *Harris v. McIntosh* [2001] 3 NZLR 721.
2678. *Maxwell v. North Canterbury Hospital Board* [1977] 2 NZLR 118; *H v. R* [1996] 1 NZLR 299; *H v. H* [1997] 2 NZLR 700: *Reekie v. Attorney-General* [2009] NZAR 304 (pin prick drawing blood); and *see Fryers v. Belfast Health and Social Care Trust* [2009] NICA 57.
2679. *Brittain v. Telecom Corporation of New Zealand Ltd* [2002] 2 NZLR 201.
2680. *H v. H* [1997] 2 NZLR 700.
2681. *Harris v. McIntosh* [2001] 3 NZLR 721.
2682. *Ibid.*
2683. *Ibid.*
2684. *Wall v. Caldow* [1964] NZLR 539.
2685. *Ellison v. L* [1998] 1 NZLR 416; *Residual Health Management Unit v. Downie* [2005] NZAR 298.
2686. *See* paras 459–460.
2687. *S v. G* [1995] 3 NZLR 681.

II. Claims for Defamation

466. The basic limitation period in defamation actions is two years, but the court has power if it thinks it just to do so to grant leave to extend the period to six years, subject to such conditions as it thinks just to impose, where it considers that the delay in bringing the action was occasioned by mistake of fact or law (other than a mistake about the limitation period) or any other reasonable cause.[2688] It is apparent that the scheme is quite similar to that which governs personal injury actions.

Examples where it was held just to grant leave are where the defendant would suffer no real prejudice as the delay was only seven months, the evidence showed that the plaintiff had always intended to sue, and in the intervening time he had other pressing matters to which he had to attend;[2689] and where there were additional defendants in the litigation anyway and the defamation cause of action was but one of several arising out of the same incidents.[2690] But leave will not be granted where the proposed action has no chance of success.[2691]

III. Claims Against an Estate

467. A cause of action in tort which subsists against the estate of a deceased tortfeasor under the Law Reform Act 1936[2692] is maintainable where proceedings in respect of that cause of action were pending at the date of death.[2693] If no such proceedings were pending, an action still can be maintained if the cause of action arose not earlier than two years before the death and proceedings are taken not later than twelve months from the date when the deceased's personal representative took out representation.[2694] However, an application may be made for leave to bring the proceedings at any time before the expiration of six years after the date when the cause of action arose, and the court may, if it thinks it just to do so, grant such leave where it considers that the failure to give the notice or the delay in bringing the proceedings was occasioned by mistake or by any other reasonable cause, or that the personal representative was not materially prejudiced by the failure or delay.[2695] Some guidance as regards the exercise of the discretion can be found in the approach that has been taken in personal injuries claims.[2696]

In cases governed by the Law Reform Act the provisions of the Limitation Act do not apply at all.[2697] In particular, the time when any cause of action arises is to be ascertained without reference to the minority of or any disability suffered by the

2688. Limitation Act 1950, s. 4(6a), (6b).
2689. *Wilson & Horton Ltd v. Lee* (1997) 11 PRNZ 550.
2690. *Outfox Total Security (New Zealand) Ltd v. New Zealand Security Industry Association Inc* [1995] 3 NZLR 122.
2691. *Rawlinson v. Oliver* [1995] 3 NZLR 62.
2692. Law Reform Act 1936, s. 3(1).
2693. *Ibid.*, s. 3(3)(a).
2694. *Ibid.*, s. 3(3)(b).
2695. *Ibid.*, s. 3(3A).
2696. *McKenzie v. Booth* [1967] NZLR 1017.
2697. Limitation Act 1950, s. 33.

plaintiff. Accordingly, where the plaintiff alleged that she had been sexually abused for a period of eleven years up to 1970 but failed due to mental disability to take any action until 1992, shortly after her abuser died, her action was statute barred. The cause of action accrued in 1970 and the period for the exercise of the court's discretion had long since expired.[2698]

§7. Laches

468. Section 4(9) of the Limitation Act 1950 provides that the statutory limits do not apply to any claim for specific performance of a contract, for an injunction, or for other equitable relief, except in so far as any provision may be applied by the Court by analogy. In *S v. G*,[2699] Gault J said that where essentially the same conduct gives rise to an alternative claim in equity, there is much to be said for the long-established analogy whereby equity follows the law. And in *Johns v. Johns*,[2700] Tipping J said in the context of a claim for breach of fiduciary duty, that there will be a bar by analogy only when the fiduciary claim parallels the statute barred claim so closely that it would be inequitable to allow the statutory bar to be outflanked by the fiduciary claim. The court must examine the underlying facts, the nature of the relationship between the parties, and the policy and purpose of the different causes of action. So where a cause of action at law against a receiver in respect of negligent conduct of the receivership was statute barred, a further and exactly coincident cause of action against the receiver based on breach of fiduciary duty was barred by analogy.[2701]

In addition, section 31 of the Limitation Act provides that nothing in the Act shall affect any equitable jurisdiction to refuse relief on the ground of acquiescence or otherwise. So a plaintiff who has been dilatory in the bringing of a purely equitable claim and has acquiesced in the wrong may be guilty of laches and barred from relief, although his or her claim is not affected by any statute of limitation. Examples where the doctrine might be invoked are where a plaintiff seeks damages in lieu of an injunction under section 13 of the Senior Courts Act 2016[2702] or for breach of duty by a fiduciary,[2703] or analogously, where the plaintiff seeks a discretionary award of public law compensation.[2704]

It has been said that the doctrine of laches applies where it would be practically unjust to give a remedy.[2705] However, no exact rule can be laid down as to when laches will or will not bar a claim. It is a question that depends in each case upon the degree of diligence that might reasonably have been expected from the plaintiff.

2698. *T v. H* [1995] 3 NZLR 37.
2699. [1995] 3 NZLR 681 at 689; and *see Re Stewart* [2004] 1 NZLR 354 at [19–21].
2700. [2004] 3 NZLR 202.
2701. *Matai Industries Ltd v. Jensen* [1989] 1 NZLR 525.
2702. *See* para. 572.
2703. *Murray v. Morel & Co. Ltd* [2007] 3 NZLR 721 at [77]–[80].
2704. *P F Sugrue Ltd v. Attorney-General* [2004] 1 NZLR 207; *Marsh v. Attorney-General* [2010] 2 NZLR 683.
2705. *Lindsay Petroleum Co. v. Hurd* (1874) LR 5 PC 221 at 239: *Welsh v. Nilsson* [1961] NZLR 644 at 659–660.

In *No. 68 Ltd v. Eastern Services Ltd*[2706] McGrath J in the Court of Appeal affirmed that laches is a separate general equitable defence that need only be addressed when statutory limitation and limitation by analogy are not available. A defendant seeking to invoke laches had to be able to show there were circumstances giving rise to an equity that on balance outweighed the plaintiff's rights. That might be difficult to do in the absence of significant prejudice. The relevant inequity would normally be founded on some change in the condition of property or the relationship of the parties over the period of delay. In the Supreme Court[2707] Anderson J questioned whether delay on its own, without actual prejudice, could defeat an equitable claim on the ground of laches.[2708] He was reluctant to endorse an unqualified principle of this kind and emphasized that a balancing of equities was needed.

§8. The Limitation Act 2010

I. General

469. In cases where the Limitation Act 2010 applies,[2709] the law has been changed in a number of substantial respects. In brief summary, time starts to run from one standard date, the expiry of the period is subject to a 'date of knowledge' which applies generally, and this date is subject to a longstop period. Special provision is made for claims involving the abuse of minors and claims in respect of personal injury caused by gradual process, disease or infection. There are also certain exceptions or modifications to the statutory periods and start dates.

II. Primary Period, Late Knowledge Period and Longstop Period

A. *Money Claims*

470. Section 11(1) provides that it is a defence to a 'money claim' if the defendant proves that the date on which the claim is filed is at least six years after the date of the act or omission on which the claim is based. This is the claim's primary period. A money claim means a claim for monetary relief at common law, in equity, or under an enactment.[2710] So in this respect the Act does not distinguish between different causes of action. Of course a money claim includes, in particular, an action in tort or for breach of contract.

A money claim's primary limitation period is subject to both a late knowledge period and a longstop period. Where a claimant has late knowledge of a claim and so the claim has a late knowledge date, and the claim is made after its primary period, it is a defence if the defendant proves that the date on which the claim is

2706. [2006] 2 NZLR 43.
2707. *Eastern Services Ltd v. No. 68 Ltd* [2006] 3 NZLR 335.
2708. *See also Hickey v. Bruhns* [1977] 2 NZLR 71; *Neylon v. Dickens* [1987] 1 NZLR 402.
2709. *See* para. 454.
2710. Limitation Act 2010, s. 12(1).

filed is at least three years after the late knowledge date.[2711] This is the date on which the claimant gained or ought reasonably to have gained knowledge of all of: (a) the fact that the act or omission on which the claim is based had occurred; (b) the fact that the act or omission was attributable (wholly or in part) to, or involved, the defendant; (c) if the alleged liability is dependent on the claimant suffering damage or loss, the fact that the claimant had suffered damage or loss; (d) if the alleged liability is dependent on the claimant not having consented to the act or omission, the fact that the claimant did not consent to that act or omission; (e) if the alleged liability is dependent on the act or omission having been induced by fraud or a mistaken belief, the fact that the act or omission is one that was induced by fraud or mistaken belief.[2712] The onus is on the claimant to prove that at the close of the start date of the primary period he or she neither knew nor ought reasonably to have known of these matters.[2713] The claimant's lack of knowledge may be attributable to causes that include fraud or mistake of fact or law.[2714]

Defamation claims are singled out for shorter periods. In this case the primary period and the late knowledge period are each two years.[2715]

Claimants thus have an extra late knowledge period running from when they discover the basis for a claim in which they can still bring proceedings. In order to prevent indefinite liability there is in addition a longstop defence. A defendant can argue that a claim which is brought more than fifteen years after the date of the act or omission on which the claim is based is barred even if the claimant was not aware of the claim at any earlier time.[2716]

B. Abuse of Minors and Disease Injury

471. Further provision is made in respect of claims involving the abuse of minors. Where a claim is in respect of the abuse of the claimant (A) when he or she was under 18 that is wholly or partly sexual abuse of A by any person, or is wholly non-sexual abuse by a parent, step-parent or legal guardian (B) or a close relative or associate of B (C), and the defendant has established or could establish a limitation defence under the 2010 Act, then the court may if it thinks it just to do so, on an application made for the purpose, order that monetary relief be granted as if there was no such defence.[2717] The court can do likewise in respect of a claim by a person of any age (A) in respect of personal injury caused by gradual process, disease or infection.[2718] In determining whether to make an order, the court must take into account the hardship to the defendant if the order were made and to A if it were not;

2711. *Ibid.*, s. 11(2), (3)(a).
2712. *Ibid.*, s. 14(1).
2713. *Ibid.*, s. 14(2).
2714. *Ibid.*, s. 14(3).
2715. *Ibid.*, s. 15. Publication online occurs each time information is downloaded, and the limitation period runs for each such publication from the time of download: *Sellman v. Slater* [2017] NZHC 2392, [2018] 2 NZLR 218 at [33]–[46].
2716. *Ibid.*, s. 11(3)(b).
2717. *Ibid.*, s. 17.
2718. *Ibid.*

the length of and the reasons for the delay on A's part; the likely effects of the delay on the defendant's ability to defend the claim and on cogency of the evidence; the defendant's conduct, including the extent to which the defendant responded to reasonable requests for information relevant to the claim; the extent to which prompt and reasonable steps were taken by A to make the claim after becoming aware that he or she was entitled to do so; the steps taken by A to get relevant expert advice and the nature of that advice; and any other matters the court considers relevant.[2719]

C. Conversion and Detinue

472. Part 3 of the Act provides for defences to certain particular types of claim. One that is presently relevant is a claim to recover converted or wrongly detained goods. It is a defence to such a claim if the defendant proves that the date on which the claim is filed is at least six years after the date of the act or omission on which the claim is based.[2720] However, if the claim is a further conversion or wrongful detention claim (i.e., one that is made in respect of goods that have been the subject of one or more earlier instances of conversion or wrongful detention) and is made by the 'original claimant', then the start date for the primary and the longstop periods is the date of the first conversion or wrongful detention.[2721] If a claim (the 'original claim') accrues to a person (the 'original claimant') in respect of the conversion or wrongful detention of goods, and before the original claimant (whether by making the original claim or taking other steps) recovers possession of the goods a further conversion or detention occurs, then the original claimant's title to the goods is extinguished if the period for the original claim ends before the original claimant makes the claim.[2722] However, this provision does not affect section 152 of the Contract and Commercial Law Act 2017 (which ensures that if goods have been stolen and the offender is prosecuted to conviction, property in the goods revests in the owner),[2723] nor claims for monetary relief in respect of a claim for conversion or wrongful detention.[2724] So if goods are stolen and there are no further conversions, the owner's claim to recover the goods is barred after six years from the date of the conversion. However, the owner does not lose title to the goods,[2725] and he or she can, therefore, exercise his or her right of recaption of the goods.[2726] If there is a further conversion the original owner loses title to the goods after six years from the first conversion, subject to the saving for section 152 of the Contract and Commercial Law Act, but can still claim damages in respect of the original conversion if the late knowledge provisions apply.

2719. *Ibid.*, s. 18.
2720. *Ibid.*, s. 29(1).
2721. *Ibid.*, ss 16(1)(b), 29(2).
2722. *Ibid.*, s. 30(1), (2).
2723. *Ibid.*, s. 30(4)(a).
2724. *Ibid.*, s. 30(4)(b).
2725. *Ibid.*, s. 43(b).
2726. As to which, *see* para. 504.

D. Claims for Contribution

473. Part 3 also makes special provision for claims for contribution. It is a defence to a claim under section 17 of the Law Reform Act 1936 by a tortfeasor (A) liable in tort to another person (B) for contribution from another tortfeasor (C) who is, or would if sued in time have been, liable in tort to B, if C proves that the date on which the claim is filed is at least two years after the date on which A's liability to B is quantified by an agreement, award, or judgment.[2727] The same applies to a claim by A, who is liable (otherwise than in tort) to B in respect of a matter, for a contribution from C where C is or would if sued in time have been liable (otherwise than in tort) to B in a coordinate way in respect of that matter. C is liable to B in a coordinate way if a common obligation underlies C's and A's liability to B, and discharge of C's liability to B would have the effect of relieving A, in whole or part, from A's liability to B.[2728]

E. Exceptions or Modifications to Periods and Start Dates

474. There are a number of exceptions or modifications to the statutory periods and start dates. In the case of a minor, the primary, longstop or Part 3 period does not start to run until the claimant turns 18.[2729] A claimant who was incapacitated at the start of or during the primary, longstop or Part 3 period may apply for a discretionary extension of the periods.[2730] 'Incapacitated' means that a claimant or personal representative is not capable of understanding the relevant issues, or is unable to give instructions to issue, defend or compromise proceedings, because of, *inter alia*, physical, intellectual or mental impairment.[2731] In deciding whether to make an order extending one of the periods, the court must take into account, *inter alia*, whether a litigation guardian was managing the claimant's affairs with respect to the act or omission concerned, the effects of the delay on the defendant's ability to defend the claim and on the cogency of the evidence, the defendant's conduct in responding to reasonable requests for information, the extent to which prompt and reasonable steps were taken after the claimant became aware that he or she was entitled to make the claim, any steps taken to obtain relevant medical, legal or other expert advice and the nature of any such advice, and any other matters considered relevant.[2732]

If after the start of a primary, longstop or Part 3 period a defendant acknowledges in writing a liability to the claimant, or makes a payment in respect of that liability, the claimant is deemed to have a fresh claim on the day after the date of the acknowledgment or part payment.[2733] The acknowledgment or part payment binds

2727. Limitation Act 2010, s. 34(1), (4).
2728. *Ibid*., s. 34(2), (3), (4).
2729. *Ibid*., s. 44.
2730. *Ibid*., s. 45(1), (2).
2731. *Ibid*., s. 46.
2732. *Ibid*., s. 45(3).
2733. *Ibid*., s. 47(1), (2).

the defendant's successors, and may be given or made by the defendant or his or her agent and to the claimant or his or her agent.[2734]

A claim's longstop or Part 3 period does not apply if the claimant proves that, because of fraud by or on behalf of the defendant, the claimant neither knew nor ought reasonably to have known of those various facts that are relevant in determining a claimant's knowledge date.[2735] 'Fraud' includes dishonest or fraudulent concealment and fraudulent breach of trust.[2736]

2734. *Ibid.*, s. 47(3).
2735. *Ibid.*, s. 48.
2736. *Ibid.*, s. 4.

Chapter 2. Plaintiff's Wrongdoing

§1. Contributory Negligence

475. A plaintiff who sues another in respect of tortiously inflicted harm, yet who has also failed to take reasonable care in looking after his or her own interests and in this way has contributed to his or her own loss, may be met with the defence of contributory negligence. The defence must be pleaded,[2737] the burden of proving it being on the defendant.[2738] If the plea is successful, the court may apportion responsibility for the damage between plaintiff and defendant under the provisions of the Contributory Negligence Act 1947.

I. The Contributory Negligence Act 1947

476. The common law lacked any mechanisms for apportioning a loss between a plaintiff and a defendant (or between two or more defendants).[2739] Rather, contributory negligence by a plaintiff operated as a complete defence.[2740] This rule had the capacity to cause obvious injustice in cases where the plaintiff's negligence played only a minor part in contributing to the damage. However, in practice, the courts tended to fix the plaintiff with sole responsibility only where his or her negligence was the substantial or predominant cause. This at least mitigated the severity of the common law. Even so, the reality in many cases, particularly those in the early part of the twentieth century involving the new phenomenon of motor traffic, was that the accident was caused by the negligence of both parties. So contributorily negligent road accident victims were frequently unable to recover any part of their loss. This 'all or nothing' approach of the common law came under increasing criticism, and reform eventually was achieved in England by the Law Reform (Contributory Negligence) Act 1945. In New Zealand, the Contributory Negligence Act 1947 followed soon afterwards, its terms being identical in material respects to the English model.

Section 3 of the Contributory Negligence Act is the key provision. This provides:

> Where any person suffers damage as the result partly of his own fault and partly of the fault of any other person or persons, a claim in respect of that damage shall not be defeated by reason of the fault of the person suffering the damage, but the damages recoverable in respect thereof shall be reduced to such extent as the Court thinks just and equitable having regard to the claimant's share in the responsibility for the damage.

2737. *Brown v. Heathcote CC (No. 2)* [1982] 2 NZLR 216 (affirmed [1986] 1 NZLR 76 (CA); [1987] 1 NZLR 720 (PC)).
2738. *Kenny v. Dunedin CC* [1920] NZLR 513; *Goldstine v. R* [1947] NZLR 588.
2739. As to which *see* para. 586.
2740. *Butterfield v. Forrester* (1809) 11 East 60; 103 ER 926.

Accordingly, the scheme of the Act is that the damage should have been caused by fault on the part of both defendant and plaintiff, whereupon the court may in its discretion apportion responsibility between them.

II. Causal Relevance

477. Negligence by the plaintiff can be disregarded if this was not a proximate cause of damage of which he or she complains. The court looks only at negligence that is causal and operative, and not at negligence that does not fall into that category.[2741] In one case, for example, the plaintiff, contrary to orders, was riding on the towbar of the defendants' traxcavator and was injured by a fellow servant who negligently drove another vehicle into the back of the traxcavator. It was held that, by his conduct, the plaintiff ran a risk not only of falling off but also of being injured in the way that had happened and he was, therefore, guilty of contributory negligence.[2742] But if his injuries had been foreign to the risk created by his negligence, the defence could not then have applied. So there was no reduction for contributory negligence when an addicted prisoner who was denied drugs on his admission to prison fell from a top bunk during withdrawal seizures and suffered serious injury.[2743] Without his addiction the injury would not have happened, but it was merely part of the history which led to his being in prison and was too remote in time, place and circumstance from the negligence of the prison staff. It is sufficient that the plaintiff's conduct should contribute to the damage he or she suffers. It is not essential that it should contribute to the event that causes the damage. So in an action by a company against an auditor, the company may be guilty of contributory negligence where it has failed to look after its own interests, even though it may not have hindered the auditor from carrying out his or her duties.[2744] Similarly, it is not necessary that in some sense a plaintiff's negligence be related to an act of conversion alleged to have been committed by the defendant.[2745]

III. 'Fault' by Plaintiff and Defendant

A. *Plaintiff's Fault*

478. 'Fault' is defined in section 2 of the Contributory Negligence Act as meaning 'negligence, breach of statutory duty or other act or omission which gives rise to a liability in tort or would, apart from the Act, give rise to the defence of contributory negligence'. In *Rowe v. Turner Hopkins*[2746] Prichard J regarded the definition as having two limbs, the first being directed to defining fault as it relates to

2741. *Griffin v. FT Wimble & Co.* [1950] NZLR 774.
2742. *Jones v. Livox Quarries Ltd* [1952] 2 QB 608.
2743. *St George v. Home Office* [2009] 1 WLR 1670.
2744. *Dairy Containers Ltd v. NZI Bank Ltd* [1995] 2 NZLR 30 at 74–76.
2745. *Ibid.*, at 114–115.
2746. [1980] 2 NZLR 550 at 555 (on appeal [1982] 1 NZLR 178 (CA)).

the conduct of the defendant and thus to the plaintiff's cause of action, and the second being concerned with and referable only to the conduct of the plaintiff. He said that this second limb means simply and logically that no act or omission of the plaintiff will entitle the defendant to a reduction in damages unless it amounts to the sort of conduct that, prior to the enactment of the Contributory Negligence Act, would have afforded a defence at common law. So also in *Standard Chartered Bank v. Pakistan Shipping Corporation*,[2747] the House of Lords held that fault means 'negligence, breach of statutory duty or other act or omission' that, in the case of a defendant, gave rise to a liability in tort and, in the case of a plaintiff, gave rise at common law to a defence of contributory negligence. Their Lordships noted that the purpose of the Law Reform (Contributory Negligence) Act 1945 (UK) was not to reduce the damages that would previously have been awarded against defendants but to relieve plaintiffs whose actions would previously have failed.

On this approach the defence of contributory negligence applies in cases where at common law the plaintiff's own negligence constituted a complete defence to his or her claim, as where both parties have been negligent. It does not apply where the defendant has committed an intentional tort in respect of which, at common law, contributory negligence was no defence. So damages are recoverable in full, notwithstanding any negligence by the plaintiff, in claims for assault and battery,[2748] deceit,[2749] conversion,[2750] or for the so-called economic torts of interference with contract, intimidation, conspiracy, and intentional interference with business by unlawful means.[2751]

Some other authorities take a different view. In particular, in *Dairy Containers Ltd v. NZI Bank Ltd*[2752] Thomas J considered that the whole of the definition of fault applies to both or either the plaintiff or defendant as may be appropriate in the circumstances. While the latter part of the definition could not apply to the fault of the defendant, it was unnecessary to go further and exclude the operation of the words 'or other act or omission which gives rise to a liability in tort' when considering the plaintiff's fault. On this view, the fault of the plaintiff includes any acts or omissions that constitute a tort or that would give rise to the defence of contributory negligence, and is not controlled by the fault that the plaintiff alleges against the defendant. Thomas J appreciated that this interpretation means that contributory negligence can apply to all torts but this, he thought, was exactly what the legislature intended. His Honour also thought that the question whether conduct 'would, apart from the Act, give rise to the defence of contributory negligence' need not be controlled by pre-Act cases. Rather, it could be argued that the common law would

---

2747. [2003] 1 AC 959; approved by the Supreme Court in *Amaltal Corporation Ltd v. Maruha Corporation* [2007] 3 NZLR 192 at [23].

2748. *Horkin v. North Melbourne Football Club* [1983] 1 VR 153; *Pritchard v. Co-Operative Group Ltd* [2011] 3 WLR 1272.

2749. *Standard Chartered Bank v. Pakistan Shipping Corporation* [2003] 1 AC 959.

2750. *Boma Manufacturing Ltd v. Canadian Imperial Bank of Commerce* [1996] 3 SCR 727.

2751. *Dellabarca v. Northern Storemen and Packers Union* [1989] 2 NZLR 734; *McIntyre v. Bianchi* [1992] 3 ERNZ 1057; *Corporación Nacional del Cobre de Chile v. Sogemin Metals Ltd* [1997] 1 WLR 1396.

2752. [1995] 2 NZLR 30 at 112.

in any event have developed to admit the defence of contributory negligence. He saw the justification for a restrictive view as having been removed once a power to apportion was admitted.

Some earlier New Zealand authorities are consistent with Thomas J's interpretation, although they lack any close discussion of the question and were decided before the more recent debates. So, contrary to decisions already cited, contributory negligence has been upheld as a defence in actions for conversion[2753] and for assault and battery.[2754] But the balance of authority favours the view that confines the defence primarily to actions alleging that the defendant acted negligently or in breach of statutory duty.

B. Defendant's Fault

479. In order for the 1947 Act to apply, the defendant's fault must constitute 'negligence, breach of statutory duty or other act or omission which gives rise to a liability in tort'. On the generally accepted view, this means that the defendant must be a tortfeasor.[2755] But tort need not be the only basis of liability. Where there is a co-extensive liability in contract and in negligence and the plaintiff brings his or her claim in negligence, the Act still applies.[2756] The existence of a liability in contract as well is immaterial.[2757] The position is the same where liability in negligence exists, but the plaintiff chooses to frame his or her action in contract.[2758] The definition of 'fault' refers only to conduct that gives rise to 'a' liability in tort and does not require that the claim actually be framed in tort. Indeed there is no objection in principle to the imposition of concurrent liability for negligence and negligent breach of contract,[2759] and so in all such cases the Contributory Negligence Act can apply.

Where a plaintiff sues only for breach of a strict contractual duty that does not depend on negligence, the Act cannot then be raised as a defence to the plaintiff's claim.[2760] However, it is still open to the defendant to put the plaintiff's responsibility in issue in terms of the cause of the loss or of the requirement that the plaintiff should act to mitigate the loss.[2761] But where a contracting party merely failed to prevent the other party from committing a breach of a strict contractual duty, then

2753. *Helson v. McKenzies (Cuba Street) Ltd* [1950] NZLR 878.
2754. *Hoebergen v. Koppens* [1974] 2 NZLR 597.
2755. *Rowe v. Turner Hopkins* [1980] 2 NZLR 550; *Dellabarca v. Northern Storemen and Packers Union* [1989] 2 NZLR 734; cp *Mouat v. Clark Boyce* [1992] 2 NZLR 559 at 564–565.
2756. *Hanmore v. Ganley* CA 158/95, 8 Sep. 1997.
2757. *Rowe v. Turner Hopkins & Partners* [1980] 2 NZLR 550 at 555.
2758. *Forsikringsaktieselskapet Vesta v. Butcher* [1989] AC 852 at 867; cp *Astley v. Austrust Ltd* (1999) 197 CLR 1.
2759. *See* para. 22.
2760. *Vining Realty Group Ltd v. Moorehouse* [2010] NZCA 104 at [64]–[67] (decision on other issues varied on appeal, sub nom *Marlborough District Council v. Altimarloch Joint Venture Ltd* [2012] 2 NZLR 726).
2761. *Lexmead (Basingstoke) Ltd v. Lewis* [1982] AC 225; *Tennant Radiant Heat Ltd v. Warrington Development Corporation* [1988] 1 EGLR 41; *Raflatac Ltd v. Eade* [1999] 1 Lloyd's Rep. 506.

even on the basis that there was also a breach of a parallel obligation in tort coterminous with the duty in contract the plaintiff was able to recover in full, because the very imposition of strict liability would be inconsistent with an apportionment of the loss.[2762]

IV. The Standard of Care

480. Whether conduct constitutes contributory negligence is a question of fact and is determined by whether the plaintiff acted reasonably in all the circumstances.[2763] 'A person is guilty of contributory negligence if he ought reasonably to have foreseen that, if he did not act as a reasonable, prudent man, he might be hurt himself; and in his reckonings he must take into account the possibility of others being careless.'[2764] The principle involved is simply that where a man is part author of his own injury, he cannot call on another to compensate him in full.[2765]

The same kinds of factors that are relevant in determining liability can also be taken into account in determining whether there is contributory negligence.[2766] They include the likelihood of danger to the plaintiff and its gravity should it happen, the social value of the plaintiff's activity, whether the plaintiff acted in the 'agony of the moment' or had an opportunity for reflection, and the ease or the burden of taking precautions against the danger. For example, the damages for a widow whose husband had died of lung cancer caused by exposure to asbestos in the course of his employment were reduced on account of the deceased's contributory negligence in continuing to smoke in notwithstanding warnings about the danger to his health.[2767] On the evidence he was not so addicted that he could not reasonably have been expected to have given up smoking, and in failing to stop he was guilty of fault that was partly responsible for his death.[2768]

In nearly all cases the question will be whether the plaintiff acted carelessly. A plaintiff who deliberately causes harm to himself or herself is unlikely to have a cause of action against another. Exceptionally, however, a cause of action may exist, in which case the plaintiff's intentional conduct may amount to contributory negligence. In *Reeves v. Commissioner of Police of the Metropolis*[2769] police officers having custody of a suicidally inclined prisoner failed to take precautions to prevent him from committing suicide. The House of Lords held that the officers were under a duty to take care to prevent the deceased from deliberately injuring himself and

2762. *Barclays Bank Plc v. Fairclough Building Ltd* [1995] QB 214.
2763. *Hooker v. Stewart* [1989] 3 NZLR 543 at 547.
2764. *Jones v. Livox Quarries* [1952] 2 QB 608 per Denning LJ at 615.
2765. *Nance v. British Columbia Electric Ry* [1951] AC 601 at 611.
2766. As to which *see* para. 141.
2767. *Badger v. Ministry of Health* [2006] 3 All ER 173; *Blackmore v. Department for Communities and Local Government* [2017] EWCA Civ 1136, [2018] QB 471.
2768. For further (random) examples, *see Southland Indoor Leisure Centre Charitable Trust v. Invercargill City Council* [2017] NZSC 190, [2018] 1 NZLR 278 (building owner not following engineer's advice); *Joslyn v. Berryman* (2003) 214 CLR 552 (passenger accompanying drunken driver); *Platform Home Loans Ltd v. Oyston Shipways Ltd* [2000] 2 AC 190 (lending money without checking financial stability of borrower).
2769. [2000] 1 AC 360.

that a fortiori this was a cause of the harm. The deceased's own conduct obviously was a cause as well, and this amounted to contributory negligence. In the circumstances it was thought to be just and equitable to apportion responsibility equally between the two causes. However, in *Corr v. IBC Vehicles Ltd*,[2770] where the plaintiff's husband committed suicide when severely depressed following a serious work injury, there was no reduction. Here the employer was responsible for the injury leading to the depression, and the husband's suicide was not a voluntary and informed decision taken by an adult of unimpaired capacity.

V. The Doctrine of Identification

481. If a person would be vicariously liable for the torts of another where he or she was being sued,[2771] then on a similar basis he or she is identified with the contributory negligence of that other when bringing an action as plaintiff.[2772] For example, where an employer's property was damaged through the combined negligence of a servant and a third party, the employer's action against the third party was met by the defence of contributory negligence on the part of the servant.[2773] Again, a principal may sometimes be identified with the contributory negligence of an agent driving the principal's car on the principal's behalf, in which case damages will be reduced to the extent of the agent's negligence. If the relationship is not one that could give rise to vicarious liability, however, the doctrine of identification does not apply.[2774] A child in the charge of an adult is not identified with that adult,[2775] nor is a husband or wife with his or her spouse,[2776] a bailor with a bailee,[2777] or a principal with an independent contractor.[2778] These claimants can recover in full, and the defendant's remedy in such cases is to make a claim for contribution from the other negligent party.[2779]

VI. Mode of Apportionment

482. Where both plaintiff and defendant are at fault, the plaintiff's damages are to be reduced 'to such extent as the court thinks just and equitable having regard to the claimant's share in the responsibility for the damage'.[2780] The 'damage' that must be apportioned is the damage of which the plaintiff is a co-cause and for which the defendant is liable. Any loss of which the defendant was a cause but for which

2770. [2008] 1 AC 844.
2771. *See* para. 373.
2772. *Mills v. Armstrong: The 'Bernina'* (1888) 13 App Cas 1.
2773. *Chaplin v. Hawes* (1828) 3 Car & P 554; 172 ER 543.
2774. *Mills v. Armstrong: The Bernina* (1888) 13 App Cas 1 at 16.
2775. *Oliver v. Birmingham & Midland Motor Omnibus Co.* [1933] 1 KB 35.
2776. *Drinkwater v. Kimber* [1952] 2 QB 281.
2777. *Pierard v. Wright* [1933] NZLR s. 120.
2778. *Morton v. Douglas Homes Ltd* [1984] 2 NZLR 548 at 581.
2779. *See* para. 586.
2780. Contributory Negligence Act 1947, s. 3.

the defendant is not liable is not included. So where loss is irrecoverable as too remote,[2781] the defence of contributory negligence operates not on the total loss but only on that part that is legally recoverable.

In deciding how to apportion the damage the courts make a comparison between the degree of responsibility of the plaintiff on the one hand and of the defendant on the other. However, a complication arises in cases where there is more than one defendant and there is a claim between co-defendants for contribution. In *Fitzgerald v. Lane*[2782] the House of Lords held that the two stages in the decision-making process, the one in the main action and the other in the contribution proceedings, should be pursued separately. Accordingly, the plaintiff's share of the responsibility should be fixed as against all the defendants together and only then should the reduced amount claimable by the plaintiff be apportioned between the defendants.

In determining each party's 'responsibility', the main emphasis is on comparative culpability or blameworthiness.[2783] This may vary widely, from trivial lapses in standards on the one hand to criminal recklessness on the other. The courts also take into account the 'causative potency' of the parties' conduct – the relative importance of the acts in causing the damage apart from the question of blameworthiness.[2784] For example, in *Helson v. McKenzies Ltd*[2785] the plaintiff left her handbag containing a large sum of money on the counter of the defendants' shop and the defendants' sales assistant, without requiring proof of ownership, handed it to an unknown person claiming it as her own. The bag was never recovered and the plaintiff sued the defendants for conversion. Her claim succeeded but her damages were reduced by three-quarters on account of her contributory negligence, the court seeing a loss of such magnitude as having been primarily caused by the plaintiff herself.

Ultimately the trial judge or jury must allocate the responsibility according to what it thinks to be 'just and equitable' in the light of the above factors. Its decision in this respect is regarded purely as a question of fact, and will not be disturbed by an appellate court unless that court is satisfied that the decision was one that could not reasonably be supported on the whole of the evidence.[2786]

§2. Assumption of the Risk

483. Where the plaintiff has voluntarily assumed the risk of an injury caused by a breach of duty by the defendant the maxim *volenti non fit injuria* applies. It means that no harm is done to one who consents. It is for the defendant to prove that the

2781. *See* paras 542–546.

2782. [1989] AC 328; *Dairy Containers Ltd v. NZI Bank Ltd* [1995] 2 NZLR 30 at 86–87.

2783. *Blackmore v. Department for Communities and Local Government* [2017] EWCA Civ 1136, [2018] QB 471.

2784. *Stapley v. Gypsum Mines Ltd* [1953] AC 663 at 682.

2785. [1950] NZLR 878.

2786. *Hibberds Foundry Ltd v. Hardy* [1953] NZLR 14; *Hoani v. Wallis* [1956] NZLR 395. In *Johnson v. Auckland Council* [2013] NZCA 662 a finding by the trial judge of 70% contributory negligence by the purchasers of a leaky home was reduced on appeal to 40%.

plaintiff consented to, or assumed the risk of, the harm.[2787] The defendant needs to show that the plaintiff was fully aware of the risk and freely and voluntarily decided to incur it.

Most of the cases involve claims for personal injury, which are barred by the accident compensation scheme. The defence still can apply in the case of other forms of damage.

I. Full Knowledge of the Risk

484. Whether a plaintiff was contributorily negligent is determined on an objective basis. The question is whether the plaintiff should reasonably have foreseen that he or she might suffer damage.[2788] But whether a plaintiff assumed the risk of injury is determined subjectively. The question here is whether the plaintiff actually possessed full knowledge of the nature and extent of the risk he ran, and then, with that full knowledge, in fact incurred it.[2789] This requirement is likely to be easier to establish in the case of existing, as opposed to future, negligence.[2790] For example, a plaintiff who was struck by a train after having passed through a gap in a dilapidated fence alongside the track was held to have assumed the risk.[2791] So here the alleged negligence in failing to maintain the fence and the acceptance of it by the plaintiff in crossing the track was before the damage happened. It is rare for a plaintiff to be held to have assumed the risk of future negligence. Arguably the defence can be applicable only in the case of an express or inferred agreement arising out of a prior relationship between the parties. An example is where the plaintiff owner lent his car to a driver known to be extremely drunk.[2792] Otherwise, he who takes the chance of encountering negligence will be met by the defence of contributory negligence.[2793]

A much litigated example concerns the question whether a passenger has assumed the risk of negligence by a drunken driver. In most cases a sufficient awareness of the circumstances and the possible consequences will not be present.[2794] However, exceptionally, the volenti doctrine may be invoked.[2795]

II. Free and Voluntary Acceptance of the Risk

485. During the nineteenth century, a workman who suffered injury as a consequence of dangerous working conditions was treated as having assumed the risk of harm. Knowledge of a risk was equated with acceptance of it. But the law was

2787. *James v. Wellington City* [1972] NZLR 978.
2788. *See* para. 480.
2789. *Heard v. New Zealand Forest Products Ltd* [1960] NZLR 329.
2790. The distinction is discussed in *Morris v. Murray* [1991] 2 QB 6.
2791. *McGinlay v. British Railways Board* [1983] 1 WLR 1427.
2792. *Walker v. Watson* [1974] 2 NZLR 175.
2793. *Morrison v. Union Steam Ship Co. of New Zealand Ltd* [1964] NZLR 468.
2794. *See*, for example, *Dixon v. King* [1975] 2 NZLR 357; *Owens v. Brimmell* [1977] QB 859.
2795. *See*, for example, *Morris v. Murray* [1991] 2 QB 6.

changed in *Smith v. Baker*,[2796] where the House of Lords held that the mere fact that a workman undertook and continued in employment known to be dangerous could not prevent his recovering damages. The employee did not have free and unfettered choice as to whether to continue to work or to leave. Since that decision it has been clear that it is not enough for the defendant to prove that the plaintiff was aware of a risk. It has to be shown that the plaintiff freely and voluntarily agreed to take upon himself or herself the risk of the harm that in fact eventuated.[2797]

Accordingly, in light of the stringency of this requirement, the plea has usually met with little success. In the drunk driving cases an awareness of danger is not normally equated with a free and voluntary agreement to bear the loss should an accident occur. The plea has rarely been invoked to bar a rescuer from recovery. If the defendant has created a dangerous situation and it is reasonably foreseeable that a person will act to rescue the person or property endangered, the rescuer's decision cannot be seen as a free and unfettered exercise of will.[2798] A visitor who comes on to land with actual knowledge of a danger does not thereby willingly assume the risk of harm arising out of the danger.[2799]

§3. Illegal Conduct

486. Misconduct by the plaintiff of sufficient turpitude may mean that a claim should fail altogether. In certain ill-defined circumstances the maxim '*ex turpi causa non oritur actio*' applies. It means 'no right of action arises from a shameful cause'. In *Gray v. Thames Trains Ltd*[2800] Lord Hoffmann recognized that the maxim expressed not so much a principle as a policy, and also that that policy was not based upon a single justification but on a group of reasons, which varied in different situations. There are indeed various justifications or arguments to be found in the cases, and

I. Reliance upon Illegal Conduct

487. In *Holman v. Johnson*[2801] Lord Mansfield said that 'No Court will lend its aid to a man who founds his cause of action upon an immoral or an illegal act.' This may be called the 'reliance' test, because it bars the plaintiff if he or she is forced to rely on his or her own illegality. So if a claim in respect of property can be made

2796. [1891] AC 325.
2797. *Bowater v. Rowley Regis Corp* [1944] 1 KB 476 at 479.
2798. *Soares v. State Fire and Accident Insurance General Manager* [1946] NZLR 51; *Russell v. McCabe* [1962] NZLR 392.
2799. *White v. Blackmore* [1972] 2 QB 651 at 662–663.
2800. *Gray v. Thames Trains Ltd* [2009] 1 AC 1339 at [30].
2801. *Holman v. Johnson* (1775) 1 Cowp 341 at 343, 98 ER 1120 at 1121.

out on the basis of ownership, and without reference to any illegality involved in the acquisition of the property, an argument based on the ex turpi defence will not succeed.[2802]

In a controversial decision of the UK Supreme Court, a claim against auditors by a one-man company for failing to detect a fraud by the company director against the claimant bank, rendering the company liable in deceit to the bank, was held to fail, because the conduct of the director was attributable to the company and it was, therefore, relying on its own fraud.[2803] However, the Supreme Court subsequently held that a company could claim against a fraudulent director what it had to pay to a third party, and that attribution of the fraud to the company was inappropriate in such a case.[2804] The same court later affirmed that there was no principle of law that the fraudulent conduct of a director was to be attributed to the company if it was a one-man company. Rather, the answer to any question whether to attribute the knowledge of a fraudulent director to a company was always to be found in consideration of the context and the purpose for which the attribution was relevant.[2805]

Dispute about what it means to say that a litigant must rely on his or her own illegality renders the reliance principle an uncertain guide. It can work arbitrarily, and its application may depend on who is bringing the action.[2806] Again, there is a question whether rules of pleading should determine the matter or whether the illegality must 'of necessity' form part of the plaintiff's case.[2807] Indeed, on the majority view in the UK Supreme Court, the reliance rule should no longer be followed.[2808]

II. Illegal Conduct the Cause of the Harm

488. The courts sometimes apply the ex turpi causa rule in circumstances where a plaintiff's unlawful conduct is seen as having caused the harm or, in a variation on the causal test, as having been 'closely connected' or 'inextricably linked' with the harm.[2809] In making this kind of inquiry they seek to draw a distinction between causing a loss and providing the opportunity for it to happen.[2810] In the present context, the question is whether the injury was truly a consequence of the plaintiff's unlawful act, in that both claimant and defendant were involved in the criminal

2802. *Tinsley v. Milligan* [1994] 1 AC 340 (HL); *Leason v. Attorney-General* [2014] 2 NZLR 224 at [129]–[130].
2803. *Stone & Rolls Ltd v. Moore Stephens* [2009] 1 AC 1391.
2804. *Bilta (UK) Ltd v. Nazir (No 2)* [2015] 2 WLR 1168; *Deloitte & Touche v. Livent Inc* 2017 SCC 63, [2017] 2 SCR 855.
2805. *Singularis Holdings Ltd v. Daiwa Capital Markets Europe Ltd* [2019] UKSC 50, [2019] 3 WLR 997.
2806. Law Commission *The Illegality Defence* (Law Commission for England and Wales, Report No. 32, 2010) at [2.13]–[2.15].
2807. Compare the views of Rimer and Vos LJJ with those of Gloster LJ in *Patel v. Mirza* [2015] Ch 271 (CA). For the decision of the Supreme Court *see* para. 491.
2808. *Patel v. Mirza* [2016] 3 WLR 399 at [110].
2809. For discussion, *see Hounga v. Allen* [2014] 1 WLR 2889 at [31]–[40], [58]–[59].
2810. *See* para. 538.

enterprise and the injury was part of the risk engendered by that enterprise,[2811] or whether it was incidental to the unlawful act and a consequence of it only in the sense that it would not have happened if the plaintiff had not been committing that act.[2812]

A causal inquiry may be relevant and helpful. But it need not follow from a conclusion that a plaintiff's illegal conduct was a cause of his or her injury that the defendant's conduct was *not* a cause. In *McCracken v. Smith*[2813] the plaintiff (M) was travelling as a pillion passenger on a trials bike, which was not designed for passengers, being ridden by the first defendant (S) at speed, on a path reserved for cyclists, and without a driving licence or insurance. Both plaintiff and defendant were injured in a collision with a minibus being driven by the third defendant (B). As regards M's claim against S, it was held that M's injury could properly be said to have been caused by his own criminal conduct even though it resulted from the negligent act of S. Although as a matter of fact the negligent act was that of S, M was jointly responsible in law for it and he could not bring a claim in respect of his own negligent act. But as regards M's claim against B, the accident had two causes – the dangerous driving of the bike and the negligent driving of the minibus. Accordingly, M could claim in negligence against B but damages would be reduced in accordance with the principles of contributory negligence so as to reflect M's own fault and responsibility for the accident.

It is apparent that M's claim against S was treated differently to M's claim against B, yet in each case the conduct involved and its causal impact were exactly the same. The claim against B can be seen as straightforward, and as regards the claim against S the true issue seems to be whether a party to a joint venture can sue another party in respect of conduct for which they are both responsible. The orthodox answer is no,[2814] but it is worth asking whether this must necessarily be so. In joint negligence cases there is something to be said for allowing the claim, by a severance of the unity of the conduct and by invoking the principles of contributory negligence.

III. Consistency Within the Law

489. In *Hall v. Hebert*[2815] the Supreme Court of Canada laid down a narrow, and convincing, test. McLachlin J maintained that the plea of ex turpi causa would bar recovery only where to allow it would undermine the integrity of the legal system, by introducing inconsistency into the law's fabric. Thus a plaintiff would not be permitted to profit from his or her illegal conduct, as where a plaintiff claimed for

2811. For example, *Joyce v. O'Brien* [2014] 1 WLR 70; *Beaumont v. Ferrer* [2016] EWCA Civ 768; *Gujra v. Roath* [2018] EWHC 854 (QB), [2018] 1 WLR 3208.

2812. For example, *Delaney v. Pickett* [2012] 1 WLR 2149.

2813. [2015] EWCA Civ 380.

2814. There are many joint venture cases where the plaintiff has failed, although the reasoning in them has varied: *see*, for example, *Gala v. Preston* (1991) 172 CLR 243; *Pitts v. Hunt* [1991] 1 QB 24; *Miller v. Miller* (2011) 242 CLR 446.

2815. *Hall v. Hebert* [1993] 2 SCR 159 at 175–177; *British Columbia v. Zastowny* [2008] 1 SCR 27; *Rankin (Rankin's Garage & Sales) v. JJ* 2018 SCC 19, [2018] 1 SCR 587 at [62]–[64].

financial loss arising from a joint illegal venture, or for exemplary damages; nor to evade a penalty prescribed by the criminal law, as where a burglar was caught due to his partner's negligence and required to pay a fine. But a wrongdoer could still recover damages insofar as this was not compensation for an illegal act but was compensation for the loss caused by the negligence of another. In *Hall* itself the plaintiff was not barred in circumstances where he was allowed by the defendant to drive the defendant's car when drunk and incapable, although the damages were reduced for contributory negligence. A plaintiff who was shot by the defendant while breaking into the defendant's shed could also recover damages although, once again, the plaintiff's criminality was treated as contributory negligence.[2816] But the plea succeeded in a case where the plaintiff killed a complete stranger after having been discharged from a mental hospital when in need of treatment, and was subsequently convicted of manslaughter. His action against the hospital failed because the damages would be, in effect, an evasion or rebate of a criminal penalty. The damage for which the plaintiff sought compensation was the detention resulting from the plaintiff's own criminal conduct.[2817] But there was no such bar to a claim against a mental health authority by a mental patient who had killed his father after his release but who was not guilty of murder by reason of insanity.[2818]

In *Gray v. Thames Trains Ltd*[2819] the plaintiff suffered major psychological harm after being involved in a train accident caused by the defendant's negligence. Following his changed mental state he later stabbed a stranger to death, and was ordered to be detained in a mental hospital after pleading guilty to manslaughter on the grounds of diminished responsibility. The House of Lords held that the defendants were not liable for loss of earnings after the date of the killing, on the basis that *ex turpi causa non oritur actio* applied. Lord Hoffmann referred to a special rule of public policy saying, in its wider form, that you could not recover for loss which you had suffered in consequence of your own criminal act, and in its narrower form, that you could not recover for damage which flowed from loss of liberty, fine or other punishment lawfully imposed on you in consequence of your own unlawful act. Here, applying the narrower rule, it was the law which as a matter of penal policy caused the damage, and it would be inconsistent for the law to require a person to be compensated for that damage.

The consistency principle also can explain some so-called exceptions to the reliance rule. For example, a claim in conversion in respect of wrongfully acquired goods which ordinarily would succeed on the basis simply of the claimant's ownership, will fail if the goods are of such a kind that it is unlawful to deal with them at all, such as obscene books,[2820] or if it appears that the goods were wanted for an illegal purpose, such as the returning of his jemmy to a burglar[2821] or a carving knife

2816. *Revill v. Newbery* [1996] QB 567.

2817. *Clunis v. Camden and Islington Health Authority* [1998] QB 978.

2818. *Ellis v. Counties Manukau DHB* [2007] 1 NZLR 196; *Hunter Area Health Service v. Presland* (2005) 63 NSWLR 22.

2819. *Gray v. Thames Trains Ltd* [2009] 1 AC 1339; applied in *Henderson v. Dorset Healthcare University NHS Foundation Trust* [2018] EWCA Civ 1841, [2018] 3 WLR 1651.

2820. *Bowmakers Ltd v. Barnet Instruments Ltd* [1945] KB 65.

2821. *R v. Collis* [1990] 2 NZLR 287 at 293.

to an intending murderer.[2822] Should a court allow such claims it would be assisting in the commission of a criminal offence, so the need for consistency with the criminal law must bar them.

IV. Plaintiff's Turpitude

490. In *Gray*, Lord Hoffmann asked whether it would be 'offensive to public notions of the fair distribution of resources that a claimant should be compensated (usually out of public funds) for the consequences of his own criminal conduct'.[2823] In *Hounga* Lord Hughes referred to the need to consider the gravity of the illegality of which the claimant was guilty and her knowledge or intention in relation to it.[2824] There are many judicial references to the question whether the plaintiff's illegal conduct is of such moral turpitude as to require recovery to be denied on the grounds of public policy.

Objection may be taken to the 'sufficient moral turpitude' test on the grounds that its content cannot be ascertained with any degree of precision and that it all depends ultimately on an ad hoc value judgment of the court concerned. In *Les Laboratoires Servier v. Apotex Inc*[2825] Lord Sumption sought to meet the difficulty by defining 'turpitude' as meaning acts which engaged the interests of the state or, to put it another way, the public interest, irrespective of the interests or rights of the parties. The paradigm case was a criminal act. In addition, the rule was concerned with a limited category of acts which, while not necessarily criminal, could conveniently be called 'quasi-criminal' because they engaged the public interest in the same way. Leaving aside the special case of contracts prohibited by law, which could give rise to no enforceable rights, the category included cases of dishonesty or corruption, some anomalous categories of misconduct, such as prostitution, and the infringement of statutory rules enacted for the protection of the public interest and attracting civil sanctions of a penal character. Torts (other than those of which dishonesty was an essential element), breaches of contract, statutory, and other civil wrongs offended against interests, which were essentially private, not public. There was no reason in such cases for the law to withhold its ordinary remedies. So in the instant case, involving the sale of a drug in England in breach of the claimant's patent rights in Canada, the illegality defence was not engaged.

Lord Sumption recognized that there might be exceptional cases where even criminal and quasi-criminal acts would not constitute turpitude, noting that some offences might be too trivial to engage the defence. But what is 'trivial' may be very much a matter of dispute. Seemingly it will be necessary to take into account factors such as the nature and gravity of the defendant's conduct and the penalty involved. So in looking to the public interest we have, perhaps, a clearer focus for the inquiry, but a judgment about the degree of turpitude involved still must be made.

2822. *Gollan v. Nugent* (1988) 166 CLR 18 at [16].
2823. *Gray v. Thames Trains Ltd* [2009] 1 AC 1339 at [51].
2824. *Hounga v. Allen* [2014] 1 WLR 2889 at [55].
2825. *Les Laboratoires Servier v. Apotex Inc* [2015] AC 430.

V. Proportionality

491. In *Hounga v. Allen*[2826] the appellant (H), when aged about 14, came from Nigeria to the UK under fraudulent arrangements made by the family of the respondent (A) in which H knowingly participated. H then worked for A, in the circumstances unlawfully, for about eighteen months before being dismissed and evicted from A's house. H brought an action complaining, *inter alia*, of unlawful discrimination relating to her employment, and the question arose whether it was barred by reason of the ex turpi causa rule.

Lord Wilson, giving the majority decision of the UK Supreme Court, recognized that the defence of illegality rested on the foundation of public policy, and said that it was necessary, first, to ask 'What is the aspect of public policy which founds the defence?' and, second, to ask 'But is there another aspect of public policy to which application of the defence would run counter?'. As regards the first question, his Lordship saw a concern to preserve the integrity of the legal system as a helpful rationale. Here an award of compensation to H did not allow her to profit from her fraud or permit evasion of a criminal penalty. It was an award of compensation for injury to her feelings consequent upon her dismissal. As regards the second question, his Lordship thought that A was guilty of 'trafficking', or her conduct was very close to it, in bringing H from Nigeria to the UK and into her home. By the Council of Europe Convention on Action against Trafficking in Human Beings, which had been ratified by the UK, each party was obliged to provide, in its internal law, for the right of victims to compensation from the perpetrators. So it would be a breach of the UK's international obligations for its law to cause H's complaint to be defeated by the defence of illegality. The public policy in support of the application of that defence, to the extent that it existed at all, should give way to the public policy to which its application was an affront.

The approach of the majority in this case appears to be inconsistent with that taken shortly afterwards in the Apotex decision by a different Supreme Court bench,[2827] leaving the law in a state of some confusion. Then, in *Patel v. Mirza*,[2828] the UK Supreme Court revisited the question and resolved the conflict broadly in accordance with the majority view in Hounga. Although this was a claim in restitution, the principles involved were clearly intended to cover tort claims.

The plaintiff (P) paid GBP 620,000 to the defendant (M) for the purposes of an illegal agreement for insider dealing in company shares. In the event, the agreement could not be and was not carried out, because the expected inside information was not forthcoming. P sued for the return of the money, and the question for the Supreme Court was whether the claim was barred by the ex turpi causa rule, on the basis that P had conspired to engage in insider trading. All nine of their Lordships agreed that P could recover his money, but they did not agree on the reasoning leading to that conclusion.

Lord Toulson, giving the majority view, recognized that the law was at a crossroads, and that the choice for the Court lay between a rule-based and a 'range of

2826. [2014] 1 WLR 2889.
2827. *See* above para. 490.
2828. [2016] 3 WLR 399.

factors' approach. There were two broad discernible policy reasons for the common law doctrine of illegality as a defence to a civil claim. One was that a person should not be allowed to profit from his own wrongdoing. The other, linked, consideration was that the law should be coherent and not self-defeating, condoning illegality by giving with the left hand what it took with the right hand. So how was the Court to determine the matter? One could not judge whether allowing a claim which was in some way tainted by illegality would be contrary to the public interest, because it would lead to inconsistency and be harmful to the integrity of the legal system, without (a) considering the underlying purpose of the prohibition which had been transgressed; (b) considering conversely any other relevant public policies which might be rendered ineffective or less effective by denial of the claim; and (c) keeping in mind the possibility of overkill unless the law was applied with a due sense of proportionality.[2829]

In the instant case his Lordship concluded that a claimant, such as P, who satisfied the ordinary requirements of a claim for unjust enrichment, should not be debarred from enforcing his claim by reason only of the fact that the money which he sought to recover was paid for an unlawful purpose. There might be rare cases where for some particular reason the enforcement of such a claim might be regarded as undermining the integrity of the justice system, but this was not such a case.

The decision in *Patel* arguably throws into doubt the continuing authority of the inconsistency argument applied in *Gray v. Thames Trains*. In *Henderson v. Dorset Healthcare University NHS Foundation Trust*[2830] the claimant, who had a history of paranoid schizophrenia, was discharged from her detention in hospital and subsequently stabbed her mother to death. She later pleaded guilty to manslaughter on the ground of diminished responsibility and was ordered to be detained in a secure hospital. She argued that it would be disproportionate to deny her claim against the hospital where her responsibility for wrongdoing was less than significant, but the English Court of Appeal held that there was no suggestion in *Patel* that *Gray* was wrongly decided, that it remained binding and that it had to be applied. Yet this seems to treat the inconsistency argument as a continuing rule of law, and leaves the potential impact of *Patel* in tort cases generally somewhat up in the air.

VI. Conclusions

492. The majority view abolishes ex turpi causa as any kind of rule, and allows considerations relating to the plaintiff's illegal behaviour to be taken into consideration together with all other factors deemed to be relevant in favour of or against

---

2829. At [82]–[101]. *See also XX v. Whittington Hospital NHS Trust* [2020] UKSC 14, [2020] 2 WLR 972 (claimant who became infertile due to defendant's negligence sought the expenses of making a lawful commercial surrogacy agreement in California, notwithstanding a statute rendering commercial surrogacy unlawful in the UK: held that the claimant would be acting lawfully and it was not contrary to public policy to award damages).

2830. [2018] EWCA Civ 1841, [2018] 3 WLR 1651. An appeal has been made to the Supreme Court.

the claim. As Lord Sumption points out in his dissenting reasoning, this is inconsistent with the very nature of the ex turpi causa plea. Its essence is that the law cannot support the plaintiff's claim, not that the merits favour the defendant. So what solution ought to be adopted in New Zealand?

So far as claims in contract are concerned, subpoint 5 of point 2 of the Contract and Commercial Law Act 2017 (formerly the Illegal Contracts Act 1970) would apply in circumstances such as in *Patel*.[2831] In tort claims it is helpful to ask, first, whether there is inconsistency between the requirements of the criminal law and the award of a civil remedy. But this narrow rule may not necessarily apply in circumstances where a claim should nonetheless be barred. For example, suppose a hitman fails to murder the proposed victim, whereupon the hirer demands his money back. Such a claim could be based upon restitutionary principles, as in *Patel*, on the basis that the principal can claim his money back from his agent without reference to the illegal purpose. Yet the decision surely would be different.[2832] The turpitude of the plaintiff's conduct must necessarily bar any relief.[2833] Accordingly, if the claim is not barred by the inconsistency principle, the courts need to ask a second question concerning the turpitude involved in the plaintiff's conduct. This, very arguably, should be whether or not the grant of relief by a court would be contrary to the public interest in the sense explained by Lord Sumption in *Apotex*.

2831. *See Horsfall v. Potter* [2017] NZSC 196, [2018] 1 NZLR 638, especially at [53]–[60].

2832. In *Patel* Lord Neuberger (at [176]) said that he would allow such a claim!.

2833. In New Zealand the claim would be covered by Part 2 subpart 5 of the Contract and Commercial Law Act 2017 (as to which *see International Encyclopaedia of Laws: Contracts (New Zealand)* (2017), paras 145–159), but our concern here is with the general principles of the common law in tort claims.

Chapter 3. Grounds of Justification

§1. Consent

I. General

493. Consent either negates liability or is a good defence to liability for an intentional tort. The consent in such cases is to the actual infliction of harm. Where there is consent merely to the risk of negligently inflicted harm, the defence known as *volenti non fit injuria* applies. Volenti raises a question about the entitlement of the plaintiff to sue rather than about the justification for inflicting consensual harm, and accordingly it has been given separate consideration.[2834]

The question of consent often arises in the context of intentionally inflicted physical injury, when the availability of a tort action in respect of conduct to which there is no, or no sufficient, consent is subject to the bar on proceedings for damages for personal injury in the accident compensation legislation.[2835] But the plaintiff may still seek to recover exemplary damages.[2836]

II. Onus of Proof

494. In the case of a claim alleging assault and battery, the Court of Appeal has said, albeit without discussion, that lack of consent is part of the cause of action.[2837] The reasoning is that a person cannot be said to be assaulted against his or her will. However, it is convenient to consider the question of consent at this point, as the same principles apply at least to some extent as where consent does operate as a defence. Certainly, as regards trespass to land and to goods and other intentional torts, it is clear that consent is a defence and that the onus of proving that the plaintiff consented to the conduct is on the defendant.

III. Nature of Consent

495. In an action for battery, if the plaintiff has consented to or permitted the contact, either expressly or impliedly, there is no liability.[2838] The principles governing consent to bodily harm in the context of a criminal prosecution were examined by the Court of Appeal in *R v. Lee*.[2839] Glazebrook J, delivering the judgment of the court, laid down the following propositions:[2840]

2834. *See* paras 483–485.
2835. *See* para. 41.
2836. *See* para. 42.
2837. *S v. G* [1995] 3 NZLR 681 at 687; cp *Department of Health & Community Services (NT) v. JWB and SMB* (1992) 175 CLR 218 at 310–311; *Non-Marine Underwriters, Lloyds of London v. Scalera* [2000] 1 SCR 551.
2838. *Dann v. Hamilton* [1939] 1 KB 504 at 515–516.
2839. [2006] 3 NZLR 42.
2840. *Ibid.*, at [312]–[316].

- Apart from sparring matches or playfights and organized matches conducted with a referee and according to established rules, consent is not a defence in relation to fighting. Those involved in sparring matches and playfights must not be acting in reckless disregard for the safety of others and must not intend to cause bodily injury for consent to be operative.
- Where grievous bodily harm is intended, public policy factors may require the judge to withdraw the defence of consent from the jury. The same applies where a perpetrator acts in reckless disregard for the safety of others. When deciding whether consent should be withdrawn as a defence on public policy grounds in such situations the judge should take into account the right to personal autonomy, the social utility (or otherwise) of the activity, the level of seriousness of the injury intended or risked, the level of risk of such injury, the rationality of any consent or belief in consent, and any other relevant factors in the particular case.

Non-organized fighting and certain other intentional harms could be treated differently in a civil case, where consent could be relevant. The public policy involved in prosecuting those fighting, or, say, inflicting harm in the course of sadomasochistic activities is different where the question is simply the recovery of damages. There may be good reason to prosecute, but not to allow a private remedy.

Participation in a sport involves consent to contacts permitted by the rules of the game, and perhaps to other contacts not involving breach of rules protecting players' safety.[2841] The minor physical contacts of everyday life, like touching a person to gain attention, may be treated as being impliedly consented to by the person concerned.[2842] To kiss one's wife or fiancée, to shake hands on meeting, or to pat a friend by way of encouragement does not involve assault because of the implicit consent.[2843] Again, a person may consent to a restraint upon his or her freedom that bars an action for false imprisonment. An example is where a passenger entered a ferry terminal through a turnstile and had to wait for the next ferry to arrive.[2844]

Consent equally may be given to an interference with goods. A defendant was not guilty of conversion where, with the consent of the owner, he obtained a stolen bicycle from the thief in order to claim a reward being offered by the owner.[2845] An owner who parked his car unlawfully in a private car park containing several notice boards warning that wheel clamps would be applied to unauthorized vehicles was held to have consented to the risk of clamping.[2846] But there was no consent where the motorist was ill and in a distressed state and did not see the notice.[2847]

There may be consent to enter land, either express or implied.[2848] An example of an implied licence is where police officers go onto land to make inquiries.[2849] If the

2841. *Zapf v. Muckalt* (1997) 142 DLR (4th) 438.
2842. *Collins v. Wilcock* [1984] 1 WLR 1172.
2843. *Police v. Bannin* [1991] 2 NZLR 237 at 244.
2844. *Robinson v. Balmain New Ferry Co.* [1910] AC 295.
2845. *Broom v. Police* [1994] 1 NZLR 680.
2846. *Arthur v. Anker* [1996] 2 WLR 602 (CA); cp *Police v. Krupinski* [1994] DCR 12.
2847. *Vine v. Waltham Forest LBC* [2000] 1 WLR 2383.
2848. *See* further para. 180.
2849. *Robson v. Hallett* [1967] 2 QB 939; *Tararo v. R* [2012] 1 NZLR 145; cp *Hamed v. R* [2012] 2 NZLR 305.

licence is withdrawn the licensee is allowed a reasonable time in which to leave.[2850] Again, there may be consent to a nuisance, but it is not a defence that the plaintiff acquired land that was already affected by the nuisance.[2851]

A person may consent to defamation, although whether the consent extends to the particular circumstances of the publication is a question of fact.[2852]

IV. Consent to Medical Treatment

496. Medical treatment to which there was no consent at all, or treatment that went beyond that to which there was consent, may constitute the tort of battery. However, any injury that this causes is likely to amount to 'treatment injury', in which case an action against the doctor is barred under the accident compensation scheme.[2853] But a claim for exemplary damages might lie,[2854] and a complaint may be made and compensation for injury to feelings awarded under the New Zealand Code of Health and Disability Consumers' Rights.[2855]

An adult patient is entitled to refuse consent to treatment irrespective of the wisdom of his or her decision or the advice of his or her doctor.[2856] Sometimes, however, a patient lacks the capacity to give or to refuse consent. Where the patient is unconscious the treatment can be justified by necessity, unless the doctor knows that no consent is given.[2857] A child of or over sixteen can give a valid consent to medical treatment,[2858] and if under sixteen or intellectually handicapped the consent may be given by the child's parent or guardian.[2859] However, a court may authorize medical procedures or treatment on the basis of what is in the best interests of the child,[2860] and in appropriate cases this authorization may override the wishes of a parent or guardian or the child himself or herself.[2861] A person of unsound mind undergoing treatment pursuant to mental health legislation is obliged to accept treatment for mental disorder[2862] and for other medical treatments necessary to prevent serious injury to himself or herself or others.[2863] In other cases, where the common law applies, the medical treatment of an intellectually incapable person is justified where it is in the best interests of the patient.[2864]

2850. *Robson v. Hallett ibid.*; *Polly v. Police* [1985] 1 NZLR 443; *Howden v. Ministry of Transport* [1987] 2 NZLR 747.
2851. *See* para. 196.
2852. *See* para. 356.
2853. *See* paras 37, 41.
2854. *See* para. 42.
2855. *See* para. 110.
2856. *Smith v. Auckland Hospital Board* [1965] NZLR 191 at 219; and *see* the New Zealand Bill of Rights Act 1990, s. 11.
2857. *See* para. 499.
2858. Care of Children Act 2004, s. 36(1).
2859. *Ibid.*, s. 36(3).
2860. *Ibid.*, ss 4, 30–35.
2861. *See Re J* [1996] 2 NZLR 134.
2862. Mental Health (Compulsory Assessment and Treatment) Act 1992, ss 58–60; Protection of Personal and Property Rights Act 1988, s. 10(1)(f).
2863. Mental Health (Compulsory Assessment and Treatment) Act 1992, s. 62.
2864. *Re F* [1990] 2 AC 1.

A doctor or other health professional is obliged to inform a patient about the risks which are involved in medical treatment, for it is the patient's fundamental right to decide whether or not to undergo the treatment.[2865] The obligation requires a doctor to disclose to his or her patient all 'material' risks. A risk is material if a reasonable person in the patient's situation would have regarded it as significant or, to the doctor's knowledge, the particular patient would have done so.[2866]

V. Duress and Fraud

497. A plaintiff who submits under duress to the infliction of a tort gives no true consent to the conduct. For example, a patient who granted sexual favours to her doctor in order to obtain the drugs to which she was addicted succeeded in an action for battery. The inequality of power between the parties, the plaintiff's dependence on the drug and the exploitative nature of the relationship meant that her consent was not voluntary.[2867]

Consent to contact with another also may be vitiated by fraud as to the harmful nature of the contact. In a criminal case, a choirmaster who induced a naive young girl to consent to sexual intercourse by telling her that he was carrying out a medical procedure that would improve her voice was held to be guilty of rape.[2868] Alternatively, it may be said that there is a duty to disclose a harmful condition, breach of which either is independently actionable or vitiates consent.

In *KSB v. ACC*,[2869] the Court of Appeal held that consent to sexual intercourse was vitiated by non-disclosure of HIV status for the purpose of establishing criminal responsibility for sexual violation or indecent assault. Ellen France J recognized that there were contrary authorities on the issue in the UK and Australia,[2870] but found the reasoning of McLachlin and Gonthier JJ in the Supreme Court of Canada in *R v. Cuerrier*,[2871] that deception in an HIV case in a very real sense went to the nature of the sexual act, changing it to a potential sentence of disease or death, to be entirely compelling. In New Zealand it was provided in the Crimes Act 1961 that a person did not consent to an act of sexual activity if mistaken about 'its nature and quality',[2872] and commentary on the question suggested that ignorance about HIV infection was not a mistake about the quality of the act, namely the intercourse, but about its consequences, that is the risk of infection.[2873] But her Honour rejected this view and held that the victim's consent was vitiated by mistake as to the nature and quality of the act and the offence of sexual violation was made out.

2865. *Montgomery v. Lanarkshire Health Board* [2015] UKSC 11, [2015] AC 1430.
2866. *Rogers v. Whitaker* (1992) 175 CLR 479 at 490.
2867. *Norberg v. Wynrib* [1992] 2 SCR 226.
2868. *R v. Williams* [1923] 1 KB 340; and *see* Crimes Act 1961, s. 128A; *R v. Cox* CA 213/96, 7 Nov. 1996; *R v. Isherwood* CA 182/04, 14 Mar. 2005.
2869. [2012] NZCA 82; and *see R v. Mwai* [1995] 3 NZLR 149.
2870. *R v. Clarence* (1889) 22 QB 23; *R v. Dica* [2004] QB 1257 (CA); and *see R v. Mobilio* [1991] 1 VR 339; *R v. B* [2007] 1 WLR 1567.
2871. [1998] 2 SCR 371.
2872. Section 128A(7) Crimes Act 1961.
2873. *Adams on Criminal Law* (B Robertson ed.), at CA128A.06(2).

Some difficult questions remain. When exactly will consent be vitiated? Should the use of a condom and/or after a degree of success with antiretroviral therapy make a difference? How big a risk must there be? In an earlier decision at first instance,[2874] where it was held that consent was not vitiated, Randerson J recognized that the problem was where to draw the line. Was a deliberate lie or misrepresentation required? What types of misrepresentation were sufficient? There was difficulty in distinguishing between non-disclosure of important facts and those that were trivial. Certainly the implications of the *KSB* decision are not at all clear.

§2. NECESSITY

I. General

498. Where the principle of necessity applies, conduct that would otherwise be a tortious interference with the person or property is lawfully justified. The onus of proving that conduct was justified by necessity rests on the defendant.[2875] At common law the defence protects a person who takes reasonable and proportionate steps to protect others from the immediate risk of significant harm.[2876] It can apply to safeguard both persons and property under threat of such harm. There are also many instances of conduct which can be justified by statute, on broadly similar bases.[2877] Necessity differs from self-defence[2878] or defence of property[2879] in that it can excuse harm being done to a person who is not personally threatening the plaintiff.

II. Protection of the Person

499. The defence of necessity is made out where a person believes in good faith and upon grounds that are objectively reasonable that his or her conduct is necessary in order to preserve human life, or to prevent serious physical harm arising to the person of another, or to render assistance to another after that other has suffered serious physical harm.[2880] There must be a situation of imminent or immediate peril.[2881] Accordingly, an invasion of the plaintiff's person may be justified by the need to preserve the plaintiff's life or health. This covers, for example, urgent treatment administered by a doctor in circumstances where the patient is unable to give

2874. *CLM v. ACC* [2006] 3 NZLR 127.
2875. *Wilcox v. Police* [1995] 2 NZLR 160 at 163.
2876. *R (Munjaz) v. Mersey Care NHS Trust* [2003] 3 WLR 1505 at [46] (on appeal [2006] 2 AC 148).
2877. *See*, for example, Search and Surveillance Act 2012, s. 14 (constable may enter land to prevent certain offending or avert emergency).
2878. *See* para. 502.
2879. *See* para. 503.
2880. *Dehn v. A-G* [1988] 2 NZLR 564 at 580 (on appeal [1989] 1 NZLR 320 (CA)); *Leason v. Attorney-General* [2014] 2 NZLR 224 at [79].
2881. *Leason v. Attorney-General* [2014] 2 NZLR 224 at [80]–[81].

his or her consent.[2882] Such treatment may be justified where the patient is unconscious,[2883] or lacks capacity to give an informed consent.[2884] The necessary treatment of mental patients can be justified by statutory powers.[2885] Again, a mental patient who has not been committed under mental health legislation and who poses a danger or potential danger to himself or others can be detained insofar as this is shown to be necessary to remove the danger.[2886] Such a patient also can be detained in seclusion to protect himself or others from the immediate risk of harm.[2887]

The withdrawal of medical life support systems or other treatments may be justified, and thus not actionable, in special cases where such a course is in accordance with good medical practice and continued treatment will not in fact benefit the patient.[2888] In a unique case, positive surgery was an act of necessity to preserve the life of one of the conjoined twins.[2889] The life of one twin could be saved if they were separated, but the operation would kill the weaker twin. Both would die within about six months without the operation. It was held that the least detrimental choice was to allow the operation.

Emergency medical treatment cannot be administered to an adult of full capacity who refuses to accept it.[2890] So an emergency caesarean operation was not authorized where the mother refused her consent.[2891] Again, a blood transfusion could not be administered to an unconscious person contrary to her clear written instructions.[2892] But a court may authorize a blood transfusion for a child, contrary to the wishes of the parents, where this is necessary to save life or prevent permanent injury.[2893] At common law there can be no justification for the force-feeding of a prisoner on hunger strike, on the ground that a prisoner of sound mind and capacity has a specific right of self-determination that entitles him to refuse nutrition and hydration.[2894] But there may be intervention in extreme circumstances, as it is provided by statute that everyone is justified in using such force as may be reasonably necessary to prevent the commission of suicide.[2895]

The necessity of saving life can also provide a proper ground for inflicting damage to another's property or for trespassing on property. Examples include throwing goods overboard to lighten a boat in a storm[2896] and, arguably, discharging oil from a ship near the plaintiff's foreshore in the belief that this was necessary to avoid a

2882. As regards consent to medical treatment, *see* para. 496.
2883. *See Malette v. Shulman* (1990) 67 DLR (4th) 321.
2884. *Re T* [1993] Fam 95.
2885. Mental Health (Compulsory Assessment and Treatment) Act 1992, s. 62. For an example in England, *see R(N) v. M* [2003] 1 WLR 562.
2886. *R v. Bournewood Community and Mental Health Trust, ex p L* [1999] 1 AC 458.
2887. *R (Munjaz) v. Mersey Care NHS Trust* [2003] 3 WLR 1505 (on appeal [2006] 2 AC 148).
2888. *Auckland Area Health Board v. A-G* [1993] 1 NZLR 235; *Airedale NHS Trust v. Bland* [1993] AC 789.
2889. *Re A* [2001] 2 WLR 480; *An NHS Trust v. Y* [2018] UKSC 46, [2018] 3 WLR 751.
2890. *Re T* [1993] Fam 95.
2891. *St George's Healthcare NHS Trust v. S* [1998] 3 WLR 936.
2892. *Malette v. Shulman* (1990) 67 DLR (4th) 321.
2893. Care of Children Act 2004, s. 37; and *see Re J* [1996] 2 NZLR 134.
2894. *Secretary of State for the Home Department v. Robb* [1995] Fam 127 at 130; cp *Leigh v. Gladstone* (1909) 26 TLR 139.
2895. Crimes Act 1961, s. 41; *R v. Roulston* (1998) 15 CRNZ 515.
2896. *Dehn v. Attorney-General* [1988] 2 NZLR 564 at 577.

shipwreck.[2897] On the other hand, a plea of necessity was rejected where the defendants had occupied empty houses belonging to the plaintiff for the sake of homeless families.[2898] Lord Denning MR cautioned that 'Necessity would open a door which no man could shut … The plea would be an excuse for all sorts of wrongdoing.' So too, three police officers were not justified in entering a house against the wishes of the occupants where the evidence did not establish sufficiently clear that the officers believed that another of the occupants was in urgent need of assistance.[2899] And damaging government property in order to expose and prevent the harm caused by the war in Iraq could not be justified on this basis.[2900]

Various statutes authorize damage to or entry on property. For example, a constable may enter premises to prevent the commission of any offence that would be likely to cause immediate and serious injury to any person or property, if he believes, on reasonable and probable grounds, that any such offence is about to be committed.[2901] There is a statutory power justifying the destruction of dangerous dogs in certain circumstances.[2902]

III. Protection of Property

500. An interference with the plaintiff's property may also be justified by the need to save other property, whether of the plaintiff, the defendant, or a third party, although a different scale of values is involved than in cases of danger to the person.[2903] Thus, a landowner is justified in driving away water from his or her land, even if the consequence is that the water goes on to and damages the land of another, where that water is not flowing naturally from higher land or is not flowing through an artificial drain that has become the place where the water is naturally deemed to go.[2904] Further examples include towing a vessel into open waters during a storm to save the vessel and the wharf to which it had been moored;[2905] and repelling a plague of locusts from the defendant's land, causing them to re-enter that of the plaintiff.[2906] But there was no sufficient necessity for the act where soil was placed on the plaintiffs' property in order to prevent subsidence after the plaintiffs had mistakenly excavated part of the defendant's land, but there was no evidence of immediate danger to the land.[2907]

2897. *Southport Corporation v. Esso Petroleum Co. Ltd* [1953] 3 WLR 773 at 778–779 (not discussed on appeal [1954] 2 QB 182 (CA), [1956] AC 218 (HL)).
2898. *Southwark London Borough Council v. Williams* [1971] Ch 734.
2899. *Dehn v. A-G* [1988] 2 NZLR 564 (on appeal [1989] 1 NZLR 320 (CA)).
2900. *Leason v. Attorney-General* [2014] 2 NZLR 224.
2901. Crimes Act 1961, s. 317(2); *Edwards v. Police* [1994] 2 NZLR 164.
2902. Dog Control Act 1996, s. 57.
2903. *Dehn v. A-G* [1988] 2 NZLR 564 at 580.
2904. *Bailey v. Vile* [1930] NZLR 829; *Dijkmans v. Howick Borough* [1971] NZLR 400; *Davis v. Lethbridge* [1976] 1 NZLR 689.
2905. *Beckingham v. Port Jackson and Manly SS Co.* [1957] SR (NSW) 403.
2906. *Greyvensteyn v. Hattingh* [1911] AC 355.
2907. *Brown v. Dunsmuir* [1994] 3 NZLR 485.

No damages in tort can be recovered in respect of harm to property where the conduct is justified by necessity, but the question remains whether a claim for restitution might be maintained. In the case of acts done for the public good, the defendant is not liable. An example is where a person, acting justifiably, pulls down the plaintiff's house in time of fire in order to stop the fire from spreading,[2908] and, by statute, no action lies in respect of any damage to property occasioned by acts done in good faith by the fire fighting services.[2909] However, at least in the case of acts done for the advancement of the defendant's own interests, arguably an order for restitution can be made.[2910] Where the act is done for the benefit of a third party, possibly the third party might be liable on a similar basis, but not where the defendant acted for the plaintiff's own benefit.

§3. Self-Help

501. Defences to conduct that would otherwise be tortious also are found in those circumstances in which a person is lawfully justified in exercising self-help in respect of the wrong of another. Self-help overlaps to a considerable extent with the principle of necessity. Generally speaking, self-help, particularly if it involves the use of force, is regarded as undesirable for the reason that it encourages breaches of the peace and is in tension with values of social order and stability.[2911]

I. Self-Defence

502. One particular form of self-help recognized at common law, and now found in legislation, is the right of self-defence, which operates as a defence to an action for battery. By section 48 of the Crimes Act 1961, an act of force is justified where it was committed in a person's own defence, or in the defence of another, and the force used was reasonable in the circumstances as that person believed them to be.[2912] 'Justified' means not guilty of an offence and not liable to any civil proceeding.[2913] The 'force' that gives rise to the defence includes threats as well as actual force,[2914] but it does not include simply acting passively.[2915] The accused should genuinely believe that he or she or another person needed defending from imminent danger of bodily harm, which may be either mental or physical harm.[2916] However,

2908. *Southwark London Borough Council v. Williams* [1971] 1 Ch 734 at 743.
2909. Fire and Emergency New Zealand Act 2017, s. 161(1).
2910. *Esso Petroleum Co. Ltd v. Southport Corporation* [1953] 3 WLR 773 at 778.
2911. *Taueki v. R* [2014] 1 NZLR 235.
2912. As to the defence of another, *see*, for example, *R v. Thomas* [1991] 3 NZLR 141; *R v. Kneale* [1998] 2 NZLR 169; *Leason v. Attorney-General* [2014] 2 NZLR 224.
2913. Crimes Act 1961, s. 42.
2914. *R v. Terewi* (1985) 1 CRNZ 623.
2915. *Bayer v. Police* [1994] 2 NZLR 48.
2916. *R v. Kneale* [1998] 2 NZLR 169. However, there must be a living person, and the defence could not be raised by demonstrators seeking to prevent women from having abortions: *Wilcox v. Police* [1994] 1 NZLR 243; *Bayer v. Police* [1994] 2 NZLR 48.

a citizen cannot take the law into his or her own hands and use force to give effect to his or her honest view that this was necessary to enforce the law in the interests of the community at large.[2917]

The test for determining whether a person was acting in self-defence or in the defence of another involves three questions:

(1) What were the circumstances as the person honestly believed them to be?
(2) In those circumstances, was the person acting in defence of self or another?
(3) Was the force used reasonable in the circumstances?[2918]

The first question is concerned with the defendant's subjective beliefs. Accordingly, there may be no civil liability where the force is inflicted in circumstances where the defendant has an honest belief that he or she is in imminent danger, irrespective of the reasonableness of that belief. It is clear that at common law there is a good defence to a claim for battery only where the belief is reasonable,[2919] so section 48 imposes an arguably inappropriate standard for a tort action. The second question poses a purely factual issue. The third question imposes an objective test of reasonableness. Broadly speaking, what constitutes reasonable force to protect oneself or another must depend on the imminence and seriousness of the threat and the opportunity to seek protection without resort to the use of force.[2920] Normally, any force should commensurate with the attack that it is intended to avert.[2921] If the force used is unreasonable and excessive then it ceases to be lawful and a plea of self-defence fails.[2922]

II. Defence of Property

503. A person may take reasonable steps in the defence of his or her property. At common law a person is justified in using reasonably necessary force to defend his or her land or chattels against a person threatening to commit or committing a trespass to that property.[2923] Where property is in real or imminent danger, the goods of another may be interfered with to preserve the property. For example, a dog could be shot for attacking sheep in circumstances where a reasonable person would have concluded that the defendant had no alternative to shooting it.[2924] The burden of

2917. *R v. Jones* [2007] 1 AC 136 at [70]–[88]; *Leason v. Attorney-General* [2014] 2 NZLR 224 at [50]–[61].
2918. *R v. Bridger* [2003] 1 NZLR 636.
2919. *Ashley v. Chief Constable of Sussex Police* [2008] 1 AC 962, where the House of Lords emphasized that there is a difference in English law between the criminal and the civil standard.
2920. *R v. Ranger* (1988) 4 CRNZ 6; *R v. Wang* [1990] 2 NZLR 529; *R v. Li* 28 Jun. 2000, CA 140 & 141/00; *Leason v. Attorney-General* [2014] 2 NZLR 224 at [50]–[61].
2921. *R v. Wang* [1990] 2 NZLR 529; *R v. Savage* [1991] 3 NZLR 155.
2922. *See*, for example, *Flint v. Tittensor* [2015] 1 WLR 4370.
2923. *Burt v. Ross* (1886) NZLR 5 SC 161; *Snell v. Mitchell* [1951] 1 NZLR 1.
2924. *Cresswell v. Sirl* [1948] 1 KB 241; and *see Hamps v. Derby* [1948] 2 KB 311. Justification for seizing or destroying aggressive dogs is now found in the Dog Control Act 1996, s. 57. The common law applies in other circumstances.

proof is on the defendant resisting the claim.[2925] Again, reasonable force can be used to retake chattels that were being wrongfully withheld from the owner.[2926] This principle seemingly can apply in all cases where chattels are in the possession of any person who is not entitled to them.[2927] However, Australian authority holds that the remedy of self-help ought to be limited to cases where the possession initially was obtained wrongfully.[2928] And certainly the remedy could not be invoked to justify the forcible removal of a person from the defendant's car where that person was there at the defendant's invitation and wished to be driven back from whence she had come.[2929]

Powers to defend property are given by statute. A person in peaceable possession of any land or building is justified in using reasonable force to prevent another from trespassing on that land or building, or to remove the other from it, provided the person does not strike or do bodily harm to the trespasser.[2930] A person in peaceable possession of a dwellinghouse is justified in using necessary force to prevent the forcible breaking and entering of that dwellinghouse if the person believes on reasonable and probable grounds that there is no lawful justification for the breaking and entering.[2931] A person in peaceable possession of goods, and anyone lending lawful assistance, is justified in using reasonable force to resist the taking of the goods by a trespasser, or to retake them from a trespasser, if the person does not strike or do bodily harm to the trespasser.[2932]

III. Recaption of Chattels

504. At common law the person entitled to possession may enter land to retake goods that have been unlawfully taken by the occupier,[2933] and may use reasonable force in doing so.[2934] But where the goods have been left on the land unlawfully, seemingly there is no right to enter to recover them:[2935] rather, the occupier can

---

2925. *Ashley v. Chief Constable of Sussex Police* [2007] 1 WLR 398 at [25]–[27] (on appeal [2008] 1 AC 962).
2926. *Blades v. Higgs* (1861) 10 CBNS 713; 142 ER 634, on appeal (1865) 11 HL Cas 621; 11 ER 1474; *De Lambert v. Ongley* [1924] NZLR 430.
2927. *De Lambert v. Ongley* [1924] NZLR 430.
2928. *Toyota Finance Australia Ltd v. Dennis* (2003) 58 NSWLR 101; followed in *Slater v. Attorney-General (No. 1)* [2006] NZAR 664.
2929. *R v. Burns* [2010] 1 WLR 2694.
2930. Crimes Act 1961, s. 56; *Taueki v. R* [2014] 1 NZLR 235 ('peaceable possession' is a possession that has been achieved other than in the context of an immediate and ongoing dispute: possession obtained and maintained before the employment of physical force the use of which the person seeks to justify); *Marsters v. R* [2014] NZCA 395.
2931. Crimes Act 1961, s. 55.
2932. *Ibid.*, s. 52.
2933. *Patrick v. Colerick* (1838) 3 M & W 483, 150 ER 1235; *Wood v. Manley* [1835-42] All ER Rep 128.
2934. *R v. Milton* (1827) 1 M & W 107, 173 ER 1097.
2935. *Stear v. Scott* [1992] RTR 226; *Lloyd v. Director of Public Prosecutions* [1992] 1 All ER 982 at 987; cp *Police v. Krupinski* [1994] DCR 12.

retain them until the owner pays for any damage done to the land.[2936] Where neither the occupier of the land nor the owner of the chattel is a wrongdoer, it may be that entry to recover the chattel can be made where the occupier has been given notice but has refused to deliver it up.[2937]

IV. Distress Damage Feasant

505. If any goods are unlawfully on land and doing damage, the person entitled to the possession of the land may seize the goods and withhold them until the owner has paid compensation for the damage. This ancient remedy is known as distress damage feasant. Its boundaries are narrowly defined. In particular, the presence of the distrained goods must be unlawful:[2938] the goods must actually be on the land when they are seized;[2939] and the goods must not at the time be in the possession of the owner.[2940] So there was no right to tow away an unlawfully parked car when the owner was actually inside it;[2941] nor could a car be immobilized by a wheel clamp when the owner was present.[2942]

The remedy of distress damage feasant is available only to secure the payment of compensation for actual damage caused by the goods. This may include the expenses reasonably incurred in removing an unlawfully parked vehicle;[2943] but overseas authority has cast doubt on this view.[2944] If the trespasser tenders reasonable compensation and the landowner refuses to accept it, the trespasser may bring an action for the wrongful detention of the chattel.[2945]

V. Impounding of Stock

506. Distress damage feasant originally extended to trespassing livestock, but a remedy now is found in statute. The occupier of land can seize and impound any stock trespassing on the land and, normally, send the stock to the nearest accessible public pound.[2946] In order to recover the stock, the owner must tender certain fees and charges[2947] and pay trespass rates.[2948] These rates, which are an alternative to

---

2936. The occupier can exercise self-help via the remedy of distress damage feasant: *see* para. 505. Alternatively, he or she can enter the land of the owner and deposit them there: *Rea v. Sheward* (1837) 2 M & W 424, 150 ER 823.
2937. *Anthony v. Haney* (1832) 8 Bing 186, 131 ER 372.
2938. *Tillett v. Ward* (1881) 10 QBD 17.
2939. *Clement v. Milner* (1800) 3 Esp 95.
2940. *Jamieson's Tow & Salvage Ltd v. Murray* [1984] 2 NZLR 144.
2941. *Ibid.*
2942. *Police v. Krupinski* [1994] DCR 12.
2943. *Jamieson's Tow & Salvage Ltd v. Murray* [1984] 2 NZLR 144.
2944. *Arthur v. Anker* [1996] 2 WLR 602.
2945. *Sorrell v. Paget* [1950] 1 KB 252 at 263; *see* para. 239.
2946. Impounding Act 1955, ss 21–22. In limited circumstances the occupier can detain stock on his or land for a short time: *see* s. 24.
2947. *Ibid.*, ss 14, 15.
2948. *Ibid.*, s. 16.

damages, are fixed by regulation according to the number and type of stock trespassing and the type of land or crops trespassed on.[2949] The occupier must elect to receive trespass rates, in which case he or she cannot claim damages.[2950] An occupier also can destroy trespassing stock in certain circumstances.[2951]

VI. Abatement of Nuisances

507. A person suffering harm from an actionable nuisance may be entitled to abate it. The remedy is available in clear and simple cases that would not justify the expense of legal proceedings, and urgent cases where an immediate remedy is required.[2952] A common example is where an occupier wishes to abate a nuisance caused by encroaching branches and roots of trees. If these can be cut back without entering the adjoining land then notice to the adjoining occupier is not required.[2953] If entry on that land is needed then, save in cases of emergency, notice is needed.[2954] Any damage done beyond that which is necessary to abate the nuisance remains actionable.[2955]

If a nuisance is abated then any future damage is avoided. However, the occupier affected may still recover damages for any past injury and for the costs of abatement.[2956] Furthermore, the occupier is not obliged to abate. He or she can choose not to do this, but to make a claim for damages or an injunction in the ordinary way.[2957] But it is possible that damages might be limited to the cost of abatement. Where tree roots owned by a highway authority were undermining a nearby building, the owner seeking damages was obliged first to give notice to the authority and the opportunity to avoid the damage by removal of the tree. Ample notice having been given, the building owner could then recover full damages from the authority.[2958]

§4. Other Matters of Justification

508. A number of other matters of justification have been considered in the context of various particular torts. For example, lawful arrest using reasonable force can justify what would otherwise amount to a false imprisonment and a battery;[2959] statutory authority is a defence to claims founded on nuisance and *Rylands v.*

2949. Impounding Regulations of 1981, Sch. 2.
2950. Impounding Act 1955, s. 27.
2951. *Ibid.*, s. 31(2).
2952. *Burton v. Winters* [1993] 1 WLR 1077 at 1081.
2953. *Lemmon v. Webb* [1895] AC 1; *Darroch v. Carroll* [1955] NZLR 997.
2954. *Lemmon v. Webb* [1895] AC 1.
2955. *Lagan Navigation Co. v. Lambeg Bleaching, Dyeing & Finishing Co. Ltd* [1927] AC 226.
2956. *New Zealand Forest Products Ltd v. O'Sullivan* [1974] 2 NZLR 80 at 83; cp *City of Richmond v. Scantelbury* [1991] 2 VR 38.
2957. *Morgan v. Khyatt* [1962] NZLR 791 (CA) (affirmed [1964] NZLR 666 (PC)).
2958. *Delaware Mansions Ltd v. Westminster City Council* [2002] 1 AC 321.
2959. *See* para. 62.

Fletcher;[2960] truth, honest opinion, and privilege were considered as defences to defamation.[2961]

2960. *See* para. 195.
2961. *See* paras 339, 342, 346, 349.

Chapter 4. Discharge of Liability

§1. Satisfaction

509. A cause of action against a tortfeasor is discharged where the obligation is fully satisfied. The rule applies as between the parties to an action and also to joint or concurrent wrongdoers. The reason is simply that the plaintiff's loss no longer exists. There is nothing left for anyone to sue on.[2962] A tortfeasor who makes only partial satisfaction of a loss may also be discharged from liability, but this will be by contract with the plaintiff, rather than by satisfaction of the full amount of the obligation.[2963] In this case an action can still be brought in respect of the unsatisfied part of the claim against other concurrent wrongdoers who caused the same damage.[2964]

§2. Judgment

510. Where an action before a court of competent jurisdiction proceeds to final judgment, the original right of action is thereby extinguished. If the plaintiff fails, he or she is estopped from asserting the same right in any other legal proceedings against that party. If the plaintiff succeeds, his or her cause of action merges in the judgment.[2965] The plaintiff may thereafter take action to enforce the judgment, but by virtue of the doctrine of res judicata he or she may no longer sue upon the original claim.

Within one cause of action there may be several issues raised that are necessary for the determination of the case. Once any such issue between the parties has been determined in an action then res judicata applies and they and their privies are precluded from litigating it again.[2966] But res judicata also can be understood in a wider sense. The decision of the High Court of Chancery in *Henderson v. Henderson*[2967] holds that it can apply not only to points on which the court was actually required to form an opinion and pronounce a judgment, but also to every point that properly belonged to the subject of litigation, and that the parties, exercising reasonable diligence, might have brought forward at the time. This latter principle is not a true case of res judicata but is founded on public policy aimed at preventing a multiplicity of actions.[2968] It has been accepted as representing the law in New Zealand on a number of occasions.[2969]

2962. *Allison v. KPMG Peat Marwick* [2000] 1 NZLR 560 at 587, 589.

2963. *See* para. 511.

2964. *Allison v. KPMG Peat Marwick* [2000] 1 NZLR 560.

2965. *Calderwood v. Nominal Defendant* [1970] NZLR 296.

2966. *See* generally *Craddock's Transport Ltd v. Stuart* [1970] NZLR 499; cp *Wall v. Radford* [1991] 2 All ER 741.

2967. (1843) 3 Hare 100; 67 ER 313.

2968. *Yat Tung Investment Co. Ltd v. Dao Heng Bank Ltd* [1975] AC 581 at 590.

2969. For example, *Bank of New Zealand v. Savril Contractors Ltd* [2005] 2 NZLR 475; *Chamberlains v. Lai* [2007] 2 NZLR 7 at [59], [71]–[72]; *Contact Energy Ltd v. Attorney-General* [2009] NZCA 351 at [85]–[87]; *IAK v. SAG* [2011] NZCA 514.

For example, a plaintiff who had brought two unsuccessful claims for defamation against the defendant arising out of the publicity attendant on the issuing of a statement of claim against him, and then instituted another action founded on the same facts but based on negligence and malicious civil proceedings, had the further action struck out on this ground.[2970] And a plaintiff bringing new proceedings could not contend that a claim was not statute barred in circumstances where the plaintiff had failed to contest the same limitation issue in earlier proceedings.[2971] But sometimes there is no sufficient connection between the two proceedings. So an action alleging economic loss caused by the defendant's negligence was allowed in circumstances where the plaintiff was the alter ego of his company and an action by the company involving similar issues had earlier been compromised.[2972] The parties had proceeded with the settlement on the basis that the plaintiff might bring a personal claim, the plaintiff had had financial and other reasons for deferring it, and the procedural history of the second action showed that the defendant accepted that it was not abusive. Again, a claim alleging negligence by an insurance broker in placing cover with a financially insecure insurer arguably was sufficiently different from an earlier claim alleging negligence in failing to pass on material information to the insurer that it could be allowed to proceed.[2973]

The maintenance of a second action that could have been part of an earlier one or that conflicted with another one is not per se an abuse of process. Later proceedings will be more obviously abusive where elements such as a collateral attack on a previous decision, dishonesty, or successive actions amounting to unjust harassment are found to be present.[2974]

§3. Accord and Satisfaction

511. The discharge of an existing liability in tort (or contract) by virtue of an agreement for valuable consideration between the injured party and the tortfeasor is known as an accord and satisfaction. The accord is the agreement by which the obligation is discharged. The satisfaction is the consideration that makes the agreement operative.[2975] So here 'satisfaction' does not mean payment of the full amount of the obligation, objectively assessed, but performance of a contractual obligation as to the amount of damages to be paid. In this case a cause of action lies only on the settlement contract and the original cause of action is extinguished.[2976] However,

2970. *NZ Social Credit Political League Inc v. O'Brien* [1984] 1 NZLR 84.
2971. *Bank of New Zealand v. Savril Contractors Ltd* [2005] 2 NZLR 475 at [109]–[110].
2972. *Johnson v. Gore Wood & Co.* [2001] 2 WLR 72.
2973. *Matthews Corp Ltd v. Edward Lumley & Sons (NZ) Ltd* (1995) 8 PRNZ 388.
2974. *Bradford & Bingley Building Soc Inc v. Seddon* [1999] 4 All ER 217, as interpreted in *Johnson v. Gore Wood & Co.* [2001] 2 WLR 72 at 90.
2975. *British Russian Gazette Ltd v. Associated Newspapers Ltd* [1933] 2 KB 616 at 644; and *see Kelliher v. Bridges* (1911) 31 NZLR 203; *Eyre v. Wilson & Horton Ltd* [1967] NZLR 769.
2976. *Allison v. KPMG Peat Marwick* [2000] 1 NZLR 560 at [131].

the compromise of one cause of action does not bar the later assertion of a different cause of action that is not encompassed by the terms of the original compromise.[2977]

In the case of joint tortfeasors an accord and satisfaction releasing one has been held to release the others,[2978] although it has been said that the rule was a trap for the unwary and that it ought to be abrogated.[2979] An accord and satisfaction with one (or more, but not all) of several tortfeasors does not release the others.[2980]

2977. *Matthews Corp Ltd v. Edward Lumley & Sons (NZ) Ltd* (1995) 8 PRNZ 388.
2978. *Brooks v. NZ Guardian Trust Co. Ltd* [1994] 2 NZLR 134 (CA), appeal dismissed [1995] 1 WLR 96 (PC).
2979. *Allison v. KPMG Peat Marwick* [2000] 1 NZLR 560 at [156]; *see* para. 565.
2980. *See* para. 584.

Chapter 5. Exclusions of Liability

§1. Introduction

512. The operation of contractual terms or of non-contractual conditions or notices seeking to limit or exclude liability in tort in general is governed by common law principle, but in certain particular cases Parliament has intervened to impose a measure of statutory control. At common law a person is free to limit or exclude liability for negligence, subject to meeting relatively stringent requirements as to giving adequate notice of the exclusion and expressing it in terms that are sufficiently clear and unambiguous. Seemingly, however, on grounds of policy, a person cannot exclude liability for his or her own fraud.[2981] As regards statute, there are controls on exclusions of liability in respect of small claims, misrepresentations inducing a contract, and statutory causes of action concerned with fair trading or with protecting consumers that cover similar ground to claims in tort for misstatement or for manufacturing defective property.

§2. Contractual Exclusions

513. A defendant may exclude his or her liability in tort by way of contract with another.[2982] An excluding term may be incorporated into the contract either by expressly including it in a signed document,[2983] or by giving reasonable notice of it to the other contracting party.[2984] A high degree of notice may be needed as regards particularly onerous terms.[2985] The words of the clause should be clear. Any ambiguity will be interpreted strictly against the interest of the party seeking to rely on the clause.[2986] In particular, a person claiming an exemption from liability for negligence must make it clear that the words of the exemption extend to include negligence. So a clause acknowledging that a purchaser of land had relied upon his own judgment and not upon any representation or warranty of the vendor was not apt to exclude antecedent tortious liability for doing building work without a permit: the clause was directed only to contractual representations or warranties actually made by the vendor and did not cover negligence.[2987] However, there need be no specific reference to negligence provided it is clear that negligence liability is being excluded.[2988]

Exclusion clauses in contracts between businesses and consumers may be interpreted more strictly than in the case of commercial contracts. The Court of Appeal

2981. *See Standard Chartered Bank v. Pakistan National Shipping Corporation* [2003] 1 AC 959 at [22].
2982. *See* generally *International Encyclopaedia of Laws: Contracts (New Zealand)*, paras 171–179.
2983. *Lestrange v. F Graucob Ltd* [1934] 2 KB 394; *Toll (FGCT) Pty Ltd v. Alphapharm Pty Ltd* (2005) 219 CLR 165; cp *Crocker v. Sundance Northwest Resorts Ltd* [1988] 1 SCR 1186.
2984. *Harvey v. Ascot Dry Cleaning Co. Ltd* [1953] NZLR 549.
2985. *Interfoto Picture Library Ltd v. Stiletto Visual Programmes Ltd* [1989] QB 433.
2986. *Photo Production Ltd v. Securicor Transport Ltd* [1980] AC 827.
2987. *Chase v. de Groot* [1994] 1 NZLR 613.
2988. *Shipbuilders Ltd v. Benson* [1992] 3 NZLR 549 at 561.

has emphasized that disputes in commercial relationships should be decided straightforwardly on what the parties have bargained for, and the courts should not transfer to the defendant what was properly a commercial risk accepted by the plaintiff.[2989]

§3. Contractual Exclusions and Third Parties

I. The Benefit of an Exclusion

514. Where there is a contract between A and B under which B excludes both B's own and also C's liability to A, the question arises whether or how C, not being a party to the contract, can rely on that exclusion. One solution is to apply the notice principle considered below.[2990] If C has given reasonable notice to A that he or she is not liable, the fact that his or her excluding notice happens to be contained in a contract or arrangement made between A and B can be seen as immaterial. For example, in *Smith v. Eric S Bush*[2991] the purchaser of a house applied for a mortgage to a building society, who instructed valuers to carry out a mortgage valuation. The mortgage application form contained a disclaimer of liability for the accuracy of the report covering both the building society and the valuer. The House of Lords held that the exclusion notice provided the valuer with a defence at common law to an action for negligence by the purchaser.[2992] Again, in *Rolls-Royce New Zealand Ltd v. Carter Holt Harvey Ltd*[2993] an owner made a contract for the construction of industrial plant with a main contractor, certain terms of which limited the liability of a subcontractor. It was held that the owner knew about and accepted the limitation, had only paid for what was to be provided under the main contract, and should not be able to improve on its bargain by direct suit. In *McKinlay Hendry Ltd v. Tonkin & Taylor Ltd*[2994] an allegedly negligent report about the suitability of land for building which was prepared by the defendant engineers for a company client could not be relied on by a subsequent owner of the land. The report was stated to have been prepared solely for the clients, and it could not be used in other contexts or for other purposes.

A further solution is provided by Part 2 subpart 1 of the Contract and Commercial Law Act 2017 (formerly the Contracts (Privity) Act 1982).[2995] Sections 12 and 13 allow a designated third party who is intended to have enforceable rights to enforce a benefit, including the benefit of an exclusion clause, in a contract between other persons. So provided C meets these requirements, he or she has a good defence. Seemingly the application of the 2017 Act and of the notice principle can overlap to a substantial extent.

2989. *DHL International (NZ) Ltd v. Richmond Ltd* [1993] 3 NZLR 10.
2990. *See* para. 516.
2991. [1990] 1 AC 831.
2992. The notice was rendered ineffective by statutory provision, which has no direct counterpart in New Zealand.
2993. [2005] 1 NZLR 324.
2994. CA 81/02, 9 Dec. 2005.
2995. *See* generally *International Encyclopaedia of Laws: Contracts (New Zealand)*, paras 194–196.

II. The Burden of an Exclusion

515. The parties to a contract normally cannot purport to place the burden of an exclusion clause on a third person. So A and B cannot rely on an agreement between themselves that one or both of them is not liable to C.[2996] But a contractual exclusion of this kind may bind the third party if he or she acted in such a way as to indicate acceptance of the stipulation.[2997] In *Rolls-Royce*,[2998] Glazebrook J said that the presence of a limitation clause in a contract between a head contractor and a subcontractor signifies clearly, if known to the owner, the subcontractor's unwillingness to do the job otherwise than subject to the limitation. The owner's acquiescence can then be deemed an acceptance of the terms under which alone the subcontractor is prepared to enter into a relationship defining its duty to the owner.

§4. Non-contractual Exclusions

516. Where there is no contract between the parties, the defendant still can attach a condition to a gift, service, or licence excluding his or her liability for negligence. For example, a licensee using a private road was bound by a clearly visible notice to the effect that all persons using the road were there at their own risk, even though she had not actually read the notice in full;[2999] and a passenger in a car was bound by an excluding notice placed prominently on the dashboard.[3000] But adequate steps must be taken to bring the notice to the plaintiff's attention. A visitor to a go-kart track was not bound by a form containing an exclusion clause that he signed on entering because he thought it was a marketing or registration form, there was limited opportunity to read it, and none of the occupier's staff drew it to his attention.[3001]

The same principle applies where a person gives information or advice to another. If the information is given subject to a stipulation disclaiming liability for it, the recipient cannot accept the advice yet at the same time reject the stipulation.[3002] Provided the disclaimer is sufficiently clear, the recipient is bound.[3003]

2996. *Ibid.*, para. 189.
2997. *Morris v. C W Martin & Sons Ltd* [1966] 1 QB 716 (CA), discussed in *Johnson Matthey & Co. Ltd v. Constantine Terminals Ltd* [1976] 2 Lloyd's Rep. 215; *Singer Co. (UK) Ltd v. Tees and Hartlepool Port Authority* [1988] 2 Lloyd's Rep. 164.
2998. [2005] 1 NZLR 324 at [110]–[113].
2999. *Ashdown v. Samuel Williams & Sons Ltd* [1957] 1 QB 409.
3000. *Birch v. Thomas* [1972] 1 WLR 295.
3001. *Le Mans Grand Prix Circuits Pty Ltd v. Iliadis* (1998) Aust Torts Reps 81-482; but *see Toll (FGCT) Pty Ltd v. Alphapharm Pty Ltd* (2005) 219 CLR 165.
3002. *Hedley Byrne & Co. Ltd v. Heller & Partners Ltd* [1964] AC 465; *see* para. 99.
3003. *See*, for example, *Taberna Europe CDO II plc v. Selskabet AF1* [2016] EWCA Civ 1262, [2017] QB 633.

§5. STATUTORY CONTROL

I. Personal Injury Cases

517. There are no special statutory restrictions on excluding liability for personal injury. However, in light of section 317 of the Accident Compensation Act 2001, there is usually no liability to exclude.[3004]

II. Property Damage and Economic Loss

518. Exclusion clauses will normally operate only as regards a potential liability for causing property damage or economic loss. The common law rules permitting this will apply unless they are ousted or rendered nugatory by specific statutory provision. There are several statutes that control the impact of exclusion clauses in certain types of claims involving a liability in tort or an analogous liability.

A. Disputes Tribunals Act 1988

519. Disputes Tribunals have jurisdiction to hear claims in contract, quasi-contract or for property damage in tort for sums up to NZD 30,000. Tribunals are required to determine a dispute according to the substantial merits and justice of the case and in doing so must have regard to the law but they are not bound to give effect to strict legal rights or obligations.[3005] In particular, they may disregard any limiting or excluding provisions in an agreement or document bearing upon the dispute between the parties.[3006] So in the case of relatively small disputes about property damage, exclusion clauses may be held to be of no effect.

B. Contract and Commercial Law Act 2017, Section 50

520. A special statutory regime in section 50 of the Contract and Commercial Law Act 2017 (formerly section 4 of the Contractual Remedies Act 1979) applies in the case of certain statements made in the course of pre-contract negotiations, although the cause of action is contractual, not tortious.[3007] Broadly, where a provision in a contract denies that any pre-contract representations were made, or that they were terms of the contract, or that they were relied on by the other party, a court is not precluded by any such provision from inquiring into the truth of the matter

3004. *See* para. 41.
3005. Disputes Tribunals Act 1988, s. 18(6).
3006. *Ibid.*, s. 18(7).
3007. *See* para. 96.

and from determining whether it is fair and reasonable to treat the clause as conclusive between the parties.[3008] In the case of a contract between commercial parties, each with separate legal advice, the court is likely to uphold the conclusiveness of a provision of this kind, at least in the absence of any fraud.[3009] But where there has been a deliberate misrepresentation, or one party is peculiarly in possession of relevant facts, or there is a disparity of bargaining power, the court is more likely to set the clause aside.[3010]

C. Fair Trading Act 1986

521. The Fair Trading Act 1986 prohibits conduct in trade that is misleading or deceptive or that is likely to mislead or deceive.[3011] Persons who suffer loss or damage caused by conduct in breach of the Act may institute civil proceedings for the amount of the loss or damage.[3012] It is clear that this cause of action covers much of the same ground as an action for misrepresentation at common law or under section 35 of the Contract and Commercial Law Act 2017.[3013] The general rule is that the provisions of the Act have affect despite anything to the contrary in any agreement,[3014] subject to a limited exception.[3015] Furthermore, the words of the 1986 Act are mandatory and it follows that any term in a contract purporting to contract out of the provisions of the Act can be of no effect.[3016] So liability under the *Hedley Byrne* principle can be excluded, but liability under the Fair Trading Act cannot.

D. Consumer Guarantees Act 1993

522. The Consumer Guarantees Act 1993 provides for an extended regime of rights and remedies in circumstances where goods or services are supplied in trade to consumers.[3017] In particular, the Act gives consumers a direct right of action against manufacturers in respect of defects in goods, which right is analogous to a claim in tort.[3018] Subject to certain exceptions, the provisions of the Act have effect

3008. Contract and Commercial Law Act 2017, s. 50.
3009. For example, *Herbison v. Papakura Video Ltd* [1987] 2 NZLR 527; *Brownlie v. Shotover Mining Ltd* unrep., CA 187/87, 21 Feb. 1992; *Hall v. Warwick Todd Ltd* (2000) 9 TCLR 448; *PAE (New Zealand) Ltd v. Brosnahan* (2009) 10 TCLR 626.
3010. For example, *M E Torbett Ltd v. Keirlor Motels Ltd* (1984) 1 NZBLC 102,079; *Snodgrass v. Hammington* unrep., CA 254/93, 22 Dec. 1995.
3011. Fair Trading Act 1986, ss 9–14; *see* para. 444.
3012. *See* para. 446.
3013. *See* para. 96.
3014. Fair Trading Act 1986, s. 5C.
3015. *Ibid.*, s. 5D.
3016. *Smythe v. Bayley's Real Estate Ltd* (1993) 5 TCLR 454; but *see* the qualifications on this proposition in *David v. TFAC Ltd* [2009] 2 NZLR 239 and *PAE (New Zealand) Ltd v. Brosnahan* (2009) 10 TCLR 626; *see* para. 448.
3017. *See International Encyclopaedia of Laws: Contracts (New Zealand)*, Part II, Ch. 5.
3018. *See* para. 448.

notwithstanding any provision to the contrary in any agreement.[3019] So a manufacturer who is in breach of one of the statutory guarantees is unable to exclude the statutory liability.

3019. Consumer Guarantees Act 1993, s. 43(1).

Part V. Causation and Remoteness of Damage

§1. Introduction

523. A defendant who is in breach of a duty in tort cannot be held responsible for loss suffered by the plaintiff unless the defendant's conduct was a cause of that loss. In making the inquiry into causation it is convenient to distinguish three questions. First, it must be determined whether the defendant's conduct was a cause in fact of the plaintiff's loss. Normally this is a minimum requirement, although in certain special cases the proposition requires some qualification. Second, if a causal link in a strictly objective sense is shown, then it is necessary to consider whether the conduct can be seen as a cause in law. It is not enough that the conduct constitutes an historical condition necessary for the harm to happen: it must also be an effective cause of the harm. The difference may be expressed as that between a *causa sine qua non* and a *causa causans*. Third, there is the question of the proximity between the cause and the damage or, in other words, of the remoteness of the damage. Assuming that the conduct was a cause, it must be sufficiently closely connected with the damage so as to justify the imposition of liability.[3020]

This arrangement cannot be regarded as set in stone. In *Deloitte Haskins & Sells v. National Mutual Life Nominees*[3021] McGechan J remarked that the question is whether there was causation in fact, of a character which the law, as a further matter of policy, will recognize. Whether one starts with a 'but for' question, and then looks for a policy (remoteness) limitation; or starts further along the line with a 'real and effective cause' question, looking back to 'but for' aspects and then onward to policy (remoteness), one will often end up at the same point. This is the law, not logic.

3020. *See* generally *Accident Compensation Corporation v. Ambros* [2008] 1 NZLR 340 at [24]–[25].
3021. (1991) 3 NZBLC 102,259 at 102,288 (appeal allowed on another point [1993] AC 774).

§2. CAUSE IN FACT

I. Indivisible Harm

524. The inquiry into cause starts with the 'but for' test: it poses the question whether the plaintiff would have suffered the loss without ('but for') the defendant's wrongdoing. If he or she would not, the wrongful conduct was a cause of the loss. If the loss would have arisen even without the defendant's wrongdoing, normally it does not give rise to legal liability.[3022]

Normally, proof that conduct was a cause in fact of loss is a minimum requirement before the defendant can be held liable for the conduct. For example, failure to treat a poisoning victim on admission to hospital did not cause his death where the victim was already bound to die;[3023] administering an anti-tetanus injection without waiting for half an hour, in accordance with recommended procedure, after a test dose was not a cause of a reaction to the serum leading to encephalitis, where the reaction only happened nine days later;[3024] deficiencies in the defendant's culvert did not cause flooding of the plaintiff's land during a storm, where the flooding would have occurred in any event;[3025] and a failure by auditors to warn the trustee of a money market company that the company was in financial difficulties was not a cause of the trustee being held liable to depositors for breach of duty as trustee because, at the time the auditors should have reported, the trustee was already liable to the depositors for the same amount as at the date of the liquidation of the company.[3026]

Where tortious acts by two or more persons combine to produce the same indivisible damage, each act may be treated as a cause of the damage (whether the acts are simultaneous or successive) and so each person may be fully liable. Thus, in the case of the house owner who sues the architect, builder, and local authority inspector for negligence in regard to a defective house, if, but for the negligence of each respondent, the defects would not have occurred, each is fully liable. Where two or more negligent drivers collide, causing damage to another person, each is fully liable if his or her negligent conduct was a cause of the harm to the third party.[3027] The same principle applies if tortious and non-tortious causes combine to produce indivisible damage. The defendant may still be fully liable for having been a contributory cause of the damage.[3028]

3022. *Kuwait Airways Corporation v. Iraqi Airways Co. (Nos 4 and 5)* [2002] 2 AC 883 at [72].

3023. *Barnett v. Chelsea Hospital* [1969] 1 QB 428.

3024. *Robinson v. Post Office* [1974] 1 WLR 1176.

3025. *Atlas Properties Ltd v. Kapiti Coast DC* 20/06/02, CA 30/02.

3026. *Deloitte Haskins & Sells v. National Mutual Life Nominees* [1993] AC 774.

3027. Each, if sued for the full amount, may seek contribution from the others: Law Reform Act 1936, s. 17 (1)(c); *see* para. 586.

3028. *Bonnington Castings Ltd v. Wardlaw* [1956] AC 613; *Dickins v. O2 plc* [2008] EWCA Civ 1144 at [40]–[48]; *Bailey v. Ministry of Defence* [2009] 1 WLR 1052; *Williams v. The Bermuda Hospital Board* [2016] UKPC 4. Compare *Ministry of Defence v. AB* [2010] EWCA Civ 1317 at [134] and [150] (exposure to ionising radiation from a series of atmospheric tests of thermonuclear devices could not be proved to have been a cause of the claimants' cancer) (on appeal *AB v. Ministry of Defence* [2013] 1 AC 78, where the approach taken by the Court of Appeal on the causation issue was confirmed).

In certain special cases the 'but for' test requires some qualification. Suppose A and B independently light fires that later combine and cause damage to C. Even though the conduct of A alone and B alone each would have caused the whole damage, neither can argue that his or her conduct was not the cause because the damage would still have happened without it. On the contrary, both are fully liable.[3029] Here the question is whether the conduct materially contributed to the harm.

II. Divisible Harm

525. The preceding principles apply where there is just one head of damage that cannot be divided up. On the other hand, if several persons each cause separate damage to the same person and it is practicable to divide up their respective contributions, each is liable only for the damage that he or she has in fact caused. Where the damage caused by each is not intermingled, there is no difficulty in making an apportionment, but where several persons contribute to the same result the test is whether the amount of each of the contributions is reasonably ascertainable. So where two dogs savaged a flock of sheep, each owner was fully liable, as the particular damage done by each dog could not be determined.[3030] But damage was apportioned where three industrial concerns polluted a river,[3031] and where successive acts of negligence caused divisible mental injury.[3032]

Similar principles apply where tortious and non-tortious causes combine to cause damage. If there is indivisible damage that otherwise would not have happened, the defendant is fully liable. So too, taking again the case of two fires that combine to cause damage, but varying the facts so that one is tortious and one is non-tortious, then the tortfeasor is liable for having made a 'substantial contribution' to the fire. But where it is practicable to determine the extent of the contribution as between tortious and non-tortious causes, an apportionment will be made. For example, where a hulk was moored alongside a barque and a few hours later a gale blew up during which the barque was damaged, the court awarded damages to compensate for the extent to which the mooring of the hulk had contributed to increase the damage.[3033] Damages were similarly divided up where damage was caused partly by a non-tortious outbreak of fire and partly by a tortious overstacking of newsprint making the fire more difficult to fight.[3034] The allowance made for the non-tortious contribution (one-third of the plaintiff's loss) was necessarily arrived at as a matter of impression and was incapable of mathematical precision.

3029. *Deloitte Haskins & Sells v. National Mutual Life Nominees* (1991) 3 NZBLC 102,259 at 102,289; *Kuwait Airways Corporation v. Iraqi Airways Co. (Nos 4 and 5)* [2002] 2 AC 883 at [74].

3030. *Arneil v. Paterson* [1931] AC 560.

3031. *Pride of Derby Angling Association Ltd v. British Celanese Ltd* [1952] 1 All ER 1326.

3032. *Rahman v. Arearose Ltd* [2001] QB 351; *Wright v. Cambridge Medical Group* [2011] EWCA Civ 699 at [80]–[84] (divisible physical injuries caused by medical negligence).

3033. *Tulloch v. Wellington Harbour Board* (1904) 23 NZLR 20.

3034. *Wilson & Horton Ltd v. A-G* [1997] 2 NZLR 513.

III. Proof of a Risk

A. General

526. Sometimes a cause of harm may not be capable of proof in the ordinary way. This may of course mean that the action fails, but in certain limited circumstances the courts have modified the ordinary rules. One such modification is found in certain decisions that hold that it is sufficient for the plaintiff to prove that the defendant caused a risk of an outcome, as opposed to the outcome itself.

B. Single Agency Rule

527. In *McGhee v. National Coal Board*[3035] the defendant negligently failed to provide workplace washing facilities, and as a consequence the plaintiff employee had to cycle home caked in brick dust. After a few days he was found to be suffering from dermatitis. The medical evidence indicated that his working conditions in cleaning out brick kilns caused the dermatitis and the fact he had to cycle home without having washed added materially to the risk he might develop the disease. It was held by the House of Lords that a finding that a breach of duty had materially increased the risk of injury amounted, for practical purposes, to a finding that the defendants' breach of duty had materially contributed to the injury. Applying this principle, the plaintiff is required to prove that the defendant's conduct was at least capable of causing or aggravating the damage,[3036] and that it did in fact materially increase the risk of that damage. On this being shown, a causal connection is treated as having been made out.

In *McGhee* proof of the creation of a risk was sufficient to prove causation in circumstances where there was only one causal agent. By contrast, in *Wilsher v. Essex Area Health Authority*[3037] the defendants' negligence in causing excessive oxygenation of the plaintiff's blood was merely one of the several factors that could have caused the onset of blindness. Their Lordships distinguished *McGhee*, on the basis that the risk in that case was from brick dust and the injury was undoubtedly caused by the dust, and so in the instant case it had to be shown that the injury was caused by oxygen and not one of the other candidates. The plaintiff could not do this and so the action had to fail. Again, in *AB v. Ministry of Defence*[3038] the UK Supreme Court thought that cancer sufferers who were alleging that the defendant put them at risk of cancer from radiation by conducting atmospheric tests of thermonuclear bombs had no prospect of establishing liability under the principle, because there was no evidence that the carcinogenic effect of radiation operated in the same way as the carcinogenic effect of other risk factors, not all of which had been identified.

3035. [1973] 1 WLR 1.
3036. *Kay v. Ayrshire & Arran Health Board* [1987] 2 All ER 417.
3037. [1988] AC 1074.; and *see Ministry of Defence v. AB* [2010] EWCA Civ 1317 at [122]–[157].
3038. [2013] 1 AC 78.

In Australia, in *Amaca Pty Ltd v. Ellis*[3039] the plaintiff died of lung cancer after having been exposed to asbestos by his employers and also having been a heavy smoker. No scientific evidence could establish why the plaintiff developed cancer. But relevant epidemiological studies established that the probability of the plaintiff developing cancer if exposed to asbestos was much lower than the probability of him developing cancer from smoking as he did. The question was which was the causative agency, and on the evidence it was more probable than not that it was smoking rather than exposure to asbestos.[3040]

On the other hand, in *Fairchild v. Glenhaven Funeral Services Ltd*[3041] the House of Lords was prepared to extend the *McGhee* principle to cover a case where the causative agency is known and there are several possible defendants. In three appeals heard together, the plaintiffs were employees who had developed mesothelioma after being exposed to asbestos dust in the course of their employment with more than one employer. Each sought damages from a former employer, alleging breach of duty in failing to protect the employee from the risk of contracting the disease. The medical evidence established that mesothelioma is caused by inhaling asbestos dust, and the risk increases according to the quantity of dust inhaled: but the condition may be caused by a single, or few, or many, asbestos fibres. Medical opinion holds that none is more probable than any other. Once it is caused, the condition is not aggravated by further exposure to asbestos. In cases of successive employments the victim may have inhaled the fatal fibres during any of the employments. There is no way of knowing which fibre initiated the genetic process that culminated in the tumour.

The House of Lords held that there were significant features to the case in favour of allowing redress to the victims. Lord Bingham expressed these in terms of six conditions:

(1) the claimants were each employed at different times and for differing periods by more than one employer;
(2) each employer was under a duty to take care to prevent inhalation of asbestos dust giving rise to the risk of mesothelioma;
(3) each employer was in breach of that duty;
(4) the victims suffered from mesothelioma;
(5) other causes of mesothelioma could be discounted;
(6) in the current state of medical science, it could not be established on the balance of probabilities which employer caused the mesothelioma.

Upon these conditions being satisfied the claimants were entitled to recover in full against any of the employers. His Lordship observed that it might be unjust to impose liability on an employer for damage it had not caused, but much greater

3039. [2010] HCA 5.
3040. Compare *Sienkiewicz v. Greif (UK) Ltd* [2011] 2 WLR 523 at [75], [90], where Lord Phillips contemplated that epidemiological data indicating significant exposure both to significant quantities of asbestos fibres and to significant cigarette smoke could satisfy the *Bonnington* test of causation (as to which *see* para. 524).
3041. [2003] 1 AC 32.

injustice would be caused by denying redress to the victims. Otherwise there would be no recovery in any case where a victim had been employed by more than one employer. Such a result would reflect no credit on the law.

C. Proportionate Liability

528. An important question that *Fairchild* did not clearly determine was the extent of each employer's liability. In *Barker v. Corus (UK) Ltd*,[3042] the House of Lords held that liability should be attributed according to the particular defendant's relative degree of contribution to the risk. Lord Hoffmann, giving the majority view, said that the justification for the normal rule that liability is joint and several[3043] is that if you caused harm, there is no reason why your liability should be reduced because someone else also caused the same harm. But when liability was exceptionally imposed because you might have caused harm, fairness suggested that if more than one person might have been responsible, liability should be divided according to the probability that one or other caused the harm. As for the quantification of the harm, it might be that the most practical method of apportionment would be according to the time of exposure for which each defendant was responsible, but allowance might also have to be made for the intensity of exposure and the type of asbestos.[3044]

D. Overview

529. In *Sienkiewicz v. Greif (UK) Ltd* and *Willmore v. Knowsley Metropolitan Borough Council*[3045] the UK Supreme Court, in a conjoined appeal, sought to clarify the nature and ambit of the special rule of causation recognized in *Fairchild* and *Barker*. In *Sienkiewicz* the claimant's mother, who died of mesothelioma, had been exposed to asbestos dust during the course of her employment with the defendant's predecessor and also to a low level of asbestos in the general atmosphere. The tortious exposure was modest compared with the environmental exposure, and increased the risk of her contracting the disease by only 18%. In *Willmore* the claimant's wife, who died of mesothelioma, had been exposed to asbestos fibres while a pupil at the defendant's school and also to low-level asbestos in the general atmosphere. The extent of the exposure caused by the defendant, although not minimal, had nonetheless been small. The Supreme Court held that in each case the claimant had satisfied the special rule of causation. The situation where only one defendant had been proved to have tortiously exposed a victim of mesothelioma to asbestos was no different to that where there were multiple claims, and the same approach should be adopted. So long as medical science was unable to attribute causation in

3042. [2006] 2 AC 572; applied in *Heneghan v. Manchester Dry Docks Ltd* [2016] 1 WLR 2036.
3043. *See* paras 581–582.
3044. In the U.K. *Barker* has been reversed by legislation in the case of claims by victims of mesothelioma: Compensation Act 2006, s. 3 (U.K.).
3045. [2011] 2 WLR 523.

mesothelioma cases, there was no place for the ordinary test of causation that, on the balance of probabilities, it was more likely than not that the defendant's breach materially contributed to the disease. Accordingly, a 'doubles the risk' test, under which the claimant needed to show that the defendant had more than doubled the risk of the deceased catching the disease, ought not to be applied. Rather, there needed to be proof of a 'material' increase in the risk, and this connoted a degree that was more than minimal. In both cases the defendants had been proved to have materially increased the risk, and the claims should therefore succeed.

In *Fairchild*, *Barker* and *Sienkiewicz* it was known that asbestos was the causative agency, but it was not known which of the possible sources was the cause.[3046] In *Amaca Pty Ltd v. Ellis*[3047] the agency was not known, for the question at issue was whether cancer was caused by asbestos exposure or smoking, and the plaintiff did not seek to argue that the risk principle should apply.

Sienkiwiewicz is a difficult decision to support, for it allows a claimant to succeed even where the probabilities were that no tort had been committed by anyone. The decision of the Supreme Court of Canada in *Clements v. Clements*[3048] may be thought to lead to a more satisfactory result. McLachlin CJ noted that the 'material contribution to risk' cases typically involved a number of tortfeasors where all were at fault and one or more had in fact caused the plaintiff's injury. The plaintiff would not have been injured 'but for' their negligence, viewed globally. However, because each could point the finger at the others, it was impossible for the plaintiff to show, on the balance of probabilities, that any one of them in fact caused the injury. In these circumstances, permitting the plaintiff to succeed on a material-contribution-to-risk basis met the underlying goals of the law of negligence. Compensation for injury was achieved. Fairness was satisfied: the plaintiff had suffered a loss due to negligence, so it was fair to turn to tort law for compensation. Deterrence also was furthered, as potential tortfeasors would know that they could not escape liability by blaming others. And the result was consistent with corrective justice: the deficit in the relationship between the plaintiff and the defendants viewed as a group that would exist if the plaintiff were denied recovery was corrected.

If limited in this way the *Fairchild* rule perhaps can prevent the injustice that would otherwise result in cases where the contribution to the harm of several defendants cannot be ascertained, but without creating serious inconsistency with the requirements of proof of cause which ordinarily apply.

E. Conclusion

530. In New Zealand, the accident compensation scheme covers employment-related diseases, including diseases contracted before the scheme came into

3046. For the insurance implications in relation to claims made under the *Fairchild* rule, *see Durham v. BAI (Run off) Ltd* [2012] 1 WLR 1267 *International Energy Group Ltd v. Zurich Insurance plc UK Branch* [2015] UKSC 33, [2016] AC 509.
3047. [2010] HCA 5; *see* para. 527.
3048. [2012] 2 SCR 181.

force.[3049] Even so, cases involving the creation of a risk of injury not covered by the scheme or of property damage are possible, and these will require a decision as to whether the risk principle ought to apply. In light of the difficulties in determining its ambit and in setting appropriate limits it may be that the courts will reject it altogether.

IV. Loss of a Chance

A. General

531. The concept of risk describes the probability of a negative outcome. Its mirror image is the loss of a chance of a positive outcome. Sometimes the courts redefine the nature of the plaintiff's loss. They award damages not for an outcome but for a loss of a chance of a benefit or of a better outcome. If the lost chance itself is recognized as amounting to damage, the plaintiff is only required to establish on the balance of probabilities that the defendant caused the loss of that chance. If the plaintiff can do this, the inquiry thereafter is simply into its value. Crucially, recovery does not depend on proof that the benefit of the chance could be assessed as being more likely than not or at least 51% in favour of the plaintiff.[3050] The question is whether the chance that was lost was 'real' or 'substantial', as opposed to the loss of a mere speculative possibility.[3051]

The circumstances in which a claim may be framed as being for the loss of a chance have not been clearly articulated. It would be possible to decide all cases in this way, which certainly is not the law. So we must determine when a chance analysis ought to be made.

B. Historical Facts

532. Where there is a dispute is as to the cause of damage occurring in the past, the ordinary rules apply. The question is whether on the balance of probabilities the defendant caused the outcome.[3052] If the test is satisfied the plaintiff recovers in full. The damages are not discounted by the extent to which the evidence falls short of 100% certainty.[3053] Once causation is established, speculative consequential loss lying in the future is recoverable according to the chance or likelihood that it might happen.[3054]

3049. *See* para. 38.
3050. *Martelli McKegg Wells & Cormack v. Commbank International NV* CA75/96, 7 Nov. 1996.
3051. *Davies v. Taylor* [1974] AC 207; *Benton v. Miller & Poulgrain* [2005] 1 NZLR 66; *McGill v. Sports and Entertainment Media Group Ltd* [2017] 1 WLR 989.
3052. *Benton v. Miller & Poulgrain* [2005] 1 NZLR 66 at [45].
3053. *Gregg v. Scott* [2005] 2 WLR 268 at [193]–[195].
3054. *A-G v. Geothermal Produce NZ Ltd* [1987] 2 NZLR 348 (loss of future profits on damaged roses).

C. Hypothetical Facts

533. We must consider now the case where it is alleged that an omission caused physical damage, involving a hypothesis as to what would have happened had the defendant acted. Here the balance of authority holds that the question of causation should be resolved in the same way as with claims involving historical fact. On the balance of probabilities, did the defendant cause the outcome? In *Hotson v. East Berkshire Area Health Authority*[3055] the defendants failed to diagnose an injury to the plaintiff's hip which had been sustained in a fall. The trial judge found that there was a 25% chance that had treatment been timeously administered, the onset of avascular necrosis would have been avoided. The House of Lords held that damages could not be awarded for that lost chance. The avascular necrosis was caused by the fall and not by the failure to treat, because the evidence showed that the plaintiff's hip was so badly injured that prompt treatment could not have prevented it. Again, in *Gregg v. Scott*[3056] the defendant's delay in diagnosing the plaintiff's cancer reduced the chance of a cure from 42% to 25%. The House of Lords held, applying *Hotson*, that the plaintiff could not show that the outcome would have been different had he been treated earlier, and accordingly the claim had to fail.

These and similar decisions decline to apply a chance analysis to negligent omissions to provide medical treatment[3057] and to other omissions where the plaintiff complains of physical injury or damage. The cases in which chance damages have either been awarded or accepted in principle tend to involve hypothetical questions as to the chance of obtaining future financial benefits or avoiding financial detriments. Examples include the loss of a chance of success in a beauty contest;[3058] the loss of a commercial opportunity;[3059] a lost opportunity to negotiate insurance cover;[3060] the loss of the chance or hope of a benefit under a will;[3061] the loss of the chance of employment;[3062] a lost opportunity to trade out of trouble;[3063] the loss of an opportunity to purchase property;[3064] the loss of a chance of a settlement of a property dispute;[3065] the loss of a chance of success in a legal claim;[3066] and a husband's lost chance of protecting his interest in the matrimonial home should his marriage later be dissolved.[3067]

3055. [1987] AC 750.
3056. [2005] 2 WLR 268; *Wright v. Cambridge Medical Group* [2011] EWCA Civ 699 at [80]–[84].
3057. *Laferrière v. Lawson* [1991] 1 ACR 541; *Tabett v. Gett* (2010) 240 CLR 537.
3058. *Chaplin v. Hicks* [1911] 2 KB 786.
3059. *Sellars v. Adelaide Petroleum NL* (1994) 179 CLR 332.
3060. *Cee Bee Marine Ltd v. Lombard Insurance Co. Ltd* [1990] 2 NZLR 1.
3061. *Gartside v. Sheffield, Young & Ellis* [1983] NZLR 37.
3062. *Spring v. Guardian Assurance plc* [1995] 2 AC 296.
3063. *Takaro Properties Ltd v. Rowling* [1986] 1 NZLR 22 (appeal to the Privy Council allowed without discussion of the point: [1987] 2 NZLR 700).
3064. *Markholm Construction Co. Ltd v. Wellington City Council* [1985] 2 NZLR 520.
3065. *Marriott v. Attorney-General* [2011] 1 NZLR 354.
3066. *Edwards v. Hugh James Ford Simey Solicitors* [2019] UKSC 54, [2019] 1 WLR 6549.
3067. *Benton v. Miller & Poulgrain* [2005] 1 NZLR 66.

The chance principle is qualified in circumstances where the court must hypothesize as to what the *plaintiff* would have done in response to the defendant's conduct. This question should be decided on the balance of probabilities.[3068] Only hypotheses as to other matters should be decided on the basis of a lost chance. In such a case, where the loss is of the chance to bring a legal claim, it is generally inappropriate to conduct a trial within a trial in order to determine whether the claim would have succeeded.[3069]

D. Indeterminate Facts

534. In *Gregg v. Scott*[3070] Lord Hoffmann and Baroness Hale drew a distinction between deterministic events in the natural world and indeterministic events involving the unfathomable actions of human agents. On this view, if an outcome is determined, the plaintiff must prove on the balance of probabilities that the defendant caused the outcome. If an outcome is indeterministic, the plaintiff must prove the defendant caused the loss of the chance of avoiding it. Whether an outcome is determined turns on its predictability. An outcome may be inherently unpredictable or it may be unpredictable because we lack full knowledge to make the prediction. The chance analysis should only be applied in the former case. An event can be treated as indeterministic if it could not have been predicted at any time in the past, it cannot be predicted in the present given unlimited time and resources, and we cannot imagine how it might be predictable in the future.[3071] For all human purposes the event is inherently unpredictable, and in these circumstances the chance that it may happen is purely objective.

A deterministic analysis gives a possible reason for drawing a distinction between physical injury and financial loss cases. Hotson and *Gregg* arguably involve deterministic events, for while our understanding of the cause of medical conditions may be incomplete, it is not impossible to imagine that they can never be predicted. So a deterministic analysis puts the risk of scientific uncertainty on the plaintiff. By contrast, the financial loss cases all involve the intervention of human agents. Hypothetical human conduct arguably involves inherent unpredictability, and in this case there may be compensation for a lost chance.

Plaintiffs normally must bear the burden of proof or the risk of non-persuasion. The assumption is that the cause of an event can be discovered by careful investigation. But where an event is indeterministic this approach cannot be taken. The risk that it is reasonable to expect the plaintiff to bear is the risk of uncertainty in the evidence, not uncertainty in the world. Accordingly, in order to cope with indeterministic cases, the courts have to make some adjustment to their world view, and the smallest concession possible is to retain causation as a deterministic concept but

3068. *Benton v. Miller & Poulgrain* [2005] 1 NZLR 66; *Perry v. Raleys Solicitors* [2019] UKSC 5, [2019] 2 WLR 636 at [20]–[25].

3069. *Perry v. Raleys Solicitors* [2019] UKSC 5, [2019] 2 WLR 636 at [31].

3070. [2005] 2 WLR 268 at [79], [220]; *and see Strack v. Grey* [2019] NZCA 432 at [49]–[53].

3071. Reece 'Losses of Chances in the Law' (1996) 59 MLR 188.

to alter the phenomenon found to have been caused.[3072] So it is only in this case that the question arises whether the defendant caused the loss of a chance.

Ultimately, the reluctance by the courts to accept the loss of a chance of avoiding physical damage as amounting to actionable damage appears to stem from concern about the implications of the argument and a fear of a significant widening of the potential liability of defendants. Indeed, it may be that there is no logical stopping point, and that accepting loss of chance damages could lead to all claims being framed in this manner. In *Gregg* Lord Hoffmann thought that the wholesale adoption of possible rather than probable causation as the criterion of liability would be so radical a change in the law as to amount to a legislative act. It would have enormous consequences for insurance companies and the health service. Again, Lord Phillips and Baroness Hale both emphasized that the change would introduce very great and unwarranted complexity into the law. So far as possible, then, their Lordships preferred to leave the traditional rule well alone.

V. Lack of Informed Consent

535. A third modification of traditional rules is found in cases concerning a lack of informed consent to medical treatment. In both *Chappel v. Hart*[3073] in Australia and *Chester v. Afshar*[3074] in the UK a surgeon who had failed to warn of a risk was held liable in circumstances where an explanation would on the balance of probabilities have caused delay, but the same treatment would have been likely to have been undertaken at a later date with a similar risk of injury. On one view, the decisions were primarily based on a policy choice to impose liability in order to ensure that the duty to obtain informed consent was respected by medical practitioners. On another, the claims were attributable to the materialization of the risk and not to the exposure to the risk. So the 'but for' test could be seen as met if the chances of the risk materializing on the later occasion were slight. Yet the argument is not convincing. It is similar to saying that a win at the casino was caused by going there on Tuesday because the chances were slight that there would have been a win had the punter gone there on Wednesday.[3075]

The principle of *Chappel* and *Chester* does not apply to claims under the accident compensation scheme alleging medical misadventure or treatment injury. Such claims must be established by proof on the balance of probability that the failure to warn caused the injury.[3076] Accordingly, any failure to warn of a small risk of medical treatment, which risk later eventuated, might not be covered for compensation yet might still be actionable at common law.

3072. *Ibid.*

3073. (1998) 195 CLR 232.

3074. [2005] 1 AC 134; compare *Correia v. University Hospital of North Staffordshire NHS Trust* [2017] EWCA Civ 356.

3075. Lord Hoffmann 'Causation' (2005) 121 LQR 592 at 602.

3076. *ACC v. Ambros* [2008] 1 NZLR 340.

VI. Causation and Quantification

536. Where successive acts of negligence operate independently from one another, both having the capacity to produce the same damage, a distinction between questions of causation and questions of quantification of damage must be drawn. In *Baker v. Willoughby*[3077] the plaintiff was knocked down by a car driven by the defendant and suffered a permanent injury to his left leg. He instituted proceedings against the defendant, but in 1967, before the action came on for trial, the same leg was amputated after he was shot by robbers. The House of Lords decided that the defendant remained liable for the injured leg even after 1967. The plaintiff's claim was for loss of amenity and earning capacity and these losses were not diminished by the second injury but would continue as long as if the second injury had not occurred. That injury accordingly was irrelevant in assessing the damages.

The decision may be contrasted with *Jobling v. Associated Dairies Ltd.*[3078] In 1973, the plaintiff slipped and injured his back when in the course of his employment, the accident being caused by the defendants' breach of statutory duty. The injury, which was permanent, reduced his earning capacity by 50%. In 1976, again before the action was heard, the plaintiff was found to be suffering from an unrelated spinal disease that rendered him totally unfit for work. It was held that the defendants' liability was for loss of earning capacity from 1973 to 1976. Damages for loss of this kind ordinarily were discounted on a speculative basis, taking into account the vicissitudes of life during the period of lost capacity. If a vicissitude had actually occurred before the trial, the court should not speculate when it in fact knew.

Baker was about the cause of a loss. The later events did not undo damage that had already been caused but, rather, made it worse. *Jobling* was about the quantification of a loss. Damages for loss of earning capacity normally would be discounted taking into account the vicissitudes of life during the period of lost capacity. Here a vicissitude had actually happened and could not be ignored.

Discounting damages for the vicissitudes of life seeks to ensure, in a rough and ready fashion, that a plaintiff is compensated for his or her actual loss. But the discount should only be made in respect of adverse contingencies in respect of which the plaintiff would not have been compensated. If the subsequent event is compensable, it is not a speculative 'loss' and is not a relevant vicissitude. In *Baker* the subsequent event was tortious and compensable and, therefore, the vicissitudes principle could not have been invoked. In *Jobling* the subsequent event was not tortious and was, therefore, a vicissitude that needed to be taken into account.[3079]

In New Zealand, cases like *Baker* and *Jobling* would be covered by the accident compensation scheme. So the concern is whether similar principles would apply in a case of property damage. Some decisions overseas have applied *Baker*,[3080] and

3077. [1970] AC 467.
3078. [1982] AC 794.
3079. In *Gray v. Thames Trains Ltd* [2009] AC 1339 the subsequent event disabling event was the claimant's own criminal wrongdoing, causing him to be imprisoned (as to which *see* para. 489). It was not a compensable intervention by someone else, and accordingly it needed to be brought into account in reduction of the plaintiff's claim for loss of earnings caused by his earlier injury.
3080. For example, *Sunrise Co. Ltd v. The 'Lake Winnipeg'* [1991] 1 SCR 3.

others *Jobling*,[3081] in both cases without distinguishing between subsequent events according to whether or not they were tortious. Perhaps, however, causal principles ought to apply to the cost of repair or replacement of property but loss of profits should be subject to vicissitudes. The physical harm is suffered immediately but profits are earned in the future. Their loss might be regarded as analogous to the loss of earning capacity occasioned by a personal injury. On this view, no discount would be made for a subsequent tortious event further damaging property, whereas the occurrence of a non-compensable event, like a natural disaster, before an award of damages was made would reduce the defendant's liability or bring it to an end.

VII. Overview

537. There are a number of ways in which the courts may deal with difficulties of proof and uncertainty, quite apart from the various modifications to the ordinary rules that are described above. These are reviewed by Glazebrook J in delivering the judgment of the Court of Appeal in *Accident Compensation Corporation v. Ambros*.[3082] Her Honour's judgment concerned proof of cause in the context of a claim for accident compensation, but the relevant principles can apply equally to common law claims.

First, there may be a shifting of the evidential burden of proof, either in the sense of the burden of adducing evidence on an issue on pain of having the trial judge determine the issue in favour of the opponent, or of the tactical burden resting on a party who appeared to be at risk of losing on a given issue at a particular point in a trial. Her Honour also approved Lord Mansfield's precept,[3083] that all evidence is to be weighed according to the proof that it was in the power of one side to have produced and in the power of the other to have contradicted.

Second, inferences of cause also can play a part notwithstanding that science cannot determine the matter. The scientific concept of causation had been developed in the context of explaining phenomena by reference to the relationship between conditions and occurrences, whereas in law problems of causation arose in the context of ascertaining or apportioning legal responsibility for a given occurrence. This difference had allowed the court to draw robust inferences of causation in some cases of uncertainty where the experts could not determine the matter.

Third, a claimant might be able to point only to a statistical link between particular events and an injury. Lord Nicholls in *Gregg v. Scott*[3084] had explained that statistics recorded retrospectively what happened to other patients in more or less comparable situations. They revealed trends of outcome and were general in nature. They did not show whether the claimant would have conformed to the trend or been an exception to it. But in practice statistical evidence of a diminution in perceived

3081. For example, *Beoca Ltd v. Alfa Laval Co. Ltd* [1995] QB 137.
3082. [2008] 1 NZLR 340.
3083. *Blatch v. Arthur* (1774) 1 Cowp 63 at 65, 98 ER 969 at 970.
3084. [2005] 2 AC 176 at [27]–[32].

prospects would, despite its imperfection, often be the nearest one could get to evidence of diminution of actual prospects in a particular case. On this basis Glazebrook J was satisfied that such evidence might be of use in the assessment of causation, but its limitations, and the risk that it might give an illusion of precision that was lacking, should be clearly borne in mind.[3085] However, such evidence could provide evidence of possibility that might translate into the requisite degree of probability, depending on the strength of that evidence and any other relevant evidence pointing to causation.

Fourth, proximity between an alleged cause and its alleged effect would always be a relevant factor, but its significance would depend on all the circumstances. Sometimes proximity alone might be deemed sufficient to prove causation, as where a person suffered an allergic reaction just after being injected with penicillin and the reaction was a known risk of the penicillin. Proximity, however, would not suffice where, for example, the reaction was not a known possible result, particularly where there were other possible causes.

§3. Cause in Law

I. General

538. Even where the 'but for' test is satisfied and conduct is a cause in fact of loss, it may be held that the conduct is not a cause in law. Sometimes, before any damage has been done, an act or an event may intervene and precipitate the damage after the defendant's wrongful act or omission has been completed. In *Sew Hoy & Sons Ltd v. Coopers & Lybrand*[3086] the Court of Appeal asked whether as a matter of 'common sense' the conduct was a cause of the harm. Thomas J described the inquiry that needs to be made in this way:

> The basic question remains whether there is a causal connection between the defendant's default and the plaintiff's loss … [T]he answer to this question will not be resolved by the application of a formula but by the application of a Judge's common sense. The Judge needs to stand back from the case, examine the facts closely, and then decide whether there is a causal link between the default and the loss in issue which can be supported by reasoned argument.

3085. Glazebrook J drew attention in this context to the key principles for evaluating statistical evidence developed by Professor Sir Austin Bradford Hill (*The Environment and Disease: Association or Causation*, 58 Proc R Soc Medicine 295 (1965)). These were: statistical association between a cause and its effect; whether the risk was seen to rise with increasing exposure; the strength of the temporal connection; the consistency of results from other epidemiological studies; analogy from other relationships similar to the putative causal relationship; whether the exposure-disease association was biologically coherent; whether removing the exposure in a population resulted in a decrease in the occurrence of the harm; whether there was a single putative cause of the harm.

3086. [1996] 1 NZLR 392.

The core problem is to distinguish between causing a loss and merely providing an opportunity for its continuance.[3087] Appeals to common sense do not take us very far. A more helpful approach is to ask whether the claimant's loss is within the scope of the risk created by the respondent's conduct. In *BNZ v. NZ Guardian Trust*,[3088] Gault J noted that the cases showed a trend in favour of analysis by reference to the scope of a duty, and inquired as to the risks against which there was a duty to protect the plaintiff. Again, in *Kuwait Airways Corporation v. Iraqi Airways Co. (Nos 4 and 5)*,[3089] Lord Nicholls remarked on the crucial importance of identifying the purpose of the relevant cause of action and the nature and scope of the defendant's obligation in the particular circumstances.

II. Intervening Third-Party Conduct

539. Where A, driving negligently, crashes his car and obstructs the highway and B, also driving negligently, later crashes into the wreckage and causes damage to C, then, in principle, A can be liable to C.[3090] In this case the risk created by A's original conduct can be seen to include the risk of someone else driving negligently and causing further harm. But suppose now that A, driving negligently, crashes into B and damages his car. B's car is taken to a repairer and is further damaged when C negligently sets the premises ablaze. Here A would not in law have caused the further damage even though but for A's conduct the car would not have been in the workshop. In other words, the risk created by the original accident would not extend to harm coming about in a way quite unconnected with the accident and the position of B's car on the road.

The risk of intervening third-party conduct may include even deliberate conduct. For example, the risk posed by the negligence of prison officers in failing to supervise borstal trainees under their charge was that the trainees might cause damage in the course of escaping;[3091] the risk posed by a decorator negligently leaving a house unlocked while out collecting materials was that a burglar might enter the building and steal some of the contents;[3092] and a solicitor should have taken more care to keep control of his client's passport, precisely because of the risk that the client might kidnap his children in the custody of his wife and take them overseas.[3093]

The same approach can be taken where the intervention is perfectly lawful. Default to a secured creditor and ultimately a forced sale were 'the very kind of things which were likely to happen' as a consequence of negligently inflicted damage to a profit-earning business.[3094]

3087. *Price Waterhouse v. Kwan* [2000] 3 NZLR 39 at 46.
3088. [1999] 1 NZLR 664 at 683.
3089. [2002] 2 AC 883 at [71].
3090. *See*, for example, *Rouse v. Squires* [1973] 1 QB 889.
3091. *Home Office v. Dorset Yacht Co. Ltd* [1970] AC 1004.
3092. *Stansbie v. Troman* [1948] 2 KB 48; *Fletcher Construction Co. Ltd v. Webster* [1948] NZLR 514.
3093. *Al Kandari v. J R Brown & Co.* [1988] QB 665.
3094. *Taupo BC v. Birnie* [1978] 2 NZLR 397.

III. Plaintiff's Intervening Conduct

540. Sometimes, following the defendant's negligence, the plaintiff's own conduct brings about the damage. Once again it is necessary to ask what was the risk posed by the defendant's negligence. In *Sew Hoy & Sons Ltd v. Coopers & Lybrand*,[3095] the plaintiff company alleged that negligence by the defendant auditors caused it to continue trading and thus to suffer further losses. The defendants argued that the alleged breaches may have given the opportunity for the trading losses to be incurred, but they had not 'caused' them in the sense required to establish liability. Rather, the cause was the conduct of the plaintiff in continuing to trade. The Court of Appeal thought that the key issue was whether it could be said that the company not only continued to trade but also continued to trade in a certain way as a result of the auditor's breach, and the way in which it traded was responsible for the trading losses. Thomas J said that the mere fact that other factors might cause trading losses, such as imprudent trading, did not mean that the losses could not be caused by identifiable features in the business activities of the plaintiff. He thought that without doubt, it was tenable to assert that the auditor's breach caused the company to refrain from taking the necessary steps to avoid the ongoing trade losses. Accordingly, the plaintiff should be required to provide further particulars identifying the respects in which the company's trading pattern reflected its belief that the company was profitable.

Examples of non-negligent conduct by the plaintiff within the risk of the defendant's negligence include a captain making for port after his ship lost its navigational equipment in a collision, resulting in its subsequently running aground;[3096] a volunteer firefighter seeking to extinguish a fire that had spread out of control from the defendant's land;[3097] a plaintiff jumping off a train when it started quickly and without warning while he was saying goodbye to a passenger;[3098] and an employee committing suicide after suffering serious injuries in a work accident.[3099]

If a causal connection is made out, the plaintiff's intervention may also be negligent, and responsibility apportioned.[3100] So where the defendant negligently parked his lorry in the middle of a dual carriageway so as to cause an obstruction, and the drunken plaintiff crashed into it, the defendant was liable for causing the crash but the plaintiff's damages were reduced by two-thirds for contributory negligence.[3101] In another example, where the defendant negligently caused the plaintiff to be locked in a public lavatory and she was injured when she trod on the toilet

3095. [1996] 1 NZLR 392. *See also Sherwin Chan & Walshe Ltd (in liquidation) v. Jones* [2013] 1 NZLR 160 (negligent failure by accountants to advise about taxation implications of company restructuring caused plaintiff to continue with existing lending arrangements and escalating levels of indebtedness, incurring a taxation liability that would not otherwise have been imposed: defendant's negligence had a 'real influence' on the occurrence of the loss).

3096. *The City of Lincoln* (1889) 15 PD 15.

3097. *Russell v. McCabe* [1962] NZLR 392.

3098. *Caterson v. Commissioner for Railways* (1973) 128 CLR 99.

3099. *Corr v. IBC Vehicles Ltd* [2008] 1 AC 844.

3100. *See* para. 482.

3101. *March v. E & M H Stramare Pty Ltd* (1991) 171 CLR 506.

roll holder while trying to climb out, the damages were reduced by 25%.[3102] And a defendant who negligently caused the plaintiff to lose a leg was also liable for further injury caused by the plaintiff tripping when manoeuvring on one leg, although the plaintiff was contributorily negligent in not using his prosthesis.[3103]

Lastly, the plaintiff's conduct may sometimes be of such importance as to be regarded as the 'real cause' of the damage. The decision of the assignee of a lease to close his shop and cease trading after discovering that the term of the lease was for ninety years, rather than the ninety-nine years that had been represented to him by the lessor, was 'extraordinary in commercial terms': the risk that he might do this was one that, if it had occurred to the lessor, would have been brushed aside as far-fetched.[3104] The placing of newspaper advertisements offering high-interest securities to the public that failed to comply with the Securities Act 1978 merely brought to investors' attention the opportunity of investing with the company. Any failure by the newspaper and the Securities Commission to ensure that the advertisements complied with the Act did not cause the losses suffered by the plaintiffs when the company went into liquidation.[3105]

IV. Other Intervening Events

541. The risk principle is not confined to harm that has come about through human intervention. It can also be applied to harm precipitated by outside forces, such as the operation of the market. In *BNZ v. NZ Guardian Trust*[3106] a trustee was charged with overseeing advances by the plaintiff bank to a property investment company, and failed to detect irregular advances by the company to its subsidiaries. Subsequently there was a fall in the market and a rise in interest rates and the company went into liquidation. It was held that the trustee was liable only for losses suffered by the plaintiff that were connected with the irregularities and the risks that they posed. It was not obliged to protect the plaintiff against all the vicissitudes of the company's future activities.[3107]

3102. *Sayers v. Harlow UDC* [1958] 1 WLR 623.
3103. *Spencer v. Wincanton Holdings Ltd* [2009] EWCA Civ 1404.
3104. *David Kimber TV & Sound Ltd v. Kaiapoi BC* [1988] 1 NZLR 376.
3105. *Fleming v. Securities Commission* [1995] 2 NZLR 514 at 525.
3106. [1999] 1 NZLR 664.
3107. The extent of a valuer's responsibility for a negligent valuation followed by a fall in the market was considered in *South Australia Asset Management Corp v. York Montague Ltd* [1997] AC 191, where the House of Lords held that the valuer was liable only for the foreseeable consequences of the information being wrong, that is for the difference between a negligent valuation and a true valuation. For an overview of this issue, *see Hughes-Holland v. BPE Solicitors* [2017] UKSC 21, [2018] AC 599.

§4. Remoteness of Damage

I. Introduction

542. A wrongful act may have all kinds of unexpected and far-reaching consequences. We have to ask whether a defendant ought to be held liable for them all, and, if not, where the line ought to be drawn. The inquiry here is into the question whether the damage should be regarded as too remote. The question arises only with respect to the unintended consequences of conduct. Those consequences that are intended by the defendant are never too remote.[3108]

There are two main tests. One allows recovery for all the direct consequences of the wrongdoing and the other restricts recovery to the foreseeable consequences. Debate as to their respective merits began in the nineteenth century and, at least as regards negligence and other torts based on fault, was eventually determined in favour of foreseeability. But in other cases the test of directness may apply.

II. Direct Consequences

543. The leading authority on the directness test is *Re Polemis and Furness Withy & Co.*,[3109] decided in 1921. Stevedores employed by the charterers of a ship negligently knocked a heavy plank into the hold, in which was stowed a quantity of petrol in tins. An explosion immediately followed that set fire to the ship and destroyed her. Arbitrators found (1) that a spark caused by the falling plank ignited petrol vapour in the hold and caused the fire, and (2) that the causing of the spark could not reasonably have been anticipated from the falling of the board, although some damage to the ship might reasonably have been contemplated. The English Court of Appeal was unanimously of the view that the charterers were liable. Scrutton LJ said that in determining whether an act is negligent, it is relevant to determine whether any reasonable person would foresee that the act would cause damage; if he or she would not, the act is not negligent. But if the act would or might probably cause damage, the fact that the damage it causes is not the exact kind of damage one would expect is immaterial, so long as the damage is directly traceable to the negligent act and not due to the operation of independent causes having no connection with the negligent act, except that they could not avoid its results. Once the act is negligent, the fact that its exact operation is not foreseen is immaterial.

3108. *Quinn v. Leathem* [1901] AC 495 at 537.
3109. [1921] 3 KB 560.

III. Foreseeable Consequences

A. The Wagon Mound Decisions

544. Critics of *Re Polemis* argued that the decision was misconceived: it was illogical and inconsistent to use the concept of foreseeability to create liability in negligence but to reject it when delimiting recovery for that negligence. Rather, culpability and compensation should go hand in hand. In *Overseas Tankship (UK) Ltd v. Morts Dock & Engineering Co. Ltd (The Wagon Mound (No. 1))*,[3110] the Privy Council took heed of this criticism. The defendants carelessly discharged oil from their ship, the *Wagon Mound*, into Sydney Harbour, which oil floated over to a wharf 200 yards away where a firm was carrying out welding operations. This work initially was stopped but it resumed after the firm's manager was told that there was no risk of fire. Two days later the oil caught fire and a conflagration developed that severely damaged the wharf and the two ships moored there. The plaintiff wharf owners sued the defendants in negligence, arguing that the damage was the direct consequences of the defendants' negligence. But the Privy Council held that the test of liability in negligence for damage done by fire was the foreseeability of the injury by fire. It was not enough that the defendants might have anticipated damage by fouling and that their carelessness was the direct cause of the damage. On the finding of the trial judge, it was foreseeable that the spillage would cause damage by fouling and pollution but it was not foreseeable that it would catch alight, and the claim accordingly failed.

Six years later, in *Overseas Tankship (UK) Ltd v. The Miller Steamship Co. Pty (The Wagon Mound (No. 2))*,[3111] the Privy Council heard a second action arising out of the same event, brought this time by the owners of the ships tied up at the wharf. The plaintiffs sued both for negligence and for public nuisance and adduced different evidence to the effect that fire was foreseeable even though the risk was a small one. Lord Reid identified a foreseeable risk as a 'real risk', being 'one which would occur to the mind of a reasonable man … and which he would not brush aside as being far-fetched'.[3112] The defendants were held liable to the owners, on the basis that there was no advantage in or justification for allowing the oil to escape, the damage could very easily have been prevented and in all the circumstances the risk was one that could not be neglected.

In summary, the test laid down by the Privy Council in these two decisions is that in cases of negligence and nuisance the defendant is liable for any type, kind, class, or character of damage that is reasonably foreseeable as liable to happen, unless the risk is so small that a reasonable man would in the whole circumstances feel justified in neglecting it.[3113]

3110. [1961] AC 388.

3111. [1967] 1 AC 617.

3112. Adopted in *Wilson & Horton Ltd v. Attorney-General* [1997] 2 NZLR 513 at 520.

3113. Compare the rule for contract laid down in *Hadley v. Baxendale* (1854) 9 Exch. 341, under which the defendant is liable for losses arising naturally, that is, according to the usual course of things, from the breach, or which may reasonably be supposed to have been in the contemplation of both parties at the time they made the contract as the probable result of the breach. *See International Encyclopaedia of Laws: Contracts (New Zealand)*, para. 243.

B. Foreseeable Kinds of Damage

545. In *Wells v. Sainsbury & Hannigan Ltd*,[3114] the Court of Appeal emphasized that the test of foreseeability does not require that all details of what happened should be foreseeable. Likewise, in *Hughes v. Lord Advocate*,[3115] the House of Lords held that 'to demand too great precision in the test of foreseeability would be unfair to the pursuer since the factors of misadventure are innumerable'. In this case there was a foreseeable risk of injury by burning, and the fact that such injury was inflicted by way of an unforeseeable explosion was immaterial. Again, in *Jolley v. Sutton London Borough Council*,[3116] the House of Lords held that the precise manner of an injury did not have to be foreseen. Here a child was injured by crushing after having jacked up an abandoned boat on the defendant's land, and it was held sufficient that there was a risk that children would meddle with the boat at the risk of some physical injury. In a further instance, in *Corr v. IBC Vehicles Ltd*[3117] the defendant's negligence caused serious injury to an employee, who later became depressed about his injuries and committed suicide. It was held that the defendant was liable for the suicide, because depression was a foreseeable consequence of the injuries and the suicide followed upon that depression. The suicide itself did not need to be foreseeable.

The same negligent act may give rise to more than one kind of risk. In *The Wagon Mound (No. 2)*, damage by fouling and by fire both were held to be foreseeable. On the other hand, loss of profits consequent upon damage done by a lorry driver to the power cable supplying the plaintiffs' factory was held to be foreseeable, but an unusual process by which a fire was caused by a power surge leading to arcing in the factory telephone system was not.[3118] Again, exposing property to the risk of theft did not cover loss of the property by arson.[3119]

If the relevant kind of damage is foreseeable, it does not matter that the defendant might not have been able to foresee the full amount or extent of that damage. In *Taupo Borough Council v. Birnie*,[3120] the defendant negligently caused a hotel to be flooded and the plaintiff owner claimed damages for loss of business profits after the flood had receded. The plaintiff was allowed to recover his whole loss even though this was particularly large because of the wide publicity given to the flooding and because the tour operators chose not to make bookings thereafter.[3121] In *Attorney-General v. Geothermal Produce New Zealand Ltd*,[3122] where the defendant damaged the plaintiff's roses by negligent spraying, damages were awarded not only for damage to the roses and loss of profits thereon but also for loss of profits on roses and orchids yet to be grown that would have been financed by the initial

3114. [1962] NZLR 552.
3115. [1963] AC 837.
3116. [2000] 1 WLR 1082.
3117. [2008] 1 AC 884.
3118. *Mainguard Packaging Ltd v. Hilton Haulage* [1990] 1 NZLR 360.
3119. *Trevison v. Springman* (1996) 16 BCLR (3d) 138.
3120. [1978] 2 NZLR 397.
3121. *See also Network Rail Infrastructure Ltd v. Conarken Group Ltd* [2011] EWCA Civ 644 (loss of revenue caused by accident having deterrent effect on future rail passengers held recoverable).
3122. [1987] 2 NZLR 348.

profits. McMullin J said that the fact that the respondents may not have known of the details of the applicants' operation and the expansion that was contemplated did not affect their liability. But there was a substantial discount for the uncertainties involved in the plaintiff's future plans.

C. Existing Physical, Mental and Financial States

546. A wrongdoer has to take the victim of the tort as he or she finds that victim. The wrongdoer thus is liable for the whole damage even though its amount is increased because of the victim's preexisting weakness or susceptibility to harm. Provided the defendant could have foreseen some damage being inflicted, it is no answer to the plaintiff's claim that a 'normal' person would not have suffered to the same extent. In *Stephenson v. Waite Tileman Ltd*,[3123] this 'thin skull' principle was accepted by the Court of Appeal. Richmond J affirmed that if the initial injury was of a reasonably foreseeable kind, type or character, then the link between the negligence and the ultimate consequences could be forged simply as one of cause and effect.

Stephenson was a case decided before the accident compensation scheme came into force, and nowadays any common law claim for personal injury normally will be statutorily barred. However, the same principle applies in the case of a person with a fragile psychological condition, where the accident compensation scheme does not provide cover.[3124] It has been held that there is no relevant difference between an eggshell skull and an eggshell personality.[3125]

If damage is done to property that is exceptionally fragile or delicate, damages similarly may be recoverable provided the kind of damage was foreseeable. An example is a case where a plaintiff landowner suffered damage to her wall caused by the pressure of surface water and soil from the defendant's property, and was met with the argument that the real cause of the damage was the inadequate construction of the wall and the lack of provision for drainage. It was held that the fact that the plaintiff's wall would only have suffered minor damage if it had been adequately constructed was no answer to the claim for the loss of the wall.[3126]

The same approach is taken where a victim is unable to prevent further damage through lack of money. In *Taupo Borough Council v. Birnie*[3127] the flooding of the plaintiff's hotel by the defendants led to a substantial loss of business and ultimately a sale by the mortgagee for a sum less than the market price that would have been obtainable on an unforced sale. The plaintiff claimed this capital loss, and the court rejected the defendant's argument that the mortgagee sale was due to the plaintiff's lack of funds. In *Attorney-General v. Geothermal Produce New Zealand*

3123. [1973] 1 NZLR 152.
3124. *See* para. 42.
3125. *Page v. Smith* [1996] 1 AC 155 at 189; *Tame v. New South Wales; Annetts v. Australian Stations Pty Ltd* (2002) 76 ALJR 1348 at [117].
3126. *McColl v. Dionisatos* (2002) Aus Torts Reps 81-652.
3127. [1978] 2 NZLR 397.

Ltd[3128] the court affirmed that foreseeability was the governing test, and McMullin J specifically drew an analogy between an applicant's financial weakness and his or her physical disability. So also, in *Lagden v. O'Connor*[3129] the House of Lords held that the test of reasonable foreseeability should apply to the economic state of a victim in the same way as it applies to the victim's physical and mental vulnerability. It required the wrongdoer to bear the consequences if it was reasonably foreseeable that the injured party would have to borrow money or incur some other kind of expenditure to mitigate his or her damages.

IV. Directness or Foreseeability?

547. The reasoning in both *Wagon Mound* cases is based on the link between liability and compensation. It suggests that where the defendant is only liable because he or she is at fault, then foreseeability of consequences is the appropriate test for assessing the remoteness issue. So foreseeability applies in cases of negligence, and *The Wagon Mound (No. 2)* confirmed that it applied in nuisance as well. Lord Reid explained that negligence in the narrow sense (by which, presumably, he meant breach of a duty to take care) is not an essential element in nuisance but that fault of some kind is almost always necessary and fault generally involves foreseeability.[3130] It could not be right to discriminate between cases of nuisance according to whether fault is or is not relevant, and as in their Lordships' judgment the similarities between nuisance and negligence far outweighed any differences, the injury in nuisance also should be foreseeable.

In *Cambridge Water Co. v. Eastern Counties Leather plc*,[3131] the House of Lords recognized that *The Wagon Mound (No. 2)* settled the law to the effect that foreseeability of harm was necessary for the recovery of damages in public and private nuisance, and were satisfied also that foreseeability of the relevant type of damage should be regarded as a prerequisite of liability in damages under the rule in *Rylands v. Fletcher.* Lord Goff said that the historical connection between nuisance and *Rylands v. Fletcher* pointed in this direction, and the conclusion also could be derived from Blackburn J's original statement of the law. In *Hamilton v. Papakura DC*,[3132] the Court of Appeal confirmed that this is the position in New Zealand as well.

The test of foreseeability extends as well to cases of strict liability, seemingly because it is more restrictive than the test of direct consequences. In *Cambridge Water* itself, Lord Goff, without seeking to explain what Lord Reid had meant by his notion of fault, advanced the orthodox view that liability in both nuisance and under the rule in *Rylands v. Fletcher* is strict, yet he accepted that foreseeability still

3128. [1987] 2 NZLR 348.

3129. [2004] 1 AC 1067; and *see Alcoa Minerals of Jamaica Inc v. Broderick* [2002] 1 AC 371; *Heslop v. Cousins* [2007] 3 NZLR 679.

3130. [1967] 1 AC 617 at 641; *see* further para. 192.

3131. [1994] 2 AC 264 at 301, 304–306; *Transco plc v. Stockport Metropolitan Borough Council* [2003] 3 WLR 1467 at [33].

3132. [2000] 1 NZLR 265 at 282–284 (affirmed [2002] 3 NZLR 308 (PC)); and *see Autex Industries Ltd v. Auckland CC* [2000] NZAR 324 at 331, 335.

should govern damages. Again, in *Hamilton*, Gault J said that once it had been shown that the damage was foreseeable, it was irrelevant that the act causing the damage was not the fault of the defendant or that the defendant acted with reasonable care and skill. The test also applies in an action for breach of statutory duty,[3133] for the republication of a libel,[3134] for cattle trespass,[3135] and for conversion, at least where committed by a person acting in good faith.[3136]

The recovery of damages for the unintended consequences of an intentional tort may be less constrained. The principle of *The Wagon Mound (No. 2)* does not limit recovery, and liability extends to all direct or natural losses in the case of an action for deceit[3137] and for injurious falsehood,[3138] and perhaps for intentional trespass to the person[3139] and to land.[3140] The policy justification for holding damage to be too remote, that the defendant not be subjected to a disproportionate burden of liability, does not apply with the same force where the defendant has intended to cause harm or to do the act constituting the tort, although without a specific intention as to consequences.

3133. *Pease v. Eltham Borough* [1962] NZLR 437 at 443: *Harris v. Lombard NZ Ltd* [1974] 2 NZLR 161 at 168 (natural consequences).
3134. *Slipper v. British Broadcasting Corp* [1991] 1 QB 283.
3135. *Gardiner v. Metcalf* [1994] 2 NZLR 8 at 11, 13.
3136. *Kuwait Airways Corporation v. Iraqi Airways Co. (Nos 4 and 5)* [2002] 2 AC 883 at [102–103].
3137. *Smith New Court Securities Ltd v. Scrimgeour Vickers (Asset Management) Ltd* [1997] AC 254.
3138. *Palmer Bruyn & Parker Pty Ltd v. Parsons* (2001) 208 CLR 388 at [65].
3139. *See* para. 51.
3140. *See* para. 176.

Part VI. Remedies

Chapter 1. General Principles

548. In most tort cases the plaintiff seeks a remedy in damages by way of compensation for the harm. Usually it is the only practicable remedy because the act has been done, the harm has been suffered, and it is not likely to be repeated. But sometimes, where harm is threatened or is continuing, the plaintiff will seek an injunction to prevent the harm or bring it to an end. Other possible remedies include restitutionary relief, a declaration as to the plaintiff's rights, non-compensatory damages including, in particular, exemplary damages, and claims for contribution between tortfeasors.

The remedies that may be available on the commission of a tort have already been considered in relation to various specific heads of liability. For example, we have discussed damages for trespass to the person,[3141] criminal proceedings, self-help, damages and injunctive relief where there has been a trespass to land;[3142] damages, an injunction and abatement as remedies for nuisance;[3143] damages and restitution in cases of conversion and detinue;[3144] damages, an injunction and an account of profits as remedies for passing off;[3145] damages, an injunction, a declaration and correction in the case of defamation;[3146] and damages and impounding for cattle trespass.[3147] The remedies for certain statutory torts have been considered as well.[3148]

The discussion of these remedies has been concerned with their special features in relation to the particular head of claim under consideration. Our focus now is more general. We will examine first the various matters of principle that a court needs to take into account when making an award of compensatory damages. We will then look at the various other remedies mentioned above, again by way of a broad overview and with a focus on general principle.

There is a right of persons to take their own remedies in limited circumstances. The topic could be discussed as an aspect of remedies, yet self-help also can operate as a defence and we have considered its various forms in that context.[3149]

3141. *See* para. 57.
3142. *See* paras 174–177.
3143. *See* paras 198–200.
3144. *See* paras 237–238.
3145. *See* paras 252–256.
3146. *See* paras 358–361.
3147. *See* para. 426.
3148. *See* paras 443, 447, 450, 452, 453.
3149. *See* paras 501–507.

Chapter 2. Compensatory Damages

§1. Overview

549. The principal common law remedy for tort is an award of damages.[3150] The purpose of an award normally is to compensate for a loss. Compensable losses may be pecuniary, that is, those that can be quantified as financial and material, and non-pecuniary, that is, those that have no quantifiable market value, such as pain, suffering, distress and loss of enjoyment of life. In the latter case in particular, the award of damages is, at best, only a rough and ready instrument for providing some measure of compensation. Exact compensation is never possible, particularly because damages are awarded in a lump sum for past, present, and future losses.

In overseas jurisdictions the topic of damages tends to be dominated by the principles that apply in personal injury actions. In New Zealand, there can be no award of damages that arise directly or indirectly out of personal injury covered by the accident compensation scheme.[3151] Accordingly, an occasion for the award of personal injury damages rarely arises. Certain forms of personal injury fall outside the ambit of the scheme,[3152] the most significant instance being mental injury, and the topic of personal injuries will therefore be addressed, albeit only in brief. But our main concern is with damages for property damage and financial loss.

Damages are not awarded solely to compensate. They may also seek, *inter alia*, to vindicate a right, deter wrongdoing, and punish a wrongdoer. Most torts are actionable only on proof of damage, but sometimes, notably as regards trespass to the person, the conduct is held to be actionable per se. Here, vindication of the right of the plaintiff to be free from the wrong is a prominent purpose. Furthermore, where there is egregious wrongdoing, the courts may award damages in order to punish the wrongdoer. These non-compensatory purposes will be considered separately later on.

Public law damages for breach of the New Zealand Bill of Rights Act 1990 may overlap with the award of damages in tort, and in this case an award of the latter is likely to be seen as sufficient.[3153] But sometimes there is no overlap and the Bill of Rights action stands alone, and sometimes a court may seek to achieve certain wider, non-compensatory, purposes, such as deterrence of public wrongdoing and vindication of the rights of the plaintiff. The principles governing the award of these public law damages were included in the earlier discussion of possible rights of action for abuse of public office.[3154]

Finally, the inquiry into damages is only necessary insofar as the plaintiff has suffered a recoverable loss. If the defendant is not responsible for a loss because the defendant owes no duty to the plaintiff or the loss is too remote,[3155] the question does not arise.

3150. *See* further Atkin, *Remedies*, in *Todd on Torts* Ch. 25 (Todd ed., 8th ed., 2019).
3151. Accident Compensation Act 2001, s. 317; *see* para. 41.
3152. *See* para. 42.
3153. *Dunlea v. Attorney-General* [2000] 3 NZLR 136.
3154. *See* para. 314.
3155. *See* paras 542–547.

§2. SPECIAL AND GENERAL DAMAGES

550. The courts draw a distinction between 'special' and 'general' damages, although they are not consistent in the meaning they give to these terms. In the context of pleading, special damage is used to signify losses that must be specifically pleaded and in respect of which, if proven, the plaintiff is entitled to be compensated, as opposed to the general damage that the law will presume from the commission of the wrong.[3156] However, the terms also are used in a more imprecise sense, so that special damage signifies damage that is capable of substantially exact pecuniary assessment whereas general damage requires assessment in the round to compensate for some form of intangible loss. So the distinction approximates that between pecuniary and non-pecuniary loss. Examples of losses for which general damages may be claimed include pain and suffering, loss of amenity, mental distress, harm to reputation, loss of freedom of movement. We will be looking in particular at the element of general damages in claims for personal injury and for property damage.

§3. QUANTIFICATION OF DAMAGE

I. Restitutio in Integrum

551. The courts must fix the amount of compensation that the victim of a tort can recover from the wrongdoer, or in other words with the quantification of the loss. The basic rule is *restitutio in integrum*: restoration to the previous position. In *Livingstone v. Rawyards Coal Co.*,[3157] Lord Blackburn put this as the governing principle:

> Where any injury is to be compensated by damages, in settling the sum of money to be given for reparation of damages, you should as nearly as possible get at the sum of money which will put the party who has been injured, or who has suffered, in the same position as he would have been in if he had not sustained the wrong for which he is now getting his compensation.

Applying the principle may be a good deal harder than stating it. A plaintiff claiming damages must be able to satisfy the court on a balance of probabilities that actual damage has been suffered and be able to prove at least in general terms what the amount of that loss is. Frequently there will be uncertainty as to what would have happened had the tort not been committed: and even if there is not, a court may face considerable difficulty in fixing the value of whatever it is that has been lost. In *McElroy Milne v. Commercial Electronics Ltd*,[3158] Cooke P emphasized that the quantum of damages in each case is a question of fact:

3156. *Ratcliffe v. Evans* [1892] 2 QB 524 at 528.
3157. (1880) 5 App Cas 25 at 39.
3158. [1993] 1 NZLR 39 at 41.

> [I hold to] the basic view that in the end the assessment of damages is a question of fact; that there is no such thing as a rule, as to the legal measure of damages, applicable to all cases; and that the ultimate question as to compensatory damages is whether the particular damage claimed is sufficiently linked to the breach of the particular duty to merit recovery in all the circumstances.

However, this does not mean that in any case the approach to be taken in calculating the quantum of the damage is entirely at large. Rather, there are guiding rules or principles that help throw light on the question and that assist the courts in achieving a degree of consistency from case to case.

II. Single Award

552. A plaintiff can sue only once for all present and future losses arising from one cause of action.[3159] Thus, a plaintiff who obtained judgment in a claim for personal injuries could not later bring a second action simply because the injuries turned out to be more serious than was thought when judgment was given.[3160] On the other hand, judgment and an award of damages for property damage suffered in a road accident was held not to bar another action for personal injuries suffered in the same accident, on the basis that the causes of action were different.[3161] This view, however, is unconvincing and has been rejected in Canada[3162] and Australia.[3163] Furthermore, an issue that should have been raised in earlier proceedings may not be raised in fresh proceedings;[3164] and if an issue has already been determined by a court it cannot be litigated again.[3165] In any event the problem can hardly arise in New Zealand in the context of separate claims for personal injury and for property damage, as there can be no common law action for personal injury caused by an accident.

There is no objection to bringing successive actions in the case of continuing or repeated torts. Where a tort that is actionable per se continues to be committed, a cause of action accrues *de die in diem* for so long as the wrongful state of affairs persists. Where a tort that is actionable only on proof of damage continues to cause new damage, a cause of action accrues as often as the damage occurs. Thus a defendant who wrongfully remains on another's land commits a continuing trespass, and a defendant who maintains a state of affairs that persistently causes unreasonable interference with a neighbour's enjoyment of land commits a continuing nuisance.

3159. *Fetter v. Beale* (1701) Ld Raym 692; 91 ER 1122.
3160. *Ibid.* In New Zealand, of course, the victim almost invariably will be covered by the accident compensation scheme, which makes provision for adjustable periodical payments: *see* para. 43.
3161. *Brunsden v. Humphrey* (1884) 14 QBD 141; and *see Darley Main Colliery Co. v. Mitchell* (1886) 11 App Cas 127 at 144, 145; *National Insurance Co. of NZ Ltd v. Geddes* [1936] NZLR 1004 at 1008; *Priest v. Mowat (No. 2)* [1937] NZLR 789.
3162. *Cahoon v. Franks* [1967] SCR 455.
3163. *Marlborough Harbour Board v. Charter Travel Co. Ltd* (1989) 18 NSWLR 223; *Tiufino v. Warland* (2000) 50 NSWLR 104.
3164. *Henderson v. Henderson* (1843) 3 Hare 100, 67 ER 313; *see* para. 510.
3165. *Tiufino v. Warland* (2000) 50 NSWLR 104.

Again, the repeated publication of the same defamatory statement gives rise to a cause of action on each publication. Similarly, a single act may cause damage to occur on several occasions, which are quite separate from and arise independently of each other, in which case it seems that successive causes of action may accrue.[3166] In cases of this kind, where a tort continues to be committed or new damage happens after an action has already been brought, fresh proceedings still may be instituted.[3167] Where, however, there is only a single tortious act with continuing consequences, such as where the defendant on one occasion inflicts lasting or permanent damage to the plaintiff or his property, only one right of action can accrue.[3168]

III. Lump Sum

553. Damages normally are awarded in a lump sum.[3169] Accordingly, where losses will continue into the future, as where the plaintiff claims for loss of future earnings or loss of future business profits, the court must make an award representing the present value of the future loss. This may well require expert professional evidence. The sum has to be discounted to allow for the fact that it is being paid early and to allow for contingencies in the future.[3170]

IV. Destruction of or Damage to Property

554. Where property is destroyed, the normal measure of damage is its value at the time and place of destruction. Where property is damaged, the loss to the plaintiff may be measured by the amount by which its value has been diminished or by the cost of repair. The courts take a pragmatic attitude and adopt whichever seems appropriate.[3171]

A. *Chattels*

555. In the case of a damaged chattel the cost of repair usually is the measure, on the basis that the cost or estimated cost indicates the amount by which the value of the chattel is reduced. Sometimes, however, the cost of repair will be much

3166. *See* para. 457.
3167. *Backhouse v. Bonomi* (1861) 9 HLC 503; 11 ER 825; *Darley Main Colliery Co. v. Mitchell* (1886) 11 App Cas 127 (HL); *Taylor v. Auto Trade Supply Ltd* [1972] NZLR 102.
3168. *T v. H* [1995] 3 NZLR 37.
3169. There may be interim payments of damages in certain circumstances: *see* HCR 2016 r 7.70; DCR 2014 rr 7.68–7.76.
3170. *See*, for example, *Attorney-General v. Geothermal Produce New Zealand Ltd* [1987] 2 NZLR 348.
3171. *Bevan Investments Ltd v. Blackhall and Struthers (No. 2)* [1978] 2 NZLR 97.

greater than the diminution in value. If the chattel has great rarity value or is unique or irreplaceable then that cost may still be awarded,[3172] but normally only its value can be recovered.[3173]

In addition, compensatory damages are available for loss of use or cost of hire of a substitute item. So too, a business losing the use of a profit-earning chattel may be able to recover loss of profits. In *Greig v. Tasman Rental Cars Ltd*[3174] the defendant's negligence caused the plaintiff's rental car to be off the road for eight and a half weeks. The defendant paid for the cost of repair, but argued that there had been no loss of income as the plaintiff had other cars in reserve that could have taken up all the available business. The Court of Appeal held that the plaintiff was entitled to a sum as general damages for the absence of the car during the period, even though no specific loss of earnings could be shown. It was considered that there was no principle of calculation of the loss capable of universal application, but the court should attempt to assess the real loss to the plaintiff. The method used was to establish whether there was a real possibility of profit-earning. The full amount of the profit then could be discounted to allow for the degree of improbability.

Some further guidance is given in *Newmans Coach Lines v. Robertshawe*.[3175] The Court of Appeal held that if loss of specific profits could not be established, a plaintiff could recover general damages for loss of use of a commercial asset. It was a matter of determining a fair figure that would in a broad and general way and after allowing for contingencies provide reasonable compensation to the particular plaintiff for the particular loss he had suffered, that is for loss of use of the asset in circumstances where he is not seeking special damages for loss of specific profits or has failed to establish such a loss. It might often be appropriate to use as a base calculation the cost of holding the individual chattel as a necessary component of the income-earning enterprise, and the resultant assessment could then be increased or reduced for the contingencies that seem fair in terms of overall income. The focus was on the asset that was damaged and the compensation was fixed as a fair measure of the value of its use to the business, including the inconvenience caused by the loss of use.[3176]

General damages for non-pecuniary loss may occasionally be appropriate, at least in 'consumer' cases. An example is where general damages were awarded for unlawful entry and repossession of a television set.[3177]

3172. *O'Grady v. Westminster Scaffolding Ltd* [1962] 2 Ll Rep 238.
3173. *Darbishire v. Warran* [1963] 1 WLR 1067.
3174. [1982] 2 NZLR 171.
3175. [1984] 1 NZLR 53.
3176. In *Beechwood Birmingham Ltd v. Hoyer Group UK Ltd* [2010] 3 WLR 1677 a car belonging to the claimant company, a dealer in cars, was damaged in an accident, and the company then hired a replacement instead of using a similar car from its own ample stock. It was held that the company was entitled to general damages for loss of use, but the sum awarded should not be assessed by reference to the spot hire rate for a vehicle of the relevant type but should be based on the interest and capital employed and any depreciation sustained over the period of repairs.
3177. *Amalgamated Finance Ltd v. Yeow* (1999) 6 NZBLC 102,639.

B. Land

556. Similar principles apply in the case of damage to land. In *Bevan Investments Ltd v. Blackhall and Struthers (No. 2)*,[3178] the Court Appeal held that damages should be measured by assessing the costs of rectifying defects, but subject to the qualification that the plaintiff should have no reasonable alternative but to carry out repairs. That the choice ultimately is based upon considerations of reasonableness is well illustrated by the decision of the House of Lords in *Ruxley Electronics Ltd v. Forsyth*.[3179] This concerned an action for breach of contract, but the same principles can apply. A swimming pool had been constructed to the wrong depth, and the cost of putting it right was GBP 21,560. The breach had no adverse effect on the value of the pool, which could still be used for diving. Their Lordships held that the expenditure needed to put right the breach was out of all proportion to the benefit to be obtained, so the damages should be measured by the diminution in value of the pool, which was nil. However, a modest sum was awarded for loss of amenity representing the plaintiff's rather less satisfactory use of the pool.

In *Ruxley*, the innocent party sought to recover the cost of reinstatement where there was no loss in value. In *Warren and Mahoney v. Dynes*,[3180] the opposite argument was presented, and once again the solution was found in what would be a reasonable course of action. In this case, a house was constructed with serious defects due to negligence by its architects and engineers. The plaintiffs sought damages on the basis of the difference in value of the house as it was and the house as it should have been without the defects. However, the defendants argued that the plaintiffs were only entitled to the cost of reinstatement and that this cost was considerably less than the diminution in value of the house. The trial judge nonetheless held that damages should be assessed on a diminution in value basis and this conclusion was upheld on appeal. There was uncertainty as to the cost of repairs, and it was not clear that the problems could be satisfactorily resolved. In these circumstances the judge was entitled to depart from the cost of repairs as the appropriate measure.

Awards of general damages sometimes are made in cases of damage to property. In a number of decisions plaintiffs have recovered damages for ill health, discomfort, stress, and anxiety arising out of defects in or damage to houses.[3181] In the case of 'leaky building syndrome' such damages are authorized by statute.[3182] General damages for stress also have been awarded, for example, in respect of a solicitor's breaches of duty in dealing with land development transactions on behalf of his client,[3183] and in nuisance for stress, anxiety, disruption and inconvenience.[3184]

3178. [1978] 2 NZLR 97; *Gunton v. Aviation Classics Ltd* [2004] 3 NZLR 836.
3179. [1996] 1 AC 344.
3180. CA 49/99, 26 Oct. 1988.
3181. For example, *Gabolinscy v. Hamilton City Corporation* [1975] 1 NZLR 150; *Young v. Tomlinosn* [1979] 2 NZLR 441; *Stieller v. Porirua City Council* [1986] 1 NZLR 84; *Chase v. de Groot* [1994] 1 NZLR 613; *Dicks v. Hobson Swan Construction Ltd* (2006) 7 NZCPR 881.
3182. Weathertight Homes Resolution Services Act 2006, s. 50; *see* para. 121.
3183. *Heslop v. Cousins* [2007] 3 NZLR 679.
3184. *Semple v. Wilson* [2018] NZHC 992, [2018] NZAR 1025.

V. Personal Injuries

557. Personal injuries claims generally are precluded by section 317 of the Accident Compensation Act 2001, so claims for common law damages can only be made in respect of the small number of cases where personal injury has been suffered as the result of a tort and there is no cover under the Act.[3185] Probably the most significant of these are claims in respect of mental injury and claims in respect of tortiously inflicted disease that is not employment-related or caused by medical treatment. In these and certain other exceptional cases damages can be claimed by the victim for his or her pecuniary and non-pecuniary losses.

A. Pecuniary Loss

558. A claimant for accident compensation receives rehabilitation expenses, and periodical payments at the rate of 80% of loss of earnings, subject to a maximum figure, with annual adjustments indexed to wage movements.[3186] In the case of a common law claim, the plaintiff can claim for medical and other expenses and for lost earnings. But as with any other claim, the damages are payable on a 'once and for all' basis by way of a lump sum. So in respect of future pecuniary losses the court must convert them into a present capital sum. This of course is likely to involve all kinds of uncertainties, and the accuracy of the result achieved by the court's calculations will depend on the assumptions on which it is based.[3187]

First, the court must determine the multiplicand – the plaintiff's net annual loss before tax[3188] and after making appropriate deductions.[3189] The capital sum is then multiplied by the number of years' purchase calculated in relation to the likely duration of the loss. Assuming the injury is permanent, the multiplier is not simply the total number of years from trial to retirement age or death. Allowance must be made for the 'vicissitudes of life', that is, for non-compensable[3190] intervening events, like illness or unemployment, that might have adversely affected the plaintiff even if he or she had not been injured by the defendant. Account also must be taken of the fact that a lump sum will produce an investment income. The aim is to produce a lump sum that, when invested, will produce an income equal to the lost income when the interest is supplemented by withdrawals of capital over the period of the multiplier.

The question arises as to whether inflation should be brought into consideration. The orthodox view is that money should be treated as retaining its value at the date of judgment, on the basis that high inflation tends to be accompanied by high rates of interest, so the higher return will offset the decline in the capital value of the fund. But the argument may not represent the reality. The Court of Appeal in the context of a claim for compensation for compulsorily acquired land has held that inflation

3185. *See* para. 42.
3186. Accident Compensation Act 2001, Sch. 1, clause 46; *see* para. 43.
3187. *Wells v. Wells* [1999] 1 AC 345 at 389.
3188. *See* para. 565.
3189. *See* para. 564.
3190. *See* para. 536.

should be taken into account, but the Crown conceded the point and the question of principle was left open.[3191] In the end it is a question of doing justice, and it may be that in most cases at least, predicting inflation trends in the future is too speculative an exercise.

A disabled plaintiff who remains in his job may be under a handicap in the labour market if he loses the job in the future. This is a compensable loss, and if satisfied the risk is a real one, the court must value this chance in light of all the circumstances.[3192]

Where an injury shortens the plaintiff's expectation of life, the plaintiff is entitled to damages for loss of earnings during the 'lost years' when, but for the accident, he probably would have remained alive and working, but with a deduction for his probable living expenses.[3193] Broadly speaking, this brings the damages in such claims into line with those where the victim is killed and a claim is made by the dependants for loss of dependency.[3194]

B. Non-pecuniary Loss

559. There is no accident compensation for pain and suffering, but claimants who meet the qualifying conditions are entitled to a lump sum for loss of amenity.[3195] At common law both heads may be claimed by way of general damages. As regards pain and suffering, a victim who remains unconscious may recover little or nothing under this head.[3196] But provided the victim is sentient an award can be made in respect of mental suffering that, standing alone, amounts to a recognizable psychiatric disorder.[3197] An award for mental suffering consequential on physical injury can cover worry about the injury and 'compensation neurosis', which will cease once an award has been determined.[3198] However, fear and anxiety without physical damage cannot be the basis of an action. So claims by employees who developed symptomless pleural plaques caused by exposure to asbestos fibres and who suffered worry as a result all failed, because their physical condition was too trivial to amount to damage.[3199]

Compensation for loss of amenity, that is, loss of faculty or the damaging effect on the plaintiff's ability to enjoy life, can provide an element of solace, even if entirely inadequate, for the victim. So one who suffers the loss of a limb or, generally, of some bodily function, or of sight or hearing or other senses, is entitled to damages. Such loss is treated as having been suffered as a matter of objective fact

3191. *Drower v. Ministry of Works* [1984] 1 NZLR 26.
3192. *Moeliker v. A Reyrolle & Co. Ltd* [1976] ICR 253.
3193. *Pickett v. British Rail Engineering Ltd* [1980] AC 126.
3194. *See* para. 560.
3195. *See* para. 43.
3196. *Wise v. Kaye* [1962] 1 QB 638; *West & Son Ltd v. Shephard* [1964] AC 326.
3197. *van Soest v. Residual Health Management Unit* [2000] 1 NZLR 179. For examples, *see Brickell v. Attorney-General* (2000) 5 NZELC 96,077; *L v. Robinson* [2000] 3 NZLR 499.
3198. *James v. Woodall Duckham Construction Co. Ltd* [1969] 1 WLR 903.
3199. *Rothwell v. Chemical & Insulating Co. Ltd* [2008] 1 AC 281; *see* para. 84; compare *Dryden v. Johnson Matthey plc* [2018] UKSC 18, [2018] 2 WLR 1109.

even if the plaintiff is not conscious and cannot appreciate the actuality of that of which he or she has been deprived.[3200] If the victim dies there can be no such award to the estate in respect of the period after death, but the courts refuse to treat a living claimant as if he or she were already dead. And, generally, the courts see it as undesirable to assess compensation based on subjective unhappiness, which would put a premium on protestations of misery.[3201]

Although non-pecuniary loss cannot be translated directly into money, the only available remedy is a monetary award and some basis for assessment has to be found. So the courts set 'tariffs' which may increase or decrease depending on the circumstances. This may at least achieve some degree of consistency, although the starting point ultimately is arbitrary and depends upon the building up of a consensus as to what is a fair and reasonable award. As the issue rarely arises in New Zealand, the courts may seek a rough guide in developments overseas.[3202]

C. Claims by Dependants

560. At common law a person who suffered financial loss on the death of another person as the result of a tort had no claim against the tortfeasor.[3203] In particular, the rule prevented claims by dependants on the death of the breadwinner, and its injustice meant that the legislature had to step in. Reform originally was achieved in England by the Fatal Accidents Act 1846 (otherwise known as Lord Campbell's Act), and the present statute is the Fatal Accidents Act 1976, consolidating earlier legislation. The equivalent legislation in New Zealand is the Deaths by Accidents Compensation Act 1952. The Act does not apply in cases covered by the Accident Compensation Act 2001, under which death benefits are payable to dependants,[3204] but it remains in force and still applies where deaths occur outside New Zealand[3205] or are otherwise outside the ambit of the Act.[3206]

The 1952 Act provides that where the death of a person is caused by a wrongful act, neglect, or default that would, if death had not ensued, have entitled the party injured to bring an action and recover damages, then the person who would have been liable to the deceased is liable to an action for damages.[3207] The action is brought by the deceased's executor or administrator for the benefit of the deceased's spouse, civil union partner, parents, and children.[3208] The court may award:

3200. *Wise v. Kaye* [1962] 1 QB 638; *West & Son Ltd v. Shephard* [1964] AC 326; *Lim v. Camden Area Health Authority* [1980] AC 174.

3201. *West & Son Ltd v. Shephard* [1964] AC 326 at 368.

3202. In England, *see Heil v. Rankin* [2001] QB 272, setting out the function of the English Court of Appeal in setting the level of awards for non-pecuniary loss. For helpful guides *see* Kemp & Kemp, *The Quantum of Damages in Personal Injury and Fatal Accident Claims* (London: Sweet & Maxwell) (looseleaf); *McGregor on Damages* (20th ed., London: Sweet & Maxwell, 2018).

3203. *Pou v. British American Tobacco (New Zealand) Ltd* [2006] 1 NZLR 661 at [7].

3204. *See* para. 43.

3205. *Mitranove v. The Ship 'Kursa'* HC, Wellington, AD 313/95, 18 Nov. 1995, J. Doogue.

3206. *Pou v. British American Tobacco (New Zealand) Ltd* [2006] 1 NZLR 661.

3207. Deaths by Accidents Compensation Act 1952, s. 4(1).

3208. *Ibid.*, s. 5.

(1) such damages as it may think proportioned to the injury resulting from the death to the persons for whose benefit the action is brought;
(2) damages in respect of the amount of actual pecuniary benefit those persons might reasonably have expected to enjoy, whether or not they were wholly or partially dependent upon the deceased; and
(3) damages in respect of medical and funeral expenses.[3209]

In awarding damages the court shall not take into account any gain to the estate or to any dependant that is consequent on the death of the deceased person.[3210]

In *Pou v. British American Tobacco (New Zealand) Ltd*[3211] the adult children of a woman who died of lung cancer brought a claim against two tobacco companies, seeking damages in respect of loss of maternal care and guidance and loss of benefits their mother would have provided but for her death. The Court of Appeal held, following earlier authority,[3212] that the Act was intended to provide compensation only for pecuniary losses, and, at least as regards adult children, the concept of pecuniary loss could not embrace loss of parental guidance and companionship. But the claim for lost services and other benefits was arguable and should not be struck out.

VI. Duty to Mitigate

561. The plaintiff has a duty to take all reasonable steps to mitigate the loss consequent on the breach, and is debarred from claiming for damage that is suffered due to his or her neglect to take such steps.[3213] The burden of proof that the plaintiff has failed to take appropriate reasonable steps is on the defendant.[3214] So the plaintiff may be expected, say, to have repairs carried out on damaged goods or property as soon as possible, and to hire a substitute in the meantime to prevent extra business loss.

Whether the plaintiff has failed to take a reasonable opportunity of mitigation is a question of fact dependent upon the particular circumstances of each case. For example, a party who became committed to the uneconomic completion of a building after relying on a negligent estimate by the builder was required to take reasonable steps to sell the property, and he was not entitled to ignore the advice in a valuer's report by asking too high a price and running the risk of the property failing to sell.[3215]

3209. *Ibid.*, s. 7(1).
3210. *Ibid.*, s. 7(2).
3211. [2006] 1 NZLR 661.
3212. *McCarthy v. Palmer* [1957] NZLR 620.
3213. *British Westinghouse Electric & Manufacturing Co. Ltd v. Underground Electric Rail Co. of London Ltd* [1912] AC 673; *Marlborough District Council v. Altimarloch Joint Venture Ltd* [2012] 2 NZLR 726 at [55].
3214. *Walop No. 3 Ltd v. Para Franchising Ltd* CA 20/03, 23 Feb. 2004; *Governors Ltd v. Anderson* CA 94/04, 16 Aug. 2005.
3215. *J & JC Abrams Ltd v. Ancliffe* [1978] 2 NZLR 420.

In the case of failed property transactions, damages normally are assessed at the date of the wrong, on the basis that the plaintiff ought to mitigate by buying a substitute property. But sometimes that may not be reasonably possible, and damages may be assessed at a later date if justice so requires.[3216]

In determining whether any proposed steps would have been reasonable, it is relevant to take into account the fact that the party in breach of duty is demanding positive action from one who may be innocent of any blame. Certainly a person is under no obligation to injure his business or property to reduce the damages payable by the wrongdoer. So it was unreasonable to expect an injured plaintiff who could no longer do the work required on his dairy farm to get rid of his milking herd and use the whole farm for running sheep and cattle.[3217] And there is no duty to embark upon a hazardous venture merely to protect the defendant from the consequences of his own carelessness.[3218] For example, the owners of a swimming pool damaged by the collapse of surrounding soil were not obliged to mitigate their claim against the architect and engineer by bringing a pioneering lawsuit against a neighbour for allegedly contributing to the damage by excessive watering.[3219]

Sometimes a plaintiff cannot afford to take steps in mitigation of a loss. The general principle is that the plaintiff cannot reasonably be required to spend money where he or she lacks the means to do so.[3220] In one older decision the House of Lords took the view that the consequences of a plaintiff's impecuniosity were not to be attributed to the defendant.[3221] But the rule was not treated as being of general application, and in any event it has now been abandoned.[3222]

It is implicit in the principle of mitigation that if mitigating steps are in fact reasonably taken, and additional loss or damage results notwithstanding the reasonable decision to take those steps, then that extra loss is recoverable in addition to any other loss.[3223] For example, an owner whose launch was damaged in a storm while moored at an unsafe berth, who then brought an action against the owner and the builder of the berth, could recover the wasted costs after he started to do repairs and it then turned out that the damage was so extensive that it was not economic to carry on.[3224] So also, it was reasonable in all the circumstances to repair a helicopter notwithstanding that, in hindsight, losses would have been minimized by selling it for parts.[3225]

3216. *Heslop v. Cousins* [2007] 3 NZLR 679; and *see International Encyclopaedia of Laws: Contracts (New Zealand)*, para. 241.
3217. *Lander v. Sorensen* [1955] NZLR 219.
3218. *Pilkington v. Wood* [1952] Ch. 770; *Treloar v. Henderson* [1968] NZLR 1985.
3219. *Warren and Mahoney v. Dynes* CA 49/88, 26 Oct. 1988.
3220. *Clippens Oil Co. Ltd v. Edinburgh and District Water Trustees* [1907] AC 291.
3221. *Liesbosch Dredger v. SS Edison* [1933] AC 449.
3222. *Lagden v. O'Connor* [2004] 1 AC 1067.
3223. *Andros Springs (Owners) v. World Beauty (Owners)* [1970] P 144 at 156.
3224. *Jaggar v. Lyttelton Marina Holdings Ltd* [2006] 2 NZLR 87.
3225. *Gunton v. Aviation Classics Ltd* [2004] 3 NZLR 836.

VII. Collateral Benefits

A. *General Principles*

562. A corollary of the principle of mitigation is that the plaintiff cannot claim for a loss that has in fact been avoided because the plaintiff received a countervailing benefit. But a difficulty lies in distinguishing between benefits that go to reduce the loss and those that are indirect or collateral and that ought to be ignored. The problem arises in the same way in contract as in tort.[3226]

Seemingly the question to ask is whether the benefit is sufficiently causally connected to the defendant's wrongdoing, or whether it arises out of an independent or disconnected transaction. In a leading contract case, plaintiffs who had been supplied with deficient turbines accepted and used them, but later replaced them with new turbines that were far more efficient than those supplied by the defendants would have been, even if they had complied with the contract. It was held that in assessing the damages the consequential gain in profits and saved expenses had to be brought into account.[3227] By contrast, purchasers who bought a defective house after a negligent misrepresentation by the vendor, and who subsequently knocked it down for the enhanced development value of the land instead of repairing it, could still recover the cost of repair from the vendor.[3228] The plaintiffs' resale of the land was no part of a continuous transaction of which their purchase was the inception, so that it could not be said that the negligence that caused damage to the plaintiffs had also caused whatever profit they made on resale.

An insurance contract is an independent transaction. It is a long-established rule that the fact that the plaintiff is insured against a loss cannot be taken into account in fixing the damages payable by the defendant.[3229] The plaintiff's foresight and prudence in taking steps to guard against a loss cannot enure for the benefit of the wrongdoer. A similar principle applies in respect of gratuitous payments made by third parties: these also are not brought into account.[3230] Again, damages were awarded against a negligent surveyor based on the difference in value of leased property with and without certain defects, this notwithstanding that the landlord subsequently remedied the defects.[3231]

B. *Betterment*

563. Another way of looking at the collateral benefit issue is by reference to the concept of betterment. The issue can arise in cases involving the repair or replacement of damaged property. In *J & B Caldwell Ltd v. Logan House Retirement Home*

3226. The closely related concept of betterment is considered at para. 563.
3227. *British Westinghouse Electric & Manufacturing Co. Ltd v. Underground Electric Rail Co. of London Ltd* [1912] AC 673.
3228. *Hussey v. Eels* [1990] 2 QB 227.
3229. *Bradburn v. Great Western Railway Co.* (1874) 10 Exch. 1; *Parry v. Cleaver* [1970] AC 1.
3230. *Naahas v. Pier House Management (Cheyne Walk) Ltd* (1984) 270 EG 328.
3231. *Gardner v. Marsh & Parsons* [1997] 1 WLR 489.

Ltd,[3232] a contract case, Fisher J recognized that allowing a plaintiff a full indemnity for a new or improved substitute item overcompensated the plaintiff, by giving it more than it would receive under the contract. However, allowing the plaintiff only the depreciated value of the item under-compensated, by overlooking the economic burdens of more immediate and more expensive replacement. The logical middle ground was to make a deduction for betterment, but only after allowance to the plaintiff for any disadvantages associated with the involuntary nature of any additional investment.

In *IT Walker Holdings Ltd v. Tuf Shoes Ltd*[3233] the Court of Appeal held that the plaintiff must prove not only that he has suffered damage, but also the amount of the damage. This might suggest that the onus is on the plaintiff to prove betterment has not occurred. However, in *Caldwell* Fisher J interpreted this as meaning that the plaintiff has the onus of proving both the presence and quantum of the loss flowing from the unexpected expenditure caused by the defendant's default, while the defendant has the onus of proving that betterment has occurred.

C. Personal Injury Claims

564. The question whether deductions should be made in respect of various kinds of collateral benefits arises in an acute form in the context of personal injury claims. In the UK the basic rule is that receipts from private sources coming to the plaintiff as a result of the injury are prima facie to be set against loss of earnings and expenses, unless they come within certain established exceptions.[3234] These are ex gratia payments,[3235] although not if made by the tortfeasor;[3236] insurance payments,[3237] provided the premiums are paid by the plaintiff and not the tortfeasor;[3238] and pensions.[3239] But sick pay is deductible from damages for lost earnings, whether or not paid by the defendant.[3240] The deductibility of social security benefits is governed by legislation.[3241]

In New Zealand, of course, there is cover for accident compensation in virtually all cases of personal injury caused by tortious conduct, barring any common law claim. The preceding principles will apply to the extent that any claim for personal injury remains possible. In such a case, unemployment benefit should be deducted from the damages.[3242]

3232. [1999] 2 NZLR 99; *Gunton v. Aviation Classics Ltd* [2004] 3 NZLR 836.
3233. [1981] 2 NZLR 391.
3234. *Hodgson v. Trapp* [1989] AC 807 at 819.
3235. *Redpath v. County Down Railway* [1947] NI 167. The donor has no claim: *Esso Petroleum Co. Ltd v. Hall Russell & Co. Ltd* [1989] AC 643.
3236. *Gaca v. Pirelli General plc* [2004] 1 WLR 2683.
3237. *See* para. 562.
3238. *Gaca v. Pirelli General plc* [2004] 1 WLR 2683.
3239. *Parry v. Cleaver* [1970] AC 1.
3240. *Ibid.*; *Hussain v. New Taplow Paper Mills Ltd* [1988] AC 514.
3241. *See* generally *Winfield and Jolowicz on Tort*(19th ed., 2014), paras 23.091–23.092.
3242. *Horsburgh v. New Zealand Meat Processors Industrial Union of Workers* [1988] 1 NZLR 698.

VIII. Taxation

565. In *British Transport Commission v. Gourley*,[3243] the House of Lords held that, in measuring damages for the loss of income or profits, the court must deduct an amount equivalent to the sum that the plaintiff would have paid by way of income tax had he or she continued to receive such yearly income. This was on the premise that two conditions were satisfied. The first was that compensation was being assessed in respect of the loss of sums that had they been received would have been subject to tax. The second was that the damages awarded to the plaintiff were not themselves subject to tax. The object of damages being to compensate the plaintiff, not to punish the defendant, it was logical to award the plaintiff not a gross sum, but a net sum, reached after deduction of his or her own liabilities to the Revenue.

In New Zealand, the *Gourley* principle initially was adopted by the Court of Appeal in *Smith v. Wellington Woollen Manufacturing Co. Ltd*,[3244] a case that similarly concerned a claim for damages in tort for loss of earning capacity. Yet the decisions demonstrated the difficulties involved in the application of the principle and, indeed, that the assessment of the amount to be deducted was likely to be more a matter of guesswork than of calculation.[3245] And eventually, in *North Island Wholesale Groceries Ltd v. Hewin*,[3246] the Court of Appeal declined to apply the rule to a claim in contract for compensation for loss of office. There were four broad considerations that led the court to this view:

(1) The employer's contractual obligation was to pay the whole of the agreed remuneration. The disposition of the remuneration by the employee was not a legitimate concern of the employer.
(2) The ascertainment of a fairly quantifiable tax burden fairly attributable to the lost remuneration was a difficult, if not hopeless, task to impose on the New Zealand courts and on those involved in settling compensation for loss of office. Tax was assessed and levied on a net global figure and, as a matter of law, it was not possible to attribute a specific amount of tax that was ultimately found to be payable to a particular income receipt. The ultimate tax liability in any particular year was affected by a variety of external considerations through tax planning possibilities, and the tax laws themselves changed from year to year. The assumptions that had to be made in applying the Gourley rule in this area involved such a high degree of artificiality and speculation as to undermine the validity of the process.
(3) Great weight should be given to the provisions in the Income Tax Act 1976 that stated that compensation for loss of office was taxable.[3247] It could not be said that to assess compensation on the basis of gross earnings enabled the individual to escape his or her fair contribution to the national revenue.

3243. [1956] AC 185.
3244. [1956] NZLR 491; *Rakena v. Richardson & Co. Ltd* [1968] NZLR 915.
3245. *See* generally *Parsons v. BNM Laboratories Ltd* [1964] 1 QB 95.
3246. [1982] 2 NZLR 176.
3247. Section 65(2)(b) (*see* now the Income Tax Act 2004, s. CE 1(f)).

(4) It was highly unsatisfactory that serious tax questions should be dealt with by employer and employee in the absence of the Commissioner. He was not bound by the approach that was taken, and there was the potential for unfairness to one side or the other if in the end the expectations of the parties as to the incidence of taxation were defeated. In the present case it was disputed whether the damages were taxable at all or on a concessionary basis. It could not be said that the Commissioner's stance could be safely predicted or what the ultimate outcome might be.

The approach taken in *Hewin* was affirmed in *Horsburgh v. New Zealand Meat Processors Industrial Union of Workers*[3248] and, more recently, in *Gilbert v. Attorney-General.*[3249]

The function of damages in contract is compensatory just as in tort, and there can be little doubt that the approach taken in *Hewitt* applies in a tort case. In any event, damages representing lost income usually will be taxable, leaving no room for the application of the *Gourley* principle. *Smith's* case has not been formally overruled, but with the arrival of the accident compensation scheme the question will rarely arise in the context of a tort action.

IX. Interest

566. Interest payments may be a particular head of special damage where they are a foreseeable consequence of the wrongdoing, as where the plaintiff has to borrow money because of the defendant's breach of duty.[3250] The amount is calculated by reference to the actual rate of interest charged.[3251]

Statute in any event now provides for the payment of interest. In every money judgment a court must award interest as compensation for a delay in the payment of money, unless the Act expressly provides otherwise.[3252] The period during which interest is payable begins on the day on which the cause of action arose and ends on the day on which the judgment debt is paid in full, unless the court specifies any shorter period in accordance with the Act.[3253] The rate of interest is calculated on a daily basis using an Internet site calculator established pursuant to the Act.[3254]

3248. [1988] 1 NZLR 698; *Equiticorp Industries Group Ltd v. R (No. 51)* (1996) 17 NZTC 12,642.
3249. (2010) 8 NZELR 72.
3250. *Lion Nathan Ltd v. CC Bottlers Ltd* [1996] 2 NZLR 385.
3251. *Lincoln Industries Group Ltd v. Angus Group Ltd* [1990] 3 NZLR 82.
3252. Interest on Money Claims Act 2016, s. 10 (1) and (2). The payment of interest formerly was governed by the Judicature Act 1908, s. 87, as to which *see Worldwide NZ LLC v. NZ Venue and Event Management Ltd* [2015] 1 NZLR 1.
3253. Interest on Money Claims Act 2016, s. 9(1) and (2).
3254. *Ibid.*, ss 12, 13.

Chapter 3. Other Remedies

§1. Restitution

567. Where the commission of a tort results in a benefit to the tortfeasor, the plaintiff may waive the tort and pursue any right he or she may have to recover that benefit in contract or by way of a restitutionary remedy. The plaintiff might do this in particular because the amount of the benefit is greater than the amount of the recoverable damages.

An example of waiver is seen where the owner of a converted chattel sues not for damages but for the proceeds of sale of the chattel.[3255] Other torts that may exist concurrently with a right to restitutionary relief and that may thus be waived include trespass to goods,[3256] trespass to land by removal of minerals, timber or fixtures,[3257] and deceit.[3258] It is not certain whether a restitutionary claim is possible whenever a tortfeasor has gained a benefit and that benefit would not have been gained but for the tort. An example might be waiver of defamation in favour of an account of the profits of the libel. However, an early decision of the English Court of Appeal confined recovery to circumstances in which the defendant had appropriated property or its proceeds.[3259] Rather more recently, the English Court of Appeal refused to grant a restitutionary remedy in the case of a nuisance by the levying of an unlawful market that infringed the plaintiff's exclusive proprietary right to hold a market.[3260] The plaintiff had suffered only nominal damage, and Nourse LJ thought that to give damages measured by the fee that it would have demanded if it had been asked for its licence to hold the market 'would revolutionise the tort of nuisance by making it unnecessary to prove loss'. It was possible that the English law of tort would in due course make a more deliberate move towards recovery based not on loss suffered by the plaintiff but on the unjust enrichment of the defendant, but the process could not begin in the instant case.[3261]

If the plaintiff obtains judgment in a restitutionary claim, his or her cause of action in tort as regards the particular defendant sued is extinguished.[3262] Equally, the plaintiff is bound to his or her election if he or she reaches a final settlement of the action.[3263] Until judgment or settlement, however, the plaintiff remains free to abandon the claim in quasi-contract and pursue the claim in tort instead.[3264]

3255. *Lamine v. Dorrell* (1705) 2 Ld Raym 1216; 92 ER 303; *Marsh v. Keating* (1834) 1 Bing NC 198; 131 ER 1094.
3256. *Oughton v. Seppings* (1830) 1 B & Ad 241; 109 ER 776; *Rodgers v. Maw* (1846) 15 M & W 444; 153 ER 924; *Neate v. Harding* (1851) 6 Exch 349; 155 ER 577.
3257. *Powell v. Rees* (1837) 7 Ad & El 426; *Dalton v. Whittem* (1842) 3 QB 961; 114 ER 777.
3258. *Hill v. Perrott* (1810) 3 Taunt 274; 128 ER 109; *Mahesan v. Malaysia Government Officers' Co-op Housing Soc Ltd* [1979] AC 374.
3259. *Phillips v. Homfray* (1883) 24 Ch D 439.
3260. *Stoke-on-Trent CC v. W & J Wass Ltd* [1988] 3 All ER 394.
3261. However, in Canada, *see Serhan Estate v. Johnson & Johnson* (2006) 269 DLR (4th) 279.
3262. *United Australia Ltd v. Barclays Bank Ltd* [1941] AC 1.
3263. *Brewer v. Sparrow* (1827) 7 B & C 310; 108 ER 739.
3264. *United Australia Ltd v. Barclays Bank Ltd* [1941] AC 1; *Thornton Hall Mfg Ltd v. Shanton Apparel Ltd* [1989] 3 NZLR 304 at 309.

§2. Injunctive Relief

I. General Principles

568. An injunction is an order of the court restraining the defendant from committing or continuing a wrongful act or, sometimes, requiring the defendant to make right a wrongful act. For example, a person whose enjoyment of land is being disturbed by a continuing nuisance, whose goodwill in a business is being appropriated by a rival or whose privacy is about to be invaded by an intrusive newspaper article may be far more concerned to stop the infringement of his or her rights than to recover damages. In these or any other cases involving the threat of or repetition or continuance of a tort, a prohibitory injunction may be issued to prevent the infringing conduct or bring it to an end. A mandatory injunction, by contrast, requires positive action to undo an infringing state of affairs.[3265]

An injunction is an equitable remedy and its issue is in the discretion of the court. Whereas damages are available as of right once the requirements for the tort have been established, there is no right to the grant of an injunction. Yet this does not mean that a plaintiff who has made out an actionable interference with his or her rights will face any particular difficulty in obtaining a remedy by way of injunction. It has been said that in this case an injunction will issue 'as of course'.[3266] For example, a landowner is prima facie entitled to an injunction to restrain a trespass by the defendant parking his vehicle on his land[3267] or running hounds across it[3268] even without proof of any particular harm. On the other hand, it has long been asserted that an injunction will not generally be granted where there is an adequate remedy in damages,[3269] which view is seemingly inconsistent with any notion that there is a prima facie right to the remedy. Certainly the courts do not accept that they ought to allow a wrong to continue simply because the wrongdoer is able and willing to pay for the injury.[3270] An approach that perhaps can reconcile these differing views is that taken in *TV3 Network Ltd v. Eveready New Zealand Ltd*,[3271] where the Court of Appeal held that an injunction should be available whenever the justice of the case so requires.

One issue that has proved controversial is the significance of any interest of the public in the continuance of the activity in question. In *Shelfer v. City of London Electric Lighting Co.*[3272] the court affirmed that the circumstance that the wrongdoer is in some sense a public benefactor is no sufficient reason for refusing to protect by injunction an individual whose rights are being persistently infringed. Yet

3265. As to which, *see* para. 569.
3266. *Shelfer v. City of London Electric Lighting Co.* [1895] 1 Ch 287; *Redland Bricks Ltd v. Morris* [1970] AC 652.
3267. *Patel v. WH Smith (Eziot)* [1987] 1 WLR 853.
3268. *League against Cruel Sports v. Scott* [1986] QB 240.
3269. *London and Blackwall Railway v. Cross* (1886) 31 Ch D 354 at 369.
3270. *Shelfer v. City of London Electric Lighting Co.* [1895] 1 Ch 287 at 315–316; *Regan v. Paul Properties DPF No 1 Ltd* [2006] 3 WLR 1131.
3271. [1993] 3 NZLR 435.
3272. [1895] 1 Ch 287; approved in *Attorney-General v. Abraham and Williams Ltd* [1949] NZLR 461.

the decision of the UK Supreme Court in *Lawrence v. Fen Tigers Ltd*,[3273] where the question of damages in lieu of an injunction was in issue, has now given greater weight to the public interest.[3274] Earlier cases show differing approaches. In *Miller v. Jackson*, the English Court of Appeal refused to grant an injunction to prevent members of a village cricket club from hitting balls into the plaintiff's garden, and two members of the court justified this on the ground that the community interest in the playing of cricket should prevail over the plaintiffs' interest in the enjoyment of their property. However, in *Kennaway v. Thompson* a similar argument made by a motorboat club was rejected, and an injunction was issued to protect neighbours from the excessive noise caused by racing motorboats. Again, in *Bank of New Zealand v. Greenwood*[3275] Hardie Boys J rejected the argument that an injunction to prevent a nuisance caused by the reflection of blinding sunlight from the defendant's building should be refused on the ground that it would have a resounding effect on building design: 'To the extent that this is an appeal to set the public interest against the private interests of the plaintiffs, then I regret that authority requires me to close my ears to it.' But he also considered that the problem could be resolved by the provision of Venetian blinds, which solution was novel in that it permitted the defendant to remove the nuisance by altering the state of the plaintiffs' own land.

An injunction will not necessarily order the defendant to cease an activity altogether. It may simply require the defendant to modify his or her activity in such a way as to cease infringing the plaintiff's rights.[3276] Where appropriate its operation may be suspended in order to give the defendant time to comply with its requirements.[3277]

An injunction will be refused if the plaintiff has acquiesced in the infringing activity. But mere delay is not enough. The plaintiff must have induced the defendant to rely to his or her detriment on the plaintiff's action or inaction and in all the circumstances it is unconscionable for the plaintiff to assert his or her legal rights.[3278]

II. Particular Types of Injunction

A. *Mandatory Injunction*

569. A mandatory injunction is an injunction ordering the defendant to carry out positive works. It is likely to be more drastic in effect than a prohibitory injunction, there is a risk that it may be used oppressively in furtherance of extortionate demands, and it may result in economic waste, as where the defendant is required

3273. [2014] AC 822.
3274. *See* para. 572.
3275. [1984] 1 NZLR 525.
3276. For example, *Mayfair Ltd v. New Zealand Properties Ltd* [1940] NZLR 190; *Bloodworth v. Cormack* [1949] NZLR 1058.
3277. For example, *Attorney-General v. Abraham v. Williams Ltd* [1949] NZLR 461; *Jerram v. Hood* [1954] NZLR 909.
3278. *Jones v. Stones* [1999] 1 WLR 1739.

to demolish a building. So the courts approach the question whether to make a mandatory order with caution. The leading decision is *Redland Bricks Ltd v. Morris*,[3279] where Lord Upjohn set out four propositions:

(1) the plaintiff must show a very strong probability that grave damage will accrue to him in the future;
(2) damages will not be a sufficient or adequate remedy if some damage does happen;
(3) the amount to be expended by the defendant must be balanced against the anticipated possible damage to the plaintiff; and
(4) the terms of the injunction must be stated clearly so that the defendant knows precisely what he has to do.

In *Redland Bricks* itself the defendants' quarrying for clay had caused subsidence in the plaintiffs' market garden, and further subsidence was likely. It was held that an injunction should be refused because of, *inter alia*, the high cost of compliance, the particular suitability of the clay on the site for brickmaking, and the availability of other land for market gardening.

B. Quia Timet *Injunction*

570. Where harm is apprehended, a *quia timet* injunction may be granted to forestall it. However, simply to assert a fear of injury is not enough. There must be proof of a very strong probability that injury will result,[3280] and that, if it occurs, it will be grave or substantial.[3281] The courts have power to issue mandatory *quia timet* injunctions, but the jurisdiction to do so should be exercised sparingly.[3282]

C. Interim Injunction

571. In cases of urgency a plaintiff may seek an immediate remedy prior to the full hearing of the action. Accordingly, he or she may make an application for an interim injunction, to take effect until that hearing takes place. The application is supported by affidavit,[3283] and the applicant is required to give an undertaking to pay damages for any loss suffered by the defendant while the injunction was in force should the application ultimately turn out to be unjustified.[3284] In *American Cyanamid Co. v. Ethicon Ltd*,[3285] the House of Lords laid down a twofold test for determining the question. The applicant must first establish that there is a 'serious

3279. [1970] AC 652.
3280. *Attorney-General (Canada) v. Ritchie Contracting & Supply Co. Ltd* [1919] AC 999.
3281. *Grocott v. Ayson* [1975] 2 NZLR 586.
3282. *Redland Bricks Ltd v. Morris* [1970] AC 652.
3283. HCR 2016, r 7.53.
3284. *SmithKline Beecham plc v. Apotex Europe Ltd* [2006] 4 All ER 1078 at [24].
3285. [1975] AC 396.

question' to be tried. If there is, the court must then decide whether the balance of convenience lies in favour of granting or refusing interim relief. The Court of Appeal in *Klissers Farmhouse Bakeries Ltd v. Harvest Bakeries Ltd*[3286] confirmed that the *American Cyanamid* test should be applied in New Zealand. Yet this approach is not to be considered as a legislative fiat laying down a set of rules to be applied in a mechanical way.[3287] In *Klissers*, Cooke P emphasized that in every case the judge has finally to stand back and ask the question where overall justice lies.

One likely concern is the adequacy of damages. Sometimes they may be inadequate because they cannot undo the harm, as where there is a permanent loss of the plaintiff's business goodwill in passing off cases[3288] or a disclosure of private information.[3289] And there may be a serious question about the ability of the plaintiff to pay damages should an injunction be granted and the defendant succeeds at the trial, which may incline the court not to grant it. Another concern is the maintenance of the status quo, and the court will seek to limit the form or terms of any injunction to the minimum required to maintain the plaintiff's position.[3290]

American Cyanamid does not totally preclude a court from a consideration of the merits of the action, but the decision has usually been treated as saying that the prospect of success is not to be looked at save as a last resort.[3291] However, there have been calls for a more flexible approach, so that where a court can come to a view on the strength of the parties' cases on credible evidence then it can do so.[3292]

III. Damages in Substitution for an Injunction

572. Lord Cairns' Act of 1858 gave the UK courts the power to award damages in lieu of an injunction. In New Zealand the relevant provision is now found in section 13 of the Senior Courts Act 2016.[3293] This provides:

> The High Court may award damages in addition to or in substitution for an injunction or specific performance.

The availability of an injunction is a prerequisite for the exercise of this jurisdiction. However, the question is whether the court *could* have granted an injunction, not whether it *would* have done so,[3294] and seemingly the power arises whenever the facts are such as to call into play the exercise of the court's general equitable

3286. [1985] 2 NZLR 129.
3287. *Consolidated Traders Ltd v. Downes* [1981] 2 NZLR 247; *Villa Maria Wines Ltd v. Montana Wines Ltd* [1984] 2 NZLR 422; [1984] 1 TCLR 224; *NZ Baking Trades Employees' Industrial Union v. General Foods Corp (NZ) Ltd* [1985] 2 NZLR 110.
3288. *See* para. 252.
3289. *See* para. 368.
3290. *Prudential Building & Investment Soc of Canterbury v. Prudential Assurance Co. of NZ Ltd* [1988] 2 NZLR 653.
3291. *Fellowes & Son v. Fisher* [1976] QB 122 at 132, 138.
3292. *Series 5 Software Ltd v. Clarke* [1996] 1 All ER 853.
3293. This provision formerly was found in the Judicature Act 1908, s. 16A.
3294. *Jaggard v. Sawyer* [1995] 1 WLR 269 at 285.

jurisdiction whether or not to grant an injunction.[3295] The damages are given in full satisfaction not only for all damages already done in the past, but also for all future damage that may occur if the injunction is not granted.[3296] And they may be awarded in substitution for an injunction even in a *quia timet* action.[3297]

In *Shelfer v. City of London Electric Lighting Co.*,[3298] AL Smith LJ stated a 'good working rule' that the jurisdiction under the Act should be exercised if it would be oppressive to the defendant to issue an injunction, and if the injury to the plaintiff's rights is small, is capable of being estimated in money, and is one that can be adequately compensated by a monetary payment. On this view the award of damages in lieu of an injunction is exceptional, but the impact of the *Shelfer* rule has been very substantially reduced by the decision of the UK Supreme Court in *Lawrence v. Fen Tigers Ltd.*[3299] Lord Neuberger thought that the court's power involved a classic exercise of discretion which should not be fettered in the way suggested. A wide range of factors could be taken into account, and in particular the public interest involved and the grant of planning permission. Lord Sumption considered that *Shelfer* was out of date. There was much to be said for the view that damages were ordinarily an adequate remedy for nuisance and that an injunction should not usually be granted in a case where it was likely that conflicting interests were engaged other than the parties' interests. These are influential views, and recent decisions accept *Lawrence* as applying in New Zealand.[3300]

§3. Declaratory Relief

573. A court has discretionary power to grant declaratory relief under the Declaratory Judgments Act 1908. A declaration may be sought in circumstances where the plaintiff is not seeking damages but wants a statement from the court that his or her rights have been infringed.

The Court of Appeal accepted in *Re Chase*[3301] that there was jurisdiction to grant a declaration as a remedy in tort. In the exercise of its discretion, however, the court declined to grant the remedy in the circumstances of the particular case.[3302] Again, in *Ashley v. Chief Constable of Sussex Police*[3303] the House of Lords recognized that a declaration was available to the court, and, in a majority decision, allowed the claim to proceed to trial.[3304]

3295. *Hooper v. Rogers* [1975] Ch 43 at 48.
3296. *Jaggard v. Sawyer* [1995] 1 WLR 269.
3297. *Leeds Industrial Co-operative Society Ltd v. Slack* [1924] AC 851.
3298. [1895] 1 Ch 287 at 322.
3299. [2014] AC 822.
3300. *Ogle v. Aitken* [2017] NZHC 1799, [2018] NZAR 1898 at [32]; *McInness v. Jones* [2017] NZHC 2781 at [25]–[26].
3301. [1989] 1 NZLR 325.
3302. *See* para. 574.
3303. [2008] 1 AC 962.
3304. *See* para. 574.

§4. NOMINAL DAMAGES

574. Some torts are actionable per se, that is, without proof of damage. Examples are assault, battery, and false imprisonment.[3305] In these cases, even though no actual damage is shown, a court may make an award of nominal damages in order, *inter alia*, to mark the wrong, support the dignity of the person and vindicate the plaintiff's right to a remedy. Such an award consists of a trifling sum to acknowledge that the plaintiff has succeeded,[3306] as opposed to a small award of compensatory damages.[3307]

The grant of a declaration and an award of nominal damages have the same effect. There is a formal distinction in that there is a right to nominal damages on proof of the infringement of a legal right, whereas a declaration is a discretionary remedy. But nothing is likely to turn on this difference.

In *Re Chase*,[3308] a claim for nominal damages for a trespass to land was held to be an abuse of procedure, where the transparent purpose of the claim was to ventilate allegations of police misconduct in relation to the circumstances in which a person had been shot dead by the police. Nor would the court exercise its discretion to grant a declaration of liability, for there had already been an inquiry and an inquest and little or nothing would be gained by further raking over of the details.

In *Ashley v. Chief Constable of Sussex Police*,[3309] where the facts were the same in material respects, the House of Lords decided that a claim for assault and battery could proceed even though the defendant Chief Constable conceded full liability to pay compensatory damages for negligence. The majority view was that the relatives' claim in respect of the death could still properly be maintained for a vindicatory purpose. By contrast, the minority took the view that the civil courts exist to award compensation, not to conduct public inquiries, and it would be an abuse to allow the action to proceed.

The decision in *Re Chase* was distinguished on the basis that all the consequences of the shooting were covered by accident compensation. However, at least since the Accident Rehabilitation and Compensation Insurance Act 1992, the bar applies only to claims for *compensation*, whatever their source.[3310] So claims for non-compensatory purposes are not covered and are not barred. The question becomes, then, whether a claim seeking nominal damages or a declaration solely for a vindicatory purpose ought to be allowed. In principle this may be possible,[3311] but a court is likely to stay the action in the exercise of its inherent jurisdiction unless it decides on balance that the action can be justified for compelling reasons of policy. But if, say, there is a claim for aggravated damages, which compensate for

3305. *See* paras 52–56.
3306. *The Mediana* [1900] AC 113 at 116.
3307. For example, *A v. Attorney-General* [2018] NZHC 986, [2018] 3 NZLR 43.
3308. [1989] 1 NZLR 325.
3309. [2008] 1 AC 962; *Breslin v. McKenna* [2009] NIQB 50.
3310. *See* para. 41.
3311. In *R (Lumba) v. Secretary of State for the Home Department* [2012] AC 245 the members of the UK Supreme Court took differing views about whether damages solely for a vindicatory purpose were allowable.

feelings of distress or outrage as a result of the particularly egregious way or circumstances in which the tort was committed,[3312] and arguably is not barred,[3313] then the action can proceed in the ordinary way.

§5. Exemplary Damages

I. Introduction

575. We have seen that the award of damages in tort normally is intended to compensate the victim. But exemplary damages are different. Their function is to punish the wrongdoer, not to compensate the victim. Whether they play a principled role in the law of civil remedies is controversial. Critics say that a form of civil punishment is being inflicted without the evidential and procedural safeguards of the criminal law. The basis upon which this punishment is imposed lacks objective foundation and is undesirably uncertain. There is no particular connection between the damages that are awarded and the plaintiff who is bringing the action. They can be described as a windfall in the plaintiff's hands. The damages, when awarded, are necessarily indeterminate. Protagonists, on the other hand, contend that civil punishment is different from criminal punishment and that it is coherent to pursue the aims of punishment through the civil law. A criminal offence is a wrong against both the victim and against society at large, with punishment being sought by or on behalf of the state. A civil wrong is a wrong against the individual victim, who seeks an exemplary award to punish an egregious wrongdoer on his or her own account. Civil proceedings have various objectives apart from compensation, including punishment and deterrence, and exemplary damages can help to achieve these objectives.

In New Zealand, as in many other common law countries, the latter arguments have prevailed. The power of the courts to make an award of exemplary damages has been accepted at least since 1873.[3314] Furthermore, they remain available in personal injury cases even after the introduction of the accident compensation scheme, although in this case they cannot be awarded in addition to compensatory damages and have to standalone.[3315] Beyond this, the circumstances in which it is appropriate to make an award remains a source of contention, in several respects.

II. Basis for Award

576. In *Taylor v. Beere*[3316] the Court of Appeal held that exemplary damages should be used to register condemnation of 'outrageous' or 'heinous' conduct by the

3312. *Attorney-General v. Niania* [1994] 3 NZLR 106.
3313. *See* para. 42.
3314. *McComb v. Low* (1873) 1 NZ Jur 49.
3315. *Donselaar v. Donselaar* [1982] 1 NZLR 97; *see* para. 42.
3316. [1982] 1 NZLR 81.

defendant and to mark the 'contumelious disregard' by the defendant of the plaintiff's rights. In this case the defendant published an innocent photograph of the plaintiff and her granddaughter in a book containing pornographic images and text. The plaintiff sued in defamation, alleging that it would appear that she had consented to the publication in that context, and was awarded both compensatory and exemplary damages.

The 'outrageous misconduct' test perhaps suggests that the kinds of cases where exemplary damages are appropriate are those where the defendant was guilty of malicious or deliberate wrongdoing. They have been awarded, for example, in claims for false imprisonment and assault,[3317] inducing breach of contract,[3318] trespass to land[3319] and, as in *Taylor* itself, defamation.[3320] In *A v. Bottrill*[3321] the Privy Council recognized that cases satisfying the *Taylor* test would usually involve intentional wrongdoing, but held that, exceptionally, negligence might qualify. However, in *Couch v. Attorney-General*[3322] the Supreme Court took a different view and overruled *Bottrill*. The remedy should, it held, be confined to cases of outrageous conduct where the defendant was subjectively aware of the risk to which his or her conduct exposed the plaintiff and acted deliberately or recklessly in taking that risk.[3323]

In cases where exemplary damages can be awarded the courts must decide on their quantum. In *McDermott v. Wallace*[3324] (a case of outrageous negligence that was decided before *Couch*), Hammond J identified six relevant considerations:

(1) whether the claimant was the victim of punishable behaviour;
(2) awards should be moderate;
(3) the means of the parties;
(4) whether any other compensation had been awarded in criminal or regulatory proceedings;
(5) whether any criminal penalty had been imposed on the defendant; and
(6) the conduct of the parties to the time of judgment, including any improper behaviour on the part of the claimant.

In some earlier personal injury claims relatively high awards were made,[3325] giving rise to the suspicion that a compensatory element was being included. However, the courts have emphasized on a number of occasions that exemplary damages cannot be used to make up for any shortcomings in the level of compensation that is

3317. *Hayward v. O'Keefe* [1993] 1 NZLR 181.
3318. *Dellabarca v. Northern Storemen and Packers Union* [1989] 2 NZLR 734.
3319. *Shattock v. Devlin* [1990] 2 NZLR 88.
3320. *Television New Zealand Ltd v. Quinn* [1996] 3 NZLR 24.
3321. [2003] 2 NZLR 721.
3322. [2010] 3 NZLR 149.
3323. So, for example, exemplary damages have been declined in claims against the police where bad faith could not be established: *A v. Attorney-General* [2018] NZHC 986, [2018] 3 NZLR 43.
3324. [2005] 3 NZLR 661.
3325. *See*, for example, *B v. R* (1996) 10 PRNZ 73 (NZD 35,000 for sexual abuse); *G v. G* (1996) 15 FRNZ 22 (NZD 85,000 for sexual assaults by husband on wife).

recoverable under the statutory scheme.[3326] Certainly the quantum of exemplary awards in more recent cases usually has been quite modest.[3327] In *McDermott* Hammond J awarded NZD 20,000 in respect of the defendant flying instructor's outrageous negligence in piloting a plane, this resulting in a crash that seriously injured his pupil. The decision accordingly has reinforced this trend.[3328] However, modesty in damages has not always been achieved in defamation claims.[3329]

III. Impact of the Criminal Law

577. An issue of general significance to the award of exemplary damages arose in four conjoint appeals in *Daniels v. Thompson*, *J v. Bell*, *W v. W*, and *H v. P*.[3330] In these cases the Court of Appeal determined that the conviction or acquittal of the defendant in a prior criminal proceeding arising out of the same matter or event prevented any subsequent recovery of exemplary damages, and that where a prosecution was likely any civil action should be stayed until the prosecution either was concluded or it became clear it would not be brought. The reason was that allowing the civil action after conviction carried the risk that the defendant might be punished twice for the same offence, and if the criminal proceedings resulted in an acquittal the defendant would still be at risk of double jeopardy. Appeals to the Privy Council in *W v. W* and *J v. Bell*[3331] were dismissed, their Lordships holding that the question was one of public policy and that it was not appropriate for them to interfere with the views of the national court.

The majority decision of the Court of Appeal therefore prevailed. But critics argued that it was unjust to victims of criminality and particularly to victims of sexual abuse, who might recover little by way of compensation under the accident compensation scheme. Parliament responded by inserting a new provision in the Accident Insurance Act 1998 aimed at reversing the Court of Appeal's decision in cases where claimants were covered by the scheme.[3332] This provision is now found in section 319 of the Accident Compensation Act 2001. It provides, in essence, that claims for damages can still be brought irrespective of whether the defendant has been charged, not charged, convicted, acquitted, or discharged of an offence involving the conduct concerned in the civil claim, but in deciding whether to make an

3326. *McLaren Transport Ltd v. Somerville* [1996] 3 NZLR 424 at 433; *Daniels v. Thompson* [1998] 3 NZLR 22 at 29; *Bottrill v. A* [2001] 3 NZLR 622 at [45]; *S v. Attorney-General* [2003] 3 NZLR 450 at [89]; *Wilding v. Attorney-General* [2003] 3 NZLR 787 at [15]; *Couch v. Attorney-General* [2010] 3 NZLR 149 at [135].
3327. The judgment in *McDermott v. Wallace* includes a schedule of the amount of the awards in previous cases, providing guidance for practitioners.
3328. Particular complications in determining quantum may arise in cases where there are or may be multiple plaintiffs: *see R (Lumba) v. Secretary of State for the Home Department*, [2012] AC 245 at [167].
3329. *See* para. 358.
3330. [1998] 3 NZLR 22.
3331. [1999] 2 NZLR 1.
3332. Accident Insurance Act 1998, s. 396.

award or the amount of the damages, the court may have regard to any criminal penalty imposed in respect of that offence. The section has affirmed the *Donselaar* principle whereby exemplary damages may be awarded in cases of personal injury covered by the accident compensation legislation,[3333] but left the circumstances in which such damages are available to be determined by the courts.[3334]

Section 319 applies where a person is seeking to recover exemplary damages for conduct that has resulted in personal injury covered by the 2001 Act or a former Act. Normally coverage under the accident compensation scheme means that a victim *cannot* sue. Here it means that the victim *can* sue. This bizarre inversion of the normal rule has come about because Parliament failed to distinguish between issues of compensation and issues of punishment. Much of the criticism of *Daniels* was really about the bar on actions for *compensatory* damages and the low levels of benefits obtainable under the Act in some cases, not about double jeopardy. And this concern was addressed to some extent in the 2001 Act, by returning to the pre-1992 position and restoring lump sums to compensate for lost amenity due to physical or mental injury.[3335] But whether or not the victims of criminal offending are now treated adequately by the statutory scheme, the issue is one of compensation for loss. It is not appropriately addressed by removing a bar to an award of exemplary damages.

The principle of *Daniels* continues to apply in cases not involving personal injury. But whether the decision should be accepted or rejected, the same principle should apply in all cases. Accordingly, it is possible that the Court of Appeal will change its stance and overrule *Daniels* in a non-accident compensation case. This would at least remove the arbitrary consequences of requiring accident compensation cover before section 319 can apply.

IV. Vicarious Liability

578. A question of considerable practical significance is whether it is appropriate for an employer to be held vicariously liable in respect of a tort giving rise to a personal liability by an employee to pay exemplary damages. In England, in *Kuddus v. Chief Constable of Leicestershire Constabulary*,[3336] the House of Lords was divided on the issue. Lord Hutton thought that the power to make an award in respect of conduct amounting to misfeasance in public office served to uphold and vindicate the rule of law and to deter wrongdoing by public officers. But Lord Scott saw an award of exemplary damages where the defendant was not a wrongdoer and the award would be met out of public funds as not adding anything at all to the deterrent effect of a finding in favour of an injured person. A defendant should not be liable to pay exemplary damages unless he had committed punishable behaviour, a principle that left no room for an award where liability was vicarious only.

3333. *See* para. 42.
3334. *Couch v. Attorney-General* [2010] 3 NZLR 149 at [87]–[90].
3335. Accident Compensation Act 2001, s. 69(1)(d), Sch. 1, pt 3. Lump sums for pain and suffering were not restored. *See* further para. 43.
3336. [2002] 2 AC 122.

In a later decision in England, the Court of Appeal took the former view.[3337] This also is the approach in Australia.[3338] But in *S v. Attorney-General*[3339] the Court of Appeal favoured the latter. Blanchard J said that it would be quite unfair to inflict a punishment upon someone who had been found not to have been complicit in the wrongdoing. The damages would not then be a reflection of the culpability of the defendant, and exemplary damages were not intended and should not be used to provide an additional monetary remedy. Furthermore, in the case of workplace injury it was debatable whether an award against an employer whose agent or employee had behaved disgracefully would provide an additional incentive to take further and effective precautions going beyond those required by an ordinary duty of care. However, the balance might possibly be different in a case in which an official of the State had deliberately, recklessly or in a grossly negligent manner, directly inflicted personal injury on the plaintiff, and whether the Crown might be held vicariously liable in such a case should be left open. On the facts it was determined that the Department of Social Welfare was vicariously liable to pay compensatory damages for sexual assaults and batteries committed by foster parents on children placed by the Department in their care,[3340] but was not liable to pay exemplary damages.

V. Direct Liability of Statutory or Corporate Bodies

579. Liability to pay exemplary damages must, then, be personal. However, in the case of a statutory or corporate body this still leaves the possibility of a direct, rather than a vicarious, liability. This matter was in issue in *W v. Attorney-General*,[3341] where the plaintiff argued that the Crown was directly liable for negligent conduct by a senior child welfare officer in failing to prevent abuse by the plaintiff's foster parents. This raised, *inter alia*, the question whether, because of her position in the Department and its relation to the plaintiff, the officer's acts and omissions should be attributed to the Department.

It was held by Blanchard J, drawing upon the rules developed for the purpose of attributing the conduct of an agent to a company,[3342] that the question in this case was: for the purpose of attributing outrageous conduct giving rise to a claim for exemplary damages, whose act ought to count as the act of the Department? It could not possibly be said that the foster parents acted as the Department, but it was arguable that the position was different in relation to the acts and omissions of the Senior Child Welfare Officer. She was the person responsible for the plaintiff's placement and supervision and she was exercising or able to exercise statutory authority in this respect. It was arguable that her acts and omissions should be attributed to the Department and that, if they were so bad as to be deserving of being marked by an award of exemplary damages, then an award should be made against the Department. However, it was not thought necessary to reach a final conclusion on this

3337. *Rowlands v. Chief Constable of the Merseyside Police* [2007] 1 WLR 1065.
3338. *New South Wales v. Bryant* [2005] NSWCA 393; *New South Wales v. Ibbett* (2006) 81 ALJR 427.
3339. [2003] 3 NZLR 450.
3340. *See* para. 390.
3341. CA 227/02, 15 Jul. 2003.
3342. *See Meridian Global Funds Management Asia Ltd v. Securities Commission* [1995] 2 AC 500.

question, as the officer's failure to pick up on and to investigate complaints of abuse was negligence, but not of such a degree as to justify an award of exemplary damages.

VI. Claims by or Against an Estate

580. A legislative bar prevents claims for exemplary damages by a deceased estate.[3343] The position as regards claims against an estate is uncertain. In principle such claims ought to be denied, on the ground that the wrongdoer is dead and cannot be punished, and the purpose of exemplary damages cannot therefore be achieved. Notwithstanding this argument, the courts occasionally have been prepared to make an award against an estate.[3344]

3343. Law Reform Act 1936, s. 3(2)(a).
3344. For example, *B v. R* (1996) 10 PRNZ 73.

Chapter 4. Multiple Tortfeasors and Claims for Contribution

§1. Introduction

581. Where two or more tortfeasors acting independently inflict different damage on the same plaintiff, each is liable only for the damage that he or she has in fact caused.[3345] But where two or more tortfeasors cause the same damage to the one plaintiff, their liability is said to be in solidum. This means that the victim can sue all or any of them and obtain judgment against each for the full amount of the loss.[3346] Of course, the plaintiff cannot actually recover damages for more than the amount of the loss: full satisfaction of the plaintiff's claim always bars further proceedings.[3347] The common law rule means that the plaintiff need not prove exactly how large a part each defendant played in causing the damage; and he or she is not prejudiced if not all of the possible defendants can be found, or are solvent, or are insured. The remedy of the person who is sued or who settles is to bring an action for contribution from any other potential defendant, seeking recovery for all or part of the sum he or she has had to pay to the plaintiff.[3348] But the risk of non-satisfaction lies with the person claiming contribution, not the plaintiff.

§2. Multiple Tortfeasors

I. Joint and Several Liability

582. At common law, tortfeasors who are liable in respect of the same damage may be either 'joint' tortfeasors or 'several' tortfeasors. Joint liability arises where there is concurrence in the act or acts causing damage, several (or concurrent) liability where there is a coincidence of separate acts that by their conjoined effect cause damage.[3349] Joint tortfeasors in law commit the same tort whereas several tortfeasors are responsible for different torts producing the same damage.

A tort is committed by several persons as joint tortfeasors either where the act giving rise to the tort is one for which both or all are responsible or where it is committed as a joint act. There is joint responsibility where a person commits a tort for which another is vicariously liable, such as where a tort is committed by an employee in the course of employment with the employer or by an agent within the scope of the authority conferred by the principal.[3350] A company and its directors may be joint tortfeasors on the basis that the actions of the directors are identified with those of the company itself, as representing its directing mind and will.[3351] Partners are jointly and severally liable to any third party for torts committed by any

3345. *Television New Zealand Ltd v. Ah Koy* [2002] 2 NZLR 616 at [31].
3346. *Coleman v. Harvey* [1989] 1 NZLR 723.
3347. *See* para. 509.
3348. *See* para. 586.
3349. *Allison v. KPMG Peat Marwick* [2000] 1 NZLR 560 at 584.
3350. *Coleman v. Harvey* [1989] 1 NZLR 723; *Brooks v. NZ Guardian Trust Co. Ltd* [1994] 2 NZLR 134 (on appeal [1995] 1 WLR 96 (PC)).
3351. *Brooks v. NZ Guardian Trust Co. Ltd ibid.*

partner either while acting in the course of business of the firm or with the authority of his or her co-partners.[3352] A joint act requires some concerted conduct in the course of a common enterprise or design.[3353] Examples are a conspiracy in which all participants act in pursuance of a joint purpose,[3354] and concerted negligence in the course of a common enterprise.[3355]

Where several publications, although independent, are to similar defamatory effect, and harm is caused by the joint consequence of all or a number of publications, the tortfeasors are deemed to have caused indivisible damage and are classified as joint tortfeasors.[3356] However, where defamatory publications are made independently of each other, each publisher is liable only for the damage done by its own publication.[3357] Further examples of several liability are where independent acts of negligence on the part of two vessels led to a collision, causing one to run into and sink a third;[3358] where a driver negligently blocked the road and another driver recklessly drove into the obstruction, injuring a passenger;[3359] where a builder put up a defective house and the local authority inspector failed to discover the defects;[3360] where an employer and a property owner both exposed an employee to danger in the course of his employment;[3361] and where separate negligence by a vendor and an auditor resulted in a company being sold at an overvalue.[3362]

II. Release of One Tortfeasor

A. Joint Tortfeasors

583. Joint or several tortfeasors are each liable in full for the entire loss. At common law there were, however, two special consequences attaching only to joint liability. One was that judgment against one tortfeasor, even if unsatisfied, barred any subsequent action against the other.[3363] The reason given was that the cause of action, being single and indivisible, merged in the judgment. This rule has long disappeared, it having been abrogated by the Law Reform Act 1936.[3364] Thus, an unsatisfied judgment against one tortfeasor is not a bar to recovery against another tortfeasor, whether their liability is joint or concurrent. The second consequence, again because liability was indivisible, was that the release of one joint tortfeasor

3352. Partnership Act 1908, ss 13, 15.
3353. For discussion of the boundaries of liability in common design cases, *see Sea Shepherd UK v. Fish & Fish Ltd* [2015] AC 1229; and *see Sellman v. Slater* [2017] NZHC 2392, [2018] 2 NZLR 218 at [116]–[118].
3354. *McIntyre v. Bianchi* [1992] 3 ERNZ 1057 at 1099.
3355. *Bourke v. Jessop (No. 3)* [1935] NZLR 246.
3356. *Television New Zealand Ltd v. Ah Koy* [2002] 2 NZLR 616 at [31].
3357. *Ibid.*
3358. *The Koursk* [1940] P 140.
3359. *Wright v. Lodge* [1993] 4 All ER 299.
3360. *Morton v. Douglas Homes Ltd* [1984] 2 NZLR 548 at 613.
3361. *Jameson v. Central Electricity Generating Board* [1999] 2 WLR 141.
3362. *Allison v. KPMG Peat Marwick* [2000] 1 NZLR 560.
3363. *Brinsmead v. Harrison* (1872) LR 7 CP 547.
3364. Law Reform Act 1936, s. 17(1)(a).

operated to release all the others.[3365] In Australia, in *Thompson v. Australian Capital Television Pty Ltd*,[3366] the High Court held in relation to equivalent legislation in the Australian Capital Territory that this rule also had been abrogated, for by abolishing the judgment rule and authorizing successive actions the legislature had severed the unity of the cause of action against joint tortfeasors for all purposes, and not simply for the purpose of precluding the application of the doctrine of merger.

In New Zealand, in *Brooks v. NZ Guardian Trust Co. Ltd*,[3367] the Court of Appeal rejected this argument and affirmed the continued existence of the release rule. Cooke P thought that the legislature in 1936 could not be attributed with an intention indirectly to abrogate the rule. Furthermore, there was much to be said for the view that release of a company should work a release of its directors also, and similarly it might be thought that release of an employer should normally imply release of his or her employee. Then, in *Robinson v. Tait*,[3368] the Court of Appeal was split. Thomas J said that when Parliament abolished the judgment rule it destroyed the concept that a victim of a tort committed by joint tortfeasors has only one cause of action and that the cause of action is one and indivisible. The release rule was an aspect of the same concept, and so section 17 had removed the substratum necessary for its operation. Blanchard J, without deciding the point, also favoured this approach. But Tipping J said that Parliament could not have intended to abrogate the release rule, and it was difficult to see how the removal of the judgment bar could be regarded as having changed the essence or nature of the cause of action. It simply removed one consequence of its unitary nature.

The release rule, while it remains, does not operate if the plaintiff 'covenants not to sue' a joint tortfeasor rather than 'releases' that tortfeasor.[3369] In this case the plaintiff's cause of action is not destroyed but is only rendered unenforceable against the tortfeasor with whom the agreement was made. The distinction was developed as a means of avoiding the rigidity of the common law rule and allowing a plaintiff to settle with a joint tortfeasor at less than the full value of a claim. It has been described by Lord Denning MR as 'arid and technical' and 'without any merits'.[3370] Indeed, in *Allison v. KPMG Peat Marwick*,[3371] Thomas J thought that the release rule itself was an absurdity and that good sense, fairness and respect for the reasonable expectations of contracting parties suggested that it should be abrogated. It was a trap for the unwary and a positive disincentive to parties to enter into bona fide and reasonable compromises. So there are good arguments in favour of reversing *Brooks* and abandoning the rule in its entirety.

3365. *Duck v. Mayeu* [1892] 2 QB 511; *Kelliher v. Bridges* (1912) 31 NZLR 203; *Eyre v. NZ Press Assn Ltd* [1968] NZLR 736.
3366. (1996) 186 CLR 574.
3367. [1994] 2 NZLR 134 (on appeal on another point [1995] 1 WLR 96 (PC)).
3368. [2002] 2 NZLR 30.
3369. *Duck v. Mayeu* [1892] 2 QB 511; *NZ Trainers Assn Ltd v. Cranson* 22 Mar. 1999, Ellis and Wild JJ, HC Wellington AP14/98; *National Insurance Life and Health Ltd v. Wayman* 7 Apr. 2000, J. Salmon, HC Auckland AP135/99.
3370. *Bryanston Finance Ltd v. de Vries* [1975] QB 703 at 723; and *see Allison v. KPMG Peat Marwick* [2000] 1 NZLR 560 at 588.
3371. [2000] 1 NZLR 560 at [156].

B. Several Tortfeasors

584. The release rule only ever applied to joint tortfeasors. But in *Jameson v. Central Electricity Generating Board*[3372] the House of Lords in effect applied it to several tortfeasors. The deceased plaintiff contracted mesothelioma from breathing in asbestos dust in the course of his employment. Shortly before his death he entered into a full and final settlement of a claim against his employers. The settlement was significantly less than the full liability value of the claim. The deceased's executors then brought proceedings on behalf of his widow against the owner and occupier of the premises where he had been working. A majority held that the earlier settlement extinguished this later claim. Lord Hope said that the effect of the compromise was to fix the amount of the claim in the same way as if the case had been pursued to judgment. The settlement could not be construed as meaning that the agreed sum was only in partial satisfaction of the claim. So the terms of the settlement extinguished the deceased's claim against any other tortfeasor.

In *Allison v. KPMG Peat Marwick*[3373] the plaintiffs settled a claim for misrepresentation against the vendors of a company and then brought an action against the company's auditors, alleging negligence in preparing the audit that was used in effecting the sale. The auditors claimed that they were entitled to the benefit of the settlement agreement between the plaintiffs and the vendors. The Court of Appeal unanimously rejected this contention. The vendors and the auditors were concurrent tortfeasors and, consistently with ordinary principle, the release of the former did not give protection to the latter.

Actual satisfaction of the full amount of a claim discharges claims against other tortfeasors, whether joint or concurrent, because there is no loss left to compensate. *Jameson* appears to be based upon a fiction, that partial satisfaction of a claim should be treated in law as full satisfaction. In its later decision in *Heaton v. AXA Equity and Law Life Assurance Society plc*[3374] the House of Lords emphasized that *Jameson* decided only that on the particular facts the sum accepted had to be taken as fixing the full measure of the plaintiff's loss: the decision did not disturb the ordinary rule that the release of one concurrent tortfeasor did not have the effect in law of releasing another concurrent tortfeasor. Indeed, in *Allison* Tipping J pointed out that a release short of full satisfaction could enure for the benefit of concurrent tortfeasors only where they were appropriately designated in terms of the Contracts (Privity) Act 1982 (now Part 2 subpart 1 of the Contract and Commercial Law Act 2017).[3375]

3372. [1999] 2 WLR 141.
3373. [2000] 1 NZLR 560.
3374. [2002] 2 AC 329; and *see McGill v. Sports and Entertainment Media Group Ltd* [2017] 1 WLR 989.
3375. *International Encyclopaedia of Laws: Contracts (New Zealand)*, para. 194.

III. Procedure

585. The normal procedure where there are several possible defendants is for the plaintiff to sue them all in the one action, in which case contribution may be sought by one of the parties concerned on application at the close of the plaintiff's action, or for the defendant who is sued to join another potential defendant as a third party, who can himself or herself join another as a fourth party, and so on.[3376] Responsibility is thus resolved in a single action. Section 17(1)(b) of the Law Reform Act 1936 discourages a plaintiff from bringing successive claims against tortfeasors liable in respect of the same damage, by providing that the sums recoverable in the later actions shall not in the aggregate exceed the amount of the damages awarded in the first action, and that the plaintiff is not entitled to costs in a later action unless there was reasonable ground for bringing the action. Non-satisfaction of the first judgment no doubt would be a reasonable ground.

Section 17(1)(b) applies to cases where there is more than one action brought by the person who has suffered damage. It does not apply where there are two or more defendants in a single action.[3377]

§3. Contribution Between Tortfeasors

I. Introduction

586. At common law there could be no action by one tortfeasor for a contribution from another.[3378] In certain circumstances there could be a claim for an indemnity in equity, where the parties shared 'coordinate liabilities' or a 'common obligation' to make good the same damage,[3379] but what exactly these expressions meant was a matter of considerable uncertainty. Certainly a wrongdoer who was not sued escaped all responsibility.

This unsatisfactory state of affairs was changed by section 17(1)(c) of the Law Reform Act 1936. The terms of this section are for the most part modelled on those contained in reforming legislation introduced in England the previous year.[3380] The English legislation has since been repealed and replaced by a new Act,[3381] but the New Zealand legislation remains largely as originally enacted. It is narrowly

3376. HCR 2016 rr 4.4–4.6.
3377. *Baxter v. Obacelo Pty Ltd* (2001) 205 CLR 635.
3378. *Merryweather v. Nixan* (1799) 8 TR 186, 101 ER 1337 (joint tortfeasors); *Horwell v. London General Omnibus Co. Ltd* (1877) 2 Ex D 365 (several tortfeasors).
3379. *Adamson v. Jarvis* (1827) 4 Bing 66, 130 ER 693; *Burke v. LFOT Pty Ltd* [2002] HCA 17, (2002) 209 CLR 282; *see* further para. 591 below.
3380. Law Reform (Married Women and Tortfeasors) Act 1935 (Eng), s. 6.
3381. Civil Liability (Contribution) Act 1978 (Eng).

drafted, in that it confines the right to seek contribution to claims between tortfeasors. Proposals for statutory reform, widening the basis upon which claims for contribution might be made, have not been implemented.[3382] Recently, however, the Supreme Court has adopted an expansive interpretation of section 17(1)(c) and also has recognized the wide availability of a claim for contribution in equity,[3383] seemingly obviating any pressing need for statutory reform. We will examine the terms of the 1936 Act before considering the ambit of the claim in equity.

Section 17(1)(c) provides:

> (1) Where damage is suffered by any person as a result of a tort (whether a crime or not) –
>
> (c) Any tortfeasor liable in respect of that damage may recover contribution from any other tortfeasor who is, or would if sued in time have been, liable in respect of the same damage, whether as a joint tortfeasor or otherwise, so, however, that no person shall be entitled to recover contribution under this section from any person entitled to be indemnified by him in respect of the liability in respect of which the contribution is sought.

This right to recover contribution is a right sui generis: it is a statutory right in the nature of an action for damages.[3384] The statutory procedure exists so that the responsibilities of defendants can be determined *inter se*.

In the following account, D1 represents the person who is claiming contribution, D2 represents the person from whom contribution is claimed, and P represents the plaintiff.

II. Entitlement to Claim Contribution

587. D1 is entitled to claim contribution if he or she is a tortfeasor who is liable for damage inflicted upon another as a result of a tort. The statute describes a person who is in substance a tortfeasor, but he or she need not be a person who has in fact been sued in tort. So contribution can be sought by a wrongdoer who was actually liable in tort even though that wrongdoer may have been sued and held liable on some other basis.[3385] However, the requirement that D1 be a 'tortfeasor' is not satisfied and D1 cannot invoke section 17(1)(c) if D1's only liability is for breach of contract[3386] or breach of trust.[3387]

3382. Contracts and Commercial Law Reform Committee, *Working Paper on Contribution in Civil Cases*, Wellington, 1983; Law Commission, *Apportionment of Civil Liability*, preliminary paper no. 19, Wellington, 1992; Law Commission, *Apportionment of Civil Liability*, Report No. 47, Wellington, 1998.

3383. *Hotchin v. New Zealand Guardian Trust Co Ltd* [2016] 1 NZLR 906; *see* paras 589, 591 below.

3384. *Collinson v. Wairarapa Automobile Assn Mutual Insurance Co.* [1958] NZLR 1 at 17.

3385. *Re Securitibank Ltd* [1986] 2 NZLR 280; *Dairy Containers Ltd v. NZI Bank Ltd* [1995] 2 NZLR 30 at 122.

3386. *New Zealand Food Group (1992) Ltd v. Amcor Trading (NZ) Ltd* (1999) 9 TCLR 184 at 199.

3387. *Fletcher v. National Mutual Life Nominees Ltd* [1990] 1 NZLR 97.

The requirement that D1 be a tortfeasor who is 'liable' in respect of damage inflicted upon another as a result of a tort obviously covers the case where D1 has been held liable to P, whether in proceedings to which D2 was a party or in separate proceedings. Where P sues both D1 and D2 in the same proceedings, D2 will be estopped from subsequently raising the question of D1's liability to P. No such estoppel arises where D2 was not a party to the proceedings, but D1 is nonetheless 'liable' in terms of the statutory language, and D2 thus is obliged to accept the judgment that P has obtained against D1.[3388] D1 also is 'liable' if he or she has settled or compromised with P, the courts taking the view that 'liable' where it first occurs in the subsection means no more than 'responsible in law'.[3389] Indeed, a settling tortfeasor can claim even where the settlement contained an express disclaimer of responsibility.[3390] However, unless D2 has admitted D1's liability in the settlement, it remains open to D2 to dispute the question and require D1 to establish affirmatively that he or she is indeed liable to P, and for that reason is entitled to claim contribution. Furthermore, D2 also can dispute the amount of D1's liability.[3391]

The proviso to section 17(1)(c) prevents recovery of contribution where D2 is only vicariously liable for D1's conduct and D1 is, therefore, liable to indemnify D2 in respect of that liability. The circumstance that is contemplated here is where an employee seeks contribution from his or her employer in respect of the employer's vicarious liability for the employee's tort, or where an agent on the same basis seeks contribution from his or her principal.[3392]

III. Liability to Make Contribution

588. D2's liability to make contribution arises where D2 is a 'tortfeasor who is or would if sued in time have been, liable in respect of the same damage'. Thus D2, like D1, must in fact be a tortfeasor. D2 cannot be liable to pay contribution to D1 if his or her only liability arises out of the breach of some other civil duty.[3393] If, however, D2 is concurrently liable to P in contract and tort then an action for contribution can be maintained.

Clearly, the word tortfeasor is used for the second time in section 17(1)(c) to embrace, although without being confined to, a person who has not yet been sued. D2 must be potentially liable as tortfeasor for the same damage.[3394] 'Liable' in this

3388. *Bitumen and Oil Refineries (Australia) Ltd v. Commissioner for Government Transport* (1955) 92 CLR 200. As to the amount that D2 may be required to pay, *see* para. 590.

3389. *Baylis v. Waugh* [1962] NZLR 44; *Re Securitibank Ltd* [1986] 2 NZLR 280; *Dairy Containers Ltd v. NZI Bank Ltd* [1995] 2 NZLR 30; *Auckland CC as Assignee of Body Corporate 16113 v. Ackland CC* [2008] 1 NZLR 838 at [50].

3390. *Baylis v. Waugh* [1962] NZLR 44.

3391. *See* para. 588.

3392. *Richardson v. O'Neill* [1959] NZLR 540.

3393. *Karori Properties Ltd v. Jelicich Austin Smith and Davies* [1969] NZLR 698; *Herrick v. Leonard and Dingley Ltd* [1975] 2 NZLR 566; *Young v. Tomlinson* [1979] 2 NZLR 441; *J W Harris & Son Ltd v. Demolition & Roading Contractors (NZ) Ltd* [1979] 2 NZLR 166; *Re Securitibank Ltd* [1986] 2 NZLR 280; *Vining Realty Group Ltd v. Moorehouse* [2010] NZCA 104 at [121].

3394. *Dairy Containers Ltd v. NZI Bank Ltd* [1995] 2 NZLR 30 at 122.

context, and by contrast to D1's position, means 'held liable in judgment'.[3395] If D2 would not at any time have been liable to P, D1's claim for contribution must fail, as where D2 would have been able to rely on an exclusion clause had he been sued by P[3396] and where D2 would have been able to rely on a defence of qualified privilege in a direct claim by P.[3397] However, D2 need not be liable to P at the time of the contribution proceedings if D2 would have been liable 'if sued in time'. The words mean that the supposed action must be treated as having been brought within time, whether or not some limitation as to time might otherwise apply.[3398] Suppose P successfully sues D1 five years after the cause of action accrued. Two years later, D1 claims contribution from D2. A claim by P against D2 at that time would be statute barred, but the claim for contribution can still proceed.

Suppose now that D2 has settled with P. Seemingly D2 should not be able to bind D1 by settling with P for an amount less than his or her share of responsibility. So Barker J could see no reason based on logic, equity, or the words of the statute why D1's right to contribution should be affected by a settlement in respect of which D1 had no control.[3399] Certainly, there has been no finding on the merits of P's claim, and the settlement neither establishes nor disproves the liability of D2.[3400] Although D2's liability to P as from the date of any settlement is discharged by accord and satisfaction, D1 can nonetheless seek to show that D2 would if sued to judgment, before the date of the settlement, have been liable to P.

D2's liability to make contribution to D1 similarly is unaffected where the claim by P against D2 has been dismissed for want of prosecution.[3401] In this case D2 has not been sued to judgment, for a dismissal for want of prosecution is simply an interlocutory order.

Where a consent judgment has been entered in favour of D2, the view of a majority in the High Court of Australia was that D2 was not a 'tortfeasor who ... would if sued have been' liable for the damage.[3402] D2 had in fact been sued, and the judgment in its favour denied it the character of a party awaiting a final determination of a suit in respect of the damage sustained by P. However, the minority thought that 'if sued' should be interpreted to mean 'if sued to judgment on the merits', so a consent judgment did not prevent D2 from coming within that description. This is the better view, for it is contrary to principle to place a plaintiff and a tortfeasor against whom contribution has been, or may be, sought in a position where they can, between themselves, deprive another tortfeasor of its statutory right to contribution. As noted, a settlement with D2 without any court order cannot do this.

Where D2 has previously been sued by P and found not liable on the merits, a claim for contribution cannot succeed. So a claim by an architect against a council

3395. *George Wimpey & Co. Ltd v. British Overseas Airways Corporation* [1955] AC 169.
3396. *Herrick v. Leonard and Dingley Ltd* [1975] 2 NZLR 566.
3397. *Osmose New Zealand Ltd v. Wakeling* [2007] 1 NZLR 841.
3398. *Campbell v. Jenkins* [1974] 1 NZLR 578 at 582.
3399. *Re Securitibank Ltd* [1986] 2 NZLR 280 at 288.
3400. *Harper v. Gray and Walker* [1985] 1 WLR 1196.
3401. *Hart v. Hall & Pickles Ltd* [1969] 1 QB 405.
3402. *James Hardie & Co. Pty Ltd v. Seltsam Pty Ltd* (1998) 196 CLR 53.

for a contribution towards the cost of repairing a defective building failed in circumstances where the council had been held not to owe a duty of care to the building owner and the owner had then abandoned its appeal.[3403] If, however, a claim has failed by reason only of the limitation defence, D1's claim is not barred for D2 would, if sued 'in time', have been liable. If P has successfully sued D2, D2's liability to P is extinguished by merger in the judgment or by payment.[3404] D2 is thus no longer 'liable' to P and again is not liable to make contribution.[3405]

IV. Liability in Respect of the Same Damage

589. The liability of D1 and D2 must be in respect of the 'same damage'. Many decisions have taken a narrow view of these words. They emphasize that the mere fact that two or more wrongs lead to a common result does not of itself mean that the wrongdoers are liable in respect of the same damage. There must be a sharing of a common liability. So there was no right of contribution between defendants where an employer had a claim against a contractor for delay in performing the contract and against an architect for negligent advice and certification of work.[3406] The contractor's breach led to disruption caused by delay and the architect's negligence had not led to any delay in performing the contract.

In *Marlborough District Council v. Altimarloch Joint Venture Ltd*,[3407] where the 'same damage' issue arose in the context of a claim for equitable compensation, the judgments show markedly different views. In this case vendors of land were liable to the purchasers for damages for breach of contract on account of misrepresentations by their agents concerning the extent of water rights associated with the land, and the local council also was liable to the purchasers for a negligent misstatement in issuing an LIM containing the same error about the extent of the water rights. The vendors sought contribution from the council, but it was held in a majority decision that no order ought to be made. Four members of the Court agreed that the test to apply was whether the liabilities were 'of the same nature and extent', but they could not agree on what this required. Tipping J (with Blanchard J agreeing) thought that the liabilities were clearly independent, because the causes of action were different and the loss was not the same. There was no coordinate liability for the same loss, no single claim for which both parties were liable, and unless the court was substantially to extend the principles of equitable contribution the vendors' claim could not succeed. McGrath J (with Anderson J agreeing) took the view that contribution could be ordered. Each party induced the purchaser to enter the contract under a mistaken belief as to the extent of the water rights, neither was misled by the other, and the errors of each caused loss of the same nature. Elias CJ did not determine the point. Her Honour considered that the liability for damages of the council was dependent on the net position reached on the liability of the vendors for

3403. *Blair& Co Ltd v. Queenstown Lakes District Council* [2010] 3 NZLR 17.
3404. *See* para. 510.
3405. *Calderwood v. Nominal Defendant* [1970] NZLR 296.
3406. *Royal Brompton Hospital NHS Trust v. Hammond* [2002] 1 WLR 1397.
3407. [2012] 2 NZLR 726.

breach of contract. Since the remedy obtained from the vendors would eliminate the loss flowing from the negligence of the council, there was no occasion for contribution between them. So, by a majority, the claim for contribution failed.

Altimarloch left the law in an undesirable state of uncertainty, but the more recent decision of the Supreme Court in *Hotchin v. New Zealand Guardian Trust Co Ltd*[3408] has placed it on a firmer foundation. The FMA alleged that the first defendant (D1) and the other directors of three companies had authorized the distribution of misleading company prospectuses, and sought compensation for the subscribers under section 55G of the Securities Act 1978.[3409] D1 argued that the trustees of the companies' trust deeds (D2) were liable to contribute to any compensation he was ordered to pay to the FMA, and joined them as third parties to the proceedings. The trustees applied to strike out the claims against them. The Supreme Court held, by a majority, that in principle D1 should be allowed to make his claim for contribution. Elias CJ said that the loss incurred by the depositors while D2 failed to act and the loss resulting from the fact that the depositors invested in a company in reliance on untrue statements in both cases was the loss of funds invested. The different basis of liability in tort was irrelevant. Once tortfeasors had a common liability to a plaintiff in respect of the 'same damage', no further commonality was needed.

Hotchin thus widens the availability of a claim for contribution under the statute, but the dispute must still be between tortfeasors. If it is not a claim in equity may be available in any event.[3410]

V. Basis for Apportionment

590. Section 17(2) Law Reform Act 1936 governs the amount of the contribution, if any, which the court should order. It provides:

> In any proceedings for contribution under this section, the amount of the contribution recoverable from any person shall be such as may be found by the Court to be just and equitable having regard to the extent of that person's responsibility for the damage; and the Court shall have power to exempt any person from liability to make contribution or to direct that the contribution to be recovered from any person shall amount to a complete indemnity.

Any order is predicated upon D1 being entitled to recover contribution. Accordingly, before making its determination, the court must first decide whether D1 is a tortfeasor liable in respect of the damage, and D2 is a tortfeasor who is, or would if sued in time have been, liable in respect of the same damage.[3411]

3408. [2016] 1 NZLR 906.
3409. Now repealed. *See* now the Financial Markets Conduct Act 2013.
3410. *See* para. 591.
3411. *Amaca Pty Ltd v. New South Wales* (2003) 77 ALJR 1509.

In making an apportionment the court must have regard both to the causative potency of the conduct and to the relative blameworthiness of the parties.[3412] A more serious fault having less causative impact on the plaintiff's damage may represent an equivalent responsibility to a less serious fault that had a greater causative impact.[3413] Ultimately what is a 'just and equitable' division of responsibility is essentially a question of fact.

Normally an apportionment will be made in relation to the amount that D1 has been ordered or has agreed to pay P. Sometimes, however, D2 may seek to challenge that amount. The High Court of Australia has suggested that if D1 has improvidently agreed to pay too large an amount or by unreasonable or negligent conduct in litigation has incurred or submitted to an excessive verdict, there is no valid reason why D2 should not say to D1 that the excess is due to D1's fault and not that of D2.[3414] It has been held, applying the principle, that D1 can recover in contribution proceedings against D2 on the basis of the full amount of any consent judgment between D1 and P only if the settlement is reasonable and, therefore, a 'just and equitable' contribution.[3415] D2 thus was obliged to contribute only to the true measure of D1's responsibility, which was held to be little more than one-tenth of the amount of the settlement.

Where P is identified with negligence by D2,[3416] D1 may plead contributory negligence by D2 in answer to P's claim. The Court of Appeal has held that D1 is not bound to do this, and may elect to seek contribution from D2 in the ordinary way.[3417] However, it has been suggested that contributory negligence should generally be determined first before turning to the question of contribution.[3418]

In cases involving vicarious liability, the correct approach is to consider the relative responsibility of the persons personally liable and to apportion liability accordingly, irrespective of whether D1 or D2 is personally or vicariously liable.[3419] However, if the contribution proceedings are between the person vicariously liable and the person for whom he or she is liable, that is, if D1 is only vicariously liable for D2, the court may direct a complete indemnity.[3420] This solution also has been adopted where D1 was only liable to P because of D2's breach of a statute[3421] and

3412. *McFarlane v. Neshausen* [1952] 1 NZLR 292; *New Zealand Apple and Pear Marketing Board v. Watts* [1967] NZLR 205 at 228, 230; *Dairy Containers Ltd v. NZI Bank Ltd* [1995] 2 NZLR 30 at 126.
3413. *Downs v. Chappell* [1996] 3 All ER 344 at 363.
3414. *Bitumen and Oil Refineries (Australia) Ltd v. Commissioner for Government Transport* (1955) 92 CLR 200 at 213.
3415. *Saccardo Constructions Pty Ltd v. Gammon (No. 2)* (1994) 63 SASR 333.
3416. *See* para. 481.
3417. *McDowell v. Attorney-General* [1963] NZLR 878.
3418. *Dairy Containers Ltd v. NZI Bank Ltd* [1995] 2 NZLR 30 at 85–87.
3419. *Dubai Aluminium Co. Ltd v. Salaam* [2003] 2 AC 366.
3420. *Richardson v. O'Neill* [1959] NZLR 540.
3421. *Harris v. Lombard New Zealand Ltd* [1974] 2 NZLR 161.

where D1 acted strictly in accordance with directions given by D2.[3422] Conversely, if D1 seeks contribution where D2 is only vicariously liable for D1, then the claim must fail.[3423]

Liability to pay contribution under the statute does not affect any express or implied contractual or other right to indemnity or contribution.[3424] On the other hand, the Law Reform Act 1936 provides that the statutory right to contribution does not render enforceable any agreement for indemnity that would not have been enforceable if section 17 had not been passed.[3425] For example, a contractual indemnity against liability in respect of a deliberate wrongful act is void, as where the indemnity was sought by a publisher in respect of his liability for publishing material known by him to be defamatory.[3426] Although there can be no recovery in contract in such a case, arguably contribution can still be sought under the Act.

The question of contribution between tortfeasors is one for the judge, not the jury (if there is one).[3427] An appellate court will not interfere with an apportionment of damages between two defendants unless, on the whole of the evidence, the court is satisfied that the judge's decision was unreasonable.[3428]

VI. Contribution in Equity

591. The principle allowing claims for contribution in equity in certain circumstances was recognized by the Supreme Court in *Marlborough District Council v. Altimarloch Joint Venture Ltd*,[3429] but it was held that it could not be invoked on the particular facts because, *inter alia*, there was no common obligation or coordinate liability. However, in *Hotchin v. New Zealand Guardian Trust Co Ltd*[3430] the Supreme Court abandoned any such requirement. Elias CJ maintained that contribution was an equitable principle which expressed natural justice in its recognition that it was unjust for the burden of meeting a loss for which others shared responsibility to be borne by one party, to the benefit of those who escaped liability. The obligations of D1 and D2 need not be identical in their source or extent. Nor was it necessary that they should have the same legal character. It was enough that the responsibility for the harm was shared. This was an inquiry that was practical and directed at the substance of the matter in the particular case. The principles upon which contribution was based were equally applicable whether under the statute or in equity. Seemingly, then the test is, quite simply, whether enforcement against one

---

3422. *Clearlite Holdings Ltd v. Auckland City Corporation* [1976] 2 NZLR 729.
3423. Law Reform Act 1936, s. 17(1)(c), proviso; *Osmose New Zealand Ltd v. Wakeling* [2007] 1 NZLR 841 at [81].
3424. *Arthur White (Contractors) Ltd v. Tarmac Civil Engineering Ltd* [1967] 1 WLR 1508; *Southland Harbour Board v. Vella* [1974] 1 NZLR 526.
3425. Section 17(4)(b) Law Reform Act 1936.
3426. *W H Smith & Son v. Clinton and Harris* (1908) 99 LT 840.
3427. *Newman Bros Ltd v. Spittal* [1947] NZLR 357.
3428. *Steel Structures Ltd v. Rangitikei County* [1974] 2 NZLR 306.
3429. [2012] 2 NZLR 726; *see* para. 589.
3430. [2016] 1 NZLR 906.

wrongdoer will diminish the liability of the other.[3431] As is recognized by Elias CJ, this gives effect to the general principles of justice underlying contribution claims, these being founded ultimately on the principle that the wrongdoer whose liability has been diminished has been unjustly enriched at the expense of the paying wrongdoer.

3431. *See Burke v. LFOT Pty Ltd* (2002) 209 CLR 282 per Kirby J.

Selected Bibliography

Atiyah. *Vicarious Liability in the Law of Torts*. London: Butterworths Ltd (1967).

Atkin. 'Defamation Law in New Zealand "Refined" and "Amplified"'. *Common Law World Review* 30 (2001): 237.

Bailey. 'Public Authority Liability in Negligence: The Continued Search for Coherence'. *Legal Studies* 26 (2006): 155.

Bailey & Nolan. 'The *Page v. Smith* Saga: A Tale of Inauspicious Origins and Unintended Consequences'. *Cambridge Law Journal* 69 (2010): 495.

Barker. 'Unreliable Assumptions in the Modern Law of Negligence'. *Law Quarterly Review* 109 (1993): 461.

Barker. 'Wielding Occam's Razor: Pruning Strategies for Economic Loss'. *Oxford Journal of Legal Studies* 26 (2006): 289.

Bell. 'The Basis of Vicarious Liability'. *Cambridge Law Journal* 72 (2013): 17.

Beuermann. *Reconceptualising Strict Liability for the Tort of Another*. Oxford: Hart Publishing (2019).

Buckley. 'The March of Negligence: Has Nuisance a Future?'. *Northern Ireland Legal Quarterly* 58 (2007): 395.

Burrows. 'Invasion of Privacy: *Hosking* and Beyond'. *New Zealand Law Review* (2006): 389.

Burrows & Cheer. *Media Law in New Zealand*. 7th edn. Wellington: LexisNexis (2015).

Burrows, Finn & Todd. *The Law of Contract in New Zealand*. 6th edn. Wellington: LexisNexis (2018).

Campbell. 'The Absence of Negligence in Hedley Byrne v. Heller'. *Law Quarterly Review* 132 (2016): 266.

Carty. 'Dilution and Passing Off: Cause for Concern'. *Law Quarterly Review* 112 (1996): 632.

Carty. 'OBG Ltd v. Allan: The House of Lords Shapes the Economic Torts and Explores Commercial Confidences and Image Rights'. *Torts Law Journal* 15 (2007): 283.

Cheer. 'The Future of Privacy: Recent Legal Developments in New Zealand'. *Canterbury Law Review* 13 (2007): 169.

Cooke. 'Remoteness of Damages and Judicial Discretion'. *Cambridge Law Journal* 37 (1978): 288.

Cooke. 'An Impossible Distinction'. *Law Quarterly Review* 107 (1991): 46.

Coote. 'Assumption of Responsibility and Pure Economic Loss in New Zealand'. *New Zealand Law Review* (2005): 1.

Cross. 'Does Only the Careless Polluter Pay? A Re-examination of the Tort of Nuisance'. *Law Quarterly Review* 111 (1995): 445.
Deakin & Randall. 'Rethinking the Economic Torts'. *Modern Law Review* 72 (2009): 519.
Degeling, Edelman & Goudkamp (eds). *Torts in Commercial Law*. Pyrmont, NSW: Law Book Co (2011).
Dias. 'Remoteness of Liability and Legal Policy'. *Cambridge Law Journal* 20 (1962): 178.
Douglas. 'The Scope of Conversion: Property and Contract'. *Modern Law Review* 74 (2011): 329.
Erbacher. *Negligence and Illegality*. Oxford: Hart Publishing (2017).
Flannigan. 'The Personal Tort Liability of Directors'. *Canadian Bar Review* 81 (2002): 247.
Fleming. 'The Law of Torts'. 10th edn. edited by Sappideen & Vines. Sydney: The Law Book Co. Ltd, 2011.
Fordham. 'Blessing or Burden? Recent Developments in Actions for Wrongful Conception and Wrongful Birth in the United Kingdom and Australia'. *Singapore Journal of Legal Studies* (2004) 462.
Fordham. 'A Life Less Ordinary – The Rejection of Actions for Wrongful Life'. *Torts Law Journal* 15 (2007): 123.
Frankel. *Intellectual Property in New Zealand*. 2nd ed. Wellington: LexisNexis (2011).
Gardner. 'The Many Faces of the Reasonable Person'. *Law Quarterly Review* 131 (2015): 563.
Gatley. *Libel and Slander*. 12th edn. London: Sweet & Maxwell Ltd (2017).
George. 'Non-delegable Duties in Tort'. *Law Quarterly Review* 130 (2014): 534.
Goodhart & Winfield. 'Trespass and Negligence'. *Law Quarterly Review* 49 (1933): 359.
Goudkamp. *Tort Law Defences*. Oxford: Hart Publishing (2013).
Green. *Causation in Negligence*. Oxford: Hart Publishing (2017).
Hart & Honoré. *Causation in the Law*. 2nd edn. Oxford: Clarendon Press (1985).
Hickman. 'The Reasonableness Principle: Reassessing Its Place in the Public Sphere'. *Cambridge Law Journal* 63 (2004): 166.
Lord Hoffmann. 'Causation'. *Law Quarterly Review* 121 (2005): 592.
Lord Hoffmann. 'Fairchild in Retrospect'. *Advocates Quarterly* 39 (2012): 257.
Holderness (ed.). *Introduction to Commercial Law in New Zealand*. 5th edn. Wellington: LexisNexis (2016).
Howarth. 'Many Duties of Care – Or a Duty of Care? Notes from the Underground'. *Oxford Journal of Legal Studies* 26 (2006): 449.
Jansen. 'The Idea of a Lost Chance'. *Oxford Journal of Legal Studies* 19 (1999): 271.
Joseph. *Constitutional and Administrative Law in New Zealand*. 4th edn. Wellington: Brookers Ltd (2014).
Kenyon. 'What Conversation? Free Speech and Defamation Law'. *Modern Law Review* 73 (2010): 697.
Koury. 'Causation and Risk in the Highest Courts of Canada, England and France'. *Law Quarterly Review* 124 (2008): 103.

Manning. 'Informed Consent to Medical Treatment: The Common Law and New Zealand's Code of Patient's Rights'. *Medical Law Review* 12 (2004): 181.
Markesinis. 'Negligence, Nuisance and Duties of Affirmative Action'. *Law Quarterly Review* 105 (1989): 104.
McBride. 'Duties of Care – Do They Really Exist?'. *Oxford Journal of Legal Studies* 24 (2004): 417.
McGregor. *Damages*. 20th edn. London: Sweet & Maxwell Ltd (2019).
McIvor. *Third Party Liability in Tort*. Oxford: Hart Publishing (2006).
Mitchell & Mitchell. *Landmark Cases in the Law of Tort*. Oxford: Hart Publishing (2010).
Moreham. 'Privacy in the Common Law: A Doctrinal and Theoretical Analysis'. *Law Quarterly Review* 121 (2005): 628.
Morgan. 'Vicarious Liability on the Move'. *Law Quarterly Review* 129 (2013): 139.
Morgan. 'Liability for Independent Contractors in Contract and Tort: Duties to Ensure That Care Is Taken'. *Cambridge Law Journal* 74 (2015): 109.
Mullany & Handford. *Tort Liability for Psychiatric Damage*. 2nd edn. Sydney: Law Book Co (2006).
Murphy. 'Rethinking Injunctions in Tort Law'. *Oxford Journal of Legal Studies* 27 (2007): 509.
Murphy. *The Law of Nuisance*. Oxford: Oxford University Press (2010).
Murphy. 'Misfeasance in a Public Office: A Tort Law Misfit?'. *Oxford Journal of Legal Studies* 32 (2012): 51.
Murphy. 'Rethinking Tortious Immunity for Judicial Acts'. *Legal Studies* 33 (2013): 455.
New Zealand Law Commission. *Invasion of Privacy: Penalties and Remedies*. NZLC R113 (2010).
Newark. 'The Boundaries of Nuisance'. *Law Quarterly Review* 65 (1949): 480.
Neyers, Pitel & Chamberlain (eds). *Emerging Issues in Tort Law*. Oxford: Hart Publishing (2007).
Nolan. 'New Forms of Damage in Negligence'. *Modern Law Review* 70 (2007): 59.
Nolan. 'Liability of Public Bodies for Failing to Confer Benefits'. *Law Quarterly Review* 127 (2011): 260
Nolan. 'Deconstructing the Duty of Care'. *Law Quarterly Review* 129 (2013): 559.
Nolan. 'Preventive Damages'. *Law Quarterly Review* 132 (2016): 68.
Nolan. 'Varying the Standard of Care in Negligence'. *Cambridge Law Journal* 72 (2013): 651.
Oliphant. 'Beyond Misadventure: Compensation for Medical Injuries in New Zealand'. *Medical Law Review* 15 (2007): 357.
Reece. 'Losses of Chances in the Law'. *Modern Law Review* 59 (1996): 188.
Rishworth, Huscroft, Optican & Mahoney. *The New Zealand Bill of Rights*. Melbourne: Oxford University Press (2003).
Scott. 'Reconsidering "Wrongful Life" in England after Thirty Years'. *Cambridge Law Journal* 72 (2013): 115.
Skegg & Paterson (eds). *Health Law in New Zealand*. Wellington: Thomson Reuters Ltd (2015).
Smillie. 'Non-natural Use'. *New Zealand Law Journal* (2011): 88.

Stanton. 'New Forms of the Tort of Breach of Statutory Duty'. *Law Quarterly Review* 120 (2004): 324.
Stanton. 'Professional Negligence: Duty of Care Methodology in the Twenty First Century'. *Journal of Professional Negligence* 22 (2006): 134.
Stevens. *Torts and Rights*. Oxford: Oxford University Press (2007).
Stapleton. 'Tort, Insurance and Ideology'. *Modern Law Review* 58 (1995): 820.
Stapleton. 'Comparative Economic Loss: Lessons from Case-Law-Focused "Middle Theory"'. *UCLA Law Review* 50 (2002): 531.
Stapleton. 'Lords A-Leaping Evidentiary Gaps'. *Torts Law Journal* 10 (2002): 276.
Stapleton. 'Cause-in-Fact and the Scope of Liability for Consequences'. *Law Quarterly Review* 119 (2003): 388.
Stapleton. 'Loss of the Chance of Cure from Cancer'. *Modern Law Review* 68 (2005): 996.
Stapleton. 'Factual Causation, Mesothelioma and Statistical Weight'. *Law Quarterly Review* 128 (2012): 521.
Strauss. 'Ex Turpi Causa Non Oritur Actio'. *Law Quarterly Review* 132 (2016): 236.
Teff. 'Liability for Negligently Inflicted Psychiatric Harm: Justifications and Boundaries'. *Cambridge Law Journal* 57 (1998): 91.
Tobin. 'Political Discussion in New Zealand: Cause for Concern?'. *New Zealand Law Review* (2003) 215.
Todd (gen ed.). *Todd on Torts*. 8th edn. Wellington: Thomson Reuters (2019).
Todd & Finn. Contract Law in New Zealand. 4th edn. The Netherlands: Wolters Kluwer (2019).
Todd. 'Treatment Injury in New Zealand'. *Chicago-Kent Law Review* 86 (2011): 1169.
Todd. 'Multiple Causes of Loss and Claims for Contribution'. *New Zealand Universities Law Review* 25 (2013): 960.
Todd. 'Applying the Ex Turpi Causa Principle in Tort Actions'. *Journal of International and Comparative Law* 1 (2014): 221.
Todd. 'Tortious Intrusions upon Solitude and Seclusion'. *Singapore Academy of Law Journal* 27 (2015): 731.
Todd, 'Personal Liability, Vicarious Liability, Non-delegable Duties and Protecting Vulnerable People'. *Torts Law Journal* 23 (2016): 105.
Todd, 'Common Law Protection for Injury to a Person's Reproductive Autonomy'. *Law Quarterly Review* 135 (2019): 635.
Trindade. 'Intentional Torts: Some Thoughts on Assault and Battery'. *Oxford Journal of Legal Studies* 2 (1982): 211.
Wilberg. 'Defensive Practice or Conflict of Duties? Policy Concerns in Public Authority Negligence Claims'. *Law Quarterly Review* 126 (2010): 420.
Williams. 'Causation in the Law'. *Cambridge Law Journal* 19 (1961): 62.
Winfield & Jolowicz. *The Law of Torts*. 19th edn. London: Sweet & Maxwell Ltd (2014).
Witting. 'Physical Damage in Negligence'. *Cambridge Law Journal* 61 (2002): 189.
Witting. *Liability for Negligent Misstatements*. Oxford: Oxford University Press (2004).
Witting. 'Duty of Care: An Analytical Approach'. *Oxford Journal of Legal Studies* 25 (2005): 33.

Woodhouse Report. *Royal Commission of Inquiry: Compensation for Personal Injury in New Zealand*. Wellington: Government Printer, 1967.

Selected Bibliography

Index

The numbers here refer to paragraph numbers.

Index

Index

Index

Made in the USA
Monee, IL
18 October 2026

66041378R10293